Bea Verschraegen (ed.)
Family Finances

Bea Verschraegen (ed.)
Family Finances

Jan Sramek Verlag

Gedruckt mit Unterstützung des Bundesministeriums
für Wissenschaft und Forschung in Wien.

Printed with the support of the
Ministry for Science and Research in Vienna

BM.W_F^a

All rights, including translations, reserved. No part of this book shall be reproduced, sotred in a retrival system or transmitted by any means, electronic, mechanical, photocopying, recording, or otherwise, without the written consent of the publisher. No liability is assumed with respect to the use of the information contained herein. Although every precaution has been taken in preparation of this book, the publisher, editor and the authors assume no responsability for errors or omissions. Neither is any liability assumed for damages resulting from the use of the information contained therein.
Publishing and rights contact see: www.jan-sramek-verlag.at

Typografic concept: Michael Karner, www.typografie.co.at
Typesetting by the publisher
Cover graphics by Tanja Jenni
Font: Arnhem
Printed in Austria (Holzhausen Druck und Medien Ges.m.b.H)
Printed on: Dito Offset 80g, 1,25

ISBN 978-3-902638-10-6

©2009, Jan Sramek Verlag KG

The ISFL 13th World Conference

Blue Danube Waltz? No time to dance
Too busy learning about family finance
I am sure we all will long remember
ISFL 13th Conference in Vienna
John Eekelaar's speech, so elegantly craft
Rivalled the music of Strauss and Mozart
Convenor Bea must be justly proud
To see such an illustrious crowd.

Participants came to this world conference
From all parts of the globe's circumference
Asia, US, Europe, Aussie, Africa in great number
Ensuring maintenance rights do not slumber
Representing every continent, creed and race
ISFL brought us to this beautiful place
To discuss family solidarity
Not forgetting the State's responsibility.

The Von Trapp Family we did not see
Sounds of Music were heard so fleetingly
Spousal support, property settlement
Took precedence over opera entertainment
You can't go cruising on Danube River
Till you learn you must maintain your lover
Your spouse, parent, children, step-children too
And adult child, if Italian, they can sue.

Even in assisted reproduction
Maintenance will become your obligation
;ame sex together cannot procreate
 ≥t the law will of them parents make
 :hild can have two parents or three
   even four, if the courts decree
   y send your daughter university?
   ι spouse, hip-hop singer's baby earn big money.

     'ren's rights may go out the door
      o-economic rights are not secure
       w, criminal constitutional, tort
        ' or all, when maintenance is sought
         ·ll-nourished on diet of financial provision
          ιre to return to our jurisdiction
)e remiss of us not to congratulate Bea
            izing such a successful affair.

                    ∞

             ·on-Ahye – Trinidad and Tobago national, resident in The Bahamas
                                             20th September 2008.

Ch.
If sc
Civil
Use a
Now,
We pr
It woul
For orga

Hazel Thom

TABLE OF CONTENTS

Authors XXIII
Preface XXVII

PART I – GENERAL ISSUES

Rainer Frank
Introductory Lecture – Family Solidarity in Support and Inheritance Law
I.	Thoughts on the Concept of »Family«	1
II.	The Right to Support	7
III.	Inheritance Law	13

John Eekelaar
Partners, Parents and Children: Grounds for Allocationg Resources across Households
I.	Introduction	23
II.	Children	25
III.	Partners	26
IV.	Parents	31
V.	Conclusion: Social or Inter-Personal Obligations?	32

Jordi Ribot
Family Law and Intergenerational Family Solidarity – Should there be Enforceable Maintenance Rights vis-à-vis Adult Relatives?
I.	Introduction	33
II.	Maintenance Obligations between Adult Relatives Revisited . .	36
III.	Legal Signalling and Developing Family Strategies	40
IV.	Conclusive Remarks: the Catalan Case	42

Elisabeth Alofs and *Renaat Hoop*
The Sustainability of Survivor and Divorce Benefits in the Adult Worker Model: Incorporation of New Social Risks
I.	Introduction: From old to new Social Risks	49
II.	The Survivor Benefit: An old Social Risk?	51
III.	Proposal for a Modern Regulation of Survivor Benefits	54

IV.	The Survivor Benefit versus the Legal Right to Alimony after Divorce	57
V.	Conclusion	66

Ruth Farrugia
State Responsibility in Enforcing Maintenance Obligations towards Children

I.	Introduction	71
II.	An Overview of the Legal Duty of the State to Intervene where Parental Responsibility is Absent or Lacking	74
III.	A Review of the State Undertaking to Share or Supplant Responsibility for the Child	76
IV.	An Evaluation of the Standard of Care Owed by the State in Replacing Parental Responsibility	79
V.	An Appraisal of Child Rights in the Enforcement of a »Basic Minimum Standard of State Care«	81

June Sinclair and *Trynie Davel*
Evolving Family Forms and the Duty of Support in South African Law

I.	Introduction	85
II.	Same-sex Partners	86
III.	Judical Extension of the Duty of Support	87
IV.	Legislation Awaited: Muslim Marriage and Heterosexual Cohabitation	92

Anton van der Linde
The Extent of the State's Duty to Support Family Life through Prevention and Early Intervention Programmes: A Reflection on the Children's Act 38 of 2005

I.	Introduction	99
II.	Prevention and Early Intervention	102
III.	National Norms and Standards for Prevention and Early Intervention Programmes	104
IV.	Court may order Early Intervention Programme	105
V.	Budgeting and Costing of the Children's Act	105
VI.	Discussion	108
VII.	Conclusion	112

Barbara Campbell
Legal Resolution Services™ and its Interface with ADR:
An Australian Perspective
I.   Introduction 115
II. *Legal Resolution Services™* 116
III. *Legal Resolution Services™* and its Place in
     Alternative Dispute Resolution Options 124
IV. Answering the Critics 130
V.   Conclusion 132

Giselle Câmara Groeninga
An Interdisciplinary Approach of Family Finances
I.   Introduction 133
II. The Interdisciplinary Approach 134
III. The Interdisciplinary Approach and the Family 135
V.   The need of Legislative Modifications beyond
     the Matrimonial Regime 139

Keum Sook Choe
Study on Legal and Financial Support for Multicultural Families in South-Korea
I.   Introduction 143
II. Statistics for International Marriages and Children 146
III. Legal and Financial Support for Multicultural Families .. 149
IV. Legal and Policy Support for »Marriage Immigrants« 158
V.   Conclusion 159

Yue FU
Expulsion of Irregular Foreign Residents from Japan:
The Right to Family Unification and the Best Interests of the Child
I.   Introduction 161
II. Foreign Nationals Residing in Japan 162
III. Expulsion of Irregular Foreign Residents and
     the »Special Permission to Stay« 166
IV. Analysis of Recent Court Decisions
     on Deportation Cases 169
V.   Conclusion 174

Ian Curry-Sumner
International Recovery of Child Support:
Are Central Authorities the way forward?
I.	Introduction	175
II.	Current Framework	176
III.	Current Problematic Areas	184
IV.	Proposed instruments	186
V.	Experience with Central Authorities	191
VI.	Conclusions	193

Adriaan P. van der Linden
What Price Should be Paid for a Child?
Financial aspects of inter-country adoption
I.	Introduction	195
II.	The Report on Inter-Country Adoption	199
III.	The Financial Aspects of Adoption	205
IV.	Conclusions	213

Katarzyna Bagan-Kurluta
Adoption in a Globalized World 215

Ann Laquer Estin
Transnational Family Finances and the United States
I.	Introduction	233
II.	Child Support in the United States	235
III.	Families Across Borders	239

Robert G. Spector
The Hague Convention on the International Recovery of Child Support and other Forms of Family Maintenance: Divergent Private International Law Rules and the Limits of Harmonisation
I.	Introduction	243
II.	Jurisdiction	244
III.	Applicable Law	248
IV.	Modifications or Variations of the Original Support Order	249
V.	Conclusion	255

Part II – Marriage and Non-formal Relationships

Ledina Mandia
Principles, Deviation therefrom and Consequences of Formal and Non-Formal Relationships
I.	Marriage as a Formal Relationship	259
II.	Cohabitation (More Uxorio) as a Non-Formal Relationship	266
III.	Conclusions	268

Dominique Goubau
Division of Family Assets and De Facto Conjugality: The Limits of a Free Choice Approach
I.	Introduction	271
II.	De facto Cohabitation in Canada	272
III.	Status and Discrimination	275
IV.	The Need for Redefining Matrimonial Property Law	277

Zdeňka Králíčková
Legal Protection of Unmarried and Divorced Mothers in the Czech Republic
I.	Introduction	281
II.	Families not Based on Marriage and as Torsos after Divorce: Why so Many?	282
III.	Underestimating Property Aspects of Family and Family Law after 1948: General Notes	284
IV.	Legal Protection of an Unmarried Mother and of her Child	286
V.	Legal Protection of Divorced Mother and her Child	288
VI.	Conclusions	290

Penelope Agallopoulou
Financial Consequences of Cohabitation between Persons of the Opposite Sex According to Greek Law
I.	Introduction	293
II.	Current Legal Situation	295
III.	Bill on Cohabitation between Persons of Opposite Sex	302
IV.	Conclusion	303

Shahar Lifshitz
A Liberal Analysis of Western Cohabitation Law
I.	Introduction	305
II.	Historical Background: Cohabitation Law in the Liberal-Conservative Debate	307
III.	The Liberal Arguments against Imposing Marriage Law on Cohabitants	309
IV.	The Counter Arguments in Favor of Equating Marriage and Cohabitation	310
V.	The Theoretical Approaches within Existing Jurisdictions	313
VI.	The Need for a New Model	316
VII.	Principle for a New Liberal Model	318

Stefano Insinga
De Facto Family and Family Enterprise in the Italian Legal System
I.	General Aspects	321
II.	Residual Nature	323
III.	Rights and Duties of the Family Members	323
IV.	Can More Uxorio Cohabitants Constitute Family Enterprise?	324
V.	Doctrine and Case-Law Orientations	325
VI.	How Could be Protected the More Uxorio Partners?	327

Margaret Briggs
The Formalization of Property Sharing Rights For De Facto Couples in New Zealand
I.	Introduction	329
II.	Framework of the Property (Relationships) Act 1976	330
III.	The Equal Property Sharing Regime and De Facto Relationships	331
IV.	Conclusion	342

Margareta Brattström
The Protection of a Vulnerable Party when a Cohabitee Relationship Ends – An Evaluation of the Swedish Cohabitees Act
I.	Introduction	345
II.	The Swedish Cohabitees Act	346
III.	Does the Design of the Act Promote its Purpose in a Satisfying Manner?	348

IV.	Does the Application of the Law Create any Special Problems?	351
V.	Does the Swedish Cohabitees Act Need Revision?	353
VI.	What can Foreign Jurisdictions Learn from the Swedish Experience of Cohabitation without Marriage?	354

Tone Sverdrup
An Ill-Fitting Garment: Why the Logic of Private Law Falls Short between Cohabitants

I.	Introduction	355
II.	Is there a Need for Statutory Intervention?	355
III.	Are Problems Solved through a Cohabitation Contract?	357
IV.	Three Statutory Models	360

Anna Stępień-Sporek
Sharing of Accruals as the Best Solution for Marriage?

I.	Introduction	369
II.	Switzerland and Germany	371
III.	Poland	374
IV.	Conclusions	377

Marija Draškić
**Financing the Romance:
Marriage Contract in the Serbian Family Act**

I.	Introduction	381
II.	Legal Property Regime	383
III.	The Regime of Marriage Contract	390
IV.	Final Remarks	392

Nigel Lowe and *Roger Kay*
**The Status of Prenuptial Agreements in English Law –
Eccentricity or Sensible Pragmatism?**

I.	Introduction	395
II.	Résumé of English Case-Law on Prenuptial Agreements	399
III.	Should The English Position Be Reformed?	407
IV.	The Reaction of Policy makers	411
V.	Conclusions	413

Paula Nuñes Correia
Matrimonial Finances in the Context of the Macanese Legal System: General Principles and Issues
I.	Introduction...	415
II.	Matrimonial Finances in the Context of the Macanese Legal System – General Principles and Issues...............	417
III.	Conclusion...	426

Gabriel García Cantero
L'Entreprise Familiale dans le Régime Matrimonial Légal Espagnol
I.	Les Aspects Commerciaux d'après la Réforme Introduite par la Loi de 13 Mai 1981 dans le Régime Matrimoniale Legal en Espagne..	427
II.	Analyse du Devoir Réciproque et Périodique qui Tombe sur les Conjoints à l'Égard de l'Information à propos de leurs Activités Économiques	428
III.	Le Statut de l'Entreprise Familiale Crée ou Fondée par un Conjoint pendant le Mariage et Moyennant des Biens Communs.......................................	430
IV.	Quelques Conclusions...................................	435

Rita Duca
Alimony in Divorce in the Italian Legal System
I.	Introduction...	439
II.	What Is the Nature of Alimony in Divorce?................	440
III.	When is Acknowledgment of the Right to Alimony Given? ...	441
III.	What Are the Criteria Followed by the Italian Courts in Deciding the ›Quantum‹ of Alimony?.....................	443
IV.	What Right Do de facto Couples Have to Alimony?..........	446

Paula Távora Vítor
Solidarity between Former Spouses – What if Guilt Has Nothing to Do with It? An Overview of the Connections between the Portuguese Divorce Reform and the Regime of Maintenance Obligations between Former Spouses
I.	Introduction...	449
II.	Guilt and Punishment and the Former Portuguese Divorce System	450

III.	What if Guilt Has Nothing to Do With It? – The Portuguese Divorce Reform and its Repercussions on Maintenance Obligations between Former Spouses	455
IV.	Some Further Conclusion-Like Remarks	459

Jan C. Bekker
An Analysis of the Rights of South African Women and Children to Maintenance from Husbands and Fathers in African Customary Marriages and Domestic Partnerships

I.	Introduction	461
II.	Problem of Proving Existence of a Customary Marriage	462
III.	The Male Heir's Duty of Support	464
IV.	Discarded Wives and Other Dual Marriages.................	466
V.	Action for Damages Caused by the Death of a Breadwinner............................	467
VI.	Women Trapped between Two Legal Cultures	468
VII.	Domestic Partnerships	470
VIII.	Maintenance of Surviving Spouses Act 27 of 1990	472
IX.	Maintenance when Courts Grant Orders for Dissolution of Customary Marriages	472
X.	The Maintenance Act 99 of 1998	473
XI	Conclusion	474

Lynn D. Wardle
Alimony on the Margins: Protecting Homemaking Service in the Public Interest

I.	Introduction: Dentifying Public Interests to Clarify the Confused State of Alimony Theory	475
II.	The Conundrum of Alimony in Family Law Theory and Practice in America	478
III.	Homemaking is Productive Labor that Promotes Substantial Public Interests	481
IV.	Many American Women Value Homemaking Service and Give It Priority	487
V.	Conclusion: Alimony Law Should Recognize the Public Worth of Homemaking Service	489

Nina Dethloff
New Models of Partnerships – Financial Consequences of Separation
I.	Introduction	491
II.	Registered Partnership	491
III.	Same-Sex Marriage	493
IV.	De facto Partnership	495
V.	Conclusion	498

Mathew Thorpe
London – The Divorce Capital of the World
I.	Introduction: The 1973 Act	501
II.	The 1984 Act Amendments	503
III.	Subsequent Legislative Inertia	507
IV.	Judicial Reform	509
V.	Parliament and the Judges	511
VI.	The European Dimension	513
VII.	Conclusion	514

Hugues Fulchiron
Des Solidarités dans les Couples Séparés
I.	Une Solidarité Minimum	520
II.	Une Solidarité Minimale	525

Part III – Children

Barbara Willenbacher
Family Finances through German Support Laws:
Effects of Child Support Priority
I.	Introduction	535
II.	The German Support Laws	536
IV.	Simulation	542
V.	Summary	544

Patrick Parkinson
The Financial Impact of Relocation Disputes:
Empirical Evidence from Australia
I.	Introduction	553
II.	Setting the Scene: The Australian Context	556
III.	Outcomes of the Relocation Dispute	557
IV.	Low Rates of Settlement	558
V.	The Legal Costs of Relocation Disputes	560
VI.	How Was the Litigation Funded?	563
VII.	The Costs of Travel	563
VIII.	Conclusion	566

Hege Brækhus
Regulation of Parenthood – Deregulation of Marriage
I.	Introduction	569
II.	Family Law Today	573
III.	Towards a Fair Family-Legislation	580
IV.	Deregulation of Marriage	582
V.	Regulation of Parenthood	583
VI.	Conclusion	586

Anna Singer
Time is money? Child Support for Children With
Alternating Residence in Sweden
I.	Introduction	591
II.	Alternating Residence	592
III.	Child Support and Alternating Residence	595
IV.	A Just Division of Child Support	599

Branka Resetar
New Child Maintenance Obligations in Croatia: More and More Being a Concern of the Public Law and Less of the Civil Law

I.	Introduction	603
II.	The Child's Right to Support Pursuant to the 2003 Family Act – Prior to the Reform of 2007	604
III.	Reform of the Child's Right to Maintenance Pursuant to the 2007 Family Act	607
IV.	Elements of the Public Law in the Field of Child Support	609
V.	Connection between Maintenance and Contacts	611
VI.	Conclusion	613

Annette Kronborg and *Christina G. Jeppesen de Boer*
The Child's Right to Two Parents:
Facilitating and Financing Joint Parenting

I.	Introduction	615
II.	Parental Authority	615
III.	The Burden of Procedures	618
IV.	Child Maintenance	623
V.	Transportation of Children	625
VI.	Concluding Remarks	627

Salvatore Casabona
Mamma Mia! The Never Ending Story of the Economic Support of the Adult Child in Italy

I.	Introduction	629
II.	The Italian Statutory Law	630
II.	The Judiciary	632
III.	Conclusion	634

Gordana Kovaček-Stanić
Child in a Single (Absent) Parent Family:
Maintenance and Family Home

I.	Introduction	637
II.	Child's Maintenance	638
III.	Family Home	644
IV.	Conclusion	646

Vesna Rijavec and *Suzana Kraljić*
The Maintenance of the Children:
Alimony Fund as the Saving Grace?
I.	Introduction	649
II.	Main Origins of Children's Maintenance in Slovenia	650
III.	Statistical Date about the Children's Maintenance	651
IV.	Problems of Non-Paying the Maintenance	653
V.	The Alimony Fund	654
VI.	Conclusion	662

Andrew Pote
Financial Provisions and Child Equality
I.	Introduction	665
II.	Financial Provsion for Children between Separated Parents	666
III.	Conclusion	670

PART IV

Part IV – Financial Planning and Responsibilty

András Kőrös
New Features of Hungarian Matrimonial Property Law in the Draft of a New Civil Code
I. Historical Antecedents 675
II. The Principles of the New Family Law Book................. 676
III. Conclusion 680

Fumiko Tsuneoka
The Economic Consequence of Divorce in Japan. Trend in No-Fault Divorce and *Rikon Isharyo* (Solatium by Divorce) Scheme
I. Introduction... 683
II. The No-Fault Divorce Regime and the Economic Consequence in Japan.......................... 684
III. Conclusion 694

Mark Henaghan
Achieving Economic Equality at the End of Marriage and Other Relationships: Not All Is Fair in Love and War
I. Introduction... 695
II. A Partnership of Equals 696
III. Achieving an Equal Result................................ 698
IV. Objections to the Disparity Provisions.................... 699
V. How the Disparity Provision Works 700
VI. The Conundrums of Compensation 702

Maria João Romão Carreiro Vaz Tomé
Elderly Dependency, Family Caretaking and Law in Portugal
I. Introduction... 709
II. Family Relationships 712
III. The Traditional Family 713
IV. Recognizing Family Look-Alikes – Quasi-Family Relationships: People That Live in a »Common Economy Relationship« (Law 6/2001 of 11th May) 716
V. Collective Responsibility Models 720
VI. Conclusion 722

Cláudia Elisabeth Pozzi
Self-Determination and State Intervention: A Balance for Protection of the Reserved Portion of the Estate in the 2002 Brazilian Civil Code in the Light of New Family Arrangements
I. Civil Law and Family in Modern Society 725
II. The Economic Protection of Families:
 The Non-Disposable Part of Patrimony 729
III. Conclusions 737

Odile Roy
Legal Protection of the Survivor of a Couple in French Family Law
I. Introduction 741
II. The Transmission of the Deceased's Possessions 743
III. The Home of the Survivor of the Couple: 746
IV. Conclusion 749

Andrea Fusaro
Legitimate Portion and other Techniques of Protection of Surviving Spouses and Children. A Comparison between Civil Law and Common Law Systems
I. Comparative Scholarship in the Area of Succession Law 751
II. Testamentary Freedom and its Possible Limitations. 752
III. Two Patterns of Protection Against Disinheritance:
 Fixed Share and Discretionary Maintenance 754
IV. Recent Developments. 756
V. Legal Transplants.. 758

Mireia Artigot-Golobardes and *Laura Alascio-Carrasco*
Family Business: The Need for a General Framework
I. Introduction 761
II. Fitting into Corporate Law:
 Corporate Challenges of Family Businesses 764
III. The Effect of Family Law on Family Businesses:
 A Difficult Overlap 768
IV. Organizing the Transfer and Future of the
 Family Business: The Effect of Inheritance Law on
 the Succession of Family Businesses 770

V.	How to Overcome Such Problems Faced by Family Businesses?	771
VI.	Conclusions	776

Roland Krause
The Planning of Succession in International Family Business. Recent Developments in Germany

I.	Challenges for Succession Planning	777
II.	Tools of Transmission	781
III.	Inheritance Tax reform of 2009	786
IV.	Conclusion	788

Bea Verschraegen
Fiddler on the Roof: On the Ambiguity of Family Finances – Concluding Lecture

I.	Who does What? Who gets What?	789
II.	Family solidarity	794
III.	Differentiation or Equalisation?	796
IV.	Marriage or Divorce: What is the greater Risk?	798
V.	Nothing but Costs!	799
VI.	Allocation of Risks and Resources	807
VII.	Modern Times or Postmodernism?	810
VIII.	Conclusions	815

Authors

- AGALLOPOULOU, Penelope; University of Piraeus, Greece.
- ALASCIO-CARRASCO, Laura; Universitat Pompeu Fabra, Barcelona, Spain.
- ALOFS, Elisabeth; Free University of Brussels / University of Antwerp, Belgium.
- ARTIGOT-GOLOBARDES, Mireia; Both at Universitat Pompeu Fabra, Barcelona, Spain.
- BAGAN-KURLUTA, Katarzyna; University of Bialystok, Poland.
- BEKKER, Jan C.; University of Pretoria, South Africa.
- BRÆKHUS, Hege; University of Tromsø, Norway.
- BRATTSTRÖM, Margareta; Associate Professor at Uppsala University, Faculty of Law, Sweden.
- BRIGGS, Margaret; Faculty of Law, University of Otago, New Zealand.
- CAMPBELL, Barbara; Campbell & Co. Lawyers, Canberra, Australia.
- CASABONA, Salvatore; Faculty of Political Science - Palermo, Italy.
- CURRY-SUMNER, Ian; UCERF, Molengraaff Institute for Private Law, Utrecht University, The Netherlands.
- DAVEL, Trynie; Professor and Head, Department of Private Law, University of Pretoria, South Africa.
- DETHLOFF, Nina; Bonn University, Germany.
- DRAŠKIĆ, Marija; School of Law, University of Belgrade, Serbia.
- DUCA, Rita; University of Palermo, Italy.
- EEKELAAR, John; Pembroke College Oxford, United Kingdom.
- ESTIN, Ann Laquer; University of Iowa College of Law, USA.
- FARRUGIA, Ruth; Advocate and Senior Lecturer, Faculty of Laws, University of Malta, Malta.
- FRANK, Rainer; Emeritus der Albert-Ludwigs-Universität Freiburg, Germany.
- FU, Yue; Research Assiciate, Graduate School of Humanities and Social Sciences, University of Tsukuba, Japan.
- FULCHIRON, Hugues; Université de Lyon, Professeur à l'Université Jean Moulin Lyon 3, Directeur du Centre de droit de la famille.
- FUSARO, Andrea; Professor of Comparative Legal Systems, Faculty of Law, Univ. Genova, Italy.
- GARCÍA CANTERO, Gabriel; Catedrático de Droit Civil, Émérite de l'Université de Zaragoza, Spain.

- Goubau, Dominique; Professor at Laval University, Quebec, Canada.
- Groeninga, Giselle Câmara; IBDFAM Brazilian Institue of Family Law, Brazil.
- Henaghan, Mark; Professor and Dean of Law, University of Otago, Dunedin, New Zealand.
- Hoop, Renaat; Free University of Brussels, Belgium.
- Insinga, Stefano; University of Palermo, Italy.
- Jeppesen de Boer, Christina G.; Utrecht University, The Netherlands.
- Kay, Roger; Storrar Cowdry Professor of Family Law, University of Chester, UK.
- Kőrös, András; Supreme Court of Hungary, Budapest.
- Kovaček-Stanić, Gordana; Faculty of Law, University of Novi Sad, Serbia.
- Králíčková, Zdeňka; Associate Professor at the Faculty of Law, Masaryk Univerzity, Brno, The Czech Republic.
- Kraljić, Suzana; Faculty of Law, University of Maribor, Slovenia.
- Krause, Roland; Lecturer, Dept. of Civil Law, Insurance Law and International Private Law, Freie Universität Berlin, Germany.
- Kronborg, Annette; Associate Professor, Copenhagen University, Denmark.
- Lifshitz, Shahar; Prof. Shahar Lifshitz, Professor, Bar-Ilan University; and Visiting Professor Cardozo Law School, New York.
- Lowe, Nigel; Professor of Law and Director of the Centre of International Family Law Studies, Cardiff Law School, Cardiff University, Wales, UK.
- Mandia, Ledina; State Attorney of Albania at the General State Attorney Office, Tirana; Pedagogue at the Law Faculty, University of Shkoder »Luigj Gurakuqi« (candidate of PhD), Albania.
- Nunes Correia, Paula; Faculty of Law, University of Macau, China.
- Parkinson, Patrick; Professor of Law, University of Sydney, Australia.
- Pote, Andrew; Chambers 13KBW, London and Oxford, United Kingdom.
- Pozzi, Cláudia Elisabeth; University of Coimbra, Portugal.
- Resetar, Branka; Faculty of Law Osijek, Croatia.
- Ribot, Jordi; Observatory of European and Comparative Private Law, University of Girona, Spain.
- Rijavec, Vesna; Faculty of Law, University of Maribor, Slovenia.

- Roy, Odile; Maître de Conférences en droit privé, Centre d'Etudes Juridiques Européennes et Comparées, Université Paris Ouest Nanterre La Défense, France.
- Sinclair, June; Honorary Professor of Law, University of Pretoria, South Africa.
- Singer, Anna; Associate Professor at Uppsala University, Faculty of Law, Sweden.
- Sook Choe, Keum; Professor of College of Law, Ewha University, South Korea.
- Spector, Robert G.; Professor of Law, University of Oklahoma Law Center, USA.
- Stępień-Sporek, Anna; University of Gdańsk, Poland.
- Sverdrup, Tone; Department of Private Law, University of Oslo, Norway.
- Távora Vítor, Paula; Family Law Center, Faculty of Law at the University of Coimbra, Portugal.
- Thorpe, Mathew; Head of International Family Justice for England & Wales and Lord Justice of Appeal.
- Tsuneoka, Fumiko; Professor of Law, Faculty of Law, Dokkyo University, Japan.
- van der Linde, Anton; University of Pretoria, South Africa.
- van der Linden, Adriaan P.; Utrecht University, The Netherlands.
- Verschraegen, Bea; Full Professor at the University of Vienna, Austria, and Bratislava, Slovakia.
- Vaz Tomé, Maria João Romão Carreiro; Portuguese Catholic University School of Law, Porto, Portugal.
- Wardle, Lynn D.; Professor of Law, Brigham Young University School of Law, Provo, USA.
- Willenbacher, Barbara; Faculty of Law, Leibniz University Hannover, Germany.

Preface

The 13th World Conference of the International Society of Family Law (ISFL) took place at the Federal Ministry of Justice in Vienna, September 16-20, 2008. The upcoming global crisis was taken as an occasion to deal with »Family Finances«. Approximately 180 participants from all over the world presented a paper. The »money issue« was also decisive when deciding how many and which contributions should be published. Therefore, a choice had to be made. It seemed important to take into account a widespread regional and thematic representation on the one hand, but also to limit the number of contributions deriving from countries that submitted numerous papers. This decision implied compromises. Thanks to Prof. *Lynn Wardle* the papers that unfortunately were not accepted for publication could be put on the homepage of the Brigham Young University (USA).

The publication of the contributions follows the schedule of the conference's program. Except for two contributions, which were written in French, all the papers are drawn up in English. The papers highlight different aspects of transfer of services, goods and financial contributions by the family members, of third parties to family members and of family members to third parties. Such transfers involve considerable transaction costs that may be questioned. Many papers demonstrate that the purpose which legal provisions or private agreements intend to achieve, might, at the end of the day, not be fulfilled. Not surprisingly, no consensus was reached regarding the question which risks should be considered as personal and/or social ones.

Many institutions and individuals supported me when I was organising this World Conference, which was held under the auspices of the Federal President of the Republic of Austria, Dr. *Heinz Fischer*. For sponsoring support I owe thanks to »Agrarmarkt Austria Marketing GesmbH«, the Federal Chamber of Labour of Vienna, to *J.-M. Bottequin*, to the Federal Ministry of Internal Affairs, the Federal Ministry of Justice, to »Österreichischer Rechtsanwaltskammertag«, to Erste Group Bank AG, the »Fachverband der österreichischen Standesbeamtinnen und Standesbeamten«, the Federation of Austrian Industrialists, Austrian Lawyers Association, Federal State Government of Lower Autria, Austrian Chamber of Notaries, the »Österreichische Nationalbank«, »Parlamentsklub der Österreichischen Volkspartei«, the Austrian Society of Attorneys, Verein der Freunde der Rechtswissenschaftlichen Fakultät and to the Austrian Federal Economic Chamber.

A report on the conference by *B. Kommenda* was published in the independent daily newspaper »Die Presse« on September 23, 2008, p. 12. The Mayor of the capital Vienna recently distinguished the convenor of the 13th World Conference of the ISFL as »successful conference convenor 2008 in Vienna«.

I owe special thanks to the Vienna Medical Academy, more precisely to Ms. *Claudia Schantl*, who was responsible for the administrative side of the conference organisation. And, among the persons who have been helping and supporting me during and after the conference, more particularly with the preparation of the publication of the conference book, Mag. *Ilse Koza* certainly deserves to be mentioned in the first place. I thank her in particular and my team in general. I also owe acknowledgments to the Scientific Council of the ISFL who supported me in the choice of the papers to be published.

Further, I would like to express my thanks to the publisher Mag. *Jan Sramek*, who assumed the task to publish this book with great care and distinction. I take it for granted that once the book is published he will feel as relieved as I will.

Finally, I hope that this book on »Family Finances« which virtually coincides with the global crisis will contribute to the understanding of multi-scalar dynamics of »Family Finances«.

Bea Verschraegen
Convenor

Part I – General Issues

Family Solidarity in Support and Inheritance Law[1]

Rainer Frank[2]

I. Thoughts on the Concept of »Family«

In speaking about »family finances«, we must first think for a moment about what »family« we are actually talking about and what priority rank this family – aside from all legal regulations – occupies in the cultural circles that practice family life.

The International Society of Family Law (ISFL) is the only world-wide society of family law. As Europeans or as those belonging to industrialized States, we therefore should not consider the theme of this conference solely from our own point of view. »Family« in China is, after all, something different from »family« in Saudi Arabia, Africa or in the USA. In the first part of my remarks, therefore, I will attempt to awaken an understanding for the fact that the theme »family finances« can only be discussed against the background of regionally defined societal i.e. family orders. Because I have lived in Asia for more than one year, it is easy for me to bring this continent into the discussion in the form of a model, Japan and Korea having long counted among the strongest groups in the ISFL in terms of numbers. Afterward, I will directly and concretely address some thoughts concerning solidarity in family law. In this regard, the laws relating to support and inheritance provide fruitful ground for comparison.

The concept of family implies the presence of children. In Nigeria the average woman brings 7.5 children into the world. Let us first be very clear about what this means: the average family in Nigeria includes, in addition to the parents, seven to eight children. In the Congo the birth rate is 6.5, in India 3 children per woman. Due to the problem of overpopulation, China is pursuing its so-called »one-child policy«. In actual practice the way this works is that each bride, at her wedding, is given a type of »child-bearing

---

1 This article was translated from the original German into English by Dr. A. Scott Loveless on the faculty of the J. Reuben Clark Law School, Brigham Young University, Provo, Utah, USA.
2 Emeritus der Albert-Ludwigs-Universität Freiburg, Germany.

permit«. When a pregnancy occurs the bride gives this permit to her doctor, who in this manner is informed whether the planned birth is legal. It is interesting that despite the threat of punitive measures in the one-child policy, the birth rate in China at 1.4 children per woman is higher than in Germany, where the current rate is 1.3 and where the State has undertaken all kinds of measures to raise the birth rate, including providing direct payments for additional children, either to the children or the parents, and other types of financial incentives. And by the way, China will likely have to deal with another rise in its birth rate in the near future: Because of the difficulty in taking care of the elderly, marriage partners who each come from a one-child family will in the future be permitted to have not just one child, but two. In a similar situation to that in China, India has undertaken great efforts including financial incentives to persuade young married couples to delay their desires for children by one year or more. Just by way of comparison: In the EU overall, the average current birth rate is 1.5 children.

Now let's just take a quick look at the meaning of marriage as a foundation for a family. In Europe we tend to be proud of the fact that people can organize their family lives in whatever manner they prefer. Anyone can, without having to fear any type of economic or social disadvantages, live together with a partner in a married or an unmarried association. Accordingly, the proportion of out-of-wedlock births in Sweden lies at more than 50%, in France and Great Britain more than 40%, and in Germany at about 25%. The situation is completely different in Asia, where marriage continues to provide the foundation for virtually every family. I am not speaking about the »Christian« marriage, but about performing whatever marriage is customary in the respective cultures and societies. Usually, this means a State-sanctioned marriage ceremony, however that may be practiced. In Japan, Korea and China, the proportion of out-of-wedlock births as a share of the total number of births clearly lies below 5% – as it was in Europe 50 years ago. And in these considerations, we should not forget the Muslims: With 1.3 billion people, they comprise approximately 20% of the world population. For them it also holds true that: »Marriage is the only way to bring families into existence.«[3] The fact that Islam allows polygamous marriages does not change this fact. We should also not lose sight of the fact that polygamous marriages in the lands of Islam have be-

---

3 Seyed Nasrollah Ebrahimi, Marriage Law of Iran under Islamic Perspectives, in: The International Survey of Family Law 2005, pp. 315, 321.

come the exception, and that polygamy from the perspective of Islam is still a better solution than a monogamous system in which adultery and unmarried cohabitation with multiple partners have become merely a private matter between the people involved.[4]

The speed with which societal value perceptions can change can be demonstrated by an example taken from the law of Germany: Art. 6 paragraph 1 of the Grundgesetz (GG or German Constitution) from the year 1949 places marriage and family under the special protection of State. In jurisprudence and legal instruction it was uncontested that the concept of »family« should be understood to mean only the married family. The developmental history of the Grundgesetz also permits no doubt that only the married family should be protected.[5] Despite these facts and subsequent to that text entering into force, the Bundesverfassungsgericht (BVerfG) (German Constitutional Court) has reinterpreted the unmodified text of the Constitution. Today it is simply outside the scope of serious discussion to suggest that Article 6 paragraph 1 of the German Constitution protects only married families and not the unmarried. The same is true for Article 8 paragraph 1 of the European Human Rights Convention (EHRC), where it states that everyone should have claim to respect for his private and family life. Today it is completely accepted that the concept »family life« is independent of the existence of a marriage. For all those who may not be familiar with the German Constitution or with the EHRC, you should understand, however, that anyone or any entity, such as the BVerfG or the European Court of Human Rights (ECHR) that decides in favor of an »open« concept of family subsequently has great difficulty in deciding who counts as part of a family and who does not. Do stepchildren, foster children, same-sex or opposite sex living partners belong to the family or not? What are the concrete requirements that qualify a given person as belonging to a family?

In view of the multitude of conceivable family models, I consider it an elementary and basic pre-condition for any discussion that we give respect to people who think differently than we do. Unfortunately, respect and tolerance all too often are given only lip service. For example, one female author writes about a much sought-for harmonization of family

---

4 See fn. 3, pp. 347, 349.
5 R. Frank, Die familienrechtliche Ordnung des Grundgesetzes (The Ordering of Family Law in the German Constitution), in: 40 Jahre Grundgesetz (Forty Years of the German Constitution), Freiburger Rechts-und Staatswissenschaftliche Abhandlungen (Freiburg Treatises on Law and Political Science), 1990, pp. 113, 121.

law in Europe as follows: »The principles of European family law should be progressive and possibly absorb the most modern solutions reached in various European countries.«[6] This sentence has little to do with tolerance. Who can tell me whether the »most modern solutions reached in various European countries« are correct or even the best? Is that which is rejected in other cultural circles false only because it does not correspond to the *Zeitgeist* of some modern, progressive European countries? Family law has always been a mirror of the societal reality, not the reverse. Besides, family law has cooperated in establishing the societal reality, at least at the periphery. I consider the sentence that the »principles of European family law« should be »modern« and »progressive« to be dangerous and of no service to the subject at hand. Personally, I clearly have more sympathy for my esteemed French colleague *Philippe Malaurie*, who expects from a jurist exemplary humility (»humilité«) and reservation.[7]

When we speak of family, another question must be asked that stands aside from all social science findings and aside from all concrete legal regulations, namely the question of what family life really means, what it means to belong to a family in a given culture. The individualism of the western world, which tends to divide the family into a profusion of individual claims against one another, often gives us a skewed perception of what the family means in other cultures. *Carbonnier*, the great French jurist and sociologist, speaks of a »pulvérisation du droit en droits subjectifs«[8] (an atomization of law into individual rights). An Asian – even today – would think differently: In China and Korea it is taken for granted that adult siblings will support one another financially, when need is great. I know from personal experience that many Asian students regularly receive monthly contributions from a brother or sister to enable them to study in Europe. The fact that children support or contribute to the support of their aged parents is an assumed part of the private care of the elderly. I often witnessed in Korea that an eldest son would take his sister into his household as long as she remained unmarried or was simply not in a position to support herself.

Permit me to clarify the typical Asian way of thinking with two examples: An English BBC correspondent who had lived in Hong Kong for 40

---

6   Antokolskaia, Family Values and the Harmonisation of Family Law, in: Maclean (ed.) Family Law and Family Values, 2005, pp. 259, 307.
7   L'humilité et le droit (Humililty and the Law), Répertoire Defrénois 2006, 703.
8   Droit et passion du droit sous la Vème République (Law and Passion under the Fifth Republic), 1966, p. 121.

years told me the following story: He had read an obituary in a Chinese newspaper. Because the correspondent knew the family of the deceased quite well, he examined with some interest the names of all those who had signed the obituary. He wondered about two names of persons of whose existence he had never heard during his time there. A friend of the family explained to him that these persons were not yet born. But when they would be born, they would carry the mentioned name and sorrow for the deceased.

A second example relates to Japan: Both Germany and Japan allow the adoption of adults. In Germany adults are adopted almost exclusively for reasons related to inheritance taxes. Through an adoption, the idea is to advance the person being adopted as a future heir into the advantageous inheritance tax class I. Because of the growing number of adult adoptions and the obvious danger of misuse, it is currently under consideration whether it would not be better to simply prohibit entirely the adoption of adult persons.[9] In Japan the number of adult adoptions is estimated at 60,000 annually,[10] an unbelievably high number. Varying from the German pattern, however, the adoption of adults in Japan is not done for financial considerations, but rather for the continuation of a family, often only in a more symbolic, spiritual sense. Aged parents who have no son or only one daughter (who belongs to the family of her husband after her marriage ceremony) seek a person in an artificial way who will later take the responsibility for tending their graves and for the care of their ancestors. In practice it is often the son-in-law who marries the only daughter – with the agreement of the parents-in-law – who is adopted. I do not wish to get into the details here, except that this example demonstrates the deep meaning of the family in Japan, even beyond death.

Now let's consider for a moment the sad picture of family law as depicted in the West even in the jurisprudential legal literature. One reads of the »right« of a woman living alone to a child, of the »right« of a same-sex couple to adopt a child, and of health insurance being required to assume the costs of artificial insemination. Children file complaints against their parents to finance their secondary education. In the famous American case of Troxel v. Granville[11] the question was whether recognition of a visitation right in the grandparents against the will of the parents

---

9 R. Frank, Rechtsprobleme der Erwachsenenadoption (Legal Problems in Adopting Adults), Das Standesamt (StAZ) 2008, 65.
10 For this information I thank Prof. Fumio Tokotani, University of Osaka.
11 530 U.S. 57 (2000).

compromised the parents' Constitutionally guaranteed right to raise their children as they wish. In Germany, many courts, including the German Constitutional Court (BVerfG), have had to deal with the reverse situation, whether the child has a right to be visited by its father.[12] The mother of an infant demands that the father who pays child support for the child but otherwise shows no interest in the child be required to visit the child at regular intervals in the presence of a psychologist. The so-called »right to know of one's heritage« is developing a number of odd branches in Germany. Thus, at the direction of the German Constitutional Court a 60-year-old mother was ordered to provide her 40-year-old daughter with the name of her father.[13] The bulk of authority holds that a decision of this kind can be enforced with monetary penalties and incarceration.[14] More recently German courts have also had to deal with cases in which parents refuse to give their child a first name or in which the parents disagree about which first name or surname a child should receive.

The increasing degree to which marriage and family issues are being reduced to matters of »legal rights« carries the germ of societal destruction. We all feel this. »Family«, in its essence, exists independent of law.[15]

I would now like to delve concretely into a few of the problems relating to the theme of our conference, »Family Finances«. In an industrial society, more than in other types, the survival of the family depends on conditions over which the family members have no influence, such as the care of the elderly, the protection given to motherhood, tax breaks, direct subsidies such as Kindergeld (government payments for having children), the availability of kindergartens, etc. Due to differences in national assumptions, family policy is not well suited for drawing comparisons in the opening session of this World Congress. I have therefore decided to limit my subsequent remarks to a few points related to private legal relationships among family members, specifically those relating to the right to support and inheritance rights.

---

12 BVerfG Zeitschrift für das gesamte Familienrecht (FamRZ) 2008, 845 with notes Luthin; OLG Stuttgart FamRZ 2006, 1060; OLG Nürnberg FamRZ 2007, 925.
13 BVerfG FamRZ 1997, 869 with discussion Frank/Helms FamRZ 1997, 1258; LG Münster Neue Juristische Wochenschrift (NJW) 1999, 726; LG Bremen NJW 1999, 729.
14 See, e.g. OLG Bremen Der Amtsvornumd (DAVorm) 1999, 722.
15 Schwab, Konkurs der Familie?(The Bankruptcy of the Family?), 1994, p. 40.

II. The Right to Support

The realities of family life in the industrial states of the European Union and North America differ only in insignificant ways. It is surprising that despite these similarities in family life, the legal regulations relating to the support of close relatives do vary quite widely.

1. Parents' Duty of Support

Let's begin with the parents' duty of support. It is of course recognized worldwide that parents are obligated to provide support for their minority-aged children. But how do things stand with respect to children who have reached the age of majority? In North America,[16] England,[17] as well as in the Scandinavian countries of Denmark, Norway and Sweden[18] the basic rule is that the duty of support ends as soon as a child reaches the age of majority, i.e. has completed the 18th year of life. It is true that the harshness of this basic rule is often softened if a course of education with which the parents agreed cannot be completed until after the age of majority is attained,[19] or when other conditions exist that appear to justify a short extension of the claim for support in an individual case.[20] Some States also set absolute upper limits, as in Denmark, where § 14 of the Child Support Law of April 1, 2002, provides that the parents may in special circumstances be required to contribute to the education of their children if the children have not yet completed their 24th year of life. But it should be well noted: »Education« in this context is something other than

---

16   Krause/Elrod/Garrison/Oldham, Family Law, 5th ed. 2003, p. 880; Krause/Meyer, Family Law, 3rd ed. 2004, p. 189.
17   Eekelaar, Family Solidarity in English Law, in: Familiäre Solidarität – Die Begründung und die Grenzen der Unterhaltspflicht unter Verwandten im europäischen Vergleich (Family Solidarity – Comparing European Approaches to the Foundation and Limits of the Duty of Support among Relatives), (Pub. Schwab/Henrich), 1997, pp. 63, 70; Lowe/Douglas, Bromley's Family Law, 10th ed. 2007, p. 967.
18   Agell, Die Begründung und die Grenzen der Unterhaltspflicht unter Verwandten in Schweden (The Foundation and Limits of the Laws on Support of Relatives in Sweden), in: Familiäre Solidarität (Family Solidarity) (see fn. 17), p. 162; Denmark: § 14 Child Support Law of July 1, 2002; Norway: § 68 Law Relating to Parents and Children of April 8, 1981; Sweden: Chapter 7 § 1 para. 2 Law of Parenting.
19   For England, e.g. Lowe/Douglas (fn. 17), p. 968; for USA *e.g.* Krause/Elrod/Garrison/Oldham (fn. 16), p. 880; for Norway § 68 Law Relating to Parents and Children; for Sweden Chapter 7 § 1 para. 2 Parenting Law; for Denmark § 14 Child Support Law.
20   For England, *compare* Lowe/Douglas (fn.17), p. 968 (»special circumstances«); for USA *compare* Krause/Meyer (fn. 16), p. 189 (»under certain circumstances costs of higher education«).

an expensive university course of study. Neither in the USA nor in England, nor in the Scandinavian States can an adult son or daughter demand the cost of a university education from the parents.[21] Parents in these countries also do not carry the risk of securing the employment or health costs of their grown children.

The legal situation is completely different in the rest of Central Europe and in the formerly socialist countries: In these countries the parents' duty to support also includes a university education, given appropriate inclination and capability in the child. In addition, after the conclusion of the education the parents are also obligated to provide support to their children if the children are not able to pursue work due to special circumstances, or if they lose their employment or fall into economic need due to illness. The fact that the national social security system can be called upon to remove some of this economic burden from the parents in such cases is a separate question. The private duty to support represents a type of catch basin for all cases where the social security system fails or develops holes.

To clarify this legal situation, allow me to reference a recent decision of a German court:[22]

A 20-year-old gymnast who had become estranged from his parents filed suit and obtained a ruling obligating his parents to pay for an apartment near his school. Each month, the parents transmitted to the son the sum set by the court to defray the son's support expenses. A short time later, the son withdrew from the school without informing his parents. The parents did not learn of this until six months later and then stopped making the payments. During the next three years the son did not pursue any type of employment. During this time, he passed his 24th birthday and successfully pursued a suit against his parents for the financing of an occupational education suitable to his inclinations and talents. The court ruled that the parents were obligated to make the desired education possible, despite their son's unstable personality structure.

---

21   Hay, US-Amerikanisches Recht (US American Law), 3rd ed. 2005, p. 154 (»The parents are not required to carry the expense of an often very expensive university course of study.«); Agell (fn. 18), p. 164 (»Under no circumstances is it the duty of the parents – even when they are peak earners – to underwrite the higher education of the child.«).
22   OLG Köln (Cologne) April 20, 2004, FamRZ 2005, 301 (case easily modified); on the basic problems of support for adult children, see Isabell Götz, Unterhalt für volljährige Kinder, Überlegungen zu einer Reform des Verwandtenunterhalts (Support of Adult Children: Considerations Toward a Reform of the Law of Support of Relatives), 2007.

2. The Child's Duty of Support

Now we come to the claim for support of parents by their adult children. The Scandinavian countries do not recognize this type of claim for support.[23] The same is true for England.[24] In the USA there are a number of individual states that recognize a duty of support from children for needy parents; but these regulations are essentially irrelevant in practice:[25] »Filial responsibility laws had never been invoked.«[26] In contrast, such support claims in the rest of Central Europe,[27] as well as in the Russian Federation,[28] Poland,[29] the Czech Republic[30] and Hungary,[31] have a long tradition, just as in most countries the duty of support from the younger generation toward the elderly is considered obvious and is often taken as an elementary component of the system for the security of the elderly, as in most Asian countries.

Those countries that have recognized a duty of support in children in favor of their parents, however, are confronted with an often hotly-contested problem: Elderly parents – particularly in the industrialized countries – often reside in expensive elder-care facilities which they cannot afford on their modest retirement incomes. Children between the ages of 50 and 60 thus bear not only a support obligation to their own parents, but also to their own children who are just completing an expensive course of university study. People in Germany speak of the »sandwich-position« of the generation of people in their 50's and 60's, because they often bear the duty of support in two directions. The decisive question here is which concrete support requirements can be charged to the grown sons and daughters for their parents. In Germany the case law has developed principles for a so-called »priority of self-support« in the duty-of-support bearers without any clear legislative direction to do so, and have also clarified that the sale of personally used grounds and personally occupied residences cannot be levied against to fulfill the duty of support.[32] In Germany as in other

---

23 In Denmark, Norway and Sweden there is no legal regulation of this issue in any form. For Sweden, see Agell (fn. 18), p. 165.
24 Eekelaar (fn. 17), p. 76.
25 Overview by Hauss, Elternunterhalt: Grundlagen und Strategien (Support of Parents: Foundations and Strategies), 2nd ed. 2007, p. 212.
26 Krause/Elrod/Garrison/Oldham (fn. 16), p. 885.
27 *E.g.* in Germany, Austria, Switzerland, France, Italy, Spain, the Netherlands.
28 Art. 87 Family Law Code (Rus).
29 Art. 128 Family Law and Guardianship Code (Pol).
30 § 87 Family Law (Cz).
31 § 61 Law on Marriage, the Family and Guardianship (Hung).
32 BGH (Highest German Civil Court) FamRZ 2006, 26 and FamRZ 2006, 1099 (priority of

industrialized States, the relationship between the private duty of support and public social assistance remains unresolved. A person finding himself in a financial emergency can, in Germany, attempt to obtain assistance in two ways: He can file suit against his own children for support payments or demand social assistance from the State. Because social assistance is given on a fundamentally subsidiary basis, the State may seek reimbursement from relatives who bear a duty of support. Whether the State attempts to secure reimbursement, however, is largely a matter of discretion. Since January 1, 2003, the agencies that provide social assistance no longer seek reimbursement from children bearing a duty of support if their personal annual income is less than €100,000.[33] However, there remains one unclear curiosity: Parents who make claims for payments against their children receive such support, even when the income of those children lies below the limit of €100,000 per year. But if the parents claim social assistance, then the children are spared from State actions for reimbursement as long as the annual income remains below the €100,000 limit.

3. The Grandparent's Duty of Support

Now let's discuss the duty of support of grandparents to their grandchildren and vice versa. States that fundamentally recognize no duty of support of parents toward their grown children and also deny the reverse duty of support owed by adult children toward their parents, also tend, obviously, to recognize no duty of support between grandparents and grandchildren. The other countries, which today comprise the great majority worldwide, also affirm a duty of support between grandparents and grandchildren.[34] It is generally true that in most industrialized States reimbursement claims by social assistance providers against duty-bearing grandparents or grandchildren are precluded, so that the problem has little practical relevance.[35] But private claims for support against grandparents are in no way meaningless, as demonstrated by the so-called supplemental liability of grandparents under German law. Not long ago the highest German Civil Court (BGH)[36] was required to make a decision in the following case:

---

    self-support); BGH FamRZ 2002, 1698 (personally used immovable assets).

33   The regulation that entered into force on Jan. 1, 2003, (Grundsicherungsgesetz) (Basic Security Law) of June 26, 2001) was recodified as of Jan. 1, 2005 to § 43 Sec. 2 Sozialgesetzbuch (Social Insurance Code) XII.

34   *E.g.*, in Germany, Austria, Switzerland, France, Italy, Spain, and also Poland, Russia, the Czech Republic, the Peoples' Republic of China, Japan, and Korea.

35   It is so, *e.g.* in Germany (discussed in detail in Hauss [fn. 25] p. 344).

36   FamRZ 2004, 800 with notes Luthin.

The son of a well-to-do married couple refused to pursue employment. He had a relationship with a married woman, from which a child was produced. The husband of the mother believed for a long time that he himself was the biological father of the child, until he learned 10 years later that the child did not come from him. He then successfully resisted the responsibilities of fatherhood and sought reimbursement from the unemployed son for 10 years of provided support, which is possible under German law. The sum in question was €50,000. Because the son was unable to pay the demanded sum, the husband of the child's mother successfully filed suit against the grandfather for payment. The Germans have a folk saying for cases of this type: »Wenn Papa nicht kann, ist Opa dran.« (»If papa cannot, then grandpa's on the spot.«)

4. Duty of Support Between Siblings

Finally, let's add a word about the duty of support between siblings. Most of those present here are probably of the opinion that in today's world there is no longer any room for a duty of support between siblings. Such a statement would likely not raise a challenge. And it is true that the USA, Canada, England, the Scandinavian countries as well as Austria, Switzerland, Germany and France reject the idea of a duty of support between siblings. But this type of duty still exists in the European States in which the family is still afforded an especially high position of respect, such as, for example, in Italy,[37] Spain,[38] Greece,[39] Portugal[40] and Turkey.[41] But there is also an entire group of formerly socialistic countries, such as the Russian Federation[42] or Poland,[43] that require a duty of support as between siblings, and this is also the case in Asia, for example in the People's Republic of China,[44] Japan,[45] and Korea.[46]

Even if the duty of support based on relational solidarity is implemented differently in individual countries, there is one line of thought which

---

37 Art. 433 Codice civile (Civil Code) (It.).
38 Art. 143 Código Civil (Civil Code) (Sp.).
39 Art. 1504 Civil Code (Grc.).
40 Art. 2009 Código Civil (Civil Code) (Port.).
41 Art. 364 Civil Code (Turk.).
42 Art. 93 Civil Code on Family Law (Rus.).
43 Art 128 Civil Code on Family and Guardianship Laws (Pol.).
44 Bergmann/Ferid, Internationales Ehe- und Kindschaftsrecht (International Law on Marriage and Childhood), under: Volksrepublik China (People's Republic of China), p. 98.
45 Art. 877 Civil Code (Jpn.).
46 Art. 974 Civil Code (Kor.) (if they live together in a common household).

many of us might find agreeable and which has been very well expressed by the Swiss Civil Code. The Swiss Civil Code distinguishes between a duty of support on the one hand and a duty to assist relatives on the other hand.[47] Parents bear a duty of support toward their under-aged children. This duty of support is – as Hegnauer phrases it – »one-sided, all-inclusive, and unconditional«.[48] Parents and children share in the same needs. In contrast, the duty of support toward relatives is a variable that depends very strongly on concrete living conditions. Adults provide help to family members when they require assistance in an emergency situation. The person in need has just as little claim to being guaranteed his former standard of living as the person bearing the duty of support is obligated to lower his own standard of living in order to provide the assistance required. In addition, the behavioral quality of the participants between or among themselves plays a not inconsequential roll here. Parents who fall into need, for example, have no claim on their children if they themselves neglected their children in earlier years. In the final analysis, the question of the extent to which relatives are considered responsible for one another (relational solidarity) in the given society will always be dispositive.

If we look for a moment at the average household size in industrialized States, we might easily arrive at the conclusion that relational solidarity will play a steadily decreasing roll in the future. The average household size in the industrialized States of Europe, North America and Asia today lies between 2.5 and 3 persons, whereas 50 years ago it lay between 3.5 and 4 persons. In the EU countries in 1960 only 15% of households consisted of just one person, whereas in 1980 that number had risen to 30%[49] and is now projected to reach 35–40%[50] by the year 2025.

---

47 *Compare* Art. 276 et seq. (»Die Unterhaltspflicht der Eltern) (»The Duty of Support Owed by Parents«) and Art. 328 *et seq.* (»Die Unterstützungspflicht«) (»The Duty of Assistance«).
48 Hegnauer, Familiäre Solidarität – Begründung und Grenzen der Unterhaltspflicht unter Verwandten im schweizerischen Recht (Family Solidarity – Basis and Limits of the Duty of Support among Relatives in Swiss Law) in: Familiäre Solidarität (Family Solidarity) (fn. 17) pp. 162, 186.
49 In the EU the average number of persons in a household in the year 1960 was 3.3, in 1980, 2.8 and in 2003 2.5 (Eurostat, Quick Statistics, Subject 3-24/2003 p. 2).
50 *Compare* Eurostat (fn. 49), p. 3.

5. Duty of Support Based on de Facto Family Relationships

Let me add one final word on the duty of support owed by persons who are connected with the person in need not by blood relationship, but by de facto relationships that are in some way similar to a family. There have been many attempts in recent years to derive a legally recognized responsibility to provide support from existing relationships that are similar to families. To this point, however, these attempts have not been generally successful. I recall in this regard the »in loco parentis doctrine«[51] and the concept of »equitable adoption«[52] in US-American law, and the duty of support owed under English law by one who had treated a child as a »child of the family«.[53] Some countries also provide a legally recognized duty of support toward step-children,[54] just as Russia recognizes, vice-versa, a duty of support of step-children toward their step-father or step-mother in cases where the step-parent provided care for the step-child as one of their own during its minority years.[55] We should also recall the attempts to derive claims of duty from the mere existence of a long-term non-marital cohabitation.[56] Without formal structures it becomes apparent, world-wide, that family law cannot work. The keys to family law are and will always be blood relationship on the one hand and marriage on the other. This is true in terms of the duty of support and also in the law of inheritance.

III. Inheritance Law

1. Inheritance Right of the Surviving Spouse

Now let's turn to inheritance law. One of the noteworthy things in this field of late is that the inheritance position of the surviving spouse has recently been substantially improved in the industrialized States, which simulta-

---

51 *Compare* Black's law Dictionary, 6th ed. 1990, under: In loco parentis.
52 *Compare* Krause/Elrod/Garrison/Oldham (fn. 16), p. 329.
53 *Compare* Lowe/Douglas (fn. 17), p. 338.
54 *E.g.*, the Netherlands (Art. 404 sec. 2 Civil Code); at present also the USA (see Engel, Stepfamily Tribulations under United States Laws and Social Policies, in: The International Survey of Family Law, 2005, p. 529; for Switzerland *see* Hegnauer, Der Unterhalt des Stiefkindes nach schweizerischem Recht (The Support of the Step-Child under Swiss Law), in: Festschrift W. Müller-Freienfels, 1986, p. 271.
55 *See* Art. 97 of the Russian Civil Code on Family Law and Art. 127 sec. 2 of the Slovenian Law of Marriage and Family Relationships.
56 *Compare* Antokolskaia, Harmonisation of Family Law in Europe: A Historical Perspective, 2006, p. 383.

neously means that the inheritance right of other relatives, especially children and grandchildren has become correspondingly worse. The reason for this development is obvious: In the modern industrial society, children usually have long since established their independent existence by the time their father or mother passes away, while the surviving spouse is usually dependent on the inheritance if he or she does not wish to endanger the previously enjoyed standard of living.

Thus, in Germany[57] today and in Switzerland[58] the surviving spouse and descendants receive half of the estate, in Austria[59] one third. In the Romance legal orders, i.e. in France, Belgium, Italy and Spain, the long-established law was that the surviving spouse received no part of the principle of the estate at all, but rather only a life estate in, a right to use, the principle of the estate. This has fundamentally changed. Since a 2001 reform in France,[60] as in Italy,[61] the surviving spouse receives half of the estate if there is one surviving child, one third if there are two or more surviving children.

The new inheritance law of the Netherlands,[62] which entered into force on January 1, 2003, has attracted international attention. According to this law, the surviving spouse becomes the sole heir, even when the deceased has left children behind. The children do receive a monetary claim, but this claim does not vest immediately. It vests only when certain events specified in the law transpire, particularly when the surviving spouse remarries. In a normal case, the surviving spouse in the Netherlands is not subjected to any kind of financial burden after the death of the decedent, enabling him or her to maintain the former standard of living unimpaired.

From an inheritance perspective, the surviving spouse in England[63] is also very well provided for. He or she receives apart from the children a »residuary interest« in the sum of £ 125,000, which in fact often means

---

57 §§ 1931 secs. 1 and 3, 1371 sec. 1 German Civil Code.
58 Art. 462 No. 1 Schweizerisches Zivilgesetzbuch (Civil Code) (Switz.).
59 § 757 Sec. 1 Allgemeines Bürgerliches Gesetzbuch (Civil Code) (Au.).
60 Art. 757 Code civil (Civil Code) (Fr.).
61 Art. 581 Codice civile (Civil Code) (It.).
62 Van Maas de Bie, Erbrecht in den Niederlanden (Inheritance Law in the Netherlands), in Süss/Haas (Pub.), Erbrecht in Europa (Inheritance Law in Europe), 2004, p. 665; Sumner/Forder, The Netherlands, in: The International Survey of Family Law, 2004, pp. 337, 361; Pintens, Pflichtteilsrecht in Belgien und in den Niederlanden (Mandatory Inheritance Shares in Belgium and in the Netherlands), in: Röthel (Pub.), Reformfragen des Pflichtteilsrechts (Reform Questions in the Law of Mandatory Inheritance Shares), 2007, p. 215.
63 Lowe/Douglas (fn. 17), p. 157.

that the surviving spouse is the sole heir. He or she also receives the personal possessions of the decedent as well as household objects (»personal chattels«), and a right of use of half of the estate (»life interest«). Finally, the Intestates' Estates Act of 1952 contains protective provisions which assure that the surviving spouse may continue to use the »family home«, at least for a transition period.

However, the inheritance right is not the only material issue pertaining to provision for the surviving spouse – the right to the goods of the marriage is also significant. Both in continental Europe and in Asia, as well as in part of the Anglo-American legal realm, a condition of property known as »community-acquired property« has become commonplace. This condition of property means that the accumulated wealth of both husband and wife during the marriage is divided in half. Thus, during her husband's life the housewife participates in the husband's accumulation of wealth, so that her inheritance right at the death of the husband becomes a type of »gravy«, i.e. an additional, second source of provision. The interplay of marriage goods and inheritance right can be demonstrated by considering US American law: In the USA there are so-called »common law states«, like New York, in which the division of goods is established by law, and so-called »community-property states«, like California, in which the wealth obtained during the marriage belongs jointly to both spouses. If one compares the situation of a surviving spouse in a common law State with one in a community-property State, it is soon apparent that the inheritance provisions are clearly better where the spouses have lived with separate property, because in those jurisdictions there is no protection of any kind for the partner in any legal goods, whereas the inheritance-based provisions in community-property States are less significant, simply because the surviving spouse is already substantially provided for on the basis of already-owned legal goods.[64]

But let's keep one thing firmly in mind: Without considering the various mechanisms for provision, the surviving spouse today – and worldwide – is substantially better protected after the death of the partner than was the case 50 years ago.

2. Inheritance Rights of the Non-Married Life Companion

The foregoing raises the question of the inheritance status of the unmarried life companion, i.e. the person whom the decedent could have mar-

---

64   *Compare* Hay (fn. 21), p. 157.

ried but – for whatever reasons – did not marry. With respect to the lively discussion concerning the legal treatment of unmarried living arrangements in the western world, it is perhaps surprising that in Europe, even there where more than 50 % of all children are born outside of marriage, as in for example Sweden and Estonia, the unmarried life companion enjoys no inheritance protection whatsoever. France, too, with 40 % unmarried births and Germany with 25 % ignore inheritance provisions for living arrangements that are only similar to marriage. One reason for this lies in the fact that it is quite easy to determine whether a person is married, but it is difficult to determine whether they live in a relationship »similar to marriage«. Countries that provide a legal inheritance right for simple life companions, such as some of the States of the former Yugoslavia or some provinces in Canada, therefore attempt to provide formal definitions to living arrangements similar to marriage by emphasizing a specific qualifying duration of living together before the rights apply (three years, five years, ten years) or by employing another factor such as the presence of jointly-produced children.[65] An additional reason why most States avoid normalizing a living arrangement similar to marriage by providing a legal inheritance right for the surviving partner lies in the consideration of the fact that it is always possible for the participants to make a will in favor of their life partner while they are still alive. They can decide for themselves how the quality of their non-marital relationship should translate into an inheritance.

3. Relational Inheritance Law

Now we turn to the legal inheritance rights of relatives. Historically speaking, for a long period of time the inheritance succession rights of relatives was not limited by any prescribed proximity of relationship. Legal heirs could be someone with whom the decedent was only distantly related and who had never even heard of his existence. The system of unlimited inheritance succession of relatives is today still valid in the USA and in Germany, but worldwide this system is becoming an ever shrinking

---

[65] *E.g.*, Kosovo (Art. 28 of the Inheritance Law: 10-year period of living together or five years with the presence of a jointly produced child). For Canada, *see* Alberta (Ferid/Firsching, Internationales Erbrecht (International Inheritance Law), line 25: 3-year period of living together, abbreviation possible with the presence of jointly produced children), British Columbia (Ferid/Firsching, line 17: 2-year period of living together), Manitoba (Ferid/Firsching, line 33: 1- to 3-year period of living together, depending on the specific question).

exception. Despite many differences, in most legal systems the circle of those who can be recognized as legal heirs with the force of law is limited to the direct posterity of the decedent, the parents and grandparents of the decedent and their direct posterity. With certain limitations this is true for Austria[66] and Switzerland[67] as well as for England,[68] the Scandinavian States,[69] Eastern Europe,[70] China,[71] Japan,[72] and Korea.[73] If there is no legal heir, the estate falls (»escheats«) to the State.

It is characteristic in the legal ranking of heirs that the laws formally distinguish ranks according to the proximity of relationship between the decedent and those recognized in the inheritance succession ranks. The quality of human relationships matters just as little as do the concrete living conditions of the heirs. If the decedent leaves behind three children, then each child inherits one-third without regard to whether he or she is rich or poor, regardless of whether the heir made personal sacrifices to take care of the decedent or was guilty of neglect. The formal strictness in the distribution of the estate does not necessarily correspond to the spirit of our time, which tends to recognize individual worthiness or uprightness. In examining the situation more carefully we do find more recently that many legal systems have incorporated compromise solutions to »dull the sharp edges« of the principle of formal strictness through weighted material elements. Thus, for example, German[74] and Swiss[75] law provide that the performance of care by a child to the decedent will later be honored by an increased share of the estate. There are now pending in Germany amendments to the German inheritance law that envision specific clarification as to the hourly reward at which the performance of care should be compensated.[76] Where the English Inheritance Act[77] contains

---

66 *See* §§ 731 *et seq.* Austrian Civil Code (according to § 741 the great-grandparents of the decedent are also included in the fourth rank of heirs.)
67 Art. 457 *et seq.* Schweizerisches Zivilgesetzbuch (Civil Code) (Switz.).
68 Administration of Estates Act of 1925, sec. 46.
69 Norway: §§ 1 *et seq.* Inheritance Law; Sweden: Chapter 2, §§ 1 *et seq.* Inheritance Law.
70 Russia: Art. 1142 Russian Civil Code; Czech Republic: §§ 473 Czech Civil Code.
71 Art. 10 Chinese Civil Code on Inheritance Law.
72 §§ 887, 889 Civil Code (Jpn.).
73 Art. 1000 Civil Code (Kor.).
74 § 2057a Sec. 1 Bürgerliches Gesetzbuch (Civil Code) (Ger.).
75 Art. 334, 334 bis Zivilgesetzbuch (Civil Code) (Switz.).
76 § 2057b sec. 2 of the draft (printed in ZErb 2008, 69) reads: »The amount of the compensation will generally be measured according to the amount provided in § 36 sec. 3 of the Elften Buches Sozialgesetzbuch (eleventh Book of the Social Insurance Code) measured at the time the care was provided.«
77 Inheritance (Provision for Family and Dependants) Act 1975.

legal protections in favor of persons whom the decedent has treated as his or her own children, we must see this simply as at attempt to replace formal criteria with material ones. The same is true in legal systems which recognize a support claim against the estate[78] for certain needy persons, particularly the spouse, because here the estate distribution depends on an economic situation of need and not simply on the simple existence of a marriage. Some legal systems establish differences in the specification of inheritance shares depending on whether a child is still in need of an occupational education.[79] In the final analysis, we should note that the attempt to include the unmarried life companion in the estate is nothing other than an effort to replace the formal criterion of the existence of a marriage with a material one, namely the lived partner relationship. One need not be a prophet in order to prognosticate that the historic, mature, formal, specific, legal inheritance succession pattern will in the future be incrementally supplemented and changed with material criteria.

4. Right to a Forced or Mandatory Share

It is contested – particularly in industrialized States – whether certain near relatives, especially the spouse, the descendants and the parents, should have a legal guarantee of a certain share of the estate if the decedent does not wish it. The existence of a so-called »right to a mandatory share« is contested because we remain to a degree uncertain about how to reconcile the principle of testamentary freedom with the principle of the responsibility of the deceased for his next of kin. Globally, there is a wide divergence of views. The Anglo-American common law[80] does not recognize a right to a mandatory share in favor of near kin any more than does the Peoples' Republic of China.[81] It is true that in England the spouse of the deceased, his children and those persons whom the decedent has treated as children can raise a claim for so-called »family provisions«, if

---

78 *E.g.*, France: Art. 767 Civil Code; Israel (Ferid/Firsching, Internationales Erbrecht, Grundzüge (International Inheritance Law, Essential Elements), line 155 *et seq.*; Austria: § 796 Civil Code.
79 Czech Republic: § 479 Civil Code.
80 Oxford Principles of English Law, English Private Law, 2nd ed. 2007, under 7.213: »Until 1938 there was almost total testamentary freedom in England and Wales.«
81 A protective provision that is similar to a compulsory share is contained, however, in Art. 19 of the Inheritance Law of the Peoples' Republic of China: »The testament must reserve a necessary portion of the estate for heirs incapable of work and without a basis for existence.«

in the will no »reasonable financial provisions« are provided for them.[82] It is also true that in the USA those individual states in which the separate goods standard is applicable as between spouses, protective provisions in favor of the surviving spouse are provided.[83] But this does not change the fact that, for example, adult sons or daughters with their own income have no legal claim to participate in the estate of their parents, either in England or in the USA, as they would in Austria, Switzerland, Germany or France.

But there is one additional problem: It was mentioned earlier that in the last 50 years the inheritance right of the surviving spouse has been strengthened worldwide. That is correct if one considers only the legal succession rankings for inheritance. That is however not true if we consider, not the legal succession ranking for inheritance, but rather examine the right to a mandatory share of the estate more closely. In many European States lawmakers even today are attempting to prevent family fortunes from flowing away into the bloodlines of another family against the will of the decedent. But that would be the case if the surviving spouse always and without exception were entitled to an absolute right to the substance of the estate and were to later remarry or leave behind children who do not descend from the decedent. For this reason the surviving spouse and children have no right to a mandatory share of the estate either in France,[84] the Netherlands,[85] Sweden[86] or the Czech Republic.[87] This does not mean that the surviving spouse is without any protection after the death of his or her partner; for in most legal systems the surviving spouse is protected by the right to married goods or has a right to continue to use the marital home or a share of the estate. But it is still astonishing that in States with the same legal traditions, the solutions to this issue diverge so significantly. In Norway, for example, the surviving spouse has

---

82 Details in Lowe/Douglas (fn. 17) p. 1105.
83 *See* Hay (fn. 21) p. 160 with evidence.
84 Art. 914-1 Civil Code (Fr.); *compare* Döbereiner, Erbrecht in Frankreich (Inheritance Law in France), in: Süss/Haas (Pub.), Erbrecht in Europa (Inheritance Law in Europe), 2004, pp. 380, 412.
85 Pintens (fn. 62) p. 219; van Maas de Bie (fn. 62) p. 689.
86 Lødrup, Pflichtteilsrecht in Norwegen und in den nordischen Staaten (Right to Mandatory Estate Share in Norway and in the Scandinavian States), in: Röthel (Pub.), Reformfragen des Pflichtteilsrechts (Reform Questions in the Right to a Mandatory Estate Share), 2007, pp. 235, 239.
87 Rombach, Erbrecht in Tschechien (Inheritance Law in the Czech Republic), in: Süss/Haas (Pub.), Erbrecht in Europa (Inheritance Law in Europe), 2004, pp. 1027, 1043.

a right to a mandatory or »forced« share of the estate, but not in Sweden.[88] In Italy[89] the surviving spouse is entitled to a share of the substance of the estate even against the will of the decedent, but not in France.[90] There can be no talk of the often-heralded European *jus commune*, at least not on the question of a right to a mandatory share of an inheritance estate.

There is also no agreement as to the circumstances that might justify a right to a mandatory estate share in favor of the spouse, children or parents. To the extent that a legal system even recognizes claims to mandatory shares, they are overwhelmingly limited to a specific quota share, generally half of the legal established inheritance share. But there are also other solutions which distinguish between whether a child entitled to a mandatory share is still a minor or has attained the age of majority.[91] In Russia, family members are only entitled to a mandatory estate share if they are incapable of working.[92] There are also many different views on the question of whether a person nominally entitled to a mandatory share can lose his or her claim to that share by specific misbehavior. Most legal systems limit misbehavior relevant to the mandatory share to a few specific, hopefully seldom-occurring cases, such as attempted murder or serious physical abuse of the decedent, falsifying of the will, and similar matters. But there are legal systems that provide for withdrawing the mandatory share if the nominally entitled person »has seriously failed in the duties owed to the decedent« (Switzerland)[93] or »habitually leads an immoral life« (Czech Republic).[94] According to § 773 a sec. 1 of the Austrian Civil Code, the decedent can even reduce the mandatory share by half if the decedent and the person nominally entitled to that share »at no time have stood in a close relationship, as conventionally exists in a family between such relatives.« In Serbia and in Kosovo until recently, a person was considered unworthy of a mandatory estate share if he avoided military service.[95]

For a person interested in comparative law, it is a joy to note that there are still areas of the law, such as the right to a mandatory estate share, in

---

88 Lødrup (fn. 86) p. 239.
89 Art. 540 *et seq.* Codice civile (Civil Code) (It.).
90 *See* fn. 84.
91 Czech Republic: § 479 Civil Code.
92 Art. 1128 Civil Code (Rus.).
93 Art. 477 No. 2 Schweizerisches Zivilgesetzbuch (Civil Code) (Switz.).
94 § 469a sec. 1 Civil Code (Cz.).
95 Pürner, Neues Erbgesetz im Kosovo (The New Inheritance Law of Kosovo), Zeitschrift für die Steuer- und Erbrechtspraxis (ZErb) 2007, pp. 159, 161.

which the worldwide solutions to the problem diverge significantly. Despite this, any conclusion drawn from these differences relating to the intensity of lived family relationships in the respective legal systems would be dubious at best. With great caution, however, one can confirm the following: The legal inheritance right of a surviving spouse in the industrialized States has been strengthened worldwide. The inheritance rankings of other relatives building on the formal blood relationship is being supplemented and corrected by material elements, in that care performed by children is honored or in that handicapped children receive a larger inheritance share than the able-bodied. Finally, the dominant individualism in the western world is also making itself felt in the law of inheritance. This means that the testamentary freedom of the decedent is being incrementally expanded to the disadvantage of his or her family members.

I am thus at the conclusion of my presentation, and hope that the conference will go well. Above all I hope that the participants will have understanding and tolerance for those who think otherwise than they do.

Partners, Parents and Children: Grounds for Allocationg Resources across Households

John Eekelaar[1]

I. Introduction

A core feature of being married is the duty of the partners to support each other. Continental family lawyers refer to it as the principle of family solidarity. When marriage was indissoluble, each party owed that duty to the other throughout their common lives. That was why, before judicial divorce was introduced in England in 1858, the ecclesiastical courts could order a husband to support his wife from whom he was separated under a decree of judicial separation.[2] The marriage still continued. But the ecclesiastical courts were not too hard on husbands. A wife could only obtain the decree (and therefore the support order) if the husband was guilty of adultery, cruelty or »unnatural offences«. And, rather than basing the husband's obligation on anything like »family solidarity«, the courts preferred to justify orders against husbands on the ground that the husbands had profited by acquiring the wife's property by marrying her. Essentially, they were only giving back to the wife what had been hers in the first place. And a »guilty« wife would get nothing at all, not even the property she had put into the marriage.[3] Still, at least you could say that it was legitimate for the courts to be involved in deciding what the obligations between married people were, even if they were living in different households.

But that could not be said when courts dissolved a marriage. Yet, when they acquired the power to do that in 1858, they were simultaneously permitted to order a husband to make monetary payments to his former wife secured on his property. This was still not a major threat to men. The courts could not make a **direct** order against their income until 1866, and had to wait until 1971 before they could order the **transfer** of any of their

---

1 Pembroke College Oxford, United Kingdom.
2 Called divorce *a mensa et thoro*.
3 On all this see *John Eekelaar* and *Mavis Maclean*, Maintenance after Divorce (1986), 5-9.

property to the wife. Even so, they could force a man make some material provision for a person to whom he was no longer related. So, on what basis should the court exercise that power? All the legislation said was that a court could make such order as »it shall think fit ... having regard to (the husband's) Fortune (if any), to the Ability of the Husband, and to the Conduct of the Parties it shall deem reasonable.«[4] But what was »fit«? It was like putting two people in a boxing ring, without any rules, and asking the referee to do what he thinks best.

I will not describe in detail how the English courts responded to this task. Suffice it to say that they used a variety of justifications for making orders. Sometimes it was a punishment for abandoning the marriage. Sometimes it was to make some recompense to a wife for property she had lost to the husband. Sometimes it was to save a wife from having to resort to prostitution. Sometimes it was to prevent her from becoming a charge on the state. On the whole, if the wife could look after herself, she would probably get nothing. Until 1971 she could certainly not expect to get any of her husband's property, even the home, even if she was looking after his children in it. If she was lucky, she might return to **her** family's home. Even after 1971 she seldom got any of his business property.[5]

Things are very different now, but change has been slow and generally disorganised, and it is still mired in uncertainty and controversy. So I want to stand back a bit and look at **possible** grounds which can confer legitimacy on the act of legally forcing one party to a broken partnership to make material provision for the other. Do not forget that the discussion is about the use of state force to require the transfer of material goods (property, income) from one household to another. We are not simply talking about the best way for people to distribute resources within their own household. So we have to remember that any forced transfer will usually compete against strong countervailing social and psychological forces which drive the holder of those resources to retain them to the benefit of the members of his or her existing household. The transaction costs in compelling transfers from one household to another can be formidable.

---

4   Divorce and Matrimonial Causes Act 1857, s. 32.
5   See *John Eekelaar*, »Post-divorce Financial Obligations« in *Sanford N. Katz, John Eekelaar* and *Mavis Maclean* (eds), Cross Currents: Family Law and Policy in the US and England (2000), ch. 18.

II. Children

If there are children, one obvious starting point, though surprisingly little used, is to view legal intervention as justified by their interests. It should be easy to accept that society can legitimately require parents to make provision for their children.[6] This does not however tell us what that provision should be, and for many years English law studiously avoided answering that question. One part of the answer must surely be a secure place for the child to live, at least where this is possible. This has in fact been a significant strand in the way English courts have exercised their property allocation powers on divorce acquired in 1971.[7] They can, and have, even done this when the parents are not married.[8]

What the right financial provision should be has proved more difficult. Some solutions base this on the amount a parent spends on children in his **present** household. But that fails to take into account any difference in the living standards between the payer's household and the one the child is in, which may be significant.[9] I have found it very difficult to find satisfying principles here. For, while it seems that a parent **should** ensure that all his children enjoy an equal living standard, this principle demands too much if a parent has children in different households. He would have to maintain all those households at the same level. But that could impose an excessive burden on the parent's current household. Also, there will be other people in those households who would benefit by such support, and to whom the parent may not owe any obligation, or at least not the equivalent obligation.

Therefore, it seems that a solution must be a compromise between a number of factors. First, there is the importance of reinforcing the primary allocation of responsibility on those who generate children to support them (apart from recognized exceptions when the responsibility is transferred to someone else, such as in adoption). This has to be traded against

---

6 *John Eekelaar*, Family Law and Personal Life (2006, 2007) pp. 67, 114-7.
7 This seems to have been less prominent in the US: see *John Eekelaar*, »Empowerment and Responsibility: The Balance Sheet Approach in the Principles and English Law« in *Robin Fretwell Wilson* (ed), Reconceiving the Family: Critique on the American Law Institute's Principles of the Law of Family Dissolution (2006), p. 438. Frequently, however, it is not possible to achieve this result because resources are insufficient.
8 *T v S* [1994] 2 FLR 883; *J v C (child: financial provision)* [1999] 1 FLR 152.
9 *Ira Mark Ellman* and *Tara O'Toole Ellman*, »The Theory of Child Support« (2008) *Harvard Journal on Legislation* 107. See generally *J. Thomas Oldham* and *Marygold S. Melli* (eds), Child Support: the Next Frontier (University of Michigan Press, 2000).

other socially-based obligations a parent may have already incurred, or may do later, for example, by taking someone else's child into their own household. Perhaps the best solution is to have a relatively simple form of assessment, say, in the form of a percentage of net income, which could be agreed to represent an indisputable minimum duty which a person responsible for the conception of the child owes towards its well-being.[10]

That does not exhaust the scope for legitimately forcing transfer of resources across households. The extent of further transfers will depend on other factors, to which I now turn.

III. Partners

It is logically possible to find a former **spouse's** obligation to provide material support for the other after the end of a marriage in the terms of the marriage itself. It could, for example, be a term in the marriage contract that, on dissolution, the property owned by each partner is to be divided between them in a certain way. Indeed, something like this is very common, especially in civil law jurisdictions. It makes sense in the case of well-informed, independent-minded, people, especially if they have the opportunity to make bespoke variations to the stipulated distribution prior to marrying. It works less well as a default mechanism for people who have given no thought to it, and of course it doesn't cover situations where the couple don't marry. As regards financial support, or the »family solidarity« principle, it could also be a written into the marriage contract that the parties should look after each other, at least to some extent, **even after the marriage is dissolved**. In fact, that can be the only basis upon which the English courts exercised their jurisdiction to make property and financial orders at least after 1971. They simply asserted that a former spouse could be compelled to meet the »reasonable requirements« of the other. They made very subjective evaluations of what they thought former spouses, especially wives, »deserved« after having been married for a certain time.[11]

---

10 The payment should be subject to a maximum amount. A parent who has resources to bring the child above that maximum should be encouraged to do that, but that should be, and be seen as being, a voluntary action undertaken for the well-being of the child. I have called the act of performing an act which exceeds one's legal obligations the exercise of responsibility in a fuller, or heightened, sense. See *John Eekelaar*, note 5 above, pp. 121-122; 129-131.
11 Cross Currents (note 5 above) 418-419; *John Eekelaar*, note 5 above, p. 144.

But who would knowingly sign up to a clause saying: »if you divorce, you agree to provide such material support for your partner as a judge may think is reasonably needed and deserved.« Yet many people, without knowing it, have done so.

Unless we are prepared to write express provisions like that into the marriage contract, it would be better not to rely on marriage as a basis for these actions. We must find something else. Here the contribution of the American Law Institute to the effort to find it must be acknowledged.[12] Its most significant step was to propose changing the basis for awarding alimony from meeting need to making compensation. In its words, this re-cast the purpose of the award »from a plea for help to a claim of entitlement.«[13] This included an entitlement to a share in property belonging to one another. This was established through a presumption that assets acquired by the labour of either during the relationship should be equally shared on separation, and that each should gain a share in the separate property of the other incrementally, over time. The Institute also proposed a compensatory award to offset loss of living standard after separation. I would summarize the rationale of this two-pronged approach as attempting to ensure a **fair return on investment of both assets and effort when the partnership ends**. Whether the return is »fair« is assessed by looking at what each put in (in terms of assets and effort), then looking at what each is left with at the end, and »if the difference between what the parties take out is greater than the difference between what they put in, then the worse off party should receive compensation for the shortfall.«[14] It is rather like looking at a balance sheet.

This type of justification is very different from the principle of family solidarity. Family solidarity is a kind of insurance against **future** risks. The earned-share and compensation approach is based on **what has already happened**. In an age of low marriage, and relatively high divorce, I believe it is no longer feasible to see marriage as an instrument for providing insurance for the period after the marriage ends. Even if you tried, it would be capricious and unreliable. I do not think there is any realistic alternative to the earned-share and compensation approach.[15] It has the addi-

---

12 *American Law Institute*, Principles of the Law of Family Dissolution: Analysis and Recommendations (2002).
13 *American Law Institute* Principles, ch. 1.
14 *John Eekelaar*, note 6 above, p. 434.
15 This seems to be the position reached in English law after the decision in *Miller v Miller; McFarlane v McFarlane* ([2006] UKHL 24). *Lord Nicholls* and *Baroness Hale* saw

tional advantage of drawing on established legal principles. The law is accustomed to deciding how individuals acquire interests in capital assets, and it is familiar with dealing with claims for compensation for losses. This is merely a new context for their application. Another advantage is that, since it is not conceptually linked to the status of the parties, it can apply whether the parties are married or not.

But both rationales envisage a certain kind of social interaction. It would surely not be right to allow someone a legal right to a share in the fruits of a friend's project on the ground that they had provided the friend encouragement and support in undertaking it, or to give them compensation because they had spent money in providing the help.[16] It would devalue acts of friendship. So I have proposed that these principles should only apply where people have adopted a »life plan« (in the sense of a plan for organizing the way we live) »as a basis upon which they followed their common life together for the long term«.[17] Where people establish a common household, it can be presumed (rebuttably) at least after a certain time that they have such a plan. If they have a relationship while living apart, it would need to be proved. Frankly, I would not be concerned whether the persons concerned were of the same sex, or were even related to one another. The concern is with principles of justice, not making statements about family structure. But that does not mean that applying the principles is easy. Far from it. I will briefly sketch where the difficulties lie.

1. The »Earned Share«

Central to the strategy is the »earned share« principle. This is based on the fact that the parties share their lives and »live and work together«.[18] If they separate, they should share the goods they have between them. But what should the shares be? It is usually said that they must be equal, and for very good reasons. Respect for individuals and gender equality demand that what each party contributes to their life together should, at least out-

---

three »strands« (*Lord Nicholls*) or »rationales« (*Baroness Hale*) underlying financial and property awards: need, compensation and »sharing«. But, as *Baroness Hale* points out (para. [140]), compensation includes meeting need (at least if the need is generated by events in the relationship, which *Baroness Hale* explicitly specifies ([138])), but goes beyond it. There therefore seem to be two primary principles: compensation and »sharing«, each of which is subject to the welfare of the children. See also *Charman v Charman* [2007] EWHC Civ 503, para [73].

16   See my discussion in *John Eekelaar*, note 6 above, ch. 2.
17   *John Eekelaar*, note 6 above, 49-50.
18   *Miller v Miller; McFarlane v McFarlane* ([2006] UKHL 24, para. 16 (*Lord Nicholls*).

side exceptional circumstances, be regarded as having equal value. But we all know the difficult cases. One party may have entered the partnership already having much more property than the other. Or one party may have received it shortly after starting the partnership either without any effort (an inheritance is the standard example), or as a result of efforts mainly made before starting it (for example, the acquisition of business assets for which almost all the work was done before marrying). Is it really thought that the contributions the other made to the joint domestic life should be put as half the value of such assets, no matter how much it is? Most systems use a variety of techniques do avoid that, usually involving excluding certain categories of property from the sharing. I am not enthusiastic about that. Partners often regard all of the property belonging to each as for the potential benefit of both. I prefer the idea that there should be entitlement to a share in **any** property belonging to a partner, **but that the extent of the share should be built up over time until its reaches equality.** [19] If, however, someone contributes **directly** to the wealth that is created, for example, by participating significantly in business activity or financially contributing to it, the share should normally be equal from the start. I call this the duration principle. The passage of time is an excellent proxy for measuring a number of factors which are important in achieving a »fair return on investment in the partnership«. They include the degree of commitment to the relationship; the value of contributions made to it which are not susceptible of straightforward economic measurement; and the extent of disadvantage undergone on separation.[20]

---

19 The time taken to reach equality could be accelerated if the person claiming the share is caring for children.
20 Another issue is whether it could be correct to apply the sharing principle to a former partner's earnings, and earning potential, after the separation. There are good reasons for grounding an award against income on a compensatory rather than an earned-share basis. One is that it is inappropriate to view a person as having a quasi-proprietal interest in the products of another's talents and effort. The scope for making claims could be endless. Worse still, such an entitlement, being of a proprietal nature, would not be subject to a duty to mitigate. It would be unaffected by whether or not the recipient made efforts to realise her own earning potential, or indeed any other financial benefit she received. That cannot be good policy.For trenchant arguments against treating such matters as property, see Ira Mark Ellman, »O'Brien v O'Brien: A Failed Reform, Unlikely Reformers« (2007) 27 Pace Law Review 949. See also Ira Mark Ellman, »Do Americans Play Football?« (2005) 19 International Journal of Law, Policy & the Family 257 at 271-275.

2. Compensation

The other basis for transferring resources is compensation. A fundamental difference between this and the earned share principle is that only in the case of compensation is the claimant under a duty to mitigate the loss, that is, to use her own efforts to lessen the disadvantage and thereby reduce the amount of the compensatory award. This is important in an age when the earnings gap between men and women is narrowing. However, while the **idea** of compensation is relatively straightforward, it is harder to decide what is being compensated. *Baroness Hale* has described the compensation as being for »relationship-generated disadvantage«.[21] Does this mean that **any** loss, or opportunity foregone, as a result of entering the relationship should be (fully?) compensated? There are strong arguments against that. In many cases the financial benefits of an »alternative life« are too speculative to provide an appropriate measure. But also, there must be a high possibility that, had the applicant not had a relationship with the respondent, (she) will have had one with another person. The »alternative life« may never have happened anyway.[22]

The compensation is therefore for exposure to the **differential risk between the parties** of the consequences of the separation.[23] This refers to the actual disparity **occurring at** the time of separation, not the losses that may have been suffered before it. Suppose a woman is earning more than a man when they separate, but she would have earned **even more** had they not entered a relationship. Surely the woman should not have a claim against the man for the cost of her lost opportunities. And if there is no disparity, so the risk has turned out even, there again seems no case for compensation. If compensation is justified, the extent to which the disadvantaged party should receive compensation should be proportionate to the disadvantage, and the length of time which the parties lived together. How this is achieved is

---

21   *Miller v Miller; McFarlane v McFarlane*, at para. 140.
22   »(The wife) has not lost a career, for that is not what she had sought. She instead lost the opportunity to have her children with someone with whom she would enjoy an enduring relationship. The most direct measure of her financial loss would compare her situation at divorce to the hypothetical situation had she married a different man.« (American Law Institute, note 11 above, section 5.05, comment e).
23   *John Eekelaar*, note 6 above, p. 52. As Lord Nicholls has said, the compensation element would be »aimed at redressing any significant prospective economic disparity between the parties arising from the way they conducted their marriage:« *Miller v Miller; McFarlane v McFarlane*, at para. 13.

a technical matter, and the American Law Institute provides one possible solution.[24]

IV. Parents

The duration principle has been criticized for applying only where a couple have lived together, or, in my version of it, have adopted a »life plan« together. It is said that a mother who cares for the father's child should be seen as contributing indirectly to his continued acquisition of wealth, even if she is no longer living with him, or has never lived with him, and they never shared a »life plan«.[25] But should she therefore be allowed to build up a share in his wealth during that period, or be compensated by him for any disparity in living standard? There are good reasons to hesitate over that. If a man has a number of children by different women, there could be multiple claims on his assets. I doubt if this could be easily handled in the legal system. The nexus between the carer's activities and the accumulation of wealth also seems remote. Unlike the case of acquisition during a partnership under a life plan, there is unlikely to have been an expectation that the carer would benefit from the accumulated assets. It also misses the point that the earned share principle is a reflection of a commitment to a common life. As far as compensation is concerned, what is being compensated? Could it be the career opportunities the mother lost by exercising care? But we don't know what she would have done if she had not mothered this child. She may well have borne another. It is too speculative. It is true that the child's carer may be relieving the father of a burden. But that can be seen as an element of his duty to the child, and that has already been considered.

---

24 The following example is based on that methodology. (i) if there are no children, the award should amount to 20 per cent of the income gap at the time of separation after a 20 year marriage, scaled down proportionately for shorter marriages, to last for a period of time equal to 60 % of the marriage duration, or longer (perhaps for joint lives) if the claimant is over 50 at separation; (ii) if there are children, the person who has taken on the majority of the child care responsibilities should receive an award equal to 30 per cent of the income gap at the time of separation after a 20 year marriage, scaled down proportionately for shorter marriages, also to last for a duration of 60 % of the marriage duration (or longer in some cases) but subject to an override where a partner leaves the other with children after a short relationship to prevent a perverse incentive for a parent to leave the other early before liability increase.
25 *Lisa Glennon*, »Obligations between Adult Partners: Moving from Form to Function?« (2008) 22 *International Journal of Law, Policy & the Family* 22.

V. Conclusion: Social or Inter-Personal Obligations?

It has been said the obligations between the couple are personal obligations, and that the approach I advocate wrongly requires one individual to pay another compensation for disadvantages that have their origin in society, and are outside the individual's control.[26] It is of course true that the greater disadvantages to which a woman may be exposed compared to those to which men may be exposed on the termination of the partnership are mostly socially caused. To that extent, the compensation places some of the consequences of social inequalities on an individual man. But the issue should not turn on conceptual purity about the nature of the obligation, but whether it is fair and just to require the better-off person to alleviate these disparate consequences to **some** degree. I think it is. First, evaluation of any compensable loss cannot be made in a vacuum. The very reason for imposing the requirement is that the social consequences of the separation bear more harshly on one person rather than the other. If the disadvantaged party were able to overcome them by her own efforts, there would be nothing to compensate. The obligation remains personal, because it does not attempt to make the obligor contribute towards improving the lot of the disadvantaged group **generally**. That is done through other kinds of obligations, for example, taxation, which *are* truly social. In the city of opera, may I end with an operatic allusion? In *Puccini's* Madama Butterfly, Lieutenant Pinkerton's betrayal of Butterfly is all the greater because of the exceptional shame it incurred for her because of her cultural background. His personal duty to her was enhanced because of the particularly acute social consequences of his breach. But that is not to make Pinkerton responsible for the cultural setting from which Butterfly came. It is not to impose a social duty on him. Butterfly could find a remedy only in her death. It must be our hope that the fulfilment of personal obligations provides a better way.

---

26 *Lucinda Ferguson*, »Family, Social Inequalities, and the Persuasive Force of Interpersonal Obligation« (2008) 22 *International Journal of Law, Policy & the Family* 61, at p. 82. »Being inter-personal in nature means that, not only is the obligation justified by reference to the nature of the parties' relationship, but it is also **limited** by it.« (emphasis in original).

Family Law and Intergenerational Family Solidarity –Should there be Enforceable Maintenance Rights vis-à-vis Adult Relatives?

Jordi Ribot[1]

I. Introduction

The legal side of intergenerational family solidarity has always been problematic. As early as the eighteenth century, *Pothier* bitterly complained about the unwillingness of children to honour their filial duties:

»*la corruption des moeurs, qui est allée toujours en croissant, et qui est aujourd'hui parvenue à son comble, rend, à l'honte de l'humanité, trés-fréquentes au palais ces demandes, qui autrefois y étoient inouies.*«[2]

The history of family support obligations shows, nevertheless, a gradual decline in the propensity of legal systems to enforce such obligations.[3] Along with sociodemographic changes and the development of modern Welfare States, the twentieth century saw maintenance obligations towards adult relatives to be repealed in a number of jurisdictions, along with their public law counterparts (*i.e.* reimbursement claims addressed by public bodies against the assisted person's relatives).[4]

Currently, for instance, Scandinavian legal systems do not recognize support duties towards members of the extended family. The only duties are those of parents vis-à-vis their minor children, which automatically finish once the child reaches a certain age, 18 or 21 depending on the countries and on the circumstances of the children.[5] In England, Section 42 of the National Assistance Act 1948 replaced the Poor Laws with a much more

---

1 *Observatory of European and Comparative Private Law*, University of Girona, Spain.
2 *Pothier* (1768), p.250.
3 See the overview provided by *Androulidakis-Dimitriadis* (1995) pp. 113-121.
4 For instance, on American Relatives' Responsibility Laws see *Britton* (1990) pp. 351 ff. More recently see also *Moskowitz* (2002) pp. 412-423.
5 *Agell* (1997) p. 173.

restricted duty to support one's spouse and minor children.[6] With regard to Scottish Law, the Family Law Act (Scotland) 1985 abolished any maintenance claim for parents from their adult children as well as from linear relatives.[7] After years of debate, the Dutch Civil Code repealed the support duties of relatives (besides parents and children) in 1970.[8] Finally, in Germany, although the civil code still lays down linear relatives' maintenance obligations in §§ 1601 ff BGB, the German social services can seek the reimbursement of allowances paid to a person in need only against her parents or children.[9]

Pointing to what appears to be the final stage of this development, Professor *Schwenzer*'s *Model Family Code* confines itself to support obligations of parents and persons in loco parentis. As she puts it, »socio-demographic developments nowadays would appear to make the unrestricted duty to support one's linear relatives inappropriate.«[10]

But is this right? The supposed demise of extended family bounds was once commonplace for sociologists. However, it is now being challenged by comparative cross-national studies showing that intergenerational family solidarity is strong even in affluent Western societies. Data provided by the OASIS Study[11] show substantial levels of intergenerational integration. Neither urbanisation nor Welfare State expansion are incompatible with feelings of filial obligations.[12] These feelings and affective relationships spanning the generations have not been weakened by geographical separation. Although the majority of older adults in most developed nations live independently of their extended families, adult children continue to be the main providers of long term health and social support to ageing parents.[13] Moreover, even in the Nordic countries involvement of families in care provision to older people is high and recent studies qualify the input of care from outside the family at the best as modest.[14]

Welfare states can relieve potential familial caregivers from care obligations and improve their chances of being active in the labour market,

---

6   *Thomas* (1989) pp. 59 ff.
7   *Meston* (1997) pp. 176-177.
8   *Breembar* (1997) p. 128.
9   Cf. § 91 I 1 Bundessozialhilfegesetz. See *Martiny / Eichenhofer* (2002) *passim*.
10 *Schwenzer* (2006) p. 166.
11 Old Age and Autonomy: the Role of Service Systems and Intergenerational Family Solidarity (2003).
12 See *Lowenstein / Daatland* (2006) p. 211. See also *Silverstein / Gans / Yang*, (2006) p.1068.
13 *Lowenstein / Daatland* (2006) p. 206 and more references therein.
14 *Rauch* (2007) pp. 260 ff. See also *Lowenstein /Daatland* (2006) p. 204.

thereby reducing care-related inequalities in general and gender inequality in particular.[15] Currently, however, most of them face serious financial and legitimacy problems which threaten this process of defamilialisation of care.[16] From the legal point of view, although it seems very unlikely that family obligations are reinstated in Scandinavia[17], in many other places a shift from public to private responsibility is encouraged and measures that emphasise private support obligations and their coercive enforcement have been adopted.[18]

A comparative overview of the legal status of support obligations suggests that reforming trends are ambivalent. Certainly, many jurisdictions repealed filial responsibility laws some years ago. But many others still keep them in law books and most of them embrace the principle of subsidiarity of welfare benefits.[19] Besides that, new family obligations are being introduced and the old ones re-enforced after having fallen into disuse. The South Dakota Supreme Court, for instance, turned again to them in 1994 in *Americana Healthcare Center v. Randall*[20] to allow a reimbursement claim addressed by a nursing home against a man after the death of his destitute mother. More recently, some voices in American legal scholarship suggest that filial responsibility laws and a Federal Filial Responsibility Statute could be the proper means for addressing the economic problems of vulnerable people, especially the elderly.[21] More generally, many authors and legislators think that the law should keep the support obligations of the relatives to be consistent with the principle that the family and not the State must be the primary care provider.[22]

The time does not seem ripe for *Schwenzer*'s proposal; or at least some of the circumstances upon which her judgment is made apparently point in the opposite direction. However, it does go to the heart of interaction between Family Law and Social Law. From the point of view of this interaction, one may wonder whether it is sensible to promote family solidarity

---

15   See *Rauch* (2007) pp. 251-3.
16   Oldham (2006) pp. 230-1. On *defamilialisation* of care, see *Esping-Andersen* (1999) pp. 147 ff.
17   *Agell* (1997) p. 173.
18   See *Moskowitz* (2002) pp. 422 ff.
19   *Ribot* (1998) pp. 1152-60.
20   513 N.W.2d 566 (S.D. 1994).
21   See *Pakula* (2005) pp. 859 ff and *Edelstone* (2002) p. 501 ff. See also *Moskowitz* (2002) p. 452.
22   Among many others see *Auletta* (1984) *passim* and *Meulders-Klein* (1993) p. 178. More recently see Oldham (2006) pp. 217 ff.

by direct or indirect enforcement of maintenance rights. The only interest at stake is relieving the State of the financial burden.[23] Besides that, does the existence of a legal obligation encourage the readiness to take care of one's relatives in need or undermine it instead?[24]

This debate about the legal expression of intergenerational family solidarity has surrounded the reforms carried out in Catalonia over recent years. When reforming Family Law at the beginning of the nineties, the Catalan legislator began to emphasise the importance of maintenance obligations and the subsidiarity of social protection. Ten years later, however, the main legal tools for enforcing the maintenance obligations of the relatives of those seeking social services and allowances have been repealed. Instead, a new Social Services Act grants access to allowances and care facilities as a subjective right, regardless of the means of applicant's relatives.[25]

II. Maintenance Obligations between Adult Relatives Revisited

1. Avant-Propos

During the twentieth century, enormous social and economic changes brought private support obligations between relatives into demise. Not all jurisdictions, however, have repealed them. To many people such a step would entail surrender to moral dissolution and endanger the family's basic social functions.[26] Besides that, public opinion tends to be in favour of the existence of enforceable maintenance rights vis-à-vis adult relatives in spite of their being rarely applied in practice. These rules express shared values as to how families must work and enshrine a symbolic character that makes them critical. Moreover, society wishes to ensure that the law can react against scandalous cases. A policy of enforcing support obligations, however, will undoubtedly trigger resentment and damage family relations.[27] As Professor *Ann Britton* put it, »having duty-to-support statutes on the books, but only enforcing them in egregious cases, is perhaps the most morally satisfying approach.«[28]

---

23 Cf. *Serverin* (1983) pp. 22-26, *Ribot* (1999) pp. 123 ff and *Van Houtte / Breda* (2005) pp. 247 ff.
24 See the groundbreaking approach provided by *Teitelbaum* (1992) pp. 773-775.
25 See below Section IV.
26 *von Munch* (1994) pp. 55-8.
27 See *Oldham* (2006) p. 228.
28 *Britton* (1990) p. 352.

2. Why do Adult Relatives Help Each Other when they Are in Need? Is it the Fear of Breaching the Law if they Don't?

People meet demands of needy relatives because they feel obliged to do so. Indeed, many studies suggest that everywhere both parents and adult children acknowledge the existence of filial responsibility as a societal expectation. Moral duty is, nevertheless, only a necessary but not a sufficient condition for adult children to provide support to their elderly mothers and fathers.[29]

Sociological scholarship stresses that intergenerational family solidarity is a multidimensional nexus of exchange relations with six bases, of which the so-called *normative solidarity* is only one among several.[30] Opportunity structures and emotional bonds also play a role; even a more substantial role. The laws of responsibility towards relatives, however, are laid down and justified on the basis of a construct of normative solidarity which is rooted exclusively in structural-functional role theory. In contrast to this approach, people are usually unaware of the extent of their legal rights/duties vis-à-vis their adult relatives. Whether they help or ask for help does not depend on the existence of a legal duty but on the combination of several factors which favourably predispose family members towards one another.[31] Contemporary families seem to look at personal affection and attachment – and not at the law, religion or morality – as the binding that secures family cohesion. Real life situations are thus increasingly becoming less duty-driven and more open to individual variation. Everywhere, legal or normative solidarities tend to give ground to *functional* as well as *effectual* solidarities. Personal care or financial assistance given or received, as well as emotional closeness or communication, tend to supersede normative solidarities as predictors of effective intergenerational family solidarity.

Normative »familiarism« is correlated with expressed »familiarism« in individuals' preferences and in policy opinions. From this standpoint, recent studies confirm that norms on filial duties come across as more prescriptive in the south (abstract and unconditional) than in the north (situational and less prescriptive).[32] By the same token, however, such correlations are weak, as is clearly illustrated by the data provided by the

---

29 *Silversten / Gans / Yang* (2006) p. 1080.
30 See the references to the theories of Bengston and others in *Lowenstein / Daatland* (2006) pp. 207-8.
31 *Silversten / Gans / Yang* (2006) p. 1071.
32 *Lowenstein / Daatland* (2006) p. 211.

Spanish sample of the OASIS study: strong filial norms do not necessarily imply that there is an agreement with the view that the family is the »natural« care provider.[33] Moreover, when circumstances change the expressions of filial solidarity also change: bearing the burden of care has visible consequences for family life; it tends to trigger more conflict than usual and has a negative impact on personal closeness and satisfaction in the lives of both family carers and the dependant person.[34]

3. *Do we really Need Legal Duties vis-à-vis Adult Relatives?*

Many years ago, Professor *Max Rheinstein* stressed that in fact only a minority of those supporting their elderly parents do it exclusively for fear of the consequences attached to the infringement of their legal duty. But he added:

> »Quite possibly there are indeed some sons for whom the fear of such adverse governmental action, legal compulsion, is a motive. Perhaps it is not the only one; but there may be some for whom other motivations might not be strong enough without their reinforcement by the motive of fear of legal compulsion.«[35]

Certainly, it was already the failure of the traditional Roman *mores* to advance filial solidarity towards needy fathers that prompted emperors, at the end of the second century AD, to use their absolute power to confer legal status to maintenance claims.[36] But the terms of the family relationship have evolved a great deal since then, as have the mutual expectations of those belonging to the same family. Conflict avoidance and personal sharing are two dimensions of connectedness which are now crucial in this particular relational context. Moreover, regarding the interaction between family and social law one must also bear in mind that whereas expectations of self-suficiency are not eroded when financial or material needs are covered by *formal* sources (such as social services, hospitals or home caring)[37] bringing claims against your own children or relatives

---

33 See *Daatland / Herlofson* (2003) p. 560.
34 See *Bazo* (2003) p. 125.
35 *Rheinstein* (1979) p. 112. See now *Oldham* (2006) p. 230 (»from a pragmatic perspective it might be argued that since the majority of people are law-abiding citizens, it is likely that the very existence of the legal duty will encourage many people to support their aging parents«).
36 *Kaser* (1971) p. 351. See also *Schiller* (1971) p. 410-15. An overview in *Van Houtte / Breda* (2005) p. 246.
37 *Hoerl* (1989) pp. 175 ff.

may well trigger conflict with (younger) generations and endanger the continuity of the relationship. That is a price too high to be paid, especially by the older generation.

4. The Political Economy behind the Principle of Subsidiarity

At the end of the day, the legal obligations of relatives are basically the pretext for a systematic disinclination to provide public care services. The principle of subsidiarity, according to which care-related problems should be resolved foremost by the family and only in cases of family failure by the society as a whole, is based upon a certain view of the role of the State vis-à-vis frail or dependent people. According to this view such a task must mainly be the responsibility of private sources, either contracted out by the individuals or provided by their families. As *Esping-Andersen* has put it

> »*strong familialism is characterized by the fact that social assistance was never upgraded because of two assumptions: it is assumed (and legally prescribed) that families are the relevant locus of social aid; and it is assumed that families normally do not fail.*«[38]

Accordingly, social services schemes are assumed not to be universal. Instead, they are selective – sometimes even stigmatising – and above all subsidiary to the relatives' maintenance obligations.

Several studies have uncovered the social costs of such policies.[39] Firstly, many potential beneficiaries give up the idea of applying for services or allowances that they do actually need.[40] Secondly, there are the hidden costs linked with restrictions to access to social services, which advocates of family care tend to overlook. Among these costs, one may mention the likelihood of conflicts arising between different generations sharing the same household and the increased risk of neglect or even abuse. Last but not least, internalising welfare responsibilities in the family is incompatible with women's demands for economic independence and careers.[41]

---

38 *Esping-Andersen* (1999) p. 90.
39 See *Serverin* (1983) *passim* and *Ribot* (1999) pp. 145 ff, and more references therein.
40 *Hoerl* (1989) p. 177 and *Britton* (1990) p. 371.
41 *Esping-Andersen* (1999) p. 174.

III. Legal Signalling and Developing Family Strategies

The shortcomings of relying upon maintenance family obligations as a public policy when developing a welfare regime are therefore clear. Some authors think, nevertheless, that the existence of a legal duty to maintain helps in terms of »legal signalling«. As *Mika Oldham* has put it
»*the existence of the obligation creates a legal tie that, in terms of signalling, locates the older generation firmly within the family.*«[42]

The problem of this approach is not only one of a certain philosophy of family relations but one of political economy behind the legal rules at stake, which includes both their *direct* and *indirect* enforcement. From that point of view, the very existence of private support obligations between extended family members anticipates the extent to which our society is willing to tackle social needs and to redistribute the costs of social risks by building individualised or familial solidarity rather than a collective one.[43] Thinking in terms of the family as a primary source of support and the formal sources as residual, tends to hide the responsibilities that the State may well legitimately bear towards its citizens. By the same token, the very existence of the support duties raises unnecessary complexities in the daily operation of social protection schemes. Experience in several jurisdictions show that the ordinary provision of services to needy persons becomes tangled when the means of the applicants are to be assessed taking into account the economic resources of those called on to maintain them according to the principle of subsidiarity.[44]

Secondly, whether you agree with the *signalling* function or not, bringing into effect the legal obligation to give support by indirect means – such as when the *means test* is applied for the provision of services or care facilities – is likely to undermine the families' strategies aimed at combining formal resources with the informal care provided by its members. The fact that the older generation is out of the *legal* picture does not mean that extended family bonds have disappeared or that they are doomed to disappear. As *Agnès Pitrou* stressed some years ago, emphasising the legal obligations of relatives hinders the development of strategies that allow vulnerable persons to receive care within the family without having

---

42   *Oldham* (2006) p. 225.
43   See again *Esping-Andersen* (1999) p. 147.
44   See *Martiny* (2000) pp. 1228 ff and *Van Houtte / Breda* (2005) pp. 251-2.

to give up the means provided by society.⁴⁵ Accordingly, there is no need to *relocate* the individual within his or her family. On the contrary, access to public services as well as financial self-sufficiency provided by public allowances and citizenship guarantees enhance the chances of all family members contributing to their family welfare, thereby reducing the strains caused to the group by economic dependence, age vulnerability or dependence.

One should recall here the distinction, made by *John Eekelaar* in another context, between enforcing (legal) obligations and encouraging responsible behaviour.⁴⁶ The State should not be interested in *imposing* family solidarity but in *promoting* the conditions for it being activated when needed. This is in line with the findings of the OASIS study. According to its conclusions the Welfare state, which is usually portrayed as institutionally individualistic, has not entirely encouraged a development of individualism in terms of support patterns.⁴⁷ Even in the Nordic countries substantial family care has not been diminished by collective responsibility through public services.⁴⁸ Likewise, welfare regimes of formerly familialistic societies seem to converge towards the mixed form in which informal and formal care play complementary roles.⁴⁹

Even those who aspire to reinforce the legal role of intergenerational family obligation concede that the wiser policy consists in setting out incentives for relatives who perform their roles as carers willingly (i.e. by means of tax reliefs, specific grants for home caring, successoral priorities in favour of carers and those providing support, etc).⁵⁰ In France, for instance, the complementarity approach has already gained ground in the case of the so-called *allocation personalisée d'autonomie* as set out by the Act 2001-647, of 20ᵗʰ of July. Under this Act the fulfilment of one's legal maintenance duties does not preclude access to the allowance but

---

45 *Pitrou* (1989) pp. 208-217.
46 *Eekelaar* (2007) p. 130-131.
47 *Björnberg / Latta* (2007) p. 442.
48 *Lowenstein / Daatland* (2006) p. 204.
49 *Daatland / Herlofson* (2003a) p. 47. This complementarity hypothesis leads to the conclusion that »more generous inputs from the welfare state enable, or trigger, families to direct their solidarity towards other roles and functions [...] and in some areas may have stimulated family exchanges, as for example where generous pensions enable older parents to support younger family members«. See *OASIS Final Report* (Ariela Lowenstein and Jim Ogg, Editors), Center for Research and Study of Aging, The University of Haifa, Israel, p. 301).
50 See *Pakula* (2005) p. 877 and *Oldham* (2001) pp. 174-7. For an overview see *Moskowitz* (2002) pp. 424 ff.

instead increases the legal rights upon the estate of the applicant. These policies are therefore fully consistent with the strategies developed by the families to provide care and help to their older or disabled members. Public support increases the resources available to the family, thereby nudging household members to involve in caring and supporting them.[51]

IV. Conclusive Remarks: the Catalan Case

Only in 1996 a new Act on relatives' maintenance obligations was passed by the Catalan Parliament as part and parcel of a broad policy to enforce family duties towards elderly people.[52] The main goal was to clarify the legal status of the potential reimbursement claims brought by the public bodies against the debtors of support obligations. Indirectly, the Act sought to relieve the Catalan Government from part of the costs of residential care and other social services. Immediately after the Act entered into force, the Department of Social Services issued a regulation to develop it regarding how to seek contribution from the relatives of a person placed in a public nursing home or otherwise financed through public funds.[53] When passing the new Family Code in 1998[54], the Catalan legislator even added a new provision allowing any legal person taking care of a person in need to bring a maintenance claim on his or her behalf against the relatives reluctant to pay the fees.[55] By so doing, the Government reaffirmed the principle of subsidiarity and tried to overcome the unwillingness of assisted people to sue their own children or relatives.

---

51 As it has been stressed in a recent official report, »le declin du principe de subsidiarité de la solidarité nationale se manifeste aussi bien pour les prestations en espèces que pour les autres formes d'aides [...] Cette evolution ne semble cependant pas avoir d'effet désincitatif sur les solidarités familiales. Les aides versées apparaissent plutôt comme un complement à l'obligation alimentaire [...] Il semble que les aides publiques augmentent le revenu final des ménages et les incitent à consacrer une partie plus importante de leur budget aux solidarités familiales«. See *La famille, espace de solidarité entre generations* (2006); Rapport au Ministre délégué à la securité sociale, aux personnes agées, aux personnes handicapées et à la famille. President du group de travail *Alain Cordier*; rapporteur *Annie Fouquet*.
52 See the overview provided in *Ribot* (1999) pp. 131-40.
53 Decree 394/1996, of 12th of December, approving the regulation of public prices of some social services and the contribution of persons using them [*Diari Oficial de la Generalitat de Catalunya* (hereafter DOGC) num. 2294, 18.12.1996; correction of mistakes published in DOGC num. 2379, 14.4.1997].
54 Act 9/1998, of 15th of July (DOGC num. 2687, 23.7.1998).
55 See art. 261 Family Code. On this provision, see *Ribot* (1999) pp.136 ff.

Ten years later, the application of this regulation seems to have been plagued with complaints and difficulties, especially among the applicants and the families of people admitted to public nursing homes. Such problems prompted a breach of the initial consensus of political parties as regards the financing of social services. Moreover, since 1998 the *mise en oeuvre* of the regulation has regularly been disapproved of by the Catalan Ombudsman in his annual report to Parliament.[56] In 2004, a special report on care provided to older people by public-funded nursing homes was released, in which a call was made to re-examine the rule forcing the relatives either to take care of the person in need at home or to contribute financially to the costs of the nursing home. The final recommendations of the Ombudsman demanded that society should openly discuss the pros and cons of such a policy and its alternatives.[57] Apparently, the long list of complaints brought up by the families of the disabled, as well as those of children and relatives of dependent people who were looking at the possibility of being admitted to one of the few public facilities available, prompted the reaction of the Ombudsman.[58]

Finally, only ten years after the Act on maintenance obligations of the relatives entered into force, following the presentation of the draft bill on social services at the beginning of 2006 there was a U-turn in policy. Although it still relied upon the principle of subsidiarity and called the relatives to contribute to the cost of some social services, the subsequent public consultation provided the opportunity to make widespread opposition to the indirect enforcement of maintenance obligations evident.[59] In fact, only the public bodies responsible for the services were keen on the rule and remembered the scarcity of the resources and the need to contain costs. Conversely, representatives of many social sectors, such as the unions, NGOs, the professional body of social workers, university departments, and official committees appointed by local authorities, as well as representatives of the families, older people and disabled persons, stood unanimously against the rule and lobbied to repeal it when

---

56 For instance, see the Report issued about the practice carried out in 2002, *Butlletí Oficial del Parlament de Catalunya* (hereafter BOPC) num. 409, 26.3.2003.
57 See *Informe extraordinari del Síndic de Greuges sobre l'atenció a la gent gran dependent a Catalunya* (BOPC num. 34, 19.3.2004).
58 See *Informe del Síndic de Greuges al Parlament de Catalunya corresponent a l'any 2005* (BOPC num. 306, 17.3.2006) (www.sindic.cat/cat/inform_anual.asp) p. 181-2.
59 An account of this consultation process can be found in www10.gencat.cat/drep/binaris/memlsc_tcm 112-34175.pdf

passing the new legislation.[60] The new Social Services Act, passed at the end of 2007, finally omitted to mention the contribution of relatives to covering the costs of certain social services.[61] Moreover, it expressly declared that their maintenance obligations should not be taken into account when assessing the financial means available to the applicant of any social service.[62]

The Catalan example may shed a light on the limits of the policy which consists in renewing the application of relatives' maintenance laws. Encouraging responsible behaviour requires both family *and* State responsibilities to be put into effect. Of course, this depends upon the extent of the redistribution of resources in a given society. At any rate, there should be no fear that devoting more resources to public care of dependent people and to supporting their carers will entail the disappearance of family bonds or of emotional closeness between family members. When families are provided with the resources they need, they honour their obligations by adapting themselves to new social realities such as gender equality and increased female participation in paid-work. Conversely, when the obligations of relatives are directly or indirectly enforced, they are poorly performed and very reluctantly received.

---

60 The opinions of the stakeholders are summarized in www10.gencat.cat/drep/binaris/informelsc_tcm 112-34170.pdf.
61 See art. 59, 65 and 66 Act 12/2007, of 11th of October (DOGC num. 4990, 18.10.2007).
62 See Transitional Provision 4$^{th.}$ Act 12/2007.

References

> Agell, Anders (1997), Die Begründung und die Grenzen der Unterhaltspflicht unter erwachsenen Verwandten in Schweden, in D. Schwab / D. Henrich (Hrsg.), *Familiäre Solidarität – Die Begründung und die Grenzen der Unterhaltspflicht unter Verwandten im europäischen Vergleich* (Bielefeld: Gieseking) pp. 163-173.

> Androulidakis-Dimitriadis, Ismene (1995), Verwandtenunterhalt im vereinten Europa, in: C. Tomuschat / H. Kötz / B. von Maydell (Hrsg.), *Europäische Integration und nationale Rechtskulturen* (Köln: Heymann) pp. 113-121.

> Auletta, Tomasso Amedeo (1984), *Alimenti e solidarietà familiare* (Milano: Giuffrè).

> Bazo, Mª Teresa (2003), Intercambios familiares entre las generaciones y ambivalencia: Una perspectiva internacional comparada, *Revista Española de Sociología* 2:121-127.

> Björnberg, Ulla; Latta, Mia (2007), The Roles of the Family and the Welfare State. The Relationship between Public and Private Financial Support in Sweden, *Current Sociology* 55(3): 415-445.

> Breembar, Willem (1997), Familiäre Solidarität in den Niederlanden. Einige Bemerkungen zum Unterhaltsrecht und seinem Verhältnis zum Sozialhilferecht, in D. Schwab / D. Henrich (Hrsg.), *Familiäre Solidarität – Die Begründung und die Grenzen der Unterhaltspflicht unter Verwandten im europäischen Vergleich* (Bielefeld: Gieseking) pp. 127-148.

> Britton, Ann (1990), America's Best Kept Secret: An Adult Child's Duty to Support Aged Parents, *California Western Law Review* 26:351-372.

> Daatland, Svein Olav; Herlofson, Katharina (2003), ›Lost solidarity‹ or ›changed solidarity‹: a comparative European view of normative family solidarity, *Ageing & Society* 23:537-560.

> Daatland, Svein Olav; Herlofson, Katharina (2003a), Family Responsibility Norms in European Countries: Contrasts and Similarities, *Retraite et Société* 38:16-47.

> Edelstone, Shannon F. (2002), Filial Responsibility: Can the Legal Duty to Support Our Parents Be Effectively Enforced?, *Family Law Quarterly* 36(3):501-514.

> Eekelaar, John (2006), *Family law and personal life* (Oxford: Oxford University Press).

> Esping-Andersen, Gøsta (1999), *Social Foundations of Postindustrial Economies* (Oxford: Oxford University Press).

› Hoerl, Josef (1989), Family, Society, and the Elderly: The Vienna Case, in: J. Eekelaar / P. Laslett (Eds), *An Aging World. Dilemmas and Challenges for Law and Social Policy* (Oxford: Clarendon Press) pp. 169-183.

› Kaser, Max (1971), *Das römische Privatrecht*, I *Das altrömische, das vorklassische und das klassische Recht* (2nd ed. München: Beck).

› Lowenstein, Ariela; Daatland, Svein Olav (2005), Intergenerational solidarity and the family–welfare state balance, *European Journal of Ageing* 2:174-182.

› Lowenstein, Ariela; Daatland, Svein Olav (2006), Filial norms and family support in a comparative cross-national context: evidence from the OASIS study, *Ageing & Society* 26:203-223.

› Martiny, Dieter; Eichenhofer, Eberhard (2002), *Empfiehlt es sich, die rechtliche Ordnung finanzieller Solidarität zwischen Verwandten in den Bereichen des Unterhaltsrechts, des Pflichtteilsrechts, des Sozialhilferechts und des Sozialversicherungsrechts neu zu gestalten? (Gutachten für den 64. Deutschen Juristentag)*, München: Beck.

› Martiny, Dieter (2000), *Unterhaltsrang und -rückgriff. Mehrpersonenverhältnisse und Rückgriffsansprüche im Unterhaltsrecht Deutschlands, Österreichs, der Schweiz, Frankreichs, Englands und der Vereinigten Staaten von Amerika* (Tubingen: Mohr Siebeck).

› Meston, Michael (1997), Unterhaltspflicht unter Verwandten in Schottland, in: D. Schwab / D. Henrich (Hrsg.), *Familiäre Solidarität – Die Begründung und die Grenzen der Unterhaltspflicht unter Verwandten im europäischen Vergleich* (Bielefeld: Gieseking) pp. 175-183.

› Meulders-Klein, Marie-Thérèse (1993), Individualisme et communautarisme: l'individu, la famille et l'État en Europe occidentale, *Droit et Société* 23/24:168-176.

› Moskowitz, Seymour (2002), Adult Children and Indigent Parents: Intergenerational Responsibilities in International Perspective, *Marquette Law Review* 86:401-453.

› von Munch, Eva Marie (1994), Reform des Verwandtenunterhalts: eine rechtspolitische Notwendigkeit oder übereilte Aufgabe der Familiensolidarität?, in: *Zehnter Deutscher Familiengerichtstag (vom 14. bis 17. Oktober 1993 in Brühl). Ansprachen und Referate. Berichte und Ergebnisse der Arbeitskreise* (Bielefeld: Gieseking) pp. 55-58.

› Oldham, Mika (2001), Financial Obligations within the Family Aspects of Intergenerational Maintenance and Succession in England and France, *Cambridge Law Journal* 60(1):128-177.

› Oldham, Mika (2006), Maintenance of the Elderly: Legal Signalling–

Kinship and State, in: F. Ebtehaj / B. Lindly / M. Richards (Eds.), *Kinship Matters* (Oxford: Hart) pp. 217-235.
> Pakula, Matthew (2005), A Federal Filial Responsibility Statute: A Uniform Tool to Help Combat the Wave of Indigent Elderly, *Family Law Quarterly* 39(3):859-877.
> Pitrou, Agnès (1987), Dépérissement des solidarités familiales?, *L'année sociologique* 37: 208-217.
> Pothier, Robert Joseph (1768), *Traités de contrat de mariage et de la puisance du mari*, in: *Oeuvres de Pothier*, tome 7e (Paris: M. Siffrein, 1822).
> Rauch, Dietmar (2007), Is There Really a Scandinavian Social Service Model? A Comparison of Childcare and Elderlycare in Six European Countries, *Acta Sociologica* 50(3): 249-269.
> Rheinstein, Max (1965), Motivation of Intergenerational Behavior by Norms of Law, in: H.G. Leser (Ed.), *Collected Works* (Tübingen: Mohr Paul Siebeck), 1979, pp. 111-137.
> Ribot, Jordi (1998), El fundamento de la obligación de alimentos entre parientes, *Anuario de Derecho Civil* 61(3):1105-1177.
> Ribot, Jordi (1999), *Alimentos entre parientes y subsidiariedad de la protección social* (València: Tirant lo blanch).
> Schiller, A. Arthur (1971), »Alimenta« in the »Sententiae Hadriani«, in: *Studi in onore di Giuseppe Grosso*, vol. IV (Torino: Giappichelli) pp. 401-415.
> Schwenzer, Ingeborg (2006), *Model family code: from a global perspective* (Antwerp: Intersentia).
> Serverin, Evelyne (1983), *La mise en oeuvre de l'obligation alimentaire familiale. Definitions de la solidarité familiale par le juge et l'administrateur* (Lyon: Université Lyon III, Institut d'études judiciaires).
> Silverstein, Merril; Gans, Daphna; Yang, Frances M. (2006), Intergenerational Support to Aging Parents. The Role of Norms and Needs, *Journal of Family Issues* 27(8):1068-1084.
> Teitelbaum, Lee E. (1992), Intergenerational Responsibility and Family Obligations: On Sharing, *Utah Law Review* 3:765-802.
> Thomas, David (1989), The Elderly in an Urban-Industrial Society: England, 1750 to the Present, in: J. Eekelaar / P. Laslett, *An Aging World. Dilemmas and Challenges for Law and Social Policy*, (Oxford: Clarendon Press) pp. 59-87.
> Van Houtte, Jean; Breda, Jef (2005), Maintenance of the Aged by their Adult Children: an Adequate Legal Institution? in: M. Maclean (Ed.), *Family Law and Family Values* (Oxford: Hart) pp. 243-255.

The Sustainability of Survivor and Divorce Benefits in the Adult Worker Model: Incorporation of New Social Risks

Elisabeth Alofs[1] and Renaat Hoop[2]

I. Introduction: From old to new Social Risks

It is widely accepted that our western welfare states are in need of substantial modification. Their social arrangements and settlements, built up during the post-war period, are based on the male, sole, breadwinner with stable employment as the focal point of policy and provide protection against risks associated with the »Social Question« that arose at the end of the 19th century.

However, fragmentation, diversity and change have come to characterise labour markets as well as families and have disrupted the profound correspondence between the prevalent form of family, the type of jobs available in the labour market and the type of social security provided by welfare states. Today, the labour force participation rate of women has risen quite dramatically and renders the breadwinner model outdated. More and more it is being replaced by the adult worker model, in which everybody is supposed to be engaged in paid work in order to secure his or her economic independence.

These significant economic, socio-demographic and cultural changes and the premises of the adult worker model raise questions about the risks a welfare state should cover and about the instruments it should use to do so.

On the one hand, some risks that are currently still provided for, are considered outdated and labelled as »old social risks«.[3] The loss of the breadwinner by death or divorce for example – a risk covered by survivor benefit schemes and legal rights to spousal support following divorce – is increasingly considered as an old (social) risk.

---

1 Free University of Brussels / University of Antwerp, Belgium.
2 Free University of Brussels, Belgium.
3 Engelen, E., Hemerijck, A. & Trommel, W. (eds.), *Van sociale bescherming naar sociale investering. Zoektocht naar een andere verzorgingsstaat*, Den Haag, Lemma, 2007, p. 311.

On the other hand, the actual socio-economic transformations – generally indicated as a shift from an industrial to a post-industrial economy and society – go hand in hand with the emergence of new situations of insecurity, new risk structures labelled as »new social risks«.[4] Taking into account the evolutive and relative character of the recognition of a need for social protection as a »social risk«,[5] these »new social risks« may today rightly call for public protection.[6] The inability for men and women to devote time to work and care activities and to freely divide these responsibilities between each other at different stages of life, constitutes such a risk in our post-industrial society.[7]

In this article we want to confront this old and new social risk. We will argue that survivor benefits were meant to compensate in some way the risk the (usually female) caregiver took in abstaining from paid work and investing all of her time in non-paid activities. There may still be a reason to maintain some kind of survivor benefit. The income (and reintegration) risk of having (partially and/or temporarily) withdrawn from the labour market which occurs in an adult worker model due to the problematic combination of labour and care, is indeed very similar. We will examine to what extent the Belgian survivor pension in its current form is capable of covering this new social risk.

We will also compare the survivor pension with the legal right to alimony after divorce. The Belgian divorce and maintenance law was recently (2007) modified so that spousal support after divorce currently is

---

4   Esping-Andersen, G., *Social Foundations of Postindustrial Economies*, Oxford, Oxford University Press, 1999; Hemerijck, A., The Self-transformation of the European Social Model(s), in: Esping-Andersen, G. et al. (ed.), *Why We Need a New Welfare State*, Oxford, Oxford University Press, 2002, p. 173-214; Taylor-Gooby, P., (ed.), *New risks, New Welfare. The Transformation of the European Welfare State*, Oxford, Oxford University Press, 2004, 248 p.; Bonoli, G., *The Politics of New Social Risks and Policies. Mapping Diversity and Accounting for Cross-national Variation in Postindustrial Welfare States*, Paper prepared for presentation at the International Sociological Association, RC 19 meeting in Paris, 2-4 September 2004.

5   Pieters, D., *Inleiding tot de beginselen van de sociale zekerheid*, Deventer/Utrecht, Kluwer, 1995, p. 63.

6   Plantenga, J., The Life Course and the System of Social Security: Rethinking Incentives, Solidarity and Risks, *European Journal of Social Security*, n° 4, p. 310, 2005; De Beer, P., Leenders, P., Plantenga, J. & Roozemond, K., *Nieuwe tijden, nieuwe zekerheden. Naar een modern stelsel van sociale zekerheid*, Utrecht, Groenlinks Wetenschappelijk Bureau, 2004, p. 25-26.

7   Bonoli, G., *o.c.*, p. 4; Taylor-Gooby, P., *o.c.*, p. 5; Trifiletti, R., *Family Policies Facing New Social Risks: Lone Parents from Northern to Southern Europe and other family policy measures in context*, paper presented at the Annual Conference of the Research Committee (RC 19), International Sociological Association, Florence, September 6-8, 2007.

limited in time and has a pure alimentary character instead of an indemnifying character. At the same time the new law takes more strongly the adult worker model into account since it aims at reintegrating the former spouse in the labour market. Since these two arrangements cover in some way a similar risk, the new characteristics of the right to alimony after a divorce may be useful as an example or source of inspiration for a modified and present-day survivor benefit.

II. The Survivor Benefit: An old Social Risk?

In most West-European countries the social security systems still grant some kind of survivor benefit. The social risk of »survival« refers to the permanent loss of the earned income of the deceased partner, leaving the family without any means of existence.[8] The survivor benefit aims at guaranteeing the surviving relatives who were dependent upon the labour income of the deceased a replacement income. The survivor benefit is thus founded on a pre-existing relationship of income dependency between people (usually the marital or other partner and the children).[9] In fact, the risk is more linked to the family configuration than it is a labour risk.[10]

This relationship of dependency results from the formerly widespread existence and social acceptance of the breadwinner regime – with a (male) breadwinner generating an income from paid labour on the one hand and a caring spouse and children »at his charge« on the other hand. It is precisely because of this traditional division of tasks that the death of the breadwinner constituted a huge social risk for the surviving relatives during most part of the last century.[11] The concomitant belief that the breadwinner should continue his obligation of support towards his dependents even after his death, constitutes the basis for the acceptance of his death as a »social risk«.[12] The same was true for the risk of getting divorced. But

---

8 Van Steenberge, J., Pensioenen, in: X., *Sociale zekerheid. Verdere ideeën*, sociura-project, Leuven, Universitaire Pers, 1994, p. 97.
9 Bod, Th., *Het pensioenbegrip. Enige beschouwingen over het pensioen en zijn rechtskarakter*, Zwolle, W.E.J. Tjeenk Willink, 1994, p. 29.
10 De Beer, P., Leenders, P., Plantenga, J. & Roozemond, K., *Nieuwe tijden, nieuwe zekerheden. Naar een modern stelsel van sociale zekerheid*, Utrecht, Groenlinks Wetenschappelijk Bureau, 2004, p. 19.
11 De Beer, P., et al., *o.c.*, p. 24.
12 Van Langendonck, J. & Put, J., *Handboek Socialezekerheidsrecht*, Antwerpen, Intersentia, 2006, p. 686.

only in the case of the decease of the breadwinner was the loss of income covered by social security since widows had fallen into their situation innocently and »deserved« the benefit, a divorcée didn't.[13] Notwithstanding the fact that the divorcée can claim a right to maintenance after divorce, some authors have suggested to provide also social security coverage in case of a divorce since it causes a similar risk as in the case of the death of the breadwinner/spouse.[14] The question as to the need of government intervention via the social security system in case of divorce rises all the more in cases of the non-payment of spousal support.[15]

Today however, the breadwinner regime seems more and more outdated. Women participate more than before in the paid labour market and ensure their own or an extra family income; they are less dependent on the earned income of their partners. Also at a policy level, the breadwinner regime is nowadays being replaced by the »adult worker model«.[16] Hence the apparently evident conclusion is that the death of the income earning partner no longer qualifies as a social risk, followed by the logical proposal to abolish the outmoded survivor benefits.

This firm conclusion however needs to be questioned. First of all, attention needs to be drawn to the fact that, even if the breadwinner model no longer seems to be pushed by the authorities, this doesn't mean that it has disappeared in practice. On the contrary, especially among the older generations there are a lot of women who have properly lived up (and still

---

13 Holtmaat, R., De reparatie van vrouwenrisico's. Naar een vernieuwend sociaal zekerheidsbeleid, in: Van Lenning, A., Brouns, M. & J. De Bruijn (eds.), *Inzichten uit vrouwenstudies: uitdagingen voor beleidsmakers*, Den Haag, SZW/Vuga, 1995, p. 238; Skevik, A., Family Economy Workers or Caring Mothers? Male Breadwinning and Widows' Pensions in Norway and the UK, *Feminist Economics*, 10 (2), July 2004, p. 95.
14 Van Steenberge, J., Pensioenen in: X. (ed.), *Sociale zekerheid. Verdere ideeën*, sociuraproject, Leuven, Universitaire Pers, 1994, p. 97; Mortelmans, D., Swennen F., Alofs, E., De echtscheiding en haar gevolgen: een vervlochten evolutie van recht en samenleving, in: Cuypers, D., Mortelmans, D. en Torfs, N. (eds.), *Is echtscheiding werkelijk win for life?*, Brugge, die keure, 2008, p. 33.
15 The service for alimony claims (»DAVO«, set up by the law of 21 February 2003) can indeed intervene by paying advances on non-paid maintenance benefits however this possibility was restricted to child support only. For the alimony paid to the former spouse, the DAVO cannot pay advances, even though the situation of (financial) need of the former spouse/parent caused by the non-payment of the alimony also influences the standard of living for the children.
16 At the level of the European Union increasing the labour force participation, and especially those of women and older workers, has become the official employment policy since the summit of Lisbon in March 2000. The so-called »Lisbon strategy« holds out the prospect of a labour force participation of 70% in the year 2010, and 60% for women.

do so) to the breadwinner model and to whom it would be unjust to remove the social protection coupled to their position as a housewife. Their acquired rights will make transitional measures inevitable.

Secondly, one should ask the question to what extent only the loss of a single income currently constitutes a risk. In the ever increasing two-earner households the loss of a second income can also constitute a risk when the livelihood of the surviving relatives gets threatened.[17] This will undoubtedly be the case when the labour income of the survivor was less than that of the deceased or, in any situation in which the survivor income is insufficient to cover the family expenses. In reality, this latter situation appears to be rather the rule than the exception since the labour force participation of women has grown but more women than men work part-time or temporarily interrupt their working career. Due to this »atypical career« of women their labour force participation cannot simply be equated with economic independency or a two-breadwinner household. The explanation for these atypical careers must be found in the difficult combination of work and care, a problem especially women get confronted with and that unanimously is described as a new social risk.[18]

Moreover, if the adult worker model should be understood as a double breadwinner model, it would completely deny the fact that, when women will participate in paid labour in the same way as men usually do (or did), a solution would have to be found for the household and care work traditionally carried out by women. In this respect awareness is growing that the solution of outsourcing these tasks knows its limits and that parents often rightly wish to keep (partly) providing for this care themselves. A modern system of social security, the social investment state, takes into account these concurrent demands of work and care and offers possibilities to combine or switch between paid work and care in a more diversified pattern of life.

It is this focus on the combining of tasks that makes it possible to see the link between the risk traditionally covered by the survivor benefit and the risk it could cover in a more up to date variant. Besides a division of earned income the breadwinner model also amounts to a(n) (implicit)

---

17 Van Steenberge, J., l.c., p. 97. This author also asks the question whether in addition to a decease, a divorce shouldn't be accepted as an equal cause of a same social risk (*Ibid.*).
18 Bonoli, G., *o.c.*, p. 4; Taylor-Gooby, P., *o.c.*, p. 5; Trifiletti, R., *Family Policies Facing New Social Risks: Lone Parents from Northern to Southern Europe and other family policy measures in context*, paper presented at the Annual Conference of the Research Committee (RC 19), International Sociological Association, Florence, September 6-8, 2007.

division of labour: it does not only determine how the family *income* is earned, notably via one fulltime worker, but also fixes the way in which the family *tasks* are performed, notably by one fulltime non-paid worker. It is precisely this division of labour and its consequences the survivor benefit »old style« provides protection for. It was assumed that since this division of labour had become irreversible from a certain moment on,[19] it was no longer justified to expect the surviving spouse to accept a modification thereof. In other words, the survivor benefit grants an income replacement to the surviving partner who, as part of a permanent cohabitation, sacrificed her own earning capacity to devote herself entirely to the domestic tasks in order to make it possible for her partner to fully commit himself to earning a family income outside the house.

Well, this kind of division of work and income within a family structure still persists in present-day society with this difference that family structures have become more diversified and the lines of division are less unequivocal. And also today, just as in the old days, the death of one of the partners counts as a disruption of this division for it makes its continuation impossible for the future. The present challenge to a modern social investment state becomes clear. The question is not whether we as a society are still prepared to subsidize the financial dependency created by the breadwinner model, but whether we are willing and able to provide coverage for the new social risk of balancing work and family life.

III. Proposal for a Modern Regulation of Survivor Benefits

The education and care of children indeed consumes time and money and goes hand in hand with a certain loss of earning capacity: either parents choose to provide the care themselves but in that situation there will be less time to earn an income, or parents choose to both stay (part-time) at work, but then they will be forced to spend a part of their earned income on childcare. On top of that, there are the material maintenance costs of raising children.

---

19 The widow (of widower) generally has to have attained a certain age, that is to say the age at which one's (re)integration into the labour market is no longer to be expected (often 40 years). This condition was often mitigated or sometimes even lifted for widow(er)s incapacitated for work and/or having raised a certain number of children or having them at charge. (Pieters, D., *o.c.*, p. 58).

As long as parents are living as a couple, there is the possibility to share these costs and care time. But as soon as one of the partners is no longer available, the remaining partner is alone. Depending on how both partners had divided work and family tasks, the lone parent will either be confronted with a loss of family income or will be obliged to outsource the care of the children, or both but to a lesser degree. It is precisely this risk rather than the loss of a breadwinner income that a present-day survivor scheme should be able to cover. The children's perspective should be central to this. It is in their interest, if one of their parents is no longer available, to secure an upbringing environment that is not disrupted by a chronic lack of time and/or money of the lone surviving parent.[20]

At the same time however the interests of the partner left behind should be taken into consideration. Because the adult worker model assumes that an adult without dependent children is self-supporting, it is important to timely restore the autonomous earning capacity of the left behind parent, for example by bringing up his or her employability to the required standards. It is obvious that a modern survivor scheme will have to do more than simply »protect«, it will also need to be »empowering«.[21] Apart from providing a direct compensation for the yet indivisible costs, society will have to invest in the future (re)integration in the labour market of the surviving partner by means of qualitative services with regard to child care, training and finding employment.

Summarizing we can say that a modern survivor scheme should cover the following risks:

a. the inability to share the costs attached to the upbringing of children with a partner;
b. the difficulty of combining paid work and care;
c. the difficulty of making the transition to a self-supporting job on the paid labour market once the care for the children has diminished or completely fallen away.

---

20 Cf. Holtmaat, R., Een paarse bladzijde in de geschiedenis van de weduwen- en wezenwetgeving in Nederland: een nieuw wetsvoorstel voor een algemene nabestaandenwet, *Sociaal maandblad arbeid*, 50, nr. 9, september 1995, p. 489.
21 Engelen, E., Hemerijck, A. & Trommel, W. (eds.), *o.c.*, p.311 and 322; Bonoli, G., *The Politics of New Social Risks Coverage*, paper prepared for the Annual meeting of the American Political Science Association, Boston, 28 August – 1 September 2002, p. 4-5; Esping-Andersen, G. et al. (eds.), *Why We Need a New Welfare State*, Oxford, Oxford University Press, 2002; Giddens, A., *The Third Way: the Renewal of Social Democracy*, Cambridge, Polity Press, 1998; Von Maydell, B., et al. (eds.), *Enabling Social Europe*, Berlijn, Springer-Verlag, 2006, p. 88.

The first of these risks could be covered, as already happens in most social security systems, by means of a special (semi-)orphan's benefit or an extra allowance on top of the common family benefits. In this way an unjustifiable drop in the living standards of the children due to the decease of one or both of the parents can be prevented.

For the coverage of the second risk a survivor benefit should be granted to make it possible for the surviving spouse to (partially) make up for the lost family income and/or the lost care work. Important in this respect is that the surviving spouse can make his or her own choice. Therefore, the benefit should be allowed to be used either as an income supplement or to pay for external care or a combination of both. Keeping the definition of the risk in mind, it goes without saying that the cumulation of this benefit with an earned income poses no problem of principle, although a maximum income limit appears useful to confine the scheme to those who need it. [22,23] The benefit will also be temporary since from a certain age[24] on it may rightly be assumed that the fulltime presence and care of the parent is no longer indispensable for the child(ren).[25] From that moment on the focal point of attention should go to the parent's (re)integration into the labour market.

To counter the last risk, the (re)integration on the labour market or the transition from a small job to a job that makes it possible to provide for oneself, a temporary adjustment benefit could be granted. The aim of this benefit is to make it possible for the surviving spouse to actively look around and to get prepared for the labour market. This adjustment benefit could not only be awarded to the spouse whose youngest child has reached the abovementioned age (before or after the death of the deceased parent) but also to surviving spouses without children who during their marriage were financially dependent upon their partner. Since this adjustment benefit intends to activate the surviving partner it could

---

22 In current schemes, as the Belgian one (cf. infra), anti-cumulation rules often work out as inactivity traps.
23 Cf.: In the United Kingdom, the bereavement benefits are not affected if the surviving partner works.
24 One could take the school age (in Belgium: 6 years) as point of reference since from that moment on most children spend most of their time at school and not at home. Obviously, other arrangements are conceivable, for instance the gradual decrease of the benefit commensurate with the increasing age of the youngest child.
25 This means that the survivor benefit can not be granted to the surviving spouse whose youngest child had already reached the fixed age limit at the time of decease of the first parent. This surviving spouse will be eligible however for the adjustment benefit (cf. infra).

be made conditional upon successfully following schooling or training, or turned into an earmarked subsidy to finance after-school child care or other transition promoting facilities.[26] If, during this adjustment period, the surviving spouse doesn't succeed in finding means of support (via personal labour or through a new marriage or cohabitation), s/he will have to rely on other (residual) social security arrangements (unemployment scheme, disability or means-tested social assistance).

IV. The Survivor Benefit versus the Legal Right to Alimony after Divorce[27]

1. *The Loss of the Breadwinner/Spouse under Private Law:*
   The Belgian Divorce Act of 27 April 2007[28]

We will contrast the Belgian survivor pension with the recently modified Belgian divorce and maintenance law and demonstrate that our plea for the conservation of a system of survivor benefits, albeit in a form and with a content adapted to the current social, economic and cultural situation as well as to the new social risks which arise out of this context, corresponds with (the premises of) this recent divorce and alimony reform.

Both the regulation concerning the survivor pension and spousal support following divorce originally assumed a marriage which was in principle lifelong and in which duties between spouses were allocated according to the traditional breadwinner model. Derived rights within the social security system (such as the survivor pension) on the one hand and the (lifelong) right to maintenance on the other hand, gave women a sort of pension and income compensation for their unpaid household work and child care after the dissolution of their marriage.

However, due to social, economic and cultural changes and the rising of the adult worker model both risks – the loss of the breadwinner/spouse by death and after divorce – have evolved in the course of time. The new social risks which a modern system of survivor benefits has to cover (cf. supra),

---

26   Cf. the Norwegian survivor system that equally includes an education benefit and a childcare benefit to encourage employment: Skevik, A., *o.c.*, p. 104-105.
27   The rules concerning the right to alimony, discussed in this article, are related to the judicial determination of the alimony. However, the basic rule is that the parties agree, on a contractual basis, about the right to and terms of any alimony after divorce.
28   The act of 27 April 2007 concerning the reform of divorce proceedings, *Moniteur Belge* 7 June 2007.

are analogous to the circumstances that follow a divorce. But whereas the Belgian survivor pension did not substantially change since its initial enactment, the divorce and alimony law was fully reformed in 2007. The Belgian (federal) legislator to some extent took into account the current social, economic and cultural changes and the related new social risks.

Whereas formerly the lifelong marriage model emphasised the public (social security) functions of marriage[29], marriage is currently considered to be a type of private agreement, with love as its foundation and which can be dissolved, with »no strings attached«, should the love disappear.[30] The divorce reform in 2007 has its basis in this socially modified concept of marriage and constitutes the (provisional) end in the continuous liberalisation of divorce law. The Belgian Divorce Act of 2007 entrenches the right to divorce and maintains only two grounds for a divorce: the divorce on the basis of the irretrievable breakdown of the marriage and the divorce by mutual consent. The fault-divorce was abolished with the aim of introducing a guiltless divorce law.

Together with the liberalisation of the procedure for and the possibility of obtaining a divorce, the consequences – and in particular the rules regarding spousal support following divorce – were thoroughly reformed. At the same time as the notion of fault was abolished in divorce proceedings (with certain exceptions), the idea of fault as the basis for the right to alimony after divorce was also deleted.[31] Consequently the Divorce Act of 2007 provides a »large basic right to post-divorce maintenance«: regarding the new article 301 of the Belgian Civil Code each former spouse in (financial) need can claim spousal support from the other (wealthier) spouse, independent of any fault of either party contributing to the breakdown of the marriage. Regarding the current purely alimentary function of spousal support (and the disappearance of its indemnifying character), its only aim is to cover the financial need or risks which occur as a result of the loss of the breadwinner/spouse. Consequently the objectives for spousal support following divorce became similar to these for a survivor benefit.

---

29 Renchon, J.-L., La nouvelle réforme (précipitée) du droit belge du divorce: le ›droit au divorce‹, *Revue trimestrielle de droit familial*, n° 4, p. 927 e.v., 934 e.v., 1059 e.v, 2007.
30 Swennen, F., Aps, F., De echtscheidingswet 2007, *Rechtskundig Weekblad*, n° 14, p. 555, 2007-08.
31 Exceptions: The spouse may be excluded from the right to alimony in case of a gross fault, partner violence or when the need of the spouse is the consequence of a unilateral decision which was not motivated by the needs of the family.

The following analysis of some of the characteristics of the right to alimony after a divorce under the reform of 2007, will show that the nature of this benefit is essentially a replacement income, which as a transitional measure has to enable a former spouse that is in need to become self-sufficient. The new maintenance regulation mainly deals with the above defined third social risk (i.e. the difficult transition from caring to employment). We will show that (some of the) reasoning and principles behind that reform can justifiably be applied to – or at least offer inspiration for – a reform of the regulation of the survivor pension. Notwithstanding the fact that the new alimony regulation is not entirely free of problems, we can learn from it for our proposal with regard to survivor benefits.

We will compare both regulations – spousal support after divorce and the survivor pension – with regard to the conditions for obtaining the benefits, as well as the duration of both benefits. We will examine systematically to what extent both regulations cover the above described new social risks. Finally, next to these current regulations we will place our proposal for a modern regulation of survivor benefits and we will analyze to what extent this proposal meets the criticism expressed with respect to the current regulations.

2. Conditions for Obtaining Compensation Benefits

As a logical consequence of the purely alimentary function of spousal support following divorce, the main requirement giving rise to this right is the financial need of the spouse. This condition of financial need implies that the former spouse is only entitled to alimony if s/he is not able to support himself – i.e. s/he does not have sufficient income and can not reasonably be expected to (be able to) gain such income. This subsidiary character of spousal support already existed before the divorce and maintenance reform of 2007, but is now more strongly emphasised assisting the former spouse to achieve independence.[32]

Similar to the legal right to alimony after a divorce, also the arrangements of survivor benefits tend to reserve the benefits to surviving relatives who most likely will be unable to provide for themselves via work and thus of whom society no longer expects a self-supporting labour contribu-

---

[32] During the parliamentary discussions it was explicitly mentioned that the former spouse has a duty to make the necessary effort to become self-supporting by seeking employment of by completing his education (Memorie van toelichting', *Parl. St.* Kamer 2005-06, nr. 51-2431/001, p. 11-19; *Hand.* Senaat, nr. 3-210 (22/3/2007), p. 64).

tion.[33] We believe that in the Belgian system of survivor pension, the principle of subsidiarity must be emphasised. The present regulation does take into account the resources of the surviving spouse. Yet the potential of the surviving spouse to acquire an income is not considered when the surviving spouse has children to care for or when s/he has reached the age of 45. These criteria according to which the surviving spouse is incontrovertibly deemed to be (permanently or temporarily) incapable of working and consequently has the right to a survivor pension, seem to be outdated, at least in part, in the current social and economic climate. We'll discuss this in detail.

2.1 Child Care

The surviving spouse, of whatever age, can claim a survivor pension if she/he has to care for at least one child. The surviving spouse is considered to do so, when s/he raises a child for whom s/he can claim child benefits; excluding some exceptions, this continues until the child has attained majority or until the end of its education. Child care, regardless of the number of children and their age, is sufficient to exempt the surviving spouse from the duty to seek employment and to entitle him or her to a survivor pension.

In this matter, the regulation concerning the survivor pension differs from spousal support following divorce. In the latter case child care does not automatically guarantee a right to alimony. Only if the need to care for a child *de facto* limits the employment options of the former spouse to the extent that s/he no longer can meet his or her financial needs, will a (temporary) right to alimony arise.

Also compared with the other sectors of the social security system, the regulation concerning the survivor pension is more generous towards a person caring for a child. Although child care indeed leads to higher benefits in several social security sectors, it rarely creates a right, as such, to any benefits – except for child benefits which (partially) cover the material cost of a child. For example, the regulation concerning the survivor pension contrasts sharply with the unemployment benefit scheme, where child care has in principle no influence on – a fortiori does not exempt the parent from – the obligation to be engaged in paid work.[34] As in the case

---

33 Pieters, D., *o.c.*, p. 56; Ogus, A. & Barendt, E., *The Law of Social Security*, London, Butterworths, 1988, 234-236.
34 According to Article 90 of the KB of 25 November 1991 a fully unemployed person who has difficulties on a social or familial plan, can obtain a temporary exemption from

when the legal right to support after a divorce is established, the unemployment benefit scheme examines whether the child care is so heavy as to create an obstacle to performing a particular job. Even if child care is a real obstacle to a particular job, the unemployed parent is not completely absolved from his duty to find employment.

Above, we indicated the risk for the surviving parent of combining child care and finding employment to be self-supporting. In the interest of the children and to avoid serious disturbance in their upbringing because of a lack of money or time on the part of the surviving parent, we emphasise that the aim of a modern regulation of survivor benefits is to cover this risk. This can be achieved, as we suggested above, by means of a benefit which compensates either the loss of income, or the loss of a caregiver and which gives the possibility to a surviving parent to use the benefit as an income supplement (if s/he fulfils the care tasks), or to purchase care (if s/he is a breadwinner), or for a combination of both (if s/he has part-time work and fulfils part-time care duties).

However, we believe that the presence and care of the parent is essential for (very) young children, but becomes less necessary for a child of a certain age. The present regulation concerning the survivor pension is based on the idea that the child is in need of care until he reaches the age of majority. This opinion seems to be no longer maintainable in the current social and economic milieu. As the (youngest) child reaches a certain age, the (fulltime) presence and care of the parent become less necessary so that s/he would be free to once again seek proper employment. For example, it seems to be more realistic to grant the survivor benefit only until the youngest child has reached the age of compulsory attendance at school (and consequently is considered to spend a large part of the day at school). From that moment the parent should be able to gradually reintegrate into the labour market and the survivor benefit can be lowered or ended. To ease the transition from care to labour a temporary benefit can be granted (cf. supra).

2.2 Age

Even without child care obtains the surviving spouse, in accordance with the present regulation, a (lifelong) right to survivor pension if s/he has

---

some duties (including the duty to work or the availability for the labour market), if they show that the exemption aims to remedy these difficulties. In such a case their unemployment benefit will be reduced to a fixed daily amount.

reached the age of 45 years. The death of the breadwinner disengages the surviving spouse of 45 years or over from ever needing to work again.

By setting the age at 45 years the legislator has assumed that the chances of a woman of 45 years finding a job or remarrying are so small that she has to be exempted from the duty to seek employment and that she should acquire a right to a survivor pension.[35] Yet, our society and our way of thinking have changed to such an extent that the rationale for the (rather low) age condition, especially when viewed in light of the adult worker model, can be questioned. The age limit of 45 years is not only strange when viewed in contrast with the current (old age) pension age, also in the framework of the active welfare state and the adult worker model, this limit seems to have a counterproductive effect.[36] Granting a survivor pension to a 45-year old surviving spouse (who was inactive on the moment of the death of the other spouse) risks discouraging his or her re-integration into socio-economic life. Moreover, it could encourage an active surviving spouse to leave the professional activity s/he was involved in at the moment of the other spouse's death.[37] The regulation concerning the survivor pension counteracts the efforts made in other sectors of the social security system, as for example in the unemployment benefits scheme, as well as in the pension sector itself (the old age pension) which seek to promote the active search for work, encourage people to remain in active employment for longer[38] and maintain higher employment rates overall. In light of the principles of the Lisbon strategy[39], the age criterion in the surviving pension regulation should be re-examined.

We believe that survivor benefits (in the form of a replacement income) are currently only justifiable when such risk occurs that care for children

---

35 A. Uyttenhove, S. Renette, E. Lenaerts, *Feitelijke scheiding, echtscheiding en sociale zekerheid*, Brugge, die keure, 2004, 181.
36 Taelemans, A., Peeters, H., Curvers, G., Berghman, J., Socio-economisch profiel van weduwen en weduwnaars met en zonder overlevingspensioen, in: Van den Troost, A., Vleminckx, K. (eds.), *Een pensioen op maat van vrouwen?*, Antwerpen, Garant, 2007, 137-154.
37 Cf. H. Peemans-Poulet, De rechten van de gezinsleden in de sociale zekerheid, Belgish tijdschrift voor sociale zekerheid, nr. 1, p. 55, 1994.
38 Cf. the measures taken in the framework of the Belgian Generation Pact which promotes the »actively ageing«, such as the reduction of social security contributions for employees of more than 45 years old, the stimulation of the right to outplacement for older employees and the increase of the age conditions concerning the interim pension etc. (cf. Kenniscentrum SD WORX (ed.), *Werken met het generatiepact*, Antwerpen, Standaard Uitgeverij, 2006, p. 71 e.v. en 93 e.v.).
39 The so-called »Lisbon strategy« holds out the prospect of a labour force participation of 70% in the year 2010, and 60% for women.

and participation in employment can only be combined with great difficulty, if at all. In our opinion, only child care (and even then only until the child reaches a certain age) can currently justify a survivor benefit. In the absence of children for which fulltime care is essential, the surviving spouse is considered, in accordance with the adult worker model, to be able to find paid work and to be self-sufficient. Yet, also in this model, temporary adaptation compensations can be offered to support the transition from care to labour in cases where child care was given in the past of to the surviving spouse without children who during his or her marriage was financially dependent upon his or her partner.[40]

3. Restriction in Time of Compensation Benefits: Reactivating Function
An important innovation of the new divorce and maintenance law concerns the time restriction of (the right to) alimony after divorce. A time restriction has to contribute to the process which will educate society that a right to alimony is not automatically acquired at a divorce. Putting a time limit on spousal support following divorce encourages the spouses to become economically independent. Moreover this restriction in time will incite future spouses to take this into account when organising their married life.[41]

The idea of the time restriction of the right to alimony after a divorce is supported by sociological research which showed that the economic decline of the spouses after a divorce is generally temporary (in the first years after the divorce).[42] Consequently, protection or compensation measures do not have to last for a lifetime. In any case such lifetime measures risk making the beneficiary (economically) dependent on the benefit. Time restricted measures must offer a temporary support to overcome the period of economic difficulties after a divorce and to allow the former spouse to rearrange his life.[43]

---

40 Cf. In the United Kingdom, a temporary bereavement allowance is paid (for 52 weeks) to the surviving partner of at least 45 years, without child care.
41 Cf. amendement nr. 29 van mevrouw Lahaye-Battheu, *Parl. St.* Kamer 2005-06, nr. 51-2341/002, p. 25.
42 Jansen, M., De financiële gevolgen van relatiebreuken: terugval en herstel bij mannen en vrouwen, in: Cuypers, D., Mortelmans, D. Torfs, N. (eds.), *Is echtscheiding werkelijk win for life?*, Brugge, die keure, 2008, p. 39-67.
43 Mortelmans, D., Swennen F., Alofs, E., De echtscheiding en haar gevolgen: een vervlochten evolutie van recht en samenleving in: Cuypers, D., Mortelmans, D., Torfs, N. (eds.), *Is echtscheiding werkelijk win for life?*, Brugge, die keure, 2008, p. 33.

Formerly, spousal support after divorce, as a consequence of the lifelong marriage model, was granted, in principle, for a life time (»win for life«).[44] Currently the right to alimony after divorce is limited in time to a period equal to the duration of the marriage. This period represents an upper limit: the judge can stipulate a shorter period. In determining the period, the judge can take into account the economic choices made by both spouses during the cohabitation (e.g. if a spouse devoted her time to the care of the household and children). The judge can deviate from the legal maximum duration of spousal support (the duration of the marriage) and prolong it in case of extraordinary circumstances. To be entitled to a prolongation of the legal duration, the alimony claimant must prove that s/he is still in need at the end of the original maximum duration for reasons outside of his or her control.[45] This implies that the claimant must demonstrate s/he made the necessary efforts to provide for his or her livelihood by looking for work, by completing a training or by claiming social security rights.[46] When the maximum duration of the right to spousal support is prolonged, the amount of the maintenance is set as a maximum (and no longer as a minimal level) at the amount which is necessary to cover the needs of the claimant.[47]

The Divorce Act of 2007 is criticised by some authors who blame the legislator for wrongfully assuming the economic independence of all spouses and to have ignored the socio-economic function of marriage for many women – in particular women with young children.[48] These authors believe that the restriction in time of spousal support has to be combined with other measures of (state) support to reinforce the economic independence of former spouses.[49] The Belgian regulation does indeed not

---

44 If the situation of one of the spouses changed drastically (of reasons out of their control) and consequently the amount of the alimony was no longer justified, the court could then reduce it.
45 Art. 301, §4, 2de lid BW.
46 Memorie van toelichting', *Parl. St.* Kamer 2005-06, nr. 51-2431/001, p. 11-19.
47 Art. 301, §4, 2de lid BW.
48 Swennen, F., Het nieuwe echtscheidingsrecht en de CEFL-beginselen inzake echtscheiding en alimentatie tussen gewezen echtgenoten, in: UCERF (ed.), *Algemene ontwikkelingen in het familierecht*, Nijmegen, Ars Aequi Libri, p. 48; Swennen, F., Aps, F., De echtscheidingswet 2007, *Rechtskundig Weekblad*, n° 14, p. 555, 2007-08; Casman, H., Nieuw echtscheidingsrecht. Toelichting voor de notariële praktijk, *Notarieel en Fiscaal Maandblad*, n° 10, p. 285, 2007; Renchon, J.-L., La nouvelle réforme (précipitée) du droit belge du divorce: le »droit au divorce«, *Revue trimestrielle de droit familial*, n° 4, p. 927 e.v., 934 e.v., 1059 e.v., 2007.
49 Casman, H., Nieuw echtscheidingsrecht. Toelichting voor de notariële praktijk, *Notarieel en Fiscaal Maandblad*, n° 10, p. 285, 2007.

necessarily provide cover (by means of alimony payment) for the period in which children born out of wedlock need (fulltime) care. Take the example of a brief marriage (e.g. 3 years), during which 2 children were born. In accordance with the Belgian regulation, spousal support is granted for a maximum of 3 years, in spite of the presence of children between 3 and 6 years old and still in need of (fulltime) care, which can complicate the combination of care and labour. The Dutch regulation on the other hand took this problem into account by setting the time restriction on a maximum of 12 years[50], assuming the less favourable situation in which a child (conceived during the marriage) is born after the divorce. It offers the beneficiary former spouse the chance to take care of the child until the latter is less in need of primary care, after which time the former spouse can undertake the necessary steps to arrange for his or her own maintenance.[51]

Similar to the right to alimony which (before the divorce reform of 2007) was granted, in principle, for the duration of the spouse's life, also the survivor pension is not restricted in time. We don't think that granting an, in principle, lifelong survivor pension still corresponds with the current social and economic milieu and the current marriage model.

We consequently integrated the principle of a time restriction for compensating benefits in our above described proposal for a new regulation of survivor benefits. The survivor benefit, which aims to compensate the loss of income or the loss of care so that the surviving spouse can balance his or her duties to work and care as s/he considers most appropriate, on the one hand, and on the other hand the adaptation compensation to support the transition from care to labour after a period of care, are both temporary. The first is only due as long as the children require fulltime care; the second only during a transitional period.

In the proposed reform we also took into account the above-mentioned criticism of ignoring the socio-economic function of marriage for many women, in particular women with young children: the right to a survivor benefit which assist the balancing act between a parent offering care and working is linked to the child's need for care (regardless of the duration of the marriage). Moreover the proposed system does not assume the im-

---

50 There is an exception when the marriage has lasted no longer than 5 years and no children are born out of wedlock in which case the right to alimony is granted for a maximum duration equal to the duration of the marriage.
51 Boele-Woelki, K., Cherednychenko, O., Coenraad, L., Dutch Report concerning the CEFL Questionnaire on Grounds for Divorce and Maintenance Between Former Spouses, http://www.law.uu.nl/priv/cefl, p. 31.

mediate independence of the caring parent after the disappearance or reduction of the care tasks. This economic independence can be reinforced gradually. During this transitional period (which is limited in time) and during which the (re)integration into the labour market can be realised, the caring parent can appeal to an adaptation compensation which will allow him or her to actively refocus on the labour market.

V. Conclusion

The characteristics of the right to alimony after divorce according to the divorce reform of 2007 reveals the nature of the benefit as a replacement income which, being a transitional measure, gives the spouse in need the chance to become financial independent in the course of a certain time. This aim results in particular from the alimentary function of the maintenance and the related condition of need and the restriction in time of the right to alimony.

If spousal support following divorce, being a private law compensation mechanism in case of the loss of the breadwinner/spouse, evolves in character to a temporary replacement income with a reactivating function, then the continuation of the regulation concerning the survivor pension (being a social security compensation mechanism covering the similar risk) in its current form becomes highly questionable. We have tried to demonstrate that the principles upon which the reform of the divorce and maintenance law has been founded can be applied to a large degree to a reform of the survivor pension in the manner that we have presented.

References

- Alfandari, E., L'évolution de la notion de risque social. Les rapports de l'économie et du social, in: Van Langendonck, J. (ed.), *The New Social Risks*, London/The Hague/Boston, Kluwer Law International, 1997, p. 29-52.
- Beck, U., *Risk Society: Towards a New Modernity*, New Delhi, Sage, 1992.
- Berghman, J., The New Social Risks: a Synthetic View, in: Van Langendonck, J. (ed.), *The New Social Risks*, London/The Hague/Boston, Kluwer Law International, 1997, p. 251-261.
- Boelaert, T., Alimentatie: tussen theorie en praktijk. Enkele beschouwingen over de tegemoetkoming van de dienst voor alimentatievorderingen, in: Cuypers, D., Mortelmans, D. en Torfs, N. (eds.), *Is echtscheiding werkelijk win for life?*, Brugge, die keure, 2008, p. 207-222.
- Bod, Th., *Het pensioenbegrip. Enige beschouwingen over het pensioen en zijn rechtskarakter*, Zwolle, W.E.J. Tjeenk Willink, 1994.
- Boeli-Woelki, K. e.a., *»Dutch Report concerning the CEFL Questionnaire on Grounds for Divorce and Maintenance Between Former Spouses«*, http://www.law.uu.nl/priv/cefl.
- Bol, J., De grondslag in de ANW: de Algemene Nabestaandenwet getoetst aan artikel 26 BuPo-verdrag en aan het ILO-verdrag 121, *Nemesis*, n° 1, p. 4-9, 1993.
- Bonoli, G., *The Politics of New Social Risks Coverage*, paper prepared for the Annual meeting of the American Political Science Association, Boston, 28 August – 1 September 2002.
- Bonoli, G., *The Politics of New Social Risks and Policies. Mapping Diversity and Accounting for Cross-national Variation in Postindustrial Welfare States*, Paper prepared for presentation at the International Sociological Association, RC 19 meeting in Paris, 2 – 4 September 2004.
- Casman, H., Nieuw echtscheidingsrecht. Toelichting voor de notariële praktijk, *Notarieel en Fiscaal Maandblad*, n° 10, p. 277-294, 2007.
- De Beer, P., Leenders, P., Plantenga, J. & Roozemond, K., *Nieuwe tijden, nieuwe zekerheden. Naar een modern stelsel van sociale zekerheid*, Utrecht, Groenlinks Wetenschappelijk Bureau, 2004.
- Engelen, E., Hemerijck A. & Trommel, W. (eds.), *Van sociale bescherming naar sociale investering. Zoektocht naar een andere verzorgingsstaat*, Den Haag, Lemma, 2007.
- Esping-Andersen, G. et al. (eds.), *Why We Need a New Welfare State*, Oxford, Oxford University Press, 2002.

› Esping-Andersen, G., *Social Foundations of Postindustrial Economies*, Oxford, Oxford University Press, 1999.
› Giddens, A., Risk and Responsibility, *Modern Law Journal*, n° 1, 1999.
› Giddens, A., *The Third Way: the Renewal of Social Democracy*, Cambridge, Polity Press, 1998.
› Hatland, A. & Skevik, A., Changes in the family, in: Van Langendonck, J. (ed.), *The New Social Risks*, London/The Hague/Boston, Kluwer Law International, 1997, p. 73-90.
› Hemerijck, A., The Self-transformation of the European Social Models, in Esping-Andersen, G. et al. (ed.), *Why We Need a New Welfare State*, Oxford, Oxford University Press, 2002, p. 173-214.
› Holtmaat, R., De reparatie van vrouwenrisico's. Naar een vernieuwend sociaal zekerheidsbeleid, in: Van Lenning, A., Brouns, M. & De Bruijn, J. (eds.), *Inzichten uit vrouwenstudies: uitdagingen voor beleidsmakers*, Den Haag, SZW/Vuga, 1995, p. 223-247.
› Holtmaat, R., Een paarse bladzijde in de geschiedenis van de weduwen- en wezenwetgeving in Nederland: een nieuw wetsvoorstel voor een algemene nabestaandenwet, *Sociaal maandblad arbeid*, n° 9, p.486-492, 1995.
› Kenniscentrum SD WORX (ed.), *Werken met het generatiepact*, Antwerpen, Standaard Uitgeverij, 2006.
› Jansen, M., De financiële gevolgen van relatiebreuken: terugval en herstel bij mannen en vrouwen, in: Cuypers, D., Mortelmans, D. en Torfs, N. (eds.), *Is echtscheiding werkelijk win for life?*, Brugge, die keure, 2008, p. 39-67.
› Knijn, T., Tussen kinderdagverblijf en verzorgingstehuis. Gezinsbeleid en levenslopen, in: Engelen, E., Hemerijck A. & Trommel, W. (eds.), *Van sociale bescherming naar sociale investering. Zoektocht naar een andere verzorgingsstaat*, Den Haag, Lemma, 2007, p. 55-81.
› Mortelmans, D., Swennen, F. en Alofs, E., De echtscheiding en haar gevolgen: een vervlochten evolutie van recht en samenleving, in: Cuypers, D., Mortelmans, D. en Torfs, N. (eds.), *Is echtscheiding werkelijk win for life?*, Brugge, die keure, 2008, p. 1-37.
› Ogus, A. & Barendt, E., *The Law of Social Security*, London, Butterworths, 1988.
› Peemans-Poulet, H., De rechten van de gezinsleden in de sociale zekerheid, *Belgisch tijdschrift voor sociale zekerheid*, n°1, p. 27-83, 1994.
› Pieters, D., *Inleiding tot de beginselen van de sociale zekerheid*, Deventer/Utrecht, Kluwer, 1995.

› Pintens, W. en Torfs, E., *Belgian Report concerning the CEFL Questionnaire on Grounds for Divorce and Maintenance Between Former Spouses*, http://www.law.uu.nl/priv/cefl.
› Plantenga, J., The Life Course and the System of Social Security: Rethinking Incentives, Solidarity and Risks, *European Journal of Social Security*, n° 4, p. 301-312, 2005.
› Renchon, J.-L., La nouvelle réforme (précipitée) du droit belge du divorce: le ›droit au divorce', *Revue trimestrielle de droit familial*, n° 4, 925-1064, 2007.
› Schmid, G., *Transitional Labour Markets: A New European Employment Strategy*, Discussion Paper FS I 98-206, Berlijn, Wissenschaftszentrum Berlin für Sozialforschung, 1998.
› Skevik, A., Family Economy Workers or Caring Mothers? Male Breadwinning and Widows' Pensions in Norway and the UK, *Feminist Economics*, n° 2, p. 91-113, 2004.
› Swennen, F., De Echtscheidingswet 2007 in een notendop, *Notariaat*, n° 9, p. 1-8, 2007.
› Swennen, F., Het nieuwe echtscheidingsrecht en de CEFL-beginselen inzake echtscheiding en alimentatie tussen gewezen echtgenoten, in: UCERF (ed.), *Algemene ontwikkelingen in het familierecht*, Nijmegen, Ars Aequi Libri, 2007, p. 43-61.
› Swennen, F. en Aps, F., De echtscheidingswet 2007, *Rechtskundig Weekblad*, n° 14, p. 554-575, 2007-08.
› Swennen, F., Eggermont, S. en Alofs, E., De wet van 27 april 2007: knelpunten van materieel recht en procesrecht inzake echtscheiding, in: Senaeve, P., Swennen, F. en Verschelden, G. (eds.), *Een evaluatie van de recente wetgeving familierecht*, Antwerpen/Oxford, Intersentia, 2009, p. 1–52.
› Taelemans, A., Peeters, H., Curvers, G. en Berghman, J., Socio-economisch profiel van weduwen en weduwnaars met en zonder overlevingspensioen, in: Van den Troost, A. en Vleminckx, K. (eds.), *Een pensioen op maat van vrouwen?*, Antwerpen, Garant, 2007, p. 137-154.
› Taylor-Gooby, P., (ed.), *New risks, New Welfare. The Transformation of the European Welfare State*, Oxford, Oxford University Press, 2004.
› Trifiletti, R., *Family Policies Facing New Social Risks: Lone Parents from Northern to Southern Europe and other family policy measures in context*, paper presented at the Annual Conference of the Research Committee (RC 19), International Sociological Association, Florence, September 6-8, 2007.
› Uyttenhove, A., Renette, S. en Lenaerts, E., *Feitelijke scheiding, echtscheiding en sociale zekerheid*, Brugge, die keure, 2004.

› Van Langendonck, J. & Put, J., *Handboek Socialezekerheidsrecht*, Antwerpen, Intersentia, 2006.
› Van Limberghen, G., *Pensioenverzekeringen*, Brussel, VUB, 2007.
› Van Steenberge, J., Pensioenen, in: X, *Sociale Zekerheid. Verdere Ideeën*, Sociura-project, Leuven, Universitaire Pers, 1994, p. 95-103.
› Viaene, J., The ›securisation‹ of social security, in: Van Langendonck, J. (ed.), *The New Social Risks*, London/The Hague/Boston, Kluwer Law International, 1997, p. 53-71.
› Von Maydell, B., et al. (eds.), *Enabling Social Europe*, Berlijn, Springer-Verlag, 2006.

State Responsibility in Enforcing Maintenance Obligations towards Children

Ruth Farrugia[1]

I. Introduction

The basic principle at law is that parents have the responsibility to maintain their children. This applies subject to the certainty that the parent is in fact the acknowledged parent and that the child is incapable of independence owing to minority or vulnerability. Family structures find their legal basis in such show of maintenance solidarity, whether voluntary or enforced. Once established, this parent-child relationship gives rise to reciprocal duties of maintenance; however, there are occasions where parents are unable or unwilling to honour them.

This paper will examine to what extent, if at all, the law supports the child in maintenance allocation. Although the law may ostensibly give children this right, the central question is whether parents are indeed compelled to honour this duty and to what extent the State is bound to supplement such obligation. Where the parent is unable or unwilling to maintain the child does the obligation shift automatically on to the State? Does the State have a responsibility to intervene where parents are not in a position to honour their commitments of maintenance towards the child? Could the best interests of the child impinge on principles of public interest or is the best interests principle automatically held paramount? Finally is it possible to arrive at a »basic minimum standard of care« due to each child?

The responses to these queries should provide valuable insight into the central theme of the conference topic, namely »whether and how the law supports the family and its members; and respectively whether the state/ economy provides sufficient means to sustain family structures, or vice versa.«

---

[1] Advocate and Senior Lecturer, Faculty of Laws, University of Malta, Malta.

It is an acknowledged premise that parents have the legal responsibility to maintain their children. Articles 3(2), 5, 18(1) and 27(2) of the United Nations Convention on the Rights of the Child all agree that States have an obligation to ensure that children receive the protection and care necessary to their well-being and development. Such undertaking is chiefly provided through the parents in carrying out their responsibilities; however the Convention places the obligation on States to ensure that parents are in fact able to respond to such a responsibility. [2]

Once a person is proved to be the parent of a child or where a legal presumption of parenthood exists, until it is disproved, that person is accorded the responsibility of maintaining the child until such time as the child attains majority.[3] Parents are also held to be liable to continue to main-

---

2   UN Convention on the Rights of the Child,
    http://www.unhchr.ch/html/menu3/b/k2crc.htm, last accessed on 06.12.2008
    Article 3 [2] *States Parties undertake to ensure the child such protection and care as is necessary for his or her well-being, taking into account the rights and duties of his or her parents, legal guardians, or other individuals legally responsible for him or her, and, to this end, shall take all appropriate legislative and administrative measures*
    Article 5 *States Parties shall respect the responsibilities, rights and duties of parents or, where applicable, the members of the extended family or community as provided for by local custom, legal guardians or other persons legally responsible for the child, to provide, in a manner consistent with the evolving capacities of the child, appropriate direction and guidance in the exercise by the child of the rights recognized in the present Convention*
    Article 18 [1] *States Parties shall use their best efforts to ensure recognition of the principle that both parents have common responsibilities for the upbringing and development of the child. Parents or, as the case may be, legal guardians, have the primary responsibility for the upbringing and development of the child. The best interests of the child will be their basic concern.* Article 27 [2] *The parent(s) or others responsible for the child have the primary responsibility to secure, within their abilities and financial capacities, the conditions of living necessary for the child's development.*
3   In Maltese law, Chapter 16 Laws of Malta, The allocation of parental responsibility is determined by a *de jure* presumption on marriage or following an acknowledgement effected *ex parte* or following a court judgment. Where the parents are married to one another at the time of the child's birth both are deemed to have equal parental responsibility. The law states that they both have parental authority over the child which equates with a number of responsibilities already cited and the right to legal usufruct over the property of the child, if applicable. Where parents marry after the birth of their child(ren) their marriage imputes the status to a child born in wedlock. According to Article 87 (1) »The acknowledgment of a child conceived and born out of wedlock may be made in the act of birth, or by any other public deed either before or after the birth.« The married mother is automatically accorded parental authority and cannot divest herself of this. The unmarried father must have attained the age of 18 before he may acknowledge his child and assume parental authority. Once he attains majority he may either acknowledge the child on the act of birth by registering the birth himself or if the act is subsequent to the birth he must inform the mother of his intention and follow procedures set out at law.

tain their adult children in cases where they remain vulnerable persons and are incapable of maintaining themselves, as in the case of a severely mentally disabled person who will never be able to provide independent maintenance.

All child rights lawyers would agree that »parental responsibility is not a goal in itself, but a function – and the primary one – in the full and harmonious development of the child.«[4] This is highlighted by Article 27 of the United Nations Convention on the Rights of the Child to be read in conjunction with Article 18[5] where parents are expected to act with the best interests of their child as their basic concern in terms of Article 5 where they must take into account the child's evolving capacities or the child's age and maturity under Article 12.

This paper looks at the responsibility of intervention by the State when the parental duty of maintenance fails. It explores the interaction between the principles of the State's primary responsibility in promoting the best interests of the child and its close competitor »public interest« which binds the State in all its decisions. In order to ground the theoretical notions fundamental to the understanding of best interest and public interests and their origin the paper includes:

a. An overview of the legal duty of the State to intervene where parental responsibility is absent or lacking;
b. A review of the State undertaking to share or supplant parental responsibility for the child;
c. An evaluation of the standard of care owed by the State in replacing parental responsibility; and
d. An appraisal of child rights in the enforcement of what I will term a »basic minimum standard of State care«.

---

4 Doek J., Council of Europe Committee of Experts on Children and families (CS-EF), Strasbourg, Dec 8 and 9, 2004, Parents and the Rights of the Child, accessed on 17.11.2008 http://www.kinderrechte.gv.at/home/upload/50%20thema/tm_jaap_e_doek_-_eltern_und_die_krk.pdf
5 Article 18 [1] op.cit., supra [2] For the purpose of guaranteeing and promoting the rights set forth in the present Convention, States Parties shall render appropriate assistance to parents and legal guardians in the performance of their child-rearing responsibilities and shall ensure the development of institutions, facilities and services for the care of children. [3] States Parties shall take all appropriate measures to ensure that children of working parents have the right to benefit from child-care services and facilities for which they are eligible.

II. An Overview of the Legal Duty of the State to Intervene where Parental Responsibility is Absent or Lacking

In order to allocate responsibility to a parent, it must first be ascertained that the person alluded to as the parent is in fact so. One would expect that unless a person undertakes to assume responsibility for a child who is not his/her own (through adoption, for example) the law does not impose it. Indeed the law only imposes parental responsibility in cases where it can be proved that there is a genetic or legal link between parent and child and then only in limited circumstances.

The principle *mater semper certa est* is applied in many civil law jurisdictions although advances in science no longer make this as clear cut as it once used to be.[6] Furthermore, the option in some jurisdictions to give birth anonymously permits mothers to renounce to parental responsibility hitherto automatically assigned to them at birth.[7] Rules on filiation are frequently subject to proof that the parent is in fact the acknowledged parent with accompanying standards as to DNA testing and verification. However a parent may acknowledge a child without any such testing and this acknowledgement would render the person responsible for the child. There is also the presumption that the child is unable to be independent owing to minority or because of a circumstance of vulnerability once the age of majority has been attained.[8]

The child-parent relationship incurs reciprocal duties of maintenance. Under Maltese law, maintenance is taken to include food, clothing, health, habitation and education (the latter inclusion in respect of children).[9] Over the years a wealth of jurisprudence has built up amplify-

---

6 With ovum implantation and assisted procreation methods it is not always a certainty that the woman who gives birth is also the woman who contributed genetic material to the child, Similarly the woman who gives birth may be carrying someone else's child with the intention of giving the child to her at birth. Maltese law does not cater for any of these eventualities and continues to recognize the woman who gives birth as the mother in terms of the maxim *mater semper certa est.*

7 France for instance applies this legislation and the Strasbourg Court of Human Rights has found no difficulty in confirming that anonymous birth is acceptable:

8 Under Maltese law, where a child has a disability which renders him/her dependent beyond the age of eighteen, parents remain liable for support and care, otherwise liability ceases on the child attaining the age of eighteen years. (Judgement of the Civil Court, First Hall, 05/11/1991: *George MALLIA v Teresa MUSCAT* nomine].

9 Laws of Malta, Chapter 16, Article 19: *(1) »Maintenance shall include food, clothing, health and habitation. (2) In regard to children and other descendents, it shall also include the expenses necessary for health and education.«*

ing the meaning of each of these components so that is little doubt of the elements which constitute maintenance and the means for their enforcement vis a vis the debtor parent.

Under Maltese Law, where there are children to the marriage [10] the spouse(s) must make provision for the care and custody (residence and contact) and maintenance of such children. Failure to do so will entail the court ordering whatever provisions are deemed suitable in the best interests of the child. Even where the spouse(s) decide on these issues, the court has the authority and responsibility to review them and may order the resubmission of the draft agreement or may make its own proposals until such time as it is satisfied that the agreement truly serves the best interests of the child(ren).[11,12]

In practice, a number of reasons may militate against the payment of maintenance by the debtor parent. The parent may be estranged from the primary carer and feel that lack of contact equates with cessation of the duty to maintain. The parent may have financial difficulties bringing up more than one child in more than one family or s/he may be unemployed or unwell and not in a position to provide for independent personal subsistence, let alone that of a child. Such motives are not cited as justification for failure to effect payment but rather as *de facto* reasons frequently quoted in the family court.

In the majority of cases, failure to pay maintenance is not an issue. More often than not, parents are only too willing to support their children well beyond the age of majority, let alone during minority/childhood. However in those cases where parents are unable or unwilling to maintain the child, it is topical to ask what legal remedies are available. The compliant parent may sue the defaulting parent on behalf of the child and on his or her own behalf since failure to pay has direct repercussions on the obliga-

---

10   Children are defined as any persons who have not attained the age of eighteen years although this applies equally to adult children who are unable to support themselves owing to disability or some other incapacity at law.
11   A recent example was a proposal agreed to by the spouses to divide the children to the marriage. The court felt such separation would be detrimental to the children, ordered a psychological report and a child advocate to hear the children's views whereupon the parents reconsidered the proposal and kept the children together (Judgement of the Court of Appeal (Civil Superior), 23/11/2004: *Pauline MUSCAT gia MALLIA v David MALLIA*].
12   Cited in Farrugia R., Juxtaposing Legal Systems and the Principles of European Family Law on Divorce and Maintenance, Orucu E. and Mair J. (eds), Intersentia, 2007, pp99-128.

tions of the compliant spouse.[13] The success of such a procedure depends on a number of factors but certainly on the cooperation and enforcement mechanisms available through the State. Furthermore, where the parent is unable or unwilling to maintain the child, it is pertinent to question whether this obligation should shift automatically on to the State.

There are a number of conventions to facilitate cross border payment of maintenance[14] however the defaulting parent must be traced and legal proceedings must be initiated by the custodial parent on the child's behalf which can and often is a time consuming and costly process in itself. During the interim, the position of the State may be to supplement maintenance where the child is shown to be in need as in the supply of social assistance or benefits. The State itself does not usually take any steps to enforce payment.

III. A Review of the State Undertaking to Share or Supplant Responsibility for the Child

According to the United Nations Convention on the Rights of the Child, the primary duty of maintenance falls squarely on the shoulders of the parents of the child, but the State carries an obligation to ensure that this responsibility is fulfilled. One could argue that the reading of Article 27 should be done in conjunction with Article 6(2) where the State has an obligation to create an environment conducive to ensuring the development of the child to the maximum extent possible.

In terms of Article 27:

> »1. States Parties recognize the right of every child to a standard of living adequate for the child's physical, mental, spiritual, moral and social development.
>
> 2. The parent(s) or others responsible for the child have the primary responsibility to secure, within their abilities and financial capacities, the conditions of living necessary for the child's development.

---

13 That spouse would have to shoulder the responsibility of maintenance completely with no contribution, even though this is due under the law.

14 Hague Convention on the Law Applicable to Maintenance Obligations towards Children 1956, Hague Convention on the Recognition and Enforcement of Decisions Relating to Maintenance Obligations 1973, Council Regulation (EC) No 44/2001: BRUSSELS I (and still a Proposal for a Council Regulation of 15 December 2005 on jurisdiction, applicable law, recognition and enforcement of decisions and cooperation in matters relating to maintenance obligations (COM(2005) 649 final].

3. States Parties, in accordance with national conditions and within their means, shall take appropriate measures to assist parents and others responsible for the child to implement this right and shall in case of need provide material assistance and support programmes, particularly with regard to nutrition, clothing and housing.
4. States Parties shall take all appropriate measures to secure the recovery of maintenance for the child from the parents or other persons having financial responsibility for the child, both within the State Party and from abroad. In particular, where the person having financial responsibility for the child lives in a State different from that of the child, States Parties shall promote the accession to international agreements or the conclusion of such agreements, as well as the making of other appropriate arrangements.«

And Article 6[2]:
»States Parties shall ensure to the maximum extent possible the survival and development of the child.«

In practice, however, does the State have a responsibility towards the child in ensuring that the maintenance accessed on his /her behalf is commensurate with that child's needs? Indeed does the State have a primary or secondary responsibility towards the child?[15] What is the State obligation, if any, where the quantum of maintenance which a parent is able to provide translates into a poverty subsistence? If all children are to have an equal start in life and a right to their present and future well-being, this may translate into state supplements to child maintenance as of right.

In practice, a number of States already respond to this concern in varying ways. They allocate children's allowance on the basis of means testing of income, they provide taxation rebates in recognition of the cost of bringing up children, they supplement schooling costs and treatment in health sectors. However such response is largely dependent on the good will and discretion of the State. The question is whether States have an obligation to provide such supplementary benefit and whether they are bound to ensure what I propose as »a basic minimum standard of maintenance« for each child under their jurisdiction. If States are bound to con-

---

15 Detrick S., The United Nations Convention on the Rights of the Child: A Guide to the Travaux Preparatoires, 1992, p.270. Detrick argues that in the drafting of the UN CRC the wording of Article 18 [1] was changed in order to clarify that the State should be regarded as having primary responsibility.

tribute towards the well-being of each and every child, then they are also accountable when those children are prejudiced through lack of maintenance. To what extent, if at all, does the State have a legal responsibility to provide for any appropriate supplement?

Ever since 1948 and the Universal Declaration of Human Rights there has been a struggle »to identify the rights of the individual vis a vis the state«[16]. While state intervention is often viewed as a necessary evil, in many international instruments its contribution is deemed a *sine qua non* desirable in the best interests of the individual. The International Covenant on Economic, Social and Cultural Rights, for instance, places »the primary responsibility on the State to ensure an adequate standard of living«[17]. It will be interesting to see how 2009 will further develop this obligation with the opening for signature of the Optional Protocol to the ICESCR eventually enabling individuals to lodge a complaint to an independent human rights body at the international level about violations of rights enshrined in the same Covenant.

Within the context of the European Court of Human Rights and its adjudication of cases under the European Convention on Human Rights, the force of its jurisprudence in recent years has encouraged States to respond to this primary responsibility issue in operating a sort of »preventative responsibility«. Prior to petitioning the Court, as a Court of last resort, State responsibility must be also identified at the international level. »A great merit of the positive obligation case law as a whole is that it encourages States to attack potential human rights violations at their roots, whether this is by the introduction of appropriate legislation...or other measures.«[18] However, its effectiveness in this particular area of law seems to remain largely untested.

Conversely, it has been advanced that Article 18(1) of the UN CRC is not only meant to protect parents from excessive intervention by the State (even if that intervention takes place with the best intentions), but also to indicate that parents cannot expect the State to always intervene if a

---

16 Mahgou, Khadeija, Parental responsibility under Article 27(2) of the UNCRC: An Islamic Shariah Perspective, paper presented at the 4th World Congress on Family Law and Children's Rights, 2005, http://www.childjustice.org/docs/mahgou2005.pdf (last accessed 10.12.2008).

17 International Covenant on Social and Cultural Rights, ICSCR Article 11, http://www.unhchr.ch/html/menu2/6/cescr.htm (last accessed 10.11.2008).

18 Jacot-Guillarmod, Oral Intervention, in Proceedings of the Sixth International Colloquy about the European Convention on Human Rights, Seville, 1985, Martinus Nijhoff, 1988, pp782–4.

problem occurs. Given the tone and wording of the preamble which refers to »the full and harmonious development of the personality« of the child, it is difficult to imagine how the UN CRC can be interpreted as minimizing State responsibility in those cases where parents require assistance in order to deliver »necessary conditions of living« or »adequate standards of living«, depending on Article 2(1) or Article 1(4).

Through Article 27(3) the State is acknowledged as having subsidiary responsibility to that of the parent(s) and is expected to deliver practical assistance through material support and assistance. The former Chairperson of the Committee on the UN CRC has clarified that such help would be necessary particularly in terms of nutrition, clothing and housing.[19]

IV. An Evaluation of the Standard of Care Owed by the State in Replacing Parental Responsibility

The law mentions a number of instances where the State undertakes to share or supplant responsibility for the child. In those cases where the child is in need of care and/or protection, the State is bound to ensure that adequate maintenance is provided to that child. Ideally the State often seeks to delegate this obligation by encouraging adoption so that another set of parents can take over the obligations of parental responsibility. However in most cases, the State ends up contracting alternative carers such as foster carers where it enters into a financial agreement which contributes to or covers the costs linked to maintenance obligations. It may also place or accommodate the child in residential care where it has a similar responsibility relating to minimum standards of care. In such cases, the State intervenes because it is invariably constrained to do so and, although disinclined to take over parental responsability, is legally bound to act. As a rule, it would be more beneficial to the child were the State to assist in keeping the family unit together and overenthusiastic state intervention has led to unwanted consequences and strong criticism from several quaters.
In the last session of the UN Committee of the CRC during the consideration of the reports submitted by States Parties under Article 44 of the Convention, the United Kingdom of Great Britain and Northern Ireland came in for strong criticism regarding the »lack of appropriate assistance

---

19   Doek J., op.cit.

in the performance of their child-rearing responsibilities, and notable those families in a crisis situation due to poverty.«[20]
The Committee expressed its concern at:
a. The insufficient investment in the staff and facilities to support children deprived of parental care;
b. The fact that children may be taken in alternative care as a result of parental low income;

The Committee therefore recommended that the State should:
a. Intensify its efforts to render appropriate assistance to parents and legal guardians in the performance of their child-rearing responsibilities; and
b. Avoid that children are taken in alternative care as a result of parental low income.«[21]

Does this approach benefit the child and affirm the right of that child to enforce a basic minimum standard of care, including its access to maintenance? When one of these eventualities applies, it is interesting to note that the State does not consistently initiate proceedings against the defaulting parent. It would appear logical to expect the State to support the child in enforcing a claim to maintenance from the parent(s). In practice it would appear that this is not done and States *in loco parentis* do not pursue any debts incurred by parents who cannot or will not pay maintenance for their children.[22] This cost is met by the taxpayer instead.

Under Maltese law, where a child is deemed to be in need of care, protection or control, that child may be placed under a care order at the order of the Minister who thereafter assumes parental responsibility for the child insofar as relates to care and custody.[23] Neglect may be one of the causes leading to such State intervention and this in itself may be the failure to supply appropriate maintenance to the child. This echoes the prac-

---

[20] CRC/C/GBR/CO/4, 3 October 2008, Committee on the Rights of the Child, Session Forty Nine, Concluding Observations re the United Kingdom of Great Britain and Northern Ireland, http://www2.ohchr.org/english/bodies/crc/docs/AdvanceVersions/CRC.C.GBR.CO.4.pdf.
[21] Op cit. supra , para 45.
[22] Even though under Maltese law the law is very clear on the remaining obligation to parents who no longer have the physical care of their child (ren): Chapter 16, Laws of Malta Article 57(1) »*Whosoever may be the person to whom the children are entrusted, the father and mother shall maintain their right to watch over their maintenance and education, and shall be bound to contribute thereto, according to law.*«
[23] Chapter 285, Laws of Malta, all articles, but in particular Articles 3, 5, 8 and 9.

tice of the United Kingdom and would doubtless elicit similar concerns from the UN Committee. In practice, numerous States seem to prefer to take a child into care than to support the parents and enable the child[24] to remain within its family, notwithstanding the long term negative effects on the child and the financial liability incurred.

However perhaps the most pressing problem in attempting to review the State's undertaking to share or supplant responsibility for the child is the seeming lack of accountability. When a State intervenes to take on responsibility for a child, the assumption is that the State is suited to do so and will be in a position to provide better prospects for that child. If this were not so then the State would have no business in moving the child at all.[25] In practice children do not always receive a better standard of care and the monitoring of care standards by an independent body accountable to Parliament rather than to the State itself is still an item on a wish list in most countries. For this reason, maintenance allocated to the child taken away from parental responsibility remains largely at the discretion of the State.

V. An Appraisal of Child Rights in the Enforcement of a »Basic Minimum Standard of State Care«

Children in most countries in the world do not enjoy independent access to civil justice.[26] They remain dependent on their parent(s) to represent them in all court proceedings. For this reason where one parent fails to provide maintenance, children rely on the other custodial parent to institute court action to try to recoup the debt.

---

24 Research shows the negative psychological and mental health repercussions of placement of children into care, particularly where stable placement is not ensured. Issues such as age on entry, duration of placement, stability and attachment all contribute to the child's present and future well-being. [Stanley (2007); Milward, Kennedy, Towlson and Minnis (2006); Schiff, Nebe and Gilman (2006) et cetera] In the research done by Stanley, children perceived care by the State as »demeaning«, but that is another story.

25 Reminiscent of the maxim : *primum non nocere*.

26 Farrugia R., Achievements in taking children's rights further in civil justice, Towards European guidelines on child-friendly justice: Identifying good principles and sharing examples of good practices as part of Council of Europe, Stockholm 2008: Building a Europe for and with Children – Towards a Strategy for 2009-2011, www.coe.int/T/TransversalProjects/Children/pdf/StockholmProgramme.pdf *or* http://www.crin.org/docs/Farrugia_en.doc

It has been shown that a child may be directly affected by a parent's failure to honour a maintenance decree and this may have repercussions on his/her present and future well being.[27] In some States this process of debt collection may carry the threat of penal sanction.[28] However this response does not satisfy the needs of the child to access food, clothing, habitation health and education requirements. Where both parents do not honour their obligation, it remains the State who must take necessary action to offset the maintenance it in turn becomes bound to provide.

In practice, how is this put into effect? Can children demand that such maintenance be provided subject to a standard objectively determined? If parents are unable or unwilling to maintain their children in a way that ensures their »*survival and development*«, almost all the States of the world have accepted to endorse this obligation.[29] The UN CRC clearly allocates to parents the primary responsibility to secure, within their abilities and financial capacities, the conditions of living necessary for the child's development. But this undertaking is subject to State assistance and

> »*where the parents are in ... need, States are expected to provide material assistance and support programmes, particularly with regard to nutrition, clothing and housing.*«[30]

The recovery of maintenance for the child from the parents or other persons having financial responsibility for the child is also an obligation placed upon the State but it is usually an obligation entered into willingly as it helps to offset the alternative burden of the State being solely responsible itself.[31] It is therefore surprising to note how the State frequently fails to follow up maintenance due to children who are in its care. Proceedings on behalf of children in care for the recovery of maintenance from defaulting parents may be foregone in the notion that they are a wasted effort but surely this cannot apply to every single case. It should be the right of

---

[27] Similarly changes in contact and residence have a very direct effect on the child's lifestyle and happiness and research shows that where children are involved in the decision making process there is always a better outcome. Skjorten K. and Barlindhaug R., The involvement of children in decisions about shared residence, International Journal of Law, Policy and the Family, 21(2007) pp 373-385.
[28] In Malta, failure to honour a maintenance decree may result in a custodial sentence in terms of Article 338 of the Criminal Code, Chapter 9 of the Laws of Malta.
[29] UN CRC Article 6(2) ratified by all states in the world except for Somalia and the USA.
[30] UN CRC Article 27.
[31] Always subject to the »*national conditions and ... means*« *of the State as referred to in the UN CRC Article 27(3).*

the child to make a decision as to whether or not to attempt to access such maintenance.[32]

Furthermore, can it therefore be a safe conclusion to assume that where children are removed from parental responsibility and placed under the care of the State they are to be guaranteed a right to a basic minimum standard of maintenance. To date it would seem that no such legal baseline has been established; however child neglect cases make such assumptions on a daily basis. If the State is to intervene then it must be in a position to offer a better alternative. Alternatively the child should not be removed from the family. However the State may always counter that in providing maintenance there are public interest issues to contend with and the child must compete with other claims on the public purse.

In a world that increasingly cites the best interests of children as paramount, such a response is unacceptable.[33] In States with a budget that permits generous allocation to a multitude of projects and concerns,[34] maintenance for children should be a priority issue both in keeping with international obligations under the UN CRC but also in acknowledgment of the fact that children are disadvantaged through poverty which in turn deprives them of their human rights.[35] States may be faced with

---

32 This depends on the maturity and understanding of the child. Asher Ben-Arieh argues in Where are the Children? Children's Role in Measuring and Monitoring their Well-Being, Social Indicators Research (2005) 74: 573–596, at page 3: *Even if children are granted only partial legal and civil rights and the partial ability to participate in decision making about their lives, then they should participate at least in the same proportion in the study of their well-being, especially since it bears so much influence on them.*

33 According to UNESCO 250 million children between the ages of 5 and 17 – or one in every six children in the world – are working http://portal.unesco.org/education/en/ev.php-URL_ID=32966&URL_DO=DO_TOPIC&URL_SECTION=201.html (10.12.2008); in Europe according to the Council of Europe 15% of children live below the poverty line http://www.coe.int/t/commissioner/Viewpoints/070709_en.asp and according to ENOC (European Network of Commissioners for Children) 19% live at risk of poverty, http://www.ombudsnet.org/enoc/resources/infodetail.asp?id=19126 (12.12.2008).

34 Save the Children, Children's Rights in the EU – A Call for Action, September 2002, p.5 »The proportion of the EU's budget which is currently spent on children is minuscule in comparison with that spent on other aspects of EU activity, and compares unfavourably with the amount spent on other social groups by the EU.« http://www.savethechildren.net/alliance/europegroup/europubs/child_rights_eu.doc

35 Rosas A., »Article 21,« in Eide and Alfredsson (eds.) *The Universal Declaration of Human Rights: A Common Standard of Achievement*, Martinus Nijhoff Publishers, 1999, at 431. Rosas points out that: *Political rights in the narrow sense cannot thrive without the principle of equality (Articles 1,2,4 and 7), and they presuppose civil rights and liberties, notably liberty and security of person (e.g. articles 3, 5 and 9) and freedom of movement, expression, assembly and association (articles 13, 19, 20). A minimum of social and economic rights also seems crucial (articles 22-26).*

the dilemma of making unpopular choices called for in deciding between issues of public interest versus the best interests of the child. However these should be viewed as complementary rather than competing goals an it is only by making choices in favor of children that the State can effectively acknowledge its full responsibility in honouring maintenance obligations towards children.

Evolving Family Forms and the Duty of Support in South African Law

June Sinclair[1] and Trynie Davel[2]

I. Introduction

The common-law duty of support rests primarily on blood relationship[3] or on marriage.[4] The reciprocal duty of support between spouses arises *ex lege* upon solemnisation of the marriage[5] and dissolution of the marriage by divorce or death terminates the duty at common law.[6] Legislation has however extended the duty of support to cover post-divorce maintenance[7] and also creates a liability for the estate of a deceased spouse to provide maintenance for the survivor, where the circumstances require it.[8] Legislation has also extended the duty of support beyond blood relationship to create a duty in favour of adopted children.[9]

---

1 Honorary Professor of Law, University of Pretoria, South Africa.
2 Professor and Head, Department of Private Law, University of Pretoria, South Africa.
3 See Van Heerden and others *Boberg's Law of Persons and the Family* 2ed (1999) chapter 10; Van Schalkwyk, »Maintenance for children«, in Davel (ed) *Introduction to Child Law in South Africa* (2000) 41, 46. The duty to support children persists even after the parent's death: *Carelse v Estate De Vries* (1906) 23 SC 532.
4 It is one of the invariable consequences of marriage that a reciprocal duty of support arises between the spouses: Sinclair assisted by Heaton *The Law of Marriage* vol 1 (1996) 415.
5 Clark, The duty of support, in *Boberg's Law of Persons and the Family op cit* note 3 at 233-235.
6 At common law the surviving spouse had no claim for maintenance against the deceased spouse's estate: *Glazer v Glazer NO* 1963 (4) SA 694 (A).
7 The court granting a decree of divorce has a discretion to include in its order a spousal agreement for maintenance or, in the absence of such an agreement, to order the payment of maintenance until the death or remarriage of the party in whose favour the order is given: section 7(3) of the Divorce Act 70 of 1979.
8 Section 2(1) of the Maintenance of Surviving Spouses Act 27 of 1990 gives a surviving spouse unable to support himself or herself a claim for reasonable maintenance against the deceased spouse's estate.
9 Section 20(2) of the Child Care Act 74 of 1983, to be replaced, see s 242 of the Children's Act 38 of 2005.

II. Same-sex Partners

Since the advent of the Constitution in 1994,[10] South African courts have been confronted with challenges to various pieces of legislation on the grounds that these Acts discriminated unfairly against same-sex couples, whom the law did not permit to marry. Several cases entailed the extension of the duty of support to same-sex couples. These are discussed below. A striking development in South African family law was the passing of the Civil Union Act 17 of 2006, which came into operation on 30 November 2006, allowing same-sex couples to marry. The Act and its interpretative problems are extensively dealt with in another ISFL publication[11] and what follows is a brief statement of the main thrust of this legislation.

The Act regulates the solemnization and registration of civil unions, by way either of marriage or civil partnership. (The choice is that of the parties, and the difference between the two forms of civil union is in name only.) It applies to all couples. Heterosexual couples may therefore elect to enter a marriage in terms of the new legislation, or in terms of the Marriage Act.[12] The opportunity for gay and lesbian couples is to »marry«, but only under the new legislation. The legal consequences of a civil union are the same as the consequences of a marriage celebrated in terms of the Marriage Act.

In the wake of the enactment of the Civil Union Act, the rights of gay and lesbian couples who do not solemnize their relationship in terms of the new legislation are not clear. Do the cases that provided these couples with protection still apply?[13] That this complex interpretive issue is not

---

10 The year of coming into operation of the Interim Constitution, which was replaced by the Constitution of the Republic of South Africa, 1996.
11 June Sinclair, »A New Definition of Marriage: Gay and Lesbian Couples May Marry«, 2008 *International Survey of Family Law* 397. See also De Vos, »The ›Inevitability‹ of Same-Sex Marriage in South Africa's post-Apartheid State« (2007) 23 *SAJHR* 432.
12 Act 25 of 1961.
13 This issue is dealt with by Sinclair *op cit* note 11 above, 406-8. And see further Bonthuys, Race and Gender in the Civil Union Act (2007) 23 *SAJHR* 526 at 540 who observes that courts may be willing to take away the rights of same-sex couples who do not marry now that the rationale for giving them those rights has fallen away, in order to adhere to formal equality between same-sex and opposite sex couples; Bilchitz and Judge, For Whom Does the Bell Toll? The Challenges and Possibilities of the Civil Union Act for Family Law in South Africa, (2007) 23 *SAJHR* 466 at 496-7 venture that it is strongly arguable that the rights of same-sex couples who do not marry are now curtailed, but that the courts may be lenient and allow some time to elapse to give these couples the chance to marry. This compromise seems unlikely merely in the interests of certainty – how much time would be an arbitrary determination. De Vos *op cit* at 462 is of the

merely academic is borne out by the fact that there has been no rush by same-sex couples to invoke their rights to marry or enter into a civil partnership.[14] Sooner or later the courts will have to determine the rights of those who remain cohabitants. Finally, it should not be overlooked that heterosexual couples who cohabit but do not marry do not enjoy the protection afforded by the courts to same-sex partners.

III. Judical Extension of the Duty of Support

The need to review law and policy in the light of a new constitutional dispensation gave prominence to the traditional boundaries of the duty of support. The courts had no trouble aligning the common law with the constitutional imperatives in a multi-cultural society.[15]

The definition of »marriage« had to be reconsidered in *Khan v Khan*,[16] where it was held that there was a legal duty to maintain a person to whom one was married according to Muslim rites, despite the fact that the marriage was in fact polygynous. The Court declared that the preamble to the Maintenance Act[17] emphasizes the establishment of a fair and equitable maintenance system premised on the fundamental rights in the Constitution. The common-law duty of support was considered a flexible concept that had been developed and extended by the courts over time to cover a wide range of relationships.[18]

At common law there were no maintenance obligations between stepchildren and stepparents.[19] In *Heystek v Heystek*[20] where the applicant sought maintenance *pendente lite* it was apparent from the applicant's itemised list that the maintenance she was seeking included items for her children from a previous marriage. The Court noted that by virtue of section 28 (1) (b) of the Constitution[21] every child in the country has a right to

---

view that legislation would be required to take away the hard-won rights of gays and lesbians developed by the courts while they could not marry.
14   See De Vos *op cit* at 463.
15   In accordance with the court's inherent jurisdiction as upper guardian of all minor children and s 8(1) of the Constitution. See also s 39 of the Constitution.
16   2005 (2) SA 272 (T).
17   Act 99 of 1998.
18   *Khan* 2005 (2) SA 272 (T) 279D-E.
19   Davel *Die Dood van 'n Broodwinner as Skadevergoedingsoorsaak* (1984) 156fn266, 472. See also *Mentz v Simpson* 1990 (4) SA 455 (A) 460A-B.
20   2002 (2) SA 754 (T).
21   Constitution of the Republic of South Africa, 1996.

parental care.[22] Inherent in the notion of parental care is the child's right to basic nutrition, shelter and basic health care services and social services[23] as well as basic education.[24] Section 28 (2) encapsulates the constitutional imperative that the child's best interests are paramount in every matter concerning that particular child.

The Court found that these considerations required an attitudinal shift from an antiquated parent-child relationship, to the rights of the child.[25] However, in *Heystek v Heystek* the parties were married in community of property and the duty of support owed by the mother to the child had to be met out of the joint estate. The stepfather became civilly liable by reason of the matrimonial property regime.[26] It could be argued that the case introduced a new child-centred approach to maintenance[27] based on the reality of relationships and the needs of children rather than a blood relationship that was determinative at common law. But it has left many questions unanswered. Does this maintenance obligation between the step-parent and stepchild cease to exist on dissolution of the marriage?[28] Is the existence of the obligation limited to marriages in community of property?[29] Is this duty sufficient to form the basis of an action for loss of support by the dependant if the breadwinner is wrongfully killed?[30]

The common-law dependant's action against the person (or his or her insurer, usually the Road Accident Fund (RAF)) who wrongfully and culpably causes the death of a breadwinner serves as an excellent example of judicial development of the law. In *Amod v Multilateral Motor Vehicle Ac-*

---

22 Parental care is not confined to natural parents, but extends to step-parents, adoptive parents and foster parents: *SW v F* 1997 (1) SA 796 (O) 802G-H.
23 Section 28(1)(c) of the Constitution and see s 28(1)(a) of the Constitution and s 50(2) of the Child Care Act 74 of 1983.
24 Section 29(1) of the Constitution.
25 At 757.
26 *Heystek v Heystek* 2002 (2) SA 754 (T). The step-parent stands *in loco parentis*, and it is unrealistic to argue that the maintenance of the household, which he then provides, stops short of the child. See also *Mentz v Simpson* 1990 (4) SA 455 (A) 460C-D.
27 Van Schalkwyk & Van der Linde, Onderhoudsplig van Stiefouer: *Heystek v Heystek* 2002 (2) SA 754 (T), (2003) 66 *THRHR* 301 at 312.
28 *Heystek* at 756.
29 See Van Schalkwyk & Van der Linde *op cit* note 27 above, at 302-305 where the authors argue that the cases to which the court referred should be contextualized properly and perhaps understood differently. They do not support the conclusion reached by the court that there is a duty of support owed by the stepfather.
30 This question is answered in the negative by Neethling, Potgieter & Visser *Law of Delict* 5 ed (2006) 259. See also Cronjé & Heaton *Die Suid-Afrikaanse Familiereg* (2004) 305-306.

cidents Fund (Commission for Gender Equality Intervening)[31] the court had to decide whether a woman married in terms of Islamic law was able to claim for loss of support via the dependant's action. The *Amods'* marriage was not registered as a civil marriage[32] but was *de facto* monogamous, contracted according to the tenets of a major religion and constituted a right worthy of protection.[33] The Supreme Court of Appeal held that the correct approach was not to ask whether the marriage was lawful at common law or not, but to enquire whether the deceased had a legal duty to support the appellant during the subsistence of the marriage.[34] The court held that it would be inconsistent with the new ethos of tolerance, pluralism and religious freedom to recognise only marriages solemnised and recognised by one faith, to the exclusion of others.[35] In this case the Court based its finding for the woman on the fact that the deceased was under a legally enforceable duty to support her in contract.[36]

This judgment signalled a remarkable development of common law, because it had been held in the past that a »mere« contractual claim to support cannot provide a proper basis for the dependant's action.[37] The only issue as yet unresolved is the question whether the outcome of *Amod* would have been any different had the marriage not been monogamous. It is submitted that, in this respect, there is in principle no difference between a customary union according to African indigenous law and a Muslim marriage and that widows in polygynous Muslim marriages should, like African customary wives, succeed in their actions.[38]

In *Du Plessis v Road Accident Fund*[39] the Supreme Court of Appeal had to decide whether a partner in a same-sex permanent life partnership was

---

[31] 1999 (4) SA 1319 (SCA).
[32] In terms of the Marriage Act 25 of 1961.
[33] Paragraph [20] at 1327G/H – H/I. See paragraph [23], where the quote from *Du Plessis and Others v De Klerk and another* 1996 (3) SA 850 (CC), 1996 (5) BCLR 658 at paragraph [86] states that the »common law is not to be trapped within the limitations of its past.
[34] Paragraphs [19] and [20] at 1327E – G/H.
[35] Paragraph [20] at 1327H/I – 1328B/C.
[36] Paragraph [25] at 1331A-B.
[37] *Nkabinde v SA Motor and General Insurance Co Ltd* 1961 (1) SA 302 (N). However, for criticism of this limitation see Davel *Die Dood van 'n Broodwinner as Skadevergoedingsoorsaak op cit* note 19 above at 435-439 and Van der Merwe & Olivier *Die Onregmatige Daad in die Suid-Afrikaanse Reg* (1989) 334.
[38] Neethling & Potgieter, Uitbreiding van die Toepassingsgebied van die Aksie van Afhanklikes, 2001 (64) *THRHR* 484; Neethling, Potgieter & Visser *op cit* note 28 above, at 259.
[39] 2004 1 SA 359 (SCA).

entitled to institute a dependant's action for his loss of support before the Civil Union Act[40] came into effect.[41] The partners in the same-sex relationship had gone through a »marriage« ceremony, before numerous witnesses. The Court accepted that they had done the best they could to publicise to the world that they intended their relationship to be similar in all respects to a valid marriage. They had lived together for eleven years, pooled their income and shared family responsibilities. Each had made a will appointing the other as sole heir. When the plaintiff was medically boarded, the deceased expressly stated that he would support the plaintiff financially and in fact did so until he died. They had tacitly undertaken a reciprocal duty of support.[42] The Court permitted the extension of the duty of support to ensure that the common law accords with the dynamic and evolving fabric of our society as reflected in the Constitution.[43] It allowed the plaintiff to claim damages from the defendant for loss of support.[44] But the Court expressly refrained from deciding whether the dependant's action should be extended to unmarried persons in a heterosexual relationship or to any other relationship.[45]

In the abovementioned case the Supreme Court of Appeal relied heavily on the decision reached by the Constitutional Court in *Satchwell v President of the Republic of South Africa*.[46] The facts were the following: In 2001 a Provincial Division of the High Court made an order declaring that the omission from the Judges' Remuneration and Conditions of Employment Act[47] of the words »or partner in a permanent same-sex partnership« after the words »spouse« was inconsistent with the equality provisions of the Constitution.[48] The Act in question[49] provided that the »surviving spouse« of a deceased judge had to be paid whatever would have been payable to the judge had he or she not died. Regulations also provided that certain allowances had to inure to the benefit of the »surviving spouse«. The ap-

---

40   17 of 2006.
41   On 30 November 2006.
42   Paragraph [14].
43   Paragraph [37]. Cf eg *Carmichele v Minister of Safety and Security and Another (Centre for Applied Legal Studies Intervening)* 2001 (4) SA 938 (CC) paragraph [43]; *Minister of Safety and Security v Van Duivenboden* 2002 (6) SA 431 (SCA) paragraph [17]; *Satchwell v President of the Republic of South Africa* 2002 (6) SA 1 (CC) paragraphs [23] and [25].
44   Paragraph [42].
45   Paragraph [43].
46   2002 (6) SA 1 (CC).
47   Act 88 of 1989, sections 8 and 9.
48   Section 9.
49   Sections 8 and 9.

plicant, a female judge, had been in a permanent same-sex relationship for more than fifteen years. She had unsuccessfully attempted to get the Minister of Justice and Constitutional Development[50] to have the Act and regulations amended so that her partner would be entitled to the relevant benefits.[51] After two years she commenced litigation, alleging that the challenged provisions violated her right to equality in that she and her partner were denied the benefits afforded to judges and their spouses.[52]

The Constitutional Court stated:[53]

»*The law attaches a duty of support to various family relationships, for example, husband and wife, and parent and child. In a society where the range of family formations has widened, such a duty of support may be inferred as a matter of fact in certain cases of persons involved in permanent, same-sex life partnerships. Whether such a duty of support exists or not will depend on the circumstances of each case.*«

The court found that »*[i]t appears probable that they have undertaken reciprocal duties of support*«[54] and thus found in favour of the plaintiff.[55]

The voluntary assumption of a reciprocal duty of support was also in issue in *Gory v Kolver NO*,[56] in which the Constitutional Court extended the application of spousal benefits under the Intestate Succession Act[57] to same-sex life partners. In *Langemaat v Minister of Safety and Security*[58] the High Court found that »*[p]arties to a same-sex union, which had existed for years in a common home, must surely owe a duty of support, in all senses, to each other*«.[59]

---

50 The second respondent.
51 The second respondent implored the applicant to be patient as he intended to effect the required changes.
52 The basis of the alleged unconstitutionality, she argued, was the omission from the impugned provisions of the words »or partner in a permanent, same-sex partnership«.
53 Paragraph [25].
54 Loc cit.
55 The Act under scrutiny here has since been repealed and replaced by Act 47 of 2001.
56 2007 (3) BCLR 249 (CC), upholding the finding of unconstitutionality in *Gory v Kolver NO* 2006 (5) SA 145 (T).
57 Act 81 of 1987.
58 1998 (3) SA 312 (TPD).
59 In this case the applicant successfully applied to the High Court to declare regulations of the South African Police Services invalid so that the same-sex partner could be registered as a dependant in terms of the Police Services' medical aid scheme (Polmed).

However, in the latter case the duty of support was not found to be based on contract.[60]

A 2008 judgment that takes the development of South African law another step forward, is *Hassan v Jacobs NO and others*.[61] Here the primary issue was whether upon the death of their husband, surviving spouses in a polygynous marriage contracted in accordance with Muslim rites are entitled to the benefits envisaged by the Intestate Succession Act,[62] (namely what in effect is a widow's portion on intestacy), and the Maintenance of Surviving Spouses Act,[63] (namely a claim for reasonable maintenance).[64] The Court held[65] that exclusion of widows of polygynous Muslim marriages from the benefits of the abovementioned Acts would be unfairly discriminatory against them and in conflict with the equality provision of the Constitution[66] and certain international human rights instruments.[67]

The Court acknowledged the fact that the constitutional validity of polygamy has not been subjected to judicial scrutiny,[68] but declared that the word »survivor« in both the Acts includes the surviving partner/s to a polygamous Muslim marriage.[69]

IV. Legislation Awaited: Muslim Marriage and Heterosexual Cohabitation

So far, we have traversed the developments in the law that have seen the formal recognition of same-sex marriages and the judicial extension of the duty of support to evolving family situations hitherto outside the ambit of family-law rules. Two situations that remain somewhat inexpli-

---

60 It therefore seems that the courts sometimes require the voluntary assumption of a »contractual« duty of support and sometimes not. This will pose a problem because it will be difficult to predict whether it is necessary to prove the factual assumption of such a duty in order to claim a specific benefit.
61 Case number 5704/2004 per Van Reenen J.
62 Act 81 of 1987.
63 Act 27 of 1990.
64 It was previously decided in *Daniels v Campbell NO and others* 2004 (5) SA 331 (CC) that the provisions of both the relevant Acts have to be interpreted to include the spouse to a *de facto monogamous* Muslim marriage.
65 Paragraph [19].
66 Section 9.
67 Eg Article 16 of the Convention on the Elimination of All Forms of Discrimination Against Women.
68 Paragraph [22].
69 Paragraphs [23.1.1] and [23.1.4].

cably neglected by the legislature, given the progressive stance taken by the courts on these matters, pertain to Muslim marriage and heterosexual cohabitation.

1. Legislative Recognition of Muslim Marriages

The reason for non-recognition of marriages celebrated according to Muslim rites is the same as that offered prior to the Recognition of Customary Marriages Act[70] for non-recognition of African customary marriages – that they are potentially polygynous. Societal mores have changed sufficiently for South Africa to accept the polygynous nature of marriage among Africans, but attempts to enact legislation to give the same recognition to Muslim marriages have failed. The failure, it should be noted, is in part a result of disagreement among senior representatives of different groupings of the Islamic faith, who grapple with the idea that a secular state should be enacting laws not consistent with the tenets of religious law.

The recognition of Muslim marriages has been under investigation by the South African Law Reform Commission for some years. In 2003 it reported on its enquiry and recommended legislation that would have seen these marriages capable of full recognition, but with some curious and complex conditions that would not apply to non-Muslim marriages.[71] Enactment of the proposed legislation, or any alternative to what was proposed, has not occurred. The courts have therefore, on a case-by-case basis, had to give effect to the Constitution's demands. The judicial extension of the duty of support to these unions has already been covered above. It is clear that this longstanding family form has not been given the attention it deserves and that the decisions of the courts adhere closely to the separation of powers, dictating that the position will not be comprehensively dealt with until there is legislation. The fragmentary result of the cases is that, for the purposes of some statutes Muslim marriages are recognised, provided that they are de facto monogamous, and for the purposes of three statutes they have been recognised in two provinces, even if they are de facto polygynous. It seems unnecessary even to comment on the absurd complexity of this situation.

---

70 Act 120 of 1998.
71 Report on Islamic Marriages and Related Matters (Project 106) July 2003, containing the draft Muslim Marriages Act. The report and the draft legislation are discussed in some detail by Sinclair and Bonthuys in 2003 *Annual Survey of South African Law* 153-63.

We eagerly await long overdue but seemingly imminent legislation to regulate Muslim marriages in a comprehensive way that will ease the tension arising out of the separation of powers and reduce the complexity of South African family law.

2. Legislative Recognition of Heterosexual Cohabitation[72]

Here is another instance where the South African Law Reform Commission has done its work and recommended legislation to regulate domestic partnerships in general, including heterosexual cohabitation.[73] But the legislature has not followed through. The difficulty of determining the rights of same-sex cohabitants now that they may marry is dealt with above. It is intended now to focus on the high incidence of heterosexual cohabitation as a neglected family form in South Africa. An aspect not always appreciated is that the migrant labour system under apartheid resulted in large numbers of rural women and children living alone while their husbands cohabited in the urban cities and towns with women whom they did not marry. It is naïve to think that the effects of this disruption on family life have evanesced. Women and children in these unformalised relationships are still vulnerable; they often cohabit for reasons of poverty. The law should recognise this fact as an added argument for regulating heterosexual cohabitation. Instead, it seems to assume that the choice to cohabit and not to marry is always a deliberate one.

The question that has challenged would-be legislators is how to regulate cohabitation. Several options were canvassed by the Law Reform Commission while it was considering domestic partnerships in general. It did grapple with the differences between those who deliberately choose not to marry (a relatively small number) and rather to cohabit, and those who make no conscious decision or cannot persuade their partners to make a formal commitment to the relationship (a much larger num-

---

[72] It is not intended to cover what circumstances constitute cohabitation in this paper, but rather to comment on the need for regulation of those relationships that it is assumed would qualify as cohabitation.

[73] Project 118 *Report on Domestic Partnerships* March 2006 contains a draft Domestic Partnerships Act (as Annexure E to the Report). The Report offers a wealth of information about the incidence of cohabitation and the consequences to which it gives rise. The Commission intended for this legislation to be enacted along with what it recommended for same-sex couples. But the legislature responded only to the latter because that is what the Constitutional Court had demanded of it in *Minister of Home Affairs v Fourie* 2006 (1) SA 524 (CC). (It was this judgment that prompted the enactment of the Civil Union Act 17 of 2006.)

ber). The option of registering the partnership in order to be within the purview of protections like the duty of support, intestate succession and property rights flowing from a marriage is contained in the legislation it recommended. Registration would be permitted only for monogamous relationships and for persons not already married. For registered partnerships courts would have the power to order maintenance, the Maintenance of Surviving Spouses and the Intestate Succession Acts would apply on termination, and property would be susceptible of division by way of the judicial discretion, as it is in some (incongruously limited) instances on divorce. Limitations on the disposal of household property and a right to occupy the joint home would apply.

The South African context, revealing high levels of poverty, low levels of literacy and high levels of dependence by women, raises the difficult issue of the position of parties in an unregistered partnership. For those who would not be likely to benefit from the registered partnership option, a decision must be made whether to confer rights upon the courts to make orders similar to those which would be available on the termination of a registered partnership. The Commission concluded that only on death or separation could a court be approached for such orders, in its discretion. No duty of support would exist during a non-registered partnership. For those (likely to remain the wealthier and educated classes) who deliberately do not register, the argument arises that legal regulation would impose obligations flowing from marriage upon cohabiting couples who do not wish to be burdened with them (surely a small number). An opt-out agreement could be considered for this category. But it was not included in the Commission's draft legislation. The sequel to the Law Commission's recommendations was the introduction and publication in January 2008 of a draft Domestic Partnership Bill very similar in its terms to the legislation recommended by the Commission.[74] Nothing has happened since then.

It is acknowledged that there is no easy solution that would satisfy the needs of all partners who cohabit. But this fact should not be an excuse for delaying the consideration and enactment of the work-product of the Law Reform Commission and, meanwhile, leaving the welfare of large numbers of vulnerable women and children unattended to.

In the absence of legislative solutions, the courts have had to deal with these inequities. A recent decision of the Constitutional Court in

---

74 See Government Gazette 30663, 14 January 2008.

Volks N O and others v Robinson[75] highlights the unsatisfactory nature of our law. After fifteen years of cohabitation which ended on the death of the male partner, the female partner claimed maintenance out of his deceased estate, alleging her entitlement to derive from the Maintenance of Surviving Spouse Act. The same Court that had found that a same-sex partner did qualify as a spouse for the purposes of this Act found that the word »spouse« could not cover the surviving partner of a heterosexual relationship. The Court conceded that there was discrimination, but found that it was not unfair, which it has to be to justify judicial interference. The couple could have married. By contrast, the unfairness that had prevailed for same-sex partners was that they could not marry (prior to the enactment of the Civil Union Act). The majority was at pains to point out that no duty of support exists between heterosexual life partners. Blame for this state of affairs was laid by the Court at the door of the legislature for failing to provide a framework of laws for the protection of heterosexual partnerships and the often vulnerable women in them. But the court was split. Three judges would not adopt such deference to the doctrine of separation of powers and found that the discrimination was unfair and based on marital status. They were much more cognisant of the evolving nature of our society, of marriage and of family life. They stressed that the woman in this partnership functioned and played the same role as a wife and had demonstrated dependency. One author aptly comments on the outcome of the case as follows:

> »*The* Volks *decision protects the institution of marriage and if heterosexual couples are excluded from the legal consequences which emanates [sic] from marriage, it is their choice. It is indeed surprising that the court when faced with the ideal opportunity to protect the vulnerability of women [sic] in domestic partnerships, in an ironical twist, acknowledges their plight, but diminishes it by passing their problem onto the legislature.*«[76]

---

75 2005 (5) BCLR 446 (CC).
76 Domingo 2005 *Annual Survey of South African Law* 169. See also the criticism of the case by Albertyn, Substantive Equality and Transformation in South Africa 2007 (23) *SAJHR* 253 at 266. This author incisively points out that the courts are »the guardians of the Constitution and are critical participants and arbiters in giving it meaning. Indeed, such is the interpretive power of the Court that it gives the Constitution meaning even as it refrains from doing so« (at 276n128).

This paper ends with an endorsement of the important contribution of Martha Minow, nearly twenty years ago.[77] Three of the judges clearly adopted her functional approach to the extension of family-law protection to include emerging and non-conventional family forms by concluding that this approach must surely be mandated by the rights to equality, dignity and non-discrimination enshrined in the South African Constitution. The existence of a duty of support for cohabitants should be based on factors such as dependence, need and contribution and not on the fulfilment of formal requirements.[78]

Cohabitation is an international phenomenon that has been dealt with by many jurisdictions. South Africa will remain out of step with modern trends and out of step with the values enshrined in its own Constitution until it fills this obvious gap in the law.

---

77 Martha Minow, Redefining Families: Who's In and Who's Out?, (1991) 61 *Colorado LR* 2.
78 See Sinclair assisted by Heaton *The Law of Marriage* (1996) 299. See also Goldblatt, Regulating Domestic Partnerships – A Necessary Step in the Development of South African Family Law, (2003) 120 *SAJHR* 610 at 625; Heaton, An Overview of the Current Legal Position Regarding Heterosexual Life Partnerships, (2005) 68 *THRHR* 662.

The Extent of the State's Duty to Support Family Life through Prevention and Early Intervention Programmes: A Reflection on the Children's Act 38 of 2005

Anton van der Linde[1]

I. Introduction

The adoption of the final Constitution in 1996 together with the ratification[2] of the *United Nations Convention on the Rights of the Child* (CRC), introduced a new legal regime affecting families, children and the interrelationship between state, family and child.[3] Legislation affecting children had to be revised in order to comply with these and other human rights documents. The South African Constitution, however, does not contain an explicit right to family life. In reply to an objection against the absence of rights with regard to the family, the Constitutional Court in *Ex parte Chairperson of the Constitutional Assembly: In re Certification of the Constitution of the Republic of South Africa*[4] remarked[5] that families are constituted, and are dissolved in such a variety of ways, resulting in the possible outcomes of constitutionalising family rights being so uncertain, that constitution-makers frequently prefer not to regard the right to marry or to pursue family life as a fundamental right that is appropriate for definition in constitutional terms. The Constitution, furthermore, clearly prohibits an arbitrary state interference with the right to marry or to establish and raise a family, while section (7) enshrines the values of human dignity, equality and freedom. On the other hand, various sections either directly of indirectly support the institution of marriage and family life. The Court,[6] for example, referred to section 28 (1)(b) which stipulates that

---
1 University of Pretoria, South Africa.
2 16 July 1995.
3 See *Sloth-Nielsen* »Ratification of the United Nations Convention on the Rights of the Child: Some Implications for South African Law« 1995 *SAJHR* 401.
4 1996 4 SA 744 (CC).
5 Par 99 807D-F.
6 Par 102 808E.

every child has the right to family care or parental care, or to appropriate alternative care when removed from the family environment. Since 1996 attempts have, therefore, been made by the courts to deal with aspects of family life under different sections of the Constitution which presumably afford indirect protection to the family.[7]

Apart from the Constitution, the importance of the »family« has recently been emphasised by the enactment of the Children's Act 38 of 2005, which came into operation in July 2007. The Preamble states that it is neither desirable, nor possible to protect children's rights in isolation from their families, as well as that the child, for the full and harmonious development of his or her personality, should grow up in a family environment. The objects of this Act are in brief to promote the preservation and strengthening of families and to give effect to the constitutional rights of children, of which the right to family care and social services seem to be relevant in the context of this contribution. These policy considerations and objects are in line with those expressed in the Preamble to the CRC. The Children's Act also contains a broad definition of »family member« and by implication the »family«, namely a parent of the child; any other person who has parental responsibilities and rights in respect of the child; a grandparent, brother, sister, uncle, aunt or cousin of the child; or any other person with whom the child has developed a significant relationship, based on psychological or emotional attachment, which resembles a family relationship.[8] This definition conforms to the CRC's view of the »family« which recognises the fact that there is a broad range of persons who may take responsibility for children.[9]

An important question relates to the duty of the states ratifying the CRC to match their pledges of protecting the family with action. Article 4 CRC proclaims:[10]

---

7   See in this regard *Dawood, Shalabi, Thomas v Minister of Home Affairs* 2000 3 SA 936 (CC), where family life was dealt with in terms of s 10 of the Constitution, namely the right to dignity.
8   Thus acknowledging a broad definition of »family«.
9   In terms of article 5 of the CRC, states are obliged to respect »the responsibilities, rights and duties of parents or, where applicable, the members of the extended family or community as provided for by local custom, legal guardians or other persons legally responsible for the child, to provide, in a manner consistent with the evolving capacities of the child, appropriate direction and guidance in the exercise by the child of the rights recognised in the present Convention«.
10 See discussion in *Reforming Child Law in South Africa: Budgeting and Implementation Planning UNICEF* Innocenti Research Centre (2007) 1-13.

> »States Parties shall undertake all appropriate legislative, administrative and other measures for the implementation of the rights recognized in the present Convention. With regard to economic, social and cultural rights, states parties shall undertake such measures to the **maximum extent of their available resources and, where needed, within the framework of international cooperation.**«[11]

In this regard the Children's Act, in keeping with article 4 of the CRC, introduced section 4 (2) which reads as follows:
> »Recognising that competing social and economic needs exist, organs of state in the national, provincial and, where applicable, local spheres of government must, in the implementation of this Act, **take reasonable measures to the maximum extent of their available resources to achieve the realization of the objects of this Act.**«[12]

The Children's Amendment Act,[13] promulgated on 18 March 2008,[14] through the insertion of Chapter 8[15] on Prevention and Early Intervention Programmes into the Children's Act 38 of 2005, can be seen as an attempt to comply with the duty imposed on the state to preserve and promote a child's right to family life. This contribution focuses on the meaning and purposes of prevention and early intervention programmes, the provision thereof, the national norms and standards they have to adhere to, the way the courts may in the future deal with these issues as well as the financial implications thereof. It also discusses the question whether these programmes can include material assistance over and above that provided by the child support and other social welfare grants. In this regard, brief mention is also made of the state's obligation to provide the socio-economic rights of children. These aspects are discussed against the background that the mutual enjoyment by parent and child of each others company constitutes a fundamental element of family life. Respect for family life implies an obligation on states to maintain and develop family ties and to act in a manner calculated to allow these ties to develop normally.[16]

---

11 Own emphasis.
12 Own emphasis. For a discussion of the meaning of this phase see par V below.
13 41 of 2007.
14 GG 30884 No 313.
15 Will come in operation at a date determined by the President.
16 See in this regard judgments by the ECtHR in *Rieme v Sweden* (1993) 16 EHRR 151 181

II. Prevention and Early Intervention

1. *Definitions*

Section 143 of the Children's Act defines *prevention programmes* as programmes designed to serve the purposes mentioned in section 144, and which are provided to families with children in order to strengthen and build their capacity and self-reliance in order to address problems that are bound to occur in the family environment which, if not attended to, may lead to statutory intervention, such as removal into alternative care. Intervention programmes means programmes provided to families where there are children identified as being vulnerable to or at risk of harm or removal into alternative vare. Both these services are intended to prevent neglect or to intervene where neglect is imminent or has already taken place.[17]

2. *Purposes and Content of Prevention and Early Intervention Programmes*

In terms of section 144 (1) these programmes must, *inter alia*, focus on preserving a child's family structure; developing appropriate parenting skills and the capacity of parents and care-givers to safeguard the well-being and best interests of their children; providing psychological, rehabilitation and therapeutic programmes for children; and avoiding the removal of a child from the family environment. Prevention and early intervention programmes *may* include assisting families to obtain the basic necessities of life; empowering families to obtain such necessities for themselves; and providing families with information to enable them to access services.[18] These programmes must involve and promote the

---

par 54-56; *Olsson v Sweden* (1989) 11 EHRR 259.
17 Frank_Costing the Children's Bill – Report: SA 5 »Situational Analysis of Early Intervention Services« 2005.
18 S 144(2). This list is not exhaustive. Typical prevention work includes (see *Costing the Children's Bill* – Report: SA 5 4-8): (a) awareness and education programmes relating to – development and capacity building of parents (life skills parenting skills, literacy skills); child safety awareness; HIV/AIDS prevention; youth development; women development (WOF – Womens Outreach Foundation); substance abuse prevention; violence against women/children awareness; info on access to social security. (b) Poverty eradication, job creation, income generation, small business development (brick-making, cooking, sewing, knitting etc); soup kitchens.
Typical intervention work includes: HIV/AIDS support to infected adults/children; marriage and divorce counselling; counselling (individual, joint, familial); Drawing up of working agreements; community work programmes such as pre-school, after-

participation of families, parents, care-givers and children in identifying and seeking solutions to their problems.[19] The emphasis is clearly on the importance of the basic family structure and the duty of the state to intervene timeously in order to avoid the removal of the child from the family environment. The desired outcome of these programmes is the preservation or creation of functional families that are safe, nurturing environments for children to grow up in.[20]

3. Strategy for Securing Prevention and Early Intervention Programmes

In terms of section 145 (1) and (2) the Minister, after consultation with interested persons, and the Ministers of Education, Finance, Health, Provincial and Local Government and Transport, must include in the departmental strategy a comprehensive *national* strategy aimed at securing the provision of prevention and early intervention programmes to families, parents, care-givers and children across the Republic. The MEC for social development must within the national strategy provide for a *provincial* strategy aimed at the provision of properly resourced, co-ordinated and managed prevention and early intervention programmes.

4. Financial Provisions and Budgeting

Section 146 (1) provides that the MEC for Social Development must, from money appropriated by the relevant provincial legislature, provide and fund prevention and early intervention programmes for that province. The provider of prevention and early intervention programmes only qualifies for funding contemplated in subsection (1) if the programmes comply with the prescribed national norms and standards contemplated in section 147 and such other requirements as may be prescribed.[21] The funding of prevention and early intervention programmes must be prioritised in communities where families lack the means of providing proper shelter, food and other basic necessities of life to their children.

---

      school, recreational; juvenile offender school / pre-perpetrator programmes; juvenile safety school; dealing with victims of domestic violence; crisis centres etc.
19   S 144(3).
20   *Costing the Children's Bill* – Report: SA 5 3.
21   S 146(3).

III. National Norms and Standards for Prevention and Early Intervention Programmes

The Minister must determine national norms and standards for prevention and early intervention programmes by regulation after consultation with interested parties.[22] The national norms and standards contemplated in subsection (1) must, *inter alia*, relate to the following services: Outreach services; education, information and promotion; therapeutic programmes; family preservation;[23] skills development programmes; diversion programmes; and temporary safe care.

The Consolidated Draft Regulations[24] pertaining to the Children's Act contain national norms and standards for such programmes.[25] It is necessary that the quality and availability of such programmes be standarized throughout the country, so that the children in need of these services are aided in the best possible manner.[26] For the purposes of section 147 (2) of the Act, the following national norms and standards must, *inter alia*, be adhered to.[27] They must, be aimed at the identification of high risk families and children; be home-based and family-centred with family members seen as the main focus; be aimed at preventing the recurrence of problems in the family environment that may harm children or adversely affect their development; address factors that put children at risk of imminent removal from their environment; address the particular needs of families in their diverse forms; and ensure that children and families are able to access documents, including birth certificates, to facilitate access to social security and other social services.

---

22 S 147(1).
23 S 147(2).
24 Not yet promulgated.
25 The role of these regulations are to flesh out and provide guidance on the provisions of the primary legislation, namely the Children's Act. They are not aimed at setting general principles, but rather implementation of the principles contained in the primary legislation. *Sloth-Nielsen* »The Children's Act Process: The Regulations« *Article 19* (2007).
26 *Costing the Children's Bill* – Report SA 5 10.
27 For the purpose hereof the norms and standards have been summarized. See however Ch 11 of the Draft Regulations 162.

IV. Court may order Early Intervention Programme[28]

Before making an order concerning the temporary or permanent removal of a child from that child's family environment, a children's court may order
a. the provincial department of social development, a designated child protection organisation, any other relevant organ of state or any other person or organisation to provide early intervention programmes in respect of the child and the family or parent or care-giver of the child if the court considers the provision of such programmes appropriate in the circumstances; or
b. the child's family and the child to participate in a prescribed family preservation programme.[29] An order made in terms of subsection (1) must be for a specified period not exceeding six months.[30] When a case resumes after the expiry of the specified period, a designated social worker's report setting out progress with early intervention programmes provided to the child and the family, parent or care-giver of the child, must be submitted to the court.[31] After considering the report, the court may decide the question whether the child should be removed; or order the continuation of the early intervention programme for a further specified period not exceeding six months.[32] Subsection (1) does not apply where the safety or well-being of the child is seriously or imminently at risk.[33]

V. Budgeting and Costing of the Children's Act

Article 4 of the CRC and section 4 (2) of the Children's Act 2005 makes it clear that states are expected to allocate and expend resources to fulfil their pledges. The allocation of resources to children to the maximum extent of their availability is key in efforts to ensure the CRC implementation.[34] Law reform and the subsequent implementation of legislation

---

28 S 148.
29 S 148(1).
30 S 148(2).
31 S 148(3).
32 S 148(4).
33 S 148(5).
34 »The Convention and Law Reform«: in UNICEF Innocenti Research Centre: Case studies: *Reforming child law in South-Africa: Budgeting and Implementation Planning* (2007) 4 wrt an earlier study by UNICEF.

through programmes requires adequate and substantial allocation of funds from governments to ensure concrete implementation and to make children's rights a reality. The role of the government begins at the macro-economic level. The Unicef Report[35] puts it in the following terms: »*Whatever the rhetoric, and however ›pro-children‹ the macro-economic policy looks, it is the state budget that gives a clear indication of governments real priorities.*« The government must be able to demonstrate that it will do as much as possible in as short a time as possible to protect children's rights, using the available resources effectively and efficiently. Governments should give priority to the rapid delivery of basic core services, improving them over time until all children's rights are fully realized. Thus, retrogressive steps of cutting back on spending for children are not acceptable.[36] The prior costing of the Children's Act is a requirement of the Public Finance Management Act.[37] Section 35 of this Act states:

»*35. Unfunded mandates. – Draft national legislation that assigns an additional function or power to, or imposes any other obligation on, a provincial government, must, in a memorandum that must be introduced in Parliament with that legislation,* **give a projection of the financial implications of that function, power or obligation to the province**«*(Own emphasis).*[38]

The Department of Social Development hired a consulting team[39] to assist in costing the Children's Bill. A 122-page report, »The Cost of the Children's Bill«, was completed in 2006.[40] The consulting team produced a full-cost scenario (what the model would cost when fully implemented) and implementation plan scenarios (allowing for a phased model). Although various different scenarios have been covered the so-called Implementation Plan Low Cost Scenario is hereby included for the sake of interest.[41]

---

35 *Ibid.*
36 Unicef report II.
37 1 of 1999.
38 S 146 creates such an obligation in the sense that the MEC for Social Development must from money appropriated by the relevant provincial legislature, provide and fund early intervention programmes for that province.
39 Cornerstone Economic Research CC.
40 Barberton »The Cost of Children's Bill – Estimates of the cost to Government of the services envisaged by the Comprehensive Children's Bill for the period 2005 to 2010 2006.« Report for the national Department of Social Development.
41 Barberton et al *Children's Bill Costing Outcome – Provincial Social Development Module –* »Activity Summary and Analysis – Implementation Plan Low Cost Scenario June 2006.« For the method of how the costing was done see the actual report fn 39.

Implementation Plan Low Cost Scenario June 2006

Cost of Activities	2008/09	2009/10	2010/11
Prevention, Intervention and Protection	R 3,415,117,316	R 4,028,057,784	R 4,703,623,965
Management	R 459,397,900	R 542,232,201	R 633,287,922
Prevention Work	R 161,158,851	R 192,616,628	R 227,937,529
Risk Assessment	R 323,586,198	R 374,761,320	R 434,132,365
Intervention Services	R 2,001,243,697	R 2,371,901,453	R 2,773,647,291
Investigations	R 341,338,921	R 395,224,743	R 457,720,310
Court Processes	R 82,714,883	R 96,008,848	R 111,472,600
Statutory After Care of other Orders	R 45,676,866	R 55,312,591	R 65,425,948

Intervention services constitute a substantial portion of the overall cost of services pertaining to children primarily due to the comparatively high level of demand for these services. However, it needs to be borne in mind that intervention services, if properly implemented, are significantly more cost-effective than drawing children deeper into the care and protection system.[42] *Budlender and Proudlock*[43] recently examined the provincial budgets for 2008/2009 and came to the following conclusions:

---

[42] The Cost of the Children's Bill 63. The costing project did establish what it would cost to implement the Children's Bill. This provides the government with a clear indication of the budgets that will need to be allocated. It also provides the basis of a detailed implementation plan p 31.

[43] »Analysis of the 2008/2009 Budget of the 9 provincial departments of Social Development: Are the budgets adequate to implement the Children's Act?« Children's Institute July 2008.

- Comparing the costing estimates to the actual budgets shows that there is a large gap between what is needed even at a minimum level and what the provincial departments are planning to provide.
- The total amount allocated in the provincial social development budgets for the three sub-programmes most closely related to children's social services covered in the Children's Act in 2009/10 is R2 923,9m (R2,9 billion).
- Costing estimates for the lowest cost scenario suggests that an amount of at least R6 billion is needed by the provincial departments of social development in the first year of implementing the Children's Act.
- Overall, the nine provinces' allocations cover less than half (about 48%) of the Implementation Plan low cost estimates over the two years (2009/10 and 2010/11).
- This indicates that major budget growth is still needed to ensure that we can implement the Act even at the lowest implementation scenario.

VI. Discussion

This position brought about by the new Children's Act is very different from the situation before. Although the idea of prevention and early intervention services is not new, the Child Care Act 74 of 1983, which has now been repealed, did not make explicit mention of the need for any prevention and early intervention services by social workers. In the Regulations to the Act,[44] mention is made that the report of the social worker to the Court[45] must contain a summary of prevention and early intervention services rendered in respect of the child and his/her family. The Regulations, however, neither contained a definition of such services, nor the contents and objects thereof. In this regard, the new Children's Act of 2005 can be seen as a revolutionary development and a step in the right direction in the sense that these programmes are explicitly required with emphasis consequently being placed on the need to keep children within the family and that removal should be seen as a measure of last resort. The emphasis, furthermore, seems to be on assisting and empowering families to support themselves through various programmes.

---

44   GN No R. 416 of 31 March 1998.
45   Contemplated in s 14(2) of the Child Care Act.

A study undertaken in South-Africa by *Matthias*[46] with regard to the position prior to the Children's Act, points out that poverty based removals will continue to occur until state maintenance of poor children is extended to situations where they can be kept with their families who can be assisted financially. In view of the child care legislation and lack of government support at that stage, she held the opinion that the emphasis was on the removal of children from the care of their families. She states:

> »*There has thus been, from the point of view of the official policy approach of the state, an imbalance which favours the ›society-as-parent‹ position.* **Not enough effort and resources have been directed to supporting children in their biological family groups.**«[47]

This conclusion was supported by her study showing a lack of preventative measures implemented by social workers, either because of their workload or due to a lack of financial resources. This problem remains applicable today where the imminent removal due to neglect or abuse stems from parental poverty. The question can thus be asked whether prevention and early intervention programmes should or could include the provision of (additional) material assistance?[48] The issue of additional material assistance touches on the question whether the parents or the state have the first responsibility with regard to the provision of children's socio-economic rights in section 28 (1) (c) of the Constitution namely the child's right to basic nutrition, shelter, basic health care services and social services, and the child's right in section 28 (1) (d) of the Constitution to be protected from maltreatment, neglect, abuse or degradation. The *Government of the Republic of South Africa v Grootboom*[49] judgment held that when children are living with their parents or families, the primary duty for their care (ito section 28 (1) (c)) falls on their families. Sec-

---

46 *Removal of Children and the Right to Family Life: South African Law and Practice* – A Community Law Centre Publication University of the Western Cape (1997) 23 to 57.
47 Own emphasis.
48 The study by *Matthias* provides an example on 22 as cited by a social worker: The Social Security Section (Pensions and Grants) refused her request for a single food voucher of R200 per month for a family that had four children which it could not feed: The section refused to pay the grant on the basis that the family had a house. It stated that, »they must sell the house«. But the family had no jobs and the house was the last thing that they had left. The state ended up removing all four children at a cost of R600 per child per month in place of a single food voucher of R200 per month that would have kept those children with their parents.
49 2000 (11) BCLR 1169 (CC).

tion 28 (1) (d) rights are, however, directly enforceable against the state. The corollary of *Grootboom*, however, is that when children are **not** living with their parents they have a direct claim to the state for their socio-economic rights.[50] This rational was recently applied to children born in public hospitals and clinics to mothers who are indigent and dependent on the state. It was thus affirmed that the protection contemplated by section 28 extends to the situation where implementation of the right to parental or family care are lacking.[51] With regard to the nature of the states obligation in relation to section 28 rights, the Constitutional Court stated that where children are in parental or familial care, the obligation would normally entail the passing of laws and creation of enforcement mechanisms for the maintenance of children and for their protection from abuse, neglect or degradation.[52] The court also mentioned the provision of maintenance/social welfare grants and other material assistance to families in need as one of the ways in which the state would meet its obligation.[53]

The problem is that although the child-support grant with regard to children between the ages of 0–14 in households earning less than R800,00 a month has been increased to R210,00, it is still inadequate. Section 144 (3) of the Children's Act states explicitly however, that prevention and early intervention programmes may include »assisting families to obtain the basic necessities of life«. What the »basic necessities« entail and whether this provision means that material assistance over and above that of the social grant can be provided, is uncertain. The emphasis, as indicated earlier, to a large extent seems to be on empowering families to support themselves. *Sloth-Nielsen*[54] provides the following helpful argument:

---

50 Sloth-Nielsen »The Child's rights to social services, the Right to Social Security and Primary Prevention of Child Abuse: Some conclusions in the aftermath of *Grootboom*: (2001) *SALJ*.
51 *Minister of Health v Treatment Action* Campaign 2002 5 SA 721 (CC) par 79. The central conclusion of *Grootboom* to section 28 (1) (c) remains unchanged after this case, however, and the states direct duty to ensure provision of shelter etc arises principally in the context of children who lack access to parental or family care; Sloth-Nielsen »Children« in Cheadle *et al* The South African Constitution: The Bill of Rights 2nd ed (2007) Ch 23-12.
52 *Grootboom* par 78.
53 *Grootboom* par 78.
54 Cheadle *et al* South African Constitutional law – The Bill of Rights 2nd ed (2007) Ch 23 13.

> »Section 28 (1) (d) does not, on the face of it, create a right which is subject to progressive realisation. Since there appear to be close links between parental poverty and child abuse in South African society, it is at least arguable, **where children's neglect stems from poverty alone, that the state should be obliged to adopt meaningful preventative measures which should include some level of financial allocation for family preservation.** The judgment in Grootboom mentions the possible establishment of social welfare programmes providing maintenance and **other material assistance** to families in need in defined circumstances, albeit that such programmes find their legal source in the context of section 27 of the Constitution (referring to the right to have access to social assistance, which the state needs only to implement progressively and within available resources.«[55]

She also submits[56] that **both** children in alternative care **and** neglected children in dire need, but being cared for by their families, have first call on state resources in the effort to protect them from neglect.

Looking for instance at an earlier interpretation of article 8 of the European Convention on Human Rights, it appears as if the state's positive obligation to maintain family life does not necessarily include material assistance. The Commission in *Andersson and Kullman v Sweden*[57] has found that article 8 does not guarantee the right to state assistance for the family, either in the form of financial support or day care facilities for children. They found, in particular, that respect for family life cannot be interpreted so as to oblige states to provide material assistance to enable a parent to take care of children at home. In *Marckx v Belgium*[58] the ECtHR, however, explicitly states the following: »Family life does not include only social, moral or cultural relations...; it also comprises interests of a material kind.« In this regard some authors are of the view that it is »very probable« that welfare provisions can be brought within the scope of article 8.[59] The question is asked whether the removal of a child from the

---

55 Own emphasis.
56 *Sloth-Nielsen* »The Child's right to social security, and primary prevention of child abuse: Some conclusions in the aftermath of *Grootboom*« 2001 *SAJHR* 210 231.
57 Appl no 11776/85 (1986) DR 46 251.
58 (1979) 2 EHRR 330 351 par 52.
59 *Duffey* »The protection of Privacy, Family life and other rights under Article 8 of the European Convention on Human Rights« 1983 *YEL* 191 193.

family home because of neglect due to poverty, can be supported by relevant and sufficient reasons where it is arguable the state which is at fault in failing to provide material assistance earlier.[60] Sections 4, 7, 19 and 27 of the CRC can certainly be helpful in this regard. A child has the right to be cared for by his parents and states have the duty to assist parents in ensuring that a child has an adequate standard of living. Institutionalisation should thus be considered only as a last resort, not only because the child has the right to be cared for by his parents, but also because it is far more expensive to institutionalise a child than to support him within the family.

VII. Conclusion

The Children's Amendment 41 of 2007, through the insertion of Chapter 8 on prevention and early intervention programmes into the Children's Act 38 of 2005, can be seen as an attempt to comply with the duty imposed on the state to promote the preservation and strengthening of families. These programmes focus on preserving a child's family structure, with the emphasis on avoiding the removal of a child from the family environment. The duty is on the state to fund these programmes. Overall, the budget documents suggest that there have been more real efforts to reflect the state's obligations as reflected in the Children's Act. The efforts do not, however, as yet cover even a fraction of the road that needs to be travelled.[61] These programmes, furthermore, have to comply with the prescribed national norms and standards contemplated in the Act. These norms and standards must relate to issues such as family preservation and the need to address factors that put children at risk of being removed from their families. Whether these programmes include possible material assistance over and above the social-welfare grants is unclear. There, therefore, still seems to be a lack of state assistance for parents who would be able to look after their own children but for a dearth (lack) of finances. There still seems to be no clear financial safety net to preserve familial units whose only problem is financial.[62]

Section 144 of the Children's Act is helpful in that it makes provision that prevention programmes may include assisting families in obtaining

---

60 Kilkelly *The child and the European Convention on Human Rights* (1999) 173.
61 Budlender and Proudlock 31.
62 See *Matthias* 23 wrt the position earlier.

the »basic necessities of life«. This, in my opinion, implies the possibility of some kind of (short term) material assistance. It can also be argued that material assistance in itself is also not excluded since the list as to what the programmes may involve, is not exhaustive. It is my submission that this view is supported by sections 7, 19 and 27 of the CRC. This is also supported by the view in the *Treatment Action Campaign* judgment[63] that the state's duty to provide children's socio-economic rights did not only arise in the context of children who were separated from parents and that the protection contemplated by section 28 extends to the situation where implementation of the right to parental or family care is lacking. The interpretation of a child's rights under section 28 (1)(d) also provides further impetus to this argument.

---

63 2002 5 SA 721 (CC).

Legal Resolution Services™ and its Interface with ADR: An Australian Perspective

Barbara Campbell[1]

I. Introduction

In this world of increased emphasis on cost effective solutions to legal disputes, with parties, governments and courts all insisting and encouraging an increase in Alternative Dispute Resolution options, using the principles of *Legal Resolution Services*™ [*LRS*™] is a surprisingly simple, economic alternative to the resolution of legal disputes. This system uses the experience of specialist lawyers and experts in the early stages or even as a first step in resolving legal disputes between parties.

The financial crisis in which so many families now find themselves, is an aspect that those of us working in the settlement of Family Law matters must genuinely examine.[2] It is therefore timely that an option is available that allows **both** parties to initially obtain good legal information from the one experienced lawyer **and** share the cost, prior to entering either an expensive, positional litigious path some lawyers unwittingly encourage or a mediated, conciliatory childfocussed resolution with their own lawyer.

This paper outlines the process and practical application of this first step approach for clients before they embark on litigation, collaboration, ongoing mediation or other settlement options.

The qualifications and experience of Settlement Facilitators is vital to the successful use of this system: Settlement Facilitators – the name given to those experts involved in *Legal Resolution Services*™ [hereinafter referred to as *LRS*™] are trained to focus the parties on identifying the **real issues** of their dispute **early** in the life of the matter.

This paper also briefly touches on new initiatives in the Australian Family Law system. This includes an Australian Court initiative: the **Less**

---

1 Campbell & Co. Lawyers, Canberra, Australia.
2 Professor Bea Verschraegen – Opening Address 13th World Conference Vienna, Austria 2008.

Adversarial Trial system [otherwise known as ›LAT‹] of hearing Family Law Matters. This is now compulsory for the hearing for Children's Cases in the Australian Family Court system and soon to be so for Property matters. This method used by Family Court Judges hearing cases when all other options have failed is less innovative to our European colleagues. Despite our system developing from the English Common Law system, LAT has been developed and adapted from the French and German judicial systems.

Whereas *LRS*™ is a **first step** approach: the hearing of a LAT matter commences on day one of a final hearing, after conferences, negotiations, mediations, offers to settle have all failed to settle the matter.

While the unifying theme of Family – single, same sex, intact or fractured unites us all in our quest for better settling Family Law disputes, focussing on a child's best interests is at the forefront of almost every jurisdiction's process.[3]

Another issue emerging throughout the world is the emergence of non-married couples in far larger numbers than 20 years ago, yet with similar breakdown statistics that those in the Family Law jurisdiction have experienced. It is notable that in some countries there is little support for so called »non-formal relationships«, yet in other countries, notably Australia as from March 2009, they are treated as almost equal to married couples. How to deal with the property of de facto couples [non-formalised relationships] is as topical in Australia as in Europe.

In Australia our *Family Law Act (1975)* has just been amended[4] to permit not only de facto couples to come under the jurisdiction of the Family Law Act but same sex couples are also included. Parties have been able to use the Family Court for children's disputes. However, save for some territories and case law developing the cross-vesting options, non-married couples have had to rely on each state and territory law to finalise their property dispute.

II. *Legal Resolution Services*™

The universality of the concept behind *Legal Resolution Services*™ is why it is adaptable for *any* legal dispute and in any jurisdiction. The option

---

3 *Family Law In Europe* Edited by Carolyn Hamilton & Kate Standley – Butterworths 1995.
4 *The Family Law Amendment (De Facto Financial Matters and Other measures) Bill 2008*.

is one that is being explored in various countries including USA[5]. It has links to many ADR practices but with some significant differences.

1. The Concept

Legal Resolution Services™ / or *LRS*™ is designed to facilitate settlement of legal disputes by providing parties *early* in their dispute, with expert, realistic, legal information and the identification of the real issues of their dispute.

The concept also allows *early* access to Consultants and Settlement Facilitators who are leaders in their field. These include experienced lawyers, barristers, retired Judges, registrars, psychologists, accountants, financial and superannuation advisers.

Accessing professionals as the first step, **and** sharing the costs of the hourly rate of the Consultant or Settlement Facilitator is a significant cost and stress-saving factor.

After having **the real issues identified** and being educated **together** by the Settlement Facilitator, parties are more aware of the issues in their dispute **and** of the law that applies to it. It is also an opportunity for **both** parties to hear from each other and from an experienced Lawyer – **early** in a dispute in a protected environment.

What the parties do after the initial consultation is open to them but knowing at all times that the Settlement Facilitator – albeit a highly experienced Lawyer – does **not** act for them, parties can then consult their own lawyer: **better able to instruct** him or her. Both parties have started with the same information. This information will include advice on all options available to a party once they have identified the issues in dispute.

2. The Process and the Model

Parties **jointly** make an approach to a *Legal Resolution Service*™ centre. Intake phone conference interviews and information provided by each party, enables identification of the area of law in dispute, and an assessment of whether parties are comfortable in the same room or require the protection of video conferencing – thus protecting and identifying parties involved in Domestic Violence.

A Pre-Action Agreement is provided to the parties for signatures and times and venues are arranged for the first conference with an appropriate Settlement Facilitator.

---

[5] Notably John Lande – see his article: *Movement to Early Case Management 2008* Ohio State Journal on Dispute Resolution.

The contracted Settlement Facilitator works with the parties to:
a. Obtain relevant information about the matter – which may include valuations and financial statements;
b. Identify the issues in dispute;
c. Provide information about the law as it applies generally;
d. Assist in mediating a settlement of the matter;
e. Advise parties of all options available to them to progress the matter towards settlement.

Once issues in dispute are identified, the parties have the option to access Experts in the area that remains in dispute, such as a Psychologist [as in a matter where children's issues are unresolvable] or a Superannuation or Forensic Accountant in property disputes.

An example where a single issue was identified at the first meeting with the Settlement Facilitator, resulted in the parties then meeting with the leading expert in Superannuation. It soon became apparent that the primary issue was how to divide the husband's considerable superannuation. In Australia, as in some other countries, we can obtain Splitting Orders permitting superannuation to be divided between parties. At the second *LRS*™ meeting the parties agreed to call in Stephen Bourke one of the country's leading expert's in superannuation splitting. Mr Bourke was able to say to both parties that he could suggest »*an option that would not normally be available in the court system but which would enable both of them to retire on exactly the same income.*« The parties paid for both the Settlement Facilitator's time, the Single Expert's report and his valuations and went off to have Terms of Settlement drawn up and executed with their own individual lawyers. The Settlement Facilitator is never involved in this last step.

With the experience of the Settlement Facilitator a range of potential outcomes is often obvious and can be made known to both parties. This enables and empowers parties to be better able to instruct their own lawyers. Often a reality check is required – carefully provided in a manner that does not inflame but often empowers. Too few clients are told: »*we serve you: you instruct us.*«

Many parties may choose to settle their matter after conferences with an *LRS*™ Settlement Facilitator but at all times independent legal advice must be obtained – even if it is to merely to draw up Consent Orders based on mediated Heads of Agreement.

3. Lawyers as Settlement Facilitators

With the sea-change away from litigation at all costs, there is an obvious use for experienced lawyers who have also examined and trained in ADR options.

A Settlement Facilitator must be: an Accredited Specialist in the area of law in dispute – in this case Family Law; or have at least 10 years experience in that area **and** have completed some ADR training.

LRS™ can use Commercial Lawyers for commercial disputes, Estate and Succession barristers/lawyers and experts for Estate disputes; accredited and experienced barristers and lawyers, psychologists and financial experts for Family Law disputes.

By using experienced lawyers only, parties are able to access the normally more expensive advice and expertise, yet pay only **half** the price by sharing the cost.

The Pre-Action Agreement signed by both parties makes it abundantly clear that the Settlement Facilitator does **not** and cannot act for either party. This in turn forces lawyers and parties to **focus** on and identify the real issues in dispute. How often is it said that a Lawyer only hears one side of the story from his or her client? The benefit of all those involved in the conference hearing and perhaps assisting in raising all issues and aspects of evidence required, cannot be underestimated.

Whether they are arbitrating, mediating, collaborating, and especially after some have been litigating, the public often think Lawyers are better placed under the sea surrounded by sharks! It is the writer's contention that most laterally-thinking, experienced lawyers make good Settlement Facilitators and many have very successful rates in focussing parties early in the process of separation, thus facilitating early settlement of their disputes.

Nancy Cameron QC re-defines advocacy in her article, *Reclaiming Advocacy*[6]. She states that lawyers must:

a. Honour process choices and agreed upon values;
b. Provide comprehensive support to the client [in the case of *LRS*™ to both parties];
c. Assist the client understand and articulate long and short term goals and interests;
d. Offer necessary support and leadership to enable the parties to resolve disputes.

---

6 »*Reclaiming Advocacy*« Nancy Cameron QC [at page 19].

While Nancy Cameron's emphasis is on Collaborative Practice techniques, these same principles apply to the running of a *LRS*™ and in effect should also apply to the servicing of a client in all legal matters.

There is a change pervading the legal profession, moving lawyers away from positional, litigious stances to a more active engagement in examining settlement options in a joint exercise and focussing on the real issues. Notwithstanding this, there is still much road to travel for some lawyers as all too often those matters that do end up in court, only then observe their lawyer focus on the real issues outside the courtroom door on the first day of the trial. The pressure of billable hours still prevents some lawyers focussing on expeditious appropriate settlement.

Why should parties on the first day and many dollars later of their final hearing, hear their Judge say (as often happens) »*why hasn't this settled?*«

Focussing the parties (as well as the lawyers) is the aim of *LRS*™.

As Professor Lande stated in his paper advocating Early Case Management:

Obviously, the sooner that participants seriously focus on cases, the sooner that at least some of them will get resolved. Early resolution has several potential benefits. Reducing the lengthy of the case is likely to reduce direct costs to the parties and courts ... Similarly, earlier resolution should generally reduce ... continuing damage to relationships and reputations. Early resolution also offers the potential of efficiency resulting from conscious efforts to streamline the process to focus only on the critical aspects of the dispute, reducing unproductive efforts such as excessive and unfocused discovery.[7]

A Settlement Facilitator is **not** just another mediator being paid at lawyers' hourly rates. What they bring to parties is legal knowledge, experience in the area, expertise and access to other experts if and when required.

One level of training that we will be using to further train and update Settlement Facilitators is Celia Burton's use of *Project Management Techniques in ADR*.[8] The innovative use of project management techniques, normally used for solving commercial disputes, is ideal for working towards legal resolutions in any type of matter. These techniques provide

---

7   John Lande *Movement to Early Case Management (2008)* at page 3.
8   Celia Burton, *The Effective use of Project Management Techniques in ADR:* AMINZ Conference August 2008.

visual data for parties so that they can more clearly see the end result and how it can be reached.

As Professor Wade of Bond University said recently – »*parties are wanting ›Value Added Mediation‹* «.[9] An example of parties wanting more than »just a mediator« was obvious in two recent phone calls to *LRS*™ from different states in Australia. One of the two potential users of *LRS*™ rang with about her De Facto property matter. She indicated that she had rung most of the mediation services in her area and ›quizzed the mediators about their knowledge of property division in a De Facto relationship‹. She found that most said they knew nothing about that area of law. This person and her partner wanted to negotiate a settlement but with someone who had expert knowledge in the area.

4. The Use of Experts and Settlement Counsel
4.1 Child and Family Psychologists

If there is an issue about children that has become intransigent a Settlement Facilitator might organise an early conference with an expert **child psychologist**. Normally this can't be done without a court Order with the attendant extra costs and delays in reaching that point. However, using the focus on Child Inclusive Settlement practices, being urged on practitioners in Australia, an *LRS*™ consultant can organise the **early joint** use of an expert in child and family psychologist to speak to both parents about what is best for their child or children. Thus this early intervention could stave off a battle over children that does nothing but harm the family.

Working with parents and encouraging them to see their dispute through the child's eyes often makes for a flash of understanding and can allow for innovative Consent Orders such as one the writer often uses. For example an Order that: *On each child's birthday and at Christmas,* **both** *parents shall spend time together with the child[ren] for a period up to 3 hours* is an option that was rarely proposed previously. Family Consultants and child experts interviewing children indicate repeatedly that a child's most common wish is to see their parents together again.[10] Even though these parents may no longer live together or even like each other or communicate properly, many are willing to admit that being focussed on the child has to be better than focussing on the past or a vindictive desire to punish the other party.

---

9   Advanced Mediation Course – Bond University August 2008.
10 Bill Hewlitt: ARCK Programme Canberra, Australia.

The writer was involved in a case that took 9 hearings and 2 appeals to convince a father that removing a baby boy from his breast-feeding mother every few days to spend an equal amount of time with him in his house, in a shared living arrangement was not good for a child of this age or even for many toddlers. One must wonder if the early receipt by the parents of joint expert intervention and advice may not have prevented both parents incurring the costs and trauma that they did.

Of course no experienced lawyer or genuine ADR operator is naïve enough to think that there are not some matters that just will not settle and which will always require a judicial decision. This is often the best option for such cases, but fortunately, a less used option. Naturally urgent cases such as impending abduction; recovery of a child taken by a parent or injunctions to prevent dissipation of property should and do immediately go to Court.

The Settlement Facilitator may also be called upon to arbitrate (if also a qualified Arbitrator) or Mediate the matter once parties have been advised to and have obtained independent legal advice.

4.2 Forensic Accountants and Valuers

Similarly, with the Settlement Facilitator identifying that valuations are in issue, the joint appointment by both parties of a forensic accountant to assess the value of a business or entity **early** in proceedings can focus parties on how to divide the property rather than later embarking on costly arguments about valuations.

4.3 Barristers as Settlement Facilitators

Very often, the involvement of experienced barristers as mediating Settlement Facilitators – after written evidence is provided to them via the initial Settlement Facilitator – settles a matter well before positions become entrenched.

As Settlement Facilitators, these barristers, with their knowledge and court experience give the parties the feeling that they are really are getting value for their money – noting that at this level they are still only paying **half** the costs they would if individually seeking counsel's opinion via their own lawyer. Many lawyers actively encourage this option and LRS™ ties in to this at an even earlier time. Some of Sydney's and Canberra's best barristers have completed the advanced mediation training and are being used by *LRS*™ and other law firms in this manner.

Whereas parties often think mediation is an option to be used only once, the early use of barristers as Settlement Facilitators especially in complex matters is an option that will encourage parties to feel that mediation by such experts is worth re-visiting and is not a »soft option«. After parties have had an initial consultation with a Settlement Facilitator, and then met with their own lawyers; having the option to return to the negotiating table with the assistance of a jointly appointed and jointly paid for barrister must result in savings of costs and earlier resolution of matters.

5. The »Where« and the »How«.

Having examined the »why«[11] and the »who«, of the concept of *Legal Resolution Service* to clients, this section will briefly examine some of the practicalities. The use of board rooms is of course an obvious choice for holding conferences but separate break-out rooms are essential in case a party becomes distressed or needs time out with the ability to access their own lawyer. The meeting rooms is set up with video-conferencing facilities, computers and whiteboard. A purpose built Settlement Centre where psychologists, accountants and lawyers all work together, is the next concept being incubated!

Already, *LRS*™ has consultants in Sydney, Brisbane and Canberra thus far and of course parties utilise their more local Settlement Facilitators.

Technological advances now provide inexpensive Video-Conferencing which all parties can access. This is linked to the *LRS*™ web site and is available to anyone with a web cam. At AU$ 15.00 [approximately €8½] an hour, video-conferencing is now incredibly affordable and enables parties who cannot or should not be in the same room to be on the same screen together along with the Settlement Facilitator.

Imagine how empowering it would be for a more vulnerable and possibly abused party to hear the bullying controlling or abusive party being given a reality check about the matter in dispute, while safe on line via video link in her own computer room. Video conferencing also enables parties to speak more freely than they may otherwise feel able to do in front of such a party.

Moreover, where distance prevents parties and a Settlement Facilitator being in the same room, each party can still »meet« together and see the other two participants at all times.

---

11 See below at *II LRS*™ *AND ITS PLACE IN OTHER ADR OPTIONS* at paragraphs 3 and following, for other reasons why *LRS*™ is a viable next step option.

Michelle Lavers, a psychologist on the *LRS*™ advisory board, is also preparing a training manual for assisting parties in coping with appearing and speaking via video link – apparently the psychology is quite different.

III. *Legal Resolution Services*™ and its Place in Alternative Dispute Resolution Options

In Australia we have instigated much early intervention in Family Law Cases. It is pleasing to see that in that other huge growth area – Estate and Will Disputes – courts are ordering the parties to Mediation at the first Directions Hearing.

The Australian Government has established 68 *Family Relationship Centres [FRCs]* all over the country, which focus entirely on assisting separating families work out how children's arrangements can best be finalised and how to cope with family disputes.

It is now **mandatory** for parties to attend an FRC or similar organisation and obtain a certificate from a designated provider before any application can be made to the Family Courts about children; unless urgent as in the case of risk to a child or recovery of a child etc. The certificate that issues to parties in conflict over their children, indicates to the court whether or not the parties have made a **genuine attempt** to settle the matter. Of course parties may settle their children's issues with the help of this mediator and S60I provider.

Mediators at *Family Relationship Centres* are not lawyers and lawyers are not permitted to attend the sessions with their own clients. What is still missing from these centres, is the ability for both parties to access early in their dispute good legal information about their matter together. Family Relationship Centres are not mandated to deal with property matters – so, after all the togetherness of mediating parenting issues or drafting parenting plans, the parties are immediately referred to individual lawyers – to fight out the property division! This often results in the mediation benefits about the children being negated or at least subsumed in the fuller litigious picture.

Even without requiring a child-focussed mediation session – parties should have the option of jointly learning about the law from experienced lawyers, and, if necessary, receiving a reality check about their case, before embarking on the costly path to litigation. It is submitted that John

Lande's Early Case Management options propounded in USA and *Legal Resolution Services™ inter alia* in Australia provide this option.

As is occurring in many jurisdictions – in children's cases before our courts – the legal profession and associated experts work together.

1. LRS™ and its Place in Mediation

Academic works on mediation – abundant as they are – differ on what matters are suited to mediation or mediatory styles : I tend to agree that by the most well-known definition – that of Folberg and Taylor (1984); – Mediation is: »*the process by which the participants, together with the assistance of a neutral person or persons, systematically isolate disputed issues in order to develop the options, consider alternatives, and reach consensual settlement that will accommodate their needs.*«[12]

The principles of *Legal Resolution Services™* are this plus the addition of expertise and if the matter requires or suggests it, an evaluative option. The warm and fuzzy approach in mediators, no longer hits it off in all cases!

Not to lessen Folberg's all-embracing definition referred to above, a list of *Indicators for Matters Suitable for Mediation*[13] prepared by leading *ADR* Professors J Wade and L Boulle of Bond University in Queensland, Australia, shows why using a Legal Resolution Services™ approach is NOT just mediation and IS suitable for ALL matters. I would respectfully suggest that both Professors would now agree that these premises are flawed! However, they provide a model against which the *LRS™* concept may be measured. The criteria for mediation as follows in the table below, appears with comments that show how the opposite indicia can also be true in a matter before a Settlement Facilitator or legal mediator, where the parties benefit from astute, expert involvement of a service that focuses the parties:

---

12 Folberg & Taylor – Definition of Mediation (1984).
13 Wade and Boulle – Advanced Mediation Course.

Mediation indicia[1]	Options That A Legal Resoution Service Can Provide
Conflict is Moderate	Even severe conflicts can be dealt with initially by a suitably qualified Settlement Facilitator – this may result in the conflict being hosed down, particularly if the initial couple of meetings result in a reality check for the most difficult party.
Parties are motivated for settlement	Parties unmotivated for settlement usually include those who want their day in court or who want to destroy the other party, make them pay, as well as those who »just want what is fair«. Sadly, some lawyers neglect to appropriately advice clients of their worst case scenario until the door of the court at a Final Hearing. They have then made substantial fees and settlement of the matter is often not an option if the other side has a reasonable position. I submit that it is those parties unmotivated to settle that benefit **the most** from the principles of a service which uses the methods of *LRS*™. It is imperative that, such an option becomes the norm for parties – an experienced lawyer as a Settlement Facilitator, is often able to move away from what can become a «mediation at all costs» blinkered approach by a non-legal mediator. Parties are often invited back to such mediation sessions even though the matter has not been advanced. Using the **experience** of a lawyer who has been at the coal-face of legal representation often identifies and prevents those using ADR options as a way of delaying settlement.

---

[1] This list of criteria is from the Bond University Mediation Course: Professor John Wade and Professor Laurence Boulle.

No severe resource shortage	With respect to the writers, this premise should be viewed as wrong. It is a travesty if impecunious clients are not able to access the expertise of a Mediator or Settlement Facilitators due to the cost. An underlying premise in using *LRS*™ so early in a matter is that it may be a conference for only one or two hours and which identifies the issues and prepares the parties for a mediation, collaborative or negotiating options. The cost – at half the experienced lawyer's hourly rate due to being shared by both parties, is thus very affordable. The only way many can involve a third party mediating the dispute is through government funded organisations. As in many countries, in Australia we have gone a long way to making sure that attending some form of negotiation with the third party is compulsory. Due to the calibre of Settlement Facilitators, those parties who fall just outside the gap which would provide them with Legal Aid, can access top Experts and experienced lawyers at half the cost. Moreover, using the video conferencing option avoids travel costs for many. This latter option will become more available and more invaluable in a country as vast as Australia.
Mediation is accepted as legitimate	Mediation or an *LRS* option, cannot be only for the ›soft‹ cases. As one of Australia's leading ADR experts, Professor Wade, admitted, »*there has been a dumbing down of mediation*«. Unfortunately many parties see mediation as a soft option – something for weaker parties – or an option for one party to bully a weaker party into a settlement that is not appropriate for them. The avoidance of the term »mediation« in discussions relating to *Legal Resolution Services*™ focuses parties towards «resolution« and away from thoughts that it is just another soft option. Paying for the expertise of experienced professionals, albeit at half the cost that individual clients would pay their lawyer, gives *LRS*™ value in the minds of parties.

Parties are relatively equal in power	This is often the gate mechanism for who can and cannot utilise collaborative or mediation options. It leaves out an enormous number of people. I contend that it is parties *unequal in power* who need the option of sitting either at the end of a camera or in the same room hearing the same information. This results in them being less likely to then move to their own lawyer with an agenda or a very one-sided story about their case.
Continuing relationship between parties	This is no longer a valid criteria for parties to attend mediation but often a reason for it being a viable option. It is most relevant in children's matters. Apart from the type of order as referred to above, a client who is a parent usually hears me say to them: »*you must get on with each other until the day your children die and hopefully that is well after you. I am sure you want to be at your children's 21st birthday their wedding and engagement parties. Children like nothing better than to look up on special days and see <u>both</u> parents in the same room focussing on them.*« If there are no children however, parties may not want nor need to continue a relationship with each other and *LRS*™ as an option, is often a way of expediting settlement and allowing the parties to move on more quickly.

2. A Pre-cursor to Collaborative Practice

While not ignoring the excellent progress the Collaborative movement has made (having trained with Stu West of USA and Marion Korn of Canada) and applauding the manner in which Collaborative Law and Practice has re-focussed many lawyers away from litigation and back to the use of settlement conferences; research is finding that the method can become very expensive especially if the focus on making fees in an era of fewer litigated matters prevails in the firms where collaboration is used. Thus, this option is often priced out of the reach of the average disputing couple.[14] If after both parties have benefitted from learning about the law as it applies to their case in a joint *LRS*™ session with one experienced lawyer, and other experts if needed, each party should be better able to instruct their own lawyers and many may choose to take a collaborative approach to settling their matter.

3. The Last Resort – Litigation

This option is hopefully a last resort for those parties who have to have their day in court. However, using the early joint session with a Settlement Facilitator at least provides parties with an unbiased reality check about the costs and pain of Litigation. Moreover imbued with the confidence to really **instruct** their own lawyers, parties are able to manage their matter with more focus on resolution rather than be coaxed into a litigious series of expensive legal manoeuvres.

4. Focussing the Client

How often do we find clients focussed on an issue that in the scheme of things is not relevant to the big settlement picture. A good settlement facilitator ventures down this mediatory path and enables these issues to be unpacked and dealt with. However, the exercise with an LRS™ practitioner also **educates** the parties in relation to what a court might see as the **real** issues. They may not be abundantly clear at the first meeting and more conferencing with the parties' own lawyers may assist, especially in complex matters.

With the use of Settlement Facilitators and Experts at this early stage it is submitted that more cases will reach the equivalent of »Day one« of a Final Hearing far earlier and at far less the cost. While *LRS*™ as an initial option, is ideal for Family Law and Estate disputes, almost any type of dispute can benefit from using *Legal Resolution Services*™ concepts and tecniques.

---

14 There is no empirical evidence that collaborative law is less costly than litigation or negotiated family law file, nor quicker...- Anne Ardagh *Repositioning the Legal Profession in ADR services: The Place of Collaborative Law in the New Family Law System in Australia* :page 243 Law and Justice Journal Volume 8 Number 1. 2008 Queensland University of Technology at page 243.

IV. Answering the Critics

One expected comment is that »*LRS*™ is just another form of mediation«. The answer is a typical lawyer's »yes and no«: but in reality probably »yes but with clout!« I contend that it is not entirely *just* mediation although it is clearly a form of Evaluative Mediation. Law Societies need to place *LRS*™ in context and one thing it is not, is a law firm acting for clients. It clearly is a mediatory option for parties.

This paper emphasises the add-on value that can result in parties accessing experienced lawyers and legal information along with the choice of appointing experts who can advise on an particular issue in dispute, **early** in their matter. At the same time sharing the costs halves the costs.

The other criticism and issue often raised, and indeed likely to be used as a sword to cut down innovations such as *LRS*™, is the claim that using lawyers to see both parties is a breach of the rules of conflict because they may well be hearing legal information from the same person. The Pre-Action Agreement signed by both parties prior to the first conference, emphasises that the Settlement Facilitators are not acting for or representing either party. Moreover, no documents emanate from the chambers or law offices other than possible Heads of Agreement for each party to take back to their own legal representative and have drawn up into a legal documentation or Consent Orders – if the party's own lawyer deems them appropriate for their client or is instructed to do so. In effect it is no different to parties attending mediation with a mediator who has also a law degree.

As there is no bar to parties having their own lawyers present at conferences, and indeed this is encouraged in smaller regions where parties may already have seen a local lawyer. Such country »GP« lawyers often do not have the specialist expertise in this particular area and are grateful for being able to bring in an experienced specialist to facilitate settlement of the matter. However, having one party only being represented when the other is not so, is discouraged.

The requirement for all Settlement Facilitators to have had some formal ADR training means that along with their legal experience of at least 10 years, plus Specialist Accreditation, they are equipped to handle the need for parties to share their thoughts, feelings and clarify the past before moving on. As Mark Stein says in his readable e-book, »*Getting Divorced Without Getting Fleeced*« once this is done, there is »*no other place to go, but the future.*«[15] Not all facts may be agreed upon but a resolution still may occure.

Just as Judges now, almost religiously focus on the future for warring parents who appear before them in the Less Adversarial Trial system, [sometimes to the detriment of permitting valuable evidence to be put before them that will enable them to properly make a decision about a parent], lawyers engaged in early Legal Resolution Services™ will also focus on the future – the immediate options for working towards resolution being the first step and not the last.

With courts and governments emphasising the use of Alternate Dispute Resolution options as a better alternative, Law Societies have to move with the times. Innovative options are developing throughout the legal world and Lawyers involvement should *not* be side-lined in the process. That said, care and caution must always be exercised in the situation where parties may not move on to see their own lawyer. Carefully written »Rules of Engagement« and the ability to notify a local court if pressure is clearly going to be used on an unrepresented party are available in the »tool box« of a Settlement Facilitator.

It is difficult to object to these early intervention innovations when governments are stating, as did Australia's Attorney General recently:

> *I want to see an emphasis on an integrated Family Law System, where family disputes are resolved outside courts wherever possible; where there are effective ways of getting entrenched cases out of courts; where situations of family violence and child abuse are managed safely and effectively.* Moreover the Attorney-General emphasised the ongoing need for bridge-building between mediators, legal practitioners and the judicial sector to help achieve these objectives.[16]

Lawyers acting as Mediators or Settlement Facilitators have clear guidelines about how much information and in what manner it is to be given – this movement towards such early intervention is occurring everywhere.

---

15 At Page 74.
16 Attorney General McClelland – opening address of the Queensland Law Society and Family Practitioners Association 18 August 2008.

V. Conclusion

The legal Resolution Services concept is simple, enthusiastically received around the world, yet not something that is in wide existence – yet. To be able to both legally and financially assist parties resolve their dispute in this area of often traumatised clients should be the aim of all lawyers.

There will always be the need for lawyers to advocate for clients – there will always be families changing, developing, disintegrating and re-grouping.

From an icon of Australian thinking – Germain Greer – recently speaking on an Australian television programme about warring groups: as applicable to warring families, and dare I say, warring lawyers: »*Quit the war and start the negotiations!*«

A Legal Resolution Service™ able to be established anywhere in the world, will focus the parties, identify the real issues and provide, early access to the experience of the legal profession and other experts at half the cost.

Legal institutions should encourage the use of an option which is less expensive, more focused and yet which uses and respects the experience of Lawyers in this most diverse and difficult field of law.

An Interdisciplinary Approach of Family Finances

Giselle Câmara Groeninga[1]

I. Introduction

It is an honour to participate in the 13th International Society of Family Law World Conference.

It is a long way from São Paulo, Brazil – to Vienna – as it is also a long time ago since Brazilian Family Law was inherited from Portugal, the *Ordenações Filipinas, Afonsinas* and *Manuelinas* – our first codes, to the 2002 Civil Code and to the proposal of the Family's Law Statute, elaborated by the Brazilian Institute of Family Law – IBDFAM– the *rationale* which I will mention briefly later.

The legal system reflects the objective and subjective identity of a nation. Besides regulating the social interactions, it also has a powerful symbolic influence on people's minds. In Brazil as in the rest of the globalized world, Family Law is facing the challenges of post-modernity trying to deal with all the changes and mutations, if one can say so, that are taking place in social and family relations.

In this paper I will focus firstly on some of these changes drawing a parallel to the way we are dealing with them in Brazilian Family Law.

The matrimonial regime will be taken as an illustrative example of the transformation that has taken place in family relations over the last century. The prevalence of a matrimonial regime bears a strong correlation with the social and historical context. I will put forward some hypotheses about subjective motivations that are underneath the choices made by the marrying couple and their consequences for the family structure.

The interpretation of these referred social changes and the couple's choices of the matrimonial regime will be made with the help of an interdisciplinary approach, mainly through the psychoanalytical lenses.

---

1   IBDFAM Brazilian Institue of Family Law, Brazil.

II. The Interdisciplinary Approach

But first we should ask the question: why an interdisciplinary approach? It is because it enables us to have a broader understanding of the complexity of human relations, which is essential nowadays. There is no doubt that family relations are the most complex ones. For instance, psychoanalysis shows us that feelings of love and hate are part of our human nature. This knowledge is not taken into account by law professionals until relationships break down and destructive feelings may steal the scene of family relations. When everything was going fairly well it was love that occupied most of the scene. The same dynamics is also valid for social relations in time of peace.

The interdisciplinary approach made a strong move in the middle of the twentieth century. The well known Frankfurt School searched for a new frame of knowledge, combining psychoanalysis and history with sociological, political and economical understanding of social interactions. The main issue dealt by the Frankfurt School, with the background of the shocking World War II, was that the ideals of the Modern Era – equality, fraternity and freedom, not only were not attained but were strongly contradicted by the reality of social, economical and political relations, to state it to a minimum. With a lighter political engagement a group of scholars of different specialties headed by the psychologist Jean Piaget got together to discuss some selected topics through the lenses of various disciplines. This was the beginning of the interdisciplinary approach.

From the second half of the last century we have experienced a change in paradigm – from the Cartesian one to the integrative one, or the paradigm of complexity as Edgar Morin – the philosopher, has put it. The Cartesian one separated and opposed reasoning and emotions, objectivity and subjectivity, civilized and primitive, north and south, eastern and western, man and woman.

Now, it is true, we are also experiencing some confusion in what is called the post-modern era, with the rearrangements of the frontiers not only geographical, social, familial, but also concerning the disciplines of knowledge. The interdisciplinary approach should sum up the contributions of some disciplines without mixing them up. In fact the result should be to strengthen their individual identities and establish their differences so that our understanding can be broadened.

III. The Interdisciplinary Approach and the Family

I shall now move on to applying the proposition of an interdisciplinary approach to the family. We depend on each other in various degrees and our humankind is essentially based on exchanges of various kinds. These range from emotional to material and economical exchanges. There are different levels of family organization that translate our exchanges. Depending on the discipline, one would see the psychological aspect of the interactions among family members, or the social bounds and roles that family members play; through the lenses of an economist the financial issues would be privileged, as well as that the law professionals would take into account the juridical division of rights and duties among the various family members.

What is important is that all these levels – psychological, social, financial and legal, are present in family relations. Thus, an interdisciplinary approach should consider them all and their interactions. Nevertheless, from my point of view, the social, economical, and legal levels are derived from our physical and psychological needs and desires. Money, finances and property, for instance, are the representatives of our need to be secure. Also depending on the context, money and property can be used to represent love or indifference and even hate. And in turn, the individual's mind and the family are strongly influenced by the economical, social and legal aspects.

Not so long ago we saw the family mainly through the lenses of the romantic, sacred and/or State ideologies. It was as if conflict, hate and also money were not part of family relations and the family was to be protected from the outside world. It was as if money – the »dirty« part of our human exchanges, was not to be mixed up with pure love family relations. Women and children – the weaker members, were to be protected from these factors.

Before the Industrial, the Communist and the Feminist revolutions, gender roles were clearly divided and mainly based upon biological traits. The man was the provider and the woman the caretaker. As in ancient Greece, the man was entitled the ágora – the public place, whilst the woman was to stay at home – in the gineseo. Objectivity, rationality and activity were almost exclusively masculine characteristics whereas subjectivity, emotionality and passivity were to be female ones. This strict division has changed a lot.

However, there are universal family characteristics, which we should search for throughout times. From the psychoanalytical and sociological point of view the family is formed on the bases of our dependent physical and emotional human nature. This dependency is bigger in our first infancy, nevertheless it continues throughout life. Our human subjective constitution is the basis for obligations as solidarity, caretaking, and even financial duties derived from our dependent nature. Moreover, the payment of alimony is also one of these derivatives.

Another important aspect of family relations is the complementary nature of the functions exerted by their members. This characteristic is based first on sexual differences – the original model of our complementary nature, and derived from those are the complementary functions and roles – as men and women, spouses, father, mother and offspring. There is an exchange among family members according to the position each one occupies. Members contribute to family life according to their role and depending on the social standards that are present in one particular time and cultural context.

We are multidetermined beings highly dependent, not only on physical aspects but also on emotional recognition and motivation.

Yet, today we are facing another revolution – we preach equanimity, we are freer than ever but we confuse equal rights with the homogenization of differences. This is what I call the »Bisexual Revolution« whereas there is an opportunity to exert personality traits independently of the gender, however there is a risk of losing the differences. From my point of view this is where the confusion lies and where a need for a change exists in the way we see the family as well as how legislation deals with it . First we had the predominance of hierarchical relations with a paternalistic character, afterwards we had the feminine revolution with a bi-hierarchical exercise of power in family life, and now we have the recognition of bisexual traits present in both genders in parallel with less prejudice about homosexuality and a strong advance in their rights.

As a consequence of this »Bisexual Revolution«, the generation gap with the differences between adults and children, between functions exerted in the family as well as those mainly distributed among gender is much subtler nowadays, although these differences are central for family composition and functioning. On one hand this »Bisexual Revolution« represents a clear advance on the freedom to exercise and to develop our personality traits; on the other hand we run the risk of homogenizing the differences that characterise us as individuals.

Going back in time we had the extended family model – it was also a time where there was not much room for individual qualities and freedom – these were sacrificed in the name of family unity. At the same time gender roles were rigidly divided.

All this cultural changes have consequences in the matrimonial regimes and in family finances.

IV. An Interdisciplinary View of the Matrimonial Regime

Until 1974 the matrimonial regime adopted in Brazil was the general partnership or community of property or assets – which is called, in Brazilian Law, Universal Community. However, from an interdisciplinary approach, this community is not only of property and assets – it is also a psychological one. The women fulfilled their needs for professional achievements by being proud of their husbands' careers and they, on the other hand, had part of their emotional realization through their wives and mothers of their children. This sort of arrangement is still in practice nowadays, but the difference is that at that time there was little freedom of choice concerning the exercise of roles within the family and in social relations. Patriarchal relations based on hierarchy dictated the norms.

After 1974 the adopted regime was the participation of acquests following the social changes and advances in women's rights.

Although Brazil had a highly patriarchal society there were quite a high number of informal unions. This reality was taken into account in the Divorce Law, in 1977, and in the 1988 Constitution. Legal recognition was given to these unions instead of denying its existence and leaving women and children unprotected.

Today in Brazil the matrimonial regime is of participation on acquests or Partial Community as it is called. Of course there is the choice of general partnership, or Universal Community; this choice bears nowadays an ideal of the traditional family where the roles and functions are divided accordingly. In these cases if divorce occurs there is a strong possibility of women facing problems in adapting to the prevalent social standards.

To add a small difficulty concerning comparative law, the 2002 Civil Code introduced the matrimonial regime of participation on acquests that differs from the Partial Communion concerning administration during marriage and division of patrimony when divorce occurs.

Let me get back to the broader scene. Much has changed in family life with all the named revolutions – Industrial, Communist, Feminine and Bisexual, in parallel with deep economic changes and modifications in the dynamics of social relations. Moreover much has changed in the way we conceptualize the family with the interdisciplinary approach and the knowledge gained by psychoanalysis. This knowledge concerns for instance: the importance of the first years of life for the development of a healthy personality, the importance attributed to the contact with both parents for the development of the child's identity, the knowledge that sexuality and gender identifications were not either directly or exclusively derived from biological characters. What was the concept and understanding of family life and the values brought by religious standards was now given a scientific, less divine and more humane perspective.

The family model has suffered a tremendous modification and the former rigid division of roles and functions has changed radically. And so has the family management of finances and marital regime. Instead of the extended indissoluble family, highly based on a patriarchal hierarchy, the model of our time is the nuclear family together with a higher value attributed to individuality.

Besides the financial issue, the *rationale* underneath the regime of participation on acquests or partial communion is also the breaking up of traditions. Nevertheless in terms of Brazil I can say that the nuclear family model and the regime of partial community and participation on acquests is still a kind of an ideal for the majority of the population that lives below what would be considered an acceptable standard.

Almost one third of our families are headed by women – they are the ones that play the role of the mother and father, of the caretaker and provider.

Whereas in the developed countries there is a high percentage of children born out of the wedlock and raised by a single parent due to cultural influences and choices, in Brazil one cannot consider this a choice but a result of factors such as:

> poverty,
> lack of social conditions
> failure in creating the consciousness of parental responsibility which could be taken as a paradox in a patriarchal society. But as I said before the patriarchal society exists for a range of the population that fits in the frame of family law.

V. The need of Legislative Modifications beyond the Matrimonial Regime

A great and necessary modification occurred with the inclusion of the informal unions by the legal system with the 2002 Civil Code. Another modification that we are facing in Brazil is the higher value placed on what we call the emotional or affective parenthood. A higher legal value is largely attributed to the social and psychological bounds in detriment of the biological one.

In a country of contrasts as is Brazil, there is a big gap between the legal system and the reality lived by families. It is true that with the 1988 Constitution this gap is smaller, yet we have a long way to go. For instance we still have a very bureaucratic system for adoption. On the other hand, we have what is called the Brazilian like adoption – *adoção à Brasileira*, an informal one in which the child is registered as if they were biological off springs of the adoptive parents. We recently had a huge campaign to legalize these adoptions.

The gap between the real situation of families and the legal system is diminishing but there is still a lot to be done. For instance, homosexual stable relationships or homoaffective ones, as we call them in Brazil, are not protected by family law, as they are in several countries.

With the 1988 Constitution and the 2002 Civil Code we had an enhanced consciousness of civil rights and an increased demand that the Courts were not able to cope with. Not only in terms of quantity but also in service quality. Furthermore there is still a gap in the legislation that does not consider the family in real terms. This situation made open clear the gap between Law, procedures and family relations. The need for a Family Statute became self evident.

The Brazilian Institute of Family Law – IBDFAM, which has an interdisciplinary approach, was founded only 10 years ago and has over 4000 members all over Brazil. This is a phenomenon that shows the need to meet an existing demand for a change and an interdisciplinary family relation approach in the legislation as well as in Court procedures. After a three year study the *Statute of the Families* was created. In spite of the difficulties of our Legislative System for the approval of laws one of the goals of the *Statute of the Families* is the discussion of the polemic issues by the civil society, which is being achieved.

We use the word families in the plural emphasising the fact that the family – the *celula mater* of the society should be considered in its plural forms according to the spirit of a real democratic society, which is not an issue that only concerns Brazil.

Regarding the marital regimes, the last thing there is to say including an interdisciplinary approach is about the separate one, which comprises the idea of independence that very seldom occurs when daily life imposes different tasks to men and women. In general the ideal of independence breaks up when there is a divorce.

In times of *homo ecconomicus* and a strong privilege put upon the market economy one final remark has to be made. One should ask whether an economical and globalized capitalistic world, that places a greater weight in consumption which is enhanced by individualism and individualized life, is still interested in the family as the *celula mater* of the society.

The tension between the family boundaries and social influence is inherent to the family existence. The family is resisting throughout times transcending extraneous ideologies that threaten its existence. Until when this will happen we do not know and this is the challenge of Family Law.

References

› ALTOÉ, Sônia (org.). *Sujeito do Direito Sujeito do Desejo – Direito e Psicanálise*. Revinter Ed. Rio de Janeiro, 1999.
› AUSLOOS, Guy. *La Compétence des Familes – Temps, Chaos, Processus*. Ed. Érès, França, 1995.
› BAUMAN, Zygmunt. *Amor Líquido – sobre a fragilidade dos laços humanos*. Rio de Janeiro: Jorge Zahar, 2004.
› BITTAR, Eduardo C. B.. *O Direito na Pós-Modernidade*. São Paulo: Forense Universitária, 2005.
› D'AMBROSIO, Ubiratan. *Transdisciplinaridade* Editora Palas Athena, São Paulo, 1997.
› DAVID-JOUGNEAU, M.. La médiation familiale: un art de la dialetique. In *Médiation Familiale – Regards Croisés et Perspectives*, Annie Babu et al ,Editions Érès, France, 1997.
› DIAS, Maria Berenice. *Manual de Direito das Famílias*. Rio de Janeiro: Editora Revista dos Tribunais, 2006.
› FACHIN, Luiz Edson. *Teoria Crítica do Direito Civil – à luz do novo Código Civil Brasileiro*. 2ª ed. Rio de Janeiro: Renovar, 2003.
› FREUD, Sigmund. Civilization and its Discontents. In the *Standard Edition of the Complete Psychological Works of Sigmund Freud*. Hogarth Press, Londres, 1974. Vol. XXII.
› GROENINGA, Giselle C. Família um Caleidoscópio de Relações. In *Direito de Família e Psicanálise – Rumo a uma Nova Epistemologia*. Coord. Giselle Câmara Groeninga e Rodrigo da Cunha Pereira. Rio de Janeiro: Imago Editora, 2003.
› GROENINGA, Giselle C. The Right to be Human: Psychoanalysis and family law – from guilt to responsibility. In *Family Life and Human Rights – Papers presented at the 11th World Conference of the International Society of Family Law*. Coordenação Peter Lødrup and Eva Modvar. Noruega: Glydendal Akademisk. 2004, pg. 265-271.
› HIRONAKA, Giselda Maria F. Novaes. *Direito Civil: Estudos*. Editora Del Rey. Belo Horizonte, 2000.
› LÔBO, Paulo Luiz Netto. Do Poder Familiar. In: *Direito de família e o novo Código Civil*. Coord. Dias, Maria Berenice; Pereira, Rodrigo da Cunha. Belo Horizonte: Del Rey, 2001.
› JAPIASSU, Hilton. *Interdisciplinaridade e patologia do saber*. Imago Editora, Rio de Janeiro, 1976.
› KLEIN, Melanie. Our Adult World and its Roots in Infancy. In *Envy and*

Gratitude and Other Works 1946-1963 Writings of Melanie Klein. The Free Press N.Y., 1984. Vol. III.
> OSÓRIO, Luis Carlos. *A Família Hoje*, Artes Médicas, Porto Alegre, 1996.
> PEREIRA, Rodrigo da Cunha. *Direito de Família – Uma Abordagem Psicanalítica*. Editora Del Rey, Belo Horizonte, 1999.
> PEREIRA, Rodrigo da Cunha. *Princípios Fundamentais Norteadores do Direito de Família*. Belo Horizonte: Del Rey, 2006.
> ROUDINESCO, Elizabeth. *Pourquoi la Psychanalyse?* Librairie Arthème Fayard, France, 1999.
> ROUDINESCO, Elizabeth. *A Família em Desordem*. Rio de Janeiro: Jorge Zahar Editor, 2003.
> SIMÃO, José Fernando. *Ser ou Não Ser: Outorga Conjugal e Solidariedade Familiar. In:* Revista Brasileira de Direito das Famílias e Sucessões. Vol 3 (abr./maio 2008). Porto Alegre: Magister; Belo Horizonte: IBDFAM, 2008
> ZIMERMAN, David, E.. *Vocabulário Contemporâneo de Psicanálise*. Artmed Editora, Porto Alegre, 2001.

Legal and Financial Support for Multicultural Families in South Korea

Keum Sook Choe[1]

I. Introduction

Korean society is facing a rise in international marriages in the current of globalization. The growing number of immigrants involved in an international marriage who are coming to Korea has led to an increasing number of multicultural families. In spite of these social changes, Korea's legal and financial support for foreign families and multicultural families are still insufficient, with more legal reforms needed and more financial aid called for. More than anything exchange on multiculturalism, human rights protection, and »social integration« is needed. Though still in the developing stage, Korea has been supporting multicultural families in many ways. Since a few years, it has given support from different sources such as the central government, local government, school and private organizations. Support has been reinforced since the »Act on Support for Multicultural Families« entered into force on September 21, 2008.

The 2006 UN Convention of International Immigrants was signed by 20 countries and enacted a legal arrangement. This convention was designed to ensure various rights of immigrants and their families, such as the right of residence and of education. However, Korea neither ratified this convention nor discussed it.[2]

On December 6 and 7, 2007, the National Human Rights Commission of Korea (NHRCK; chairperson Ahn, Kyong-Whan) cooperated with the British Embassy in Seoul, Yeungnam University, and Chonnam National University to organize international seminars on this subject. Professor Michael Keith and Commissioner Leonie McCarthy of Britain's Commission on Integration and Cohesion were the guest speakers. The seminar's topic was »Promoting Human Rights in the Local Community in a

---
1 Professor of School of Law, Ewha Womans University, South Korea.
2 Lee Ji-hun, Assessment of Multi-Cultural Policy and Future Tasks, the Seminar for Promoting Human Rights in Local Communities, National Human Rights Commission of Korea and Chonnam Univ. of Korea, December 6 and 7, 2007, p.28.

Multicultural Era«. Invited guests[3] were the commissioners of the Commission on Integration and Cohesion, which was established on the recommendation of the Secretary of State of the Communities and Local Government of the UK in 2006. The commission conducts case studies to integrate and harmonize residents from diverse cultures, and provides the U.K. government with policy advice. The numbers of multicultural families are also increasing in Korea's local government districts, calling for exchange, harmonization and integration between the culture of the multicultural families and that of Korea. Therefore, the U.K. local government's example was important for Korea.

1. Act of Support for Multicultural Families

1.1 Enforcement of the »Act on Support for Multicultural Families« in Korea

First, Korea established the »Proposed Standard Ordinance to Support Resident Aliens« enabling local governments to enforce several policies to help multicultural families. Most recently, the »Act on Support for Multicultural Families« (Act No. 8937) was elaborated, and put into effect on September 21, 2008.

1.2 The purpose of the Act and the legal definition of multicultural families

Article 1 of the Act defines its purpose as follows: »The purpose of this act is to help improve multicultural family member's quality of life and social integration by enabling them to maintain a peaceful and stable family life«.

Article 2 of the Act provides the legal definition of »multicultural families«. Legally, there are two definitions for multicultural families in Korea.

The Basic Act for the Treatment of Foreign Residents in Korea states in No. 3 of Article 2 that a multicultural family is a family comprised of a person (marriage immigrant) who married to a Korean citizen and a person (for example, their child) who has had Korean citizenship since birth as stated by Article 2 of the Korean Nationality Act.

According to Article 4 of the Korean Nationality Act, a multicultural family is a family comprised of a person (a naturalized citizen) who has

---

[3] Prof. Michael Keith (Commission on Integration and Cohesion, Commissioner) Theme Speech: Interaction at Neighborhood Level: Strategic Approaches Can Bring Success.

been conferred citizenship and a person (for example, his/her child) who, according to Article 2 of the same Act, has acquired Korean citizenship since birth.

The range of definition of multicultural family in Article 2, No. 3 of the Basic Law for the Treatment of Foreign Residents in Korea is narrow. Multicultural families are legally defined by marriage. This term excludes cohabiting families or single mother/father households and other similar groups who are in actual need of protection. Therefore, the provision of this Act should, in my opinion, expand the definition of the multicultural family.

1.3 The »Act to Supervise Marriage Agencies« in Korea

An act on the supervision of marriage agencies was made on December 14, 2007 (Act No. 8688) and was put into effect six months later as of June 14, 2008. This Act defines in Article 2 No. 4 that »International Marriage Agencies« are marriage agencies that deal with marriages between Korean citizens and foreigners« and states that international marriage agencies must be subject to regulations in order to lessen any damages caused by a multicultural marriage.

2. *Policy and Financial Support in Central Government*

The central and local government has declared policy-making for multicultural families as a major issue for the Korean society and is providing financial support for its enforcement. Although many departments are involved in the work, it is mostly entrusted to the Ministry of Gender Equality (formerly the Ministry of Gender Equality & Family), the Ministry of Education, Science and Technology, the Ministry for Health, Welfare and Family Affairs (formerly the Ministry of Health and Welfare) and the Ministry of Justice.

Financially, the budget of the Ministry of Education, Science and Technology for »education plan to support students of multicultural families« was about $ 70 million from 2009 to 2012 (according to the report of the Ministry, 2008. 10), and the budget (2008) of the Ministry of Gender Equality for multicultural families was about $ 22,300,000 (22,300,000,000 Won / 2008.1), 471.8 % increase from 2007 (about $ 3,900,000 (3,900,000,000 Won / 2008.1). The Ministry for Health, Welfare and Family Affairs (formerly the Ministry of Health and Welfare) has proposed a fund[4] for a »Service

---

4 The Ministry of Health, Welfare and Family Affairs, Department of Multicultural Families.

to Provide Information to Marriage Immigrants in Advance« in April 2008, with the fund of about $ 100,000.

3. Support from NGOs

Private organizations are active in Korea. A large number of marriage immigrant family support centers as private organizations are helping marriage immigrants and multicultural families. Such organizations numbered 38 in 2007. With the government increasing funding in 2008, the number of private organizations is expected to rise to 80.[5] The Ministry of Gender Equality has provided Marriage Immigrant Support Centers with $ 2,800,000 in 2008, 115.4% more than the year before.

II. Statistics for International Marriages and Children

1. Statistics for International Marriages

According to data from the National Statistical Office's >current status of international marriages over the last 3 years, there were 309,700 marriages between Koreans and foreigners in 2006, about three times more than 12,300 marriages in 2000. However, the numbers had decreased by 8,.% (that is, by 3.400 marriages) compared to the 43,100 marriages in 2005.

> In 2006, the number of marriages to Korean men was 30,208.[6] It had decreased by 972 (3.1%) compared to 2005. In 2007, however, the number is expected to be high due to the increase and mediation of marriage agencies.[7]

> In 2006, there were 9,500 marriages to Korean females. It had decreased by 20.6% compared to 2005.

---

5 Budget of the Ministry of Gender Equality and Family (June 2008).
6 25.594 in 2004, 31.180 in 2005.
7 Data of the National Statistical Office of Korea in 2006.

1.1 Statistics for Foreign Women Who Married Korean Men (by Nationality) [8]

	Marriages 2006	Percentage	Deviation from the previous year
China	14,608	48.4	-29.2
Vietnam	10,131	33.5	74.0
Japan	1,484	4.9	18.2
Philippines	1,157	3.8	16.0
Mongol	594	2.0	5.9
Cambodia	394	1.3	151.0
USA	334	1.1	17.2
Uzbekistan	314	1.0	-5.7
Others	1,192	3.9	5.0
Total	30,208	100.0	-3.1

---

8 Data of the National Statistical Office of Korea in 2006.

1.2 Statistics for Foreign Men Who Married Korean Women (by Nationality)[9]

	marriages 2006	Ratio in %	Deviation from previous year
Japan	3,756	39.6	2.3
China	2,597	27.4	-48.5
USA	1,455	15.3	3.0
Canada	308	3.2	8.1
Pakistan	152	1.6	-30.6
Australia	139	1.5	36.3
England	138	1.5	30.2
Germany	129	1.4	51.8
Others	808	8.5	-20.6
Total	9,482	100.0	-20.6

2. *Statistics for the Children in Multicultural Families*
2.1 Present Status of Children of International Marriage Households
> Children of international marriage households presently enrolled in school in 2006: 7.998 (Elementary School/Primary Education 85%, Middle School 11,6%, High School 3,5%)
> In international marriage households, families in which the mother is a foreigner are the majority, taking up 83,7% (6.695 households).[10]

---

9 Data of the National Statistical Office of Korea in 2006.
10 Survey of Samsung Economic Research Institute, April 3, 2007 (Yonhap News). Regionally, Gyeonggido has 1.852 (23,1%), Seoul 12,2%, Cheonnam 11,8%, Cheonbuk 9,1%, Gyungbuk 6,0%.

2.2 Present status of migrant workers
> Among the foreigners registered in the Ministry of Justice, 17,287 are of school age (7–18 years old), with only 1,574 of them attending a regular school (7.800 of them attend a foreign school).
> The percentages of foreign students are as follows: Japan 24.4% (386 students), Mongolia 21.3% (338 students), USA 17.2% (273 students) and China 2.8% (45 students). [11]

III. Legal and Financial Support for Multicultural Families

1. Reinforcement of Legal Support

The »Act on Support for Multicultural Families« (Act No. 8937) was established on March 21, 2008 and entered into force on September 21, 2008.

Previously, the Korean government made a »Proposed Standard Ordinance to Support Resident Aliens« so that local governments would enforce more policies to help multicultural families. When the application of the Act will become more effective, support for multicultural families will increase.

2. Reinforcement of Financial Support

2.1 Central Government

The budget for multicultural families of the Ministry of Gender Equality (2008) was about $ 22,300,000, which is 471.8% more than 2007, The budget for multicultural families of the Ministry of Gender Equality (the name was changed from Ministry of Gender Equality and Family in 2008) has increased notably in 2008 in comparison to the year before. In certain category (Visiting Education Service for Learning Hangul/Korean Alphabet) there has been a 2,700% increase in comparison to 2007. The following table refers to this.

---

[11] Data of the Ministry of Justice, 2006. Among them, the majority are attending school in Seoul (35%) and Gyeonggi (31%).

Budget Comparison for Marriage Immigrants Policy
(Ministry of Gender Equality and Family, 2008. 6)

	2007 (US dollar)	2008 (US dollar)	Increase Rate
Visiting Education Service for Learning Han-geul (Korean Alphabet)	about 200,000	about 5,600,000	2,700%
Visiting Child Care giving Assistance Service	about 1,900,000	about 11,100,000	484.2%
Supporting Center for Marriage Immigrant Family (The number)	about 1,300,000 (38 centers)	about 2,800,000 (80 centers)	115.4% (110.5%)
Marriage Immigrant Child Care giving Information Share Space (New Business)		about 200,000	Pure Increase
Total Budget	about 3,900,000	about 22.300,000	471.8%

The Ministry of Education, Science and Technology has the »support plan« to strengthen educational capacity of students and their parents of multicultural families, and to increase public comprehension about social multiculturalism. The Ministry has had 4 policies and 14 action plans and its budget for »education plan to support students of multicultural families« was about $ 70 million from 2009 to 2012 (according to the report of the Ministry, 2008. 10).

As mentioned above, the Ministry of Health, Welfare and Family Affairs (formerly the Ministry of Health and Welfare in 2007) proposed a fund[12] for a »Service to Provide Information to Marriage Immigrants in Advance«, with the fund for the work about $ 100,000. The Ministry of Health, Welfare and Family Affairs provided this fund because when some women from countries such as Vietnam, the Philippines or China came to Korea as marriage immigrants, they often had little or no information on Korea or of their marriage partners. This resulted in some becoming victims of frauds. At some times these women would come to Korea for marriage, but be forced into prostitution or into entertainment establishments instead. Or they would have problems in the marriages, resulting in divorce.

2.2   Local Governments
As local governments also need to carry out policies for multicultural families, they have recently formed budget plans, which have found backup.

For example, the Ministry of Education and Science designated a fund of about $ 1,094,000 for the »Education for Children of Multicultural Families and Cross-cultural Awareness Education Programs«. Of the total financial aid, $ 974,000 is reserved for the educational aid for multicultural children in local governments of city and province.

3.   Reinforcing the Duties of State and Local Government

Article 3, paragraph 1 of the »Act on Support for Multicultural Families« defines the duties of the state and local government. Namely, »(t)he state and the local government must produce the necessary system and conditions for the stable family life of multicultural family members and establish measures to that end.«

According to this Act, the state and the local government must establish policies and make the necessary system.

4.   Important Policies and Implementations
4.1   Research on Actual Conditions

The Minister for Health, Welfare and Family Affairs must conduct research on the actual conditions of multicultural families every 3 years and officially announce the findings. The results will be used to understand the actual conditions of multicultural families and establish policies to support them. (Article 4, Paragraph 1 of the Act) This provision of

---

12   The Ministry of Health, Welfare and Family Affairs, Department of Multicultural Families (April 2008).

the Act was made because statistical data on multicultural families are still insufficient, making their actual conditions difficult to understand. Illegal immigrants have the greater problem of not appearing in the statistics. A well-developed multicultural family statistics for marriage and divorce, children, Korean language education support, and domestic violence would be a basis for better financial support and policy making. Statistical data should expand into more categories than the present, and continue for the long term. It is also problematic that the ministry for surveying multicultural families is continually changing, and that the responsibility is divided into different ministries/departments. It is important that one ministry/department continues to survey the actual conditions of multicultural families.

4.2   Promoting Understanding of Multicultural Families
The state and local government must prevent social discrimination and prejudice towards multicultural families. They should also provide necessary measures to help society accept and respect cultural diversity through education in understanding multiculturalism and through the diffusion of public information (Article 5 of the Act).

Central and local governments are now carrying out diverse multicultural education programs. Education to change the Korean people' perspectives on multicultural families is needed first of all, because Koreans still have some discriminatory and unfriendly attitudes toward foreigners. Education to help multicultural families understand Korean culture, language, family and other aspects are also needed. Presently, the provinces have more marriages between foreign women and Korean men than the city does, and though the numbers of multicultural families are increasing, there is still a little understanding of them.

In 2008, the Ministry of Gender Equality promoted various programs to help marriage immigrants from their entry into the country to the time they are raising families. As examples they began education on Korean alphabet, family, culture, child support, family relations, and couple education. The Ministry has developed an education service that visits foreign women in provinces, such as the »Finding and Going Hangeul/Korean alphabet Education Service« and the »Finding and Going Child Education Support (for children between the ages of 0–12).« Since 2008, the Ministry of Justice has carried out a policy to support education for professionals in a multicultural society. This professional training education has the added aspect of changing the prejudicial perspective of Koreans.

For an example in local government, one can refer to the multi-culture education in the Gangwon-do Office of Education, namely programs for parents in multicultural families, programs for pre-school children, and school programs (elementary, middle, and high schools). The program contents involve Korean language education, culture education, and home-stay programs.

More effective visiting programs such as the Ministry of Gender Equality's »Finding and Going Service« should be established.

4.3 Providing Information on Living and Supporting Education

The state and local government must provide marriage immigrants with the basic information needed to live in Korea. They can also give necessary aid in education for social adaptation, job education and training, and so on (Article 6, Paragraph 1 of the Act).

4.4 Measures to Maintain Equal Family Relations

The state and local government must promote family counseling, couple education, parent education, family life education, and other forms of education so that multicultural families can maintain a democratic and gender equal family relation. In this case, they should strive to offer a professional service system that takes cultural differences into account.

4.5 Protection and Support for Victims of Domestic Violence

Legal Support

Domestic violence is a notable problem in multicultural families. To prevent this, the establishment of an act is needed. Although domestic violence is also existent in Korean families, it is much more difficult to prevent them in multicultural families because the women may experience language barriers and difficulties getting help in the Korean society. This makes support for these women more necessary than ever. To prevent domestic violence in multicultural families, the more provisions of this Act is needed. More legal provisions are needed because it enables more budget support, and because the state and local government is then able to create and implement more policies to protect these women. Based on this foundation, the activities of various nongovernmental organizations are called for in order to prevent domestic violence.

> - The state and local government must strive to prevent domestic violence within multicultural families (Article 8, Paragraph 1 of the Act). The state and local government should establish or support domes-

tic violence counseling centers for multicultural households in order to find cases of domestic abuse and to help these people through programs that prevent domestic violence (couple counseling, education for multicultural families). They have to employ more welfare workers to visit and help the victims in multicultural families to prevent another domestic violence.

> The state and local government must strive to extend domestic abuse counseling centers and shelters with interpretation (of the language) services to protect and aid marriage immigrants who have suffered domestic abuse (Article 8, Paragraph 2 of the Act). Interpretation services are given because women who have suffered from domestic violence are often unable to give an accurate description of the abuse in the Korean language. Interpretations are given from the women's native language into Korean. Because interpretations require fees, they are still held on a small-scale. However, these services should be expanded in the future.
> The state and local government may provide the necessary interpretation (of the language) services legal counseling and administrative aid for hearing statements and confirming facts at the time of the domestic violence. This is to prevent the marriage immigrant from being put in a disadvantageous position due to communication difficulties or insufficient information on the law on divorce in the context of domestic violence (Article 8, Paragraph 3 of the Act). This provision's problem is that the expression implies that such interpretation services do not necessarily need to be given. The word »may« should be revised to »must«. Despite the drawback of cost, the problem of multicultural family members being unable to communicate is so great that interpretation services are inevitable.

Policy and Financial Support
The prevention of domestic violence is provided by multicultural family support centers, which are private organizations. There were 80 multicultural family support centers nationwide in 2008. This will be explained later.

4.6 Healthcare support for before and after childbirth
The state and local government may provide education on nutrition and health, and send helpers before and after childbirth and offer health check-ups and interpretation (of the language) during the check-ups

(Article 9 of the Act). The state and local government may provide foreign wives of multicultural families with education on nutrition and health, send them helpers before and after childbirth, and offer them health check-ups with interpretation services available. The purpose is to ensure that marriage immigrants can give safe and healthy births.

4.7 Childcare and Education
Legal Support
> - The state and local government shall not discriminate against children of multicultural families in implementing childcare and education (Article 10, Paragraph 1 of the Act).
> - The state and local government must provide measures for educational support so that children of multicultural families can adapt to school life. Furthermore the superintendent of Educational Affairs of the municipality or local government may support children of multicultural families through extracurricular and after-school educational programs (Article 10, Paragraph 2 of the Act).
> - The state and local government may endeavor to give childcare and education support to children of multicultural families before they enter school. The government may also give aid in the form of textbooks, academic help, and other necessary help to improve language skills (Article 10, Paragraph 3 of the Act).

Policy and Financial Support
A large problem for marriage immigrants and their children is that they experience difficulty in education because they are not familiar with the Korean language. The Ministry of Education and Science is giving special effort to overcome this problem.

The Ministry of Education and Science and Technology is undertaking the »Education for Children of Multicultural Families and Multicultural Awareness Education Programs« in various ways. The funding for the work is about $ 1,094,000 of the national treasury (private subsidies).
> - City and province funding for the education of multicultural children: $ 974,000.
> - Budget for maintenance of research school on multicultural education in 2007: $ 120,000.

Support Projects
- Programs for overcoming isolation in school education and social life
 (e.g. On-line education, Korean language-based acquisition of the mother language (for children of migrant workers), support for Chinese, Mongolian, and other foreign schools, programs to overcome maladjustment at school).
- Programs for children of multicultural families to establish their identities as members of Korean society
 (e.g. Individual and group counseling, strengthening the role of family, understanding each other's culture properly).
- Programs to overcome cultural prejudice for the general public (students included
 (e.g. 1:1 solidarity projects, cultural festivals, multicultural experience programs, club activities.).
- Programs based on people built through a community network
 (e.g. Support for university clubs, mentoring by university students who are teachers-in-training, use of military volunteering, full use of retired teaching staff, use of international marriage immigrants as after-class school instructors etc.).
- Programs to help care and educate infants and children
 (e.g. Korean language instruction for pre-school children and their parents).

4.8 Designating Multicultural Family Support Centers
Legal Support
- The Minister of Health, Welfare and Family Affairs may designate, when necessary, a corporation or an organization with the professional staff and facilities needed to support multicultural families as a multicultural family support (Article 12, Paragraph 1 and of the Act). The state and local government alone may not be able to carry the responsibilities of these policies by themselves; they should designate nongovernmental organizations as multicultural family support centers. The government can give financial or administrative aid to these centers.
  a.) Carry out support services including education and counseling
  b.) Offer information and publicity for multicultural family support services.
  c.) Link together multicultural family support institutions and organizations
  d.) Promote other services needed to support multicultural families.

Support centers must hire professionals who have knowledge and experience in related fields to work in education and counseling for multicultural families (Article 12, Paragraph 3 of the Act).

The state and local government can, within their budget, give assistance to the support centers designated in Paragraph 1 by subsidizing the entire, or part of the expenses for each work specified in Paragraph 2 (Article 12, Paragraph 4 of the Act).

Policy and Financial Support
Private organizations are very active in Korea. A large number of »marriage immigrant family support centers« are helping marriage immigrants and multicultural families. The Ministry of Gender Equality and Family gave $ 2,800,000 to support centers for marriage immigrant families in 2008, 115.4 % more than the previous year.[13]

Formerly many of these organizations worked as »support centers for marriage immigrant families«. The Act continues to support them now as »support centers for multicultural families« (Supplementary Provision, Paragraph 1 of the Act).

5. Other Policies and Actions

5.1. Providing services in various languages

The state and local government must strive to provide services in different languages. This will ease marriage immigrants' difficulties in communicating and make the services more accessible (Article 11 of the Act).

5.2 Educating public service personnel on support services for multicultural families

The state and local government may educate public service personnel who work in supporting multicultural families. This is to promote understanding of multicultural families and to attain a higher standard of professionalism (Article 13 of the Act).

5.3 Treatment of spouses and children

The above Acts apply to members of multicultural families who have lawfully married Korean citizens and are raising children of the said marriage (Article 14 of the Act).

---

13   Budget of the Ministry of Gender Equality and Family (June 2008).

5.4 Support from Private Organizations, etc.
Legal Support
The state and local government can subsidize a part or all of the expenses needed by a group or individual in doing support work for multicultural families. They can also give administrative support for undertaking such work (Article 16, Paragraph 1 of the Act).

The state and local government can support marriage immigrants in forming and managing/operating organizations for mutual aid (Article 16, Paragraph 2 of the Act).

Policy and Financial Support
Thanks to these Acts, more private organizations will be founded, and the central and local government will reflect this in the allocation of budget and in their policies.

IV. Legal and Policy Support for »Marriage Immigrants«

1. Reinforcement of Legal Support

Persons involved in international marriages usually have a limited time to meet their spouses through the mediation of agencies before deciding on marriages and entering Korea. When some young women of Vietnam, the Philippines, China, Bangladesh and Mongolia want to get married to Korean men, they use the mediation of marriage agencies in many cases, and at the time of meetings of men and women through the mediations of marriage agencies, they have to decide whether to marriage or not in a short time. So they have little information of the Korean men and Korean culture. Therefore they experience difficulties in adapting to life in Korea after marriage. Insufficient information and lack of mutual understanding between spouses have also led to cases of domestic violence or divorce. Therefore, the »Act on the Supervision of Marriage Agencies« (proclaimed on December 14, 2007, Act No. 8688) was elaborated and entered into force on June 14, 2008.

Article 10 of this Act obliges marriage agencies to put their contract in writing and to fully explain the content of the contract. Also, Article 12 prohibits any false or exaggerated contents or announcements. Violation of this Act can be punished by law.

2. Policy and Financial Support for Marriage Immigrants

The Ministry of Health, Welfare and Family Affairs announced a proposal for trust fund[14] for a »Service to Provide Information to Marriage Immigrants in Advance« in April 2008.

The time period for the project is from May to November of 2008 (seven months from the contract day) and the total funding is about $ 100,000. The work involves opening call centers to prospective marriage immigrants from areas where cases of damage are rising, and in providing immigrants with information on Korea through educational programs before they leave their countries.

V. Conclusion

Thus far, we have examined how Korea supports multicultural families through the legal system, policies and finances. As Korea is evolving into a multicultural society, policies for multicultural families must be developed on various levels and carried out with cooperation from all sides. The question of »multicultural families« is not just the issue of one country, but an international one.

Co-operation for »multicultural families« must happen between two countries and also. Many women from countries such as Vietnam, the Philippines, China, Mongolia and Bangladesh have been coming to Korea for immigration through marriage or for work. Therefore it is necessary for Korea as well as the countries involved to develop policies and activities to protect multicultural families. National governments and nongovernmental organizations should collaborate internationally. If professors, researchers and activists who study or work with multicultural families also cooperate internationally, it will yield even better results. A solid legal system must be developed in particular, with central government, local government, schools, and private organizations providing policy and legal support.

Above all, it is important that each country understands multicultural societies and the idea of multiculturalism, and keeps an open mind in supporting multicultural families.

---

14 The Ministry of Health, Welfare and Family Affairs, Department of Multicultural Families (April 2008).

Expulsion of Irregular Foreign Residents from Japan
The Right to Family Unification and the best Interests of the Child

Yue Fu[1]

I. Introduction

The purpose of this paper is to analyze how the right to family unification and the best interests of the child are taken into consideration by reviewing recent court decisions on cases regarding the deportation of irregular foreign families from Japan.[2] The right to family unification as stipulated in Art. 17 (1) and Art. 23 (1) of the International Covenant on Civil and Political Rights (hereinafter referred to as ICCPR) and the best interests of the child as stated in Art. 3 (1) of the Convention on the Rights of the Child (hereinafter referred to as CRC), to which Japan is a signatory, are upheld in reaching court decisions.

There are many irregular foreign nationals residing in Japan, and many of them form a family and settle in Japan for a long period of time. As the Japanese Immigration Control Administration plans to take strict measures to reduce the number of irregular foreign residents by half from its level in 2003 to 2008, many irregular foreign families are facing forced expulsion. Sometimes the parents are deported to different countries because they have different nationalities, and the child who was born and raised in Japan has to be deported with one of the parents. In this context, the right to family unification and the best interests of the child are often argued upon expulsion of irregular foreign residents.

In this paper, I will analyze how the right to family unification and the best interests of the child, which are invoked by the irregular foreign families based on ICCPR and CRC to support their cases to stay in Japan, are

---

1 Research Assiciate, Graduate School of Humanities and Social Sciences, University of Tsukuba, Japan.
2 In this paper, I use the words »irregular foreign nationals« and »illegal foreigners« equivalently and interchangeably, and the same for the words »expulsion« and »deportation«. Foreign nationals include stateless persons.

taken into consideration by recent court decisions on deportation cases of irregular foreign families in Japan.

Before analyzing the court decisions (IV), I would like to introduce the situation of foreign residents in Japan by using statistics (II), briefly explain the law and the procedure of deportation, and the »Special Permission to Stay« regarding irregular foreign residents in Japan (III).

II. Foreign Nationals Residing in Japan

1. Increase in Number of Foreign Residents in Japan

Under the influences of economic globalization and mixed marriages[3], more and more foreign nationals established their livelihood and form families in Japan. The statistics on the registered foreign nationals (see, graph 1 on the next page) indicates the number of foreign nationals who stay in Japan for a long time.[4] As of the end of 2007, the number of registered foreign nationals set a new record of more than 2.1 million which marked nearly three times as many than twenty years ago and reached 1.69 % of the total Japanese population[5].

2. Registered Foreign Nationals by Major Nationality

Registered foreign nationals residing in Japan came from 190 different countries or place of origin. Until the late 1980s, most foreign residents were from former Japanese colonies. They had immigrated or had been brought by force to Japan from former Japanese colonies, such as the Korean Peninsula and Taiwan, before or during WWII. Since 1992, these people were granted the »Special Permanent Resident« status.[6] They

---

[3] There were approximately one out of fifteen couples that, one or both are foreign national(s), had registered their marriage in Japan through the fiscal year of 2006. Population Survey Report published by the Ministry of Health, Labor and Welfare at http://www.mhlw.go.jp/toukei/saikin/hw/jinkou/tokusyu/gaikoku07/index.html (15 December 2008).

[4] In accordance with the Alien Registration Law (http://www.moj.go.jp/ENGLISH/information/tarl-01.html, 15 December 2008), every foreign national who has entered Japan must be registered within 90 days after his / her landing (Art.3 of the Alien Registration Law). However, more than 90 % of the total foreign nationals who entered Japan as »Temporary Visitors« and leave Japan within 90 days without being registered.

[5] The number of registered foreign nationals as of the end of each year, and the number of Japanese population as of 1 October each year.

[6] Solidarity Network with Migrants Japan, *Living together with migrants and ethnic minorities in Japan: NGO policy proposals*, Gendaijinbun-sha (2007), pp. 8–9.

are so called »old comers« compared to the »new comers« who came to Japan later under the effects of globalization. The statistic (below graph 2) shows that while the people from Korea gradually decreased[7], the number of people from China, Brazil, the Philippines and Peru has continued to increase significantly.

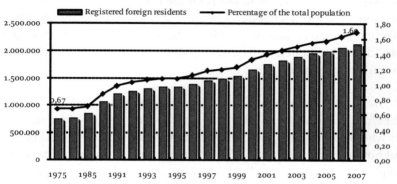

Registered foreign residents in Japan

*According to the statistics of the Immigration Bureau, Ministry of Justice.
http://www.immi-moj.go.jp/toukei/index.html (15 December 2008).

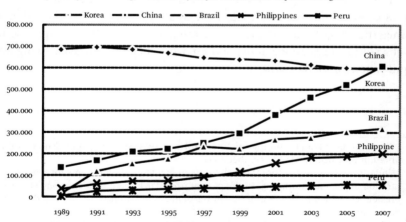

Graph2: Registered foreign residents by major nationalities or place of origin

* Created by the author according to the statistics of the Immigration Bureau, Ministry of Justice.
http://www.immi-moj.go.jp/toukei/index.html (15 December 2008).
* Korea indicates the people from Korean Peninsula, namely North Korea (DPRK) and South Korea (ROK).
* China includes the people from China (PRC), Hong Kong and Taiwan (ROC).

---

7   One of the reasons to explain the declining number of registered Korean is naturalization.

The amended Immigration Control and Refugee Recognition Law (hereafter referred to as the Immigration Control Law) enforced in 1990 that favors Japanese descendants to provide them a »long-term resident« status and unrestricted rights of employment, has especially attracted many Japanese descendents from Brazil and Peru coming to Japan. On the other hand, since the number of Chinese people coming to Japan for the purposes of study or technical training continuously increases, by the end of 2007, Chinese overtook Koreans for the first time and marked the largest number of foreign nationals in the total[8]. However, a large number of irregular foreign residents are living in Japan and most of them have not gone through the alien registration process and hence are not included in the official statistics.[9]

3. Irregular Foreign Nationals Residing in Japan

The Immigration Bureau estimates that there are 150,000 foreign nationals who have stayed in Japan beyond the permitted periods of stay without obtaining an extension permission or a new status of residence (see graph 3 on the next page)[10]. The number has declined notably in recent years because of various measures against illegal foreign residents such as intensified detection, and also owing to the prolonged economic slump in Japan.[11] In addition, it is estimated that about 30,000 foreign nationals have been smuggled to or illegally entered Japan.[12] Thus, the total number of irregular foreign residents is estimated at approximately 180,000, namely around 10% of the total number of foreign residents. Since the irregular foreign residents are persons who live in Japan without a status of residence, most of them work illegally to make a living for quite a long period of time.

---

[8] The third Basic Plan for Immigration Control at http://www.moj.go.jp/ENGLISH/information/bpic3rd.html (15 December 2008).

[9] Under the Alien Registration Law, the foreign residents should apply for alien registration at the local authority. In the case of irregular foreign residents, »no status of residence« which indicates of irregular residence is mentioned on the issued foreign resident's registration card.

[10] The number was estimated by the Immigration Control Bureau. The third Basic Plan for Immigration Control at http://www.moj.go.jp/ENGLISH/information/bpic3rd.html (15 December 2008).

[11] Ibid.

[12] Ibid.

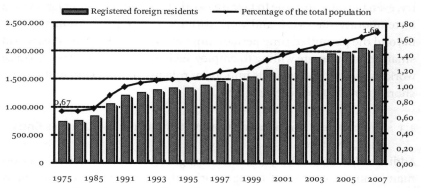

*According to the statistics of the Immigration Bureau, Ministry of Justice. http://www.immi-moj.go.jp/toukei/index.html (15 December 2008).

4. Backgrounds of Irregular Foreign Nationals Residing in Japan

4.1 Japanese Immigration Policy: »No Unskilled Workers Accepted«

Foreign nationals who wish to come to Japan to work legally should have a »Status of residence« listed in the Immigration Control Law, such as professor, engineer, artist, and so on[13]. So called »unskilled workers« are not accepted under the Japanese immigration policy and law. In other words, the Japanese government maintains the professionally-segmented status system rather than accepting foreign workers in general even if the demand for less skilled workers exists in the labor market.[14]

4.2 High Demand of Workers in Japanese Labor Market

Despite the fact that the demand for workers in the Japanese labor market remains high, the Japanese immigration policy consistently maintains the precondition that unskilled workers are not accepted.[15] As a result, due to the economic gaps between Japan and its neighboring countries, and a high excess supply of workers in these Asian countries, people from the Philippines, Thailand and South Korea come to Japan to benefit from job opportunities and higher levels of wages in the labor market. Natural-

---

13 The Appended Table I of the Immigration Control Law at http://www.cas.go.jp/jp/seisaku/hourei/data/icrra.pdf (15 December 2008).
14 Solidarity Network with Migrants Japan, *Living together with migrants and ethnic minorities in Japan: NGO policy proposals*, Gendaijinbun-sha (2007), pp. 10–13.
15 The third Basic Plan for Immigration Control at http://www.moj.go.jp/ENGLISH/information/bpic3rd.html (15 December 2008).

ly, for those who are not able to obtain a legal status to work they would try, even illegally, to come to Japan to work. Most of them enter Japan with a »temporary stay« visa, and work without a work permission and stay beyond the permitted time period. Employers especially in medicine and small companies are willing to employ such workers at low wages. These workers play an increasingly important role in the reduction of the labor shortage in the Japanese economy.

4.3 The Japanese Immigration Control System: Mainly Controls Entry and Departure

Additionally, since the Japanese immigration control system focuses mainly on the control of foreign nationals' entry and departure, many irregular foreign nationals find their partner to marry, have children who are born in Japan and settle with their families in Japan for years. However, since they live in Japan without a legal status and are not allowed to work legally, they are subjects of potential expulsion under the Japanese Immigration Control Law. Indeed, the Japanese immigration control administration plans to take tough measures to reduce the number of irregular foreign residents.

III. Expulsion of Irregular Foreign Residents and the »Special Permission to Stay«

1. Policy of Expulsion of Irregular Foreign Residents

Japan's The immigration policies are based on two basic pillars: one is to accept »favorable foreigners« for Japan, and the other one is to expel »unfavorable foreigners«, based on the precondition of »no skilled workers accepted«.[16] In addition, reflecting the sociopolitical backgrounds such as »counter-terrorism« since »9.11« in 2001, and the »worsening security« campaign, the cabinet meeting for crime prevention which was held in December 2003, set a target to »decrease illegal foreigners staying in Japan by half over the next five years«.[17] According to the third Basic Plan for Immigration Control issued by the Ministry of Justice in 2005[18],

---

16 Solidarity Network with Migrants Japan, *Living together with migrants and ethnic minorities in Japan: NGO policy proposals*, Gendaijinbun-sha (2007), p. 10.
17 Ibid.
18 The third Basic Plan for Immigration Control at http://www.moj.go.jp/ENGLISH/information/bpic3rd.html (15 December 2008).

the Ministry of Justice with relevant administrations will take strong and effective measures in order to expose and deport irregular foreign residents.

2. Subjects of Deportation

According to the Immigration Control Law, any foreign national who has illegally entered Japan, has stayed beyond the permitted period of stay, worked without a work permission, has committed drug offences, or has fallen under any other conditions as stipulated in Art. 24 of the Immigration Control Law may be deported forcibly from Japan. There were 45,502 foreign nationals who violated the Immigration Control Law and underwent deportation procedures in 2007.[19]

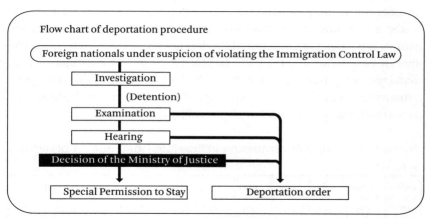

* Created by author according to the flow chart by the Immigration Bureau at http://www.immi-moj.go.jp/english/tetuduki/taikyo/taikyo_flow.pdf (15 December 2008)

3. Deportation Procedure

In case of a detection of a foreign national who is a subject under Art. 24 of the Immigration Control Law, following the investigation and examination, when the decision by the Ministry of Justice finds the violation, basically the irregular foreign national would be deported from Japan. However, in case the irregular foreign resident desires to stay in Japan for a variety of reasons, they may declare their wish during the deportation procedure, and the Ministry of Justice then delivers the decision whether to grant the »Special Permission to Stay« or not. When the administra-

---

19 Ibid.

tive procedure is exhausted, the irregular foreign resident may file a suit in court requesting to revoke the deportation order and arguing that the decision by the Ministry of Justice is illegal for not granting the Special Permission to Stay.

4. Special Permission to Stay

Article 50 of the Immigration Control Law stipulates that the Ministry of Justice may grant the irregular foreign resident a »Special Permission to Stay« under its discretion. The third Basic Plan for Immigration Control refers that »special permission to stay has been granted to illegal foreign residents who have close links with Japanese society or who, from a humanitarian standpoint, would suffer from deportation«.[20]

The Special Permission to Stay has been granted to an increasing number of irregular foreign residents as depicted below. This amounted to about one third of deportation cases[21]. According to the immigration control report in 2007, »[m]ost of the foreign nationals who received the Special Permission to Stay had established close relationships such as marriage with Japanese nationals and had, in fact, settled down in Japan in many respects«[22]. Nonetheless, a significant share of the illegal foreign nationals residing in Japan have been subject to deportation.

Number of the Special Permission to Stay (SPS) and number of deportations (Dep)

Year	1998	1999	2000	2001	2002	2003	2004	2005	2006	2007
SPS	2.497	4.318	6.930	5.306	6.995	10.327	13.239	10.834	9.360	7.388
Dep	45.699	50.381	45.145	35.380	33.788	35.911	41.926	33.192	33.018	27.913

*Created by the author according to the statistics of the Immigration Bureau, Ministry of Justice. Immigration Control 2008 at http://www.moj.go.jp/NYUKAN/nyukan80.html (15 December 2008).

Hereinafter, I will analyze the recent court decisions on cases which were brought by irregular foreign families requesting to revoke the deportation order and arguing that the decision by the Ministry of Justice is illegal for not granting the Special Permission to Stay which is against their right

---

20 Ibid.
21 Immigration Bureau, Ministry of Justice, *Immigration Control Report 2007*, pp. 42–43 at http://www.moj.go.jp/NYUKAN/nyukan68.html (15 December 2008).
22 Ibid, p. 42.

to family unification and against the best interests of the child together with other grounds.

IV. Analysis of Recent Court Decisions on Deportation Cases

1. Positive Attitude to Respect the Family Life and the Interests of the Child

There are some court decisions which take the right to family unification and the best interests of the child into consideration, in cases where the deportation orders are issued to irregular foreign residents without granting the Special Permission to Stay by the Ministry of Justice. The court indicated that it is legitimate to respect the benefits of the family unification, when the Ministry of Justice exercises its discretion (under the Immigration Control Act) based on Art. 17 (1) and Art. 23 (1) of ICCPR.[23] Therefore, in case that one of the spouses is a Japanese national and their life is base in Japan, the family unification should be viewed as an important factor.

1.1 Relationship to a Japanese Spouse or a Japanese Child

In the court decisions on deportation cases, the right to family unification is deemed as an important factor for granting the Special Permission to Stay in case the irregular foreign resident has a marital relationship with a Japanese national or has a parental relationship with a Japanese child. For example, in the case[24] which was brought forward by a Thai woman who married a Japanese man and had three children and had stayed legally in Japan for nine years but then stayed illegally for another nine years since she was imprisoned for drug offences. The court stated that »in judging whether to grant the Special Permission to Stay, the authority weighted the plaintiff's serving time for drug offences too heavily, but did not make adequate considerations of the fact of the plaintiff's marriage to a Japanese man and her relationship to their three Japanese children.«

In this case, the court indicated the following points as positive factors upon granting the Special Permission to Stay: (i) the plaintiff's marital relationship with a Japanese man, (ii) her relationship to their three minor children who are Japanese nationals, and (iii) her established relation to

---

[23] Nagoya District Court Decision on 9 February 2006 (*Hanreitaikei* database ID: 28110958).
[24] Tokyo District Court Decision on 28 August 2007 (*Hanrei Jihou* No.1984, p. 18 / Database of *Hanreitaikei* ID: 28140047).

Japanese society. Especially the first and the second factors merit special considerations from the humanitarian aspect. Although the right to family unification is not mentioned in the decisions specifically, I consider the right of family unification is respected through the protection of marital status and ensuring the child's welfare.

1.2 Respect to the Family Life and the Interests of the Child

There are two cases, one with regard to a Korean family that stayed in Japan for 6 years[25] and another with regard to an Iranian family that stayed in Japan for 10 years,[26] respectively at the time of the decision by the Ministry of Justice in which the Special Permission to Stay was not granted to those families. The courts stated the fact that, the foreign nationals who had stayed in Japan peacefully for a long time as a good citizen and established the basis of their life, confirming positive criteria for granting the Special Permission to Stay. Therefore, the courts decided that the decision made by the Ministry of Justice ignored this criterion and are illegal. At the same time, the courts judged that the changes in the family life, especially the burden on the children, compared to the risk to national interests when the authority grants the Special Permission to Stay to the families, must be tremendous.

In these two cases, the court decisions valued the families' long and peaceful life in Japan and took the interests of the children to live and study in Japan into account. Therefore, as the result, it could be consider that their right to family life or the right to family unification was protected.

2. Neglection of the Right to Family Unification and the Best Interests of the Child

The right to family unification is rarely considered for irregular foreign families composed of only foreign nationals. On the contrary, additionally to the two cases mentioned above, there are more decisions that censure the conducts of the irregular residents such as »illegal work«, »illegal over-stay« and »faked purpose of stay« upon entry that harmed the »national interests« of Japan, rather than to weigh their peaceful life in Japan and their contributions to the Japanese society.[27]

---

[25] Tokyo District Court Decision on 17 October 2003 (*Hanreitaikei* database ID: 28090050).

[26] Tokyo District Court Decision on 19 September 2003 (*Hanrei Jihou* No.1836, p. 46 / Database of *Hanreitaikei* ID: 28082829).

[27] Tokyo District Court Decision on 5 November 2004 (*Hanrei Times* No.1216, p. 82 /

2.1 Separation of a Family upon Expulsion

The decisions in deportation cases can result in two common outcomes: separation of a family or child separation. If the parents have different nationalities, there would be a separation of the family upon deportation since in general, the irregular foreign residents would be deported to the country of her/his nationality.

For instance, in the case[28] of a family where the husband has a Turkish nationality and had stayed in Japan for 11 years and where the wife has a Philippine nationality and had stayed in Japan for 7 years, and their three year old child was born in Japan and has the same nationality as her mother. Despite the fact that the child was born in Japan and the whole family set their base of life in Japan for a long time, the court accused them that the strong tie between the irregular foreign family and the Japanese society was created on the continuous situation of illegal over-stay. Moreover, the fact that working in Japan for a long term is nothing but illegal work. Even if the family members are deported to different countries, the court pointed out that one cannot claim that it is extremely difficult to reunite the family again in one of their countries of origin and their three year old child might adapt in a new environment easily. Furthermore, the court mentioned that although the child would be separated from the father temporarily, there would not be a serious psychological or physical impact as long as the child stays with it's mother.[29]

On the other hand, in another case, the court argued that the general terms in Japan, that the child is better off with the mother,[30] should not be forced to foreigners, for justifying the deportation of the three year old child with the father.[31] As the consequence, it could be strongly consi-

---

Database of *Hanreitaikei* ID:28101395), Tokyo District Court Decision on 23 March 2007 (*Hanreitaikei* database ID: 28130871), Nagoya District Court Decision on 9 Februafy 2006 (*Hanreitaikei* database ID: 28110958), Osaka High Court Decision on 31 August 2006 (*Hanreitaikei* database ID: 28112504), Nagoya District Court Decision on 31 August 2005 (*Hanrei Times* No.1250, p. 110 / Database of *Hanreitaikei* ID: 28102154), Kobe District Court Decision on 10 October 2003 (*Hanreitaikei* database ID: 28091726).

28 Tokyo District Court Decision on 23th March 2007 (*Hanreitaikei* database ID: 28130871).
29 Ibid.
30 Regarding to the welfare of the child, the court decisions referred that it is considered in Japan that the child should be with the mother, at least till three years old. Tokyo District Court Decision on 23 March 2007 (*Hanreitaikei* database ID: 28130871) and Nagoya District Court Decision on 31 August 2005 (*Hanrei Times* No.1250, p. 110 / Database of *Hanreitaikei* ID: 28102154).
31 Nagoya District Court Decision on 31 August 2005 (*Hanrei Times* No.1250, p. 110 / Database of *Hanreitaikei* ID: 28102154).

dered that it is clear that the right to family unification, upon expulsion of the irregular foreign residents, is not guaranteed in Japan, not at the administrative decisions and rarely in the court decisions.

2.2 When the Special Permission to Stay is only Granted to the Child

While whether to grant the Special Permission to Stay is examined individually by the Ministry of Justice, as well as in the court decisions, there are some cases where the Special Permission to Stay is justified for the child, although the Special Permission to Stay is not granted to the parents[32].

In the case brought in by a Filipino family where the parents with four children who had lived in Japan for 15 years, only the eldest daughter's claim for the Special Permission to Stay was recognized.[33] In this situation, the family had to make the decision to live separately in Japan and the Philippines, or be deported to the Philippines all together.

In this case, regarding the fifteen year old girl who was born in Japan, the court judged that (i) one cannot declare her responsibility for over stay; (ii) she has been spending her life just as other Japanese children do, familiar with Japanese custom and culture, on the other hand; (iii) it would be very hard for her to live in the Philippines where the language and living customs are totally different; and (iv) she strongly wished to continue to study in Japan and work in Japan. Thus, taking these factors into consideration, the decision by the Ministry of Justice not to grant her the Special Permission to Stay was judged illegal.

However, the fifteen year old girl's Special Permission to Stay was denied in the appeal court for the reason that, if she were to stay in Japan alone, there was no financial proof to live in Japan when the parents are deported and there is no legal status on the assumption for her under the current Immigration Control Act[34]. Thus, it seems like there would not be a family separation in reality, because the whole family would be expelled to their country of origin even though there are justifications and interests for the child to stay in Japan.

---

[32] Tokyo District Court Decision on 19 July 2006 (*Hanreitaikei* database ID: 28111700) and Tokyo District Court Decision on 5 November 2004 (*Hanrei Times* No.1216, p. 82 / Database of *Hanreitaikei* ID: 28101395).

[33] Tokyo District Court Decision on 5 November 2004 (*Hanrei Times* No.1216, p. 82 / Database of *Hanreitaikei* ID: 28101395).

[34] Tokyo High Court Decision on 13 April 2005 (*Hanrei Times* No.1175, p. 106 / *Hanreijiho* No.1890, p. 27 / *Hanreitaikei* database IDi ID:28100832).

2.3 Responsibility of the Family Unification

Some of the court decisions address that in case the family members are deported to different countries due to their different nationalities, the family reunification should be achieved by the family's own efforts under their own responsibility.[35] Furthermore, there was a court decision which argued that the responsibility for the separation of a family in the deportation cases should be taken by the family itself because they have made the choice to marry one who has a different nationality.[36]

2.4 Protection of the Best Interests of the Child upon Expulsion

Regarding the best interests of the child, in some recent court decisions of deportation cases, the interests of the child to continue the education in Japan, the detriments when the child is deported to the country of nationality, and the child's own will have been taken into account.[37] However, those factors are examined based on the precondition of the deportation of the parents. Therefore, in most cases, despite the fact that the child is not responsible for staying irregularly in Japan, and while the child is familiar with Japanese customs and culture but does not speak the language of his/her country of nationality, and there are interests to stay and study in Japan which are worthy of protection, the Special Permission to Stay for the child is denied. This happens under the logic that the best interest of the child is to be in the custody of the parents and therefore the child should be deported with the parents.

Moreover, the magic word »adaptability« is used to justify the deportation of the child together with the parents. This means that even if there are some obstacles when the child is deported to the country of its' nationality, the child would easily adapt to a new environment and learn the new language quickly. This word must be magic because it was applied

---

35 Tokyo District Court Decision on 23 March 2007 (*Hanreitaikei* database ID ID: 28130871), Nagoya District Court Decision on 31 August 2005 (*Hanrei Times* No.1250, p. 110 / (*Hanreitaikei* database ID: 28102154) and Kobe District Court Decision on 10 October 2003 ((*Hanreitaikei* database ID: 28091726).
36 Nagoya District Court Decision on 31 August 2005 (*Hanrei Times* No.1250, p. 110 / (*Hanreitaikei* database ID: 28102154).
37 Tokyo District Court Decision on 19 July 2006 (*Hanreitaikei* database ID: 28111700), Fukuoka High Court Decision on 7 March 2005 (Hanrei Times No.1234, p. 73 / Database of *Hanreitaikei* ID:28100727), Tokyo District Court Decision on 5 November 2004 (*Hanrei Times* No.1216, p. 82 / *Hanreitaikei* database ID:28101395), Tokyo District Court Decision on 17 October 2003 (*Hanreitaikei* database ID: 28090050) and Tokyo District Court Decision on 19 September 2003 (*Hanrei Jihou* No.1836, p. 46 / *Hanreitaikei* database ID: 28082829).

to children who were about two years old, as well as to a child who was fifteen years old in court decisions.

V. Conclusion

When there is a conflict between the national interests violated by irregular foreign residents and the interests of the family life of irregular foreign residents upon expulsion cases, the family life of irregular foreign residents should be protected from the human rights point of view, and the related clauses of ICCPR and CRC should be interpreted according to the purposes of the conventions. Especially, for those irregular families composed of members with different nationalities, if they have lived in Japan for an extended period of time and have integrated into Japanese society without committing crimes other than the violation of the Immigration Control Law, their right to family unification and the best interests of the child should be considered from the human rights point of view.

In most court decisions, guaranteeing the best interests of the child was considered as expulsion of the child from Japan together with the parents rather than to protect the children's best interests to stay in Japan together with the parents. Moreover, upon the expulsion of the irregular foreign families, the separation of the family is not dealt with as a human rights violation under the responsibility of Japan. I strongly argue that ignoring the child's interests to stay in Japan based on the parents' responsibility for being illegal residents in Japan is a clear discrimination of the child on the basis of the status or the activities of the parents which is prohibited under Art. 2 of CRC. It is evident that the Japanese government has not adopted the spirit and legal obligations of the ICCPR and CRC to which it was a signatory.

International Recovery of Child Support: Are Central Authorities the way forward?

Ian Curry-Sumner[1]

I. Introduction

As Europe continues to develop and society continues to change, existing legal frameworks need to be adapted to deal with legal and social problems of the future. One such field is child maintenance. In 2005, 33,890 children were involved in divorce proceedings in The Netherlands (in 57% of all divorces),[2] 136,332 in the UK (53%)[3] and approximately 87,000 in France (65%).[4]

With Europe witnessing a steadily increasing divorce rate,[5] these figures are only set to rise. Similar problems are equally manifest with respect to separating unmarried couples,[6] to whom an ever increasing number of children are born. Furthermore, European countries have been witness to a shift in focus from ex-spousal maintenance to child maintenance,[7] ensuring that child maintenance is increasingly the only surviving financial obligation of any intimate relationship post-separation.[8]

---

1 UCERF, Molengraaff Institute for Private Law, Utrecht University, The Netherlands. This contribution was made possible by an imovational research grant from the Dutch Scientific Organisation.
2 Centraal Bureau voor Staistieken (CBS), online database, 2007.
3 Office of National Statistics (ONS), »Divorces: Couples and children of divorced couples, 1981, 1991 and 2001-2005«, *Population Trends,* 2005, No. 125.
4 Z. Belmokhtar, *Les divores en 1996. Une analyse statistique des jugements prononcés. Etudes et statistique Justice,* 1999, Ministère de la Justice, No. 14; C. Martin and A. Math, »A comparative study of child maintenance regimes: French report«, London: Department of Work and Pensions, 2006.
5 Eurostat, *Europe in figures,* Luxembourg: European Commission, 2007, p. 70.
6 K. Kiernan, »European perspectives on union formation«, in: L. Waite, C. Barhrach, M. Hindin, E. Thomson and A. Thorton (eds.), *Ties that bind: Perspectives on marriage and cohabitation,* Hawthorn: Aldine de Gruyter, p. 40-88.
7 J. Eekelaar, *Regulating Divorce,* Oxford: Clarendon Press, 1991, p. 90.
8 J. Teachman and K. Paasch, »Financial impact of divorce on children and their families«, *Future of Children,* 4/1994, p. 63-83.

These trends have culminated to ensure that child maintenance has become one of the top governmental topics in recent years.

Another important and associated trend is the proliferation of international families. More than 5% of persons in the EU (c. 19 million) do not possess the citizenship of the state in which they live.[9] Furthermore, according to official statistics, the net migration to the EU in 2004 totalled more than 1.8 million.[10]

Alongside this migration, approximately 4% of those entering into marriage are of differing nationalities.[11] These two distinct, yet interrelated developments (on the one hand the increasing importance of child maintenance and the internalisation of families on the other), have coalesced to ensure that an ever-increasing number of child maintenance payments involve transnational elements.

After describing the various international and European instruments currently operating with respect to child maintenance (section III), attention will be devoted on the problems experienced in this field (section IV) that have led to the calls for change (section V).

In the two new instruments proposed, namely the Hague Maintenance Convention and the European Maintenance Regulation, both have chosen to introduce a system of Central Authorities. Section VI will focus on the experience of such a network from other international and European instruments.

II. Current Framework

Before dealing with these proposed instruments, attention will first be paid to the existing instruments in this field. These can be divided into two main categories:
> Those operating at the international level (section III.1) and
> those operating at the European level (section III.2).

---

9   Eurostat, *The social situation in the European Union 2004*, Luxembourg: European Commission, 2005.
10 Eurostat, *Europe in figures*, Luxembourg: European Commission, 2007, p. 76.
11 SEC (2005) 1629, p. 6.

1. International Framework[12]

1.1 1956 New York Convention[13]

64 States are at present party to the 1956 New York Convention.[14] Although work had originally been undertaken by UNIDROIT, the Convention was eventually drafted by the United Nations Economic and Social Council and signed on the 20th June 1956. Unlike other instruments in this field,[15] this Convention does not contain any substantive rules relating to the recognition and enforcement of maintenance determinations. Instead, the convention establishes a global network of agencies aimed at regulating the administrative aspects of the recovery of transnational maintenance obligations.

The system established by the 1956 New York Convention is, at first glance, relatively straightforward. Each States Parties must designate a body (or bodies) to act as a transmitting and/or receiving agency (in practice these are often referred to as the »contacts«). A maintenance creditor in a contracting state is, therefore, able to contact the transmitting agency in the state of his or her residence.[16] The transmitting agency must then communicate this claim to the receiving agency in the contracting state of the maintenance debtor's residence.[17] The receiving agency is then obliged to »take all appropriate steps for the recovery of maintenance, including the settlement of the claim, and, where necessary, the institution

---

12 Another important convention has also been concluded outside of Europe, namely Inter-American Convention on Support Obligations of 15th July 1989 (also known as the Montevideo Convention).
13 New York Convention of 20th June 1956 on the Recovery Abroad of Maintenance.
14 Algeria, Argentina, Australia, Austria, Barbados, Belarus, Belgium, Bosnia and Herzegovina, Brazil, Burkina Faso, Cape Verde Islands, Central African Republic, Chile, Colombia, Croatia, Cyprus, Czech Republic, Denmark, Ecuador, Estonia, Finland, France, Germany, Greece, Guatemala, Haiti, Holy See, Hungary, Ireland, Israel, Italy, Kazakhstan, Kyrgyzstan, Liberia, Luxembourg, Mexico, Moldova, Monaco, Montenegro, Morocco, The Netherlands, New Zealand, Niger, Norway, Pakistan, Philippines, Poland, Portugal, Romania, Serbia, Seychelles, Slovakia, Slovenia, Spain, Sri Lanka, Suriname, Sweden, Switzerland, FYR Macedonia, Tunisia, Turkey, Ukraine, United Kingdom and Uruguay. Furthermore, the following States have signed the Convention, yet not subsequently ratified it: Bolivia, Cambodia, China, Cuba, Dominican Republic and El Salvador. For up-to-date information regarding ratifications visit: http://untreaty.un.org/English/access.asp. It is therefore worth noting that Bulgaria, Latvia, Lithuania and Malta are the only EU Member states currently not participating in the 1956 New York Convention.
15 See sections III.1.a and III.2.
16 Article 2 (1), 1956 New York Convention.
17 Article 2 (2), 1956 New York Convention.

and prosecution of an action for maintenance and the execution of any order or other judicial act for the payment of maintenance.«[18]

On the surface, it would appear that this Convention bestows Contracting States with a smooth-running, well-oiled machine. Yet, upon closer inspection, it would appear that a large number of States Parties do not even fulfil their basic obligations under the Convention, leading to severe operational problems.[19] However, due to the nature of the Convention (i.e. its rather technical and organisational structure), it is generally only referred to in passing in case law.[20] The oft-heard complaint concerning the operational problems was the main reason for the Hague Conference to undertake steps to modernise the legislation in this field.[21] The effective functioning of the administrative co-operation established by the 1956 New York Convention is reliant upon the efficient operation of the legal procedures according to Article 6 of the Convention. However, the various national acts implementing this convention display enormous differences, leading to a vast array of diverse procedures.[22]

1.2   1958 Hague Convention[23] and 1973 Hague Convention[24]

19 States are at present party to the 1958 Hague Convention[25] and 22 States are party to the 1973 Hague Convention.[26] Although the 1973 Hague Con-

---

18   Article 6 (1), 1956 New York Convention.
19   W. Duncan, The Development of the New Hague Convention on the International Recovery of Child Support and Other Forms of Family Maintenance«, *Family Law Quarterly*, 38/2004, p. 663-687, at p. 666.
20   D. Katanou, »Übereinkommen über die Geltendmachung von Unterhaltsansprüchen im Ausland – New Yorker-Unterhaltsübereinkommen«, *Familie, Partnerschaft, Recht*, 6/2006, p. 255-258, at p. 256. For example, OLG Schleswig, 14th May 1975, *Die deutsche Rechtsprechund*, 1977, No. 140.
21   D. van Iterson, »Het functioneren van de Alimentatieverdragen«, *Tijdschrift voor Familie- en Jeugdrecht*, 6/1999, p. 127-130, at p. 127.
22   Further operational problems in relation to the 1956 New York Convention arise in relation to the substantive scope of the Convention. Different States Parties have interpreted the Convention differently with regards the applicability of the Convention to legal aid cases: D. van Iterson, *ibid*, at p. 128.
23   Hague Convention of 15 April 1958 concerning the Recognition and Enforcement of Decisions relating to Maintenance Obligations towards Children.
24   Hague Convention of 2 October 1973 on the Recognition and Enforcement of Decisions relating to Maintenance Obligations.
25   Austria, Belgium, Czech Republic, Denmark, Finland, France, Germany, Hungary, Italy, Liechtenstein, Norway, The Netherlands, Portugal, Slovakia, Spain, Sweden, Switzerland, Suriname and Turkey. Furthermore, Greece and Luxembourg have both signed the Convention without subsequent ratification. For up-to-date ratifications visit: http://www.hcch.net.
26   Australia, Czech Republic, Denmark, Estonia, Finland, France, Germany, Greece,

vention declares that it shall replace the 1958 Hague Convention, this only applies as regards those States Parties that are party to the 1973 Convention.[27] According to both Hague Conventions, a maintenance decision or settlement made in one contracting State may be recognised and subsequently enforced in another contracting State. However, unlike the 1958 Hague Convention, the 1973 Hague Convention is not restricted to child maintenance claims, but instead extends to maintenance obligations arising from »a family relationship, parentage, marriage or affinity, including a maintenance obligation towards an infant who is not legitimate.«[28] According to Articles 4, 7 and 8, 1973 Hague Convention, an indirect jurisdictional test is imposed as a prerequisite to recognition of a child maintenance award. Moreover, even if an award has been made by a judge in accordance with these provisions, recognition may nonetheless be refused if recognition would be manifestly incompatible with the public policy of the State addressed, the decision was obtained by procedural fraud, the proceedings between the same parties and having the same purpose are pending before an authority in the state addressed, or that the decision is incompatible with a decision rendered between the same parties and having the same purpose, either in the State addressed or in another state.[29]

Italy, Lithuania, Luxembourg, The Netherlands, Norway, Poland Portugal, Slovakia, Spain, Sweden, Switzerland, Turkey, Ukraine and the United Kingdom. Furthermore, Belgium has signed the Convention without subsequent ratification and the Ukraine has acceded without it having entered into force. For up-to-date ratifications visit: http://www.hcch.net.

27 As a result a complex situation has arisen with the 1958 Convention being applicable with regards relations between Austria, Belgium, Hungary, Liechtenstein and Suriname, on the one hand, and the Czech Republic, Denmark, Finland, France, Germany, Italy, The Netherlands, Portugal, Slovakia, Spain and Sweden, on the other. However, the latter group of nations has also ratified the 1973 Hague Convention. Therefore, for claims as between the latter group, the 1973 Convention is applicable. For Estonia, Greece, Lithuania, Poland, Ukraine and the United Kingdom, the 1973 Convention is only valid insofar as the other country has also ratified the 1973 Hague Convention.
28 Article 1, 1973 Hague Convention.
29 Article 5, 1973 Hague Convention.

2. European Framework[30]

2.1 1968 Brussels Convention[31]

Although in 2001, the Brussels I Regulation[32] came to replace the 1968 Brussels Convention for 14 Member States,[33] this was not the case for Denmark.[34] Consequently, questions of jurisdiction between Denmark and the other EU Member States continued to be governed by the Brussels Convention. However, on the 19th October 2005, the European Community concluded an agreement with Denmark ensuring that the Regulation is also to be applied in relation to Denmark.[35] The agreement entered into force on the 1st July 2007. Accordingly, the 1968 Brussels Convention has for all intents and purposes been replaced by the Brussels I Regulation for all intracommunity cases subsequent to 1st July 2007.[36] Accordingly, this paper will not deal with the content of the 1968 Brussels Convention.

2.2 Lugano I Convention[37] and the Lugano II Convention

The Lugano I Convention is currently in force as between all EU Member States (including Denmark) and the members of the European Free Trade Association (excluding Liechtenstein).[38] The general Lugano regime is

---

30   This paper will not discuss the 1990 Rome Convention, which has not and more-than likely, will never come into force.
31   Brussels Convention on Jurisdiction and the Enforcement of Judgments in Civil and Commercial Matters 1968.
32   See *infra* section 4.2.3.
33   The Brussels I Regulation has been extended to the new Member States that acceded in 2004 and 2007.
34   This Danish opt-out was based on the 1997 Protocol No 5 on the position of Denmark annexed to the Treaty on European Union and to the Treaty establishing the European Community, OJ C340, 10.11.1997.
35   K. Boele-Woelki, »Katern: Internationaal Privaatrecht«, *Ars Aequi*, 2005, p. 5370-5372.
36   The scope of the Brussels I Regulation is circumscribed by Article 299 EC, which defines the territorial scope of the Regulation. The 1968 Brussels Convention, on the other hand, as an international convention extends to certain overseas territories belonging to various Member States, including certain French overseas territories, as well as the Dutch territory of Aruba. Since those territories are not part of the European Union, the Brussels I Regulation does not apply to them and the Brussels Convention continues to apply to them: ECJ Opinion, 27th February 2006, Opinion 1/03, §15. These issues will, however, remain outside the scope of this paper.
37   Lugano Convention on Jurisdiction and the Enforcement of Judgments in Civil and Commercial Matters 1988. The terms Lugano I and Lugano II have been coined for ease of reading. One should be careful not to confuse these terms with those publications in which Lugano II is used to refer to the draft convention to mirror the current provisions of the Brussels IIbis Regulation.
38   That is to say Iceland, Norway and Switzerland.

almost identical to that of the original 1968 Brussels Convention. However, with the coming into force of the Brussels I Regulation, the two regimes have become slightly divergent. As a result, discussions were opened to revise the Lugano I Convention.[39] In March 2007, a final text was agreed upon and the Convention was signed on the 30th October 2007. As soon as this convention enters into force,[40] the differences between the Lugano II Convention and the Brussels I Regulation will be minor, especially with regards the recognition and enforcement of child maintenance awards.

According to the Lugano II Convention, a »judgment given in a State bound by this Convention shall be recognised in the other States bound by this Convention without any special procedure being required.«[41] The only exceptions to this principle are those listed in Articles 34 and 35. The grounds are extremely restrictive and non-recognition is only permitted if it would be contrary to public policy,[42] the decision was given in default of appearance, or the defendant was not served in sufficient time,[43] it would be irreconcilable with a previous judgment from the State in which recognition is sought,[44] it would be irreconcilable with a previous judgment from a different State bound by the Lugano Convention or a third State, provided the earlier judgment is recognised in the State addressed,[45] or the State (bound by the Lugano II Convention) where recognition is sought has, prior to the entry into force of the Lugano II Convention undertaken not to recognise judgments given in other states bound by the Lugano II Convention against defendants domiciled or habitually resident in a third State where the judgment could only be founded on an exorbitant ground of jurisdiction.[46, 47]

---

39   A. Markus, »Revidierte Übereinkommen von Brüssel und Lugano: Zu den Hauptpunkten«, *Schweizerische Zeitschrift für Wirtschaft- und Finanzmarktrecht*, 5/1999, p. 205; M. Jametti Greiner, »Neues Lugano-Übereinkommen:« Stand der Arbeiten«, *Internationales Zivil- und Verfahrensrecht*, 2/2003, p. 113; K. Boele-Woelki, »Katern: Internationaal Privaatrecht«, *Ars Aequi*, 2006, p. 5502-5505.
40   This is not expected until 1st January 2010, at the very earliest. See for press release, http://www.bj.admin.ch/bj/en/home/themen/wirtschaft/internationales_privatrecht/lugano_uebereinkommen/0.html.
41   Article 33, Lugano II Convention.
42   Article 34 (1), Lugano II Convention.
43   Article 34 (2), Lugano II Convention.
44   Article 34 (3), Lugano II Convention.
45   Article 34 (4), Lugano II Convention.
46   Article 35 (1), Lugano II Convention, in conjunction with Articles 3 (2) and 68, future Lugano II Convention. The exorbitant grounds of jurisdiction referred to in Article 3 (2) are subsequently listed in Annex I to the Lugano II Convention.
47   A further ground for non-recognition is contained in Article 35 (1) with regards those

Like its earlier counterpart, the Lugano II Convention aims to ensure that the court seized shall not undertake a review of the original court's grounds of jurisdiction, except in extremely rare and clearly defined cases.[48] The enforcement provisions according to the Lugano II Convention are almost identical to those set forth in the Brussels I Regulation.[49]

2.3 Brussels I Regulation[50]

Along identical lines to the Lugano II outlined above, according to the Brussels I Regulation a child maintenance judgment[51] granted or issued in one EU Member State will automatically be recognised[52] in all other Member States,[53] save for limited exceptions.[54] Nonetheless, even under

---

decisions that conflict with the jurisdictional rules laid down in Sections 3, 4 or 6 of Title II, Lugano II Convention. However, these provisions do not affect child maintenance claims and therefore have not been dealt with here.

48 Although the Lugano I Convention also permits non-recognition on four jurisdictional based grounds not found in the Brussels I Regulation (Article 54B (3) and 57 (4), as well as Art. Ia and Ib, Protocol 1), these are generally not relevant for the recognition of child maintenance awards, and have therefore been excluded from the scope of this paper. Moreover, only two of these grounds will remain under the Lugano II Convention (Art. 54B (3), Lugano I is to be found in Art. 64 (3), Lugano II, and Art. 57 (4), Lugano I in Art. 67 (4), Lugano II). Art. Ia, Protocol 1 ceased to have effect on the 31st December 1999, and Article Ib, Protocol 1 has been removed altogether.

49 The only difference relates to Article 50 (2), Lugano II Convention which provides that »an applicant who requests the enforcement of a decision given by an administrative authority in Denmark, in Iceland or in Norway in respect of maintenance may, in the State addressed, claim the benefits referred to in [Article 50] paragraph 1 if he presents a statement from the Danish, the Icelandic or the Norwegian Ministry of Justice to the effect that he fulfills the economic requirements to qualify for the grant of complete or partial legal aid or exemption from costs or expenses.«.

50 Council Regulation (EC) No. 44/2001 of 22 December 2000 on jurisdiction and the recognition and enforcement of judgments in civil and commercial matters.

51 A judgment is defined in Article 32 as »any judgment given by a court or tribunal of a Member State, whatever the judgment may be called, including a decree, order, decision or writ of execution, as well as the determination of costs or expenses by an officer of the court«. This has also been held to include provisional decisions (which is obviously important with respect to child maintenance claims). See, for example, ECJ, *Van Uden/Deco-Line*, 17th November 1998, C-391/95 [1998] I ECR 7091 and ECJ, *Mietz/Internship*, 27th April 1999, C-99/96 [1999] I ECR 2277.

52 This normally means that a decision will be granted the same effects of *res judicata* as a domestic judgment: ECJ, *Hoffmann v. Krieg*, 4th February 1988, C-145/86 [1988] ECR 645. See also the Jenard Report, Art. 26.

53 Article 33, Brussels I. Article 53(1) does impose a requirement that a copy of the judgment is delivered by the party seeking recognition in order for the receiving authority to confirm its authenticity.

54 Article 34 and 35, Brussels I. See N. Bala, J. Oldham and A. Perry, »Regulating cross-border child support within federated systems: The United States, Canada and the

the Brussels I regime, it is still necessary to obtain a declaration of enforceability in the country where enforcement is sought.[55] Articles 38 through 56, Brussels I Regulation contain a number of rather technical provisions, although nonetheless highly important, with regards this exequatur procedure.[56] The exequatur procedure is regulated by the law of the Member State is which enforcement is sought,[57] except for those issues dealt with expressly by the Brussels I Regulation.[58]

2.4 European Enforcement Order Regulation[59]

One crucial shortcoming of the regime laid down by the Brussels I Regulation and Lugano II Convention, is the need for a separate enforcement procedure (known as an *exequatur procedure*). Especially with regards child maintenance claims, where the sums of money to be paid although relatively small can be of enormous importance to the maintenance creditor, this procedure is regarded as a great obstacle to the proper functioning of the recovery and enforcement system. As a result, the European Commission put forward proposals to create an easier and more efficient system for non-contentious claims.[60]

This Regulation, which has been in force since the 21st October 2005, is based upon the principle of mutual trust in the administration of jus-

---

European Union«, *Transnational Law and Contemporary Problems*, 15/2005, p. 87-107 at p. 102. For a detailed explanation of the grounds for refusing recognition, see M. Zilinsky, *De Europese Executoriale Titel*, Kluwer: Deventer, 2005, p. 92-123.

55   Article 38 (1), Brussels I.
56   These rules include, for example, the competent authority to which the enforcement application should be submitted (Article 39 (1), in conjunction with Annex II, Brussels I), the competent authority to which an appeal against the declaration of enforceability may be lodged (Article 43 (2), in conjunction with Annex III, Brussels I) and the appeal procedure for a subsequent appeal (Article 44, in conjunction with Annex IV, Brussels I). The party wishing to enforce must produce a standard form completed by the issuing competent authority, alongside the judgment itself (as provided for in Article 54, in conjunction with Annex V, Brussels I). For a more detailed discussion of the *exequatur* procedure, see M. Zilinsky, *ibid*, p. 125-142.
57   Article 40 (1), Brussels I.
58   *Carron v. Germany*, C-198/95 [1986] ECR 2437.
59   Council Regulation (EC) No. 805/2004 of 21 April 2004 creating a European Enforcement Order for uncontested claims. For general information regarding the EEO Regulation, see T. Rauscher, *Der Europäische Vollstreckungstitel für unbestrittene Forderungen*, GPR Praxis Schriften zum Gemeinschaftsprivatrecht: Munich, 2004; A. Stadler, »Kritische Anmerkungen zum Europäischen Vollstreckungstitel«, *Recht der Internationalen Wirtschaft*, 11/2004, p. 801-808.
60   COM (2004) 173 final.

tice.[61] Operating alongside Brussels I by providing a speedier and more efficient mechanism for the enforcement non-contentious claims, the EEO Regulation authorises the court making the original judgment[62] to provide a requesting claimant[63] with a certificate indicating that all the conditions of the EEO Regulation have been satisfied.[64] This EEO certificate then ensures that the judgment may be enforced in all other EU Member States without the need for an *exequatur procedure*. Only in extremely limited circumstances is a judge confronted with an EEO certified judgment permitted to undertaken a jurisdictional test.[65]

III. Current Problematic Areas

According to both the Hague Conference and the European Union, the current system of maintenance enforcement is suffering from numerous problems. It is, nonetheless, possible to categorise the problems that have been identified by these supranational organisations. At the current stage of this research project, it is not possible to provide a complete inventory of **all** current problematic aspects. However, it is possible to provide a summary and categorisation of the most pressing issues.

Firstly, a recurring problem is that the creditor is often unaware of his or her rights with respect to transnational maintenance recovery. Many maintenance creditors believe, incorrectly, that they have no chance of receiving maintenance payments if their ex-partner has emigrated, or do not even wish to pursue the case. Secondly, from the extensive reports

---

61 Since it is based on Title IV, EC Treaty, the EEO Regulation does not apply to judgments, decisions and authentic instruments from Denmark (Article 2 (3), EEO Regulation).

62 Article 6, EEO Regulation. A relevant judgment is one that satisfies the conditions as laid down in Articles 2 (i.e. in the field of civil and commercial matters, including child maintenance) and Article 3 (i.e. an uncontested claim). A claim is regarded as uncontested if the debtor has expressly agreed to it (Article 3 (1) (a) and (d)), if the debtor has refrained from objecting to it (Article 3 (1) (b)), or if the debtor has neither appeared nor been represented at the court hearing, provided that such conduct amounts to a tacit admission under the law of the State of origin (Article 3 (1) (c)).

63 It is explicitly stated in both in COM (2002) 159, as well as COM (2003) 341 that the EEO certificate must be *requested* by the *maintenance creditor*. The judge is not permitted to provide this certificate *ex officio*.

64 Article 5, EEO Regulation.

65 Article 6 (1) (b), EEO Regulation. This is only permitted if the jurisdiction of the original judge conflicts with sections 3 (matters relating to insurance) or 6 (exclusive jurisdiction), Brussels I Regulation.

compiled by the Hague Conference, it is clear that at present the national enforcement agencies do not transmit all the documents required by the foreign agency. This occurs for numerous reasons, not least of which because the transmitting agencies are often unaware of the documents that are required by the receiving agency.

Furthermore, as in every international case, translations are highly problematic. According to Article 17 (5), 1973 Hague Convention, the party seeking enforcement of the decision must furnish a translation of various documents, including (a) the decision, (b) any document needed to prove that the decision is no longer subject to the ordinary forms of review, (c) if rendered by default, any document required to prove that the notice of the institution of proceedings was properly served, and (d) where appropriate, any document necessary to prove that he/she obtained legal aid or exemption from costs. As a result of this requirement, a lot of material, sometimes even unnecessarily, requires translation, causing delays in the transmission procedure.[66]

No system of administrative cooperation is provided for according to the Hague Conventions. Although the absence of such provisions is perhaps to be accounted for due to the existence of the 1956 New York Convention, the heterogeneous nature of these sources can and does indeed cause operational problems.[67] This is especially the case because the role of the transmitting agency can be very different in each contracting state. In some jurisdictions the agency is a department of a ministry, in others an independent governmental agency and in others simply a location to which documents and files must be sent.

Fourthly, each contracting state is under an obligation to ensure that the relevant authorities perform the tasks assigned to it. Although less relevant for transnational claims between European States, the operation of the 1956 New York Convention has been disrupted by the fact that many jurisdictions have failed to perform even the basic duties entrusted to them according to the Convention.[68] However, if when this occurs, no action is available for the maintenance creditor or the transmitting agency

---

66 General Conclusions, §14.
67 Hague Conference, »Maintenance Obligations. Note on the desirability of revising the Hague conventions on Maintenance Obligations and including in a new instrument rules on judicial and administrative co-operation«, (1999) Preliminary Document No. 2, p. 12, §15b.
68 Hague Conference, *Towards a new global instrument on the international recovery of child support and other forms of family maintenance,* (2003) Preliminary Document No. 3, p.15.

to ensure that these tasks are in fact executed. Fifthly the current regulatory framework has caused certain issues in relation to the modification of maintenance decisions. Since the 1958 and 1973 Hague Conventions contain no rules on direct jurisdiction, it would appear that the question which authority (alongside the authority in the country of origin) is competent to modify a maintenance order is left unanswered. However, it has been suggested that Article 7 (1), 1973 Hague Convention, in providing rules indirectly recognising the competency of the authorities in the State where the debtor has his or her habitual residence, allows the authorities in this State to also modify an order.[69]

Finally, there is the recurring problem of the wandering debtor. Although obviously not really a problem of the debtor, one of the main problems in the effective enforcement of maintenance claims emanates from the inability of the authorities to locate the debtor. If the maintenance creditor lives not where the maintenance debtor has moved to, the whole recovery procedure could be severely delayed, and possibly even frustrated altogether.[70] The same also applies to gaining information regarding the debtor's assets and income.[71]

IV. Proposed instruments

1. *European Maintenance Regulation (EMR)*[72]

An investigation into the possibility of creating common procedural rules aimed at simplifying and accelerating the settlement of cross-border maintenance disputes was placed on the European agenda at the meeting of the European Council in Tampere on 15th and 16th October 1999.[73] This was reaffirmed in the Hague Programme[74] and led to the adoption

---

69 M. PELICHET, »Note on the operation of the Hague Conventions relating to maintenance obligations and of the New York Convention on the Recovery Abroad of Maintenance«, (1995) Preliminary Document No. 1, §95.
70 SEC (2005) 1629, p.4.
71 SEC (2005) 1629, p.4.
72 Council Regulation (EC) No. 4/2009 of 18th December 2008 on Jurisdiction, Applicable Law, Recognition and Enforcement of Decisions and Cooperation in Matters relating to Maintenance Obligations.
    This contribution was written before the publication of the European Maintenance Regulation. Although references have been amended, extensive discussion of the Chapter is not possible.
73 COM (2005) 649, p. 2.
74 3rd March 2005, Official Journal, C53.

by the European Council and European Commission of a common Action Plan.[75] Most recently, the shared will to move forward in such an important area as maintenance obligations was highlighted at the informal meeting of Justice and Home Affairs Ministers in Dresden on 15th and 16th January 2007.[76]

At the same time, the European Commission commissioned a study on the recovery of maintenance claims, and on the 3rd November 2003, a first expert meeting took place aimed at identifying the principal aspects for inclusion in a future Green Paper. The Green Paper was published on the 15th April 2004[77] and a public hearing scheduled for 2nd June 2004.[78] These developments culminated with the publication by the European Commission on the 15th December 2005 of a proposal for a Council Regulation on Jurisdiction, Applicable Law, Recognition and Enforcement of Decisions and Cooperation in Matters relating to Maintenance Obligations.[79]

The Regulation was passed on the 18th December 2008 and will enter into force on the 18th June 2011. The Regulation will make important changes to the existing framework regarding the enforcement of child maintenance orders. When in force, the EMR will entirely revoke the existing regime as laid down by the Brussels I Regulation and the EEO Regulation, with regards **all** maintenance obligations.[80] Perhaps the greatest change is with respect to the current *exequatur* procedure as required for contentious claims and non-contentious claims not falling within the scope of the EEO Regulation. Although, as stated above, the EEO Regulation has abolished the *exequatur* procedure for uncontested child maintenance claims, the EMR will abolish the exequatur procedure in relation to **all child maintenance claims**,[81] subject to the condition that the judgment is enforceable in the Member State where it was issued, it will be recognised **and enforced** without an intermediate measure being re-

---

75 Document of the Council of the European Union, No. 9778/2/05 REV 2 JAI 207.
76 PRES/2007/77, 2794th Council Meeting, Luxembourg, 19th-20th April 2007.
77 COM (2004) 254.
78 The consultation is available at: http://europa.eu.int:8082/comm/justice_home/ejn/maintenance_claim
79 COM (2005) 649.
80 Article 68 (1), EMR. See further, G. Smith, »The EU Commission's Draft Regulation on Maintenance Obligations«, *International Family Law,* 2006, p. 72-76, at p. 73; K. Boele-Woelki, »Katern 98: Internationaal Privaatrecht«, *Ars Aequi,* 2006, p. 5440-5441; K. Gebauer, »Vollstreckung von Unterhaltstiteln nach der EuVTVO und der geplanten Unterhaltsverordnung«, *Familie, Partnerschaft, Recht,* 6/2006, p. 252-255, at p. 254-255.
81 Article 17 (2) EMR. This is subject to that Member State having ratified the 2007 Hague Protocol.

quired.[82] This will also be the case, notwithstanding an appeal permitted by national law. Furthermore, any review as to the substance of the decision will not be permitted during the enforcement procedure.[83] Nonetheless, the enforcing Member State will be able to limit the impact of the order to those assets which are deemed to be attachable in that State.

Moreover, as a result of the EMR, a future maintenance creditor will only need produce a copy of the decision to be enforced, as well as a standardised extract as listed in Annex I to the Regulation.[84] Consequently, **no translation** of the foreign decision will be required.[85] At this moment in time, no indication is provided with regards to whom the enforcement procedure should be addressed. Since enforcement of a foreign maintenance claim in The Netherlands, for example, can be executed by the *Landelijk Bureau Inning Onderhoudsgelden* (LBIO), the question remains whether the choice of execution form lies with the maintenance creditor or whether the EMR will provide a list of authorised competent authorities for the execution of the judgment.

As stated in recital 31, the EMR provides for the creation of a network of Central Authorities in all Member States. These »new« authorities are to provide for the exchange of information to ensure that debtors are located and their assets properly evaluated and assessed.[86] According to Article 41 (2), EMR a maintenance creditor will be provided with the possibility of being represented by the central authority of the Member State on the territory of which the court seised in a matter relating to maintenance is located or the central authority of the Member State of enforcement.[87] Further comprehensive details regarding the proposed co-operation mechanisms are, however, absent, since it is hoped that this will be coordinated with the forthcoming Hague Maintenance Convention.

In the original proposal, these new central authorities, in providing access to information to facilitate the recovery of child maintenance could

---

82 Only extremely limited possibilities for refusal or suspension of enforcement exist according to Article 21, EMR. By virtue of the word »only«, this list of refusal grounds is also exclusive.
83 Article 42, EMR.
84 Article 20 (1), EMR.
85 Article 20 (2), EMR..
86 Proposed Article 50, EMR.
87 All services provided by the Central Authority will also need to be provided free of charge to the maintenance creditor: Article 44 (1), EMR. To aid the process by which these claims may be processed, the maintenance creditor will also be provided with the opportunity to proceed through the court of the place of his or her habitual residence, which will assist in ensuring that the co-operation operates properly.

have been required to provide, at least, the administration and authorities in other Member States access to the following areas: tax and duties, social security, population registers, land registers, motor vehicle registrations and central banks.[88] According to the final text, this list is not mentioned.

2. Hague Maintenance Convention (HMC)[89]

In 1995, a Special Commission was established to identify the problems associated with the working of the international instruments in the field of maintenance obligations. Although, a number of clear, identifiable problems were uncovered, the Special Commission took the view that a major reform of these instruments was not necessary.[90] Nonetheless, discontent with the functioning of the current international instruments did not subside and in April 1999 a special commission was held to examine the practical operation of the 1956 New York Convention, as well as the 1958 and 1973 Hague Conventions.[91] As a result of this special commission, work commenced on the drafting of a new international instrument to deal with the international recovery of child support and other forms of family maintenance.[92] The Convention was concluded in The Hague on the 23rd

---

88 Proposed Article 44 (2), EMR. This provision did not, however, require Member States to create new records: Proposed Article 44 (3), EMR. However, the simple fact that access to these records may be required in transnational cases has already raised questions of privacy. A number of safeguards are already in place, see Proposed Articles 45-47, EMR. However, this has not silenced all calls for review: Opinion of the European Data Protection Supervisor on the Proposal for a Council Regulation on jurisdiction, applicable law, recognition and enforcement of decisions and cooperation in matters relating to maintenance obligations, *Official Journal*, 2006, C-242/14. This issue would appear to have been solved with reference to Directive 95/46/EC.
89 2007 Hague Convention on the International Recovery of Child Support and Other Forms of Family Maintenance.
90 In general it was felt that this area suffers from a certain degree of *overkill*. Alongside the global instruments mentioned in this paper, many regional international conventions also exist, such as the Inter-American Convention on Support Obligations (Done at Montevideo, 15th July 1989). This Convention has been ratified by Argentina, Belize, Bolivia, Brazil, Costa Rica, Ecuador, Guatemala, Mexico, Panama, Paraguay, Peru, Uruguay (and further signed, but not ratified by Colombia, Haiti and Venezuela). There are furthermore hundreds of bilateral agreements between States, e.g. the United States of America and The Netherlands Bilateral Agreement for the Enforcement of Maintenance (Support) Obligations, signed at Washington 30th May 2001 and entered into force 1st May 2002.
91 The Commission also investigated the operation of the 1956 and 1973 Hague Conventions with regards the applicable law in maintenance obligations. These Conventions fall outside the scope of this paper.
92 The first round of talks commenced in May 2003, the second in June 2004, the third in April 2005, the fourth in June 2006, the fifth in May 2007. A diplomatic session

November 2007. At present, only the United States of America and Burkina Faso have signed.

According to the preparatory work conducted by the Hague Conference, it was clear that in order for a future Convention to be successful, Contracting States must have confidence in the enforcement mechanisms in place in reciprocating States. Unlike the EMR, a child maintenance order falling within the substantive, geographical and temporal scope of the HMC,[93] will only be recognised if it satisfies the indirect jurisdictional test conditions laid down in proposed Article 17, HMC. This Article provides for a compromise between those jurisdictions (e.g. the EU) that adhere to the creditor's jurisdictional principle and other states (e.g. the USA) that adhere to a fact-based approach, whereby the jurisdiction of the court of origin is tested according to the jurisdictional rules of the requested court.[94] Although the enforcement procedure itself is to be governed by national law,[95] a number of common enforcement measures have been proposed.[96]

Like the EMR, the HMC also opts for a centralised system of central authorities designated by each Contracting State.[97] The exact delineation of the functions, duties and obligations of these Central Authorities has been crucial to the ongoing discussions during the meetings of the Special Commission.[98] The concept of Central Authorities emanates from the existing system of central authorities established under the auspices of the 1980 Hague Convention on the Civil Aspects of International Child Abduction. A number of discussions have already presented serious problems in relation, for example, to the role the Central Authority will play in relation to the facilitation and monitoring of enforcement procedures

---

is scheduled to take place from the 5th–23rd November 2007. For information regarding the initial developments, see W. Duncan, »The development of the new Hague Convention on the international recovery of child support and other forms of family maintenance«, *Family Law Quarterly*, 38/2004, p. 663–687.

93   Article 2, 3 and 55, HMC.
94   See, for example, the explicit reference to the creditor's jurisdictional principle in Article 17 (1), HMC and the explicit reference to the fact based approach in Article 17 (3), HMC.
95   Article 30 (1), HMC.
96   Article 30 (2), HMC: (a) wage withholding, (b) garnishment from bank accounts and other sources, (c) deductions from social security payments, (d) lien on or forced sale of property, (e) tax refund withholding, (f) withholding or attachment of pension benefits, (g) credit bureau reporting and (h) denial, suspension or revocation of various licenses (for example, driving licenses).
97   Article 1 (a), HMC.
98   Articles 5–8, HMC.

and assisting in obtaining provisional measures, such as freezing a bank account.[99]

V. Experience with Central Authorities

Both instruments have laudable aims with respect to the proposed administrative co-operation system. Both instruments set forth a system whereby the formalities that need to be followed are simple and cost-effective, whereby the amount of money spent in attempting to enforce and recover a claim is proportionate to the amount of maintenance actually recovered. Furthermore, any procedures should be able to take account of the variety and diversity in national child maintenance systems, both with regard to the determination, as well as the enforcement of such claims. And finally, any system should attempt to ensure tat the maintenance creditor is provided with a rapid conclusion of their case. There are few us who would not wish to support these aims. The ultimate discussion is, however, how best to achieve these aims.

Although both proposals involve the creation of a network of Central Authorities, as yet little attention has been paid to the actual effectiveness of such a system. Will this network be sufficient to deal with the current problems? Is it actually the best possible administrative network or organisation for these problems? It has been assumed that because such a network has functioned successfully in other areas, such as international adoption and child abduction, it will, therefore, be suitable to this area too.[100] However, child maintenance cases are fundamentally different since they involve an ongoing, long-term relationship. Furthermore, the volume of cases in this field is very different the volume of cases in the field of adoption or abduction.

This organisational structure is, however, nothing new. It has been utilised in numerous international instruments. It would, therefore, seem expedient to investigate the experience of such an administrative system in other fields of law. At present, this research project has focused on the experience in six Hague conventions that have established a system of Central Authorities, as well as four Regulations at European level. These

---

99 A procedure that is available for example according to the proposed EMR: Article 35, EMR.
100 Hague Conference, *Hague Preliminary Draft Convention on the International Recovery of Child Support and Other Forms of Family Maintenance*, (2007) Preliminary Document 32, p.20, §71.

instruments can be divided into two main fields of law, namely family law and procedural law.[101]

With this track record and history with the organisational structure of central authorities, it is interesting to note that from examining the evaluative reports of all of these instruments, a system of Central Authorities has far from solved all of the issues of any given problem. The same may also be true of child maintenance, especially when one considers that child support recovery is characeised by the exceptionally high volume of cases and the long duration of maintenance claims, when compared to the other fields where central authorities have been utilised.

Since each central authority remains an operating organ within a national legal system, the discrepancy in the application of the rules will remain. Obviously, with a European regulation, the rules are to be applied uniformly, but procedural uniform application in practice will be very difficult to ensure when the organs themselves will have different legal positions in the national legal systems, as already explained. Although space restrictions prevent a full discussion of all of the issues that will remain with a system of central authorities, it is important to be aware of the crucial defect of such a system, that being in the location of the debtor and the ascertainment of the debtor's assets.

Even if each country in the EU has created a central authority responsible for incoming and outgoing maintenance claims, the transmitting agency will still need to transmit the claim to the relevant foreign agency

---

[101] Convention of 15th November 1965 on the service abroad of judicial and extrajudicial document in civil or commercial matters, Convention of 18th March 1970 on the taking of evidence abroad in civil or commercial matters, Convention of 25th October 1980 on the civil aspects of international child abduction, Convention of 29th March 1993 on the protection of children and co-operation in respect of inter-country adoption, Convention of 19th October 1996 on jurisdiction, applicable law, recognition, enforcement and co-operation in respect of parental responsibility and measures for the protection of children and the Convention of 13th January 2000 on the international protection of adults. In the European Union the four Regulations are Council Regulation (EC) No. 1393/2007 of the European Parliament and of the Council of 13th November 2007 on the service in the Member States of judicial and extrajudicial documents in civil or commercial matters and repealing Council Regulation (EC) No. 1348/2000, Council Regulation (EC) No. 1206/2001 of 28th May 2001 on cooperation between the courts of the Member States in the taking of evidence in civil or commercial matters, Council Regulation Council Regulation (EC) No. 2201/2003 concerning jurisdiction and the recognition and enforcement of judgments in matrimonial matters and in matters of parental responsibility, repealing Regulation (EC) No. 1347/2000 and Council Regulation (EC) No 2006/2004 on Consumer Protection Cooperation .

in order to ensure effective recovery. If the maintenance creditor has no idea where the debtor is residing, the fundamental problem of locating the debtor will remain. Bearing in mind the principle of free movement of persons in the EU, locating a wandering debtor is obviously an acute problem and is a problem that is only set to worsen.

VI. Conclusions

Over the coming years, it is this author's intention to investigate this issue further with respect to the other ways in which the current international recovery problems in the European Union can be solved using alternative organisational structures. One option to some of the problems that will remain after the introduction of central authorities would be to provide more guidance with respect to the legal status of the central authorities.

I personally feel that moving towards a central parent locator system would be advantageous to all. Obviously, any step would have to be made in close cooperation with the European Data Protection Supervisor, but is not outside the realms of possibilities, since Europol already operates according to these lines. The ultimate goal of a single European Maintenance Agency with branches in the various Member States is also a possible solution, although one which at present is perhaps too ambitious. Nonetheless, these options should not be disregarded prematurely.

What Price Should be Paid for a Child?
Financial aspects of inter-country adoption

Adriaan P. van der Linden[1]

I. Introduction

As is the case in many countries, inter-country adoption is continually the focus of attention in the Netherlands. On the one hand, newspapers are reporting of (financial) exploitation related to adoption, while on the other hand the Dutch adoption lobby manages time and time again to convince members of parliament to urge the government to relax adoption rules with a view to enabling more people (without children) to adopt a child, as quickly and easily as possible. It is obvious that the interests of the adults are put first, while the child's best interest is dragged in by head and shoulders, if at all.

International law, however, has explicitly acknowledged with regard to inter-country adoption that the child's best interest should prevail and that this form of adoption can only be accepted as a last resort. Both points of departure – the interest of the child and adoption as a last resort- are the most important considerations in the Hague Adoption Convention[2] as well as in article 21 of the Convention on the Rights of a Child, which stipulates that Member States must ensure that the child's best interest is put first when adoption is considered.[3]

The adoption scandals which featured prominently in Dutch media were met by strong reactions and have undoubtedly caused the ideas on inter-country adoption to change fundamentally. Until recently, attention was primarily and particularly focused on the simplification of the adoption process, while the aim was to relax or even dispense completely with

---

1   Utrecht University, The Netherlands.
2   Convention on Protection of Children and Co-operation in respect of Intercountry Adoption, The Hague 29 May 1993.
3   Convention on the Rights of the Child. Verdrag inzake de rechten van het kind. The convention was adopted by the UN General Meeting on 20 November 1989 and became operative on September 2nd 1990.

age limits. The reverse is true now: there is a call for stricter regulation and more controls in the adoption process. At the same time, there is a trend, which started between 2000 and 2005, of a decrease in the number of foreign children available for inter-country adoption in the Netherlands.[4] This reduction continued in 2007. If the number of children available for inter-country adoption drops, there is a risk that new sources are tapped into. This happens particularly in African countries such as Ethiopia, Mali, Uganda and South Africa. On the other hand, fewer children from Asia, China and Vietnam are coming our way.

June 2006 saw the Dutch Justice Minister submit a bill for the amendment of the Placement of Foreign Children for Adoption Act (PFCAA) for review by relevant partners and interested groups.[5] As a result of the reactions to this bill and the developments described above, the Minister created a committee in 2007 that was to present recommendations on two main issues, including the future of inter-country adoption in the Netherlands.[6] This contribution only addresses the latter part of the Kalsbeek Committee's review.[7]

The Kalsbeek Committee presented its recommendations to the Justice Minister in a report on inter-country adoption.[8] In its report, the

---

[4] This trend can be observed worldwide and also applies to countries such as Canada, Denmark, France, Norway, Sweden and Switzerland. Source: International Social Service, »Diversification of countries of origin and an increase in the age of adopted children against a background of inter-country adoption that continues to be tense«, Monthly Review No 7-8/2008, July/August 2008, Editorial, p. 2-3 and »The global reduction of inter-country adoptions that started in 2005 and that has persisted in 2007«, Monthly Review No 7-8/2008, July/August 2008, Practise, p. 5.

[5] Amendments of Book 1 of the Dutch Civil Code in connection with the shortening of the adoption process and amendment of the Placement of Foreign Children for Adoption Act when two same sex spouses adopt together.Second Chamber, 2005-2006, 30 551.

[6] Regulation of 26 September 2007, no. 5507329/07/6, with respect to the creation of a Committee on lesbian parenthood and inter-country adoption (Dutch) Staatscourant 5 October 2007, no. 193, p. 6. The Committee's chair is Mrs. Ella Kalsbeek, former junior minister of justice and member of parliament. The committee's members are experts in the field of Family and Juvenile law, private international law, behavioural sciences and administrative law.

[7] The other part concerns particularly the legal position of the lesbian ›duo-mother‹. In its report Lesbian Parenthood (*Lesbisch Ouderschap*, only available in Dutch), which the committee published on 31 October 2007, its major proposal is to allow the possiblity of creating a duo- mother by allowing a woman to recognise the child of her female partner. At the moment the recognition of a child is available to biological and social fathers only.

[8] Report inter-country adoption. »All things of value are defenceless« (*Alles van waarde is weerloos*), Ministry of Justice, The Hague 29 May 2008. There is also an English translation available.

Committee discusses how to strike a balance between, on the one hand, the best interests of children who are eligible for adoption and, on the other hand, the desire of prospective adoptive parents to start a family, as well as the related responsibilities and roles of the authorities. The Committee focused on the arguments in parliament and society in favour of relaxing age limits in adoption and on the decreasing number of foreign children available for adoption. Its recommendations are infused with what is best for the child. In addition to the child's best interest, the Committee also considered the best interests of the other parties in the adoption triangle: the prospective adoptive parents and the biological parents.

The report's motto is: »Everything valuable is defenceless«. This famous line in Dutch poetry was written by Lucebert, a well-known poet, painter, artist and lithographer.[9] The Committee has applied the motto to the most relevant aspects of the adoption process. The value of a child as a human being is obvious, or at least should be. Then there is the vulnerability, the defencelessness of a child who may be an orphan or who may have been put up for adoption and the value of a child for prospective adoptive parents who would like to start a family, which has not come to them naturally. And last, but certainly not least, we must not forget the biological parent who is often forced, due to poverty or pressure from her social environment, to give up caring for the child or who simply does not dare to care for it.

The report gives 26 recommendations aimed at reducing the vulnerability of the inter-country adoption process in order to allow only those inter-country adoptions that satisfy the requirements laid down in the Convention on the Rights of a Child and the Hague Adoption Convention.

I will briefly discuss these recommendations in the following chapter of this contribution and finish it in the third chapter with the focus on the financial aspects of inter-county adoption.

---

9 Lucebert is a pseudonym for Lubertus Jacobus Swaansdijk, who lived from 1924 to 1994. The line of poetry comes from the verse »The very old sings« (*De zeer oude zingt*) (1974).

II. The Report on Inter-Country Adoption

1. Adoption in General[10]

The first two chapters of the Kalsbeek Committee report focus on the process of inter-country adoption in general. Many children all over the world live in poverty, without adults to provide them with the necessary care and without any hope for improvement. All over the world children are placed in homes, while research shows that growing up in a home may be harmful to a child's development. The question then arises what is really in the best interest of these children. The Convention on the Rights of a Child (CRC) and the Hague Adoption Convention are based on the axiom that a child should be cared for in a family setting, where possible in the country of origin. This implies the return of the child to his parent(s), placement in a foster family or domestic adoption. Permanent residence in a family setting is preferred to staying in a home. In this context, the principle of subsidiarity means that inter-country adoption is the last resort.

The worldwide objective should be that the need for inter-country adoption is minimised for future generations of foreign children. Consequently, inter-country adoption should neither undermine the subsidiarity principle, nor hinder or restrain constructive local developments. People could become dependent on the income generated by inter-country adoption, for example, or such income may discourage efforts aimed at abolishing the stigma of unmarried motherhood.

The vulnerability of the individual child and the importance, for children as a group, of preventing irregularities and exploitation in inter-country adoption make it necessary not only to create adequate rules but also to actually enforce them. It is beyond dispute that children are particularly vulnerable in inter-country adoptions. A child who is orphaned or abandoned by his parent(s) no longer has any actual, emotional and legal ties with his parents and their families, rendering it defenceless. This reason alone should be enough for adoptions to be carried out with due care. Another reason is that worldwide the number of people seeking to adopt a foreign child in order to start a family exceeds the number of children, particularly young, healthy ones, available for adoption. It makes inter-country adoption prone to irregularities and there is the risk of an

---

10 See for the prevailing Dutch rules on (inter-country) adoption, A. P. van der Linden »Law on Adoption« (*Adoptierecht*) Monographs Family, Youth and the Law, part 3, The Hague 2006 (in Dutch only).

economic law becoming the guiding principle: »demand precedes supply«. The government must ensure that the preconditions which guarantee the best interests of all parties in the adoption triangle are satisfied in society. This also pertains to the way in which (adoption) children come to the Netherlands.

2. The Adoption Process

The third chapter of the report addresses several aspects of the adoption process that succeeds the receipt of an adoption certification. The adoption certification is a written statement issued by the Justice Minister in which he grants the applicant(s) permission, in principle, to adopt a foreign child (section 2 PFCAA). The adoption of a foreign child is not allowed in the Netherlands without the adoption certification.

Inter-country adoptions from Non-Member States are not governed by the same procedures as inter-country adoptions from Member States. Although adoptions from Non-Member States are also governed by the basic principles and guarantees of the Hague Adoption Convention, there are material procedural differences with Convention adoptions, which are considered undesirable. The adoption procedures for Non-Member States must therefore be tightened and improved in view of the child's best interest, for example by introducing a statement of approval by the Dutch Central Authority for every non-Convention adoption, authorisation per country and the Dutch Central Authority's power to instruct.

2.1 Do it Yourself Adoptions

Do-it-yourself adoptions, as referred to in section 7a PFCAA, is also discussed. The prevailing practice in the Netherlands entails that prospective adoptive parents themselves contact authorities, persons or institutions in the country of their choice, through whom they seek to adopt a child (also called »the contact«). Although the process has been tightened in the Quality Framework,[11] there is some concern as to the supervision of do-it-yourself adoptions . Moreover, some prospective adoptive parents requesting permission for a do-it-yourself adoption select a country of origin of which the adoption system is completely unknown, while the Dutch Central Authority has little time and resources to investigate that

---

11 Quality Framework Licence holders Inter-country adoption, The Hague: Minstry of Justice, June 2008. The Justice Minister submitted it to the Second Chamber on 15 July 2008, TK 2007-2008, 31 265, no. 8.

particular adoption. Furthermore, the Dutch Central Authority only verifies the amount to be paid for the services provided in relation to do-it-yourself adoptions in the country of origin in advance and on the basis of an estimation, which increases the risk of inappropriate flows of money. Other objections with regard to do-it-yourself adoptions adoption services concern those cases where the child to be adopted is matched with the intended adoptive parents before the do-it yourself adoption services are applied for and before the contact in question is approved. Section 7a PFCAA does not preclude such a course of events. As this puts more pressure on the process, it is obviously not a desirable situation. Moreover, the Hague Adoption Convention is based on the principle that the child's best interests are best served by full-scope adoption services, which provide professional support at each phase of the adoption process. This is not the case with the partial adoption services. The rules for do-it-yourself adoption services allow prospective adoptive parents to seek contact with the person or institute responsible for the potential adoptive child, such as an orphanage, prior to the matching, while this person or institute also decides in which home the child will be placed for adoption. That is in violation of article 29 of the Hague Adoption Convention.

Although there may be good reasons to opt for do-it-yourself adoption services, the Committee is of the opinion that do-it-yourself adoption services should be abolished in view of the best interests of the child. The reasons are the risk of inadequate supervision, the greater risk of irregularities and because do-it-yourself adoption services undermine the basic principles of the Hague Adoption Convention.

The recently published »Quality Framework for Inter-Country Adoption Licence Holders« mentions the high quality standards and professionalism of the licence holders.[12] It justifies the government's support towards maintaining these standards and therefore a structural subsidy to the licence holders would be appropriate.

In order to maintain the high quality of the adoption process, the licence holder must monitor the adoption process at all times and have extensive know-how, as this improves the efficiency and professionalism of his organisation. Even though the Quality Framework is a step in the right direction, the present statutory minimum requirement of one adoption

---

12 During its consultations the Kalsbeek Committee has been able to consult the latest concept of the Quality Framework, as a result of which it could anticipate on it before its publication date.

every two years is too small to create an efficient and professional organisation. A small organisation runs the risk that it may not be able to survive under certain circumstances if it realises a small number of adoptions only. Conversely, a more substantial licence holder may not experience the same pressure to complete an individual adoption in order to survive as an organisation. This is the reason for the recommended legal requirement of at least thirty adoption procedures per year.

Chapter 3 of the report also discusses the accelerated process for a preliminary placement order, the stricter supervision of the financial aspects of the adoption process and the need for the Dutch delegation in countries of origin to be alert with respect to the inter-country adoption situation in that country.

The possibility of international supervision is also addressed. A major obstacle in the creation of an international supervisory body is that the views on the process of inter-country adoption in Europe are very different indeed. Countries such as France, Italy and Spain would like to increase the adoption capacity, whereas the Scandinavian countries and the Netherlands are reluctant to do so. It is interesting to note that the European Parliament stated on 16 January 2008 that a common policy should be formulated to facilitate (inter-country) adoption in the European Union, but then again it also observed European Union countries organise the support to the child's natural parents and their youth welfare work in such a way that inter-country (European) adoption is not required. The Dutch government should place inter-country adoption on the European agenda with a view to achieving, wherever possible, a common vision on inter-country adoption.[13]

2.2 Age Limits

The fourth chapter of the report addresses age limits and the required suitability of prospective adoptive parents. It is a fact that every adopted child has lost at least one person, but more often than not, more than one. That is the reason why it must be avoided that adopted children run a bigger risk of losing their parents or other important family members such as grand-parents at a significantly younger age than children who are not adopted. It is in the child's interest to imitate the natural situation as closely as possible when it comes to the age of the adoptive parents

---

13 The Council of Europe's Committee of Ministers adopted the new Convention on adoption on 7 May 2008, which will be available for signatories in November 2008.

and the age difference between the adoptive parents and the child to be adopted. The setting of age limits is not discriminatory. The argument often used in favour of raising age limits is that women today postpone motherhood until they are somewhat older. Such evidence is hardly convincing because the majority of the Dutch first-borns in a family are born to women in the age of 27-32 years. Women beyond forty who have a baby are an exception.

The Committee supports a hard age limit of 48, provided the age limit of a child, as required in the adoption process, is raised from six to eight and the maximum age difference between the prospective adoptive parent and the child to be adopted is set at 40. The 48-years' limit should also apply to the partner in the case of a single-parent adoption. The advantage of a hard age limit is that it provides a clear demarcation and it also helps to mitigate the expectations of prospective adoptive parents. It may be possible, however, that such a limit is not in the adoption child's best interest if it means that his biological brother or sister cannot be adopted by the same adoptive parents. There is good reason, therefore, to make the law flexible in this respect.

Raising the maximum age of adoptive children upon arrival in the Netherlands from six to eight years (i.e. up to and including their seventh year), could mitigate complaints from countries of origin, which often find it difficult to accept that older children are apparently not welcome in the Netherlands, whereas there is a place for them in families in other receiving countries such as Sweden, Italy or the United States. [14] From a scientific point of view, a child's development does not suffer from raising the age to eight years. We must not forget, however, that the maximum age difference between the intended adoptive parent and the child to be adopted should not exceed 40. The current exception laid down in article 3 paragraph 2 under a of the Guidelines for the Placement of Foreign Children for Adoption 2000, which implies that a child who is two years and a day old can be placed with older adoptive parents, should therefore be abolished. A prospective adoptive parent of, let's say, 45 would then no longer be able to adopt a two-year old child, as he could do now, but only a

---

14 Worldwide the trend can be observed showing that the age of children on the moment of adoption is increasing. The percentage of adopted children older than five was in 2006 19% and in 2007 23%. Source: International Social Service, »The global reduction of inter-country adoptions that started in 2005 and that has persisted in 2007«, Monthly Review No 7-8/2008, July/August 2008, Practise, p. 6. See also the Editorial in the same issue.

child aged five or older. This adjustment will give a larger number of older children the opportunity of growing up in a family setting.

There is a number of prospective adoptive parents in the Netherlands who feel that the present home study is intrusive and that it should be limited to, e.g., consultation of the Judicial Documentation Register and a medical examination. Their opinion denies the special importance of the specific background of adoption children, which makes it imperative that adoptive parents meet special requirements. Moreover, the home study is mandatory under article 5 of the Hague Adoption Convention.

The requirements regarding the suitability of prospective adoptive parents and any age limits should also apply to the spouse, registered partner or life companion of the person who wants to adopt in case of a single parent adoption. After all, this partner is a permanent member of the family in which the adoption child will be raised.

The growing number of special needs children and the fact that prospective adoptive parents do not always know in advance whether their request for a child who is mentally and physically healthy will be honoured and the increased availability of older children means that the mandatory adoption training course given by the Adoption Facilities Foundation should be based on the adoption of a special needs child and/or older child. This course also prepares prospective adoptive parents for other aspects of inter-country adoption. In addition to the mandatory adoption information and preparation training course, the Video Interaction Support provided by the Adoption Facilities Foundation should become mandatory for families with whom an adoption child was placed recently. This preventive Video Interaction Support has been part of the follow-up care since 2000 and is well-established and accepted by the Dutch adoption field. The method applies video-feedback and is based on empirical evidence. Furthermore, preventive support helps to reduce the cost of curative care later on. The growing number of special needs children and older children make it all the more obvious that adequate attention for adoption related problems by the Minister for Youth and Family and the provinces is a pressing issue.

Regardless of whether a child is raised in a traditionally closed or a more open adoption situation, openness about adoption is essential. The Child Welfare Council should explicitly discuss the preparedness to be forthright about relinquishment and adoption with the prospective adoptive parents; the results of this discussion should be taken into consideration when making the recommendation.

2.3 Waiting Lists

The fifth chapter addresses the waiting list in the adoption process up until the granting of the adoption certification and the adoption capacity (the number of children eligible for adoption in the Netherlands). It also discusses foster care as an alternative to inter-country adoption and the cost of adoption for (prospective) adoptive parents.

The fact that there are more prospective adoptive parents than foreign children available for inter-country adoption causes a bottleneck in the adoption process. This bottleneck should preferably be located at the beginning of the process by using a waiting list rather than during the mediation phase, i.e. after the adoption certification has been granted. After all, the licence holders will be under greater pressure to complete an adoption as quickly as possible, for example because the age limit is approaching, after the adoption certification has been granted. This may result in an increase of irregularities. The consequence of the waiting list could be that there is a considerable lapse of time between the first registration and the decision regarding the adoption certification. In some cases, the adoption certification is refused because a prospective adoptive parent has reached the age limit. The child's interest, however, should be put before the interest of prospective adoptive parents, even if this implies that some will not be granted an (extension of the) adoption certification due to their age.

Prospective parents' expectations as to the possibilities of adopting a child should be managed optimally. This would reduce the number of people who apply for an adoption certification, put themselves on the waiting list and withdraw later on. The information supplied by the Adoption Facilities Foundation, the Dutch Central Authority, the Child Welfare Council and the licence holders already points out the difficulties involved in realising the adoption of a foreign child and the reasons for this. Matters that spring to mind are the low number of children eligible for adoption, age, special needs children and requirements made by the countries of origin which can be far-reaching, such as demands with respect to the prospective parent's weight. The supply of information should focus on this. It is definitely **not** the government's job to facilitate an increase in the number of children eligible for adoption in the Netherlands.

2.4 Foster Care as an Alternative?

As an alternative to adoption it may be worth considering foster care as a solution for the shortage of foster families, which would also enable prospective adoptive parents to start a family sooner. Study has shown that waiting lists are a problem in foster care, but these are not really caused by a shortage of foster parents. The demand for foster care is, however, expected to rise. In anticipation of present bottlenecks and future developments, the government should examine whether the recruitment of prospective adoptive parents for foster parentage would boost the number of potential foster parents and shorten the waiting list for prospective adoptive parents. Any further steps, such as the introduction of the weak adoption for a permanent placement within a foster family with the perspective of permanent care could also be examined.

The cost of inter-country adoption is high and many people who would like to adopt a child refrain from doing so due to financial restrictions, certainly now that adoption expenses are no longer (partly) tax deductible. This is not a desirable situation and therefore (prospective) adoptive parents should be compensated. The amounts of compensation paid in Norway and Denmark (€ 4,760,- en € 5,400,-, respectively) may serve as an example. The payment should, however, be conditional upon the completion of the recognition process of section 7 Private International Law Adoption Act, including the conversion of a weak adoption into a strong adoption (regardless of whether it is a Convention adoption or a non-Convention adoption), as a result of which the adopted child would have the Dutch nationality at the time of the compensation payment.

III. The Financial Aspects of Adoption

The third chapter of this contribution focuses on the financial aspects of inter-county adoption. Until now, it has proven to be nearly impossible to make clear arrangements in the inter-country adoption practice on the costs related to inter-country adoption. Practices should be more transparent than they are now, and that applies to the states of origin as well as to the receiving states.[15] As many of the sending states are poor and suffer from the consequences of poverty, there is a greater risk of inter-country adoption becoming a »commodity trade«. Those involved in the adoption process are faced with an extensive range of costs, expenses and fees at

---

15 See International Social Service, »On the shared responsibility of receiving States and States of origin in the setting of inter-country adoption costs«, Monthly Review No 6/2008, June 2008, Editorial, p. 1-2.

every stage of the inter-country adoption process: translation fees, administrative expenses, cost for medical examinations (of the adoptive parents and adoptive children), costs charged by the children's homes and other »supplying« institutions, and travel and accommodation expenses.

Adoption is sometimes a source of income and there are cases of inter-country adoption being exploited for financial gains. One may wonder whether subsidies to licence holders or the compensation of the cost incurred by adoptive parents in connection with inter-country adoption are a good idea.

1. Adoption as a Source of Income

As already indicated earlier, the adoption process is vulnerable for many different reasons. The »demand« largely exceeds the »supply« and it is understandable and almost inevitable that this situation leads to exploitation. This particularly holds true for the financial aspects of the inter-country adoption process.

Firstly, some organisations are willing to pay substantial amounts for an adoption child and in some countries, such as India, inter-country adoptions are more profitable than domestic ones.[16] Children are then placed in the countries with the highest bid. Countries that are willing to pay higher prices for a child, such as Spain, France, Italy and the USA are increasingly offered more and more children, whereas the well-behaved countries such as the Netherlands and the Scandinavian countries are offered fewer children. Roelie Post refers in her book to a statement by the World Bank in 2000 that a child is worth money: »bankable.«[17] In a way, adoption is a money-making industry.[18] This is a branch in which a lot of money can be made by perceiving children as commodities. This is worsened by the fact that the distance between the sending and the receiving

---

16 R. Post: »Some adoption NGOs selected babies at the maternity wards, and placed them in a foster family until their adoption was arranged. These foster families received a much higher salary than those hired under the normal Romanian foster family scheme. As a result, foster families for children that were not meant for intercountry adoption had become hard to find.« R. Post (2007), p. 50.
17 R. Post, present at the »Conference on Children Deprived of Parental Care: Rights and Realities, Unicef/World Bank, Budapest, Hungary, 22-24 October 2000, organized by Unicef and the Worldbank, wrote this in het book »Romania, for export only, The untold story of the Romanian ›orphans‹ «, 2007, p. 71. See also D.M. Smolin, Child Laundering: How the Intercountry Adoption System Legitimizes and Incentives the Practices of Buying, Trafficking, Kidnapping, and Stealing Children, The Wayne Law Review, 2005, Volume 52-113, p. 175.
18 R. Post, infra note 16 p. 274.

state in inter-country adoptions is often large, which effectively means a final and irreversible separation. [19] In this context the word »commodification« is often used.[20]

In relation to inter-country adoption, the economic principle that demand precedes supply is substantiated by the demand of prospective adoptive parents for adoption children. The urgency felt by some prospective adoptive parents to adopt and the fact that money can be made through adoption may lead (or tempt) people to undertake inter-country adoptions without due consideration of the obvious interest of the child.

Secondly, inter-country adoption can also be a source of income on which people or institutions depend. This leads to the unnecessary continuation of inter-country adoption. William Duncan says the following in this regard: »A tricky matter in many countries of origin is the practice of using the adoption process between countries as a way to ensure certain financial contributions to the activities and the development of youth welfare work in these countries.«[21] A Swedish report adds:

> »Just as fast as the adoption costs rise as a result of the competition between receiving states, there is also the risk of creating reliance on the income from the inter-country adoption work in the children's countries of origin. If people are willing to pay substantial amounts on top of the compensation for the actual cost, it may become financially more attractive to make children available for inter-country adoption than to promote domestic adoptions or placement in foster families. These cases of inter-country adoption may hinder positive local developments, which is unacceptable. This practice means that there is a risk that inter-country adoptions contribute to the continuation of structures with archaic ideas about women and illegitimate or disabled children that are unacceptable for Sweden. Such a development is not acceptable under any circumstance. It is of the utmost importance that all parties who are involved in inter-country adoption maintain high ethical standards in adoption activities. Inter-country adoption must be

---

19 M. Strathern, Partners and Consumers: Making Relations Visible, in: A.D. Schtift (ed), The logic of the Gift, New York 1997, p. 302; B. Yngversson (2004), p. 212-214; S. Howell (2007), pp. 48.
20 M. Strathern (1997), p. 302. See also B. Yngversson (2004), p. 212 and K. Lovelock (2000), p. 929.
21 W. Duncan, The Hague Convention on Protection of Children and Co-operation in Respect of Intercountry Adoption, Its birth and prospects, in: Intercountry Adoption, Developments, trends and perspectives, P. Selman ed., London 2000, p. 49.

placed in a wider context than is the case now; until now it was mainly regarded as an alternative way of forming a family.«[22]

Rumania is a well-known example of a country which regarded inter-country adoption as a source of income. About ten years ago it was using a so-called »point system«. Adoption organisations could earn points, the number of which depended on how much was paid for the improvement of youth welfare work. The number of points was related to the number of children available for inter-country adoption. An American report commented on this practice as follows: »In practice, it does provide much needed financial support for critical child abandonment prevention and family reunification services. But the resources generated by the use of the point system come with a price. The point system inherently fails to put the best interest of the individual children involved in the adoption process first. Instead, the point system puts the goal of generating and coordinating resources for child welfare programs first. As a result of the point system, domestic adoptions and local social services – particularly child welfare services – have become inextricably linked to inter-country adoption. Most of our study participants confirmed that the point system discourages adoption of Romanian children by Romanian families.«[23]

Thirdly, bribes occur throughout the adoption process in many ways. For example, midwives in Guatemala would receive $ 50 to register the birth of a non-existing child by using the false name of the mother. By paying $ 50 to another woman, the latter would pose as the mother of a (usually stolen) child. She would be told to take the child to Guatemala City in order to »relinquish« her child for adoption. The woman would sign all required official deeds.[24] As a result of this abuse, the Netherlands suspended the adoption of children from this country.[25] It is thus customary in some countries of origin to pay a small amount to the persons or institutions involved in the adoption. The payment of bribes to foreign officials is, in principle, liable to punishment in the Netherlands (sections

---

22 Adoption – but at what price?, Summary of the report of the enquiry into Intercountry adoption and a compilation of adoption research, Stockholm, p. 2003, pp. 13, 14.
23 Michael W. Ambrose en A.M. Coburn (authors), Report on Intercountry Adoption in Romania, January 22, 2001. See also R. Post (2007), p. 31 et seq. p. 84 et seq.
24 United Nations, Economic and Social Council, Commission on human rights, Rights of the child, Report of the Special Reporter on the sale of children, child prostitution and child pornography, O. Calcetas-Santos, Addendum, Report on the mission to Guatemala, 27 january 2000, E/CN.4/2000/73/Add2.
25 See Parliamentary Papers II 2000-2001, 27 256, no. 8.

177, 177a and 178a Dutch Code on Penal Law). The use of local agents or representatives to effect the actual payment of the bribes may also be qualified as a punishable act in the Netherlands. This also applies to licence holders. Nevertheless, the Dutch Public Prosecution Service does not instigate prosecution proceedings in cases of so-called »facilitation payments«, small amounts »to make things easier«, aimed at encouraging government officials to perform their job.[26] Licence holders should be allowed to pay such »facilitation payments«, where this is customary in particular countries. However, this should only be acceptable for payments that are minor and considered acceptable.[27] Adoptions from Cambodia to the Netherlands were put on hold in 2003 after the local Dutch delegation reported cases of bribery to the Dutch Central Authority.[28] The Dutch delegation made an extensive report on the matter, in which it concluded that according to some reports the adoptive parents had to call in on 16 departments where they were expected to pay $ 100 on each

---

26 Indications of investigation and prosecution of official corruption abroad, Staatscourant. 2 July 2007, no. 124, p.14: »The OESO convention does not regard modest payments for ›facilitation‹ as payments to obtain and keep any commercial or other illegal advantage«. This type of »facilitation payments« is therefor not covered by the treaty obligation to make bribe of foreign officials punishable. (...) For the criminal liability by virtue of sections 177a and 177 of the Dutch Code of Penal Law the purpose of the bribery of the official is irrelevant. This makes »facilitation payments« punishable strictly speaking. The Prosecution Service does not regard it opportune to adopt a more stict prosecution policy with respect to foreign officials than is required by the OESO treaty. It means that acts that qualified as ›facilitation payments‹ according to the OESO convention will not be prosecuted. The factors listed below can serve as examples for this prosecution policy. A criminal investigation may be required to answer the question whether one or more of these factors justify a decision to prosecute. Factors against prosecution:
 • The official involved acted or omitted to act as a result of a statutory obligation.
 • The payment may not in any way distort competition.
 • The amounts are, absolutely as well as relatively, small.
 • The payments are made to lower ranking officials.
 • The gift must be openly recorded in the company's books and should not be concealed.
 • The foreign official must have taken the initiative with respect to the gift.
 • T International companies should be under any doubt that hiring a local agent/representative/consultant also makes them punishable.«
27 In connection with this, see also the Dutch national ombudsman Mr. Oosting, ›Report of the Investigation into supervision on the Meiling Foundation in relation to possible abuse with respect to adoption from India during 1995-2002 (*Verslag van een onderzoek naar het toezicht op de Stichting Meiling in verband met de mogelijke misstanden met betrekking tot adoptie uit India in de periode 1995 – 2002, in Dutch*), The Hague, September 2007, p. 12, which gives a similar opinion.
28 See Parliamentary Papers II 2003-2004, 28 457, no 7.

occasion. The rule of thumb, and according to a statement by an adoption parent: »the higher the bribe, the faster the process...«[29]

The media are flush with examples in which the relinquishment of a child takes place in an inappropriate manner. »An Albanian gang was accused of having taken away a three-year old boy from his parents in the Albanian harbour town Dürres in exchange for a TV set. The little boy was delivered to a childless Italian couple in Calabria for €5,000. (...)«[30]

It is particularly single mothers who can be pressurised into relinquishing their child. In her dissertation, Pien Bos writes that her research has demonstrated that adoption as intervention to take children from homes actually encourages the relinquishment of children. The mothers who participated in her research explained how today s legal adoption system put them under pressure to relinquish their child. [31]

2. *Financial Abuse of Inter-Country Adoption*

Inter-country adoption is susceptible to undesired and irregular manipulation due to the prospect of financial gains when children are put up for inter-country adoption. Fortunately, this is acknowledged worldwide. Article 21 CRC explicitly states that Member States must take appropriate measures to ensure that inter-country adoption does not lead to improper financial gains by those involved. By virtue of article 4 of the Hague Adoption Convention the consent of the persons, institutions and authorities involved in the country of origin must not be obtained against payment or in exchange for any other consideration. This must be established by the competent authorities in the countries of origin. Section 20 paragraph 3 of the PFCAA stipulates that a licence holder may not pay a disproportional amount for services supplied in connection with the mediation. This provision is enforced by requiring the licence holder to supply information on his relations with institutions abroad (section 20 paragraph 4 of the PFCAA).

Supervision from the Netherlands on the enforcement of the said provision of the Convention and other legal requirements should be tightened. It is of the utmost importance that licence holders are fully transparent with regard to the funds flowing from the Netherlands into the countries

---

29 The Royal Netherlands Embassy in Bangkok, International child adoption in Cambodia, a situation report, May 2003, p. 10.
30 De Volkskrant, 30 september 2003.
31 P. Bos, Once a mother, Relinquishment and adoption from the perspective of unmarried mothers in South India,(dissertation), Nijmegen 2008, p. 275.

of origin and how these funds are spent. This should not only apply to the amounts paid by licence holders to countries of origin, but also to those amounts paid directly by prospective adoptive parents to persons or institutions in the country of origin. The Quality Framework for Inter-Country Adoption Licence Holders gives more detailed rules on the information to be provided by licence holders. Meticulous monitoring of the Framework's test criteria is essential to ensure proper insight into the financial situation of the contacts abroad.[32] It is a fact that the monetary flow always starts at the prospective adoptive parent and ends abroad. As the licence holder is the party that liaises with the authorities, persons or institutions abroad and is also a determining factor in the adoption process, every licence holder is also responsible for monitoring the flows of money of such a foreign contact. This not only applies to the funds flowing from the licence holder to his contact, but, in principle, also to the funds flowing from the prospective adoptive parent directly to the contact, including any other allocation of those funds by the foreign contact.

It would be advisable that foreign contacts submit an auditor‹s report. The problem is, however, that many countries are not familiar with audits and the auditor's report as is customary in the Netherlands.

3. Subsidies for Licence Holders

Dutch licence holders are legal persons who have been granted a permit to offer mediation services in connection with the placement of a foreign child with a view to his adoption (sections 1, 15 and 16 PFCAA). The Kalsbeek Committee has studied whether the creation of a subsidy for licence holders would improve the quality of the adoption process. The Committee pointed out that restraint should be exercised with respect to granting subsidies to licence holders. After all, subsidies may lead to the government actually promoting inter-country adoption, which is not considered the government‹s task in the Netherlands.

On the other hand, subsidies for licence holders may enable the government to direct the adoption process. The PFCAA, however, in addition to other instruments, already provides adequate directive instruments. Consequently, a subsidy aimed at preventing licence holders from processing adoptions that do not satisfy the conditions laid down in statutes and treaties in order to raise their »turnover« levels, will not be required.

---

32 Quality Framework for Licence holders Inter-country Adoption, The Hague: Ministry of Justice, June 2008. p. 27-29.

On the other hand, it is important that the government provide financial support to ensure that the standards of quality and professionalism as set by the Quality Framework for Inter-Country Adoption Licence Holders are met and enforced. This means that a structural subsidy for licence holders aimed at enforcing quality standards is appropriate after all. If the government fails to offer licence holders the required facilities, there is a risk that the licence holders will charge the costs related to scaling-up and quality standards to the prospective adoptive parents. That would be absolutely undesirable because these costs are already high. The government should not grant such a subsidy, however, before the licence holder has completed an average of 30 adoption procedures per year.

4. Cost Compensation for Adoptive Parents

The cost of inter-country adoption is high and many people who would like to adopt a child cannot do so due to financial restrictions, certainly once adoption expenses are no longer (partly) tax deductible in the Netherlands.[33] This is less desirable and that is why it is recommended that (prospective) adoptive parents are compensated in some way. Some people regard inter-country adoption as a form of child protection, which would imply government compensation for the cost incurred. It's true, adoption is aimed at the protection of a child but that does not make it a child protection order. It is an autonomous legal instrument which creates legal family ties and, as a result, has legal consequences that continue to apply after the child has come of age.[34] The reason for compensation, if any, of the adoption parents is therefore not that adoption is a child protection order.

---

33 Prospective adoptive parents pay € 900 for the mandatory training course and the Minstry of Justice annually supplements the deficits by € 300,000. Home studies by the Child Welfare Council cost € 4.8 milion every year. Mediation services by the licence holders range from € 5000 to 30,000, to be paid by the prospective adoptive parents (in Denmark on average € 10,400 and Norway on average € 11.800). The (personnel) expenses of the Central Authority are €600,000 annually. The activities of the Inspection Youth Welfare Work in this respect are € 100,000 annually. The programme mininstry Youth and Family pays an annual subsidy of € 650.000 to the Video Interaction and support and follow-up care. The central government also pays € 3.7 milion annually by virtue of section 39 of the Act on Income Tax as a result of the tax deductability of adoption expenses, which will be abolished on 1 January 2009. Furthermore, the Ministry of Foreign Affairs pays for the activities in the field of inter-country adoption.

34 See also: Independent Panel of Family Law Experts of EU Member States, Summary of opinion on the matter of adoptions, Brussels, 19 May 2004, not published but included in: R. Post, Romania, for export only, 2007, p. 147 as far as relevant.

One can think of different modalities for this compensation. If the government wants to compensate adoption parents, it must do it in such a way as to ensure that the quality of the adoption process is maintained under any circumstance. One of the debits is the amount of € 900,- for the mandatory information training course. More than half of the applicants for an adoption certification withdraw after having received this bill. The receipt of the bill apparently makes many prospective adoptive parents wonder whether they wish to pursue the adoption process. That decision must be made as early as possible in the process. Considering the current waiting list, the € 900,- bill is an appropriate threshold which would disappear if prospective adoptive parents were granted compensation in this phase of the adoption process.

Another modality would be making government funds available to licence holders as a result of which the prospective adoptive parents would be charged less by the licence holders. But that would in fact imply that licence holders would be granted a subsidy to cover a part of their expenses, which is not desirable. The Kalsbeek Committee is in favour of compensating the adoptive parents after the arrival of the adoptive child in the Netherlands. This is what happens in countries such as Norway and Denmark. The amounts paid out in these countries are € 4,760.- and € 5,400.- respectively. A similar amount would be appropriate in the Dutch situation. The payment should be subject, however, to the completion of the recognition procedure of section 7 Private International Law Adoption Act, including the conversion of a weak adoption into a strong adoption (regardless of whether it is a Convention adoption or a non-Convention adoption), which means that the adopted child has the Dutch nationality.[35]

IV. Conclusions

The trend in the Netherlands is that fewer prospective adoptive parents apply for inter-country adoptions. Gradually, more and more people are opting for foster care rather than adoption. The existing waiting lists are causing more prospective adoptive parents to withdraw because they realise that their chance of adopting a foreign child is slim. While the number of adoptions grew annually until 2005, there has been a decline

---

35 In the meanwhile Dutch government has decided to give adoptive parents € 3700,- from January 1, 2009. See Parliamentary Papers II 2008-2009, 29 689 and 31 265, no 231.

since then. These data make prospective adoptive parents readjust their expectations, as they become more aware of their slim chance of adopting a child. About 95 % of the prospective adoptive parents regard adoption as a way to start a family. The remaining 5 % opt for adoption for idealistic reasons: they want to offer a child a good and reliable home.

As demand exceeds supply in inter-country adoption, there is a risk of »child trafficking«. As set out earlier, this easily leads to financial exploitation. Adoption is a source of income to many and poor mothers are forced to »sell« their child.

Financial exploitation therefore needs to be tackled. To combat exploitation it is above all essential that all parties involved in inter-country adoption strictly adhere to the rules of the Convention on the Rights of a Child and the Hague Adoption Convention. Therefore, restricted subsidies to licence holders and compensation payments for adoptive parents (after completion of the adoption) can be justified in view of the aim of processing solely »clean« adoptions.

Furthermore, it is imperative that the practice of do-it-yourself prospective adoptive parents, who make their own contacts with authorities, persons or institutions in the country of origin of their choice in order to »acquire« an adopted child, be abolished. Government supervision of every individual adoption process should be tightened. All this with a view to these children's primary interest.

And finally, there is always the awareness that these »solutions« are not the be all and end all and remain liable for misuse. Therefore, preferred solutions still focus on: facilitating the return of children to their own parent(s), improving the status of single mothers, promoting adoptions in the country of origin and, as is the trend in the Netherlands, encouraging prospective adoptive parents to seriously consider foster care.

Adoption in a Globalized World

Katarzyna Bagan-Kurluta[1]

In Roman times and in the 19th century adoption was an institution to pass property or or to have an heir; the family relations produced by it were of mere importance. In modern times adoption is an essential instrument of imitation of family life for children – orphans. The main aim is to provide them new, stable families, the main principle is the best interest of a child. In that sense a lack of economic importance of adoption is connected with the will of childless people to adopt for any cost and sometimes with a lack of state money to cover the cost of living of orphans.

The regulation of intercountry adoption and its relation to domestic adoption may be influenced by the divison of countries according to adoption practice: into those that »import« or »export« children. The former, including well-developed countries such as the U.S.A.[2], Canada and other Western European countries, is characterized by relatively small number of children waiting to be adopted; the number of potential adopters, however, is big, which tendency is proved by data related to adoptions completed in 1960: in the U.S. – 130 000, in Great Britain – 18 000, in Germany – 8 000, and in France – 4 000. What is more, in late 90's of the last century, in Germany there was one child to 25 couples ready to adopt.[3] The lack of children for adoption in Ireland is shown by the number of completed procedures: in 1981 there were 1191 adoptions, and only 648

---

1 University of Bialystok, Poland.
2 On the other hand this state is also a source of children for intercountry adoptions. Because of lack of data concerning a number of children leaving USA in connection with adoption, it is only possible to state that they mostly go to Canada and Europe. According to Canadian Adoption Council, during a period 1993-2002 Canadians adopted 786 American children: D. Rachford, Statistically Speaking: Intercountry Adoption, Political Sensitivity, and the United States, 25 Child. Legal Rts. J. 2005, p. 66.
3 A. Ładyżynski, Uwarunkowania weryfikacji, przygotowania i przeprowadzenia procesu adopcyjnego w wybranych krajach, in: K. Ostrowska, E. Milewska (ed.), Adopcja. Teoria i praktyka, Centrum Metodyczne Pomocy Psychologiczno-Pedagogicznej Ministerstwa Edukacji Narodowej, Warsaw 1999, p. 108-111.

in 1991, with 380 children adopted by their relatives. A new adoption act introduced in 1991[4] resulted in over 300 applications for adoption of Romanian children, submitted by Irish families. The latter group comprises poorer, high birth rate countries, where the opportunities for adoption are better. This is due to significant number of orphans (social orphans included), who arouse lower interest (for example, Asian or South American countries[5]).

The initial sharpness of the division into richer (importing) and poorer (exporting) countries was questioned because of South Korea that, despite its relatively strong economic position, was still treated as a source of children for American adoptive parents. Another factor that weakened the established division were transformations inside the communist countries and the resulting demise of the bloc. Russia, formerly considered an empire, is now – along with China – a source country of most children adopted abroad.[6] Other countries sending large quantities of children were Bulgaria and Romania, with Poland ranking among the first twenty countries with the highest rate of children export.[7] So, it is difficult to speak of a clear-cut division into two groups (especially when taking into account the countries where adoption is either illegal or not regulated by law, being inconsistent with the Koran) – the division that allows for permanent attribution to one group or another.

As shown by information recorded by American Department of State and Canadian Adoption Council, 2005 saw a slow down in intercountry adoption procedures (Haiti, Moldavia, Philippines, Russia) and temporary (Azerbaijan, Belarus, Georgia, Sierra Leone, Ukraine) or permanent (Cambodia, Guatemala, Romania) resignation from these procedures

---

4 1991 Adoption Act (No. 14/1991), Irish Legislation http://www.bailii.org/ie/legis/num_act/1991/zza14y1991.1.html#zza14y1991s10 (12.07.07).
5 Intercountry adoptions are also for these states a source of big income. According to J. G. Stein (A Call to End Baby Selling: Why the Hague Convention on Intercountry Adoption Should Be Modified to Include the Consent Provisions of the Uniform Adoption Act, 24 »Thomas Jefferson Law Review«, 2001-2002, p.65), it is $ 15-20 mln per annum for South Korea, $ 5 mln for Guatemala, Honduras has earned $ 2 mln during the first 9 months of year 1991.
6 M. Pereboom, The European Union and International Adoption, http://www.adoptionpolicy.org/pdf/4-28-05-MPereboomTheEUandInternationAdoption.pdf. (12.03.07), N. B. Graff, Intercountry Adoption and the Convention of the Rights of a Child: Can the Free Market in Children Be Controlled?, 27 Syracuse J. Int'l L.& Com., 2000, p. 406.
7 E. Holewińska-Łapińska, Prawne przesłanki kwalifikowania »rodziców adopcyjnych« a praktyka sądowa w sprawach o przysposobienie, in: K. Ostrowska, E. Milewska (ed.), op. cit., p. 38.

due to changes in law in the countries where formerly many children were adopted.[8] On the other hand, at the turn of the 21st century there was a steady increase of intercountry adoptions to richer countries. This tendency is exemplified by Sweden, where such adoptions started on a small scale in the 50's of the 20th century – in 1969-2004 at least 40 thousand children entered Sweden, with about 800-1100 children adopted per annum at the turn of and in the first decade of the 21st century.[9] In some countries the changes in law were followed by the change of adoption policy into a more liberal one, which was motivated by large disproportions between the number of children living in orphanages and the number of adoptions (in Croatia, for example, in 2002 only 135 children out of 1500 staying in orphanages were adopted[10]). The multitude of Romanian children adopted by American, Canadian, French and Italian families is the result of Nicolae Ceausescu's regime and his anti-abortion and pro-life policy (including the lack of legal regulation of adoption[11]) and the period following his death when it came to daylight that thousands of abandoned and ill children, often infected with HIV through blood transfusion, had been stranded in streets or vegetating in guardianship centres[12]. Between 1989 and 2003, 8300 immigrant visas (of which 2594 only in 1991) were issued to Romanian orphans coming to the States, and 600 – to Canada in 1995-2001[13]. Romania's efforts to join the European Union involved the necessity of its children's policy to be revised. In December 2000, the Romanian Prime Minister Nastase announced the suspension of intercountry adoption. On June 21st, 2001 the Romanian Adoption Committee placed a one-year moratorium on intercountry adoption due to corruption. Pursuant to two ordinances issued by the Romanian government

---

8 *Adoption Council of Canada*, http://adoption.ca/ (8.05.07).
9 Å. Saldeen, The Children's Ombudsman, Adoption by Homosexual Partners and Assisted Reproduction, in: A. Bainham, The International Survey of Family Law, 2004 Edition, Published on behalf of the International Society of Family Law, Jordan Publishing Limited, Bristol 2004, p. 440.
10 D. Hrabar, The Protection of Weaker Family Members: The Ombudsman for Children, Same-Sex Unions, Family Violence and Family Law, in: A. Bainham, The International Survey of Family Law, 2004 Edition, Published on behalf of the International Society of Family Law, Jordan Publishing Limited, Bristol 2004, p. 112-113, 115-117,120-121.
11 O. A. Djużewa, Problemy zakonodatielstwa o mieżdunarodnom usynowlienii, »Gosudarstwo i Prawo« 1995, no. 6, p. 41-42.
12 M. Pereboom, op. cit.
13 Data according to: US Department of State http://www.travel.state.gov./family/adoption resources 02.html, *Adoption Institute* http://www.adoptioninstitute.org?FactOverview/international.html and BC Families of Adoptive Children http://www.bcadoption.com/articles/intercountry/romania.htm.

in the same year, child protection was made one of the priorities of the governmental program for years 2001-2004, implemented in relation to Romania's integration in the EU. Also, it was allowed to carry out intercountry adoption proceedings under extraordinary circumstances (such as these involving children with special needs), provided that adoption is for the benefit of a child. During the next two years Romania prepared a package of draft laws referring to the protection of children's rights and adoption. New adoption law was approved in May 2004 and stipulated that intercountry adoption can only be possible among relatives in the second degree of kinship. In the meantime, during the secrecy of adoption information came out of proceedings being in progress of 105 Romanian children to be adopted by Italian families. Similarly, when the ordinance of conditional intercountry adoption was still binding, 1115 such adoptions were completed (384 children were adopted by adoptive parents from the U.S., 230 – from Italy, 224 – from Spain, 73 – from France, 49 – from Israel and 44 – from Germany)[14].

In Poland intercountry adoptions were reported at the turn of the 60's of the 20th century – they were often intrafamily adoptions[15], particularly done by foreigners of Polish origin, or Polish citizens living abroad[16]. Obviously, it would be hard to assume that such adoptions, especially involving moving abroad (to the western countries) might have appeared as early as during the Stalinist regime, since orphans were then treated as state-owned children and trained to become »janissaries of communism« who would not need neither family upbringing nor family ties[17] – a consequence of post-revolutionary idea of the primacy of social over family education[18]. The number of adoptions went up in the 70's of the 20th cen-

---

14 Data according to: Romania & International Adoption. Press Information, Joint Council on International Children's Services, http://www.jcics.org/JCICSPressInformationRo.pdf. (13.03.07).
15 M. Kolankiewicz, Adopcja, in: M. Kolankiewicz (ed.), Zagrożone dzieciństwo. Rodzinne i instytucjonalne formy opieki, Warsaw 1998, p. 233.
16 E. Mądrzycka, K. Olejniczak, Praktyka sądów w zakresie spraw z wniosków cudzoziemców i obywateli polskich zamieszkałych za granicą o przysposobienie obywateli polskich, »Biuletyn Ministerstwa Sprawiedliwości« 1960, no. 5-6, p. 39-55 and Przysposobienie dzieci polskich przez cudzoziemców, »Palestra« 1960, no. 9, p. 3.
17 M. Łopatkowa, Miłość i bezpieczeństwo – elementarne potrzeby dziecka w aspekcie prawnym, społecznym i wychowawczym, in: J. Komorowska (ed.), Dziecko we współczesnej Polsce, Tom II, Warsaw 1991, p. 45.
18 I. Andrejew, Oceny prawne karcenia nieletnich, Warsaw 1964, p. 75, A. I. Gojchbarg, Pierwyj kodeks zakonow RSFSR, »Proletarskaja rewolucja i prawo« 7/1918, p. 6, A. Zieliński, Sądownictwo opiekuńcze w sprawach małoletnich, Wydawnictwo Prawnicze, Warsaw 1975, p. 22.

tury; hence the belief, as it may seem, that it was then that they appeared in Poland[19] – while in other countries adoption became international after World War I[20] (however, a substantial rise in number of intercountry adoptions in the world was observed towards the end of World War II, it was connected with participation of the American troops in the conflict and, consequently, interest of American families in adopting orphans from Europe (Germany, Italy, Greece) and Asia (Japan, China): mostly out of sympathy.[21] According to the Polish Ministry of Justice, it appears that over several years (the 70's and 80's of the 20th c.), the number of intercountry adoptions done in Poland rose significantly, although general number of adoption judgments remained steady until mid 80's.[22] Figures show an abrupt rise in intercountry adoptions in 1987 and 1989 with their peak in 1991, and gradual drop after 1993, which by the doctrine is connected to Poland's ratification of the Convention on the Rights of the Child in 1991 and with a change of internal laws referring to adoption centres.[23]

---

19 A. Zieliński, Przysposobienie międzynarodowe, »Studia Iuridica« XXI/1994, p. 219.
20 R. Pawłowska, Wybrane elementy przysposobienia w polskim prawie prywatnym. Rys historyczny, »Zeszyty Naukowe Wydziału Humanistycznego Uniwersytetu Gdańskiego«, Pedagogika. Historia wychowania, 1988, no. 17, p. 69.
21 J.H.A. van Loon, International co-operation and protection of children with regard to intercountry adoption, »Recueil des Cours« 1993, VII(244), p. 229 and J. H. A. van Loon, Report on intercountry adoption. Preliminary Document No 1 of April 1990, w: Hague Conference on private international law, Proceedings of the Seventeenth Session 10 to 29 May 1993, Tome II. Adoption – co-operation, SDU Publishers/The Hague, Netherlands/1994, Annex C, p. 37-39.
22 A. Zieliński, Przysposobienie międzynarodowe, »Studia Iuridica« XXI/1994, p. 219, J. Szymańczak, Adopcja. Kancelaria Sejmu. Biuro Studiów i Ekspertyz, Information no. 70, I. Lewandowska, Adopcje – kontrowersje, niepokoje, wątpliwości, »Gazeta Prawnicza«, no. 16 (533) 1986.08.16, p. 5. Because the number of the judgments is not equally even with the number of adopted children (one judgment can be a base for adoption of more than one child - brothers and sisters), the number of children adopted in Poland was as it follows: in 1989 – 4289, 1990 – 4299, 1991 – 3827, 1992 – 3468, 1993 – 3281, 1994 – 3069, 1995 – 2978 (A. Zieliński, Przysposobienie międzynarodowe, »Studia Iuridica« XXI/1994, p. 223). To compare: in 1991 over 5 mln. adopted children lived in USA and there were 140 to 160 thousands judgments issued each year: J. S. Loomis, Adoption by Homosexuals, 18 »Ohio Northern University Law Review«, 1991-1992, p. 647.
23 A. Bałandynowicz, Adopcja formą kompensacji sieroctwa społecznego, in: K. Ostrowska, E. Milewska (ed.), op. cit., p. 25, M. Kolankiewicz, op. cit., p. 235.

Year	The number of decisions concerning placement of a child in a orphanage	The number of petitions to adopt a child	The general number of adoption judgments	The number of court judgments of intercountry adoption	Percentage of intercountry adoptions in relation to all adoptions	The number of children who left orphanages as a consequence of adoption
1951			6258			
1952			6100			
1953			6478			
1955			2719			
1957				about 60		
1958				about 60		
1959				about 60		
1960			2795			
1963			3942			
1965			1991			
1967		3816	3800			
1969		3561				
1970			1992	about 40		
1971		3794				
1973			3119			
1974			3164	57	2	
1975			3111			
1976			3700			
1977			3294	68		
1978			3354	72		
1979			3704	86		
1980		4096	3572	93	2,6	
1981		4112	3484	65	1,86	
1982		4189	3711	60	1,41	
1983		4133	3517	100	4,71	
1984		4094	3474	125	3,59	
1985		3934	3419	136	4	
1986		4094	3461	168	4,85	
1987		4000	3481	259	7,4	

1988		4035	3343	261	7,8	
1989		4289	3599	412	11,4	
1990	31684	4249	3629	506	13,9	828
1991	31986	3827	3360	523	15,6	952
1992	31007	3468	3021	480	15,8	1064
1993	29538	3281	2810	404	14,3	967
1994	29284	3069	2600	274	10,5	878
1995	29731	3054	2495	238	9,5	848
1996	30277	3008	2519	248	9,8	926
1997	30777	2877	2441	205	8,3	850
1998						1088

Was the rise in intercountry adoptions caused by Poland's opening-up or rather by the need of seeking methods of providing children with surrogate family environment also abroad? Perhaps the said rise was influenced by worsening financial situation of many Polish families, which in turn encouraged interest in the institution of foster family subsidized by the state, at the expense of adoption for which such financial assistance was not provided. It was also then that the lengthiness of proceedings concerning deprivation of parental authority for parents of children staying in orphanages was criticized[24], as well as »haste and eagerness« of proceedings concerning intercountry adoptions. It was at the same time pointed out that guardianship centres should primarily aim at tailoring most optimal form of care for each child rather than satisfying expectations of childless families and searching for a child who matches their dreams.[25] Perhaps it was Polish reality of the 80's and 90's that encouraged growing interest in Polish children as potential subject of adoption relationship – or subject of transaction, as press often had reported it.[26] After 1983, when the number of intercountry adoption actions

---

24 G. Pisarski, Trzeba wybrać złoty środek, »Gazeta Prawnicza« 1989, no. 13, I. Lewandowska, W kolejce po dziecko, »Gazeta Prawnicza« 1984, no. 24.
25 I. Lewandowska, Adopcje – kontrowersje, niepokoje, wątpliwości, »Gazeta Prawnicza«, no. 16 (533) 1986.08.16, p. 5, Z. Wasilkowska, Prawna ochrona rodziny, in: D. Graniewska (ed.), Socjalne i prawne środki ochrony macierzyństwa i rodziny, Warsaw 1976, p. 158, J. Zaporowska, J. Mazurkiewicz, Coś zróbmy, coś zaróbmy, »Rzeczpospolita«, 14/11/1995, J. Zaporowska, J. Mazurkiewicz, Dywagacje bez końca, »Rzeczpospolita«, 02/10/1995, I. Wagner, Reakcje instytucjonalne wobec sieroctwa społecznego i adopcji, Częstochowa 1995/1996, p. 76.
26 For instance: Jak się sprzedaje polskie dzieci. Adopcja dolarami podszyta, »Express Wie-

rose, Poland, as a source of white children available for adoption was considered a »rather rich adoption market«.[27] On the other hand, according to government figures of 1985, there were relatively few court orders of deprivation of parental authority (18 232 orders of deprivation, 6 281 of suspension and 139 629 of limitation of parental authority)[28]. At the end of 1994 and the beginning of 1995 the press[29] gave wide coverage to a debate concerning child trafficking and its relation to intercountry adoption arranged to bring financial benefit. The debate was provoked by the reports of two Polish lawyers charged with criminal offence of participating in child trafficking and accepting material profits[30].

The claim that adoption may be connected with child trafficking is based on the results of research concerning south-eastern European countries and carried out by International Organization for Migration (IOM) and NEXUS Institute to Combat Human Trafficking (NEXUS Institute), as well as the controversy over procedures of placing children for adoption in the U.S., and adoption-related figures. The fact that child trafficking is a large-scale business is shown by UNICEF reports: it has been documented that over 1.2 million of children are trafficked every year. According to the American Department of State, 600–800 thousand people half of them children – are trafficked to the U.S. annually.[31] 1999's report issued by the U.N. on Guatemala illustrates how trade mechanisms work in intercountry adoption: only in 1999, 1500 Guatemalan children were sold abroad, which figure constituted 95% of all adoptions there.[32] Many such cases were preceded by illegal actions, including newborn registration by a woman who had not given birth to the child (with false particulars of a mother), theft or purchase of a child whose age matched the registered baby, providing a false mother to renounce parental rights and give consent to adoption, at the same time handing the child over to

---

czorny«, 30.01.1992, Niemowlę – towar poszukiwany, »Dziennik lubelski«, 6.07.1993, Polak za pieniądze. Zostać Niemcem lub Francuzem, »Super Express«, 15.06.1993.
27 Ż. Semprich, Los nie zawsze szczęśliwy. Instytut Wymiaru Sprawiedliwości alarmuje, »Rzeczpospolita«, 10.07.1998.
28 M. Łopatkowa, Miłość i bezpieczeństwo – elementarne potrzeby dziecka w aspekcie prawnym, społecznym i wychowawczym, in: J. Komorowska (ed.), Dziecko we współczesnej Polsce, Tom II, Warsaw 1991, p. 52.
29 »Rzeczpospolita«, »Gazeta Wyborcza«, »Palestra«.
30 H. Pasek, Adwokaci i handel dziećmi, »Rzeczpospolita«, 22.09.1994, Dzieci za dolary, »Gazeta Wyborcza«, 22.09.1994.
31 K. Schulte, Statistically Speaking: Child Trafficking, Current Concerns, and the United States, 25 Child. Legal Rts. 2005, p. 55.
32 J. G. Stein, op. cit., p.66-69, 77.

a guardianship institution that went on with further adoption proceedings.[33] There were also reports on the practice of falsifying children's particulars in mid 90's of 20th c. in Argentina[34] and Peru, where after 1984 many dishonest lawyers took up child trafficking.[35] As for Ecuador, up to 1990 remarkable difficulties were reported in domestic adoptions, with intercountry adoption being extremely easy[36].

State	Price for a child received by a mother	»Black market« price for a child
Philippines	$ 40	
El Salvador	$ 65	
Sri Lanka	$ 50	$ 1 000 - $ 5 000
Guatemala	$ 50	
Peru	$ 40	
Romania	$ 200	$ 5 000 - $ 10 000
Ecuador		$ 8 000 - $ 10 000

Table according to: C. Maldonado, A. Marques, L. Hayes Vertulfo, B. Cordero, C. Valdez, op. cit., p. 201, 206, »Expreso Newspaper«, Guayaquil, Ecuador, February 16, 1992 and »Time Magazine« Statistics 1990.

Child trafficking observed in Russia was of slightly different nature: the practice allegedly involved American agents to recruit pregnant women, paid $ 15.000 fee by adoption agencies, and the women who came to the

---

33 K. M. Wittner, Curbing Child-Trafficking in Intercountry Adoptions: Will International Treaties and Adoption Moratoriums Accomplish the Job in Cambodia?, 12, »Pacific Rim Law & Policy Journal«, 2003, p. 601, according to: Report on the Mission to Guatemala, Commission on Human Rights, 56th Sess., Agenda Item 13, w: 4 U. N. Doc. E/CN.4/2000/73/Add.2 (2000).
34 C. P. Grosman, D. B. Inigo, Adoption of children in Argentina by local citizens and foreign nationals, in: Jaffe E. D. (ed.), Intercountry adoptions. Laws and Perspectives of »Sending« Countries, Martinus Nijhoff Publishers, Dordrecht/Boston/London 1995, p. 164-165.
35 E.W. de Sztrancman, I. Sztrancman Waisblack, Peruvian foreign adoptions, in: Jaffe E. D. (ed.), Intercountry adoptions. Laws and Perspectives of »Sending« Countries, Martinus Nijhoff Publishers, Dordrecht/Boston/London 1995, p. 185-187.
36 C. Maldonado, A. Marques, L. Hayes Vertulfo, B. Cordero, C. Valdez, Adoption in Ecuador, in: Jaffe E. D. (ed.), Intercountry adoptions. Laws and Perspectives of »Sending« Countries, Martinus Nijhoff Publishers, Dordrecht/Boston/London 1995, p. 200-201.

U.S. to deliver their babies and left the country alone.[37] The relations of corruption and child trafficking were true also of Brazil of the 90's. The Brazilian social services revealed a series of cases in which judges coerced biological mothers to stop contacting their children. As a result, the mothers were deprived of their parental authority and the children were available for adoption. The majority of said cases referred to children who came from north-eastern region of the country, were white or of German (or European) origin. Furthermore, according to the Brazilian federal police, at that time there were 1500 legally adopted children to 3000 of those illegally leaving the country.[38] According to the research on human trafficking, there emerged a new (if not just recently discovered) practice of infant trafficking with the purpose of illegal adoption to be completed in various EU countries.[39] Among the scrutinized cases of children trafficking in Bulgaria, Moldavia, Romania, Albania, Bosnia and Herzegovina, Croatia, Macedonia, Serbia, Montenegro and Kosovo, there were 8 documented cases of human trafficking with the aim of placing a child for adoption, all of which took place in 2004 and involved Bulgarian citizens. Other similar cases were revealed by Italian, Greek and French police and involved pregnant Bulgarian women taken to other countries to deliver their babies there and hand them over to criminal organized groups specializing in adoption arrangements. Apart from proceedings being under way outside Bulgaria, the Bulgarian border protection services saw to 30 cases of children trafficked for adoption to the EU countries. Despite the fact that these figures refer to a relatively small number of children coming from one country exclusively, it may be assumed that this is only the tip of the iceberg, with many other cases of not necessarily Bulgarian children hidden beneath. There are mentions by the very author of said research of actions pending in the cases of: a child sold by a mother in Moldavia, eight children (7 Albanian and 1 Belarusian) taken to Italy for adoption, allegations regarding child trafficking in Bosnia and Herzegovina for adoption in Germany and Austria, or an Albanian child sold for adoption to Italy.[40]

---

37 J. G. Stein, op. cit., p. 66-69, 77.
38 D. Carvalho da Silva, The legal procedures for adopting children in Brazil by citizens and foreign nationals, in: Jaffe E.D. (ed.), Intercountry adoptions. Laws and Perspectives of »Sending« Countries, Martinus Nijhoff Publishers, Dordrecht/Boston/London 1995, p. 129.
39 R. Surtees, Child Trafficking in Southeastern Europe: Different Forms of Trafficking and Alternative Interventions, 14 »Tulane Journal of International & Comparative Law«, 2005-2006, p. 459.
40 R. Surtees, op. cit., p. 478.

In the United States the adoption controversy refers mainly to private institutions and individuals acting as agents along with state establishments authorized to perform activity of the kind. On the one hand, it is pointed out that parental constitutional right to decide on the upbringing and future of their children entails the possibility of selecting and providing adoptive family for their children without a public institution as an intermediary[41], and, provided such actions are under judicial supervision, everybody should be allowed to perform them[42]. On the other hand, participation of a public institution, or state-authorized agency is supported by the principle that it is in the interest of the state, in connection with *parens patriae,* to think of children first, even at the expense of breaking or weakening family ties with their biological parents[43]; another argument to back the point is the belief that »adoption via a private adoption agent« is synonymous with »black market adoption«[44]. The latter opinion is actually proved correct in American literature on the subject of child trafficking: you can meet there with the claim that American agencies in general have their employees overseas to recruit children for adoption in Latin America, Asia and Europe and pay them at least $ 10.000 for a child without even taking into account the way the child was recruited. [45] The laws of most American states allow placing children in adoptive families without participation of an authorized agency if the child is adopted by a spouse of the parent or by other family member and such adoption by a non-related person is only allowed in some states[46]. However, in the states where it is impossible to follow these procedures by the parties that are not related to one another, the law permits adoption agreements between biological and potential adoptive parents; such agreements result

---

41 Survey of New Jersey Adoption Law, 16 Rutgers L. Rev., 1961-1962, p. 403.
42 R. I. Aaron, Proposals For Truce In the Holy War: Utah Adoption, 1970 »Utah Law Review«, p. 325.
43 Survey of New Jersey Adoption Law, op. cit., s. 403, the judgments: In re Jacques, 48 N.J. Super. 523, 138 A.2d 581 (CH. Div. 1958), Richard v. Collins, 45 N. J. Eq. 283, 17 Atl. 831 (E&A. 1889), and the regulation of 1953 New Jersey Revised Statutes (art. 9.2-9 to 12).
44 R. I. Aaron, op. cit., s. 325, A Road with Good Intentions. Following An Adoption Proceeding, 2 Child. Legal RTs. J., 1980-1981, p. 26.
45 D. M. Smolin, Intercountry adoption as child trafficking, 39 »Valparaiso University Law Review«, 2004-2005, p. 288.
46 In the beginning of 90's, parents were allowed to place a child in a non-related adoptional family chosen solely by them or in cooperation with lawyer, physician, nurse or social worker in 44 states and District Columbia. In 6 states (Colorado, Connecticut, Delaware, Massachusetts, Michigan, Minnesota) it was not allowed: J. S. Loomis, op. cit., p. 633.

in adoption proceeding carried out by an authorized agency[47]. Also, the majority of state statutes forbid child trafficking, at the same time reducing adoption-related costs that may be borne by adopters[48]. Acceptable costs usually include: agent fees (for agencies: 7 to 10 thousand dollars or more, for private individuals – about 20 thousand dollars), lawyer or advisor fees, reimbursement of medical expenses (incurred for the child and the child's biological mother)[49], the cost of living of expecting mother during her pregnancy.[50] Despite authority by law to incur reasonable costs by adopters, adoption should never be regarded as commercial transaction in which the mother or the agent sells product – the child – for financial profit. This being so, using adoption as a means for making unjustifiable profits is prohibited. Consequences of illegal steps taken in specific cases of child trafficking, however, are still a matter of dispute. On the one hand, courts generally refuse to withdraw the consent for adoption[51], while on the other – they order sanctions against child traffickers. However, the judgment awarded in 1994 against a lawyer who, acting as an adoption agent gave a biological mother the sum of $ 12.000 for giving her five children (including pre-born twins) up for adoption implies that such sanctions are of rather disciplinary character[52]. It is therefore difficult to speak of imposing disciplinary sanctions such as exclusion from a legal corporation, against people who do not perform legal professions or who do not institutionally deal with adoption issues. In American reality the question of child trafficking usually applies to domestic adoptions, with intercountry adoptions taken into account only when a foreign judicial decision is not recognized as final in the United States, which in turn results in the necessity of making an appropriate decision by an American court. In

---

47 D. E. Abrams, S. H. Ramsey, A Primer on Adoption Law, 52 »Juvenile and Family Court Journal«, Summer 2001, p. 29.
48 For instance according to §7-105 of Vermont Statutes it was forbidden to: pay, receive or demand money for child placement in adoptional family, parent's, legal representative's or agency's consent for adoption, renunciation of looking for an adoptional family by an adoptional agency and recruitment of pregnant women living outside the state in order to gain their children for adoption, http://198.187.128.12/vermont/lpext.dll?f=templates&fn=fs-main.htm&2.0. (2.03.07).
49 J. H. Hollinger, Introduction to Adoption Law and Practice, §1.05[3][a], in: J. H. Hollinger, Adoption Law and Practice, 2000.
50 D. E. Abrams, S. H. Ramsey, op. cit., p. 30, D. M. Smolin, Intercountry adoption as child trafficking, 39 »Valparaiso University Law Review«, 2004-2005, p. 320-323.
51 D. E. Abrams, S. H. Ramsey, op. cit., p. 30-32.
52 In re Thacker, 881 S.W.2d 307 (Tex. 1994) and Thacker v. State, 889 S.W.2d 380, 384-85 (Tex. Ct. App. 1994).

the latter case there is little likehood that the American court is informed about child trafficking practice. As it may seem, facts about child trafficking may show up in the course of legal action (pending on the territory of a foreign country) or may be disclosed by biological parents – but this seems highly doubtful, as it is them who participate in the trade and seek profit. However, sometimes the racket comes to daylight or is prevented, as it happened in Andhra Pradesh, India[53]. The business of double (if not triple) child trafficking probably started in 1995, but two other scandals involving the employees of numerous orphanages in Andhra Pradesh, American and Canadian adoption agencies and parents – members of the nomad tribe of Lambada broke in 1999 and 2001. Both cases concerned commercial transactions in which children were made available for adoption, entered into by the parents of unwanted girls and the representatives hired by orphanages; the price of a child in 1999 varied from $ 15 to $ 45. Then, the child was again subject of a deal – this time between the hireling and the orphanage, $ 220 to $ 440 for a child. Later, orphanages successfully placed the children for adoption; the price now increased to $ 2.000 – $ 3.000. In 1999 at least 228 children were sold in this way. Two years later the children were freed from orphanages and attempts were made to bring them back to their homes. Unfortunately, the whole thing was far from being successful since some children died, and some were not welcomed by their biological parents. What is more, in the course of criminal action taken in relation to the described practice, it turned out that some children were snatched and their particulars were altered. In the light of the fact that in one of orphanages, in a group of 60 other children there was one who had corneas removed from both eyes, a suspicion arose as to true intentions of the perpetrators[54].

In a globalized world there are still doubts concerning adoption (especially its intercountry form): should it be a sort of business to organize adoptions, what should be the role of a state in this business, does the traditional division into the poor (exporting children) countries and wealthy (importing them) countries still exist, can the poor state make any efforts to send children abroad for adoption – even selling them or letting future adopters to pay for certain services of its institutions – if it is not able to protect them by giving them new homes, can adoption still be treated as

---

53 D. M. Smolin, Intercountry adoption as child trafficking, 39 »Valparaiso University Law Review«, 2004-2005, p. 288.
54 D. M. Smolin, The Two Faces of Intercountry Adoption: The Significance of the Indian Adoption Scandals, 35 »Seton Hall Law Review«, 2004-2005, p. 455.

a transaction and connected with child trafficking etc. Thinking about these doubts we should consider a role of international conventions and the possibility that the new regulations will improve the image of intercountry adoption (e.g. concerning open adoptions, double authorization of adoption agencies, post adoption reports, registration of adopted children, possibility of reimbursement of costs of adoption)? The most important international instrument of cooperation is still the Hague Convention of 29 May 1993 on Protection of Children and Co-operation in Respect of Intercountry Adoption.[55] Although probably the biggest number of children was adopted to the USA, the Hague convention was not applied there until April 1, 2008 (when it entered into force) – so the effects of its application should be seen in the next years. Analysis of the data from the last fourteen years concerning the number of intercountry adoptions to the United States shows that their number in 2007 (18,748) is over twice bigger than it was in 1994 (8,333)[56]. While in 1994 the biggest number of adopted children came to the USA from South Korea (1,795), in 2007 it was China and 5,453 children being adopted.

Twenty countries »exporting« children (the biggest number of children adopted to USA in two periods: 2000–2006[57] and 1994–1999[58])

2000	2001	2002	2003	2004	2005	2006
China (06)	China (06)	China (06)	China (06)	China (06)	China (06)	China (06)
Russia	Russia	Russia	Russia	Russia	Russia	Guatemala (03)
South Korea	South Korea	Guatemala (03)	Guatemala (03)	Guatemala (03)	Guatemala (03)	Russia
Guatemala (03)	Guatemala (03)	South Korea	South Korea	South Korea	South Korea	South Korea
Romania (95)	Ukraine	Ukraine	Kazakhstan	Kazakhstan	Ukraine	Ethiopia

---

55 Although a text of a new (revised) European Convention on the Adoption of Children was just presented.
56 Taking into consideration 20 countries, where the biggest number of children had been adopted from.
57 According to: The Evan B. Donaldson Adoption Institute, International Adoption Facts 2002, http://www.adoptioninstitute.org/FactOverview/international.html (22.03.07) and U.S. Department of State: http://travel.state.gov/family/adoption/stats/stats_451.html (22.03.07).
58 According to: U.S. Department of State http://travel.state.gov/family/adoption/stats/stats_451.html. (22.03.07)

Vietnam	Romania (95)	Kazakhstan	Ukraine	Ukraine	Kazakhstan	Kazakhstan
Ukraine	Vietnam	Vietnam	India (03)	India (03)	Ethiopia	Ukraine
India (03)	Kazakhstan	India (03)	Vietnam	Haiti	India (03)	Liberia
Cambodia	India (03)	Colombia (98)	Colombia (98)	Ethiopia	Colombia (98)	Colombia (98)
Kazakhstan	Colombia (98)	Bulgaria (02)	Haiti	Colombia (98)	Philippines (96)	India (03)
Colombia (98)	Bulgaria (02)	Cambodia	Philippines (96)	Belarus (03)	Haiti	Haiti
Bulgaria (02)	Cambodia	Philippines (96)	Romania (95)	Philippines (96)	Liberia	Philippines (96)
Philippines (96)	Philippines (96)	Haiti	Bulgaria (02)	Bulgaria (02)	Taiwan*	Taiwan*
Haiti	Haiti	Belarus (03)	Belarus (03)	Poland (95)	Mexico (95)	Vietnam
Mexico (95)	Ethiopia	Romania (95)	Ethiopia	Mexico (95)	Poland (95)	Mexico (95)
Ethiopia	Belarus (03)	Ethiopia	Georgia (99)	Liberia	Thailand (04)	Poland (95)
Thailand (04)	Poland (95)	Poland (95)	Cambodia	Nepal	Brazil (99)	Brazil (99)
Poland (95)	Thailand (04)	Thailand (04)	Taiwan	Nigeria	Nigeria	Nepal
Moldova (98)	Mexico (95)	Georgia (99)	Poland (95)	Thailand (04) and Brazil (99)	Jamaica	Nigeria
Bolivia (02)	Liberia	Mexico (95)	Thailand (04)	Romania (95)	Nepal	Thailand (04)
6/20	5/20	7/20	9/20	11/20	8/20	9/20
8/20	9/20	8/20	8/20	9/20	10/20	10/20

> white with black letters – states, which are not signatories of the Hague Convention of 29 May 1993 on Protection of Children and Co-operation in Respect of Intercountry Adoption;
> light grey with black letters – states/parties of the Hague Convention of 29 May 1993 on Protection of Children and Co-operation in Respect of Intercountry Adoption (date of entering into life in brackets);
> grey with white letters – states which are the parties of the Hague Convention of 29 May 1993 on Protection of Children and Co-operation in Respect of Intercountry Adoption now, but they were not during the year analyzed (date of entering it into life in brackets);
> *Taiwan – (there is no information if the adoptions took place in China or in Taiwan -children were born in Taiwan);

- *italics* – number of states/parties of the convention in relation to the number of all examined states;
- **bold** – number of states which are not the signatories of the convention in relation to the number of all examined states:

1999	1998	1997	1996	1995	1994
Russia	Russia	Russia	China (06)	China (06)	South Korea
China (06)	**China (06)**	**China (06)**	Russia	Russia	Russia
South Korea	South Korea	South Korea	South Korea	South Korea	**China (06)**
Guatemala (03)	Guatemala (03)	Guatemala (03)	Romania *(95)*	Guatemala (03)	Paraguay *(98)*
Romania *(95)*	Vietnam	Romania *(95)*	Guatemala (03)	India (03)	Guatemala (03)
Vietnam	*India (03)*	Vietnam	India (03)	Paraguay *(98)*	*India (03)*
India (03)	Romania *(95)*	*India (03)*	Vietnam	Colombia *(98)*	Colombia *(98)*
Ukraine	Cambodia	Colombia *(98)*	Paraguay *(98)*	Vietnam	Philippines *(96)*
Cambodia	Colombia *(98)*	Philippines *(96)*	Colombia *(98)*	Philippines *(96)*	Vietnam
Colombia *(98)*	Philippines *(96)*	Mexico *(95)*	Philippines *(96)*	Romania *(95)*	Romania *(95)*
Bulgaria (02)	Ukraine	**Bulgaria (02)**	**Bulgaria (02)**	Brazil *(99)*	Ukraine
Philippines *(96)*	Mexico *(95)*	Haiti	Brazil *(99)*	**Bulgaria (02)**	Brazil *(99)*
	Bulgaria (02)	Latvia *(02)*	Latvia *(02)*	Lithuania *(98)*	**Bulgaria (02)**
	Haiti	Brazil *(99)*	Lithuania *(98)*	Chile *(99)*	Lithuania *(98)*
	Ethiopia	Ethiopia	Georgia *(99)*	Mexico *(95)*	Poland *(95)*
	Brazil *(99)*	Lithuania *(98)*	Mexico *(95)*	Ecuador *(96)*	Mexico *(95)*
	Thailand *(04)*	Poland *(95)*	Haiti	Ethiopia	Chile *(99)*
	Poland *(95)*	Bolivia *(02)*	Poland *(95)*	Japan	Honduras
	Latvia *(02)*	Hungary *(05)*	Chile *(99)*	Latvia *(02)*	Haiti
	Bolivia *(02)*	Cambodia	Thailand *(04)*	Thailand *(04)*	Ethiopia
3/12	*5/20*	*4/20*	*4/20*	*2/20*	*0/20*
5/12	**7/20**	**6/20**	**4/20**	**5/20**	**7/20**

Examination of the data proves that the number of international adoptions to the USA was bigger each year, the same can be said about the number of states/parties of the Hague convention in a group of twenty states where children were adopted from. Should we believe that lately more and more decisions regarding intercountry adoptions were made in the best interest of an adopted child? Should we believe that a best interest of a child standard has nothing in common (and will never have) with child trafficking? According to the information that the national regulations regarding intercountry adoption were changed in several countries during the last years and news about recent authorization of American adoption agencies[59] we should at least hope so.

---

59 http://www.travel.state.gov/family/adoption/stats/stats_451.html (6/10/08).

Transnational Family Finances and the United States

Ann Laquer Estin[1]

I. Introduction

Our children live in a newly global world, in families that form and extend and dissolve across international borders.[2] If it takes a village to raise a child, for some children that village is now a global one. This global village links individuals who reside in different countries, speak different languages, and live within different cultures and legal systems. In this global village, protection for children is a complex problem, which demands the cooperation of authorities from around the globe at every level of government.

Who are these new global families? They may result from migration, when individuals or family members move across national boundaries either temporarily or with the intention of settling permanently. They may be formed by international couples, with roots in different countries, who marry or come together in more fleeting relationships. They may result when parents in one nation look across borders to undertake an intercountry adoption. Family members may live together in one place, or be widely dispersed around the globe. Some families or solo migrants maintain strong ties of culture, religion, or nationality to their place of origin, while others assimilate quickly and adopt new ways in their new homes.

The diversity of families and family stories in the new global village presents unique challenges for child support. Social norms and legal requirements vary substantially around the world, even among nations with similar legal and economic systems. Each country with a tie to a particular family may have different conceptions of what relationships give rise to

---

1   University of Iowa College of Law, USA.
2   Prepared for the International Society of Family Law 13th World Conference, Vienna Austria, Sept. 16-20, 2008. I served as an observer on behalf of the ISFL during the final rounds of negotiations for the Family Maintenance Convention in The Hague in May and December 2007. My thanks to the University of Iowa College of Law for financial support that allowed me to take on this responsibility.

family support obligations, and different procedures for establishment and enforcement of such obligations. Because of these differences, the project of coordinating child support enforcement across borders has proved to be a significant challenge.[3]

Under existing multilateral treaties, a large group of nations have agreed on rules for recognition and enforcement of child support orders across international borders.[4] These agreements are important, but they do not provide mechanisms for cooperation between governments to assure that support orders are actually established and enforced. Against this landscape, the new Hague Convention on the International Recovery of Child Support and other Forms of Family Maintenance (Family Maintenance Convention)[5] is an important step forward. The treaty, intended to extend and improve on several earlier generations of multilateral international child support agreements, is the result of more than five years of work by the Permanent Bureau and member countries of the Hague Conference on Private International Law.[6] As with earlier treaties, the new convention requires member states to recognize and enforce most child and spousal maintenance orders entered in other member states. In addition, where child support is concerned, the convention implements a

---

3 For a comparative assessment of child support laws, see Mavis Maclean and Andrea Warman, *A Comparative Approach to Child Support Systems: Legal Rules and Social Policies, in* Child Support: The Next Frontier (J. Thomas Oldham and Marygold S. Melli, eds, 2000) and J. Thomas Oldham, *Lessons from the New English and Australian Child Support Systems*, 29 Vand. J. Transnat'l L. 691 (1996).

4 The most important of these is the New York Convention on the Recovery Abroad of Maintenance, June 20, 1956, 268 U.N.T.S. 32-47 (1957); The New York Convention has 56 parties; see http://untreaty.un.org/sample/EnglishInternetBible/partI/chapterXX/treaty1.htm (last visited Dec. 7, 2008).

There are also two sets of Hague Conventions in force, concluded in the 1950s and in 1973. The more recent of these are the Convention on the Recognition and Enforcement of Decisions Relating to Maintenance Obligations, Oct. 2, 1973, 1021 U.N.T.S. 209 (1973) and Convention on the Law Applicable to Maintenance Obligations Toward Children, Oct. 2, 1973, 1056 U.N.T.S. 27 (1973). These are in force in twenty-two and fourteen countries respectively. The 1973 treaties succeeded and superseded the 1956 treaties, which are the Convention on the Law Applicable to Maintenance Obligations Toward Children, Oct. 24, 1956, 510 U.N.T.S. 161 (1962) (14 Contracting States) and the Convention Concerning the Recognition and Enforcement of Decisions Relating to Maintenance Obligations Toward Children, April 15, 1958, 539 U.N.T.S. 27 (1962) (20 Contracting States). Detailed information is available on the web site of the Hague Conference on Private International Law at www.hcch.net.

5 Convention on the International Recovery of Child Support and other Forms of Family Maintenance (2007).

6 See generally William Duncan, *The New Hague Convention on the International Recovery of Child Support and Other Forms of Family Maintenance*, Int'l Fam. L. 13 (Mar. 2008).

system of administrative cooperation between Central Authorities designated by each member state. This approach makes the new convention a significantly more ambitious project than what was envisioned by prior multilateral agreements. With this essay, my goal is to explore what the new Family Maintenance Convention might mean both for the United States and for children around the world.

II. Child Support in the United States

For the United States, participation in prior multilateral child support agreements was made difficult by differences between the common law and civil law systems and our federalist constitutional tradition, in which the state governments have primary responsibility for family law.[7] The state courts have a tradition of recognizing and enforcing foreign support orders on the basis of comity,[8] however, and individual states began years ago to address child support issues through reciprocal arrangements with foreign jurisdictions.[9] Since 1996, the federal government has also entered into bilateral agreements with other nations for reciprocal support enforcement.[10] Important features of these bilateral agreements were incorporated into the new Family Maintenance Convention, including the requirement that services needed for establishment and enforcement of a child support order must be provided at no cost to the applicant in international cases.

When the new Family Maintenance Convention was concluded at The Hague in November 2007, the U.S. was the first nation to sign, signaling

---

7 See Gloria Folger DeHart, *Comity, Conventions and the Constitution: State and Federal Initiatives in International Child Support Enforcement*, 28 Fam. L.Q. 89 (1994); David Cavers, *International Enforcement of Family Support*, 81 Colum. L. Rev. 994 (1981).
8 E.g. Nichol v. Tanner, 256 N.W.2d 796 (Minn. 1976); Office of Child Support v. Sholan, 782 A.2d 1199 (Vt. 2001).
9 See Gloria F. DeHart, International Enforcement of Support and Custody: Reciprocity and Other Strategies 12-21 (1986).
10 This is authorized by 42 U.S.C. §659a. The current list of »foreign reciprocating countries« at the national level includes Australia, Canada, Czech Republic, El Salvador, Finland, Hungary, Ireland, Netherlands, Norway, Poland, Portugal, Slovak Republic, Switzerland and the United Kingdom, and negotiations with other countries are underway. For more information, see http://www.acf.hhs.gov/programs/cse/international/. A number of other nations have entered reciprocity agreements at the state level, which in now expressly authorized by 42 U.S.C. §659a(d). Nations with state-level arrangements in some states include Austria, France, Germany, Greece, Israel, Jamaica, Mexico, South Africa and Sweden.

its intention to ratify and implement the Convention as soon as possible.[11] The treaty was transmitted by President George W. Bush to the Senate for its advice and consent to ratification on September 8, 2008.[12] Once Congress enacts a federal implementing statute, the states will need to enact parallel legislation, which has already been prepared.[13] There is real enthusiasm for the treaty within the state and federal governments and among the organizations and agencies that carry out the work of domestic child support enforcement. United States participation in negotiation of the Convention helped assure that the new international regime will be compatible with our domestic program of interstate child support enforcement. On the most optimistic scenario, federal implementing legislation could be enacted in 2009, and the United States would be in a position to present its instruments of ratification to the Hague Conference two years later.[14]

The strong United States support for the new Family Maintenance Convention is remarkable, for a number of reasons. One is our general and recent history of standing apart from international treaty regimes on matters ranging from private international law and human rights to global warming and the International Criminal Court. Another is the particular difficulty of formulating national and international family policy that is consistent with our constitutional traditions.[15] In light of these factors, what explains the U.S. enthusiasm for the new Convention?

Vigorous child support enforcement has been strong national priority in the United States for the past thirty years. There are both fiscal and more idealistic explanations for these policies. New child support legislation is regularly enacted in Congress by large and bipartisan majorities.[16]

---

11 Margot Bean, Commissioner of the U.S. Office of Child Support Enforcement, signed the treaty on behalf of the United States at the closing of the Hague Conference Diplomatic Session on November 23, 2007.
12 Treaty Document No. 110-21.
13 At the state level, implementation will be achieved through amendments to the current Uniform Interstate Family Support Act (UIFSA). These amendments were approved by the Uniform Laws Commission in July 2008. See http://www.nccusl.org/Update/DesktopModules/NewsDisplay.aspx?ItemID=208. The amended UIFSA text is available at http://www.law.upenn.edu/bll/archives/ulc/uifsa/2008am_approved.htm.
14 This reflects the legislative timetable of the states, which would be required to enact the 2008 UIFSA amendments in order to implement the Convention.
15 See Ann Laquer Estin, *Sharing Governance: Family Law in Congress and the States*, 18 Cornell J. L. & Pub. Pol'y (forthcoming 2009).
16 See generally Ann Laquer Estin, *Federalism and Child Support*, 5 Va. J. Soc. Pol'y & L. 541, 545-48 (1998).

These reforms have created a system that provides a wide range of services without cost for establishing paternity and establishing and enforcing child support orders. Today, the domestic support enforcement program is enormous, with 15.8 million cases in fiscal year 2007 and total collections of almost $ 25 billion. Two thirds of the total cost of this program is paid by the federal government, and a portion of the funds collected is used to reimburse the costs of public assistance payments for children provided by the federal government.[17] Historically, fiscal considerations have been a strong motivator of the program, but support enforcement services are available to families whether or not they are eligible for public assistance benefits.

As a matter of public policy, the U.S. legislation emphasizes the private obligation of parents to support their children. The system is designed to make determination of parentage, establishment of a support order, and collection of support payments »automatic and inescapable«.[18] If a child support debtor is employed, and has income or assets that can be identified, establishment and enforcement of a support order is almost guaranteed. For parents who have the ability to pay, yet still manage to evade these obligations, the law provides stringent sanctions including the possibility of federal criminal prosecution, and measures such as revocation of passports or drivers and professional licenses.[19]

In its efforts to assure that all parents provide for their children, the U.S. system reflects a policy that is also found in Article 27(4) of the United Nations Convention on the Rights of the Child. That provision requires states parties to »take all appropriate measures to secure the recovery of maintenance for the child from the parents of other persons having financial responsibility for the child, both within the State part and from abroad.«[20] This more idealistic perspective is particularly evident in in-

---

17   In 2007, $ 1 billion of the $ 25 billion collected went to reimburse public assistance payments; the balance went directly to children and families. Detailed information is available on the web site of the Department of Health and Human Services at www.acf.gov./programs/cse/.
18   Paul K. Legler, *The Coming Revolution in Child Support Policy: Implications from the 1996 Welfare Act*, 30 Fam. L.Q. 519 (1996).
19   The same general policies extend to all families, rich and poor, but these laws obviously have different implications for families with adequate financial means than for those families above or below the poverty line.
20   Art. 27(4) continues: »In particular, where the person having financial responsibility for the child lives in a State different from that of the child, States Parties shall promote the accession to international agreements of the conclusion of such agreements, as well as the making of other appropriate arrangements.«

ternational cases, where bilateral agreements and the new Family Maintenance Convention seem more likely to serve individuals and families than to help governments recover social welfare costs. In its support for the Family Maintenance Convention, the United States has adopted the same child-focused perspective reflected in our slow but steady progress toward joining other important Hague Children's Conventions – the 1980 Convention on the Civil Aspects of International Child Abduction and the 1993 Convention on Intercountry Adoption in 2000[21] – and several other international agreements formulated to protect children against particularly serious abuses.[22]

III. Families Across Borders

The contemporary Hague Children's Conventions reflect a new approach to private international law and the possibilities of international legal cooperation. This potential may be most dramatic with the Family Maintenance Convention, which contemplates a very substantial level of coordination among the authorities of participating member states. In contrast with other areas of international law, these agreements are not intended to accomplish political, economic or strategic objectives. Their purpose is to foster the best interests of children and families, and to implement this new vision, governments must be prepared to prioritize children's needs.

For the United States, participation in the Family Maintenance Convention will allow the possibility of recovery from support obligors located abroad for the benefit of children who reside in the United States. This

---

21 See the International Child Abduction Remedies Act (ICARA), Pub. L. No. 100-300, 102 Stat. 437 (1988) (codified at 42 U.S.C. §§ 11601 et seq.), and the Intercountry Adoption Act, Pub. L. No. 106-279, 114 Stat. 825 (2000) (codified at 42 U.S.C. §14901 et seq.). The process of ratification and implementation of these treaties extended over many years, particularly with respect to the Adoption Convention, which the U.S. was finally able to ratify in December 2007. Ratification of the Family Maintenance Convention should move more quickly for several reasons: there is already a significant federal role in child support enforcement, the current bilateral agreements have established a template that will facilitate implementation of this treaty, and representatives of state and local child support enforcement authorities were closely involved with the treaty negotiations.

22 The U.S. has ratified two Protocols to the Convention on the Rights of the Child addressing the involvement of children in armed conflict and the sale of children, child prostitution, and child pornography, as well as the International Labor Organization Convention on the Worst Forms of Child Labor.

is also true of the bilateral child support agreements the United States has already signed. With some partner countries, there may be relatively equal financial flows coming into and out of the United States. But if the new Convention works as intended and anticipated, it should be especially important for improving the circumstances of children in less wealthy families and less wealthy nations of the world. This could happen in two ways: by providing a new stream of financial support in some cases, and by establishing new and more effective systems for support enforcement across the board.

Three factors are particularly significant to understanding the potential of the Family Maintenance Convention to provide significant benefits for children beyond the borders of the United States. The first is the change in family structures that has resulted from globalization and migration. The second factor is the ongoing commitment of the Hague Conference to expanding its membership and providing support for implementation of the Children's Conventions among new member countries. The third factor is the design of the Convention and the features that are intended to foster cooperation and make cross-border support enforcement efficient and affordable.

1. The Role of Globalization

For many generations, the United States has been a nation of immigrants, and our population remains highly diverse and international. As of 2003, about 12 % of the U.S. population was foreign-born. There are also an estimated 6 million Americans living abroad, not including government employees and members of the armed services. These numbers suggest that international child support laws are potentially relevant to millions of international families with ties to the United States.

At the present time, the United States does not have good statistics to indicate what the ratio of incoming to outgoing applications for support under the Family Maintenance Convention is likely to be. Nonetheless, it appears that that there is already a net flow of funds out of the United States in international support cases,[23] and this trend is likely to increase if the new convention is widely ratified. The more broad and diverse the

---

23 Data from Texas made available to the Drafting Committee preparing revisions to UIFSA indicated that of 1000 international child support cases processed in that state in the first seven months of 2007 there were more than 900 incoming requests for support and fewer than 100 outgoing cases. See http://www.law.upenn.edu/bll/archives/ulc/uifsa/brooks_stats.pdf.

range of nations participating in the new system, the more substantial this trend will be.[24]

In light of globalization, the redistributive potential of the new convention should be clear. Around the world, migration patterns reflect the pull of stronger economies and more attractive opportunities for employment in wealthier and more highly developed nations, including the United States and other countries that are long-standing members of the Hague Conference. Among the more recent members and new participants in the work of the Conference are many countries that are more likely to send workers abroad while some family members remain behind. A broadly applicable international child support enforcement regime could help facilitate the transfer of funds from family members who live and work in wealthy countries to family members in other parts of the world. Like the international remittances that workers send voluntarily to families, child support payments will shape and reflect international family networks.[25] Payments can foster communication between parents and children left behind, and reinforce these connections and relationships in positive ways.

2. Transformation of the Hague Conference

The Hague Conference today includes a much broader membership than it did when it was founded in 1955 by a group of 15 western European nations and Japan. By 1980, the Conference had 26 member countries, including a large number of European nations, Australia, Canada, the United States, as well as Egypt, Israel, Turkey; Argentina and Venezuela.[26] Today, the Hague Conference has 69 members and has relationships with another fourteen countries that have status as observers. More than 80 countries participate in one or more of the Hague Children's Conventions. The current membership reflects a richer and more complex diversity of cultures and languages, and legal, economic and political systems.

---

24 More than 60 nations participated in negotiating the Family Maintenance Convention, including both member countries of the Hague Conference and other countries invited to participate as observers.

25 See The World Bank, Global Economic Prospects 2006: Economic Implications of Remittances and Migration (2006) (reporting that developing countries' remittance receipts totaled $ 160 billion in 2004, more than twice the amount of official aid). Currently, there are large transaction costs involved in sending these funds. Use of the Hague system could be far cheaper and more efficient than channels now used to send funds to family members abroad.

26 For a list of member countries of the Hague Conference with dates of membership, see http://www.hcch.net/index_en.php?act=states.listing.

As it has grown, the Conference has made its treaties and proceedings available in a wider range of languages and has searched for financial support to permit representatives from less wealthy nations to participate in its meetings. Through these efforts, a record number of delegations from across the globe participated in the negotiation of the Family Maintenance Convention.[27] The Hague Conference has fostered broad participation in the Children's Conventions through ongoing projects including development of judicial training, guides to good practice, and technical assistance for implementing the conventions. This combination of increased membership and new collective efforts to support member countries in carrying out their treaty responsibilities has helped to shift the focus of the Children's Conventions and expand the numbers of children they can reach.

3. Administrative Efficiencies and Free Legal Assistance

The new system of cooperation envisioned by the Family Maintenance Convention contributes to its potential to serve many more of the world's children. Building on innovations in many countries, including but certainly not limited to the United States, the Convention will incorporate mechanisms to facilitate international case processing and administrative cooperation.[28] The Convention was crafted with the goals of taking full advantage of current technology and allowing for further advances in such areas as conversion and transmission of currency, electronic transmission of evidence, and participation in proceedings by electronic means.

Most importantly, the Convention includes an express obligation to make legal or administrative assistance available at no cost in international child support cases.[29] The United States insisted on this point, which reflects the current practice in our domestic system and our bilat-

---

[27] All of the Hague members and any country that participated in the proceedings may sign and ratify the new Convention. Art. 58.1. provides that the Convention is open for signature and ratification »by the States which were Members of the Hague Conference on Private International Law at the time of its Twenty-First Session and by the other States which participated in that Session.« To encourage broad participation, Art. 58.2. also provides that any other State or Regional Economic Integration Organization may accede to the Convention after it has entered into force.

[28] During the several years of negotiations, a »Forms Working Group« worked to develop standardized forms and procedures that will eliminate (or minimize) problems of translation and promote expedited processing.

[29] See Art. 14.2.

eral international agreements. The question of free legal assistance was contested in the negotiations, because the obligation to provide free legal assistance in incoming support cases will make the Family Maintenance Convention more difficult for some Hague Conference members to implement. Without this obligation, however, the new Convention would not represent an improvement on the prior multilateral treaties that provide for recognition and enforcement without providing means to carry this out. Although some nations may hesitate to invest the resources necessary to implement the new Family Maintenance Convention, many will be able to realize concrete financial benefits well beyond the initial costs to develop the infrastructure required for ratification or accession.

These two innovations – streamlined procedures and free legal assistance – work together to make the Convention much more likely to provide real assistance to a substantial number of the world's children. Under the existing multilateral agreements, a party who wishes to establish or enforce a child support order must navigate a foreign set of laws and procedures, often in addition to barriers of language or culture. With these practical and financial obstacles, the existing frameworks are only useful for those with sufficient resources to retain counsel to pursue their claim. Conversely, with access to advanced information and communication technologies, and the obligation to provide streamlined procedures and legal or administrative assistance, the new regime will create a real and attainable remedy for all children, and not only those in families with relatively substantial means.

Like its predecessors, particularly the Child Abduction Convention and the Intercountry Adoption Convention, the new Family Maintenance Convention moves far beyond the traditional work of private international law. This progression has been quite deliberate over the past twenty to thirty years, as the Conference has worked steadily to become a center for international judicial and administrative cooperation toward the goal of protecting families and children. Collectively, the Hague Children's Conventions have two goals: first, to embrace the wide global diversity of laws concerning children, and then to build bridges between those differences. In the United States and throughout the new global village, the Family Maintenance Convention presents us with a wonderful opportunity to act together to help children who live everywhere.

The Hague Convention on the International Recovery of Child Support and other Forms of Family Maintenance: Divergent Private International Law Rules and the Limits of Harmonisation

Robert G. Spector[1]

I. Introduction

The negotiations for the Maintenance Convention came to a conclusion at The Hague last November. The United States took the extraordinary step of immediately signing the Convention and the ratification process has begun. The President sent the Convention to Congress in October, 2008. The negotiations on the maintenance convention were far more challenging than the 2000 Protection of Incapacitated Adults Convention or the 1996 Convention on the Protection of Minors.[2] With regard to private international law, all States generally have the same approach to jurisdiction, applicable law and enforcement of judgments in cases concerning measures for the protection of minors and incapacitated adults. In the are of maintenance, the negotiations were difficult because there are great differences in the private international law systems of the United States and the rest of the world.

The United States has a federal system of government where some of the functions are performed by the national government and others are performed by the individual unit states. Domestic relations issues, including the subjects of marriage, divorce or dissolution of marriage, maintenance, division of marital property, custody and access to children, as well as other areas of parental responsibility, are almost exclusively within the control of the individual states.[3] However, the United States

---

1 Professor of Law, University of Oklahoma Law Center, USA.
2 There were many difficult topics during the negotiations on the Maintenance Convention, not the least of which was the issue of costs, which almost derailed the entire Convention.
3 The federal government does plays a peripheral role in some family law areas that are of national concern. For example, pursuant to the Full Faith and Credit Clause of the United States Constitution, the federal government may regulate the effect that the judgments and the laws of one state have in another state. See the discussion in Scoles E./Hay

Supreme Court may limit a state's control. Even if a federal court were to have jurisdiction over the parties on an independent federal ground, such as diversity of citizenship,[4] the federal court will abstain from deciding issues of domestic relations when it finds that individual state courts are a more appropriate forum.[5] Since each individual state is solely competent to decide cases involving problems of domestic relations, like maintenance issues, they relate to each other in the same way as independent countries. Therefore, it has become necessary to develop some method to determine which state will have jurisdiction to decide the various family law issues, the law applicable to those issues, and to determine which family law judgments shall be enforced by other states.

II. Jurisdiction

1. Direct Rules of Jurisdiction

In the United States, family law cases are subject to three different jurisdictional standards. First, jurisdiction to enter a judgment of divorce or dissolution depends on the relationship between one of the parties and the forum.[6] Second, jurisdiction over measures to protect minors, such as custody or access, depends on the length of time the minor has been habitually resident in the state. If the minor has been a resident of the state for six months, jurisdiction to determine the minor's custody and access, as an original matter, is normally present.[7]

P/.Borchers P,/Symeonides S. Conflict of Laws, 4th ed ed. St. Paul 2004 pp. 1257-1337.. In another example, the federal government passed the »Defense of Marriage« Act, Publ. L. No. 104-199, § 3 (a),110 Stat. 2419 (1996)(codified in 1 U.S.C. § 7), which authorized the individual states to refuse to recognize a same-sex marriage performed in other states. That law also provides that for federal law purposes, such as federal income taxation and social security, a marriage shall be defined as one man and one woman.

4   28 U.S.C. §1332 (2005).
5   *Barber v. Barber*, 62 U.S. 583 (1858); *Ex parte Burrus v. Burrus*, 136 U.S. 586 (1890).
6   If one party is domiciled in the state that grants the divorce, all other states must much give recognize the divorce under the Full Faith and Credit Clause of the United States Constitution.. Williams v. North Carolina [I], 317 U.S. 287 (1942). The United States does not recognize divorce jurisdiction based upon nationality. By statute, most states have a durational residency requirement, usually six months, before the state will grant a divorce. The case of *Sosna v. Iowa,* 419 U.S. 393 (1975), upheld the constitutionality of these statutes.
7   Uniform Child Custody Jurisdiction and Enforcement Act § 201. , II Yearbook of Private International Law pp.75-99 (Sarcevic and Voken eds, Swiss Institute of Comparative Law (2000).

The third jurisdictional issue concerns the ability of a court to enter a maintenance order. In this jurisdictional area, the United States Supreme Court has interpreted the United States Constitution to mandate an entirely different approach to jurisdiction. Instead of focusing on the relationship between the creditor/child and the forum, the court adopted the approach used in tort and contract cases and focused on the relationship between the defendant/debtor and the forum. In cases involving monetary awards, such as maintenance cases, the jurisdictional standards dictated by the Constitution are based on the relationship between the defendant/debtor, and the forum. A state is always allowed to exercise jurisdiction over defendants who are residents of the state.

The case of Kulko v. California determined this approach.[8] The parents lived in New York and divorced in Haiti. The mother moved to California and the father returned to New York. The children ultimately came to live with their mother. The mother sued the father for maintenance in California. The father resisted, arguing that California did not have personal jurisdiction over him.

The United States Supreme Court agreed. It noted the due process clause of the Fourteenth Amendment to the United States Constitution requires that the defendant have minimum contacts with the forum. Purchasing the ticket to send his daughter to California did not satisfy this requirement. The mother argued that California should have jurisdiction because it had substantial interests in protecting the welfare of its minor residents. The court responded that:

> »These interests are unquestionably important. But while the presence of the children and one parent in California arguably might favor application of California law in a lawsuit in New York, the fact that California might be the ›center of gravity‹ for choice-of-law purposes does not mean that California has personal jurisdiction over the defendant. And California has not attempted to assert any particularized interest in trying such cases in its courts by e.g., enacting a special jurisdictional statute.«[9]

In response the Uniform Interstate Family Support Act (UIFSA), (in force in all American states) § 201, enacted a particularized statute that asserts personal jurisdiction in an extended list of cases where the child is in the

---

8   436 U.S. 84 (1978).
9   436 U.S. at 98.

forum state and the defendant/debtor resides outside the state. The section asserts jurisdiction to the limits of the constitution. The listed bases of jurisdiction are:
a) the individual is personally served with a legal citation within the state;
b) the individual submits to the jurisdiction of the state by consent, by entering a general appearance, or by filing a responsive document that has the effect of waiving the objection to the state's jurisdiction;
c) the individual resided with the child in the state;
d) the individual resided in the state and provided prenatal expenses or support for the child;
e) the child resided in the state as a result of the acts or directives of the individual;
f) the individual engaged in sexual intercourse in the state and the child may have been conceived by that act of intercourse;
g) the individual asserted parentage in the state's putative father registry.

Conspicuously absent from the list is the exercise of jurisdiction based on the habitual residence of the creditor. The notion that a creditor can sue for maintenance at the place of the creditor's habitual residence, or at the creditor's option, at the habitual residence of the debtor, is normal approach elsewhere.[10] It is difficult to harmonize two such disparate approaches to jurisdiction.[11] Therefore the Special Commissions, noting that the real problem was the recovery of maintenance, ultimately concluded that the Convention could survive without direct rules of jurisdiction.[12]

2. Indirect Rules of Jurisdiction

An indirect rule of jurisdiction is a rule that indicates when a judgment will be enforced. The United States makes no distinction between direct and indirect rules of jurisdiction. Therefore, under UIFSA, American

---

10 Council of the European Union, Regulation on Jurisdiction and the Recognition and Enforcement of Judgments in Civil and Commercial Matters, No.44/2001 of 22 December 2000, Art.5.2. The discussions at the Special Commissions indicated that, with the possible exception of Korea, the United States is the only country that does not accept the principle of allowing the maintenance creditor to sue at home.
11 See the discussion in *Robert G. Spector, Toward an Accommodation of Divergent Jurisdictional Standards for the Determination of Maintenance Obligations in Private International Law*, 36 Fam.L.Q. 273 (2002).
12 See William Duncan, The Development of the New Hague Convention on the International Recovery of Child Support and Other Forms of Family Maintenance, 38 Fam. L. Q. 663 (2003).

courts will enforce a support order if jurisdiction is proper under Section 201. Conversely, if none of the jurisdictional bases of Section 201 are present, then the court cannot enforce a maintenance decision .

Again, there is a dichotomy between the United States and other countries. This is the main reason why the United States could not accede to the 1973 Hague Convention on the Recognition and Enforcement of Decisions Relating to Maintenance Obligations. Some of the indirect jurisdictional rules of Articles 7 and 8 of the 1973 Convention would be unconstitutional in the United States, including recognizing a maintenance judgment from the country of the creditor's habitual residence. Some of the jurisdictional rules of UIFSA would, no doubt, be found to be exhorbitant to the states that are parties to the 1973 Hague Convention, such as »tag« jurisdiction. The same may be true of jurisdiction based upon sexual relations that took place in the state and that may have resulted in the conception of the child at issue. This could result in a court asserting jurisdiction when neither the maintenance creditor nor the debtor habitually reside in the state.

This dichotomy presented a very difficult problem for the Special Commissions drafting the new maintenance convention. The United States proposed that recognition and enforcement of a foreign maintenance decision should not be conditioned on specific rules of indirect jurisdiction, but should be recognized if, under the facts and circumstances of the case, jurisdiction would have been proper under the law of the state addressed.[13]

Ultimately the Special Commissions were able to compromise and adopted a combined approach in Article 20. This article has specific rules for the recognition of maintenance orders, including those from the habitual residence of the creditor. However, a state is allowed to take a reservation to that particular section. If a state does then it shall enforce a maintenance order if, under the facts and circumstances of the case jurisdiction would have been proper under its own law.

This article of the convention also contains a proposal that is featured in the United States' bilateral arrangements. It provides that where a state has taken reservation to recognizing a maintenance decision based solely on the habitual residence of the creditor and where such state is the ha-

---

[13] See the discussion in Robert G. Spector, Toward an Accommodation of Divergent Jurisdictional Standards for the Determination of Maintenance Obligations in Private International Law, 36 Fam.L.Q. 273 (2002).

bitual residence of the debtor that state has an obligation to establish a maintenance decision against the debtor.

This compromise successfully harmonizes the difference between those countries that recognize maintenance decisions based on the habitual residence of the creditor and those countries that require jurisdiction over the debtor. But, this successful harmonization only applies to principles of recognition regarding to the original maintenance decision. As will be explained, there are significant problems with regard to recognition of modifications or variances of the original decision.

III. Applicable Law

Unlike civil law countries, the United States and the other common law systems, apply the law of the forum in matrimonial cases for the establishment of support orders. Common law countries have no experience with applicable law rules in family law cases and especially in child support. The administrative tribunals established to decide most child support cases in the United States are highly specialized. The administrative law judge and the attorneys who appear in these cases are trained in the support law and procedures of their particular states. The administrative law judge hearing these cases processes 20 to 40 cases a day. Local cases, interstate cases, and international cases are all a part of the mix. If the applicable law rule required the judge and the attorneys to apply the law of some other state, then the entire system would interminably slow down and would delay support when it is needed most. The law governing the establishment of child support has to be far more concerned with the efficient administration of justice than at arriving at the absolutely correct result in a particular case. Therefore, applicability of local law is the only way to insure an efficient operation of the administrative system.[14] However, states will never refuse to recognize a foreign order because of an error in the applicable law.

The First Special Commission established a Working Group on the Law Applicable to Maintenance Obligations. The report of the Working Group concluded that compromise was not possible between the common law and civil law States and therefore recommended that the Convention not

---

14 Indeed the strongest opposition to any applicable law rules came from countries like Australia and Norway which have solely administrative systems.

include an applicable law article, but that an optional protocol on the applicable law be drafted. The Protocol was successfully concluded during the diplomatic session. The United States will not ratify the Protocol.

IV. Modifications or Variations of the Original Support Order

In the United States, two main rules exist regarding modifications of the maintenance obligation. Section 205 of UIFSA contains the basic rule. That section provides that the state which issued the original support order retains continuing exclusive jurisdiction to modify the order so long as the state is the residence of the debtor, the individual creditor, or the child. If all of the parties and the child no longer reside in the issuing state, then the issuing state no longer has an appropriate nexus with the parties or the child to exercise jurisdiction to modify its child-support order.[15] However, if the parties agree, then they may designate some other state to assume jurisdiction over the support order.[16] And that state would become the state with continuing exclusive jurisdiction over the support order.

Sections 611 and 613 contain the second rule. If the creditor, debtor and the child leave the state that issued the original support order, then that state loses the ability to modify its own order. If all parties now reside in another state, then section 613 provides that the new state may modify the original order and it may also assume continuing exclusive jurisdiction over the support order.

A different approach prevails if both parties leave the state that issued the original order and each moves to a different state. In that case, section 611 provides that a state may modify a child support order of another state if the person seeking the modification is a nonresident of the state and the state would have jurisdiction over the nonmoving party under the

---

15   Even though the issuing state may not modify its own order, all states must enforce the order, including the issuing state, until such time that a state with jurisdiction modifies the order.
16   This designation may include the original issuing state. Section 205 provides that even if the issuing state is not the residence of the obligor, the individual obligee, or the child for whose benefit the support order is issued, the parties may consent in a record or in open court that the tribunal of the original issuing state may continue to exercise jurisdiction to modify its order. The designated state must have personal jurisdiction over at least one of the parties to the case. The parties cannot simply designate a state that has no relationship to either of them.

standards set forth in section 201. Thus if the debtor is seeking a downward modification of the order, then it must be done in a state with jurisdiction over the creditor, which will usually be the creditor's state of residence. If the creditor is seeking an upward modification, then it must be done in a state with jurisdiction over the debtor, which will usually be where the debtor resides.

This restriction on the jurisdictional grounds otherwise available under section 201 attempts to achieve a rough justice between the parties in the majority of cases by preventing a litigant from choosing to seek a modification in a local tribunal to the marked disadvantage of the other party. For example, a debtor visiting the children at the residence of the creditor cannot be validly served with a citation accompanied by a motion to modify the support order. Even though section 201 authorizes such personal service on the debtor in the obligee's home state and such service is consistent with the United States Supreme Court's holding in *Burnham v. California*,[17] the motion to modify does not fulfill the requirement of being brought »by a petitioner who is a non resident of this state.« Thus both parties are prohibited from seeking a hometown modification. Under the system in place for the original order, in those instances in which the parties began in the same state, the party who moves from the issuing state is the one who bears the burden of litigating in a foreign forum. But when both parties move, the individual who is seeking the modification bears the burden to litigate in a distant forum. When there is a valid order in existence, the person seeking to change it bears this burden.

Certain aspects of the original support order are not modifiable. These aspects include the duration of the order, the accrual of interest on arrears, and the existence and satisfaction of other obligations under the support order.[18]

There is a special rule for some foreign countries in section 615. If a child support order has been issued by a foreign country and that country will not or cannot modify its own order pursuant to its laws, then a state of the United States may modify the order and bind all persons who are sub-

---

17 495 U.S. 604 (1990).
18 The above rules are applicable to modification of a maintenance decision where the maintenance is ordered for a child. A special rule applies to spousal-only maintenance orders. Those orders can only be modified by the state that issued the original order. UIFSA Section 211. Thus if State A issues an order requiring the debtor to pay an amount for child support and a separate amount for spousal support, the child support can be modified according to the above procedure, but the spousal support could only be modified by the state that issued the order.

ject to its jurisdiction under section 201. This situation arises when there is a support order from a foreign country which would have continuing exclusive jurisdiction under UIFSA but, under its own law, cannot modify the order. This could occur where the foreign country's law requires both parties to be present for a modification but cannot force the absent party to return. Without a special rule the United States could not modify the order because the foreign country would have exclusive continuing jurisdiction and the foreign country could not modify the order because it could not compel the absent party to return. When this happens, a state of the United States that has jurisdiction over the parties may modify the foreign order.

Conspicuously missing from the grounds for modification is the option given by civil law countries of the European Union to the creditor to modify the support order where the creditor is habitually resident or, at the creditor's option, where the debtor is habitually resident. This dichotomy between European and United States rules on modification was the most difficult problem to harmonize. Currently the only provision in the convention on modification is Article 18 which provides:

1. Where a decision is made in a Contracting State where the creditor is habitually resident, the debtor may not bring proceedings for a new or modified decision in any other Contracting State as long as the creditor remains habitually resident in that State.

2. The previous paragraph shall not apply –

a) where there is agreement between the parties as to the jurisdiction of that other Contracting State in writing or evidenced in writing;

b) where the creditor submits to the jurisdiction of that other Contracting State either expressly or by defending on the merits of the case without objecting to the jurisdiction at the first available opportunity; or,

c) where the competent authority in the State of origin cannot, or refuses to, exercise jurisdiction to modify the decision or make a new decision.

This Article is relatively uncontroversial since it involves the fact pattern where both systems agree on the determination of where the modification proceeding should be brought. When the maintenance decision is made in the state where the creditor is habitually resident and the creditor continues to reside there, then that state is the appropriate state for any proceeding for modification. Under UIFSA the restriction on the debtor is appropriate because the state of the creditor's habitual residence has continuing exclusive jurisdiction. The solution is also appropriate under the civil law rules since the modification proceeding would take place where the creditor habitually resides.

The exceptions to the general rule contained in section 2 of Article 18 generally comport with the UIFSA rules. Section 205 of UIFSA allows the parties to agree that another state shall assume continuing exclusive jurisdiction over the support order. However, UIFSA requires that the parties must file the consent with the court of the new state assuming continuing jurisdiction. The same is required if all the parties move from the state that issued the original order, but the parties agree to allow the issuing state to retain continuing jurisdiction. Unlike Article 18 of the proposed convention, UIFSA does not allow a new state to assume continuing exclusive jurisdiction where one party defends on the merits without raising the jurisdictional issue.

The major problem is that Article 18 only covers the situation where the creditor remains in the original state. There are a large number of fact patterns that are not covered by Article 18. First, consider the situation where a married couple habitually resides in Texas and divorces in Texas with a child support order issued by a Texas tribunal. Suppose the creditor and the child move to France and wish to modify the support order. Under the current Brussels regulation, jurisdiction to modify would be proper in France since that is the habitual residence of the creditor. Under UIFSA, if the debtor has not moved, only Texas would have jurisdiction to modify the order. It is certainly possible for an European Union country to modify an American support order when the creditor seeking the modification is habitually resident in the European Union country. However, if the debtor still resides in the American state that entered the order, then the United States will not recognize the European Union order, even though countries of the Europe Union would undoubtedly recognize it. This runs contrary to the overriding theory of UIFSA: there should be one and only one support order in existence at any given time.

The second situation is a variation of this problem and occurs when the creditor, child, and debtor leave the original issuing state. For example, suppose the child and creditor move from Texas to France and the debtor moves to another state within the United States, such as Oklahoma. Under the Brussels regulation, modification would be proper in France since France is the habitual residence of the creditor. However, under UIFSA section 613, because all parties left Texas, the state that originally issued the order, the support order can only be modified in a state where the petitioner is a nonresident and where jurisdiction is proper over the respondent. The UIFSA solution would require the debtor to modify the order in France and the creditor to modify the order in Oklahoma. If the creditor obtained a modification in France, then the United States would not recognize the modification. The only solution that would avoid two orders would require compliance with the UIFSA system. If the creditor modifies in Oklahoma, then the United States would recognize the modification under UIFSA and France would recognize it because French law allows the creditor to modify where the debtor resides. Both France and the United States would also recognize a modification instituted by the debtor in France. The United States would recognize it because it comports with the UIFSA system. France would find the modification proper in France because it is the habitual residence of the creditor.

The third situation is the case where a married couple habitually resides in and then divorces in France. France issues a support order for the child. Assume that the creditor and the child move to Texas and the debtor remains in France. Under the current Brussels regulations, Texas has jurisdiction to modify the order since it is now the creditor's habitual residence. However, under UIFSA, Texas would decide that it had no jurisdiction because France had continuing exclusive jurisdiction over the support order. The only way that a modification of the support order could be recognized under both system is if the creditor returns to France to seek a modification. This would be proper under UIFSA which provides that France has continuing exclusive jurisdiction. French law would also find this permissible since the creditor has the option of suing at the place where the debtor habitually resides.

A fourth situation is where France issues a support order against a resident of the United States. Assume that the United States would recognize the order under Article 16 of the draft of the proposed convention. The creditor then moves to Italy from France and wishes to obtain a modification of the French support order. Under the Brussels regulation the creditor may obtain a modification in Italy. However, since UIFSA section 613 will only recognize modifications that take place in a state where the petitioner is a nonresident and therefore the modification in Italy would not be recognized in the United States. Again in order to avoid two orders, the creditor would have to obtain a modification in Texas. Article 18 does not address any of these fact patterns.

There was one potential compromise that was raised. It would be to require states to recognize modifications in those situations where the original order was recognized and where the state making the original support order would recognize the modification. In other words recognition of the original support order would also entail recognition of those situations where the state that issued the original order would or would not allow the order's modification. Thus if France issued the original support order and the United States recognized the order, then a modification of the order made where the creditor habitually resided, or, at the creditor's option, where the debtor habitually resided would receive recognition in the United States. Conversely, if the United States issued the original order and France recognized it, then such recognition would obligate France to acknowledge any modification that the United States, as the original issuing state, would recognize. Such a rule would also have to require that a state not recognize a modification which was not made in accordance with the modification rules of the state that originally issued the order. Unfortunately the compromise was rejected by both the United States and the European Union, with the result that the Convention almost totally fails to address modification issues.

The failure to arrive at a compromise on modification scenarios has put a major hole in the Convention. Not deciding modification problems leads the international support system to one of two undesirable results. The first is that, for a large number of cases, there will be two valid support orders in existence. This result negates UIFSA's major purpose to eliminate this problem. The second result is that, to avoid duplicate enforceable orders, creditors will have to modify where the debtor habitually resides. This means that creditors of limited resources would face significant burdens in pursuing a modification.

Whether these undesirable results can be avoided depends solely on whether the Convention's system of administrative cooperation works as proposed. Article 10 of the Convention provides that an application through the Central Authorities of the countries includes an application from either a debtor or a creditor to modify an extant maintenance order. Therefore it is possible, through the central authority system to arrange to have the case brought in the legal system that would result in one order that would be enforceable everywhere.

Thus in first situation discussed above the creditor could ask the central authority of the European country to send an application for modification to the central authority in the United States. The United States would recognize the modification because it was made by the state with continuing exclusive jurisdiction. The European Union country would recognize the modification because under its regulations the creditor has the option to file where the debtor is habitually resident. The same result would occur in the other scenarios.

Whether this can be done in a cost effective way will depend solely on the process of administrative cooperation through the central authorities. If the system works as designed, it may prove to be cost effective. However, this will push many cases into the State child support system and further reduce the role of private bar in handling international child support cases.

V. Conclusion

The drafting of the new Hague Convention on Child Support and Other Forms of Family Maintenance was very challenging. Attempting to develop a compromise between two different systems of private international law called for a delicate blend of two significantly different approaches. Though the Special and Diplomatic Commissions succeeded in crafting an approach that permits the recognition of the some decisions across international borders, it was unable to achieve a perfectly blended, all encompassing solution, especially in relation to child support modification.

Part II – Marriage and Non-formal Relationships

Principles, Deviation therefrom and Consequences of Formal and Non-Formal Relationships

Ledina Mandia[1]

Family relationships have been an important part of the Albanian legislation since the ancient times. The marriage is the most important institute of the family law, meanwhile, cohabitation was made known as an institute of family law for the first time by the Family Code of 2003, because of the fanatic mentality.

I. Marriage as a Formal Relationship

The act and the institute of the marriage are very important, not only on the social view, but also on the legal view. The marriage is considered like a social fact, which to have the legal value, should be realized in accordance with the legal order in general and the special law, which regulate the family relation in particular.

There is not a definition of the marriage in the recent Family Code 2003, nor in the other family codes in Albania[2], but under the doctrine, it was considered as a constant union between a man and a woman by aiming at creating the family and life's reproduction.

Under the recent Family Code, marriage is considered as a legal cohabitation between a man and a woman. The 1st Article of the New Family Code of 2003 states:

> »*Marriage, as a legal cohabitation, is founded on the moral and legal equality of the spouses, in the mutual sentiment of love, respect and understanding, as the basis of unity in the family. Marriage and family enjoy special protection from the state.*«

---

1 State Attorney of Albania at the General State Attorney Office, Tirana; Pedagogue at the Law Faculty, University of Shkoder »Luigj Gurakuqi« (candidate of PhD), Albania.
2 Family Code of 1928, 1965, 1982.

On this framework, the general principles of the relationships between the spouses are as follows:
- The marriage enjoys the protection of the State;
- Within marriage men and women have reciprocal rights and obligations;
- Equality of the spouses;
- Reciprocal love and respect;
- Marriage between persons of different sex;
- Common life (residence);
- Loyalty, support, cooperation between the spouses

Deviation from such a kind of principles is a fact. The consequence is the divorce.

1 Conditions of the Marriage

The spouses can marry if they fulfill the principal conditions of the marriage under the law in force, considering it as a valid marriage.

In contrary, in case of non fulfillment of the principal conditions and the existence of the impediments, the marriage will be void.

Under the Albanian family law doctrine, principal conditions of marriage are considered as follows:

a) Natural Conditions: difference of the sexes; age of the future spouses; the medical examination;
b) Contractual Condition: the free will and the ability to marry;
c) Moral Conditions, related to the impediments under the Family Code.

1.1 Natural Conditions

Difference of the Sexes

The Constitution of Albania in the 53th article promulgates the right of each person to marry and to create family. In the meaning of articles 8 & 12 of the European Convention on Human Rights, family life is considered as the relationship during marriage and outside of the marriage[3].
According to article 7 of the Albanian Family Code the marriage can be concluded between a man and a woman.

---

[3] Albania ratified the Convention on Human Rights in 1996. This Convention has an important place in the legal system of Albania, on the same level as the Constitution.

In the Family Code, such a condition is obligatory. The morality of the Albanian society, the legal heritage and the legal system, don't allow the marriage between the people of the same sex.

Age of the Future Spouses
Article 7 of the Albanian Family Code states:
> »Marriage can be concluded between a man and a woman who are 18 years or older.
> The court in the location where the marriage is to be concluded may, for sufficient reasons, allow marriage prior to this age.«

For the first time man and woman are treated equally concerning the age of marriage.[4] There is not a maximum age as a barrier for getting married.

The court by its decision, allows the marriage prior to this age in the cases of the woman's pregnancy, giving birth to a child or other cases when found appropriate.

Medical Examination
Under the law in force, people who suffer from certain diseases are prohibited to marry. Article 12 of the Family Code states:
> »A person who suffers from a mental illness or lacks the mental capacity to understand the nature of marriage cannot enter into matrimony.«

However, there is not a provision in the Family Code, stipulating that the medical examination before the marriage is ordinary.

1.2 Contractual Condition
Article 8 of the recent Family Code states:
> »Marriage is concluded in front of the civil registration office clerk, upon the free consent of the future spouses.«

The expressed free will of the future spouses is very important at the moment of the marriage act. Both, future spouses should be present to marry each other and give their consent personally. Neither of them can be represented by another person.

---

4 In the other Civil Codes of Albania the age for marriage was 16 years old for the woman and 18 for the man.

The Albanian law does not recognize the institute of the pre-marriage and that of the engagement.

1.3 Moral Conditions, Related to the Impediments under the Family Code

Monogamy
Article 9 of the recent Family Code states:
»*A previously married person cannot conclude a marriage, unless the previous marriage has been voided or terminated.*«

Only the marriage between a man and a woman is allowed and stipulated by law[5].

1.4 The Impediment of the Marriage under the Provision of the Recent Family Code, Related to the Affinity.

Under the article 10 of the recent Family Code, predecessors and descendants, brother and sister, uncle and niece, aunt and nephew, and first cousins may not join in matrimony. But, the court can allow the marriage of first cousins[6] for sufficient reasons.

According to the article 11 of the recent Family Code, father in law and daughter in law, mother in law and son in law, stepparents and stepchildren cannot join in matrimony, even when the marriage, which created that relationship has been declared void, has ceased or has been dissolved.

According to article 13 of Family Code, a guardian and a ward under their supervision may not enter into matrimony during the time the guardianship is in effect.

According to article 14 of Family Code, the marriage between an adoptive parent and the adoptee and their descendants, the adoptee and the spouse of the adoptive parent, between the adoptive parent and the spouse of the adoptee, between adoptees, as well as between adoptee and the children of the adoptive parent is forbidden.

2. Reciprocal Rights and Obligations of the Spouses

The marriage should be considered concluded when the marriage act is signed by both future spouses. From this moment, the marriage creates the rights and the duties for both spouses.

---

5   Article 7 of Albanian Family Code.
6   Case of the pregnancy of the woman; when is given birth to a child.

Under the recent Albanian Family Code, the rights and duties of the spouses rely on the principle of the equality between the spouses and are classified by their nature in personal and property rights.

2.1 Personal Rights of the Spouses

Article 50 of the recent Family Code states:
>»Within marriage men and women have the same rights and obligations.
>Marriage partners have a mutual obligation of loyalty, for moral and material support, and for cooperation in the interest of the family and cohabitation.«

Personal obligations as loyalty, cooperation in the interest of the family, common contribution during the matrimonial life, the joint support for the children are considered as important personal obligation of the spouses, which are regulated with imperative provisions in the Albanian Family Code.

According to the article 53 of the recent Family Code, the marriage obliges both spouses to maintain, edify and educate their children, bearing in mind the capacities, natural predispositions and the desires of the children.

Also, the spouses are obligated to contribute to the needs of the family in accordance with their conditions and abilities, even if the contribution by the spouses for marital obligation is not stipulated in the marriage contract.[7]

On the other hand personal rights as the choice of the surname, profession, nationality or residence are considered as permissive obligations.

The spouses, when concluding a marriage, have the right to choose as a common surname one of their surnames or to keep their own surnames. The surname should be registered in the marriage register.[8]

A child shall have the common surname of the parents. When the parents have different surnames, all children shall have the same surname, as specified by the agreement of the parents. If an agreement cannot be reached, the children shall have the surname of the father[9].

---

7   Article 54 of Albanian Family Code.
8   Article 51 of Albanian Family Code.
9   Article 52 of Albanian Family Code.

The choosing of the profession is free under the Constitution of Albanian, and still remains as a permissive obligation under the Family Code. Each of the spouses can freely pursue a profession and manage their income from employment or other means, in accordance with the respective marital property regime, after contributing to the marital obligations.[10]

Common residence of the spouses is an imperative obligation, although the choosing of the residence is permissive.

The spouses are obligated to live together during all their matrimonial life. If, it is necessary to change their common residence they need the consensus of the other spouse. Article 55 of the recent Family Code states:

> »Spouses have an obligation to have a common residence.
> The residence of the family shall be selected by the spouses by a mutual agreement.
> In case of disagreement, either of the spouses can petition the court, which, after hearing the opinion of the spouses and, if there are any, the opinion of children older than fourteen years, shall attempt to reach a solution through settlement.
> If a settlement cannot be reached the court shall devise a solution that it deems most appropriate for the needs of the family.«

The right to moral and material support required in this Code is considered to have been withdrawn when a spouse leaves the family home without cause and refuses to return.

Under the 56th article of the Family Code, the court, in the case of unfulfilled obligations originating from the marriage, based on the circumstances, can order to the necessary extent a seizure of the goods spouses who has left.

Collaboration between spouses and the agreement to resolve the everyday situations in the family is obligatory under the recent Albanian Family Code. Every action/decision of a spouse should be approved by the other spouse, in the cases requested by law.

However, under the article 60 of the Family Code, each of the spouses can perform legal transactions that are related to the maintenance of the family or the education of children individually, without the approval of the other spouse. Obligations incurred by one spouse constitute the mutual obligation of both spouses.

---

10 Article 63 of Albanian Family Code.

Mutual obligations may not be incurred for extravagant expenses, taking into consideration the lifestyle of the family, the benefits of the transaction performed, and the good faith or malicious intent of third party contractors.

In the recent family code for the first time, provisions concerning the protection of the family relationships have been provided.

It is a fact that in the Albanian family relationships, cases of the family abandonment, domestic violence, irresponsibility of the spouses against the family members have been found.

The so-called »*Urgent measures*« are applied in case the spouses clearly fail to fulfill their obligation and put at risk the interests of the family. In such cases, the court, upon request of the other spouse, can approve urgent measures regarding the spouses.

The extent of such urgent measures must be specified and must not exceed 3 years[11].

Another measure was provided against the domestic violence, in cases of the abusing spouse during the matrimonial life. The only provision is the so called »*Measures against violence*«. Article 62 of recent Family Code states:

»*A spouse, who is subjected to violence, has the right to request that the court order as an urgent measure the removal of the spouse, that perpetrated violence, from the marital residence.*«

Since 2003, when the Family Code was adapted, there is not any court decision as a consequence of the above mentioned provision. This provision remains not applied, meanwhile the cases of domestic violence, almost between spouses increase every day.

Also, this provision doesn't realize the whole protection of family relationships.

Another specific law is adapted, the law on »The Measures against the violence in the family relations«, which intends to protect a lot of people in family relations, including those called cohabitants or ex-spouses.

2.2 Property Rights of the Spouses

The spouses are obliged to support and maintain each other. This is a personal obligation of the spouses with property character.

---

11   Article 61 of Albanian Family Code.

Support of obligation is promulgated in the title II of the Family Code. A spouse, who is incapable of working and without sufficient means to live, has the right to request alimony from the other spouse.

A request for alimony should be made in the petition for the dissolution of the marriage.

Also, this request may be submitted within 6 months from the date the decision for the dissolution of marriage becomes final, if the conditions for the incapacity to work or insufficiency of means to live existed during the marriage[12].

Concerning the personal properties of the spouses, each of them has the right to manage on his own without the consent of the other spouse.

Concerning the properties made during the marital life, the recent Family Code for the first time stipulates the marital property regime of the spouses.

The marital property regime of spouses is stipulated by law, in the absence of a specific agreement by the spouses designating their own regime[13].

Apart from the marital regime selected, spouses cannot avoid their rights and obligations originating from the marriage, their parental responsibilities and the rules of legal administration and guardianship.

II. Cohabitation (More Uxorio) as a Non-Formal Relationship

The cohabitation, differently from the marriage, is divested from every kind of formality.

In the Albanian traditional family, cohabitation has been unacceptable for the society.

In terms of protecting the family relations, the state applied a fine to the man who cohabitated with a women. After 90' such a provision was abrogated, but the cohabitation was not known as a legal institute.

Only under the recent family Code of 2003, Cohabitation was stipulated by law. Cohabitation is determined as a factual union between a man and a woman living as a couple, with a common life that is stable and continuous in nature[14].

---

12 Article 199 of Albanian Family Code.
13 Article 66 of Albanian Family Code.
14 Article 163 of Albanian Family Code.

There are not principal obligatory conditions required by law like in a marriage, but there are some elements that are necessary to qualify a relationship as cohabitation under the law.
> *The age of the partners*
  The age is not required, but the fact they will continuously live together as a couple and will undertake duties and responsibilities implies that they should be 18 years old;
> *The common residence between a man and a woman*
  The principle of monogamy should be respected during cohabitance. The cohabitation between the partners of the same sex is not known as a family relationship. The stability in this kind of relationship is required;
> *The free and whole consent of the partners*
  The free consent/will of the partners is an important element of the cohabitance. The obligatory cohabitation is illegal and punished by law. The continuity of partners' relationship for the future depends on their decision.

In the Albanian Family Code the rights and obligations of the cohabitant partners are not determined, nor the consequences of the deviations they are from.

There are not personal rights of the cohabitants as in the case of marriage.

However, cohabitation is considered as a family relationship and as such the relation is protected by the state. On this framework, law »On measures against the domestic violence« considered the cohabitant partners and ex-cohabitant partners as subject of that law.

Cohabitant partners face obligations, only in case they sign an agreement in the presence of a public notary, whereby they determine the consequences resulting from cohabitation in relation to children and assets acquired during the cohabitation.[15]

Even if any kind of agreement is not signed, in any case the general principles of the Albanian Family Law should be applied as following:
> Marriage and family enjoy special protection from the state.[16]
> Parents have the duty and right to ensure the proper care, development, well-being, education and edification of children born from

---

15 Article 164 of Albanian Family Code.
16 Article 1 of Albanian Family Code.

marriage or out of wedlock.The state and society must offer to families the necessary support to care for their children, in order to prevent their maltreatment and abandonment, and to preserve the stability of the family.[17]
> Children born out of wedlock have the same rights and responsibilities as children born in wedlock.[18]

III. Conclusions

Recently for the first time in Albania, Cohabitation is known as a legal institute, meanwhile marriage as an old institute deriving from the ancient times.

The Albanian legislation stipulates the general principles of the family law that can be applied during the cohabitation and the marriage.

There is a doctrinal and legal determination of cohabitation and the marriage, but for the marriage all the conditions to conclude the marriage and the duties of the spouses are stipulated by law, meanwhile, for the cohabitation the duties and rights of the cohabitant partners are not stipulated by law.

Although the general principles could be applied for the cohabitant partners, there is a lack of legal regulation concerning the cohabitation institute.

There are no conditions for the persons who cohabitate; the cohabitant partners are not registered and as a consequence they can't have special protection by the State. In Albania there are no data of the persons who cohabitate and of the cohabitant partners who stipulate their rights of the property or their parental rights by notary act.

Concerning the marriage, known as an old institute, although all the principles, the duties of the spouses are stipulated by law, there is a lack of the application of the law in general.

There are no cases, whether the spouses have decided to stipulate their regime of the property by contract or separation. There is also a lack of the action of the state structures to guarantee the matrimonial relations, even in the case of a legal cohabitation between a man and a woman.

Despite the strengthening of the legal structures, the elaboration of the

---

17 Article 3 of Albanian Family Code.
18 Article 4 of Albanian Family Code.

cohabitation institute in the family code and other laws related to that concerning the conditions for the cohabitation, duties/rights of cohabitant partners and the consequences after the resolution of the cohabitation will be very important in the future.

Division of Family Assets and De Facto Conjugality: The Limits of a Free Choice Approach

Dominique Goubau[1]

I. Introduction

When people decide to live in a conjugal relationship outside any legal framework such as marriage or some kind of civil union or registered partnership, they apparently choose to avoid the legal consequences of that relationship, in particular economic/financial consequences. Yet an important question arises: does or should the law impose in some way protective rules upon separation for the disadvantaged unmarried spouses, particularly regarding the division of family assets?[2] Do we still consider this as being a private matter as we did for many years, or do we actually face a public issue, considering the fact that a growing number of people live with no legal status and considering also the fact that we may not pass in silence anymore over the fact that in many cases there are economic disadvantages to one of the partners arising from the relationship or its breakdown. Those consequences undoubtedly occur whatever the legal status of the parties involved. Some countries have extended their family assets provisions to unmarried couples. The central argument of my paper is that mandatory division of family assets upon separation should not be anymore a consequence of status but rather a consequence for spouses or partners of having children together. Free choice should be

---

1 Professor at Laval University, Quebec, Canada.
2 The legal literature on this topic is abundant; see e.g. W.H. Holland, »Has the Time Come to Bridge the Gap ?«, in *Special Lectures of the Law Society of Upper Canada, Canada*, Toronto, 1994, 369; D. Goubau, »La notion de conjoint: la loi et la société avancent-elles au même pas?«, *Actes de la XVIe Conférence des juristes de l'État*, Cowansville, Les Éditions Yvon Blais Inc., 2004, 39-60 ; N. Bala and R. Jaremko Bromwich, »Context and Inclusivity in Canada's Evolving Definition of the Family«, (2002)16 *International Journal of Law, Policy and the Family*, 145-180; D. Goubau, »La conjugalité en droit privé : comment concilier »autonomie« et »protection«?«, dans *L'union civile. Nouveaux modèles de conjugalité et de parentalité au 21e siècle*, dir. P.-C. Lafond et B. Lefèvre, Cowansville, Les Éditions Yvon Blais, 2003, 153-163; M. Jarry, *Les conjoints de fait au Québec : vers un encadrement légal*, Cowansville, Les Éditions Yvon Blais, 2008.

the paramount consideration when only adults are concerned, whereas a protective approach should prevail if children are involved. This could be an interesting way in balancing two fundamental values: protection of those who need it and autonomy for those who are capable of it.

When dealing with this issues, some authors answer in the classical way by stating that choice must be paramount and that the individual autonomy principle must prevail[3]. As Justice Bastarache from the Supreme Court of Canada wrote in the seminal Walsh case »people who marry can be said to freely accept mutual rights and obligations. A decision not to marry should be respected because it also stems from a conscious choice of the parties«[4]. This reasoning is simple and it is clear: if people choose to live outside any legal status, their choice should be respected and one should restrain from imposing any obligation on them. Other observers answer to this question by emphasizing that there is actually an urgent social need for the implementation of protective measures in favour of the disadvantaged partners, especially women with children. This issue is not a new one as it arose more than thirty year ago in many western countries. But what has changed indeed is the social context as we actually witness dramatic changes in conjugal behaviour and as the number of marriages is crumbling in many western societies. The Canadian and Quebec's experience may be of some interest in this particular debate.

II. *De facto* Cohabitation in Canada

The 2006 Census of Population from Statistics Canada (a Federal Agency) gives us interesting figures. Whereas de facto couples represent 13,4 % of all couples in Canada (excluding Quebec), *de facto* cohabitation is the principal distinctive feature of family structures in the province of Quebec where 34,6 % of all couples live outside any legal status. This figures rise up to 60 % when partners are between 25 and 40 years old.[5] That makes Quebec one of the world's front runners in terms of de facto cohabitation. As a matter of fact, marriage is decreasing. In 1972 there were 54 000 marriage celebrations in the province of Quebec (with a population of 6,1 million)

---

3 For example, C.P. Prémont and M. Bernier, »Un engagement distinct qui engendre des consequences distinctes«, in Barreau du Québec, *Développements récents sur l'union de fait*, Cowansville, Les Éditions Yvon Blais, 2000, p. 1.
4 *Nova Scotia (Attorney General) v. Walsh*, [2002] 4 S.C.R. 325.
5 http://www.stat.gouv.qc.ca/donstat/societe/demographie/struc_poplt/202.htm.

and in 2006 this numbers fell to 22 000 celebrations (for a population of 7,7 million).[6] Furthermore, about 60 % of the children born in Quebec during the year 2005 are born out of wedlock.[7] And everyone agrees that this numbers are actually on the rise. If the law is to reflect reality, this new figures can not be ignored by lawmakers.

As family behaviours changed, the law changed quickly too. A major trend in Canadian public law, for several years now, is to give married and unmarried couples, hetero or same-sex, the same rights and obligations.[8] There is a growing awareness of the functional similarities between married and unmarried families. The outcome of this awareness is an equation of the legal position of all couples, regardless their status, in the field of public and social law and in the field of parent/child relations. As far as the relations between individuals and the State or between parents and children are concerned, the law makes no difference anymore amongst married, unmarried, hetero or same-sex couples, neither in Canadian federal law[9], nor in provincial laws[10]. That is the result of successful constitutional challenges and, for most provinces, extensive legislative reforms. It is revealing that when in its 2007 report on family policies, the Family and Childhood Council of the Government of Quebec refers to »family diversity«, it refers only to families with one, two or more parental figures but it does not even mention the distinction between married or unmarried couples[11]. In the field of public and social law, the issue is not status but rather how to define *de facto* cohabitation. Most statutes provide with a definition. For example, the Quebec's *Interpretation Act* reads as follows:

> »The word ›spouse‹ includes a de facto spouse unless the context indicates otherwise. Two persons of opposite sex or the same sex who live together and represent themselves publicly as a couple are de facto spouses regardless, except where otherwise provided, of

---

6 http://www.stat.gouv.qc.ca/donstat/societe/demographie/etat_matrm_marg/501a.htm
7 http://www.stat.gouv.qc.ca/donstat/societe/demographie/naisn_deces/naissance/410.htm
8 W. H. Holland and B. E. Stalbecker-Pourney (ed.), *Cohabitation: the law in Canada*, Toronto, Carswell, 1990 (looseleaf, updated).
9 *Modernization of Benefits and Obligations Act*, Statutes of Canada 2000, c. 12.
10 See for example, *An Act to amend various legislative provisions concerning de facto spouses*, Statutes of Quebec 1999, c. 14.
11 Gouvernement du Québec, Conseil de la famille et de l'enfance, *La politique familiale au Québec : visée, portée, durée et rayonnement*, Québec, 2007.

> how long they have been living together. If, in the absence of a legal criterion for the recognition of a de facto union, a controversy arises as to whether persons are living together, that fact is presumed when they have been cohabiting for at least one year or from the time they together become the parents of a child.«[12]

The equalization of status has been extended to some private law dimensions of marriage. In all Canadian provinces, but Quebec, support obligations have been extended to unmarried couples. For example, in Ontario, recognition that cohabiting couples are subject to the spousal support regime occurred as early as in 1978.[13] But a major difference still exists regarding property division upon separation, divorce or death. All Canadian provinces have passed legislation providing for an equitable distribution of family property upon marriage breakdown otherwise than according to ownership. Those statutes differ in some ways, including what »property« is subject to division, when a right to claim a division of family property arises, and whether the rights granted are debtor-creditor rights or proprietary rights in the family assets.[14] In most provinces, parties are free to contract out of the statutory regime or to restructure the statutory regime by domestic contract if they believe that the regime does not meet their particular needs. The spouses have an opting-out right. Yet in Quebec the partition of the family patrimony is mandatory for married couples and there is no opting-out right in that province. In most provinces, as is the case in Quebec, this distribution rights extend only to married couples and to registered partners (or »civil union spouses«), leaving an opting-in right for *de facto* spouses. But in some few provinces, legislators extended the definition of »spouse« to include persons who have cohabited in a marriage-like relationship continuously for a given period of time, which means that in those provinces (Saskatchewan and Manitoba, for example[15]) there are but slight differences anymore between married and unmarried couples regarding private law matters.

Where there is no such an extension, unmarried couples must rely on remedial constructive trust and unjust enrichment to obtain quasi-matrimonial property rights. As justice Bastarache wrote in the Walsh case:

---

12   *Interpretation Act*, R.S.Q. c. I-16, s. 61.1.
13   *Family Law Reform Act*, S.O. 1978, c. 2.
14   J.G. McLeod and A.A. Mamo, *Annual Review of Family Law 2007*, Toronto, Carswell, 2007, 467.
15   *Family Property Act*, S.S. 2001, c. 51; *Family Property Act*, C.C.S.M. c. F25.

»Persons unwilling or unable to marry have alternative choices and remedies available to them. The couple may choose to own property jointly and/or to enter into a domestic contract that may be enforced.

[...] For those couples who have not made arrangements regarding their property at the outset of their relationship, the law of constructive trust remains available to address inequities that may arise at the time of the dissolution.[16]«

And there is indeed a significant body of caselaw, including from the Supreme Court of Canada[17], based on those mechanisms, that extends such rights to unmarried couples. But such cases require a detailed examination of the circumstances around acquisition of property as well as of the intention and conduct of the parties during cohabitation. That makes it for claimants a difficult path to walk on, which is not often a path to success.

III. Status and Discrimination

The exclusion of married couples from a right to automatic division of family assets brought Ms. Walsh to challenge, in the late nineties, the constitutionality of the Nova Scotia's *Matrimonial Property Act* which, as it then was, extended only to married spouses. After ten years of cohabitation, she wanted to share her partner's property. Therefore she sought that Nova Scotia's family property statute was discriminatory and, as such, unconstitutional. A few years before, in 1995, the Supreme Court opened the door to such a claim when it decided in *Miron v. Trudel*[18] that marital status may indeed constitute an analogous ground of discrimination under section 15 of the *Canadian Charter of rights and Freedoms*.[19]

The Supreme Court of Canada rendered its decision in the Walsh case in 2002[20]. The Court ruled that it is constitutionally permissible to exclude unmarried couples from the scope of marital property statutes. This decision surprised many lawyers because, as mentioned earlier, a

---

16 *Nova Scotia (Attorney General) v. Walsh*, [2002] 4 S.C.R. 325, par. 58.
17 *Peter v. Beblow*, [1993] 1 R.C.S. 980.
18 *Miron v. Trudel*, [1995] 2 R.C.S. 418.
19 *Canadian Charter of rights and Freedoms*, R.S.C. (1985). App. II, n. 44.
20 *Nova Scotia (Attorney General) v. Walsh*, [2002]4 SCR 325.

major trend in Canadian public law for several years now is to give same rights to married and unmarried couples, hetero or same-sex. And there is also a significant trend in the case-law extending many rights and obligations of the married spouses in private law to the unmarried spouses. For example, the exclusion of cohabiting couples from the scope of the spousal support divisions of the Alberta Domestic Relations Act[21] was successfully challenged in a case of the Alberta Court of Appeal[22] on the ground of the equality section of the Canadian Charter of rights and Freedoms. But when it comes to automatic division of assets, things are different. In the Walsh case, the Supreme Court ruled that for matrimonial property statutes to exclude unmarried couples was not unconstitutional because spouses are free to marry or not, and thus to accept or to refuse mandatory division of family assets. In other words, the signal given by the Canadian Supreme Court is that the individual autonomy principle must prevail in domestic property matters and that the dignity of individuals dictates that their personal choices be respected as far as sharing of property is concerned:

»*Where the legislation has the effect of dramatically altering the legal obligations of partners, as between themselves, choice must be paramount. The decision to marry or not is intensely personal and engages a complex interplay of social, political, religious, and financial considerations by the individual. While it remains true that unmarried spouses have suffered from historical disadvantage and stereotyping, it simultaneously cannot be ignored that many persons in circumstances similar to those of the parties (...) have chosen to avoid the institution of marriage and the legal consequences that flow from it.*«[23]

Yet some fact finding studies tend to show that the decision to marry or not is not often shared by both spouses or partners.[24] And one may be surprised by the Supreme Court's opinion, as a majority of it judges said exactly the opposite some years earlier, underlining the fact that

»*people who make a conscious decision not to subscribe to the institution of marriage may very well be motivated by very personal*

---

21   *Alberta Domestic Relations Act*, R.S.A. 1980, c. D-37.
22   *Taylor v. Rossu*, (1998) 39 R.F.L. (4th) 242.
23   *Nova Scotia (Attorney General) v. Walsh*, [2002]4 SCR 325. par. 43.
24   See, eg, H. Belleau, *L'union de fait et le marriage au Québec: analyse des differences et les similitudes,* Montréal, INRS Urbanisation, Culture et Société, 2007-2, novembre 2007.

beliefs which have nothing whatsoever to do with the contractual rights and obligations that incidentally attach to that status.«[25]

It is important to notice that in the Walsh case, the Supreme Court based its decision heavily on the fact that provincial legislation provides that an unmarried cohabitant or common-law partner enjoys already some kind of protection if needed because she or he may apply to a court for a maintenance or support order. In this context, according to the Supreme Court, the dignity of common law spouses cannot be said to be affected adversely. That makes this decision interesting in light of Quebec's law where there is no such maintenance right between unmarried spouses. Yet the maintenance provisions of the Quebec's Civil Code are actually challenged before the Superior Court whereas an unmarried wife seeks a declaration of unconstitutionality of the relevant sections that exclude unmarried spouses from the partition of the family patrimony and from spousal support. It will be interesting to see if the Superior Court of Quebec will be eager to decide what the legislator has constantly refused to decide, namely to extend matrimonial rights and obligations to people who are supposed to have chosen to avoid those legal consequences.

IV. The Need for Redefining Matrimonial Property Law

By refusing to extend the legal status of married couples to unmarried couples, provincial legislators bring Canadian family law into a new era. The scope of matrimonial law has dramatically changed with the figures of unmarried couples rising. When years ago, the law imposed economical consequences on marriage and on marriage breakdown, the purpose of the law was to reach most of the people since the majority of the couples where married. Conjugality has been governed by marriage for centuries. But now that, particularly in Quebec, marriage is less popular (to say the least), the aim of matrimonial law seems to change. And the matrimonial property law could well miss its traditional target as a growing number of citizens escape from mandatory property division rules. They are left to individually negotiable obligations, if any, with the risks entailed.

---

25 Miron v. Trudel, [1995] 2 R.C.S. 418 (par. XV of Justice L'Heureux-Dubé's majority opinion). Also, C. Smart, »Stories of Family Life : Cohabitation, Marriage and Social Change«, (2000) 17 Canadian Journal of Family Law, 20.

Contract and trust law principles govern for a large part the financial consequences of unmarried cohabitation. As a result, status still matters in Quebec and in many other parts of Canada when dealing with obligations between adult partners. But if, as the Supreme Court of Canada stated in the Walsh case, »choice must be paramount«, one must not forget that adult choices may cause important collateral damage, in the first place when children are involved.[26] The »free choice« argument is not convincing at all from a child's perspective. The consequences of a free choice should at least be limited to those who make a choice, the adults, not the children. One can not ignore that division of property has an impact on children, especially if the custodial parent does not benefit from any distribution. That's why time has probably come for matrimonial property law to make a distinction, not between couples with or without a legal status, but between couples with children and childless couples. Matrimonial property rules would apply to the former while the latter would be free to contract in the way they think is good for them.

Some observers put forward the idea that the law should go even further and impose on *de facto* spouses a same status as that of married spouses. Among the arguments that favour the implementation of a restrictive and protective legal framework, is the idea that many married women, regardless of education, are often unaware of their rights and that they live with the illusion that they are every bit as protected as are married women. This lack of awareness seems to be confirmed both by testimonies of attorneys representing unmarried women as by various fragmentary fact-finding studies.[27] Yet the price for this proposal is an important loss of individual liberty in a field where, paradoxically, freedom has been at the very heart of recriminations over these past thirty years. In this respect, one may even say that in our contemporary society the concept of freedom henceforth represents an essential constituent of conjugal relations, which is the epitome of privacy. If misunderstood laws and illusory protection are, as some tend to believe, confirmed facts, then why hesitate from first implementing effective programs to make information freely available? In today's society characterized by omni-

---

26 D. Goubau, G. Otis et D. Robitaille, »La spécificité patrimoniale de l'union de fait : le libre choix et ses dommages collatéraux«, (2003) *Cahiers de Droit*, 3-51.
27 Chambre des notaires du Québec/Ipsos Descarie, *Perception du mariage et de l'union libre. Rapport de recherche*, Montréal, 2007. But one study shows that the more women are educated, the more they choose not to marry : H. Belleau, *L'union de fait et le mariage au Québec: analyse des differences et des similitudes, op.cit. supra*.

present and all-powerful sources of information, should it not be imperative to enlist these means before sacrificing individuals' rights in the field of intimate relations?

This, although, does not mean that one should deny the fact that conjugal relationships are also quite often the scene of power and subordination to which many women still succumb as victims. The tenant of »absolute privacy« is no more valid than that of universal and mandatory protection based upon a postulate of generalized victimization of women. The presumption of women's autonomy is every bit as erroneous as that of their systematic dependency. Adequate means of legal protection are therefore necessary. And they do exist, even if imperfect and perfectible. On this issue, a majority bench of Canadian Supreme Court justices set forth in the Walsh case an idealized perception of the efficacy of measures as those based upon the theory of unjust enrichment. An analysis of contemporary case-law indeed demonstrates that while the courts regularly accept this type of reasoning, the awards granted are usually pitiful. Yet before abandoning such recourses in favour of forced massive protection to the detriment of liberty sought by an increasing number of men and women, might one not consider making an effort to perfect such means? One may say that the importance of what is at stake here amply justifies such an effort. The Supreme Court of Canada bases its reasoning on the existence of a recourse for unjust enrichment, thereby demonstrating that common-law spouses do benefit from a type of protection that makes non discriminatory their exclusion from the benefit of legislation granting a *de facto* right to the sharing of family property. One means among others to address the issue of disadvantaged common-law spouses following separation could therefore be to acknowledge the reasoning of Supreme Court justices and in doing so, apply to common-law spouses with far more flexibility and understanding than is currently the case the rules of compensation as it is the case for married people. The need for protecting the family and women in precarious dependency speaks loudly for enhanced equality of treatment in these issues. But this does not mean that status should never matter anymore. When no children are involved, spouses should be free to decide what the financial consequences of their relationship will be. Upon separation the law provides for remedial measures, such as constructive trust, unjust enrichment and maintenance rights. Those measures should be applied with fairness and effectiveness. Yet when partners are parents too, status should be put aside for the sake of children.

Legal Protection of Unmarried and Divorced Mothers in the Czech Republic

Zdeňka Králíčková[1]

I. Introduction

This paper explores the influence of political, social, and economic changes of family structures in the Czech Republic.[2] The study deals with statistic figures and looks for the reasons of the many informal relationships in the Czech Republic. As such families are very unstable this paper mainly focuses on the bad social and economic situation of de facto family torsos: very often unmarried mothers with new-borns or very small children. As the divorce rate is very high in the Czech Republic the economic situation of unmarried mothers is compared to the supposedly »much better« financial conditions of divorced mothers with minor children.

Presenting a comprehensive study with respect to historical aspects this paper also analyzes changes in Czech Family Law, especially in connection with legal aspects of financial protection of incomplete families: families of unmarried mothers or divorced mothers and their under-age children. It is generally known that due to the idealistic approach of communist ideology and doctrine, the property issues in legal regulation of both families based on marriage and families not established by marriage were neglected. Today we still face the consequences.

As the full reform of Czech Family Law in the new Civil Code has been discussed for almost 20 years along with great expectations by most experts, as well as a continuing adoration of the old law, the final lines of this paper are devoted to an introduction to the designed law.

---

1 Associate Professor at the Faculty of Law, Masaryk Univerzity, Brno, The Czech Republic.
2 On this issue see S. *Radvanová:* The state of the Czech family and the family law at present [in Czech]. Právní praxe, 1999, No. 2-3, pp. 94-102, A Portrait of a Family (on the background of the legal order) [in Czech]. Zdravotnictví a právo, 2004, No. 2, pp. 15-22 and other publications by the same author. For the Czech reality in details, see *J. Haderka:* The Czech Republic – New Problems and Old Worries. The International Survey of Family Law. The Hague – Boston – London: Martinus Nijhoff Publ., 1996, pp. 181-197.

II. Families not Based on Marriage and as Torsos after Divorce: Why so Many?

As mentioned above, this paper is focused mainly on families not based on marriage and families after the break-down of the marriage as a result of the current development of the Czech society. The problems are listed as follows:
> adoration of the phenomenon of a single life style,
> an increase of the amount of children born out of wedlock (34.5% in 2007),
> quite a lot of children with the status of the father unknown (28% in 2007),[3]
> an increasing number of de facto families, quite a high cohabitation **natality** and – surprisingly – alarming instability of such families,
> postponing the decision to get married (the age of brides 28.6, the age of grooms 31 in 2007),
> a low number of new marriages (about 5 to 1 000 inhabitants: 57 157 in 2007) and very low marital **natality** (65.5% in 2007),
> marital instability and a high divorce rate (49% divorces to 100 marriages: 31 129 in 2007),
> granting the individual custody of minor children mainly to their mothers (90%),
> diversity of incomes, turbulences on the labour market, unemployment, polarisation of the society, a high rate of family debts, etc., problems with the enforcement of maintenance.

It creates many problems especially for single mothers, for divorced mothers and for children in fatherless families as well as for the whole society, including the state budget and social benefits. To get a better picture of the Czech society, let us have a look at some figures from the Yearbook of the Czech Statistical Office.[4]

---

3   In the number of the children born out of wedlock.
4   For details see www.czso.cz from 15. 7. 2008. Some figures are available in English.

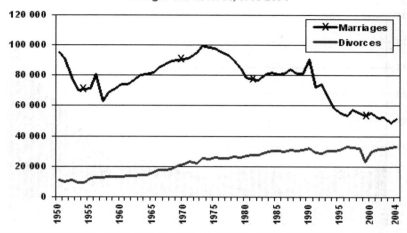

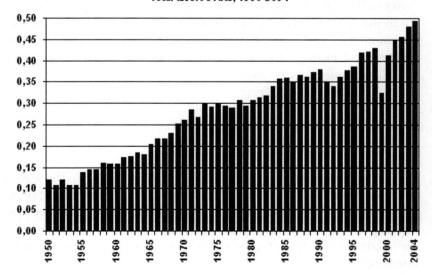

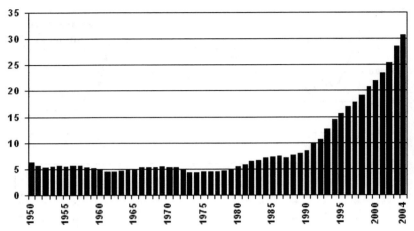

Percentage of extra-marital births, 1950-2004

As for the reasons why there are so many informal relationships, de facto families, quasi-marital unions, free forms of cohabitation – mainly heterosexual with minor children, and great instability of any relationships, we can say that they are miscellaneous. Are they connected to the crisis of traditional values in Europe or to the communist past of the Czech republic? These questions are not easy to answer, especially for lawyers.

Regarding the reasons why the economic and social situation of family torsos is quite bad, the answers may be found in the retrospect to the communist and the post-communist reality and to the communist doctrine and ideology based on underestimating property aspects in family and family law after 1948.

III. Underestimating Property Aspects of Family and Family Law after 1948: General Notes

The Czechoslovak Family Law was designed according to the Soviet pattern in many aspects. The »independent« Act on Family Law (1949) and the Act on the Family (1963 – further only AF) abandoned the traditional family law institutions and vulgarised some of them. The Civil Codes (1950, 1964 – further only CC) were not based on traditional values either.

The maintenance duty between the spouses and ex-spouses was taken as exceptional. As Olga A. Khazova says:
»*The Soviet family model knew no ›housewife marriage‹ and ›the right‹ of a woman to claim maintenance from her husband merely because of her status as wife was abolished as ›a bourgeois survival of the past‹ which would be ›incompatible with the ideology of proletarian State.‹*«[5]

It is not surprising that Senta Radvanová, in her studies, speaks about the phenomenon called »*feminisation of poverty*« and about increasing economic gaps between children living with both parents and children living only with one parent, mainly with the mothers.[6]

The euphoria and enthusiasm of the early 1990´s could have led to revolutionary changes in Czech Family Law. Unfortunately, the development in the Czech Republic was different from the countries of the former Soviet Union where all 15 republics cancelled the law designed according to the Soviet pattern and passed a new one.[7] In the Czech Republic, only the so-called Great Amendment of the Act on Family was passed in 1998.[8]

---

5 For details see *O. A. Khazova:* Family Law in the Former Soviet Union: More Differences or More in Common. *M. Antokolskaia (ed.):* Convergence and Divergence of Family Law in Europe. Antwerpen – Oxford: Intersentia, 2007, pp. 98-99.
6 See *S. Radvanová:* Maintenance duty with question marks [in Czech]. Právo a zákonnost, 1990, No. 8, pp. 440 ff.
7 Towards this see *M. Antokolskaia:* New Russian Family Law [in Czech]. Právní praxe, 1999, No. 2/3, pp. 141, and *O. A. Khazova:* Family Law in the Former Soviet Union ... op. cit., pp. 97 ff.
8 The so-called *Great Amendment to the Act on the Family* made by the Act No. 91/1998 Coll. was preceded by an *amendment* in the form of the Act No. 234/1992 Coll. which is very limited with respect to its size but is of key importance from the point of view of its content: the possibility to enter a marriage in a church was reinstated into the legal order of the federation (Art. 4a-4b of the Family Act), including the relatively problematic retroactivity (cf. Art. 4c of the Family Act).
As for the *Civil Code* amendments important for the family law it is necessary to mention the so-called *Great Amendment* made by the Act No. 509/1991 Coll. which significantly touched upon the issue of community property of spouses by enabling the so-called modification contracts and by adjusting the common use of a flat by a married couple, when substituting it with the traditional notion of »tenancy«. By this, however, the amendment did not fully break the rigidity of property rights – as for married couples in general, or as for the dwelling of the spouses in particular. The Civil Code was amended by the *Great Amendment to the Act on the Family* made by the Act No. 91/1998 Coll., too. Joint ownership by spouses (only things) was changed into Community of property of spouses with much bigger scope.

As Jiří Haderka aptly called it, it was only »*a half-hearted law reform.*«[9] Fortunately, some positive changes were made in the sphere of maintenance and marital property law in 1998. We should mention the most important points: (a) when considering the liable party the court shall consider the entire property situation of the liable person, including potentiality (Art. 96/1 AF), (b) when determining the extent of maintenance for the child based on the »same living standard«, the possibility of creating »savings« for the child from the maintenance with no limits (Art. 85a/2 AF), (c) the extension of maintenance duty for unmarried mothers of children for 2 years (see Art. 95 AF), (d) the establishment of the so-called »sanctioning« maintenance between ex-spouses based on the »same living standard« for 3 years following the divorce (Art. 93 AF), (e) the extension of the scope of the community of property of spouses (see Art. 143 CC) and (f) more autonomy of will between the spouses (Art. 143a CC).

IV. Legal Protection of an Unmarried Mother and of her Child

Polls and statistics show that more and more people wish to live with a partner without a marriage in the so-called factual cohabitation, or even without a partner all together. To a large extent this is a reaction to the previous closed society where the family life based on marriage considerably prevailed as a way of life. Under the communist regime, only older people – divorced or widowed – lived as unmarried couples. That is why there is neither a legal definition of cohabitation nor a catalogue of rights and duties of unmarried couples in the Act on Family.[10]

---

9 For details see *M. Zuklínová:* What is new in the Family Act [in Czech]. Právní praxe, 1998, No. 5, p. 258, and *J. Haderka:* On the origin and basic problems of the Family Act Amendment of 1998 in Czech. Právní praxe, 1998, No. 5, pp. 269 - 297.

   See *J. Haderka:* A Half-Hearted Family Law Reform of 1998. International Survey of Family Law. Bristol: Jordan Publ., 2000, pp. 119-130.

   On problems of the development in the post-communist countries, see materials from the conference held in Prague in 1998, organised by the *International society of family law*, especially the introductory paper; see *J. Haderka:* Basic features of the legal regulation of the family law in the post-totalitarian states of Central and Eastern Europe [in Czech]. Právní praxe, 1999, No. 2/3, pp. 71-93.

   For the general view on the communist family law, compare *M. Mladenović, M. Janjić-Komar, C. Jessel-Holst:* The family in Post-Socialist Countries. International Encyclopaedia of Comparative Law. Vol. IV, Chap. 10. Tübingen 1998, pp. 3-151.

10 Let us note that *no community of property* similar to joint property of married spouses may arise between unmarried spouses on the basis of a law or a contract (Art. 136/2 CC). If unmarried spouses have lived together in a factual long term union, each of

If the de-facto partners manage their finances together by informal agreement their needs are factually satisfied within that framework. The problem is that barely a couple has an agreement. Therefore, when problems arise or after the extinction of such an informal relationship, the economically weaker party of the couple has no legal entitlement towards the other partner, not even when they have a minor child.

It is alarming that quite a lot of women (mainly with the basic education and low income) decide to stay single with the child's legal status of »father unknown« in order to profit from the state social benefits scheme. Sometimes they are not familiar with the special legal protection of an unmarried mother with a new-born child and – the legal protection of her child:

a) To avoid the difficult social and economic situation of a pregnant unmarried woman and to prevent her from (sometimes) abandoning the new-born child,[11] the law (Art. 95/2 AF) grants her the entitlement in court prior to the child's delivery, towards the man whose paternity is probable: (i) the costs of her maintenance, (ii) the costs related to pregnancy and child delivery and (iii) the costs of the expected child's maintenance for a time span of 28 weeks, however not in the

---

them acquires property into his/her own *individual ownership* and may dispose of this property without the consent of the other spouse. If they obtain something together, *co-ownership with shares* may arise between them like among other persons. If not stipulated by the law or agreed by the parties otherwise the *portions* of the property owned by them are *equal* (Art. 137/2 CC).

Unlike married spouses *no common tenancy of a flat* shared by unmarried couples may arise *by operation of the law*. The other spouse may only live in the flat as *a close person* or as *a family member* (Art. 115 and Art. 116 CC).

Only upon the death of the tenant the tenancy of the flat may pass by operation of the law to the surviving person supposing he/she proves that he/she lived with the dead partner *for three years* prior to his/her death and he/she does not have a flat of his/her own (Art. 706/1 CC). As for co-operative flats it holds that in the case of the death of the tenant the tenancy passes to an heir of the share. If there is *no will* the situation of the surviving de facto partner is rather *difficult*.

On this issue see *M. Zuklínová:* Question marks on another (i.e. non-marital) co-habitation from the point of view of family law [in Czech]. Právní rozhledy, 1999, No. 6, pp. 295 – 299.

11 On fierce critical comments see *M. Hrušáková, Z. Králíčková.:* Anonymous and secret motherhood in the Czech Republic – a utopia, or reality? [in Czech]. Právní rozhledy, 2005, No. 2, p. 53ff.

On the history, the contemporary state and, unfortunately, the future of the boxes for abandoned children see *M. Zuklínová:* Several notes on the legal questions on the so-called baby-boxes [in Czech]. Právní rozhledy, 2005, No. 7, pp. 250 and following. Compare further the conclusion, not very favourable for the Czech Republic and its legislative practice.

scope of »the same living standard« but only as »necessary maintenance«, which »pushes« the unmarried mother after the child's delivery to establish the child's legal fathership and to demand the proper maintenance. The court may rule that the probable father will be obliged to reimburse the necessary amount in advance. It is of no relevance whether the parents of the child live together or not.

b) In addition, the Act on Family provides for the entitlements of an unmarried mother towards her child's legal father only to a very limited extent. It has no relevance whether the child's mother lives with his/her father or not (Art. 95/1 AF). According to the law the child's »legal« father to whom the mother is not married is obliged to (i) contribute »reasonably« to cover the costs for her maintenance in the period of two years and to (ii) reimburse her expenditures related to her pregnancy and confinement. The mother may claim the costs as stated if and only after the child has been delivered and paternity legally established either by the common affirmation of the parents or by the court ruling.

Regarding the maintenance duty towards the child, the child has the right to enjoy the living standard of it's parents (it does not matter whether they are married or not) until he/she gets a chance to manage his/her maintenance by himself/herself (see Art. 85 AF). That is why the mother can claim the child's maintenance in the scope of »the same living standard«, including the costs towards the child's father incurring from purchasing the necessary items for the child such as a baby pram, a baby cot, baby clothing, etc.

V. Legal Protection of Divorced Mother and her Child

Unlike the law of many West European countries the law of the former communist countries did not regulate the duty to maintain the divorced spouse with a (very) small child as an usual effect of divorce. This conception was due to an almost full-employment of women in the former Czechoslovak Socialist Republic from the early 1950s. The after-divorce maintenance duty was considered exceptional. Therefore the Act on Family in its original wording (1963) recognized the divorced spouse's right to be maintained in such a situation only when the spouse was not able to support himself or herself. The entitlement was limited to the so-called »necessary« maintenance and to the period of five years following

the divorce with the option for the judge to prolong the duty to maintain in special cases. The limits were cancelled in 1982. The so-called Great Amendment of the Act on Family of 1998 brought about big changes:[12]
a) General legal regulation of post-divorce maintenance is still based on the »state of need« and is not limited in time. The key precondition for claiming the duty to maintain between the divorced spouses is that one of the spouses is not able to support himself/herself after the divorce. That is all. The former spouse who is not able to provide the maintenance for himself can ask the other one for the rent of »reasonable« maintenance (Art. 92 AF). The court practice holds »reasonableness« as considered in relation to abilities and possibilities and the whole property situation of the liable divorced persons, the living standard during the marriage, the length of the marriage, the care of children – and health condition, age, property conditions etc. of the entitled divorced persons. There are no tables, percentages fixed by law, etc. The allowance must not be settled when it is contrary to the principle of good morals. It is to be proved by the liable person. Therefore, along with determining maintenance, the court also considers reasons leading to the breakdown of the marriage.
b) The law regulates specifically the so-called »sanctioning« maintenance (Art. 93 AF). In exceptional cases, the former spouse who, did not cause prevalently the breakdown of the marriage by violating the matrimonial duties and who suffered a serious (non-proprietary) loss by the divorce, can require a maintenance in the scope of »the same living standard« from the other former spouse – i.e. such an amount so that the material and cultural living standards of both spouses could be principally the same, i.e. as if no divorce occurred. This provision is connected to the new regulation of divorce (see Art. 24a and 24b AF) and mainly to the problem called feminisation of poverty. Such an extended maintenance may be granted for no more than three years following the divorce. In determining the extent of maintenance the court does not examine whether the divorced spouse is able to support himself or herself.

---

12 See *Z. Králíčková:* Maintenance duty between divorced spouses according to the Great Amendment to the Act on the Family being in force since 1. 8. 1998. [in Czech]. Právní rozhledy, 1998, No. 8, pp. 389 – 393.

Let us note that property rights of a minor child after the divorce of his/her parents are secured by other provisions of the Act on the Family. The law provides that if the spouses have minor children a »special« court determination of the after-divorce parental care (individual, common, alternative custody) and maintenance liability has to precede the divorce itself (Art. 25 AF). Regarding the maintenance both parents have to contribute to the child's maintenance according to their abilities, possibilities and general property conditions so that the child can enjoy the same living standard as his/her parents (see Art. 85 AF).[13] However, sometimes it remains »law in book«. For some mothers it is very difficult to prove the high living standard of the father and to demand »the same living standard« and »savings« for the child.[14]

VI. Conclusions

As it was said above, the full reform of Czech Family Law within a new Civil Code has been discussed for almost 20 years. There were some attempts in the history after 1989.[15] In 2001 the new Government approved the

---

13   In evaluating the liable party‹s abilities, possibilities and property conditions, the court shall examine whether the liable person has *not given up a more advantageous job or gainful activity or property benefit* without an important reason and eventually whether he or she does not undergo inadequate property *risks*. In determining the maintenance the court shall take into account *justified needs of the entitled person*. In determining the *extent* of the maintenance duty the court shall consider parents´ *personal care* of the child as well. The parent‹s duty to maintain their children exists *unless the children are able to earn their living on their own* (achieving the age of 18, 21 or 26 by the child is not relevant for this purpose).

14   That is why the above mentioned Great Amendment to the Act on Family (1998) established the *presumption of income* of the liable parent to »*improve*« *a minor child's position* (new Art. 85a AF). The law provides that a *parent* having *an income* other than from employment, i.e. subject to income tax, *must prove* his or her income before court submitting documents necessary for an evaluation of his or her property conditions and enable the court to find out also other facts necessary for its decision by making accessible data protected pursuant to special Acts. If the *parent fails to fulfil this duty* his or her *average monthly earning shall be presumed* to amount to the 12.7 multiple of the life minimum necessary for ensuring the maintenance and other fundamental personal needs of this parent pursuant to the Act on Living and Subsistence Level (in 2008 it is about 40 000 Czech crowns). If the property condition of the liable parent allows so, *creation of savings* ensuring in particular preparation for the future profession may also be considered a child‹s justified need.

15   Compare *J. Švestka, F. Zoulík, M. Knappová, J. Mikeš:* On the development and the contemporary state of re-codification of the Czech civil law [in Czech]. In: The issues of re-codification of private law [in Czech]. Acta Universitatis Carolinae, Iuridica, 2003, No. 2/3, p. 39.

legislative intention of the new Civil Code that was followed by the Draft. Since then, the Draft has been a topic of comments, analyses and conferences. Family law rules form the second part of the work.[16]

When looking at the explanatory note on the Draft, the creators' efforts aiming at making discontinuity with the communist law and at the creation of a code in harmony with European cultural standards is perceivable at the first sight – especially in the sphere of maintenance and marital property law, topics which were suppressed by the communist doctrine.[17] The family and (post-)partnership solidarity and private law responsibility are the key values the Draft is based on.

---

16 On the subject matter of the law compare *K. Eliáš, M. Zuklínová:* Principles and starting points of the new private law code [in Czech]. Praha: Linde 2001.
17 See the explanatory note, I. general part, pp. 1 and following, and the partial explanatory notes to the individual clauses of the Second Part – Family law, pp. 92 and following of the Draft for the Civil Code. Part One to Four. Draft of the working committee. Praha: Ministry of Justice, without reference, without year (spring 2005) [in Czech]. [Main compilers: *K. Eliáš* and *M. Zuklínová*]. Then, see the 2008 ′version of the Draft – www.justice.cz (15. 7. 2008).

Financial Consequences of Cohabitation between Persons of the Opposite Sex According to Greek Law

Penelope Agallopoulou[1]

I. Introduction

By cohabitation I mean a relationship between a man and a woman which has a tendency to be stable. Cohabitation between same-sex couples is outside the scope of this paper.

In Greece the level of cohabitation is one of the lowest of all the member states of the EU. It should be noted, of course, that it is increasing year by year, mainly among young people[2]. This is accounted for by the fact that Greece, along with Ireland, has one of the highest marriage rates in the EU and there are comparatively few children born out of wedlock. Nevertheless, the number of couples living together out of wedlock is also increasing. In Greece marriage today is usually the culmination of a previous long-term relationship rather than the start of a new period in the life of the newlyweds. Recent statistics also support the assertion that the institution of marriage is changing in Greece.

In spite of the fact that cohabitation is generally accepted in Greece as a social phenomenon, it is still, as of September 2008, not regulated by law[3]. Cohabitation is thus confronted as *a de facto* situation, which is nei-

---

[1] University of Piraeus, Greece.
[2] Although the average cohabitation in the European Union is 9%, in Greece it is only 1%. It is also important to note that amongst the under 30s, although the average in the European Union is 28%, in Greece it is only 7% (See *P.Agallopoulou*, Cohabitations, in the collective Volume edited in honor of Prof. Apostolos Georgiadis, Vol. I, 2007, p.5; *K. Kasearu*,The case of unmarried cohabitation in Western and Eastern Europe, 2007, p. 2, in site: http://www.eui.eu/Personal/Dronkers/Divorce/ Divorceconference2007/Kasearu.pdf ; *B.N.Adams*, Families and family Study in International Perspective, in Journal of Marriage and Family 66 (2004), p.1081. As far as births out of wedlock are concerned, they continue to increase in the European Union, reflecting the growing popularity of cohabitation but, in Greece, in the year 2006, the percentage was only 5,28% of all births (http://epp.eurostat.ec.europa.eu).
[3] Cohabitation has been recently regulated by Law 3719/2008. On this issue see *infra*, esp. section III.

ther permitted nor prohibited by the law. The provisions of the Greek Civil Code concerning cohabitation are the following:
a) the disposition of article 1444 § 2, according to which in case of divorce »the right of maintenance shall cease if the ex-spouse entitled thereto re-marries or if he/she cohabits permanently with somebody else in a free union.«
b) The dispositions of articles 1455 ff. on medically assisted human reproduction, which provide that all kinds of medically assisted reproduction are also permitted for cohabitants[4]. It is important to emphasize that according to the dispositions of the Civil Code on medically assisted reproduction, which were introduced by law 3089/2002, married and unmarried couples and even single women have the right to enjoy medically assisted methods in order to procreate.

Cohabitation contracts between the cohabitants regulating their relationship during and after their cohabitation are valid according to the general principle of the freedom of the parties to enter into contracts (Art. 361 CC). This is so because, as already mentioned, cohabitation is not a relationship contrary to morality or the public policy. Naturally, it is not possible by such an agreement to impose guarantee clauses or the application of the dispositions of Greek family law.

Greek family law does not contain any specific dispositions concerning the consequences of cohabitation. According to the prevailing opinion of legal scholars the dispositions of the Civil Code concerning marriage could be applied, by analogy, during cohabitation[5].

In view of the shortcomings of the current legal situation, a Bill on the cohabitation of persons of opposite sex has been prepared by a preliminary committee, but, as of September 2008, has not yet been voted by the

---

[4] Arts. 1455 ff. have been introduced into the Greek Civil Code by Law 3089/2002 on medically assisted human reproduction.

[5] *M.Stathopoulos-Chr.Stambelou*, Introductory remarks to articles 1350-1371, in Ap. Georgiadis – M. Stathopoulos, Commentary on the Civil Code (collective work), Vol. VII (2nd edition) 2007, no 14ff; *Agallopoulou*, op.cit., p.14; *Th.Papachristos*, A Manual of Family Law, (3rd edition) 2005, p.192; *G. Koumantos*, Family Law, volume I, 1988, p. 19 ff.; *I. Androulidaki-Dimitriadi*, The influence of cohabitation on the right to maintenance in the »Essays in honour of Professor G. Michailidis-Nouaros« 1987, p. 65 ff.; *P. Nikolopoulos*, Common Life in family Law, in Nomiko Vima (Law Journal, hereinafter:NoV), 1994, p. 1133. But see also: *A. Gazis*, Introductory remarks to family law, in Ap. Georgiadis-M. Stathopoulos, op. cit., Vol. VII (1st edition) 1991, no. 75.

Greek Parliament.[6] This Bill provides for the conclusion of cohabitation contracts as well as their termination. It also regulates relations between the cohabitants, both during their contract and after its termination, as well as issues regarding their children.[7]

II. Current Legal Situation

1. Legal Consequences during Cohabitation

As I have already mentioned Greek family law does not contain any specific dispositions concerning the consequences of cohabitation between the cohabitants during cohabitation. The weaknesses of the law are covered by the legal scholars and case-law.

According to the prevailing opinion of legal scholars the dispositions of the Civil Code concerning marriage could be applied, by analogy, during cohabitation.[8]

More specifically: It concerns the dispositions about the obligation to cohabit (article 1386 CC), the obligation to decide jointly on any matter pertaining to conjugal life (article 1387 CC), the obligation to contribute jointly, each according his/her resources, to the needs of the family (Art. 1389 CC), and the presumptions in the matter of movable property (Art. 1398 CC)[9].

Gifts between cohabitants are valid if all the formal and substantive requirements for their validity have been met (Arts. 496–498 CC). Fur-

---

6   The Bill has been voted and enacted into law on the 26th November 2008 (See Law 3719/2008 on Reform on the law relating to the family, the child, the society and other provisions).
7   This Bill does not concern cohabitation between persons of same sex. Although marriage, far less cohabitation, between persons of same sex is not permitted by Greek law, the mayor of the small island of Tilos performed two marriages between persons of same sex. Although there has been much debate about the legality of these marriages, they are non-existent according to Greek law.
8   See *supra* note 5.
9   ➤ Movable property in the possession of or held by one or both spouses shall be deemed for the benefit of the creditors of each of the spouses to belong to the spouse who is indebted to them. This presumption shall not hold in the case of the interruption of life in common.
    ➤ Movable property in the possession of or held by both spouses shall be presumed in the relationships between themselves to belong to both in equal parts.
    ➤ In the relationships of the spouses between themselves and between the spouses and their creditors it shall be presumed that movable property destined for the personal use of one of the spouses belong to this spouse.

thermore the content of the donation must be consistent with law and morality.

A question posed in the case of cohabitation is the following: do juridical acts concluded by one of the cohabitants with a third person in connection with the current needs of their household bind the other cohabitant? I assume that the other cohabitant is responsible only if he/she has approved the juridical act concluded between his/her companion and a third person according to the dispositions of a pseudo-representative (*falsus procurator*). Furthermore, I assume that it is not necessary to give an approval each time one of the cohabitants concludes a contract with a third person, because given the fact that there exists a cohabitation, it is assumed that power of attorney has tacitly been given by one cohabitant to the other who concluded the juridical act.[10]

2. *Legal Consequences after Interruption of Cohabitation by the Unilateral Will of one of the Cohabitants*

After the interruption of cohabitation by the unilateral will of one of the cohabitants, given that, in a long-term relationship the situation formed is similar to marriage, I feel that some dispositions of the Civil Code concerning the dissolution of marriage should be applied. More specifically:

2.1 Claim to Participate in the Increments

Given that one of the cohabitants has made a contribution to the increase of the assets of the other in various ways, such as the provision of capital to acquire movable or immovable property, the provision of a home, work in the house or the provision of work in the office or the business, it is reasonable to accept a similar application of the regulations of the Civil Code concerning the claim to participation of one spouse in the increase of the assets of the other spouse, accumulated during the cohabitation, provided of course that he/she is able to prove that this increase of assets is also due to his/her own contribution (Art.1400, 1 and 2 CC).

I should also add that because it is difficult to prove the contribution of one spouse to the assets of the other, the Greek Civil Code establishes a rebuttable presumption by which such contribution is limited to one third (⅓) of the increase. But, given the fact that, as already mentioned, such a presumption is rebuttable, if it is proved that the contribution was greater, the claim will also be higher. If, on the contrary, it is proved that

---

10 *Agallopoulou*, op.cit., p.14 ff; *I. Androulidaki-Dimitriadi*, The Cohabitation, 1984, p.183.

the contribution was less or that there was no contribution, the claim will be limited accordingly or disallowed altogether (Art. 1400, 1 and 2 CC). The application by analogy of the above dispositions of the Civil Code in cohabitation is accepted by the legal scholars and a part of case-law.[11]

2.2 Regulation of the Use of the Family Home and Distribution of Movable Property

I also feel that in the case of interruption of the common life of the spouses 'the appropriate application of the provisions of the Civil Code concerning the regulation of the use of the family home[12] (Art. 1393 CC)[13] and the distribution of movable property between spouses[14] (Arts.1394-1395 CC) is possible[15].

---

[11] See *Agallopoulou*, op.cit., p.17; *Androulidaki-Dimitriadi*, The Cohabitation, op.cit, p. 152 ff.; *G. Koumantos*, op. cit., p. 20; *Nikolopoulos*, op.cit., p.1133. See also decision 206/1991 of the Rhodes Court of First Instance, in Elliniki Dikaiosini (Law journal, hereinafter: EllDni 1995, 725 with a positive comment by *P. Nikolopoulos*. See also the following court decisions, which do not accept a similar application of the assessment of participation in the goods acquired during the cohabitation: 204/1999 of the Kozani Court of First Instance, in NoV 2000, 1446, with negative comments by *E. Kounougeri-Manoledaki*, in EllDni 2003, 919; 778/2004 of Athens Court of First Instance, in Data bank of the Athens Bar Association. See also *P. Nikolopoulos*, Developments in Case-Law Regarding Increments of the Spouses, (2nd ed.), 2004, pp. 38ff.; *Papachristos*, op.cit., p.190.

[12] In the case of the interruption of communal life, the court may, insofar as is required by considerations of indulgence regarding the special circumstances of each of the spouses and the interest of the children, grant to one spouse the exclusive use of the whole or part of the immovable property that is used as the main abode of the spouses (family home), independently of which of them is the owner or has the right of use. The decision of the court is subject to review when circumstances so require. If the right of use of the family home arises from a service relationship between one of the spouses and a third party the granting of use thereof to the other spouse by the court pursuant to the conditions laid down in the preceding paragraph may only take place with the consent of the third party (Art. 1393 CC).

[13] See: *Agallopoulou*, op.cit., p.17; *M. Stathopoulos – Ch. Stambelou*, op.cit., no 14; *Androulidaki-Dimitriadi*, op.cit., p. 158; *Koumantos*, op.cit., p. 20.

[14] In the case of the interruption of communal life, each of the spouses shall be entitled to recover the movable property belonging to him/her even if this was used by both or by the other spouse alone. He/she shall, however, be under an obligation to allow the other spouse to make use of the household items that are absolutely necessary to him/her for his/her separate residence if for reasons of indulgence the circumstances so require (Art.1394 CC). In the case of the interruption of communal life, the spouses shall apportion the use of the movable property belonging to both in accordance with their personal needs. If they disagree, the apportionment shall be made by the court, which may award reasonable compensation for the use it grants (Art.1395 CC).

[15] *Agallopoulou*, op.cit,p.17; *M. Stathopoulos-Ch.Stambelou*, op.cit., Introduction to arts 1350-1371, no.14; *T.Papazissi*, in Georgiadis-Stathopoulos, Commentary on the Civil Code , Vol. VII, op.cit., Introductory remarks to articles 1394-1395, nos. 22 ff.; *Androulidaki-Dimitriadi*, op.cit., pp.146 ff.; *Koumantos*, op.cit., p. 20; *Nikolopoulos*, op.cit.,p. 1133.

2.3 Claims in the Case of Collaboration between Cohabitants

After the interruption of cohabitation by unilateral will, in cases where one of the cohabitants has worked in the enterprise of his/her companion without being paid we must distinguish whether or not a contract of work has been concluded between the cohabitants before the breakdown of the relationship. If a contract has been made the cohabitant who has worked can bring an action against his/her companion based on that contract. Alternatively, he/she can bring an action based on the dispositions concerning enrichment without just cause (Arts. 904 ff CC)[16].

In cases where the cohabitants have created a business together, it is possible after the breakdown of the relationship to proceed to dissolve the business, and after the settlement of debts and the restitution of the contributions, liquidate and distribute the remaining balance between the parties. In cases where the partners do not agree on the distribution one of them can ask for it, by launching a special action[17].

In cases where the cohabitants have not created a business together but have created a common capital, I assume that a *de facto* company has been created between them and is therefore argued that concerning the distribution of movable property, articles 1394–1395 of the Civil Code are applicable by analogy.

2.4 Claim of the Mother of a Child Born following the Cohabitation

Although the Greek Civil Code does not include a special disposition concerning the children of cohabitants, it is evident that in the case of cohabitation the procedure for the judicial acknowledgement by a father of a child born out of wedlock is easier.

---

16 See *Agallopouloui*, op.cit., p. 18; *Androulidaki-Dimitriadi, op.cit*, p. 136;. From the case law see: 1244/1964 of the Athens Court of Appeal, in Armenopoulos (Law Journal, hereinafter Arm) 1965, 310; 266/1965 of the Court of Cassation, in NoV 1966, 17; 181/1969 of the Athens Court of First Instance, in Epitheorissis Ergatikou Dikaiou (Law journal, hereinafter EED) 1969, 376; 2693/1970 of the Athens Court of Appeal, in EED 1971, 300; 6690/1975 of the Athens Court of Appeal, in NoV 1976, 328; 194/1990 of the Court of Cassation, in NoV 1991, 548; 1356/1992 of the Court of Cassation, in EllDni 1995,345; 544/1995 of the Court of Cassation, in EllDni 1996, 314. Contra: 1051/1975 of the Athens Court of Appeal, in EED 1975, 1325; 274/1986 of the Athens Court of Appeal, in EED 1987, 79; 1704/1990 of Thessaloniki Court of Appeal, in Arm 1990, 345.
17 See *Agallopoulou*, op. cit., p.18 ff. See also the decision 119/2000 of Kerkyra Court of Appeal, in Dikaio Epihiriseon kai Eterion (Law Journal) 2001, 867.

In the case of acknowledgement, whether voluntary or judicial, the child has in all matters the position of a child born in marriage with regard to both parents and their relatives (Art. 1484 CC).

Concerning the financial obligations of the father towards the mother of the child it should be noted that according article 1503 of the Civil Code: if, following the cohabitation a child was born, which was acknowledged judicially by its father, the mother has the right to ask for the restitution of the expenses occasioned by the childbirth and for maintenance in so far as she is unable to provide for her own maintenance for 2 months before the childbirth and 4 months after or, in the event of special circumstances, one year at most. Naturally, she has to claim these amounts if they have not already have been paid by the father.

If the paternity is very probable and the mother is without resources she may ask the court, even before lodging an action for acknowledgment, to order, as a provisional measure, the prepayment by the father to the child each month of a reasonable amount for the maintenance owed to the child (Art.1502 CC).

3. Legal Consequences of Cohabitation in the Case of Death of one of the Cohabitants

The problems arising in the case of death of one of the cohabitants are the following:

3.1 Possibility for the Survivor to Inherit a Part of the Estate of the Deceased by a Will

The disposition of the will of a cohabitant by which he/she bequeaths a part of his/her estate to his/her companion is valid except in the case where this disposition results in contempt of his/her next of kin. This is the case where, without a valid reason, he/she has left his/her next of kin a very small part of his/her estate.[18]

The disposition of a will by which the deceased has left his/her companion a sum of money as remuneration for the sexual relationship they had is also considered void.[19]

---

18 See decisions: 1117/1974 of the Court of Cassation, in NoV 1975, 720; 821/1977 of the Court of Cassation, in NoV 1978, 669; 52/1990 of Thesprotias Court of First Instance, in Arm 1991, 143; 13/1991 of the Court of Cassation, in NoV 1993, 528; 1411/1998 of the Court of Cassation, in Arm 1998, 1488.
19 See *Agallopoulou*, op. cit., p. 20; *Androulidaki-Dimitriadi*, op. cit., p. 168; *A. Gazis - K. Kerameus*, Invalidity of adoption and of a will in the case of lacking capacity and oppo-

3.2 Regulation of the Use of the Family Home

According to the prevailing opinion of the legal scholars, in the case of death of one of the cohabitants, if the cohabitation was of long duration, the dispositions concerning the family home in the case of marriage are applicable by analogy.[20]

3.3 Request for Compensation to the Surviving Companion in the Case of Violent Death

In case of death the survivor does not have the right to ask for compensation (Art. 928 CC).[21]

With regard to medical and funeral expenses the surviving partner is not obliged to pay for them. In cases where he/she has paid for them[22] and is not an heir of the deceased, he/she has the right to claim their reimbursement from the heir by application of the dispositions of voluntary agency (Arts. 736 ff. CC). In cases where the survivor is an heir of the deceased he/she should pay the expenses in proportion to his share of the estate of the deceased (Art. 1885 CC).

Concerning the reparation for moral suffering caused to the survivor by the death of his/her companion, the consistent judicial precedent has for several years accepted that the survivor can claim such reparation by application of article 932 of the Civil Code. The case-law was based on the interpretation of the last sentence of article 932 CC which implies that »in the case of the death of a person such monetary reparation may be allotted to the victim's family on account of moral suffering«. It was admitted

---

sition to morality (Consultation), in NoV 1987, 324; From the case law see: 1021/1969 of the Athens Court of Appeal, in NoV 1970, 571; 299/1974 of the Court of Cassation, in NoV 1974, 1287; 1174/1974 of the Court of Cassation, in NoV 1975, 720; 579/1976 of the Court of Cassation, in NoV 1976, 1085; 821/1977 of the Court of Cassation, in NoV 1978, 669; 1311/1982 of the Court of Cassation, in NoV 1983, 1343; 1439/1986 of the Athens Court of First Instance, in Archeio Nomologias (Law Journal) 1988, 147.

20 According to the disposition of article 612 $ 2 CC »In a case where the leased thing was used during the lifetime of the lessee as family home in the meaning of article 1393 (Art. 1393 CC concerns the use of family home) and at the time of the lessee's demise his or her spouse is alive, the rights and obligations arising from the lease contract devolve exclusively on the surviving spouse who however shall have the right to terminate the lease at any time subject to notice given in accordance with the provisions of the proceeding paragraph« (that is that the termination shall take place by notice given at least three months in advance and shall be effective for the end of a calendar month). See *Androulidaki-Dimitriadi*, op. cit., p. 188.
21 See *Agallopoulou*, op. cit., p. 21.
22 Expenses are paid by the heirs (Arts. 1901 § 1 and 1831 CC).

by case-law that the cohabitant is also included within the meaning of the word »family«[23].

However, I realized with surprise that this point of view was not shared by some recent Greek case-law, in particular by decisions of the Greek Court of Cassation according to which »cohabitation is a *de facto* family relation which is improper and lies in the margins of legal life«[24].

3.4 Right to a Pension

Two years' married cohabitation is a necessary requirement for the recognition of the right to a pension either by the Greek Social Security Organisation or by the Greek state.[25]

There is disagreement, however, on the calculation of the two-year period: The judicial precedent of the Council of the State accepts that in calculating the two years, the long-term cohabitation of the couple should be taken into account, without a marriage having taken place, assuming that it was prevented by a legal hindrance.[26]

In contrast, the case-law of the Audits Court has accepted that the mere cohabitation of the couple before the contracting of a marriage should not be taken into account in calculating the two-year period of married cohabitation.[27]

---

23 See *I. Spyridakis*, Note to Athens Court of Appeal 618/1976, in NoV 1976, 725; *K. Pantelidou*, The meaning of family in the article 932 § 3 of the Civil Code, in Arm 1982, 402; *Ap. Georgiadis*, Law of Obligations, 1999, p. 614. From the case law see 193/1976 of Karditsa Court of Fist instance, in NoV 1977, 776; 668/1979 of Heraklion County Court, in Arm 1980, 116.

24 See Decisions 434/2005, 1735/2006, 1141/2007 of the Court of Cassation, in Data bank »Nomos«. Cf. however decision 1837/2007 of the Court of Cassation, in NoV 2008, 76, which, provided that the parties are engaged to be married, accepted that the fiancé »was tied by love and respect to her partner« and as a result of his sudden death suffered »deep pain and intense distress and as such deserves adequate financial compensation«.

25 See, respectively, art. 28 § 7, case b, of the emergency law 1846/1951, as modified later by art.1 of law 208/1974 and art. 5 § 1, case a, of the presidential decree 1041/1979.

26 See decisions of the Council of State: 2295/1987, in Deltio Ergatikis Nomothesias (Law Journal , hereinafter DEN) 1988, 310 ; 4337/1988, in DEN 1990, 370 ; 2566/1998, in Data bank »Nomos«; 816/2003, in NoV 51, 1995; 816/2003, in NoV 2003,1995; 288/2004, 3848/2004, 467/2005, 2175/2005, 290/2006, 739/2006, 1317/2007,2007/2007 in Data bank »Nomos«.

27 See decisions of the Superior Special Court: 44/1991, in Epitheorissis Dikaiou Kinonikis Asfalisis (Law Journal, hereinafter EDKA) 1991, 616 ; 31/1999, in EDKA 2000, 351; 680/2005, in EDKA 2005,680.

III. Bill on Cohabitation between Persons of opposite Sex[28]

In view of the shortcomings of the current legal situation, a bill on the cohabitation of persons of opposite sex prepared by a preliminary committee was approved by the Inner Cabinet but, as of September 2008, has not yet been voted by the Greek Parliament. The above-mentioned bill concerning the cohabitation of persons of opposite sex provides for the conclusion of cohabitation contracts (in the form of notarial deeds) and their termination. This agreement shall enter into force as soon as a copy of the contract is submitted to the registry of the place of residence. This document is filed in a special archive.

This bill was welcomed by many unmarried couples living together and by a number of academics[29] but also drew criticism.[30]

The above mentioned bill regulates relations between the cohabitants, both during their contract and after its termination, as well as issues regarding their children. This bill would grant heterosexual couples living together almost the same rights as married couples. Children born to unmarried couples would also have all the rights, hereditary and otherwise, of children born to married parents.

More specifically concerning the financial relations between the cohabitants, the following should be noted:

1. Property Relations

The bill provides that the cohabitants can, by their contract, regulate their property relations and specially the fate of the assets they will acquire during their cohabitation. If they have not reached such an agreement each partner, following the interruption of their contract, has a claim against the other, provided of course that he/she is able to prove that the increase of assets is also due to his/her own contribution[31]. No provision is made, however, for rebuttable presumption, as in the case of marriage.

In the case of death of one of the cohabitants, the claim to the increment of the assets accumulated during cohabitation does neither arise to the benefit of the heirs of the deceased cohabitant nor can it be part of the

---

28 This Bill has been recently enacted into law. See *supra* note 6.
29 *Th. Papachristos*: Cohabitation Contract: the rival of marriage or an alternative form of cohabitation, in Efarmoges Astikou Dikaiou (Law Journal), 2008, 393.
30 *K.Pantelidou*, Critical Comments on the Bill »Cohabitation Contract« in Efarmoges Astikou Dikaiou, op.cit., 2008, 386.
31 Art. 6 of the Bill concerning cohabitation between persons of opposite sex.

deceased's estate, but the surviving cohabitant may exercise the claim in question against the heirs of the deceased.

This claim shall be prescribed two years after the termination of the contract.

2. Maintenance after the Termination of the Contract

The contract to cohabit freely may include an agreement by which the obligation to maintenance is assumed, either by one or the other party or mutually, in the case of the inability of one party to maintain himself/herself from his/her own income or property, after the termination of the contract. The obligant is relieved from his/her duty to support his/her partner if, in view of all his/her obligations, he/she cannot afford it without endangering his/her own maintenance. An agreement cannot be reached for maintenance that tends to enrich the other party. This obligation does not fall upon the heirs of the obligant. The agreement is also invalid if the contract is terminated *ipso jure* by the marriage of the surviving partner to a third party[32]. Finally, this agreement does not apply in case of dissolution of the cohabitation due to death of one of the parties. In this case the survivor has a succession right on the estate of the deceased.

3. Right of Inheritance

On the termination of the contract because of death of one of the cohabitants the survivor is called an heir in intestacy with the relatives of the first rank (e.g. descendants of the deceased) to 1/6 of the estate and with the relatives of the other ranks (e.g. parents, siblings, grand-parents) to 1/3 of the estate. If there are no relatives of the deceased the surviving cohabitant is called an intestate heir to the entire estate.[33]

The surviving cohabitant has also right to a forced share in the estate. The forced heirship share is ½ of the intestate succession share.

IV. Conclusion

Turning to a brief assessment of the above-mentioned bill, which was enacted into law on the 26th November 2008[34] and does not concern

---

[32] Art. 7 of the Bill concerning cohabitation between persons of opposite sex.
[33] Art. 12 of the Bill concerning cohabitation between persons of opposite sex.
[34] See *supra* note 6.

cohabitation between persons of same sex, I consider that it is of dubious usefulness. The preamble to the bill states that the basic idea informing it is that the cohabitation contract is an alternative form of permanent cohabitation and not a form of »loose« marriage. It goes on to state that the cohabitation contract does not preclude the existence of free cohabitation entered into without such a contract. In this case this form of cohabitation will continue to have the same legal significance that it has today.

I wonder, then, what its usefulness is. It lies somewhere between marriage, which is an institution, and free cohabitation, whose one characteristic feature is the strong desire on the part of the cohabitants to remain outside the scope of legal regulation. Moreover, taking into account that the new regulation does not provide for the application, by analogy, of the provisions on marriage in the case of cohabitation, many issues remain unsettled as, for example, the use of the family home after interruption of cohabitation, the request for compensation to the surviving companion in the case of violent death and the right to a pension.

A further issue which arises out of the new regulation is the following: When there are forms of cohabitation that do not involve the drawing up of a contract, how can their consequences be regulated in the event of their termination either by the will of the cohabitants or by death? In these cases, I believe that the courts will not accept the application by analogy of the provisions relating to marriage, asserting that the cohabitants, by not drawing up a contract, did not wish to incur the same consequences as in the case of marriage.

In recent years the phenomenon of the cohabitation between persons of opposite or the same sex has become accepted in Greece. There are new models of families. This is why it is necessary to protect and respect the freedom of the cohabitants on the one hand and their fundamental rights on the other hand by eliminating the differences between such relationships and unions based on marriage. Accordingly, I believe that in the modern age, it is clearly incumbent on Greece to regulate the cohabitation between homosexuals by law, as happens in a large number of other countries.

A Liberal Analysis of Western Cohabitation Law

Shahar Lifshitz[1]

I. Introduction

The second half of the 20th century witnessed dramatic transformation and liberalization of the Western world's conception of family law.[2] Prominent scholars have described this transformation as a shift in the perception of marriage from a public institution to a private contract between couples.[3]

One of the outstanding products of this liberal transformation is the regulation of the economic relationship between unmarried cohabitants. Traditionally, Western law sharply distinguished between marriage and cohabitation obligations and even invalidated contracts in which the cohabitants explicitly assumed marriage-like commitments.[4] The last decade of the 20th century, however, was characterized by a trend to narrow the gap between the mutual obligations of cohabitants and those of married partners.[5]

Conventional wisdom depicts this trend as liberal and contractual while its opposition is viewed as conservative and moralistic.[6] The new restatement on family dissolution in the United States, as well as legislation and cases in New Zealand, Canada, Israel, Sweden and other

---

[1] Prof. Shahar Lifshitz, Professor, Bar-Ilan University; and Visiting Professor Cardozo Law School, New York.
[2] See Marry A. Glendon, *The Transformation of Family Law - State Law and Family in the United States and Western Europe (1989)*. (Describes the liberalization of western family law in the last decades of the 20th century.).
[3] See John Witte, *From Sacrament to Contract – Marriage, Religion, and Law in the Western Tradition (1997)*. (Argues that the contractual model of marriage emerged in the second half of the 20th century.); Jana B. Singer, *The Privatization of Family Law*, 1992 WIS. L. REV. 1443. (Describes the privatization process that transforms marriage from a public institution to a private arrangement.).
[4] See *infra* part 2.
[5] See *infra* note 11.
[6] See *infra* note 8.

jurisdictions,[7] may reflect the next liberal step of almost total equalization in the regulation of the relationship between unmarried cohabitants and between married partners. This paper breaks with conventional wisdom by presenting a liberal case against equalizing the mutual obligations of cohabitants and married partners. An initial version of a liberal distinction between marriage and cohabitation obligations appears already in legal scholarship and rests on a contractual basis.[8] The existing version of the liberal argument is not convincing, however, as it does not contend with counter-arguments (**extra-contractual, relational and same-sex**) which support imposing marriage law on cohabitants.[9] This paper, on the other hand, deepens and broadens the philosophical basis of the liberal case for distinguishing between marriage and cohabitation and considers the counter-arguments. More importantly, it suggests an innovative legal model that distinguishes between different types of cohabitants' obligations and different kinds of cohabitants and thus enjoys the benefits yet avoids the problems of existing approaches.

Structurally the article continues as follows: Part I begins with the **conventional story of the confrontation between conservatives and liberals**. The former support a status-based distinction between marriage and cohabitation commitments, while the later favour contractual equation of those commitments. Part II continues with **liberal arguments (contractual and pluralist) against imposing marriage law on cohabitants**. Part III responds **with three counter-arguments (extra-contractual, relational and same-sex)** in favor of equating the mutual commitments between married and cohabitant partners. Part IV links various arguments and theoretical approaches to concrete legal models present in western countries. Part V exposes the weaknesses common to all models and demonstrates the need for a new model. Part VI presents the principles for a new liberal model.

---

7   Regarding the recent trend that equates marriage and cohabitation commitments, see *infra* Part IV. (4).
8   See Ruth Deech, *The Case Against Legal Recognition of Cohabitation*, 29 INT'L & COMP.L.Q. 480 (1980) (Opposes the modern trend to apply marriage law to cohabitants; based on a liberal-individualistic perspective); David Westfall, *Forcing Incidents of Marriage on Unmarried Cohabitants: The American Law Institute's Principles of Family Dissolution*, 76 NOTRE DAME L REV.1467, 1471 (2001) et seq. (Criticizes the American Law Institution's principles for equating marriage and cohabitation.).
9   But See Marsha Garrison, *Is consent necessary? An evaluation of the emerging law of cohabitant obligation*, 52 UCLA L. REV. 815 (2005) (Criticizes the emerging trend of equating marriage and cohabitation and contends the counter arguments).

II. Historical Background: Cohabitation Law in the Liberal-Conservative Debate

Historically, the legal discussion regarding cohabitants was divided between a conservative approach that distinguished marriage from cohabitation, and a liberal approach that narrowed the gap between the legal status of married and cohabitant partners. The position of most western jurisdictions until the final decades of the 20th century represented the most conservative extreme toward cohabitation. Motivated by moral condemnation of non-marital conjugal relationships and public policy considerations in favor of marriage,[10] traditional family law fought against cohabitants in various ways.[11] Regarding the economic relationship between cohabitants, this policy led traditional law not only to reject the application of marriage law to cohabitating partners but even to invalidate explicit contracts between cohabitants.[12] Influenced by the liberal transformation of western family law during the second half of the 20th century, most jurisdictions now respect spouses' private choices and validate explicit contracts in which cohabitants assume marriage-like commitments.[13] Furthermore, during the last decade of the 20th century a variety of legal doctrines[14] such as implied contract theory,[15] restitution,[16]

---

10 See Thomas Oldham & David S. Caudill, *A Reconnaissance of Public Policy Restriction upon Enforcement of Contracts Between Cohabitants*, 18 FAM. L.Q. 93, 97 (1984) at 106 »Because of the perceived immorality of these relationships, even express contracts between cohabitants were not enforced.«
11 See Jane Lewis, *Family Policy in the Post-War Period*, CROSS CURRENTS - FAMILY LAW AND POLICY IN THE US AND ENGLAND 81, 82-90 (Sanford, N. Katz et al. eds., 2000) (The legal avenues for discouraging cohabitation included excluding cohabitants from marriage rights, defining children born outside of marriage as illegitimate, and in some states, even criminalizing cohabitation.)
12 See Harry G. Prince, *Public Policy Limitations on Cohabitation Agreements Unruly Horse or Circus Pony*, 70 MINN. L. REV.163 (1985).
13 See Harry Willekens, *Long Term Development in Family Law in Western Europe*, THE CHANCHING FAMILY: FAMILY FORMS & FAMILY LAW 47 (Oxford, J. Eekelaar & T. Nhlapo eds., 1998) ; Wolfman Muller-Freinenfels, *Cohabitation and Marriage Law – A Comparative Study*, 1 INT. J. L. & FAM. 259 (1987).
14 SEE J. MEE, THE PROPERTY RIGHTS OF COHABITEES (Oxford, 1999) (A comparative description of the legal method used for recognizing cohabitants' rights.)
15 See the classic Marvin v. Marvin, 557 P. 2d 106 (1976). (Applies the marriage commitment to cohabitants; based on the implicit contract theory.)
16 See Kaiswe v. Felming 745 N.E.2d 144 (Ill. App. Ct. 2000).

unjust enrichment,[17] and constructive trust[18] were used to impose marital commitments on cohabitants. In conventional legal discourse, substantive general liberal principles such as freedom of choice[19] and state neutrality[20] joined the current liberal tendency to favor private-contractual models of spousal regulation[21] in order to support imposing marriage law on cohabitants. Beyond the liberal approach, those who equated marriage and cohabitation assumed that these institutions differ in their formal form but involve substantially the same attitudes and orientations. They adopted a functional policy[22] and argued that the mere formal difference between marriage and cohabitation does not justify distinguishing between the two institutions.[23] As Professor Frances Olsen argues »If marriage is seen as nothing more than what the parties agree to and if the parties' agreement is all that is enforceable by the courts, a couple's agreement should not be less enforceable just because it does not include formal marriage.«[24]

---

17   See Robert C. Casad, *Unmarried Couples and Unjust Enrichment: From Status to Contract and Back Again?*, 77 MICH. L. REV. 47, 55 (1978); Jeffrey L. Oakes, *Comment, Article 2298, the Codification of the Principle Forbidding Unjust Enrichment, and the Elimination of Quantum Meruit as a Basis for Recovery in Louisiana*, 56 LA. L. REV. 873 (1996); Watts v. Watts, 405 N.W.2d 303, 316 (Wis. 1987) (Holds that unmarried cohabitants can bring claims that rest in either contract or equity, such as unjust enrichment or partition.)
18   See Shuraleff v. Donnelly, 817 P.2d 764 (Or. Ct. App. 1991).
19   See the rhetoric of Pashman, J., concurring at Kozlowski v. Kozlowski, 403 A.2d 902, (N.J. 1979) at 909 »The decision to cohabit without marriage represents each partner's voluntary choice as to how his or her life should be ordered, a choice with which the state cannot interfere.« See also in the context of Australian law H.A. Finlay, *Defining the Informal Marriage*, 3 U.N.S.W L. J. 279 (1980).
20   See A.M. van de Wiel, *Cohabitation outside Marriage in Dutch Law*«, MARRIAGE AND COHABITATION IN CONTEMPORARY SOCIETIES 212,215 (Toronto, John M. Eekelaar & Sanford N. Katz eds., 1980). (The principle of neutrality is also central to Sweden's approach to cohabitation. see, for example S. Danielsen, *Unmarried Partners, Scandinavian Law in the Making*, 3 OXFORD J. LEGAL STtudies 59,65 (1983).
21   See Jana B. Singer, *The Privatization of Family Law*, 1992 WIS. L. REV. 1443.
22   See Martha Minow, *Redefining Families: Who's In and Who's Out?*, 62 COLO L REV 268 (1991) (Argues for legal recognition of functional families outside the traditional legal categories, including adult couples in informal unions.)
23   See Milton C. Regan, Jr., *Unmarried Partners and the Legacy of Marvin v. Marvin: Calibrated Commitment: The Legal Treatment of Marriage and Cohabitation*, 76 NOTRE DAME L. REV. 1435, 1437 (2001). (Describes anti-formalist objections to the distinction between marriage and cohabitation).
24   See Frances E. Olsen, *The Politics of Family Law*, 2 LAW AND INEQUALITY: A JOURNAL OF THEORY OF PRACTICE 1, note 45 (1984).

III. The Liberal Arguments against Imposing Marriage Law on Cohabitants

In contrast to conventional wisdom, this section presents a liberal case against equalizing cohabitation and marriage and offers two main arguments: contractual and pluralistic.

1. The Contractual Argument

The liberal-contractual argument refutes the characterization of cohabitation as an implied contract in which marriage law can be applied.[25] According to the liberal-contractual argument, the choice not to marry reflects the partners' opposition (or at least that partner who refuses to marry) to bear the legal status of marriage. One of the key reasons for avoiding the legal status that marriage confers relates to the economic burdens imposed on married persons who decide to separate from their spouses. Therefore the liberal approach, which emphasizes an individual's intentions, respects one's decision not to marry and does not impose quasi-marital obligations on such an individual.[26]

Beyond speculation about the meaning of the choice not to marry, the contractual argument is supported by empirical findings which point to systematic differences in the lifestyles of married and cohabiting partners. These findings suggest that generally, the level of commitment between married couples is higher than that of cohabitating couples.[27] According to this contractual argument, the law should reflect these differences.[28]

---

25 See Margaret F. Bring, *Domestic Partnership and default rules*, in RECONCEIVING THE FAMILY: CRITICAL REFLECTIONS ON THE AMERICAN LAW INSTITUTE'S PRINCIPLES OF THE LAW OF FAMILY DISSOLUTION 269 (Rabin F. Wilson ed., 2006) (»Parties who didn't want to get married but wanted to cohabit would find themselves with a set of responsibilities on dissolution that they didn't want to assume.«)

26 See Garison, *supra* note 8, at 857 »Conscriptive cohabitation laws do define attributes of personhood ... under the compulsion of the State' by imposing obligations on those who have not chosen them.«

27 See Steven Nock, *A Comparison of Marriages and Cohabiting Relationships*, 16 J. FAM. ISSUES 53 (1995). (Based on empirical studies, describes substantial distinctions between the elements of cohabiting relationships and those of married spouses.)

28 See Garison, *supra* note 8, at pp. 839-845 (Based on an extensive survey of sociological research, demonstrates that cohabitants and married couples behave differently and that these differences appear to reflect underlying differences in attitude.)

2. The Pluralist Argument

While the contractual argument focuses on partners' hypothetical wishes, the pluralist argument focuses on the law's need to create different types of institutions in order to support the diversity of spousal lifestyles. To achieve this, the law must treat cohabitation and legal marriage differently. Philosophically, the pluralist argument is based on modern liberal approaches that emphasize individual autonomy. It emphasizes that individual autonomy expresses itself not only in the absence of formal limitations regarding an individual's choices, but also in the existence of a range of options. The modern liberal approaches emphasize the liberal state's duty to create a range of social institutions that enable the individual to make genuine choices among various alternatives.[29]

The application of these approaches to cohabitation law may lead to surprising conclusions. Imagine a world in which the law distinguishes between marriage and cohabitation. In such a world, a couple in a spousal relationship – perhaps a relationship that is even characterized as a sociological marriage – may choose a high level of legal commitment (i.e. legal marriage), a lower level, or no such commitment at all (i.e. cohabitation). Such a framework would offer individuals a range of options.

On the other hand, imagine a legal world which, in accordance with the supposedly liberal position, equates the status of cohabitants to that of married couples. In such a world, couples who desire to maintain an intimate relationship that can be characterized as sociological marriage are automatically subject to the system of marriage laws. Such a framework does not offer couples social institutions with meaningful differences or the possibility for making genuine choices.

IV. The Counter Arguments in Favor of Equating Marriage and Cohabitation

1. The Extra-Contractual Counter-Argument

The extra-contractual counter-argument focuses on gender differences that might result in exploitation and injustice. This argument contests the contractual argument with extra-contractual considerations that jus-

---

[29] See JOSEPH RAZ, THE MORALITY OF Freedom (Oxford, 1986). (Designs a modern liberal theory based on the principles of freedom and individual autonomy.)

tify applying marriage law to cohabitants.³⁰ These include protection for economically weaker members of the family, mostly women; »equitable« considerations aimed at preventing exploitation or unjust enrichment; fairness; gender equality; public aspects of the spousal relationship such as concern for children growing up in the family, and so on. ³¹ According to this counter-argument, these extra-contractual considerations justify imposing a marriage commitment on cohabitants.

Furthermore, the contractual argument implicitly assumes that the choice not to marry is a joint decision made by equal partners. While this premise of equality corresponds to an idealist vision of a desirable world, it hardly reflects the concrete gender reality.³² In the real world, significant differences exist between men and women in their economic capacity, business experience, patterns of negotiation management, and status in the marriage market.³³ Consequently, in many cases the choice not to marry reflects a unilateral decision made by the powerful partner rather than a joint decision made by both partners.³⁴

---

30 See Grace G. Blumberg, *The regularization of no marital cohabitation: rights and responsibilities in the American welfare state*, 76 NOTRE DAME L. REV. 1265, 1299-1303 (2001) (Suggests status model regulation of cohabitants' relationships in order to protect weaker members of the family.) See also Ira M. Ellman, *Contract Thinking Was Marvin's Fatal Flaw* 76 NOTRE DAME LAW REV. 1365 (2001). (Criticizes the contractual perspective of Marvin v. Marvin and suggests an extra-contractual perspective to cohabitation law.)

31 See Law Comm'n of Canada, *Beyond Conjugality: Recognizing and Supporting Close Personal Adult Relationships* Ch 2 (2001) »Parliament's goal is to achieve some other outcome - like the support of children, the recognition of economic interdependence, the prevention of exploitation - that is connected to, but not exactly congruent with, the marriage relationship.«

32 See DEBORAH L. RHODE, JUSTICE & GENDER - SEX DISCRIMINATION & THE LAW (1989) (Describes the tension between »sameness« feminism, which presumes actual equality between men and women, and »difference« feminism, which considers the differences between men and women).

33 See Marcia A. Neave, *Resolving the Dilemma of Difference: A Critique of The Role of Private Ordering in Family Law*, 44 U. TORONTO L. J. 97 (1994); See also B. Cossman, *A Matter of Difference: Domestic Contracts and Gender Equality«* 28 OSGOODE HALL LAW JOURNAL 303 (1990) (Both explain how differences between men and women, both in economic circumstance and in negotiation patterns, make private ordering dangerous for women.)

34 Regarding the fear that unequal lifestyles combined with the freedom to leave will cause women serious injury see M.D. Newcomb, *Cohabitation, Marriage and Divorce among Adolescents and Young Adults*, 3 JOURNAL OF SOCIAL AND PERSONAL RELATIONSHIPS 473 (1986). See also American Law Institution *Principle of The Law of Family Dissolution: Analysis and Recommendations*), s. 6.02 cmt a (2002) (Argues that cohabitation reflects strong social or economic inequality between the partners, allowing the stronger partner to resist the weaker partner's preference for marriage.)

2. The Relational-Contract Counter-Argument

The second counter-argument opposes the factual premise that cohabitants intentionally reject marriage law. It argues that in many cases cohabitation is not the outcome of an active conscious decision not to marry, but rather the natural continuation of the cohabitants' existing lifestyle.[35] Furthermore, even when the decision not to marry initially reflects an aversion to marriage law, one should not disregard the changing circumstances that cause spouses to re-evaluate their life plans and mutual commitments, albeit in an informal way. Based on relational contract theory,[36] this argument emphasizes the implied commitment inherent in long-term cohabitation relationships, even in the absence of a formal commitment.[37]

3. The Same-Sex Couple's Counter-Argument

The last counter-argument focuses on same-sex couples who are still disqualified from marrying in most western jurisdictions.[38] It argues that in such cases the basic assumption of the contractual argument – namely that choosing to live as cohabitants reflects the couples' rejection of marriage law – is not relevant.[39] The case of same-sex couples has been a dom-

---

35 See Grace G. Blumberg, *Cohabitation Without Marriage: A Different Perspective*, 28 UCLA L. REV. 1125, 1135-1136 (1981) (Presents sociological findings that reject the thesis that the cohabitation lifestyle reflects a repudiation of the legal obligations entailed by marriage.)

36 See Ian R. Macneil, *Contracts: Adjustment of Long-Term Economic Relations Under Classical, Neoclassical and Relational Contract Law*, 72 NW. U. L. REV. 854 (1978). (The relational contract theory treats contracts characterized by ongoing personal relationships as *relational* contracts, as opposed to discrete *transactional* contracts that are characterized by the fact that they deal with an isolated transaction between two strangers. According to this theory, if a contract is closer in character to a relational contract its treatment under the law must be based *less* on the express arrangements and initial intentions of the parties, and *more* on their behavior and the informal understanding between the parties.)

37 See Elizabeth Scott, *Domestic Partnerships, Implied Contracts and Law Reform*, in RECONCEIVING THE FAMILY: CRITICAL REFLECTIONS ON THE AMERICAN LAW INSTITUTE'S PRINCIPLES OF THE LAW OF FAMILY DISSOLUTION 331 (Rabin F. Wilson ed., 2006). (Criticizes the ALI's basis in the status model and suggests replacing it with a relational contract model.) See more generally Elizabeth S. Scott & Robert E. Scott, *Marriage as Relational Contract*, 84 VA. L. REV.1225 (1998). (Applies relational contract theory to the long-term commitment inherent in marriage.)

38 See Lyne D. Wardle, *same sex marriage and the tragedy of the commons: A response to »conservative case« for same sex marriage*,22 BYU JOURNAL OF PUBLIC POLICY 441,443-447 (2008) (A comparative survey of the status of same-sex marriages throughout the world.)

39 See T.S. Kogan, *Competing Approaches to Same Sex Versus Opposite Sex, Unmarried Couples in Domestic Partnership Laws and Ordinances*, 2001 B.Y.U.L. REV. 1023, (The trend to equate marriage and cohabitation is best defended in terms of the long-term interests of gay and lesbian individuals.)

inant force in the movement to equate marriage and cohabitation regulation.[40]

V. The Theoretical Approaches within Existing Jurisdictions

Our survey of the various arguments and theoretical approaches reveals that ironically, the contractual argument and model on the one hand, and the extra-contractual argument and the status model on the other hand, justify both the distinction and the equation of marriage and cohabitation. This leads to a discussion of the following legal models for the regulation of the economic relationship between cohabitants.

1. The Status Model Distinction between Marriage and Cohabitation
The traditional model that invalidates even explicit contracts between cohabitants[41] is not very popular.[42] Yet there are still some modern jurisdictions that, based on the status model and supported by public-oriented considerations for privileging marriage, restrict cohabitants' mutual commitments.[43]

2. The Contractual Distinction between Marriage and Cohabitation
The contractual argument against imposing marriage law on cohabitants serves as the ideological basis for **the explicit contract model**. This model

---

40 See Blumberg, *supra* note 29, at 1268-69 (Same-sex couples have been the dominant force in the movement to regularize non-marital cohabitation.) See also Elizabeth Scott, *Marriage, cohabitation and collective responsibility for dependency* 2004 U. CHI. LEGAL F. 225, 238 »Today, the most compelling arguments against privileging marriage over non-marital unions are made on behalf of same-sex couples.« (Interestingly, in Israel the case of couples who are disqualified to marry for religious reasons has played an important role in defining cohabitation as alternative to marriage.) See Shahar Lifshitz, *The External Rights of Cohabitating Couples in Israel*, 37 ISR. L.REV. 346, 389-394 (2003).
41 See *supra* notes 1.
42 See Hewitt v. Hewitt 77 Ill.2d 49, 394 N.E.2d 1204 (Ill., 1979) at 1208 »There are major public policy questions involved in determining whether, under what circumstances, and to what extent it is desirable to accord some type of legal status to claims arising from such relationships. Of substantially greater importance than the rights of the immediate parties *is the impact of such recognition upon our society and the institution of marriage.*«
43 See the description of the germane case at Ilona Ostner, *Cohabitation in Germany - Rules, Reality and Public Discourses*, 15 INTERNATIONAL J. OF L. POLICY & THE FAMILY 88, 96 *et seq* (2001). (The German constitution's preference for marriage limits the ability to equate marriage and cohabitation.)

rejects the premise that ongoing »marriage-like« relationships reflect an implied marriage contract.[44] Consequently, it recognizes economic obligations between cohabitants only when the parties have entered a formal and explicit agreement.[45]

3. The Contractual Equation between Marriage and Cohabitation

Further developing the implied contract model, in the celebrated Marvin v. Marvin case the court set a precedent in applying marriage-like commitment to cohabitants' relationships even in the absence of an explicit agreement between the partners.[46] There is considerable ambiguity, however, as to the circumstances in which the implied contract theory should be applied.[47] In light of this background, I believe that the relational contract theory has the potential to breathe new life into the implied contract model. According to the relational version of the implied contract model that was unofficially adopted by a few courts in the United States,[48] the implied contract is not limited to cases where there is concrete and specified understanding regarding the legal aspects of the relationship but extends also to broader understanding between the partners regarding their mutual commitment. Continuing in this line of thought, Professor Elizabeth Scott recently suggested that the law should presume a contractual obligation in order to apply marriage law to cases in which couples have lived together for over five years.[49]

---

44 See Tapley v. Tapley, 449 A.2d 1218, 1219 (N.H. 1982); (We realize that couples enter into these unstructured domestic relationships in order to avoid the rights and responsibilities that the State imposes on the marital relationship.)

45 See Morone v. Morone, 50 N.Y.2d 481, 488, , 595, 413 N.E.2d 1154, 1157 (1980) (Upon dissolution of a non-marital living arrangement, the mutual rights of the spouses should not exceed recovery on theory of express contract.) Regarding legislation that adopts the explicit written contract model see Minn. Stat. Ann. §513.075 (West 2002)

46 See Marvin *supra* note 14, at 110. »In the absence of an express contract, the courts should inquire into the conduct of the parties to determine whether that conduct demonstrates an implied contract, agreement of partnership or joint venture, or some other tacit understanding between the parties.« See generally J. THOMAS OLDHAM, DIVORCE, SEPARATION AND THE DISTRIBUTION OF PROPERTY 1.02 (2002) (Lists decisions following Marvin.)

47 See Ann L. Estin, *Ordinary Cohabitation*, 76 NOTRE DAME L. REV. 1381, (Analyzes the diversity of results of the implied contract theory.) See also Scott 2006, *supra* note 36, at 335 »Court often concludes that that the parties' understanding were too indefinites for contractual enforcement.«

48 See Scott, id, at 335 »A few courts have implicitly suggested that living together in long-term marriage-like unions is evidence of the parties' intentions to undertake marriage sharing like of property.«

49 See Scott, id, at 342-348.

4. The Status Model Equation between Marriage and Cohabitation

Motivated by extra-contractual consideration and supported by the same-sex argument, the new Restatement on family dissolution in the United States,[50] as well as legislation and cases in New Zealand,[51] Canada,[52] Israel,[53] and other western jurisdictions,[54] adopts a status model for equating marriage and cohabitation. This model applies marriage-like commitments to cohabitants without the need to argue for explicit or implied contract. In addition, according to the status model cohabitants who wish to free themselves of marriage commitments must provide a written agreement that is subject to strict judicial review.[55]

Our analysis of the existing approaches is summarized in the following table:

---

50 See ALI, *supra* note 32 , Ch 6 (Imposes marriage commitments on cohabitants.)
51 In New Zealand, financial support and property division claims are recognized when unions of three years duration dissolve. See Property (Relationships) Amendment Act § 2E, 2001 (NZ). See also Bill Atkin, *The Legal World of Unmarried Couples: Reflections on »De Facto Relationships« in Recent New Zealand Legislation*, VUW LAW REVIEW (forthcoming, 2008)
52 See the following argument of the Canadian law commission: »Individuals in close personal relationships who are not married ... may have many of the characteristics of economic and emotional interdependency that ought to give rise to rights and responsibilities. To fail to include these individuals may undermine the state's interests in recognizing and supporting the full range of committed, mutually supportive personal adult relationships.« Law Comm'n of Canada, *Beyond Conjugality: Recognizing and Supporting Close Personal Adult Relationships*), Ch.3 pt.1, 4 (2001). See also Garrison, *supra* note 7, note 224 and the accompany text. The Canadian Law Reform Commission has also noted that conscriptive laws are »generally heralded as a way for governments to prevent the risks of exploitation inherent in a contractual model.«
53 Regarding the trend in Israeli law to equate marriage and cohabitation see Shahar Lifshitz, *An outsider perspective on American Same-sex Marriage Debate*, 22 BYU JOURNAL OF LAW AND POLICY, 359 372-378 (2008).
54 See Blumberg, *supra* note 29, at 1299-1303 (A comparative survey of the legal systems that adopt the status model.)
55 See Westfall, *supra* note 7, at 1479 et seq. (Criticizes the ALI for its limitation on cohabitants' ability to contract out marriage law commitments.) See also Atkin, *supra* note 50, at note 48 (The New Zealand Property (Relationships) Act 1976 subjects cohabitants' contracts to a unique fairness review.) See Lifshitz, *supra note* 52, at note 81-83 (Addresses the limitation of cohabitants' freedom of contract in Israel.)

Table I: Summary of the Existing Approaches

Model	Representative	Ideology	Distinction / Equation	Validity of Contract
Status Distinction	Traditional position *Hewitt v. Hewitt* German law (mild version)	Moral hostility to cohabitants Public-policy preference for marriage	Distinction	Invalidation of even explicit contract
Contractual Distinction between Marriage and Cohabitants	The NY Cases (the explicit contract model)	Contractual arguments	Distinction	Validation only of explicit oral/written agreements to apply marriage law
Contractual Equation between Marriage and Cohabitants	Original Marvin and most of its followers	Implied contract theory	Dependent on the existence of implied contract	Validation of agreements between cohabitants either to apply or to reject marriage law
	Few of Marvin followers Scott	Relational counter-argument	Equation	
Status Equation of Marriage and Cohabitation	Israel New Zealand ALI	Extra-contractual and same-Sex counter-arguments	Equation	Validation of explicit agreement to opt out of marriage law but subjects such agreements to strict supervision

VI. The Need for a New Model

Our discussion thus far has demonstrated three central points. First, liberal-contractual considerations such as state neutrality, freedom of choice, and freedom of contract oppose the traditional status approach that invalidates even explicit contracts in which cohabitants assume marriage-like commitments. Second, the contractual and pluralist arguments expose the non-liberal aspects of imposing marriage commitments on cohabitants. Third, the counter-arguments demonstrate the extremely problematic nature of regulating cohabitation law solely on the basis of the contractual argument and the explicit contractual model.

Do the counter-arguments then put an end to the debate regarding the proper regulation of cohabitants' relationships as is often assumed by legal scholars? The following analysis suggests they do not. I argue that though persuasive to some degree, the counter-arguments fail to refute the essence of the liberal argument against equating marriage and cohabitation. I further demonstrate that ironically, the relational contract and the status model that developed under the influence of the counter-arguments as alternatives to the explicit contract model, fall victim to the same traps as the explicit contract model. Hence they too should be rejected as an ideal solution to our problem.

First, like the explicit contractual model, the relational and status models also focus on one subgroup of cohabitants. (The status model focuses on gap powered cohabitants, while the relational contract model focuses on cohabitants who maintain their original lifestyle.) However these models ignore or deny the existence of other subgroups (such as egalitarian cohabitants who intentionally reject marriage-like obligations). Yet, just as it would be problematic to assume that all cohabitants are disinterested in legalizing their spousal relationships, (as the contractual approach asserts), so too is it problematic to adopt the opposite policy that ignores cohabitants who have rejected or not yet assumed marriage commitment in their relationships. What is required, therefore, is a differential model that accounts for different subgroups of cohabitants.

Second, normatively, just as the contractual approach is justly criticized for ignoring the extra-contractual considerations, so too the status model ignores the importance of consent and parties' autonomy for liberal regulation of cohabitants' law. Thus, at least at present, each approach focuses on specific considerations and fails to offer a suitable balance among the different considerations.

The narrow perspective of the status model becomes even more obvious when it bases itself on the same-sex couple's counter-argument. This counter-argument is relevant only to those couples, such as same-sex couples, who are not eligible to marry. Yet the case of same-sex couples has been a dominant force in the movement to equate marriage and cohabitation regulation in general.

Furthermore, even the gender equality perspective, which served as a cornerstone in the extra-contractual arguments, does not justify the status model. Apparently, the need to protect women may justify deviation from the partners' explicit or implied agreement in the appropriate cases. Yet, it is hard to ignore the costs of such protection in situations when this protection apparently clashes with the parties' choices. Indeed, such protection implies that (1) women in a spousal relationship are always the weaker partner and (2) women are unable to care for themselves or assert their rights and are therefore in need of legal protection. Thus, even those who hold that existing differences between men and women raise concern that contractual thought and a formal egalitarian approach may lead to unjust outcomes, cannot ignore the costs of such protection. From a gender perspective the challenge to lawmakers is to develop a model which protects women without implicit harm to their agency. Thus far, neither the contractual models nor the status model meet this challenge.[56] The disadvantages of the existing approaches highlight the need for a new framework in which to integrate the partial views outlined above. Based on the innovative pluralist argument detailed above, the last part of this paper offers the cornerstones for a new liberal-pluralist model of cohabitation law.

VII. Principle for a New Liberal Model

Despite the substantial differences among them, the existing approaches are trapped in the following dichotomy: According to **one option**, cohabitation and marriage relationships are substantially **identical** and thus the law should equate their regulation. According to the **second option**, cohabitation and marriage are **different.** Marriage is the **preferable** relationship and the law should reflect this preference by **distinguishing** marriage and cohabitation regulation. What is missing in the current discourse is a third option which refers to and designs marriage and cohabitation as two equally respected options while still distinguishing their regulation.

To this point, the pluralist approach enters into the picture as an alternative to the existing approaches, emphasizing the liberal state's responsibility to create a variety of spousal institutions.

According to the pluralist approach, marriage and cohabitation should be separate legal institutions. Thus, the pluralist approach rejects the

---

[56] The tension between the need to protect women as the weaker economic partner and the need to promote a message of equality is very typical in modern family law. See Rhode *supra* note 31. While in other contexts certain proposals have sought to bridge these two extremes, thus far in the case of cohabitation each argument and model has taken an extreme position.

status model with its complete merger of marriage and cohabitation commitments. At the same time, influenced by the counter-arguments, the pluralist approach also rejects the opposite policy that denies any commitment between cohabitants. Instead of these »all or nothing« approaches, the pluralist approach suggests a careful design of cohabitation as a separate social and legal institution with rights and duties that draw on the philosophical foundations that justify its separate existence. Hence the pluralist model offers a selective application of elements of marriage law to cohabitants. The model further offers criteria to determine which aspects of marriage law should be appropriately applied to cohabitation.

The first criterion distinguishes between **channeling and responsive** components of marriage law. This distinction balances between the ex-ante aspiration to design marriage and cohabitation as separate social institutions and the ex-post response to situations in which during the cohabitation period, cohabitants' lifestyles and needs resemble those of married partners. Thus, according to the pluralist model the components of marriage law whose principal function is to encourage specific kinds of behaviors or to express society's ethos regarding marriage properties should not apply to cohabitation. In contrast, »responsive« provisions of marriage law, such as provisions that seek to protect weaker and dependant family members, should be applied to cohabitants. Second, based on the original rationale of marriage law, the pluralist model distinguishes between components of **a contractual nature** and those of an **extra-contractual** nature. In cases in which marriage law itself is based primarily on the expressed and/or presumed intention of the parties, it may not be appropriate to impose marriage law on those who have chosen not to marry. In contrast, in cases in which marriage law is based on extra-contractual considerations such as justice, prevention of exploitation, or protection of children, it would be appropriate to impose such law on cohabitants. The third criterion distinguishes between **community** and **autonomy based** components of marriage law. It suggests that cohabitation law should recognize the commitments between the couples as individual. In contrast, cohabitation law should reject regulation that prefers the »we« aspects of spousal relationships over the »I« aspects and it should especially reject limitations to the couples' right of exit. Follow-up research to this paper applies the principles outlined above and, based on the three criteria discussed, considers which aspects of marriage law (especially inheritance, marital property law, alimony, compensation for career losses and marital contracts) should be applied to cohabitants.[57]

An additional, unique feature of the pluralist approach is its sensitivity to the variety of cohabitants' relationships. Thus, contrary to current legal approaches, the pluralist model distinguishes among trial marriage, regular cohabitation, relational cohabitation, exploitation cohabitation and same-sex cohabitation. It tailors a unique package of rights and duties for each subcategory of cohabitants.

First, the model posits an »entry requirement« in order to screen couples who are trying out their relationship. According to this model, the trial should not be regulated by cohabitant law, but rather by regular civil doctrines such as contract law and un-just enrichment. Second, this model offers innovative distinctions between regular and relational cohabitants. The former are entitled to the basic package of cohabitant law that mainly includes the responsive, extra-contractual and autonomy based components of marriage law. The latter are entitled to the extended package, which reflects their relational commitments, closer, albeit not identical, to marriage law. The distinctions between these types are based on the relationship's duration and other criteria that shed light on the relational commitment between the partners. Third, this model distinguishes between exploitive situations and egalitarian decision-making between cohabitants. In the egalitarian situation, the model respects cohabitants' formal agreement and, in some circumstances and in regard to certain topics, even respects the informal understanding that deviates from the conventional cohabitation law. In cases where there is a gap between the economic powers, which the model defines as »susceptible for exploitation«, the model demands a formal agreement – subject to strict review – in order to opt out of cohabitation obligations. Finally, the model distinguishes between same-sex and different-sex couples and argues that in the case of the former, cohabitants' commitments should parallel marriage law.

In summary, this paper offers an alternative, innovative theory and model for cohabitation law. While the paper provides a solid foundation for the model, further research is still needed to elaborate on its detailed application.

---

57 See Shahar Lifshitz, Married against their will? Towards a pluralist regulation of spousal relationships. Washington and Lee Law reviews (Forthcoming 2010).

De Facto Family and Family Enterprise in the Italian Legal System

Stefano Insinga[1]

I. General Aspects

The family enterprise is regulated by article 230-*bis*[2] of the Italian Civil Code amended by the act n. 151/1975, that modified the Italian family system.

This article is the only one regulating family work and patrimonial relationships between people bound by kinship and affinity.

Before family law reform, family members working inside family enterprise could not have any legal rights, because this work was gratuitous and family could not receive any legal retribution.

In fact family cooperation was based on solidarity and on the emotional relationships and therefore characterized by gratuitousness.

---

1 University of Palermo, Italy.
2 Unless there is another kind of relationship, the family member that works constantly inside the family or in the family enterprise has the right of maintenance according to the patrimonial condition of the family. He benefits from the family company profits, from the goods that are purchased thanks to these profits and from the company increases, according to the quantity and quality of his work. The decisions on the use of the profits, on the extraordinary management, on the production policy and closing down of the enterprise are made by majority by the family members that participate in the company itself. The family members that don't have full capacity of action are represented in the election by those who exercise legal power on them.
Women's labour is considered equal to men's.
Under provisions of first paragraph, a family member is the spouse, the relatives within the third degree and the in-laws within second degree. A family enterprise is that where the spouse and the above mentioned relatives work.
The right of participation mentioned in the first paragraph is non-transferable, unless the transfer is made in favour of the family members mentioned in the previous paragraph with the agreement of all the participants. It can be cleared with money if labour stops (for whichever reason) and in case of enterprise alienation. The payment can take place in several times determined by the judge.
In case of hereditary division or move of the company, the participants mentioned in the first paragraph are entitled with the right of pre-emption on the company. The provision of the article is applied as far as it is consistent.
The tacit family communions in the exercise of agricolture are ruled by uses that must not appose to the previous norms.

So, article 230-*bis* is a reaction to the presumption of gratuitousness work developed inside family communities and wants to eliminate the freedom in the relationships between family members and the owner of the enterprise.

The purpose of this rule is to supply a right legal protection to the family workers who, even though working inside the enterprise could not claim anything from the family entrepreneur.[3]

Cooperation between spouses, third degree relatives and second degree affinity are paramount characters of family enterprise.

The indispensable requirement in order to create a family enterprise is the familiar *status*, the work in the enterprise and for the family.

Inside family enterprise we can find two figures: the first is a family member working continuatively in the family enterprise and he receives all the rights amended by article 230-*bis*; the second much discussed figures is a family member working not in the enterprise but for the family (ex. housework); even in this case one has the right of maintenance, according to the patrimonial family condition. He participates to the enterprise increases and to the enterprise start-up, in proportion to the quantity and quality of his work.[4]

The purpose is to recognize the value of housework, considering that one can succeed in his entrepreneurial work, thanks to his spouse who deals with home activities.

The housework made by a spouse is not enough to recognize to her all the family enterprise rights. Two conditions are needed: the first is to give the proof of constant and continuing work; the second is to give the proof of the enterprise increases that spring from her work, in order to quantify the fee of participation and the enterprise increases that concern her[5].

So, family cooperation, housework or enterprise work, as it has been ratified on article 230-*bis* of the Italian Civil Code, has to be continuative.

The doctrine intends »continuative« as synonym of regularity, referring to the time and work stability. So we cannot consider participating to the family enterprise those who work occasionally.

---

3   See G. PALMERI, *Del regime patrimoniale della famiglia*, in *Comm. cod. civ. Scialoja-Branca* (ed. by F. Galgano), sub. *art.* 230-*bis*, Bologna, 2004, p. 20.
4   M. DOGLIOTTI-A. FIGONE, *L'impresa familiare*, in, AA.VV., *Il diritto di famiglia* (by) T. Auletta, L. Bruscaglia, M. Dogliotti, A. Figone, IV, II, Torino, 2004, p. 596.
5   In this way, Tribunale di Milano, May 21st, 2006, in *Riv. crit. di dir. lav.*, 2006, III. comment by G. Cordedda, *Lavoro nella famiglia e partecipatione allimpresa familiare: due facce di due medaglie differenti*.

But »continuative« does not mean »exclusiveness« of family work. This means that family cooperation does not have to be full-time which signifies that one can develop work outside the family but family work has to be predominant.

II. Residual Nature

Family enterprise has a residual nature and it is a non-pactional institute that does not provide an agreement between parties.

Doctrine and case-law have specified that, for its subsistence, continuative and co-ordinate cooperation are necessary in the enterprise. So the article 230 is ruled out in all the cases in which there is a work contract between the owner and his family.[6]

It means that if the family members do not constitute a specific work relationship, with a work contract, they are obliged to submit to the family enterprise discipline.

III. Rights and Duties of the Family Members

Article 230-*bis* assigns specific rights to family participants, in fact the rule recognizes them patrimonial and instrumental rights like participation to management decisions.

The first right that is recognized to family workers is the maintenance. It's an identical right for each family members (but not necessarily it has an identical entity for each one) and it is given according to the patrimonial family condition. The difference from the other important right (profit right and business increases right), is that this second right is variable, because it is considered proportionally to the quality and quantity of each family work.

Right of maintenance is not even conditioned by the real enterprise trend. It must be given to each family member even if the enterprise does not have any profit. The other way round, profits are parcelled out only if the enterprise has produced them.

---

6   L. BALESTRA, *I Soggetti dell'impresa familiare,* in P. Cendon (ed), *La Famiglia,* Padova, 2004, p. 493.

The decisions on the use of the profits, on the extraordinary management, on the production policy and closing down of the enterprise are made by majority by the family members that participate in the firm.

IV. Can *More Uxorio* Cohabitants Constitute Family Enterprise?

A very much discussed issue concerns the *more uxorio* relationships. Is it possible to create a family enterprise between people not linked by a formal act?

It's a question that involves the notion itself, characteristics and perspectives of the *de facto* family fact.

In a legal system, like ours, in which there are many *more uxorio* relationships we ask ourselves if it is the case to extend the 230-bis effects on these *more uxorio* couples.

The major obstacle towards a real juridical recognition of the phenomenon and the cause of the suspicious behaviour of the expert is the notion of the *de facto* family itself, where there is not an unique tendency and where there is not any legislative reforms.

According to the predominant orientations, we have two characterizing elements of the *de facto* family: the first is a subjective element and it consists in the »*affectio*«, that is the participation of one partner in the life of the other one and *viceversa;* the second is an objective element: the constant cohabitation (so based on a strong and serious engagement), without any formal act.

In our legal system, the *de facto* family is not recognized as a juridical entity, so the doctrine orients itself into three different directions: analogical application of legitimate family; private autonomy; introduction of a specific legislation. So, the *de facto* family partners, in order to regulate their relationships, find some solutions on typical and atypical contractual instruments, in fact their relationships are not object of legal guardianship and remain regulated by private agreements between cohabitant people.

In Italy, there has been a great debate with the purpose of understanding if *de facto* family can find place inside family enterprise rules. The question, even after an important doctrine debate, has not achieved a predominant tendency.

The interpretative problems are not linked to the terms used in the legal rule but to the creation of instruments to protect non formal unions, without legal bind.

In this way, my survey aims to verify the possibility if the *more uxorio* cohabitant can receive the recognition of citizenship inside family enterprise, thanks to an analogical and broad interpretation of the 3° comma, art. 230-*bis*.

V. Doctrine and Case-Law Orientations

The difficulty of interpreting the law does not arise from the terms that are used but from the need to built (forms of) protection for those unions that are not formalized by the bond of matrimony.

The predominant tendency, above mentioned, excludes the extension of family enterprise rule to *de facto* family.[7] Part of this doctrine refers to the literal element of the rule. This tendency of thought says that article 230-*bis* mentions clearly a »spouse«, and he is the subject of the specific family and married status created by marriage.

»Spouse« is a technical term. It's impossible to refer it to subjects not linked by legal marriage.

Another part of the doctrine has excluded the opening towards the *de facto* family, not for the literal element, but for the logical-juridical consequences that this opening could bring. Who thinks that the cohabitant position can be identical to that of the spouse, could extend by analogy, the legal discipline for married couples to the simple cohabitant couples.

In Italy, we have just two sentences of the 80's and 90's that have legislated in a different way from the predominant tendency.

The first is one from Ivrea Court[8] in 1981, in which, through a careful sociological survey of family evolution, arranged by industrial revolution, judges asserted the possibility to create a family enterprise between *more uxorio* cohabitants.

The case submitted to the judge concerned a cohabitation that had lasted about 30 years during which *the more uxorio* cohabitants had got a rural firm. The labour provided by the lady consisted of housework (invoices and receits showed expenses for constructions works and for the repairs of household appliances) and of cultivation of a ground (for which there were specific bills registered in both cohabitants' name and concerning the purchase of manure and seeds).

---

7   M. A. INNOCENTI, *Famiglia di fatto e impresa familiare*, in *Il Civilista*, 2007, 1, Milano, p. 67.
8   In this way: Tribunale di Ivrea, October 10th, 1981, in *RDa* 1983, II, p. 464.

In that occasion the quantity and quality of her labour inside family enterprise was considered important and of equal value if compared with her partner's labour, in order to acknowledge her several rights.

The verdict has reconsidered in this way under the notion of spouses and kinship not only the married family but also that family granted but the stability of *affectio* and solidarity between man and woman that cooperate on the same level in the management of their family company.[9]

The second is one from Turin Court[10] in 1990, it was an attempt for a new opening towards the *de facto* family, in order to give them relief and juridical dignity.

They are an important but isolated opening towards a first recognition of the *de facto* family inside family enterprise legal rule and for their strong opening, they were deeply criticized, above all because they had compared *de facto* families to legitimate ones.

In doctrine, the people who agree with this tendency and support an overcoming of the formal aspect, think that the identical conditions and ratio existing in *more uxorio* cohabitant must lead necessarily to the recognition of a family enterprise based on a *de facto* family.

More uxorio cohabitation is grounded indeed on steady affections and on a spiritual and material communion, too.

But in 1994, the Supreme Court, trying to stop every doubt, asserted that article 230-*bis* has a special could not be interpreted analogically[11].

The debate that has arisen is still open at present, even if, lately both jurisprudence and legislator have showed they want to review the discipline of family enterprise.

An important verdict of the »*Corte di Cassazione*« (Italian Supreme Court), nO. 5632 dated May 15th, 2006, established that any work and assistance activities made in a family environment in favour of the cohabiting partner usually arise from bonds of solidarity and affection that already existed.

---

9 A. MASCIA, *Famiglia di fatto: riconoscimento e tutela* in *Diritto civile professionisti*, Matelica, 2004, pag. 140.
10 In this way Tribunale di Torino, November 24th 1990, in *Giur. it.*, 1992, Vol. I, p. 428
11 In this way, Cass. Cov, Sez. lav. May 5th 1994, n. 4204, in *Giur. it.*, 1995, Vol. I, p. 845. The sentence ratifies that »*predominant element of family enterprise is not the work inside the enterprise, not the affective bonds, but the definite family in its main members...there is no possibility of assimilation between marriage and more uxorio cohabitating, because they are antithetical concepts...marriage is a fundamental law institute, from which constant consequences arise. Cohabitation is a fact situation, chosen by people that want to detract from marriage legal duties*«.

These bonds are usually alternative to the typical bonds of a work relationships based on reciprocal performances such as dependent work, while sometimes we can consider the same relationship inside the family enterprise and also in refer to the de facto family, as this one is an atypical social unit with constitutional importance according to art. 2^{12} of the Constitution.

The *more uxorio* cohabiting people cannot currently build a family enterprise and cannot benefit of the tutelage granted by article 230-*bis* of the Italian Civil Code.

This is due to the case-law that considers family enterprise only if there is a legal family and that marriage charges the spouses with precise consequences, while cohabitation is a precarious situation.

VI. How Could be Protected the *More Uxorio* Partners?

Both case-law and doctrine do not want to extend to *more uxorio* cohabitation the article 230-bis and therefore the *more uxorio* cohabitants can be protected by other institutes.

Some people think that this tutelage can be found in the obligation field (and not in the family or labour-law), except for those rare cases in which there is a subordinate job relationship.

The instruments that can be used in this field are of pactional and preventive kind. They are the stipulation of a company contract or of a cohabitation contract (with no-pactional nature) like natural obligation and unjustified enrichment.

Only the latter seems to be appropriate to supply some sort of payment for the work offers by the »weaker« partner[13].

This is an institute ruled by article 2042 of the Italian Civil Code by which the person enriched is obliged to restore or make good to the other the amount or the extent of his enrichment. This institute has allowed as general remedy the unjustified enrichment which can be used also as subsidiary action, when the damaged subject cannot do anything else to remove the prejudice.

---

12 Art.2: »*The Republic recognizes and guarantees the inviolable rights of man, as an individual, and in the social groups where he expresses his personality, and demands the fulfilment of the intransgressible duties of political, economic, and social solidarity*«.
13 L. BALESTRA, *I soggetti dell'impresa familiare*, cit., p. 520.

In our case we must consider that the work offered by cohabitant partners, although its nature is of pure kindness, it also has an important economical value. They are made above all by the weaker partner to satisfy a moral and social duty.

This however does not mean that the weaker partner wants to become poorer by giving up any payment. Actually the partner who offers this work does not expect remuneration in the strict sense of the word. He expects from the other partner the same social and moral duties, on whose base he has supplied work.

Unjustified enrichment is used as legal basis when a part claims compensation. Unjustified enrichment can be illustrated as: the owner of the enterprise made a profit thanks to the partner's work and if the profit is »unjustified« and has »no legal basis« it shall be returned.

The partner has, in this case, lost something that he owns. To be able to claim the owner for compensation, the loss of the partner must also be a benefit for the owner. The purpose of this rule is to equalize the transaction between the two subjects.

As a consequence, we must consider the relationship between the partners of an economic kind.

It's a residual remedy for the *more uxorio* tutelage. Tutelage that actually is relegated at the border of the society.

The Formalization of Property Sharing Rights For De Facto Couples in New Zealand

Margaret Briggs[1]

I. Introduction[2]

The Property (Relationships) Amendment Act 2001 is one of the most important family law statutes enacted in New Zealand in recent years. In particular, it marks a watershed in the legislative recognition of property rights for unmarried cohabitants in informal, unregistered relationships – referred to in New Zealand as de facto couples. Before the introduction of the Property (Relationships) Amendment Act, property disputes between de facto couples were resolved by general principles of contract, property and trust law. By contrast, property disputes between married couples were governed by the Matrimonial Property Act 1976, which treated marriage as a partnership of equals and applied an equal property sharing regime to the matrimonial property. However, significant changes in the composition of the traditional family unit in the last few decades of the twentieth century, including increasing numbers of couples living in de facto relationships, led the New Zealand Parliament to conclude that the Matrimonial Property Act 1976 no longer fully accommodated the sorts of informal living arrangements that were becoming widespread in the general community.[3] According to Parliament, property disputes between de facto couples also warranted legislative intervention.

The Property (Relationships) Amendment Act came into force on 1 February 2002 and significantly amended the Matrimonial Property Act 1976. It now applies to de facto relationships that end on or after that

---

1 Faculty of Law, University of Otago, New Zealand.
2 The author thanks Professors Mark Henaghan and Nicola Peart, Faculty of Law, University of Otago, and Professor Bill Atkin, Victoria University of Wellington, New Zealand, for their helpful comments and suggestions.
3 The trend towards cohabitation outside marriage is common to many western countries. See K Kiernan, »The Rise of Cohabitation and Childbearing Outside Marriage in Western Europe« (2001) 15 International Journal of Law, Policy and the Family 1.

date.[4] The Matrimonial Property Act was subsequently renamed the Property (Relationships) Act 1976 (hereafter the PRA) to recognise the range of relationships now covered by the legislation.[5] Following the enactment of the Civil Union Act 2004, the PRA was further amended to include registered civil unions (heterosexual and same-sex).[6]

The effect of the PRA is that the equal property regime now extends to married couples, civil union partners and de facto partners.[7] But of the three categories of relationships included in the PRA, de facto relationships sit apart from the other two. Whereas marriages and civil unions are distinct legal states, de facto relationships are informal, unregistered and determined entirely on the basis of questions of fact.[8] This paper will examine the wisdom of including de facto relationships in the PRA. While the Act has made the legal position for many de facto couples more clear and predictable on the breakdown of the relationship, that is not so in all cases. There are several problems with including de facto relationships in a property sharing system originally tailored to meet the property needs of married couples. The paper will begin with a brief outline of the central features of New Zealand's relationship property regime. It will then examine the issues raised by including de facto relationships within the PRA, before concluding with a brief consideration of the lessons to be learned from New Zealand's foray into equal property rights for informal, unregistered de facto relationships.

II. Framework of the Property (Relationships) Act 1976

The PRA is a code that applies to all property transactions between married couples, civil union couples and de facto couples (in relationships of three or more years' duration) instead of the rules and presumptions of the common law and equity,[9] unless the couple elects to contract out of

---

4 Section 4C. Many people opposed the legislation, arguing that the proposed law would erode the special status of marriage and devalue it as the preferred institution for enhancing strong family life.
5 Property (Relationships) Amendment Act 2001, s 5(1).
6 Civil Union Act 2004, s 4.
7 Provided the de facto partners have lived together for three or more years: s 14A.
8 See further, N Peart, »De Facto Relationships (or Maybe Not) in New Zealand« June [2008] IFL 113.
9 Section 4.

the Act.[10] It is a deferred property sharing regime with the result that conventional common law and equitable property rules apply during the relationship. When the parties separate or divorce, the rules in the PRA come into operation. The parties' assets are then classified as either relationship property or separate property.[11] Property acquired during the marriage, civil union or de facto relationship which the parties own individually or jointly, as well as property which is intended for their common use and benefit, is relationship property and is shared equally between them, unless one of the narrow exceptions provided for in the Act applies.[12] Property not acquired during the relationship or in contemplation of it, or acquired by gift or inheritance but not intermingled with other relationship property, remains the separate property of the owning party. It is the contribution to the relationship rather than the contribution to the property that determines the property rights between the parties. Both partners are presumed to have contributed equally to the relationship and share the relationship property equally. All forms of contributions, both domestic and non-domestic, are treated as equal.[13] Nor is any distinction made between different types of relationship property. The family home and chattels and other relationship property are all subject to equal division.[14] This is of particular significance to de facto partners who, under the general principles of contract and property law, often found it difficult to obtain a share of the non-domestic property.[15]

III. The Equal Property Sharing Regime and De Facto Relationships

In many cases, the inclusion of de facto relationships within the Act will present few problems. However, not all informal domestic relationships are straightforward, and it is the more complicated cases that are testing the new law. The following discussion identifies some of the main prob-

---

10 The PRA enables couples to contract out of the provisions of the Act: s 21. They can make an agreement regarding the status, ownership and division of their property at the start of their relationship, or at a later stage, such as at separation, in order to settle their respective relationship property entitlements.
11 Sections 8, 9, 9A and 10.
12 Sections 13, 14, 14AA, 14A.
13 Section 18.
14 Section 11.
15 It was often difficult to prove contributions to property other than the family home. This included property interests such as partnerships and businesses.

lems generated by including de facto relationships within the equal property sharing system.

1. The Statutory Definition of »de facto Relationship«

A de facto relationship is defined in s 2D(1) as a relationship between two persons who are both aged 18 years or older, who live together as a couple and who are not married to, or in a civil union with, one another. In determining whether two persons live together as a couple for the purposes of s 2D (1), all the circumstances of the relationship are to be taken into account. This includes any of the matters listed in s 2D(2) that are relevant in a particular case. The factors to be taken into account are:

a) the duration of the relationship;
b) the nature and extent of common residence;
c) whether or not a sexual relationship exists;
d) the degree of financial dependence or interdependence, and any arrangements for financial support, between the parties;
e) the ownership, use, and acquisition of property;
f) the degree of mutual commitment to a shared life;
g) the care and support of children;
h) the performance of household duties;
i) the reputation and public aspects of the relationship.

The Court is also entitled to have regard to such matters, and to attach such weight to any matter, as may seem appropriate to the Court in the circumstances of the case.[16]

In the seven years since the Act came into force, there have been numerous cases on s 2D,[17] suggesting that the provision is difficult to apply in practice. Section 2D vests in the court a large measure of discretion, which inevitably leads to uncertainty. Some of the main problems with the definition are discussed below.

---

16 Section 2D(3)(b). A de facto relationship ends if the de facto partners cease to live together as a couple or one of the de facto partners dies: s 2D(4).
17 Conservatively, there are at least 100 cases at Family Court or High Court level that examine the law as it now relates to de facto partners' property rights. At the time of writing, however, the Court of Appeal and the Supreme Court have yet to rule on these issues.

1.1 Different Definitions in Different Statutes

One problematic factor is that another important New Zealand statute, the Interpretation Act 1999, defines de facto relationships quite differently to s 2D of the PRA. The Interpretation Act provides that a de facto relationship is »a relationship in the nature of marriage or civil union«.[18] That definition was inserted in 2005, four years after the enactment of the PRA. While it does not apply to the PRA, it applies to other statutes that do not contain their own definition of de facto relationship.[19] The result of the two different definitions is that a couple might be in a de facto relationship in certain facets of their lives (eg a property dispute involving the PRA) but not in a de facto relationship in other aspects of their lives (eg for welfare benefit purposes under the Social Security Act 1964).[20] This is hardly satisfactory for the parties concerned or indeed for the government administrators, lawyers and courts whose job it is to interpret the legislation. Because the definition was not inserted in the Interpretation Act until 2005, however, it must be supposed that it was a deliberate departure from s 2D of the PRA rather than a drafting oversight. The confusion generated by the different definitions requires legislative reconsideration.

1.2 The Age Criterion

A further example of the different qualifying criteria in the PRA is to be found in 2D (1) (a) which requires that both partners are 18 years or older. This is in contrast to age limits specified in other legislation. For example, minors may marry at 16 with the consent of the parent or guardian.[21] The definition of de facto relationship in the Interpretation Act 1999[22] also specifies the age of 16 years or older. The legislative intent behind the different age restrictions is not obvious. The effect of the requirement is that the PRA does not recognize the relationship until the younger of the two partners turns 18. If a relationship ends before the younger partner turns 18, the Act will not cover any property disputes. Or where, for example, partners live together from the age of 16 to the age of 20, s 2D will only recognize the relationship from the time the younger partner turns

---

18 Section 29A(1)(a), inserted by s 4 Interpretation Amendment Act 2005.
19 Eg, the Social Security Act 1964, the Child Support Act 1991, the Domestic Violence Act 1995 and the Income Tax Act 2007. See *Ruka v DSW* [1997] 1 NZLR 154 (CA) for an interpretation of the term »relationship in the nature of marriage«.
20 By contrast, this would not be the case for marriage or civil unions.
21 Marriage Act 1955, s 18.
22 Section 29A(1)(c).

18.[23] While most very young partners are unlikely to have much property to dispute,[24] it seems illogical to exclude a section of the population from the PRA for no good reason.

1.3 »Living Together as a Couple«

The principal difficulty with s 2D is to determine whether a de facto relationship in fact exists in a given situation. The definition is neither straightforward nor easy to apply in individual cases. The list of criteria in s 2D(2) is not exhaustive, and operates more as a guide than a set of rules. The court is entitled to have regard to such matters, and to attach such weight to any matter, as may seem appropriate in the circumstances of the case.[25] None of the nine factors is essential to the existence of a de facto relationship, either on its own or in combination with other criteria. Rather, the only critical factor is that the partners live together as a couple – a matter virtually incapable of objective verification. Thus it is a question of fact, evidence and degree whether a couple is in a de facto relationship.

The New Zealand courts have commented on the provision on several occasions.[26] In the leading case of *Scragg v Scott* the High Court noted that the approach to s 2D(2) must be broad, with various factors to be weighed up in an evaluative task, similar to those the Courts are frequently called upon to undertake when drawing conclusions from circumstantial evidence.[27] The task necessarily requires the application of common sense and it is the cumulative weight of all factors whether specified in the Act or not which is decisive.[28] A brief case study of four recent decisions demonstrates that the question of whether a couple is living together as a couple requires an unavoidably high level of subjective assessment dependent on the combination of indicia unique to that couple's circumstances.

The case of *C v S*[29] shows that even a very lengthy relationship may not necessarily be a de facto relationship. There, the Court found that a rela-

---

23 Such a de facto relationship will be one of short duration and the requirements of s 14A must be satisfied in order for property sharing to take place. See further, *Brookers Family Law – Family Property* (Wellington, Brookers, 2008) PR2B.
24 That will not always be the case. For example, some young people become the recipients of substantial inheritances.
25 Section 2D(3)(b).
26 For analyses by the High Court see *S v M* 17/4/07, Gendall J, HC Wellington CIV-2006-485-1940; *Benseman v Foster* (2006) 25 FRNZ 803, also reported as *Benseman v Ball* [2007] NZFLR 127.
27 (2006) 25 FRNZ 942; [2006] NZFLR 1076, at para 64.
28 (2006) 25 FRNZ 942; [2006] NZFLR 1076, at para 64.
29 *C v S* 28/9/06, Judge Smith, FC Dunedin FAM-2005-012-157.

tionship of 20 years' standing never became a de facto relationship. While the parties were lovers and had an intense and emotional relationship for much of the time, when both were free to share a residence, they did not do so, nor did they ever develop any financial interdependence. During the entire association between C and S, S was married to another woman with whom he had two children. His wife was apparently aware of her husband's long-term involvement with another woman but, for whatever reason, elected to tolerate the situation.

In *Scragg v Scott*, on the other hand, the Court was prepared to find a de facto relationship. The parties met in 1990 and did not finally end their relationship until 2002 or 2003. The most unusual aspect of their relationship was that they lived separately for much of the time – the respondent mainly in New Zealand, and the appellant mainly in Guam where he ran a business. When they were together in the same country, they shared a residence, but the longest period the parties ever resided together was about nine months in Guam. They had a sexual relationship but they were not monogamous. They kept their finances largely separate apart from a property investment they entered into in 1996. Ms Scott had no obvious means of income, and the Court inferred that Mr Scragg helped to support her financially. The Court held that despite the intermittent nature of their common residence, the cumulative weight of all the factors provided sufficient evidence that they lived together as a couple for the period between 1996 (when Ms Scott invested settlement monies from her former marriage in investment properties in Australia and Mr Scragg gave her $10,000 to assist with the purchase), and 2002 (when Ms Scott discovered Mr Scragg was living with another woman in Guam). The Court found that »[t]hey presented to the outside world generally as a couple.«[30]

Perhaps the most worthwhile thing to be derived from a comparison of cases on s 2D, it is that no two relationships are the same. It might be argued that *Scragg v Scott* and *C v S* were not so different (except for the intermittent shared residence in *Scragg v Scott*) as to warrant different outcomes, but in view of the subjective nature of the court's task, it is difficult to isolate precisely which factors tip a case one way or the other.

---

30 Para 65. The Court also observed, at para 41, that »[c]ouples may cohabit from time to time where, for example, one party has to spend long periods away from home for reasons of occupation, or is a member of the Armed Forces, or a merchant seafarer or otherwise«.

Allison v Scott[31] is another recent case where the Court found in favour of a de facto relationship. There, the couple met in late 1999 and the relationship ended when Mr Scott died in an accident in June 2005. They both had children from previous relationships and, out of a concern for the children, decided not to move in together too soon. Nonetheless, the parties were in a sexual relationship, often visited each other's homes and gradually began to intermingle their finances. Although Ms Allison did not move permanently to Mr Scott's home until September 2004, the Court held that they began living together as a couple more than a year before that – in or around June 2003. This finding was based on the rather thin reasoning that it was at that point that they began to mingle their finances and start to renovate Mr Scott's house. Another important factor was that Ms Allison was pregnant at the time Mr Scott died in June 2005 and gave birth in September 2005.

The arguably generous reading of the s 2D criteria in *Scragg v Scott* and *Allison v Scott* may be contrasted with *C v A*.[32] The facts in *C v A* were similar in many ways to those in *Allison v Scott*, but in *C v A* the Court found no de facto relationship. C and A had both been married and both had children from those relationships. A died in an accident in 2005 before C, with whom he had been having a relationship for the past four years, had moved in with him. As was the case in *Allison v Scott*, the couple in *C v A* were worried about the possible reactions of their children. This, together with their religious beliefs as Jehovah's Witnesses, led to their decision to postpone moving in together. However, in 2004, A purchased a house for them both to live in, which C helped to decorate and furnish, moving some items of her own furniture into the property. On balance, the Court formed the view that that they were not living together as a couple and were not in a de facto relationship. According to the Judge, they did not live together and apart from their sexual relationship and emotional connection they had not intermingled the practical aspects of their lives relating to their households, their finances and their children.[33] The main point of difference between *Allison v Scott* and *C v A* was the shared residence in *Allison v Scott*. That would also appear to be the main difference between *Scragg v Scott* and *C v S*.

31　*Allison v Scott* 31/5/07, Judge Smith, FC Dunedin, FAM 2006-045-58.
32　*C v A* (2007) 26 FRNZ 389 (FC).
33　*C v A* (2007) 26 FRNZ 389 (FC), para 80.

From this examination of just four cases, it may be seen that outcomes can differ widely, indicating the very high level of fact sensitivity in this area of the law. In the borderline cases, the outcome will depend almost entirely on the court's subjective assessment of all the circumstances.

In conclusion then, the broad discretion in s 2D is an awkward inclusion in legislation that has stripped so many other discretions away from the judiciary. By comparison, the court has little or no discretion on the issue of the division of the relationship property. While there are some provisions that allow a departure from equal sharing,[34] these provisions are designed to apply in exceptional cases only. None relates to a discretion so central as that found in s 2D, where the court must rule on the status of the relationship, which in turn, either qualifies or disqualifies entry to the Act's inflexible equal sharing rules. Such an uncertain access route into a rigid code can turn the process into an expensive gamble for potential applicants.

1.4 Duration of the de facto Relationship

As the cases discussed above illustrate, even if a de facto relationship exists, it is also important to identify its duration. When did it begin and when did it end? Unlike marriages and civil unions, there is no public record of de facto relationships and so it can be difficult to specify a commencement date. A de facto relationship ends for the purposes of the Act if the de facto partners cease to live together as a couple or if one of them dies.[35] The length of the relationship is relevant for a number of reasons. In the first place, marriages, civil unions and de facto relationships of short duration (less than three years) are not treated alike. A marriage or civil union of short duration[36] is covered by the PRA, whereas a de facto relationship of less than three years is not covered unless the court is satisfied that there is a child of the de facto relationship, or that the applicant has made a substantial contribution to the de facto relationship, and that failure to make an order would result in serious injustice.[37] The dates of commencement and termination are thus important to a great many de

---

34 Eg, s 13. Note also, s 15 which empowers the court to award compensation for economic disparity.
35 Section 2D(4).
36 For marriages of short duration see s 14. For civil unions of short duration see s 14AA.
37 Section 14A. If the de facto relationship of short duration is not covered by the PRA, general principles of law apply. This might require the claimant to argue the existence of a constructive trust to obtain a share of the assets accumulated during the relationship. See, eg *Lankow v Rose* [1995] 1 NZLR 277 (CA).

facto relationships, not merely those where it is doubtful that the relationship meets the s 2D criteria.

Section 2B of the Act complicates matters further, providing that if a marriage was immediately preceded by a de facto relationship between the husband and the wife, the de facto relationship must be treated as if it were part of the marriage. The period of the de facto relationship is taken into account in determining the length of the marriage with the result that a marriage that has lasted less than three years may not be a short duration marriage. For example, a two-year marriage, preceded by a four-year de facto relationship will be treated as a six-year marriage. Again, therefore, it is crucial to identify whether a de facto relationship existed and if so, its commencement and termination dates.

Even if the de facto relationship is longer than three years and therefore covered by the Act, its commencement and/or termination dates are still very relevant in terms of the classification of the property as relationship property or separate property. For example, property (other than the family home and family chattels[38]) acquired before the relationship began usually remains the separate property of the partner who acquired it, unless the property was acquired in contemplation of the relationship.[39] As the cases discussed under the previous heading show, identifying when the relationship began can be a complicated exercise. Problems can also arise where separation occurs many years later when the partners' recollections of the early days of their relationship are clouded by the passing of time.[40]

2. The PRA Applies Retrospectively and is an Opt-Out Scheme

The Act applies to all de facto relationships of three or more years' duration ending on or after 1 February 2002.[41] The Act operates retrospectively, with the effect that the actions of de facto couples before 1 February 2002 now have legal consequences that may not have been anticipated at the

---

[38] Section 8(1)(a),(b).
[39] Section 8(1)(d).
[40] Eg, *Boyd v Jackson* 6/3/03, Judge Inglis QC, FC Napier FP041/363/01, where the parties had lived together before their marriage in 1982, but 20 years later neither was able to recall when their de facto relationship began. See also *Scragg v Scott* (2006) 25 FRNZ 942; [2006] NZFLR 1076. There, the parties' relationship had initially commenced as early as 1990, but the Court found that their de facto relationship had developed gradually and had begun by 1996.
[41] Section 4C. It does not apply to de facto relationships that ended before 1 February 2002.

time of those actions. To impose a legislative scheme on de facto couples ex post facto has few merits, particularly in view of the general statutory prohibition against retrospective legislation. It appears especially unwarranted in those cases where the parties made property arrangements before the PRA applied to them and which are now liable to be overturned. For example, a transfer some time before the Act came into effect of the family home into trust as a protection against a claim from one's partner, could now be set aside under the Act, or perhaps result in an award of compensation.[42] This leads to a related issue, namely, that the Act is an opt-out scheme, not an opt-in scheme.

The PRA applies to all marriages, civil unions and de facto relationships (of more than three years' duration) provided the parties have not contracted out of the Act.[43] A similar scheme operated under the Matrimonial Property Act 1976. Parliament evidently regarded the extension of the existing statutory regime to include de facto relationships as the most practical solution. As foreshadowed above, however, the inclusion of de facto couples in the existing scheme overlooks the fact that it was not a genuine option for all those couples already in relationships before the Act came into force. It might be argued, however, that couples could have contracted out of the Act before it came into force if they did not want it to apply to them. Parliament adopted the PRA on 29 March 2001, but the Act did not come into force until 1 February 2002. One of the reasons for the 10-month delay was to provide the chance to educate the public about the new law and to allow de facto partners to arrange their property affairs accordingly.[44] In addition, the contracting out provisions came into force on 1 August 2001 – some six months before the rest of the Act took effect – with the purpose of allowing de facto partners to contract out in advance. While it is not known how many couples responded to that opportunity, it

---

42 See N Peart, M Briggs, and M Henaghan (eds), *Relationship Property on Death*, (Wellington, Brookers Ltd, 2004) 30. This calls attention to a drafting error in the PRA related to bundling de facto relationships into an existing Act originally designed for married couples. Under s 44 the court may set aside dispositions made in order to defeat an applicant's rights under the PRA. But where the disposition was made before the PRA was enacted (ie, before the statute applied to de facto relationships), it is illogical to subsequently impute an intention to defeat relationship property rights. This drafting error indicates that the decision to deal with de facto relationships within the PRA rather than in a separate statute was hurried through without adequate attention to detail.
43 See Part 6, PRA.
44 See the commentary to the Matrimonial Property Amendment Bill and SOP No.25 (109-3) 13.

is clear from the growing number of cases on s 2D, that many couples did nothing or, at least, their efforts in this regard came to nothing.[45]

Even for those people who have entered de facto relationships since the Act came into force, it is doubtful that the publicity in 2001 and 2002 is still effective seven or eight years later. Furthermore, given the uncertainty of the de facto relationship definition in s 2D, many people may not even be aware they are in a qualifying de facto relationship. By the time they do become aware of their status as a de facto partner, it may be too late to reach a mutually satisfactory contracting out arrangement. The same arguments cannot be made in respect of marriages or civil unions. In contrast to de facto relationships, marriage has always carried some proprietary consequences – even if only to impose long-term maintenance obligations on separation. Spouses can reasonably be deemed to expect consequences will flow from the change of status. Similarly, a civil union is a registered relationship and the parties will usually have put their minds to the property sharing consequences of entering the union. Whereas people formally opt-in to marriages and civil unions, they generally only drift into de facto relationships. This may make all the difference to a person's awareness of their property rights and obligations. To apply an opt-out property sharing regime to de facto relationships is problematic: one must first know there is a law from which he or she must opt-out.

3. Comparison with Other Legal Systems

When looking for a suitable definition for de facto relationship, New Zealand took as its template for s 2D the definition of de facto relationship already in use in the Australian state of New South Wales in its Property (Relationships) Act 1984, as amended in 1999. But in a number of material respects, the New South Wales statute is quite distinct from the New Zealand PRA. The New South Wales legislation only applies to people

---

45 Anecdotal evidence obtained from family law practitioners suggests that many de facto relationships broke down during this time when couples were unable to agree on contracting out terms. In its recent Report on *Cohabitation: The Financial Consequences of Relationship Breakdown*, the UK Law Commission took the view that »agreements entered into before the enactment of legislation should not be capable of being valid opt-out agreements because parties should be able to take this step only in full knowledge of the terms of the legislation.« The Commission recommended a period between the legislation being enacted and implementation of the scheme during which cohabitants should be able to make an opt-out agreement: Law Com No 307 (July 2007, London) 116, para 5.71.

in de facto relationships or other domestic relationships.[46] In Australia, property disputes between married couples are dealt with separately in the Family Law Act 1975 (Commonwealth). By contrast, the New Zealand PRA has taken the definition out of its original context by translating it into a statute that covers marriages, civil unions and de facto relationships. Nor should it be overlooked that the New South Wales law does not impose an equal sharing regime on de facto relationships and other domestic relationships. Rather, the court has a wide discretion to make such orders adjusting the interests of the parties in the property as to it seems just and equitable having regard to the financial and non-financial contributions of the parties to the acquisition, conservation or improvement of any property, and to the contributions made by either party to the welfare of the other party or a child of the parties (including homemaking contributions).[47] Whereas the New Zealand PRA gives the court virtually no scope to depart from equal sharing, the New South Wales legislation thus provides a broad discretion.

No other western legal system has gone as far as the New Zealand PRA. Most other schemes, whether already in force or currently at the recommendation stage, are based on a model that separates the property interests of unmarried cohabitants from spouses or those in registered relationships. These schemes also give the courts a discretion regarding the division of property. In its recent report on the financial consequences of the breakdown of relationships between cohabiting partners, the English Law Commission concluded that reform was necessary to address inadequacies in the current law in that jurisdiction.[48] Unlike the New Zealand model, however, the Commission recommended a separate statutory regime for cohabitants on separation that would not equate cohabitants with married couples or give them equivalent rights. The scheme would look at the economic consequences of the contributions made by the parties during the relationship, rather than automatically applying to all cohabitants who satisfied the eligibility criteria.[49]

---

46 A domestic relationship is defined as a de facto relationship or a close personal relationship (other than marriage or a de facto relationship) between 2 adults whether or not related by family, who are living together, one of whom provides the other with domestic support and personal care: s 5.
47 Property (Relationships) Act 1984 (NSW), s 20.
48 Law Commission (UK): *Cohabitation: The Financial Consequences of Relationship Breakdown* (Law Com No 307, July 2007, London).
49 Like the PRA, the Law Commission did not seek to create a formal registration system before rights would accrue.

IV. Conclusion

This paper has argued that New Zealand's decision to integrate de facto relationships into an existing property regime originally designed to address property disputes between married couples on divorce was a bold and, in some respects, imprudent move. New Zealand has gone further than other legal systems in its recognition of equal property rights for de facto partners. It is a regime that puts a premium on identifying a qualifying de facto relationship. But the s 2D definition is shrouded in uncertainty and has opened the door wide to litigation. Already, it is proving difficult to apply to the wide variety of informal relationships that couples find themselves in either by accident or design.

In some cases, including those discussed in Part III, there is no bright line whether or not the parties really were living together as a couple for the purposes of s 2D. At a practical level, it is to be hoped that the courts proceed with care when interpreting s 2D, lest the definition develops in a different direction than Parliament intended. How New Zealand's senior appellate courts deal with the issue when it eventually comes before them will be significant, although of course it would be wrong to be too confident that we will be able to distil general principles in light of the fact specific nature of the inquiry.[50]

It may be noted that s 1N of the PRA contains four guiding principles designed to assist in the interpretation of the Act. The last of these is »the principle that questions arising under the Act about relationship property should be resolved inexpensively, simply and speedily as is consistent with justice.«[51] Paradoxically, the definition of de facto relationship in s 2D seems to be achieving the opposite result – if the volume of litigation is anything to go by.

When one compares legal developments in other countries to those in New Zealand, it becomes apparent that New Zealand has adopted a rather more experimental approach to resolving relationship property disputes between de facto partners. As has been discussed, the property consequences flowing from the breakdown of informal relationships in jurisdictions such as New South Wales in Australia, are dealt with separately from formal relationships. The United Kingdom proposal indicates a similar preference. In New Zealand, the PRA covers everyone: married

---

50 See S Jefferson, »De facto or ›friends with benefits‹?« (2007) 5 NZFLJ 304, 307.
51 Section 1N(d).

couples, civil union couples and de facto couples. From such a cursory comparison it would, of course, be wrong to jump to the conclusion that New Zealand has taken a wrong turning in its treatment of de facto partners' property rights. But if nothing else, this must give New Zealand pause for thought: are we the only jurisdiction to have achieved the correct legal balance?

The Protection of a Vulnerable Party when a Cohabitee Relationship Ends – An Evaluation of the Swedish Cohabitees Act

Margareta Brattström[1]

I. Introduction

In recent decades, there has been an almost worldwide increase in the number of couples living together without getting married. In Sweden, this development began already in the 1960s. As a result, the *Cohabitees (Joint Homes) Act*[2] was introduced in 1988. In 2003, it was replaced by the *Cohabitees Act*.[3] The new Act contains some clarifications and applies to all cohabitees, irrespective of their sex. Nowadays, it is estimated that every third couple living together in Sweden is unmarried. Moreover, a majority of newborn children have an unmarried mother, many of whom cohabit with the father of the child outside of marriage.[4]

In this article, the Swedish *Cohabitees Act* (2003: 376) will be evaluated. I will first provide the background to the law and present its main principles (Part 2). Subsequently, I will discuss four questions: Does the design of the law promote its purpose in a satisfying manner? (Part 3); Does the application of the law create any special problems? (Part 4); Does the Swedish Cohabitees Act need to be revised? (Part 5); What can foreign jurisdictions learn from the Swedish experience of cohabitation without marriage? (Part 6).

---

1 Associate Professor at Uppsala University, Faculty of Law, Sweden.
2 Cohabitees (Joint Homes) Act (1987:232).
3 Cohabitees Act (2003:376). The Swedish Ministry of Justice has produced an information sheet about the Cohabitees Act in English which may be found at <www.regeringen.se/content/1/c4/34/44/a6c7b981.pdf>.
4 A. Agell and M. Brattström, *Äktenskap, Samboende, Partnerskap*, Fourth edition, Iustus Förlag 2008 pp. 18–20.

II. The Swedish Cohabitees Act

The overall purpose of the Swedish Cohabitees Act is to provide a minimum level of protection for a financially vulnerable party upon the dissolution of a cohabitee relationship.[5] The legislator has stipulated the grounds for the Act by referring to the everyday life of cohabitees, who tend to interlace their finances without regulating the situation in an agreement. This practice has made it necessary to provide protection for the financially vulnerable party. The protection consists of a right to share the home that has been jointly built up. Swedish law offers limited protection for cohabitees in comparison to the protection it provides for spouses and registered partners.[6] Another difference is that, unlike spouses and registered partners, cohabitees never have maintenance obligations towards one another – neither during nor after the relationship. The differences between cohabitees, on the one hand, and married or registered partners, on the other hand, are the result of a conscious choice; since the right of cohabitees to share property is limited, from a practical point of view, to only include the indispensable.[7] The protection for a vulnerable party in a cohabitee relationship is established by the main principles of the Swedish Cohabitees Act.

When two people live together on a permanent basis as a couple, and share a household, they are cohabitees, irrespective of the sex of the couple.[8] During the relationship, each cohabitee remains the sole owner of all of his or her property, with sole administration rights, regardless of the type of property or the time and manner of acquisition.[9] All debts re-

---

[5] Prop. (Government Bill) 2002/03:80 (Ny sambolag) p. 25. The *travaux préparatoires* to the Swedish Cohabitees Act, SOU 1999:104 (Nya Samboregler), contain an English summary of the investigator's work (pp. 27-36). The summary may be found at <www.regeringen.se/sb/d/108/a/1237>.

[6] When marriage or registered partnership is entered into, each party's property shall, under the main rule, become so-called *marital property* (in Swedish: *giftorättsgods*), forming a part of the deferred community property regime, Swedish Marriage Code Chapter 7, Section 1; and the Registered Partnership Act (1994:1117) Chapter 3, Section 1. The value of all of the marital property shall be shared equally between the spouses or registered partners upon dissolution of the matrimonial property regime.

[7] Prop. (Government Bill) 1986/87:1 (om äktenskapsbalk m.m.) p. 99.

[8] Swedish Cohabitees Act, Section 1. The Act is not applicable if one, or both, of the cohabitees is married or is a registered partner.

[9] There are, however, certain limitations on a cohabitee's possibility to dispose of his or her property: Swedish Cohabitees Act, Section 23. A cohabitee may not, without the consent of the other cohabitee, sell, give away, mortgage/pledge, or let the joint home. Nor may a cohabitee, without the consent of the other, sell, give away, or pawn joint household goods. The consent of the other cohabitee may be replaced by a court decision.

main a cohabitee's own debts. The protection provided for a vulnerable party, pursuant to the Swedish Cohabitees Act, only becomes available if a cohabitee demands a division of property when the relationship ends. A relationship ends upon separation or death of one of the cohabitees.[10] The request must be made no later than one year after the cohabitee relationship has ended. It is the value of the joint dwelling and household goods **acquired** for joint use by one, or by both, of the cohabitees that can be shared.[11] However, the dwelling and the household goods must be **remaining** when the relationship ends. The values of other assets such as savings, cars or items for leisure purposes cannot be subject to division under the Swedish Cohabitees Act.[12]

When the division of property takes place, the cohabitees' shares shall first be calculated.[13] When calculating these shares, a deduction shall be made from each cohabitee's property, sufficient to cover the debts which that cohabitee had.[14] The value of the assets shall then be divided equally between the cohabitees.[15] Exceptions to the fifty-fifty share rule may be made if this would lead to an unreasonable result, particularly with regard to the duration of the relationship.[16] In special cases, such as after very short cohabitee relationships, an adjustment may be made so that each party simply retains his or her own property.

On the basis of the shares calculated for the cohabitees, the property is then to be distributed.[17] The main rule is that the cohabitee whose assets exceed half of the total divisible mass, can choose whether to surrender property to the other cohabitee, or to pay a corresponding sum of money instead.[18] It should be underlined, however, that this is subject to a special rule: the cohabitee in greatest need of the dwelling or household goods is entitled to receive it, even if he or she did not own the property, provided that it is reasonable.[19] The cohabitee who does not receive the dwelling,

---

10 Swedish Cohabitees Act, Section 8.2.
11 Swedish Cohabitees Act, Sections 3, 8 & 14.
12 Swedish Cohabitees Act, Sections 3 & 7.
13 Swedish Cohabitees Act, Section 12.
14 Swedish Cohabitees Act, Section 13. A creditor's claims on a cohabitee, which carry a preferential right in that a cohabitee's property that is not a dwelling or household goods, shall only be covered by that kind of property in so far as payment cannot be obtained out of his or her other property.
15 Swedish Cohabitees Act, Section 14.
16 Swedish Cohabitees Act, Section 15.
17 Swedish Cohabitees Act, Section 16.1.
18 Swedish Cohabitees Act, Section 17.
19 Swedish Cohabitees Act, Section 16.2. A tenant-owner (condominium) or tenancy

will have a right to other property from the joint home to the same value, or a corresponding sum of money. The cohabitee »in greatest need« of the dwelling is usually considered to be the cohabitee who, following the separation, will have custody of the children or, in the case of joint custody, the actual care of the children. As a result, that cohabitee will most likely be considered »in greatest need« to stay on in the dwelling. In addition, other factors such as the cohabitee's age and health, and his or her prospects of obtaining a new home, may be taken into consideration in this context.[20]

Cohabitees who wish to keep their financial affairs completely separate, may conclude an agreement to the effect that the rules on division of property contained in the Swedish Cohabitees Act shall not apply to their cohabitee relationship.[21] They may also agree that certain property shall not be included in the division of property. The agreement shall be in writing and signed by the cohabitees.[22] Such an agreement may be entered into before, as well as during, the cohabitation. If the agreement is held to be unreasonable in view of the subject matter of the agreement; the circumstances when it was drawn up; circumstances subsequently arising; and in view of the overall circumstances, it may be adjusted or completely disregarded in the division of property.[23]

III. Does the Design of the Act Promote its Purpose in a Satisfying Manner?

The Swedish Cohabitees Act becomes applicable without any procedure or consent, when the couple moves in together and the requirements of the Act are met.[24] This creates a good starting point for promoting the Act's primary purpose: to provide a minimum level of protection for a financially vulnerable party.

---

right that was not acquired for joint use but which nevertheless has been used jointly, is not, of course, included in the division of property. But there is a special rule which gives the cohabitee in most need of the dwelling a right to take it over from the other cohabite: Swedish Cohabitees Act, Section 22. However, if the cohabitee's have no children, there must be extraordinary reasons for taking it over. The party taking over the dwelling shall fully compensate the other for the value of the dwelling.

20 A. Agell and M. Brattström, *Äktenskap, Samboende, Partnerskap*, Fourth edition, Iustus Förlag, 2008, pp. 207-208 and 276-277.
21 Swedish Cohabitees Act, Section 9.
a22 The agreement will not be registered and does not need to be attested.
23 Swedish Cohabitees Act, Section 9.3.
24 Swedish Cohabitees Act, Section 1.

The level of protection offered is, however, dependent on the value that can be shared. It is the joint dwelling and household goods, acquired for joint use, that is shared, irrespective of which party owns the property.[25] In many cases the protection will grow during the relationship, since couples create their joint home. When the family grows, they may move to a larger home and furniture will be replaced on an ongoing basis. As a result of an improved financial situation, both the home and furniture will often become more valuable. After a long cohabitee relationship there are usually assets of considerable value to be shared, and the protection of the vulnerable party will be secured. It should be mentioned that an adjustment can be made if equal sharing leads to an unreasonable outcome for the party who owned most of the property to be shared.[26]

If the dwelling and household goods have not been acquired for the purpose of joint use, there will be nothing to share upon the dissolution of the cohabitee relationship. The requirement of »acquired for joint use« may also limit the value that will, in the end, be included in the division of property. This can occur when a couple starts cohabiting in a dwelling that one of them owned prior to the cohabitation relationship. Even if the couple has shared the mortgage repayments and other costs there will be no value to be shared when the relationship ends, since the dwelling was not acquired for joint use. The situation will be to the contrary, as mentioned above, if the cohabitees move in to a new dwelling together. Another example where there may be no value to be shared is if property has been given to one of the cohabitees as a gift. Such property will, most likely, not be seen as acquired for joint use.[27] Even in these situations, there can, of course, be a vulnerable party upon the dissolution of a relationship, but the Swedish Cohabitees Act does not contain any protection for that party if there is nothing to share.

---

25   Swedish Cohabitees Act, Sections 5 & 6.
26   Swedish Cohabitees Act, Section 15. In the Swedish Supreme Court decision NJA 2003 p. 650 the relationship ended after four and a half years. During the last two years, the cohabitees had lived in an apartment owned by them both, in different shares. When they bought the apartment, the male cohabitee paid most of the purchases price (with money he had inherited from his dead wife). The Supreme Court found it fair that the female cohabite received 25% instead of 50% of the value of the apartment.
27   See also, Swedish Cohabitees Act, Section 4. When a third party, who has donated or bequeathed property to a recipient, upon condition that the property shall be the recipient's separate property, the property cannot be shared between two cohabitees. As a rule, all property replacing separate property is regarded as separate property of the owner.

However, the Cohabitees Act is not the only way to share assets between cohabitees when the relationship ends. The general principles of the law of obligations and property are applicable to cohabitees. As a result, cohabitees may enter into legal transactions with each other, or acquire property jointly and become joint owners. In Swedish case law, the principle of caveat (»hidden«) joint ownership of property has developed. Caveat ownership may occur when only one of the cohabitees holds the title to the property, if it has been acquired for the cohabitees' joint use. However, the cohabitees must have intended that the property be jointly owned by them, and the cohabitee not holding the title must also have made a financial contribution to the acquisition.[28] A recent Supreme Court decision, NJA 2008 p. 826, confirms that caveat ownership between cohabitees can arise in respect of real estate used only for recreational purposes. Caveat ownership has proven to be particularly useful when a cohabitee relationship ends, allowing assets that have been jointly built up to be shared between the cohabitees, even if the property in question is not connected to the dwelling or household goods. General rules contained in the Swedish Act on Joint Ownership[29] are applicable when cohabitees – or others – are joint owners, which means that the property may be sold at a public auction when one of the owners requests it, and the sales amount will be shared between the owners. When cohabitees are not joint owners, but one of them has made it possible for the other cohabitee to build up great assets that will not be shared in accordance to the Swedish Cohabitees Act, the general principle on compensation for unjustified enrichment can, in theory, be used. However, this principle is rarely used in practise. This, in my opinion, is not satisfactory, since it limits the protection available to a financially vulnerable party.

In a situation where cohabitation is dissolved by the death of one of the parties, the Swedish Act does not provide any inheritance rights for the surviving cohabitee. However, the surviving cohabitee is protected by special rules found in the Swedish Cohabitees Act. Firstly, the surviving cohabitee alone has the right to decide whether or not a division of property shall take place.[30] The heirs of the deceased cohabitee are not

---

28 See Swedish Supreme Court decisions NJA 1980 p. 705; NJA 1981 p. 693; and NJA 1982 p. 589, which have all contributed to the development of the principles and requirements in relation to the so-called caveat joint ownership between spouses and cohabitees.
29 Lag (1904:48) om samägande, p. 1.
30 Swedish Cohabitees Act, Section 18.

entitled to make such a request. This means that the surviving cohabitee can decide that each side retains their property, which will benefit the surviving cohabitee if he or she owns the major part of the joint dwelling and household goods. Secondly, the surviving cohabitee is protected by a right, upon division of the joint dwelling and household goods, to retain an amount of the property equivalent to twice the so-called basic amount sum.[31] This protection is, however, not far-reaching; at the moment amounting to approximately 80 000 Swedish kronor (8 000 Euros), and an application presupposes that there is property, to the value of this sum, to divide between cohabitees (by way of joint dwelling or household goods). It has been argued that this amount »would protect the small nests from shattering«.[32] But even in this situation, one could ask whether the Act promotes its purpose to provide a minimum level of protection for a vulnerable party on the dissolution of the cohabitation. The guaranteed sum of 80 000 Swedish kronor to be paid from the joint dwelling and household goods, can be compared to the average amount of assets in a decent estate, which is 500 000 Swedish kronor (50 000 Euros).[33] A deceased person's most valuable asset is usually the dwelling.

IV. Does the Application of the Law Create any Special Problems?

As mentioned above, only the joint dwelling and household goods, acquired for joint use, are included in a property division between cohabitees. If the cohabitees have redecorated and improved a dwelling, instead of moving to a larger home, the joint dwelling will not be included in a property division, unless it was acquired for the purpose of joint use from the beginning.[34] It can be difficult for cohabitees to understand the difference in outcome if they choose to improve a home instead of moving to a new one.

Another prerequisite for sharing the value of a dwelling and household goods is that the property in question is remaining when the relationship ends. If the cohabitees have been living in a house that would have been shared in a property division, but subsequently move to a rented apartment, which in Sweden does not have any economic value, the amount

---

31 Swedish Cohabitees Act, Section 18.2.
32 Prop. (Government Bill) 1986/87:1 (om äktenskapsbalk m.m.) pp. 109–110.
33 M. Brattström and A. Singer, *Rätt arv*, Second edition, Iustus Förlag 2008 p. 80.
34 See Swedish Supreme Court decision NJA 2004 p. 542.

received from the sale of the house is not included in a property division, since money and savings are excluded from the Swedish Cohabitees Act. This may come as a negative surprise for the cohabitee who did not own a share of the house.

Both of the situations mentioned above reflect the most common problem with the Swedish Cohabitees Act: Many cohabitees believe that the Act gives them more protection than it actually does. It should be kept in mind, however, that the purpose of the Cohabitees Act is only to provide a minimum level of protection for a financially vulnerable party, by sharing the value of a home that has been jointly built up. If cohabitees want something else, they are expected to get married or make agreements in accordance with the general principles of the law of obligations and property.[35] However, possibilities for cohabitees to extend the rules applicable to married couples through agreements instead of marriage are very limited. Cohabitees cannot agree to include property in a future division other than the joint dwelling and household goods acquired for joint use.[36] The possibility of securing the situation for the surviving cohabitee is also limited. If the first deceased cohabitee leaves children, the children have a mandatory right to inherit from the parent, a right which can only be partly overridden by a will.[37] This is also the case when the children are the cohabitees' joint children. Had the parents been married, the entire estate of the deceased spouse would have gone to the surviving spouse.[38] A child does not inherit parents who are married, until both spouses are deceased. In other areas of law, cohabitees and spouses are treated equally; in respect of tax laws and social laws for instance, particularly where cohabitees have children together. Keeping this in mind, one can easily see how difficult it can be for cohabitees to understand how the law regulates their relationship. The legislator claims to be aware of the never ending need for clear and accessible information about the Swedish Cohabitees Act.[39] Whether or not information has reached those in need of information, however, is a completely different question.

---

35 Prop. (Government Bill) 1986/87:1 (om äktenskapsbalk m.m.) pp. 99 & 107–108.
36 See Supreme Court decision NJA 1997 p. 227
37 Swedish Code of Inheritance (Ärvdabalken), Chapter 2, Section 1 & Chapter 7, Section 1.
38 Swedish Code of Inheritance (Ärvdabalken), Chapter 3, Section 1.
39 Prop. (Government Bill) 2002/03:80 (Ny sambolag) p. 42. The *travaux préparatoires* to the Swedish Cohabitees Act, SOU 1999:104 (Nya Samboregler) p. 32 & pp. 245–249.

V. Does the Swedish Cohabitees Act Need Revision?

Things can always be improved. During the last few years, a question that has been discussed in Sweden is whether the assets which can be included in a property division between cohabitees, ought to be increased – for the purpose of improving the financial protection for a vulnerable party. It has been suggested that cars and other motor vehicles, such as motor boats and snow scooters, should be covered by the Cohabitees Act, since this kind of property is often equally as important for the finances of the cohabitees as the dwelling and household goods.[40] To date, the proposal has not materialized because it has been considered problematic with reference to the purpose of the law.[41] Instead, the government – in March 2003 – promised a new investigation would be undertaken for the purpose of analyzing what property shall be shared between cohabitees when a relationship ends.

In my opinion, the most urgent reform is to give cohabitees an improved possibility to secure the situation for the surviving cohabitee. The number of dissolutions of cohabitation by death of one of the cohabitees is increasing, and many of the cohabitees have children together. Statistics show that 55 per cent of the newborn children in Sweden have an unmarried mother.[42] We also know that an unmarried mother, in most cases (86 per cent), lives together with the father of the child. Where small children are involved, there is often a great need to secure a surviving cohabitee's right to inheritance as a measure of creating a safe situation for the children to grow up in. In Denmark, Sweden's neighboring country, cohabitees have recently been given the right to put a surviving cohabitee in the same position as a surviving spouse, by a will.[43] This has made it possible for a surviving cohabitee to inherit the deceased cohabitee as though the couple were married. In my view, Sweden ought to introduce the same possibility in its law.

---

40 The *travaux préparatoires* to the Swedish Cohabitees Act, SOU 1999:104 (Nya Samboregler) pp. 29–30 & 199–202.
41 Prop. (Government Bill) 2002/03:80 (Ny sambolag) p. 32.
42 Tabeller över Sveriges befolkning 2007 p. 216. The source can be found at <www.scb.se/templates/PlanerPublicerat/ViewInfo.aspx?publobjid=6636&lang=SV>.
43 L 100/2006-07 Førslag till Arvelov. Norway, another neighboring country to Sweden, is also planning to improve the situation for a surviving cohabitee by conferring a right to inherit.

VI. What can Foreign Jurisdictions Learn from the Swedish Experience of Cohabitation without Marriage?

Creating rules that regulate unmarried cohabitation is, in a way, an impossible mission; the situations that must be covered include many different kinds of couples. There are those who are in the beginning of a relationship, only testing out what it is like to live together, and there are those who are cohabiting because they do not want to get married. Moreover, there are those who simply have not had the time to get married, or who have not given marriage a thought. There are also cohabitees who are under the mistaken impression that the result of cohabiting and marriage is the same. The Swedish approach – to provide a minimum level of protection for a vulnerable party upon the dissolution of a cohabitee relationship – may be seen as a sufficient solution for handling different kinds of cohabitees, with different aims and needs. However, one must remember that the Swedish system only offers a **minimum level** of financial protection and the value of the protection depends on what property is to be shared in the individual case. One could also consider whether the Act should distinguish between dissolution upon separation, and dissolution upon the death of one of the cohabitees.

An Ill-Fitting Garment: Why the Logic of Private Law Falls Short between Cohabitants

Tone Sverdrup[1]

I. Introduction

The general law of property and trust has a tendency to produce unfair and arbitrary outcomes for cohabitants upon termination of their relationship.[2] The most obvious reason for this is that cohabitants tend to live as interdependent entities in terms of work, investment and consumption, and unlike market relationships the exchange of services is not dependent on any closure of contracts, and services are not mutually conditioned upon a counter-service during the relationship. This article calls attention to some vital characteristics of cohabiting relationships which cause the logic of private law to fall short, and discusses the consequences for legislation in the area.

II. Is there a Need for Statutory Intervention?

With reference to research findings in several countries, Professor *Marsha Garrison* has pointed out that cohabitants are far less likely to pool monetary resources and share them jointly, as opposed to married couples.[3] *Garrison* finds that this behavioural difference reflects divergent

---

[1] Department of Private Law, University of Oslo, Norway.
[2] See for example THE LAW COMMISSION FOR ENGLAND AND WALES, *Cohabitation: The Financial Consequences of Relationship Breakdown* (Consultation Paper No. 179) Part 4 and AMERICAN LAW INSTITUTE, *Principles of the Law of Family Dissolution* (2002) § 6.03 Reporter's Note to comment b at p. 930-935. See also K. BOELE-WOELKI (ed.) *Common Core and Better Law in European Family Law*, EFL Series, No. 10, Intersentia, Antwerp (2005), Part Three: Informal Long-Term Relationships p. 243 ff. and the national reports in J.M. SCHERPE/ N. YASSARI (Hrsg.) *Die Rechtsstellung nichtehelicher Lebensgemeinschaften* (2005) p. 208 ff.
[3] M. GARRISON, Marriage Matters: What's Wrong with the ALI's Domestic Partnership Proposal, in R.F. WILSON (ed.), *Reconceiving the Family. Critique on the American Law Institute's Principles of the Law of Family Dissolution* (2006) p. 310.

relational attitudes between unmarried and married couples and that this divergence should affect legal policy. When cohabitants prefer – or unconsciously assume – separate finances, she argues that lawmakers should refrain from intervening with statutory regulations.

As I see it, cohabitants are not capable of maintaining separate finances over a long period of time, despite the will to do so. Cohabitants live as a financially interdependent entity even when they do not pool and share money jointly. Together, they form a work unit, as well as a consumption and investment unit, and for these reasons the financial position of one party can hardly avoid being affected by the other. The most widespread example of this is the unbalanced division of labour in terms of child care and housework in families – an imbalance that is common even in countries where the life-long housewife is a thing of the past. A cohabitant who only works part-time outside the home seldom has any surplus income to invest – her entire salary goes to cover household expenses for the family.

Even when both cohabitants earn the same amount of money, it is not uncommon that one cohabitant pays the mortgage and the other covers the household expenses. Such a division of labour is often the result of a practical arrangement and bears no significance whatsoever as a sign of intended ownership. In most jurisdictions, however, payment of the purchase price or title is decisive for the ownership of the house – indirect contributions in the form of payment of household expenses are not recognised (see IV. below).

In most relationships the two cohabitants do not earn the same amount of money. Nevertheless, they eat the same food, go on the same holidays and share common financial responsibilities towards their children. They form a **consumption unit.** In these situations the person with the higher income will pull the total consumption expenses upward. If the parties operate an independent money-management system and share household expenses equally, the cohabitant with the lowest income will in many cases not have much money left for investments. Even when cohabitants do not pool and share money, the financial position of one party can hardly avoid being affected by the other's.

A fundamental economic adaptation between the parties lies solely in the fact that most cohabitants must be content with one dwelling; it is in the nature of family life that both parties live in a single family home. If only one of them owned the house before they started to cohabit, the other in most cases will not make future investments (savings) in a house. If one of the cohabitants brings a house, a car etc. into the relationship, the basic investments are already available to the family. In this situation it is natural for the cohabitants to apply most of their disposable income to current expenses. The party without property will benefit from the other party's investments during the union, but will sustain considerable losses if nothing is saved when the cohabitants part company after many years. In order to preclude the non-owning party's coming out of a dissolved union empty-handed, the said party must set aside part of his or her income during the relationship in the event of a possible breach. Court cases indicate that non-owning cohabitants do not make these provisions. Cohabitants live in a community of life, one of the consequences of which is that they form a consumption unit. They adjust the level of consumption to each other and to the fact that basic investments such as a family home are already available, and do not take the long-term legal effects into account.

On the economic level, these adaptations are the essence of living together in a unit – they comprise the »logic of cohabitation«. Behavioural differences in terms of, for example the desire to operate individual money-managing systems, might well reflect divergent relational attitudes between unmarried and married couples, but these will be mere ripples on the surface when compared to the economic undercurrents that govern behaviour in a couple relationship.

III. Are Problems Solved through a Cohabitation Contract?

Not many cohabitants contract »pre-nuptial« agreements aimed at regulating financial consequences upon termination of a union.[4] Public information about the importance of making such arrangements does not seem to help – at least not in Scandinavia – where unmarried cohabitation has been common for more than three decades.[5] This should come as no surprise. The closing of a contract implies mutual commitment and in limiting one's own freedom in such a way both parties would expect to

---

[4] AMERICAN LAW INSTITUTE, *Principles of the Law of Family Dissolution* (2002) § 6.02, comment a, at p. 914.

[5] In 1997 about 20 % of the Norwegian cohabiting couples had contracted an agreement, cf. NOU 1999: 25, *Samboerne og samfunnnet*, (Official Norwegian Report on Cohabitation and Society) p. 71. See also T. NOACK, *Cohabitation in Norway: An accepted and gradually more regulated way of living*, International Journal of Law, Policy and the Family, 2001, p.108 and p. 112.

derive some benefits. For several reasons this is far from the case in many cohabiting relationships.

In commercial relationships, a contract is the prerequisite for an effective exchange of goods and services. A transaction occurs in which one receives nothing without providing something in return. In a family, the transfers of goods and services are normally not mutually conditioned. In cohabitation relationships the exchange of services and goods is not dependent on any closure of contracts. Rather than being contractually conditioned, in a number of cases, the service would **lose** value if it were conditionally dependent on a counter-service. Nevertheless, concepts of reciprocation seem to exist in many relationships – cohabitants appear to expect an overall balance between service and counter-service during the relationship. Likewise, there is reason to believe that many cohabitants expect an overall balance between their own contributions during the relationship, and reciprocal returns upon termination. The norm is to »pay at the exit«.

It is difficult to agree on a »price« when nothing yet has been exchanged. Let us suppose that the two cohabitants at the beginning of their relationship consider contracting equal co-ownership of the family home in order to ensure predictability in the event the relationship fails. They also feel that equal ownership should presuppose balanced future contributions – directly or indirectly – to the acquisition of the house. They do not know whether one of them will receive an inheritance in the future that will be used to pay off the mortgage, or whether one of them will spend his or her income to buy a cabin rather than pay off the mortgage. This lack of knowledge about future contributions is another impediment to the formation of cohabitation contracts.[6]

In the market both parties expect a transaction to result in profit. In cohabitation relationships, however, one of the parties will by definition lose money when signing a contract that regulates the financial consequences upon termination. As a cohabitation contract determines the division of their future assets, it is a »cake« that is divided. The closure of such a contract is a zero-sum game, in which one will lose and one will win. In many cases the two cohabitants are also well aware of who is to lose and who is to gain from the contract. There is no »veil of ignorance« to use Rawls' expression.[7] The fact that one of the parties will inevitably

---

6   T. SVERDRUP, *Stiftelse av sameie i ekteskap og ugift samliv* (Co-ownership in Marriage and in Unmarried Cohabitation), 1997, p. 201 ff.
7   J. RAWLS, *A Theory of Justice*, (rev. edition 1999), p. 118 ff.

suffer a financial loss from a cohabitation contract is of course a serious impediment to contract formation.

The function of a commercial contract is to unite the two parties and provide reliability and predictability to the relationship, and these functions are partly absent when it comes to cohabitation contracts. As opposed to commercial contracts, a cohabitation contract is not necessary to establish any relationship between the parties. As mentioned, it is difficult to find a suitable »price« in advance to include in such a contract; the contract does not always ensure predictability and – last, but not least – one of the parties will by definition lose money when signing the contract. In my view it is understandable that such contracts are infrequently made. Cohabitation contracts are not a realistic alternative to statutory intervention.

Many of those opposed to statutory intervention claim that the couple should have freedom of choice, i.e. the cohabiting couple should decide themselves whether to regulate their relationship or not. As I see it, this argument shrouds the entire issue. The question is not whether **the couple** should have freedom of choice, but whether **the cohabitants** should have such freedom. It takes two to make an agreement, the reluctant party has the right of veto. The freedom of choice exists only for the party opposed to making a contract – not for the other party. The expression »freedom for the couple«, conceals the fact that the whole issue is about contracting within the couple. It is not about couple autonomy, but about individual autonomy.

Furthermore, the expression »freedom of choice« presupposes in a way that legal regulation does not exist beforehand. This of course is not the case. The financial consequences upon termination are already regulated by the general law of property or trust. The only reason why another, presumably much fairer, regulation should entail any lesser freedom than that already existing, is based on consideration for status quo. This argument, however, is weakened by the fact that many unmarried couples seem to be unaware of the financial consequences of a relationship breakdown.[8]

---

8   *Jo Miles* points out that the British public is curiously affected by the, legally erroneous, belief hat, »simply by virtue of living together« cohabiting couples enjoy the same legal status as married couples, J. MILES, Financial Relief Between Cohabitants on Separation, K. BOELE-WOELKI/ T. SVERDRUP (eds.) *European Challenges in Contemporary Family law*, 2008, p. 276. Americans seem to entertain the same, erroneous belief, according to the AMERICAN LAW INSTITUTE, *Principles of the Law of Family Dissolution* (2002) § 6.02, comment a, at p. 914. My impression is that the same belief is shared by many Norwegians.

IV. Three Statutory Models

When choosing among various statutory models for division of assets upon relationship breakdown, I posit two primary considerations or objectives: The statutes should provide a certain balanced apportionment between contributions rendered during the relationship and returns upon termination of the relationship. There should, however, be no »mathematical« justice. Secondly, in consideration for the couple's children, the provisions should be set up in such a way as to avoid disagreement and conflicts between the cohabitants. Since cooperation between the parents after relationship breakdown is vital for the well-being of their children, the best interest of the child is perhaps the most important consideration when drafting legal statutes for division of assets upon relationship breakdown. The motto for any statutory intervention should therefore be: »keep it simple«.

With these considerations as a starting point, I will discuss three basic models for statutory regulation – a **retrospective** model measuring the parties' direct and indirect contributions to the acquisition of property, a **future-oriented** compensation for disadvantages and benefits caused by the relationship, and thirdly, a model in which **the relationship itself** provides the basis for rights and obligations.

1. *A Retrospective Model, where Division of Property is Based on the Parties' Direct and Indirect Contributions to the Acquisition of Property.*

Co-ownership based on indirect contribution is the most prominent example of such a retrospective model. The granting of compensation to avert unjust enrichment, common in many jurisdictions, is another example that falls within this category.

A broad doctrine acknowledging indirect contribution within the framework of a remedial constructive trust has been adopted in some common law jurisdictions but not in England.[9] Among the Scandinavian countries, Norway is the only jurisdiction where co-ownership is established on the basis of the cohabitants' indirect contribution in the form of domestic work or payment of current expenses.[10] As long as the co-

---

9   S.M. CRETNEY, J.M. MASSON, R. BAILEY-HARRIS and P. J. PROBERT, *Principles of Family Law*, 8. ed. (2008) p. 138–141.
10 T. SVERDRUP, Compensating Gain and Loss in Marriage: A Scandinavian Comment on the ALI Principles, in R.F. WILSON (ed.), *Reconceiving the Family. Critique on the American Law Institute's Principles of the Law of Family Dissolution* (2006) p. 472 ff.

habitants have not agreed upon who is to be deemed the owner of the particular items of property, co-ownership is based on what the parties contributed to the acquisition of the property.[11] Not only direct, but also indirect contributions are acknowledged. (Norwegian Supreme Court Reports 1978, p. 1352 and 1984, p. 497). A homemaker's indirect contributions in the form of care for small children are sufficient in the majority of cases to make her an equal co-owner of the common residence or other items of mutual and personal use bought by the breadwinner with income earned during the same period of time. If the children are of compulsory school age and the homemaker still works full-time at home, her work will normally constitute a lesser contribution. Indirect contributions in the form of covering the family's current expenditures are acknowledged as well.

Co-ownership based on indirect contributions has the advantage that the party who has not paid for an item of property is not left vulnerable in bankruptcy cases. This model, however, is not suited for settlements after relationship breakdown. The model implies an increased level of litigation because the outcome is not easily predictable in many cases. More importantly, since the model is largely based on factual indices, it invites disputes and conflicts on a grand scale. An unlimited number of facts and incidents are subject to dispute. Experience from Norwegian court cases concerning compensation and co-ownership show that few natural delimitations exist in this respect: Who paid for the bath tub and the mortgage instalments ten years ago? Who performed the various household tasks, etc.?

Moreover, the model invites disputes concerning judicial classification. As services are not mutually conditioned upon a counter-service during the relationship, concepts like **gift, loan** and **sale** lose some of their meaning. Since the parties' **intentions** relating to these dispositions are diffuse, there are no distinct demarcation lines between these legal categories during cohabitation. In hindsight, in the attempt to de-

---

[11] In Norway, ownership is obtained regardless of title, and a legal enforceable agreement relating to land does not have to be in writing, although this is normally the case. If both cohabitants have made a direct financial contribution to the purchase sum of an item of property for mutual personal use, there is a presumption that the spouses have made a tacit agreement of co-ownership even if one of the cohabitants is the buyer. This presumption is rebuttable – specific circumstances might suggest that the financial contribution was a gift or a loan, cf. T. SVERDRUP, *Stiftelse av sameie i ekteskap og ugift samliv* (Co-ownership in Marriage and in Unmarried Cohabitation), 1997, p. 141 ff, 318-320.

termine intention, one finds oneself looking for something that does not exist. Let us suppose that the female cohabitant entrusts an amount of inheritance money to the disposal of her male cohabitant, thus enabling him, by pooling the inheritance with his own funds, to purchase a boat. Often, it would be unnatural for her to state explicitly that her contribution was not meant as a gift or a loan, and to insist on a contract formalising co-ownership. An explicit agreement is not always in harmony with the basic rule of confidence that prevails both in marriage and cohabitation. In a family, it is often unacceptable or unnatural for one of the parties to formulate reciprocity explicitly and, for example, to say »I will not look after the children unless I become co-owner of the house« or »I will not be responsible for the debt unless I become co-owner of the car«.

As mentioned above, in a number of cases, a contribution would lose its value if it were conditioned upon a counter-contribution. More importantly, even in situations where an explicit agreement is acceptable and natural, the conditions are not always clear. If asked whether the amount was intended as a gift or a loan, the female cohabitant in the example above would typically respond that this depends on the circumstances, and on what services are exchanged between the parties in the future. If her partner paid for the children's education with his inheritance money, she would for example consider it a gift etc. The reluctance to freeze one item in such a delicate and fluid system of balance is understandable. Rational behaviour is to keep such questions open. These concepts of contract law were primarily developed with a view to market relationships. The concepts are based on the logic of private law, which falls short when applied to cohabitants living communally – the legal system is an ill-fitting garment. This promotes conflicts as well. Experience shows that cohabitants feel alienated when factual indices and the parties' intentions are decisive and central features in the settlement upon termination. The devil is in the details, and fact-finding is indeed the devil in settlements upon termination of cohabiting relationships.

Not only procedural, but also substantial objections can be made to this retrospective model. Since only assets created during cohabitation are subject to division, the model does not take into account the situation mentioned earlier, where the favourable financial position of one cohabitant at the beginning of the cohabitation is an impediment to capital accumulation in a family home during the relationship.

2. Future-Oriented Compensation for Disadvantages and Benefits Caused by the Relationship.

In the Australian states, the court is given the discretionary power to divide property upon termination (strong discretion).[12] The proposal from the Law Commission for England and Wales (2007) falls within this category as well (weak discretion).[13] One could also place the Model Family Code proposed by Professor *Ingeborg Schwenzer* in this category if one emphasizes the exceptions, although her model as a whole mainly resembles model 3, since she proposes equal division of assets acquired during the relationship as the main rule.[14]

The future-oriented model has several advantages compared to a retrospective model: Facts from the past are not allowed to predominate, and the needs of the cohabitants might be better attended to. However, fact-finding is predominant in this model as well. New points of conflict arise, as the parties' contributions to the relationship, retained benefits and economic losses must be assessed. In addition, the causal relationships between contributions, benefits and losses must be established. In my opinion, conflict-promoting fact-finding is prominent in this model, as well.

In the causal reasoning it is tempting to fall back on rationales that are not germane to the specific communal relationships in which cohabitants live. The Law Commission of England and Wales, for example claims that buying groceries does not result in a retained benefit, where the respondent was able to pay the mortgage without that contribution being made«.[15] Does this mean that coverage of consumer expenses does not constitute an indirect contribution to the acquisition of the house in cases were the respondent had inherited money that he, hypothetically,

---

12 O. JESSEP, Legal Status of Cohabitants in Australia and New Zealand in J.M. SCHERPE / N.YASSARI (Hrsg.) *Die Rechtsstellung nichtehelicher Lebensgemeinschaften* (2005) p.529 ff.
13 THE LAW COMMISSION FOR ENGLAND AND WALES, *Cohabitation: The Financial Consequences of Relationship Breakdown* 2007 (Law.Com. No 307) para 4.32 – 4.42.
14 I. SCHWENZER, *Model Family Code* (2006), p. 47 ff. (Model Family Code Articles 1.22, 1.27, cf. 1.28).
15 »Qualifying contributions would only give rise to relief where they had resulted in a retained benefit or an economic disadvantage. For example, carrying out routine maintenance work on property in one's spare time, without adding to its value, would not give rise to relief. Nor would buying groceries where the respondent was able to pay the mortgage without that contribution being made.« THE LAW COMMISSION FOR ENGLAND AND WALES, *Cohabitation: The Financial Consequences of Relationship Breakdown* 2007 (Law.Com. No 307) para 4.45.

could have used to pay off the mortgage? If so, a financial loss is inherent in the comparative situation. A rationale of this type, in my opinion, is untenable. The purpose is not to find out what would most probably have happened in the alternative instance, but to trace the economic significance of the covering of the household expenditure for the acquisition. In order to establish a causal connection **sine qua non** in these cases, the rest of the respondent's financial assets must be kept constant in the comparative, hypothetical situation.

In a case where the non-owning party had looked after the family's children, thereby enabling the homeowner to stay in work or to work longer hours, the Law Commission argues that it is unlikely the applicant would be able to show that work done in the home had been a **cause** of a retained benefit in the other party's hands:

> »It would theoretically be possible for an applicant to claim that his or her domestic contributions have conferred a retained benefit on the respondent in the form of savings or increased earning capacity. The applicant might, for example, contend that, by looking after the family, he or she had enabled the respondent to build up savings or to advance a career. However, such a contention would be very difficult to uphold because of the need to establish causation. The applicant would have to prove what the respondent would have achieved had the applicant not made his or her contribution. This would be extremely difficult as there are so many variables: for example, the respondent could argue that he or she would have been able to deal with household tasks by engaging professional domestic help. Accordingly, it would only be in exceptional circumstances that domestic contributions could be shown to have conferred a retained benefit, and we expect that they would more often give rise to claims of economic disadvantage.« (Law Commission, para 4.48)

In my view it is not difficult to establish a causal connection in the example mentioned above. Consider first childcare. The care of parents and others is not fully substitutable. The reason is not that one kind of child care is necessarily better than another. There are divergent opinions on this matter in society, and the legal system should therefore take the parents' choice of childcare as a given point of departure. Thus, the amount of contact between children and their parents should be kept constant in the comparative situation.[16] Furthermore it must be presupposed that the person working outside the home should have just as much **spare time** in the hypothetical situation where work outside and inside the home is divided equally. Again, the purpose is not to find out what likely would have happened in the alternative instance, but to trace the economic significance of domestic labour for the acquisition. If leisure is kept constant, one sees that the respondent (father) would have had to reduce his working hours if the mother had not performed some of his half-share of the childcare. From this point of view, she has enabled a portion of his earnings, and if these additional earnings result in savings or greater pension benefits or earning capacity, there is a causal connection **sine qua non** between the domestic work and the retained benefit.

A different result occurs with household chores, since such work can be substituted more easily by market services without significantly changing the character of the service. The housewife's labour could therefore be regarded as a freeing of capital for the respondent, which in most cases would entail a lower retained benefit. However, if most of the household chores were to be substituted over a longer period of time, the distinctive character of that particular relationship would change substantially, and freeing of capital is no longer an obvious alternative.[17]

In a similar way, the drafters of the American Law Institute's Principles are of the opinion that it is difficult to show that a homemaker, performing housework, has contributed to the other spouse's earning capacity although this difficulty does »not cast doubt on the observation that, in assuming that role, the homemaker incurs a significant economic loss.«[18] The drafters state that because »there are many cases in which the facts would not suggest that the claimant contributed to the potential obligor's earning capacity, the contribution rationale would leave many awards

---

16 This is also the position of the Norwegian Supreme Court when establishing co-ownership on the basis of indirect contributions in the form of childcare. The Court speaks of the freeing of time and not of the freeing of capital when children are concerned, *Norwegian Supreme Court Reports* 1975 p. 220, 1976 p. 694, 1980 p. 1403 and Rt. 1983 p.1146.
17 The Norwegian Supreme Court has regarded household chores in both when establishing co-ownership, cf. *Norwegian Supreme Court Reports* 1978 p.1352 (both time and capital) and 1979 p.1463 (time).
18 AMERICAN LAW INSTITUTE, *Principles of the Law of Family Dissolution* (2002) § 5.04 comment b, at p. 808. With childcare, the contribution side is recognized. See AMERICAN LAW INSTITUTE, *Principles of the Law of Family Dissolution* (2002) § 5.05, comment e, at p. 841.

unexplained.«[19] In this reasoning, the drafters posit a hypothetical situation where the husband (breadwinner) is **single**:

> »*Such cases do not usually suggest that the trial court examine each particular case to determine whether the obligor might avoid or reduce the award by showing that he would have done as well without his spouse.*«

And furthermore:

> »*Such a contribution is, however, difficult to show. It is clear that married men earn more than single men. The problem for the researchers is to determine whether their earning advantage results from a) marriage itself [or other factors]*«[20]

In my opinion, the question is not whether the breadwinner would have done as well without his spouse or cohabitant, but whether he would have done as well if he had borne his share of homemaking tasks in the family, as discussed above.[21]

The causal reasoning presented by the Law Commission and the American Law Institute does not take into account that the parties live in a communal relationship and argues as if the parties were entities completely detached from each other. Due to the fact that cohabitants tend to live as interdependent entities, such a perspective does not conform to reality.

To sum up: The conditions set down in the future-oriented model provide solid justifications for division of assets upon termination, but they are ill suited to serve as legal criteria in specific cases. The criteria lead

---

19 AMERICAN LAW INSTITUTE, *Principles of the Law of Family Dissolution* (2002) § 5.04 comment b at p. 808.
20 AMERICAN LAW INSTITUTE, *Principles of the Law of Family Dissolution* (2002) § 5.04 comment b at p. 823.
21 Another question concerns which factors should be kept constant in this comparative situation. If the spouses (or cohabitants) have agreed upon the division of labour — and a strong presumption that they have agreed should exist if they have practiced this division of labour for some years — their existing quality of life, in terms of spare time and standard of homemaking should be taken as a given when assessing the homemaker's contribution to the other party's earning capacity. By taking spare time and the standard of homemaking as givens in cases where the division of labour is agreed upon, a breadwinner would have had to reduce his working hours if the homemaker had not performed some of »his« share of the homemaking. In other words, a causal connection exists between household tasks and earning capacity, cf. T. SVERDRUP, Compensating Gain and Loss in Marriage: A Scandinavian Comment on the ALI Principles, in R.F. WILSON (ed.), *Reconceiving the Family. Critique on the American Law Institute's Principles of the Law of Family Dissolution* (2006) p. 472 ff.

to extensive fact-finding and causal rationales which generate disagreements and disputes between the cohabitants – conflicts that could seriously harm the future relationship between the cohabitants. Primarily out of consideration for the children of the relationship, this should be avoided. As pointed out earlier, the best interest of the child should be the foremost consideration also when considering how to divide assets upon termination.

3. The Relationship in itself Provides a Basis for Obligations and Rights.

Among the countries practising such a model are New Zealand and Sweden. In New Zealand a dwelling used for family purposes – acquired before or during the relationship – is treated by the Property (Relationship) Act 1976 as »relationship property« and is usually divided equally, even in cases where it was owned by one of the cohabitants prior to the relationship, and even if inheritance money was used to pay off the mortgage. The same rule applies to chattels (e.g. car, furniture, boat) used mainly for family purposes. Other items, like bank accounts or shares owned by one of the parties prior to the relationship, or later inherited, fall within the category of separate property and are likely to remain with the owning cohabitant.[22] Only cohabiting relationships of at least three years' duration are generally covered by this Act.

In Sweden the value of the family home and household goods is divided equally upon termination as long as the items are acquired for joint use – regardless of whether the house is financed with inherited funds or gifts. Other items are not subject to equal division.[23]

The American Law Institute's Principles of the Law of Family Dissolution (2002) falls under this category as well. According to these Principles, assets acquired during the relationship are generally divided equally between the cohabitants.[24] This is also the main rule in *Ingeborg Schwenzer*'s Model Family Code.[25]

---

22   B. ATKIN, Reflections on New Zealand's Property Reforms 'Five Years On', in B. ATKIN (ed.), *The International Survey of Family Law 2007 Edition*, p. 217 ff. and O. JESSEP, Legal Status of Cohabitants in Australia and New Zealand in J.M.SCHERPE/N.YASSARI (Hrsg.) *Die Rechtsstellung nichtehelicher Lebensgemeinschaften* (2005) p.542 ff.
23   The Swedish Cohabitation Act 2003, section 3, cf. section 4. See also E. RYRSTEDT, Legal Status of Cohabitants in Sweden, in J.M.SCHERPE/N.YASSARI (Hrsg.) *Die Rechtsstellung nichtehelicher Lebensgemeinschaften* (2005) p. 415 ff.
24   AMERICAN LAW INSTITUTE, *Principles of the Law of Family Dissolution* (2002) § 6.03.
25   I. SCHWENZER, *Model Family Code* (2006), Articles 1.22, 1.27.

Cohabitants form a work unit, as well as a consumption and investment unit – even in cases where they keep their finances separate. They live in a financially interdependent unit where the financial position of one party can hardly avoid the influence of the other's. When the cohabiting relationship in itself affects the parties' finances, it would appear logical that the relation in itself should also provide the basis for obligations and rights.

Fact-finding is not as predominant in model 3 as in the other models. I would suggest a version of model 3 where only assets acquired during the relationship are subject to equal division in relationships of shorter duration – for example, from two to five years. One then avoids the thresholds effects encountered when property acquired before the relationship is divided in all relationships falling under the provisions of the Act – as in the case of New Zealand. Such a division could be limited to the family home and household goods, or include more, or all, assets. However, if only the value of assets acquired during the relationship is subject to division in relationships of longer duration, fact-finding will become predominant in this scheme as well, as the issue of whether current assets can be traced back to pre-relationship assets or inheritance will be crucial to the financial outcome. Just as importantly: If assets acquired only during the relationship are subject to division, one does not take into account the fact that a favourable economic position of one cohabitant at the beginning of the relationship is an impediment to accumulation of capital during the relationship – this typically occurs when one cohabitant owns a house before the relationship started, cf. II above. Problems of this kind are avoided if pre-relationship assets, inheritance and gifts are divided according to a durational factor – for example, 20% of the net value is divided after 5 years, 50% after 12 years and 100% after 25 years.

In theory, the assessment of contributions, benefits or losses of the parties inherent in both the retrospective and the future-oriented models may potentially lead to fair and accurate settlements. In practice, the outcomes are not so predictable and provide fertile soil for disputes between the cohabitants about the events that occurred during the relationship and about future outcomes. These two models also provide fertile soil for the cohabitant's lawyers, not only in terms of facts and causal connections, but also in terms of legal concepts such as gift, loan and equity of the individual parties, since the intent behind these private law dispositions run counter to the logic of cohabitation relationships. In my opinion the cohabitational relationship in itself should provide the basis for obligations and rights.

Sharing of Accruals as the Best Solution for Marriage?

Anna Stępień-Sporek[1]

I. Introduction[2]

The rules on matrimonial property determine the financial relationships of spouses. It is therefore important that marital property law fulfils the expectations of the spouses and guards the interest of each spouse, as well as gives the spouses significant contractual freedom, particularly if they decide to start a commercial activity. The great challenge for the legislator is to choose an appropriate standard statutory regime because most spouses do not make alternative arrangements regarding their matrimonial property regime[3].

The possible way out for the legislator could be the introduction of the sharing of accruals. It can be a statutory regime or a contractual regime. The latter can be used if a country has a strong and sufficient attachment to a different regime[4]. In such a situation, it is easy to choose the sharing of accruals regime because it combines some of the advantages of two opposite regimes: separation of property and community of property. The first one guarantees the equity of the spouses[5] and the second one gives each spouse a fraction in marital property. Sharing of accruals is a compromise.

---

1 *University of Gdańsk, Poland.*
2 Many thanks to Margaret Ryznar for editing support.
3 This task is complicated because the expectations and needs of each married couple are different. It will not be an exaggeration to say that it is impossible to find the solution that meets all these expectations. But the legislator should undertake all measures so as to work out the best result. I mean that the introduced statutory regime should be the answer to the needs of the most marriages.
4 A good example of a long tradition of one leading regime, namely the community of property, is in Poland.
5 Actually it is only a formal equity because the professional and financial status of each spouse is different. It is also still the case that lots of women spend more time taking care of children and family home. See D. Henrich, Eheliche Gemeinschaft, Partnerschaft Und Vermögen im europäischen Vergleich: die deutsche Sicht in: D. Henrich, D. Schwab, Eheliche Gemeinschaft, Partnerschaft und Vermögen im europäischen Vergleich, Bielefeld 1999, p. 361.

In Poland, family law has gone through important changes, particularly in the past decade. One of the main reasons for this is the increasing commercial activity of spouses, which revealed the weakest points of regulation and the fact that the statutory regime of community of property is out of date with its rules of management and liability. That system of matrimonial property befitted the institution of so called »socialist marriage«[6] and was not a satisfactory solution for modern spouses.

For this reason, the Civil Law Codification Commission started its work on the reform of family law. In preparing the new legislation, the Commission took into account the sharing of accruals as a possible statutory regime. The main reason in support of the sharing of accruals was that it is known in many countries and is the standard statutory regime in some of them (e.g. Germany). The adherents of the regime emphasized that it is an optimal solution for spouses conducting business and it does not weaken the grounds of maintenance of the family.[7] Finally, sharing of accruals has become a contractual matrimonial regime because it was suggested that the new legal regime could be misunderstood by the society who has become accustomed to community of property.[8]

My article will be divided into two parts. The first one will concern »model solutions« of sharing of accruals. I use this expression because the regulations analysed below guided the Polish legislator and were the source of model provisions on the subject of the new regime.[9] It should be mentioned that there are more examples of the regulations concerning the sharing of accruals, but it is not possible to present them all in this paper so only a few could be selected. The second part of my contribution will consider the Polish solution. In both sections, I will discuss the characteristics of the regime in order to be able to point out the advantages and disadvantages of the examined system of marital property.

Before I start, it should be emphasized that the basic idea of the sharing of accruals is that during the marriage each spouse has his or her own estate and remains the sole owner of it. In general, there is no liability for

---

6   D. Lasok, Polish Family Law, Leyden 1968, p. 89
7   T. Smyczyński, Kierunki reform Kodeksu rodzinnego i opiekuńczego, Kwartalnik Prawa Prywatnego no 2, 1999, p. 314
8   T. Smyczyński, Projekt ustawy zmieniającej małżeńskie prawo majątkowe, Studia Prawnicze no 3-4, 2000, p. 154
9   It should be stressed that the regulations described below are based on the same general pattern but they differ in many aspects. E.g. in Germany and Switzerland the rule of the separation of goods during marriage is not absolute in contradistinction to Poland.

the acts or debts of the other spouse.[10] The dissolution of the regime is very important. At this moment the accrual of each spouse becomes available to the other party. The above mentioned construction makes the system attractive for spouses. As mentioned, it combines the best features of community of property and separation of property,[11] taking into account the case wherein one spouse runs the common home while the other one earns money. This fundamental conception is developed by the regulations in different countries.

II. Switzerland and Germany

The statutory regime in Switzerland is the deferred community of acquisitions (*Errungenschaftbeteiligung*).[12] It comes into operation automatically when the spouses marry and do not make any alternative settlement with regard to their matrimonial property regime. It was introduced in 1988 by the law which also abolished the concept of the head of the household and stated the equality between spouses.[13]

This regime is a combination of the separation of property during the marriage with a distribution of goods, upon dissolution of the marriage, gained by each spouse during the marriage.[14] Each spouse has his or her own separate property but it is divided into two parts, namely personal property (*Eigengut*) and gained property (*Errungenschaft*). Personal property includes the property owned individually at the time of wedlock and the property inherited personally during the marriage. The gained property contains all property acquired during the duration of the statutory regime. It may include income from labour or acquired property. Some

---

10 The exceptions are contractual rights from contracts concluded for the expenses incurred for the daily family life.
11 E.g. in Poland there are the same rules concerning the management in case the spouses choose the total separation of property or the sharing of accruals. See J. Strzebińczyk, Nowelizacja przepisów Nowelizacja przepisów kodeksu rodzinnego i opiekuńczego w zakresie małżeńskiego prawa majątkowego (cz. II), Rejent no 9, 2004, p. 93.
12 See A. Büchler, Family Law in Switzerland: Recent Reform and Future Issues – an Overview, European Journal of Law Reform no 3, 2001, p. 277.
13 See A. Büchler, Family Law in Switzerland: Recent Reform and Future Issues – an Overview, European Journal of Law Reform no 3, 2001, p. 278.
14 B. Graham-Siegenthaler, International Marriage and Divorce Regulation and Recognition in Switzerland, Family Law Quarterly no 3, 1995, p. 689; C. Hamilton, A. Perry, Family Law in Europe, London 2002, p. 673.

other examples of this kind of property are given in art. 197 ZGB[15]. In case of doubt about whether property is personal or gained, there is a presumption in favour of gained property. The parties may agree upon another division of acquisitions or even the distribution of accruals by providing that chattels connected with the commercial activity of the spouse leading a business or exercising a profession remain his or her personal property.

The Swiss regulation concerning the distribution of gains is well-developed. A few stages of the distribution can be distinguished. The first step is the classification of the property among spouses and their personal or gained property. The next stage consists of two actions. The first one is to reduce each property with claims, expenses and expenditures made on the property of the other spouse. The second one is to increase the property of each spouse with donations made during the five years before the dissolution of the statutory regime and with the value of property sold in order to reduce the claim concerning sharing of accrued gains (*Beteiligungsanspruch*). The last level is the sharing of gains accrued by each spouse. Each spouse[16] is entitled to one-half of the difference between his or her net family property (gained property) and that of the other spouse. By a marriage contract, the spouses may, within certain limits, deviate from the above mentioned equal distribution. It should be added that the matrimonial property regime is dissolved retroactively to the date when the petition for divorce was submitted.

During the marriage, each spouse is able to manage his own property solely. He or she is able to contract debts and is liable for them.[17] However, there are some limits for each spouse.[18] The reasons for these limits are the necessity of protecting the family home and of protecting the sufficiency of the economic basis for the family. If the spouse wants to sell the family home, he or she is obliged to get the consent of the other spouse.[19] The same rules concern the disposition of a share in property belonging to both spouses and guaranteeing a loan. It is also possible to make a motion to the court so as to mandate consent of one spouse for the other

---

15 Schweizerisches Zivilgesetzbuch vom 10. Dezember 1907 (SR 210).
16 In case of the death of one spouse, his or her heirs are entitled to a share in accrued gains.
17 See art. 201-202 ZGB.
18 See K. Boele-Woelki, Matrimonial Property Law from a Comparative Law Perspective, Amsterdam 2000, p. 20 and P. Gottwald, D. Schwab, E. Büttner, Family and Sucession Law in Germany, The Hague – London – Boston 2001, p. 108.
19 See art. 169 ZGB.

spouse's actions when those actions influence the economic position of the family.[20]

Similar solutions are found in German law. The statutory regime in Germany is the community of surplus (*Zugewinngemeinschaft*).[21] The name is misleading because there is not actually any community property.[22] It should be also stressed that spouses do not automatically share assets acquired during marriage. Therefore, the standard statutory regime should be called the sharing of accruals[23] or the community of increase.[24]

The main reason for introducing this system is that all assets acquired during marriage should be the property of both spouses because, although many changes have occurred in family arrangements, it is often still the case that the wife is a homemaker and the husband conducts a business or works. Analogous to Swiss regulation, each spouse administrates his or her own property. The freedom in management is, however, limited. If a spouse wants to dispose of his or her whole property[25] or household goods, the consent of the other spouse is mandatory. In some situations, it can be appointed by the decision of the court. Like in Swiss law, the grounds for such solutions are the necessity of protecting the family and its financial situation. It should be pointed out that each spouse is obliged to inform the other spouse about the situation of his or her property, which is especially important in the context of the future claim concerning the equalization of the accruals upon dissolution of the regime.

The claim of sharing of accrued gains arises *ex lege*. For accruals to be equalized, it is necessary to compare the value of the property of each spouse at the beginning of the regime (*Anfangsvermögen*) and at the end

---

20 See art. 178 ZGB
21 If spouses do not want the discussed regime, they can conclude a special agreement and chose the community of property (*Gütergemeinschaft*) or the separation of property (*Gütertrennung*).
22 See J. Gernhuber, D. Coester-Waltejen, Famielienrecht, München 2006, p. 359 and L. K. Thiele, The German Marital Property System: Conflict of Laws in a Dual-nationality Marriage, California Western International Law Journal no 12, 1982, p. 84.
23 See G. Robbers, An Introduction to German Law, Baden-Baden 2006, p. 283.
24 D. Coester-Waltjen, M. Coester, Study on Matrimonial Property Regimes and the Property of Unmarried Couples in Private International Law and Internal Law. National Report – Germany, p. 7.
25 § 1365 (1) BGB. The disposition of the whole property sometimes means the transfer of one thing which is worth a lot of money. See P. Gottwald, D. Schwab, E. Büttner, Family and Sucession Law in Germany, The Hague – London – Boston 2001, p. 111.

of it (*Endvermögen*)[26]. Both the starting value of property and its end value are presumed to be at least zero. The obtained surplus is divided. The final value should be increased with the value of assets distributed gratuitously by one of the spouses or in a prejudicial way to the other spouse.[27] The initial value should be established according to an inventory made by spouses. If such an inventory has not been made, the final value is regarded as the value of the surplus. The special regulation is dedicated to the situation of the end of the regime upon death. In such a case, the fraction of the surviving spouse in the inheritance increases in an additional quarter share of the estate of the deceased (*pauschalierter Zugewinnausgleich*)[28].

III. Poland

The regime of sharing of accruals was introduced to Polish law on 20th January 2005[29] and is now an optional (contractual) regime.[30] It can be introduced by the spouses in a marriage settlement, which can be concluded during the marriage or before it by prospective spouses. The literal translation of the name of this regime is the separation of property with the equalization of surpluses *(rozdzielność majątkowa z wyrównaniem dorobków)*. The Polish regulation is not very well-developed,[31] especially when compared to the laws mentioned above.

The essential idea of the regime is realised by the rule that during the regime each spouse has his or her own separate property. In comparison to Swiss law, the separate property is not split into two parts.[32] Separate property of each spouse is managed solely by him or her and each spouse is free to dispose of his or her property. Contrary to the foreign systems of marital property mentioned above, the consent of the other spouse is not necessary in any case. Although the spouse should inform the other spouse of

---

26 See § 1373-1378 BGB (Bürgerliches Gesetzbuch vom 18. August 1896 – RGBl. S. 195).
27 See § 1375 BGB.
28 See § 1371 (1) BGB.
29 Act of 17th June 2004 concerning changing of the Family and Guardianship Code and other acts (Dz. U. nr 162, poz. 1691).
30 It should be added that it is not a completely new solution in Polish law. After the Second World War it was a statutory regime. That regulation was changed in 1950.
31 The new system of marital property is regulated by art. 51^2-51^5 k.r.o. (Kodeks rodzinny i opiekuńczy – The Family and Guardianship Code of 25th February 1964 - Dz. U. nr 9, poz. 59 with amendments).
32 A regulation similar to the Swiss one was in force in Poland until 1950.

his or her actions, the law does not provide any provisions concerning this kind of obligation. During the marriage, the situation of the spouses is the same as if they had chosen the regime of separation of the property.[33] Special provisions relate to the dissolution of the regime. The consequences of dissolution distinguish this regime from the system of the separation of property.[34] The reasons for dissolution of the regime is a marriage settlement introducing another regime, divorce, legal separation, bankruptcy, incapacitation or a decision of the court establishing separate property.

The key notion in the dissolution of marriage is »surplus«, which is the increase of the property of each spouse in the period after the introduction of the regime and before the dissolution of marriage.[35] The surplus is obtained when the final value of property is larger than the initial value. In practice, some difficulties may appear in establishing the surplus because spouses are not obliged to prepare an inventory. The spouses are not allowed to change the meaning of the notion »surplus«, but are free to modify some rules of the calculation of the surplus.[36] There is potential danger that spouses modify those rules which make the equalization of surpluses useless.[37] If they have not done it, statutory rules are applied.

According to these statutory rules, goods obtained before the beginning of the regime, inherited property, gifts, non-transferable rights, compensation for bodily or moral harm, claims for payment and rights of an author[38] should not be taken into account in calculation of the surplus. On the other hand, the final value of property should include gifts made by one spouse (apart from gifts to the common descendants of spouses and tiny customary gifts), services performed in favour of the other spouse's separate property and expenses made in favour of the other spouse's separate property.[39]

---

[33] The Polish regime of sharing of accruals is characterized by the fact that the rules regarding the total separation are used. See art. 51^2 k.r.o.

[34] J. Strzebińczyk, Nowelizacja przepisów kodeksu rodzinnego i opiekuńczego w zakresie małżeńskiego prawa majątkowego (cz. II), Rejent no 9, 2004, p. 93.

[35] See M. Sychowicz in: H. Ciepła, B. Czech, T. Domińczyk, S. Kalus, K. Piasecki, M. Sychowicz, Kodeks rodzinny i opiekuńczy, Komentarz, Warszawa 2006, p. 286. The increase in value of chattels is important in the proceedings of equalization of accruals when it is larger than inflation.

[36] G. Bieniek, Umowne ustroje majątkowe, Rejent nr 9/2005, p. 125.

[37] M. Sychowicz in: H. Ciepła, B. Czech, T. Domińczyk, S. Kalus, K. Piasecki, M. Sychowicz, Kodeks rodzinny i opiekuńczy, Komentarz, Warszawa 2006, p. 284.

[38] See art. 51^3 § 2 k.r.o.

[39] See art. 51^3 § 2 k.r.o.

As a rule, the claim of equalization amounts to half of the surplus which the other spouse has made in excess of the claiming spouse's surplus. Important is that the amount of the claim is not limited expressly to the value of the assets existing at the time of the termination of the regime.[40] It is a good solution to some extent. The debtor is not able to reduce tactically his or her assets in the time between the moment he has learned about the prospective termination of the regime and the actual end of it.

The equalization of surpluses means that the spouse with the smaller accruals has those accruals subtracted from the surplus of the other spouse. It can be made by payment or *in natura*. The spouses should establish the way of equalization. If not, the court chooses the method of equalization. The claim of equalization may be reduced because of important reasons (grave reasons),[41] such as when one spouse earns money and keeps the family house while the other spouse does nothing despite being able-bodied. In other words, the reduction of the claim is possible when one spouse significantly and negligently fails to carry out his or her obligation arising from marriage.

The equalization is made with regard to the assets of each spouse on the last day of the regime. However, it is taken according to the prices of the day when the surplus is distributed.[42] The actual values, the value of assets at the beginning of the regime and the worth of assets at the end of it, are compared. If you take into consideration that all assets acquired before marriage should be passed over, the initial value is, as a rule, equal to zero.[43] There is some doubt whether the surplus is calculated on the basis of the net value of assets, which is not resolved by the regulation. It seems, however, that only the net value shows actual growth of the property of each spouse.

In case of the death of one spouse, the equalization of accruals is made between heirs and the surviving spouse. The heirs may claim the reduc-

---

40 Cp. § 1378 BGB.
41 See art. 51⁴ § 2 k.r.o. The phrase »important reasons« has similar meaning to the »gross inequity« known in German law. Polish law does not provide the exclusion of the claim of equalization. Cp. J. Gernhuber, D. Coester-Waltjen, Familienrecht, Familienrecht, München 2006, p. 349.
42 See art. 51³ § 3 k.r.o. Such rule guarantees that inflation is not taken into account. See M. Sychowicz in: H. Ciepła, B. Czech, T. Domińczyk, S. Kalus, K. Piasecki, M. Sychowicz, Kodeks rodzinny i opiekuńczy, Komentarz, Warszawa 2006, p. 286.
43 The spouses can change the rules of calculation of surplus. They are able to change the principle that states that the assets obtained before the beginning of the regime are not property taken into account during estimation of surplus.

tion of the equalization claim if the deceased spouse brought a lawsuit against the other spouse for annulment of the marriage, for legal separation or for divorce. This rule may lead to the curiosity that in the case of bringing a lawsuit by the surviving spouse who was actually guilty of the irretrievable and total breakdown of marriage, the reduction of equalization is not possible. Polish law does not provide the solution regarding the simultaneous death of both spouses.

The problematic issue is also the prescription of claim for equalization of surplus. The construction used in Polish law is that the claim is not enforceable after ten years, but the beginning of this period starts on the day of the dissolution of marriage. The dissolution of the regime does not mean the end of marriage, especially if the spouses have made a settlement choosing another regime.[44] This consequence can be dangerous for the creditors of the spouses.

IV. Conclusions

Sharing of accruals can be a good solution for marriage. The recent changes in family relationships and the formal equality of spouses have decreased the number of families in which one spouse is a breadwinner while the other one is a housekeeper. However, even if the wife starts working, there is still the case that her income is lower than the income of her husband because, for example, she is not as flexible as he is or she has to spend more time fulfilling maternal duties. On the other hand, her husband would not be able to earn as much money if he was not relieved of household tasks. That is why it is necessary to guarantee the wife a share in the income obtained by her husband. Obviously, the roles of the spouses can be fixed in a different way such that the wife earns money while the husband is responsible for the family, home and children. The examined regime is therefore a good example of giving a spouse who is unable to increase in number his or her separate property a fraction in the gained accruals. At the same time, the regime protects assets of the »weaker« spouse from the creditors of the other spouse.

The other advantages of the regime are sole administration of the property of each spouse and elimination of liability for the acts and debts of

---

44 See M. Sychowicz in: H. Ciepła, B. Czech, T. Domińczyk, S. Kalus, K. Piasecki, M. Sychowicz, Kodeks rodzinny i opiekuńczy, Komentarz, Warszawa 2006, p. 349.

the other spouse. These features allow a spouse to do business or professional activities without the disturbance connected to the necessity of obtaining the consent of the other spouse for these acts. The next important thing is that the other spouse is protected because he or she does not incur property consequences of the wrong decisions of the spouse during his business or professional doings. The creditors of the other spouse have no recourse against the separate property of the spouse.

Although sharing of accruals has a large number of advantages, it should be kept in mind that there are some disadvantages for the creditors of the spouses and for the spouses themselves. For example, the creditors are unable to assess the size of the claim concerning the equalization of accrual.[45] The question is whether these disadvantages are enough to choose another regime to govern the financial relationships of spouses. In my opinion, they are not and I would recommend this regime for marriage. Although it is not perfect, especially in Polish law, it could be a good solution for spouses.

To make the regime attractive to spouses, it is vital to give a list of conditions which should be fulfilled by the regulation. It should be established by the legislator that before spouses decide to introduce the regime they should prepare an inventory. Naturally the spouses should be interested in making the inventory, but without certain regulation in this field they may fail to do it. The freedom in management of the property during the regime should not be absolute. Family law should protect not only the creditors of the spouses, but also the family. It means that at least the basic needs of the family should be guaranteed by the law. The spouse should not be able to transfer the family home and other sufficient goods without the consent of the other spouse. The legislators should follow the German or Swiss solutions to these problems, but the spouse should be able to start a commercial activity and to conduct his or her own business without spousal consent. It seems that the best way to achieve this is to compare the value of the transaction to the total property of spouse. If the proportion shows that the transaction is significant to the property of spouses, it should be made only with the consent of the other spouse. The moment of equalization of accrued gains should be established in such a way that will guarantee that the spouse is not able to transfer his or her property depriving the other spouse of the possibility of equalization. The claim of equalization of surpluses should terminate after a fixed period of

---

45 See J. Gernhuber, D. Coester-Waltjen, Familienrecht, München 2006, p. 364

time and the starting point of that period should be the day of dissolution of the regime.

The above mentioned postulates are based in particular on Polish regulation[46] and should be treated as facilitating the discussion regarding which regime benefits families most. The problem is still complex. However, this debate could promote a better regime and give spouses the opportunity to make well-informed decisions.

---

46 It should be mentioned, however, that in the Resolution (78) 37 on Equality of Spouses in Civil Law (Adopted by the Committee of Ministers on 27 September 1978 at the 292nd meeting of the Ministers' Deputies), the Committee of Ministers of the Council of Europe recommends »*to ensure that where the operation of law provides for the sharing of the property acquired during the marriage and, where applicable, the property belonging to one of the spouses, the legal provisions protecting the rights of the spouses in such property, for example, the prohibition of gifts of great value, should be the same for both spouse*«. Another important recommendation in the resolution grants each spouse »*an equal right to be informed of the extent of the property belonging to the other spouse where the law requires such information to be given*«.

Financing the Romance: Marriage Contract in the Serbian Family Act

Marija Draškić[1]

I. Introduction

Property relations of spouses or extramarital partners are an integral part of all marital and extramarital relationships, although most people are not immediately aware of this fact. Namely, spouses and extramarital partners rarely think about the property and legal aspects of their relationship, especially at a time when those relations are harmonious and when there is no conflict between them. Conversely, when those relations become disturbed, when a divorce happens or living in an extramarital cohabitation ends, dispute of property issues between former partners move to courtrooms, where lengthy, costly and exhausting legal proceedings start, which – in general – end in the discontent of both parties. Thus the possibility of concluding a marriage contract, introduced in the Serbian legislation for the first time by the new Family Act, offers the opportunity of adjusting the property relations between spouses and extramarital partners to the real needs and interests of participants in these relations before disputes occur. It also preserves the property from unnecessary diminution, caused by paying court tax fees and lawyer services, and, finally, promotes legal security for both partners in the marriage or the extramarital cohabitation and of all third parties, by the legal certainty of mutual property relations.

The marriage contract in Serbian law has an interesting legal history that can be divided into three main periods.

1. The First Period

This period pertains to the time when the marriage contract was a legal institution known to old Serbian civil law. Namely, according to the Civil code of the Kingdom of Serbia, enacted in 1844 – which integrated, to a great extent, provisions from the Austrian Civil code, and which was

---

[1] School of Law, University of Belgrade, Serbia.

applied on the territory of Serbia until the Kingdom of Yugoslavia ceased to exist in 1946, after the World War Two – spouses were allowed to regulate their property relations by mutual agreement.[2] The freedom of contracting was limited, on the one hand, by the general provision pertaining to all contracts according to which a contract must not be contrary to moral order and *ordre public*. On the other hand, it was not possible to change mandatory rules on personal relations between spouses by a marriage contract, namely, to limit or exclude the husband's dominion, abolish legal incapacity of a married woman, limit or abolish the husband's right to represent the wife.[3] The Serbian civil code did not prescribe any special form of marriage contract, thus making all these contracts informal until September 11th 1930 when the Act on Public Notary entered into force which obliged the spouses to conclude the marriage contracts in the form of a public record document or in the form of a document verified by the court.[4]

2. The Second Period

In this period (1946–2000) – which coincides with the existence of socialist Yugoslavia as well as its dissolution through the wars in the early 1990s – the marriage contract was not allowed under Serbian law. Namely, the regime of community property was the mandatory legal property regime, which meant that spouses were forbidden to make a contract which would change the legal regime of community property.

3. The Third Period

Finally, in the third period, the one that marks the beginning of Serbia's transition and economic convergence towards conditions of real market economy, the imperative legal property regime, which functioned earlier in spousal property relations, loosened. Thus, the Serbian Family Act of 2005 provides for parallel existence of two property regimes in the marriage: 1) the legal property regime, which became dispositive instead of imperative and 2) the regime of marriage contract.

---

2   See Serbian Civil code (1844), Art. 759.
3   See Serbian Civil code (1844), Art. 107.
4   See Act on Public Notary, (1930), Art. 52.

II. Legal Property Regime

The legal property regime encompasses community property and separate property of the spouses.

1. Concept of Community Property

The Community property is the property that the spouses have acquired through work during their cohabitation in the marriage.[5] Therefore, the notion of community property is defined by two main facts: (i) work and (ii) cohabitation of spouses.

1.1 Work

Community property arises from individual or joint work of spouses, which is its basic characteristic. In addition to that, the relationship between work and community property can be direct or indirect. A direct relationship between work and acquisition of community property exists when the work in question has direct financial effects expressed through appropriate gain. An indirect relationship between work and acquisition of community property corresponds to work that does not have financial gain as an immediate result, but provides the opportunity for the other spouse to earn more. Furthermore, the notion of work does not imply just work that directly or indirectly leads to augmentation of the community property, but also work that contributes to maintaining the community property, namely ensures that diminution of community property is less than it would have been otherwise. Finally, work performed by spouses does not need to contribute equally to the acquisition of the community property, and property acquired through work is considered community, even if one spouse's contribution was obviously disproportionately less.

---

5   See Family Act, Art. 171/1 (Official Gazette if the Republic of Serbia, No. 18/2005). The concept of property is, however, one of the hardest and least understandable categories of civil law. From the middle of the 19th century, debates on the concept of property in the European legal space are dominated by the so called classical theory of the renowned French legal authors *Aubry* and *Rau*. According to their theory, a person's property encompasses all his goods without any difference, present and future, assets and liabilities. As professor Stanković put it vividly, property conceived in this way is a pure product of speculative reason, a concept that could be compared to an imaginary vessel, which could be full of money, or empty, or full of receipts for amounts owned. In all three cases it denotes the same. On the classical theory, its numerous interpretations and its criticisms, see in more detail in Stanković, O. – V. Vodinelić, Uvod u građansko pravo, Beograd, 1995, pp. 144–160. See also Vedriš, M. – P. Klarić, Osnove imovinskog prava, Zagreb, 1983, p. 80.

This provision does not jeopardize the legal regime of community property, but in case of division, it gives the right to the court to award monetary compensation to the lesser earner in the marriage according to the value of his/her work. Finally, it is also possible to initiate the process of proving that the work of one spouse did not in any way contribute to the acquisition of the community property.[6]

Besides property that spouses have acquired through work during their cohabitation in the marriage, community property also includes:

a) income from community property, both resulting from work or generated by the property without any work (i.e. rental, interest rate, dividends, etc.);
b) income from separate property, if it was acquired through spousal work;
c) assets furnished from community property;[7]
d) restitutions awarded on different legal grounds for assets from community property (for instance, compensation for damage, restitution for expropriated real estate, insurance amount for destroyed or damaged assets, etc.);
e) restitutions which were awarded for work of one of the spouses, but do not constitute an income (financial allowance as compensation for a lost income due to inability to work, terminal wage, awards, honors, scholarships, etc.);[8]
f) royalties, patents and other intellectual property rights;[9]

---

6 »The fact that immovable property was acquired for the duration of the marriage does not necessarily have as its consequence that the property thus acquired is the community property of the spouses. Namely, the property is community, if it has been acquired through the work of both spouses. But not if it has been through the work of only one of them, while the other spouse spent his earnings on drinking, having fun with his friends, support of another woman and his son, as it had been established in this particular case.« See the ruling of the Supreme Court of Croatia Gž. 836/80 of December 4, 1980, Court Practice Review, Contribution Naše zakonitosti, No. 18/1981, ruling No. 105.

7 This is a case of the so called 'real subrogation', which means that property rights were transferred from the item that has been substituted to the item acquired by this substitution (subrogation) by a direct substitution of items or property values.

8 As opposed to that, awards and honors that were not awarded for a spouse's work, but represent a recognition for a personal characteristic (e.g. talent, courage, devotedness), are included in separate property. As for the scholarships, they can also be part of separate property of the spouse who acquires them, if they have no other purpose than to secure learning or studying and if they do not result in any kind of obligation towards the scholarship giver.

9 See Family Act, Art. 173. For more details on this interesting issue of the nature of author property rights as an integral part of the community property see Pekiž, B., Umetniško delo – skupno premoženje zakoncev?, Pravnik, No. 3-4/1988, p. 249.

g) property acquired through games of chance (i.e. lotto, sports booking, lottery), unless the spouse who got the winnings proves that he/she invested separate property in the game;[10]
h) property acquired through a contract of support for lifetime.

1.2 Cohabitation

The notion of community property, on the other hand, includes only those property rights and obligations that were acquired during the cohabitation in the marriage. Conversely, what was acquired through work after the permanent ending of a marital cohabitation – despite the fact that it was obtained while the marriage was still legally valid – as well as what was acquired before cohabitation was established, constitutes separate property of each spouse.[11] Therefore, the crucial criterion for the concept of community property is the existence of marital cohabitation at the time when the acquisition of property took place. Thus the ending of a marital cohabitation does not change the legal nature of the property acquired before the cohabitation ended in the form of credit having the character of joint obligation (i.e. by bank loan);[12] likewise, the establishment of a marital cohabitation does not affect separate property acquired before its

---

10   See Family Act, Art. 172.
11   In judicial practice pertaining to the interpretation of cohabitation, one can also find rulings as the following: »Community property of spouses consists only of property acquired by common work during marriage, but not the property the spouses acquired after the disruption of marital relations and the breach of the economic union, despite the fact that at the moment the property was acquired the marriage was legally valid, and spouses were living together, but their economic union was reduced to contributions for support of the spouse and the children, as well as to the sharing of the housing rent and reimbursements for the provision of municipal services.« See the ruling by the Supreme Court of Bosnia and Herzegovina Gž. 1531/76 of June 20, 1977. Quoted after Draškić, M., Praktikum za porodično pravo, Beograd, 1989, ruling No. 632.
12   The standpoint that an item obtained through a loan raised for the duration of the cohabitation is to be considered a common item only in the amount that corresponds to the sum of loan repaid for the duration of cohabitation is incorrect. Namely, irrespective of which of the spouses repaid the loan after the cohabitation ceased, the item acquired by this loan during the cohabitation is a common item, since the obligation resulting from the loan also remains a common obligation. The cessation of the cohabitation and the divorce of the marriage do not alter the legal relations resulting from the common obligation; the party that had repaid for the other party the loan either fully or partially, is entitled to request from the other party a remuneration for settling the obligations of the other party, namely, by a legally binding request, but that does not alter the real property relation.« See the ruling by the Supreme Court of Croatia Gž. 3598/70 of March 2, 1972, Court Practice Review, Contribution Naše zakonitosti, No. 1/1972.

start, despite the fact that the obligations are fulfilled by both spouses.[13] A short term interruption of the marital cohabitation does not affect the community property obtained during that time.[14]

2. Legal Nature of Community Property

Title holders of community property are spouses from both valid and void marriages. The main characteristic of the legal nature of community property is the fact that the co-owner's or co-creditor's share of each spouse in community property is not determined. Therefore, title holders of community property, unlike joint property owners or proprietors *d'etage*, do not possess neither ideal nor real share in community property; instead, their rights spread equally to everything that was acquired during their marital cohabitation. Community property rights thus exist under a specific legal regime, which is valid until the community property is divided.[15] In order to safeguard this regime it is in particular stated in the Family Act that each entry into public record of rights on immovable property always pertains to both spouses – even when only one spouse is entered – as co-owners of unspecified shares.[16]

3. Managing and Disposing of Community Property

Spouses manage and dispose of their community property jointly and consensually. A spouse may not dispose of his/her share in the community property nor may he/she burden it with legal acts *inter vivos*, but can dispose of it in his/her will even before division, although only to the degree that does not infringe the other spouse's share of community property.[17] Inability of the spouse to dispose individually of his/her own share in community property results from the legal nature of community property, i. e. from the fact that the shares of the spouses in community property are unspecified. However, spouses may conclude a contract entrusting

---

13 »A residence bought by one spouse before the marriage was concluded represents his/her separate property, despite the fact that later, during cohabitation, the other spouse participated in the repayment of the loan for that residence«. See ruling by the Supreme Court of Croatia Gž. 2429/78 of March 29, 1979, Court Practice Review, Contribution Naše zakonitosti, No. 15/1979, ruling No. 53.
14 See, in the same sense, the ruling by the Supreme Court of Macedonia Rev. 1356/86 of December 16, 1986, Court Practice, No. 1/1988, ruling No. 69.
15 It is assumed that the shares of the spouses in the community property are equal only if the division of the community property is performed by the court. See Family Act, Art. 180/2.
16 See Family Act, Art. 176/2.
17 See Family Act, Art. 174/3.

one of them to manage and dispose of their entire community property or some parts of this property.[18]

4. Division of Community Property

The division of community property is to be considered as a determination of the co-owner's or co-creditor's share of each spouse in community property. The division of community property may take place for the duration of the marriage or after its termination.

The right to demand a division of community property belongs to: (i) spouses, (ii) heirs of a deceased spouse and (iii) creditors of a spouse whose claims could not be settled from the spouse's separate property.[19]

In terms of division options of community property, two solutions exist: (i) spouses agree on division of community property (consensual division) or (ii) division of community property is carried out by the court (court division).

4.1 Consensual Division

Given the complexity and sensitivity of the division of community property, a spousal agreement on each other's share in acquisition of community property is, without any doubt, welcome, as the most desired option for resolving this complex problem. Within the consensual division all modalities known to law are allowed. Therefore, spouses can agree:

---

[18] There is no prescribed form for this type of contract, except in the case of a contract by which the other spouse is authorized to dispose of the immovable property, which is also registered in the public record of rights on immovable property. See Family Act, Art. 189. On the one hand, this is a consequence of the rule that a form prescribed by law for a particular contract is also valid for the authorization to conclude such a contract, and on the other hand, of the fact that a written form is prescribed for a legal transaction pertaining to immovable property transactions. See Art. 90. of the Law on Obligations (Official Gazette of the SFRY, No. 29/1978) and Art. 4. of the Law on Transactions of Immovable Property (Official Gazette of the Republic of Serbia, No. 42/1998). Thus also Sudžum, 1982, p. 196. An opposite opinion, according to which the authorization contract whereby one spouse authorizes the other to conclude a contract on a transaction of immovable property does not have to be in a written form, as this is not prescribed by provisions of the Family law, and provisions of Family Act are *lex specialis* for all questions of Family law, is supported by Janković, M., Komentar Zakona o braku i porodičnim odnosima, Beograd, 1981, p. 242. Same also Gams, A., Bračno i porodično imovinsko pravo, Beograd, 1966, p. 76. For more details on the form of authorization in the case of formal contracts see Perović, S., Formalni ugovori zaključeni preko punomoćnika, Anali Pravnog fakulteta u Beogradu, No. 2–3/1961, p. 221.

[19] See Family Act, Art. 181.

a) to change the regime of community property into a regime of joint ownership with specified, ideal shares of co-ownership,
b) to perform a real division, in which certain items within the community property will be allocated to one spouse, while other items will be awarded to the other spouse, or
c) to award all items within the community property to one of the spouses, while the other spouse receives a financial compensation, based on his/her share in acquisition of community property.

The agreement on a division of community property pertaining to immovable property must be concluded in a written form, due to the general rules on the form of contracts.[20]

4.2 Court Division

In the case of inability of spouses to reach an agreement on the division of community property, the division is to be made by a court. In that case, the legal assumption is that the shares of both spouses are equal, but each spouse has the right to contest this assumption and provide proof showing that his/her share is larger than the one of his/her counterpart.[21] The

---

20 See Art. 4. of the Law on Transactions of Immovable Property. It is interesting that the judicial practice recognizes the existence of a written agreement on the division of community property when the spouses reach an agreement on the division within the divorce proceedings, and when such an agreement is entered in the record of the main hearing: »The agreement on the division of community property reached by the parties within the divorce proceedings, which is entered in the record of the main proceedings, represents a valid contract on the division of community property.« See the ruling by the Supreme Court of Serbia Gzz. 427/76, Collection of court rulings in the field of civil law 1973–1986, Beograd, 1986, ruling No. 1094.
21 See Family Act, Art. 180/1–3. The French Court of Cassation delivered an interesting ruling while deciding on the division of community property of spouses. Namely, although in this specific case the provision of the Swiss Law – according to which the husband should receive 2/3 and the wife 1/3 of the community property – should have been applied according to the provision of the French Private international law, the Court of Cassation divided the property into equal shares, applying directly Art. 5 of the Protocol No. 7 with the European Convention on Human Rights, assessing that this provision represents an integral part of the French public order. Namely, Art. 5. of the Protocol No. 7 prescribes that the spouses have equal rights both regarding all mutual civil rights and obligations, as well as regarding their children. Such a provision made the Court of Cassation conclude that spouses must have equal rights in all matters, including the division of community property. It is, of course, going to be interesting to see whether other national courts will also interpret the aforementioned provision in the same way within the context of property relations between spouses. If such a thing should happen, the provision of national laws regulating property relations between spouses that are in contradiction with the principle of absolute equality in the division

larger share of one spouse in acquisition of community property depends on his/her realized income, household activity, child care, care and/or maintenance of property and all other considerations which are of importance to maintaining or increasing the value of community property.[22]

5. Concept of Separate Property

The separate property is the entire property of each spouse that does not fall under the regime of community property. Therefore, separate property is defined as property acquired before conclusion of marriage, as well as property acquired during marriage if it was not the result of work. More precisely, separate property is:

> Property which a spouse had at the moment the marriage was concluded, regardless of the legal ground on which it was acquired (i.e. through work, heritage, game of chance, etc.);[23]
> property which a spouse has acquired during marriage, but not through work, rather obtained it as a gift, heritage or other form of gratuitous acquisition;[24]

---

of community property could not be applied any more. So far, the European Court of Human Rights did not have a chance to state its opinion on the scope of such a provision. See the ruling by the French Court of Cassation of February 24, 1998. Cited after Jakšić, A., Evropska konvencija o ljudskim pravima – komentar, Beograd, 2006, p. 329.

22 The judicial practice rightly assessed that the contribution of a woman performing household duties can not be established in comparison to the value of the earnings of a maid: »The work of a spouse – housewife, mother, or other work that, as a rule, can not always be expressed in terms of money when participation in community property is being established, is evaluated freely, beyond the framework of monetary calculations, on the basis of contribution in the creation of the community property of spouses.« See the ruling by the Supreme Court of Slovenia Pž. 785/72 of February 23, 1972, Collection of court rulings, Beograd, 1973, Vol. 18, No. 4, ruling No. 484. Same also in the ruling of the Federal Supreme Court, Rev. 2010/60 of September 17, 1960. From Court archive.

23 See Family Act, Art. 168/1.

24 See Family Act, Art. 168/2. Separate property consists, thus, also of items bestowed as a gift to both spouses, or inherited jointly by both spouses. Spouses gain joint property rights on these items, rather than community property rights, as these items have not been acquired by work. Spouses become co-owners on equal shares, unless the donor or testator appropriate the shares differently, or the nature of the gift (jewelry, clothing, footwear) or the circumstances under which the gift had been bestowed (birthday, graduation, beginning of army service) infer that the gift had been bestowed to only one spouse. Thus also Gams, 1966, pp. 55–56, Sudžum, 1982, p. 242, Stanković – Orlić, 1989, p. 226. The judicial practice expressed the same opinion: »Items acquired on the occasion of engagement or marriage can not be considered to be community property, as they have not been acquired by work during marriage, put parties can agree as to the division of such items.« See the ruling by the Federal Supreme Court Rev. 1371/59 of January 29, 1960, Bulletin of the Supreme Court of Yugoslavia, No. 2/1960, p. 6.

- property which is awarded to the spouse on the basis of division of community property;
- property which the wife has brought into marriage in the form of dowry;[25]
- income from separate property if it was not acquired through work (for example, interest rate, rent, dividends, etc.).

6. Managing and Disposing of Separate Property

Each spouse independently manages and disposes of his/her separate property.[26] That means that a spouse can, in regards to his/her own property, conclude all legal acts known to law. The only restriction in disposing of separate property is stipulated when community property is insufficient for settlement of obligations undertaken to satisfy the daily needs of cohabitation in marriage. In that case, in order to provide sufficient funding, separate property must be used.

III. The Regime of Marriage Contract

The new Family Act (2005) has returned the legal concept of marriage contract in the Serbian law after 60 years. This concept established a right of spouses, or future spouses, to change the legal regime of community property and conclude a contract by means of which they can *pro futuro* regulate property relations regarding their existing or future property.[27] The same contract can be concluded by extramarital partners on the basis of the general rule which provides that provisions of this Act govern-

---

25 Dowry is property which according to the Serbian Civil code (1844) parents or third parties gave to the husband in order to ease the burden of supporting the family.
26 See Family Act, Art. 169.
27 As the regime of community property is no longer the imperative legal property regime in Serbian Family law, the spouses are free to conclude all legal transactions pertaining to their separate properties (e.g. contract of gift, contract of sale, contract of exchange, authorization contract etc.), but also all other contracts pertaining to the regime of community property (e.g., marriage contract, contract on management and disposition of community property, contract on division of community property, authorization contract etc.). In other words, spouses are forbidden to conclude only contracts that violate the imperative norms of Family law in general. Namely, it means that spouses can not conclude, for example, a contract by which one spouse declines in advance his/her right to legal support, right to revoke a contract on management and disposition of community property, or a contract by which one of the spouses is relieved from the duty of leading a common life, etc.

ing property relations between spouses will apply accordingly to property relations between cohabitees.[28] This pertains to provisions on community and separate property, as well as to provisions related to marriage contract. Extramarital cohabitation thus has to be a real and longer cohabitation of extramarital partners between whom there are no marriage impediments.

The type of marriage contract is not specifically legally regulated in Serbian law, as it is the case in certain foreign legal systems (i.e. French law offers to future spouses several types of marriage contracts, but also provides them with the opportunity to create their own property regime). Therefore spouses are free to define marriage contracts themselves or with the help of their legal counselors (for example, they can agree that everything each of them obtains through work during their cohabitation in marriage remains to his/her separate property, thus completely annulling the regime of community property; they can agree to keep the regime of community property, but specify their shares by the contract; they can establish new criteria for the acquisition of community and/or separate property; they can define their legal responsibility for personal or joint obligations etc.).

A marriage contract has to be concluded in a written form and has to be notarized by a judge (it is most likely that in the near future this duty will be performed by the public notary – once Serbia adopts a Public Notary Act), meaning that the judge is required to read the contract to the spouses prior to its certification, and advise them that such a contract excludes the legal regime of community property.[29] If the marriage contract refers to immovable property, it has to be additionally registered in the public registry of realty.[30] Both of these conditions – which entail that the marriage contract must be in the form of a public document – are envisaged, on the one hand, to protect the interests of the spouses by warning them on legal consequences which take effect once the exclusion of community property regime takes place, and on the other hand, to protect the interests of third parties and inform them that the regime of community property is not applicable, namely that it has been modified in comparison to the legal regime of community property.

---

28 See Family Act, Art. 191/2.
29 See Family Act, Art. 188/2.
30 See Family Act, Art. 188/2-3.

IV. Final Remarks

In legal literature pertaining to the new legal concept of marriage contract in the Serbian Family Act, criticisms of its introduction have already appeared. The most frequent objections that have been voiced are the following:
> - the legal norms on the marriage contract in the Family Act are insufficient;
> - the legislator did not define mechanisms to protect the economically weaker partner, i. e. did not provide for the right of the judge to assess the marriage contract on the basis of legal consequences that will result from it;
> - finally, it has been said that a marriage contract is contrary to Serbian tradition and as such disturbs the harmony of emotional relations which are forming between partners about to conclude marriage.

In regards to this criticism, the following can be said:
> - It is true that only one article of the Family Act has been devoted to the marriage contract, but by the general rule of article 196 of the Family Act, referral has been made to the law that governs property law relations and the law that governs obligations regarding all questions pertaining to property relations between spouses and extramarital partners that are not defined in the Family Act. According to that stipulation, the rule on general limitation of freedom of contract from the Act on obligations provides that every contract must not be contrary to *ius cogens*, *ordre public* or *bonnes moeurs* (good habits) and moral order. Also, all other provisions of this Act that pertain to the object and basis of the contract, ability to conclude the contract, breach of the contract, annulment of the contract (fraud, duress, error, usurious contract etc.), convalidation, conversion, etc., and that encompass over 100 articles of the Act on obligations – will be accordingly applied to the marriage contract as well;
> - as to the suggestion that the judge who certifies the marriage contract should be given the right to influence its content, in order to protect the financially weaker partner, this can not be accepted, because in that case little or nothing would be left of the freedom of contracting, as the most important principle of the law on contracts. On the other hand, protection of the financially weaker partner can be achieved by provisions concerning alimony of the spouse and/or extramarital

partner, as well as by the provision of the Family Act according to which relinquishment of this right to support does not have legal effect (article 8/2);
- finally, it is utterly untrue that the marriage contract is contrary to Serbian tradition, given the history of marriage contract in the Serbian Civil code from the 19th century that was mentioned earlier. As to the objection that negotiations preceding the conclusion of a marriage contract can endanger love between partners and harmony of their relationship, it is my opinion that, on the contrary, property relations are an integral part of all human relationships, including the love relationship, both marital or extramarital, and there's no point in shutting the eyes in front of such a fact and denying its existence. A conclusion of a marriage contract is not an obligation for anyone; this contract will be acceptable to couples that have a considerable property or expect to acquire it during their common living or simply want to clarify any possible dilemma and uncertainty in their mutual relations in future. In any case, their number will be significantly low. Finally, if it is possible to fall in love over something valuable (»romancing the stone»), why would it not be possible to protect the very same love through voluntary and common financial arrangement (»financing the romance»)?

The Status of Prenuptial Agreements in English Law – Eccentricity or sensible pragmatism?

Nigel Lowe[1] and Roger Kay[2]

I. Introduction

The status of prenuptial agreements, which are not binding in English law, is a rich source of debate. In 2007, the Court of Appeal in *Charman v Charman*[3] suggested *obiter* that they should be enforceable; a Private Member's Bill to do just that was introduced into the House of Commons by Quentin Davies MP[4]; a differently constituted Court of Appeal seemed to take the law further in *Crossley v Crossley*[5] and the Law Commission announced that pre-nuptial agreements would form part of their tenth programme of reform. The Commission had recently considered in some detail, in *Cohabitation: The Financial Consequences of Relationship Breakdown*[6], the conditions under which opting out might be effected from the proposed financial and property regime on cohabitation breakdown. Further, as we were writing, the Privy Council was considering an appeal from the Isle of Man inter alia on the enforceability of a prenuptial agreement and has now given its judgment.[7]

Although there seems broad agreement that prenuptial agreements should be given some effect, there is no agreement on exactly what that effect should be, and on what basis. As the Law Commission said:

---

[1] Professor of Law and Director of the Centre of International Family Law Studies, Cardiff Law School, Cardiff University, Wales, UK.
[2] Storrar Cowdry Professor of Family Law, University of Chester, UK.
[3] [2007] EWCA Civ 503, [2007] 1 FLR 1246.
[4] Namely, the Prenuptial Agreements Bill, which had its First Reading in July 2007 but lapsed in October 2007.
[5] [2007] EWCA Civ 1491, [2008] 1 FLR 1467.
[6] Law Com (307).
[7] *MacLeod v MacLeod* [2008] UKPC 64, [2009] 1 FLR 641.

> »...the reluctance to allow parties to live with the consequences of the agreement they have made on the basis of legal advice is something of an English eccentricity.«[8]

We consider first the current position and then debate whether that position is indeed mere English eccentricity or sensible pragmatism. To put this debate into context we first clarify terminology, then explain the general background to the English position before concentrating specifically on the status of prenuptial agreements. We conclude with arguments about whether or not the law should be reformed.

1. Clarification of Terms

At the outset it will be useful to clarify terms. By »prenuptial agreement« (also referred to as »antenuptial agreement«) is meant an agreement made before marriage concerning what is to happen to all the parties' assets in the event of a divorce or separation. Although there must now be the equivalent »pre-civil partnership agreements«[9] there has yet to be an established phrase for such agreements. One (perhaps frivolous) suggestion[10] is that they can be referred to as »pre-reggies« (as opposed to »pre-nups«); others[11] refer to them as »pre-cips«. Prenuptial agreements must be contrasted with »antenuptial settlements« (which are variable under MCA 1973, s 24) which seek to regulate the spouses' financial affairs upon and during their marriage but which do **not** contemplate the dissolution of the marriage[12] In turn these agreements are to be contrasted with »post separation agreements«, which are commonly negotiated during the divorce process, and which, though not binding,[13] are positively encouraged. Finally, all the above, are to be contrasted with »cohabitation contracts« which govern the parties' position during and after cohabitation and in which neither marriage nor civil partnership is contemplated.

---

8 Law Com (307) at 5.19.
9 Since 5 December 2005 same sex couples in the UK have been able to enter into civil partnerships: Civil Partnership Act 2004.
10 C Barton, »The FMA Annual Conference«, [2005] *Fam Law* 992 at 994.
11 S Harris-Short and J Miles *Family Law, Text, Cases and Materials* (2007) at 551.
12 Per Wall J in *N v N (Jurisdiction: Pre-Nuptial Agreement)* [1999] 2 FLR 745 at 751-2.
13 See *Soulsbury v Soulsbury* [2007] EWCA Civ 969, [2008] Fam 11.

2. General Background to the English Position

To put the English position on prenuptial agreements into perspective some explanation of the general system for dealing with matrimonial property is required. In contrast to many (if not most) continental European legal systems, English law has never developed a special regime for dealing with family assets and consequently has no notion of community of property. Indeed in general (though see below in the context of *Miller v Miller; McFarlane v McFarlane*)[14] it recognises no special concept of »family property« at all. Consequently whenever ownership of family assets are strictly in issue whether it be in the context of marriage or cohabitation regard is had to the ordinary rules governing property law which in England and Wales rest upon the doctrine of separation of property.

Grafted onto this basic position are the court's wide distributive powers conferred by Parliament through the Matrimonial Causes Act 1973 (as amended) (hereafter »MCA 1973«) which can be exercised upon the ending of the marriage through divorce and now, through the Civil Partnership Act 2004, upon the dissolution of the civil partnership. Under these powers the court can make property adjustment orders (including the out and out transfer of ownership from one spouse to the other or even to any child of the family); it can order the property to be sold and direct to whom the proceeds should be paid; it can order the one-off payment of lump sums; it can order the sharing of pension rights and it can order continuing maintenance payments (known under English law as »periodical payments«) both in favour of the former spouse and of any child of the family.

Not only are these powers wide ranging, effectively covering all aspects of family assets, but their exercise is subject to minimal statutory control. All the 1973 Act (through s an 25A) directs the court to do is

1.) in deciding whether and how to exercise its powers »to have regard to all the circumstances of the case first [note, not paramount] consideration being given to the welfare while a minor or any child of the family who has not attained the age of eighteen«;
2.) when exercising its powers »to consider whether it would be appropriate so to exercise those powers that the financial obligations of each party towards each other will be terminated as soon after the grant of the decree as the court considers just and reasonable« [the »clean break« principle]; and

---

14 [2006] UKHL 24, [2006] 2 AC 618.

3.) when exercising its powers: to have regard to each party's current and potential income, earning capacity, property and other financial resources, their (and their children's) financial needs, the family's standard of living before the marital breakdown, the spouses' age and any disability, the duration of the marriage, each party's contribution (past, present and future) to the welfare of the family (including looking after the home or caring for the family) and each party's conduct insofar as it would be inequitable to disregard it.

Notably absent from the statutory guidance is any statement of what the overall object of the court's powers is. It was with this in mind that the House of Lords in *White v White*[15] held that the underlying object was to achieve a fair outcome between the parties as judged against the yardstick of equality and without being biased in favour of the money-earner as against the home-make and the child-carer. This approach (which, at a stroke, removed the so-called »glass ceiling« of any awards) has since been further refined by the House of Lords in *Miller v Miller; McFarlane v McFarlane*, above. That judgment recognised three principles upon which the redistribution of resources from one party to another following a divorce was justified, namely

> the **needs** (primarily housing and financial) generated by the relationship between the parties. This is often where the search for fairness begins and ends since in most cases the available assets are insufficient to provide adequately for the needs of two homes;
> **compensation** for relationship-generated disadvantage – women in particular may still suffer a disproportionate financial loss upon marital breakdown having sacrificed their careers looking after the home and family; and
> **sharing** of the fruits of the matrimonial partnership of equals (sometimes referred to as »entitlement«).

Although there is debate[16] about the extent to which »non-matrimonial« property (that is, property brought into the marriage, other than that used as or to provide for the matrimonial home, and property acquired by gift or inheritance during the marriage) should be taken into account at

---

15   [2001] AC 596.
16   Compare, for example, Lord Nicholls with Baroness Hale in *Miller v Miller; McFarlane v McFarlane*.

any rate in short marriages, that should not mask the basic fact that more or less **all** the spouses' assets, however and whenever acquired, are subject to the court's extraordinarily wide powers and are therefore at risk of being redistributed. This risk, one might have thought, makes the need to recognise prenuptial agreements all the more pressing (although at the same time it also makes it understandable why they are not binding). Yet, as will be seen, English law almost alone not only in Europe but also among other common law jurisdictions, has hitherto refused to recognise such agreements as binding.

II. Résumé of English Case-Law on Prenuptial Agreements

There is no formal statutory prohibition against the making nor indeed the enforcement of pre-nuptial agreements. Section 34(1) of the MCA does, however, provide that insofar as a »maintenance agreement« (defined, inter alia as »any agreement in writing made between **two parties to a marriage**« (s 34(2)) purports to »restrict any right to apply for an order containing financial provisions« it is void, though it also states that »any other financial arrangements contained in the agreement shall not thereby be rendered void or unenforceable«.[17] Strictly, prenuptial agreements fall outside the scope of s 34 since they are made before the marriage and are not therefore made between spouses. However, it is implicit that the prohibition extends to all agreements **whenever made** that purport to oust the court's jurisdiction. In any event, s 34(1)(a), a re-enactment of a series of provisions going back to s 1(2) of the Maintenance Agreements Act 1957, reflects the House of Lords' decision in *Hyman v Hyman*[18] that no spousal maintenance agreement can preclude a spouse from applying for financial relief in divorce proceedings. Based upon the premise that the court's power to order the husband to maintain his former wife after divorce was intended to protect not only her but also any third party dealing with her and indirectly the state since it may have had to support her, it was held to be contrary to public policy to permit to oust the court's jurisdiction. Put another way, as Lord Atkin said in *Hyman*, the »wife's right to future maintenance is a matter of public concern which she cannot barter away«. So

---

17 For the similar provision concerning maintenance agreements between civil partners – see the Civil Partnership Act 2004, Sch 5, para 67.
18 [1929] AC 601.

stated, it is evident that the wide ratio of *Hyman* is that no matter when it is made an agreement cannot oust the court's jurisdiction. At any rate, it is generally taken as read that prenuptial agreements are not binding. As Wall J said in *N v N (Jurisdiction: Pre-Nuptial Agreement)*[19]:

> »*The attitude of the English courts to antenuptial agreements... has always been that they are not enforceable.*«

Illustrative of this standpoint is *F v F (Ancillary Relief: Substantial Assets)*[20], which seems to be the first reported English decision on prenuptial agreements (though in that case they were called »antenuptial contracts«). Thereunder an agreement drawn up in Germany, the wife of a millionaire would have been restricted to receiving the equivalent of a pension of a German judge, a result which Thorpe J (as he then was) dismissed as being »ridiculous«. Although he acknowledged that

> »*contracts of this sort are commonplace in the society from which the parties come*«, Thorpe J considered that in »*this jurisdiction they must be of very limited significance*«.

In *MacLeod v MacLeod*[21] the Privy Council, having exhaustively reviewed the relevant authorities, concluded that it was not open to them »to reverse the long standing rule that ante-nuptial agreements are contrary to public policy and thus not binding in the contractual sense.« In the Board's view »the difficult issue of the validity and effect of ante-nuptial agreements is more appropriate to legislative rather than judicial development.«[22]

Despite these decisions and notwithstanding other judicial comments prior to *Macleod* that prenuptial agreements are not enforceable,[23] it would be a mistake to think that English courts simply dismiss their relevance. Indeed, simply to ignore a prenuptial agreement could be thought

---

19   Above at n 12. In fact, the decision was especially strict since Wall J considered that the public policy argument applied to individual clauses even if they could be severed from the rest of the agreement and that there was no power to compel the parties to implement part of the agreement.
20   [1995] 2 FLR 45.
21   [2008] UKPC 64, [2009] 1 FLR 641 and noted at [2009] Fam Law 178.
22   See respectively, paras [31] and [34]. For a more extensive discussion of the decision, see A Meehan »Agreements and Ancillary Relief after *S* and *Macleod v MacLeod*« [2009] Fam Law 206.
23   See, for example, *C v C (Variation of Post-Nuptial Settlement)* [2003] EWHC 742 (Fam), [2004] 2 FLR 1 in which Wilson J commented »Even nowadays, notwithstanding the law's growing respect for properly negotiated prenuptial agreements, it is impossible to argue that they can succeed in ousting the jurisdiction of the court«.

to violate Article 8 of the European Convention on Human Rights as being an interference with the right to respect for private and family life. Even before *N v N*, referred to above, there had been indications that such agreements were a material consideration in deciding how property may be distributed after the divorce. In *N v N (Foreign Divorce: Financial Relief)*[24], for example, a case involving Swedish nationals, it was held that while their prenuptial agreement was not conclusive in England (as it was in Sweden) it was nonetheless a material consideration to which the court should have regard in applying the criteria set out in the MCA 1973. More strikingly still, in *S v S (Divorce: Staying Proceedings)*[25] Wilson J said that there was a danger that the words of Thorpe J in *F v F* (referred to above) might be taken out of context. Looking to the future his Lordship added[26]

> »There will come a case... where the circumstances surrounding the prenuptial agreement and the provisions therein contained might, when viewed in the context of other circumstances of the case prove influential or even crucial. When other jurisdictions, both in the USA and in the European Union, have been persuaded that there are cases where justice can only be served by confining parties to their rights under prenuptial agreements, we should be cautious about asserting the contrary. I can find nothing in s 25 to compel a conclusion so much at odds with personal freedoms to make agreements for ourselves, that escape from solemn bargains, carefully struck by informed adults is readily available here. It all depends.«

Although Wilson J's comments were obiter, the clear thrust of the post-2000 case-law has been to confirm the basic proposition that prenuptial agreements **are** a material consideration in the post-divorce redistribution of property exercise either as part of »all the circumstances« or as »conduct« (according to Connell J in *M v M (Prenuptial Agreement)*[27] it does not matter which) which the court is directed to take into account under s 25 of the MCA 1973.

1. Some Illustrative Post-2000 Decisions

In *M v M (Prenuptial Agreement)* (above) the parties were Canadian. The woman became pregnant and the man was opposed to her having an

---

24 [1997] 1 FLR 900.
25 [1997] 2 FLR 100.
26 Ibid, at 103.
27 [2002] 1 FLR 654 at 661.

abortion. She refused to have the child unless they married. But having undergone an acrimonious and expensive divorce from his first wife, the man refused to marry her unless she signed a prenuptial agreement he had had drawn up by his lawyers, under which the wife would receive £ 275,000 in the event of a divorce. Despite being advised by an independent experienced matrimonial lawyer not to do so the woman signed the agreement since that was the only way she was able to ensure that marriage went ahead as planned. The marriage lasted five years by which time the husband's net worth was about £ 7.5 million. The wife sought £ 1.3 million. Connell J commented:

> »The circumstances of this case illustrate vividly that the existence of a prenuptial agreement can do more to obscure rather than clarify the underlying justice of the case..... In my view it would be as unjust to the husband to ignore the existence of the agreement and its terms as it would be to the wife to hold her strictly to those terms. I do bear the agreement in mind as one of the more relevant circumstances of this case, but the court's overriding duty remains to attempt to arrive at a solution which is fair in all the circumstances, applying s 25 of the Matrimonial Causes Act 1973.«

He accordingly ordered the husband to pay the wife £ 875,000 which because of the prenuptial agreement was »a more modest award than might have been made without it«.

In *K v K (Ancillary Relief: Prenuptial Agreement)*[28] the wife became pregnant and her mother pressured the husband to marry. Both parties came from wealthy backgrounds, the husband having wealth of around £ 25 million and the wife being a beneficiary of trusts valued at some £ 1 million. According to the prenuptial agreement, signed after each took legal advice, but without the husband making full disclosure, if the marriage ended within five years, the wife was to receive £ 100,000 from the husband (to be increased by 10% p.a. compound) and the husband was to make reasonable financial provision for any children. The agreement made no provision for periodical payments for the wife. The marriage ended after 14 months and the wife sought a lump sum of £ 1.6 million and periodical payments of £ 57,000 p.a. for herself in addition to the £ 15,000 p.a. for their child. The husband offered a £ 120,000 lump sum (plus £ 600,000 to provide a

---

28 [2003] 1 FLR 120.

home in which she could bring up the child). Given that the husband had agreed to marry the wife under pressure and upon the understanding that no capital claim in the event of an early termination of the marriage would be governed by their agreement, it was held that entry into the agreement constituted »conduct which it would be inequitable to disregard« under s 25 (2) (g) of the 1973 Act. Accordingly, it was decided that the capital element of the agreement should be upheld. However, it was thought wrong to confine provision to the wife to the husband's offer, since it failed to recognise her role as the child's mother. The court awarded the wife periodical payments of £ 15,000 p.a. It also ordered a lump sum of £ 1.2 million to be paid so as to provide the wife and child with a house that bore some relationship to the husband's standard of living.

In *Ella v Ella*[29], the parties, who had dual British/Israeli nationality, married in Israel in 1996 having made a prenuptial contract that provided for Israeli law to apply to any questions concerning their property and provided for separation of property with future assets belonging exclusively to the spouse creating them. The spouses made their marital home in London but in 2006 the marriage ran into difficulties and the wife petitioned for divorce in London. The husband countered by petitioning in Israel and in due course the Rabbinical court issued a consent order under which it would first determine the question of jurisdiction. Subsequently, on the husband's without notice application, the Israeli court ruled that it had exclusive jurisdiction. The husband then sought a stay of the English proceedings. At first instance the husband succeeded, Macur J holding that in reaching the decision the prenuptial agreement was a »major factor«. The Court of Appeal agreed. As Charles J (with whom Kay LJ agreed) said:

> »I agree with the submission made on behalf of the wife that absent the prenuptial agreement, this would be an English case and the husband would not be able to show that Israel was clearly the appropriate forum. The judge clearly recognises the connecting factors connecting the family to Israel. In my judgment the judge was right to conclude that, taken together with those factors, the prenuptial agreement is a major factor in this case, and in my view it is one that results in Israel being clearly the more appropriate forum«.

---

29 [2007] EWCA Civ 99, [2007] 2 FLR 35.

Ella is interesting on a number of counts: it was the first *Court of Appeal* decision in which a prenuptial agreement has been held to be relevant; it provided a rare example of a decisive role played by such an agreement notwithstanding that the wife did not take independent legal advice before making the agreement (though in this respect it was acknowledged that the wife might not be deprived of a remedy in the English courts under Part III of the Matrimonial and Family Proceedings Act 1984).

Ella was different from the previous two decisions inasmuch as it concerned jurisdiction rather than the quantum of the award. But any doubts that the Court of Appeal would take a different attitude to quantum issues were quashed by *Crossley v Crossley*.[30]

That case concerned the enforceability of a prenuptial agreement made in England between two independently wealthy English parties (the man's fortune was in the region of £ 45 million and the woman's, £ 18 million). Both parties had been married before – the wife (who was 50) in fact three times previously and the husband (who was 62) once before as well as having lived in a long-term relationship; and both had children from their previous relationships. The parties met in June 2005, became engaged in September and, before their marriage in January 2006 and after negotiations between their experienced lawyers, signed a prenuptial agreement in November 2005, by which they agreed that in the event of a divorce neither would be entitled to financial assistance from the other. The marriage did not last: the parties separated after 14 months and the wife sought a divorce five months after that. It was in summary a short childless marriage between two independently wealthy people who, on their lawyers' advice had signed a prenuptial contract not to make a financial claim on each other in the event of a divorce. As Thorpe LJ put it (at para [15]) »if ever there is to be a paradigm case in which the court will look to the prenuptial agreement as not simply one of the peripheral factors in the case but as a factor of magnetic importance«, this was such a case.

Although the clear implication of *Crossley* was that the wife would effectively be held to her agreement, it is important to appreciate that the Court of Appeal did **not**, even in these circumstances, hold that the prenuptial agreement was **binding** (rather that it was likely to be **the** key factor in determining how the discretion under s 25 should be exercised) nor did they in fact hold that the wife would be limited to terms agreed upon for that was to be decided at a future hearing. Instead, what the Court of Ap-

---

30   [2007] EWCA Civ 1491, [2008] 1 FLR 1467.

peal did was to uphold the trial judge's (Bennett J) ruling that rather than the parties filing full documents and questionnaires as would be normal (as provided for by the Family Proceedings Rules 1991 (»FPR«), r 2.61B), the wife should show cause why her claims for financial relief should not be resolved within the terms of the prenuptial agreement).[31] In fact Mrs Crossley withdrew her application so that the case never proceeded to a substantive hearing.

Notwithstanding the relative narrowness of *Crossley*, it is of significance not least because it was a *Court of Appeal* decision on a quantum issue and one involving Thorpe and Wall LJJ both of whom had not long previously been dismissive of the relevance of prenuptial agreements (see respectively their decisions in *F v F* and *Re N*, discussed above). Indeed Wall LJ remained cautious saying that he limited his decision »strictly to the facts of this particular case«. Thorpe LJ, on the other hand, referred to the decision as being in accord »with a developing view that prenuptial contracts are gaining in importance in a particularly fraught area that confronts so many parties separating and divorcing«.

Although *Crossley* has generated considerable discussion (though given its facts, even in English terms, the decision was not all that surprising and to those steeped in the civil law tradition, it would barely merit a raised eyebrow), it did not alter the basic English stance that prenuptial agreements are not binding but may be taken into account when making ancillary relief orders. This is further illustrated by the subsequent decision, *NG v KR (Pre-Nuptial Contract)*[32], which concerned the relevance of a prenuptial agreement made between a French man and a German woman who married in London and by which each agreed that neither would have a claim upon the other in the event of the divorce and that German law would govern the contract. The agreement (which was found as a fact to have been binding both in Germany and in France) had been prepared by a German notary instructed by the woman's mother but a disclosure clause was struck out on the woman's instructions before being forwarded to the man for signature. The man had, at best, one week's no-

---

31 This »show cause« procedure is known as a *'Dean v Dean* application' after the case of the same name see [1978] 3 WLR 288. This ruling was held in the circumstances to be a sensible cost saving management decision and which was proportionate to the parties' financial resources (which is the overriding objective of FPR r 2.51D.
32 [2008] EWHC 1532 (Fam), [2008] Fam Law 948. Note, leave to appeal to the Court of Appeal has been granted, see *Radmacher v Granatino* [2008] EWCA Civ 1304, [2009] Fam Law 183.

tice of the agreement and had therefore no realistic opportunity to seek independent advice. He signed it in the August before their marriage in November. At the time of their marriage the husband worked as an investment banker earning around $ 470,000 p.a.. She, on the other hand, had assets worth about £ 100 million. After eight years, during which time they had two children, the parties separated. Some three years prior to that the husband gave up his job to read for a D Phil at Oxford University and estimated his earning prospects as researcher at £ 30,000 per year. At the time of the hearing he had no assets and indeed debts of £ 800,000 (£ 600,000 of which were for court costs). He now sought in ancillary proceedings to their divorce £ 6.9 million pounds plus a sum to purchase a house in Germany (the wife had obtained a relocation order in previous proceedings) to enable him to see the children until they were 21 and £ 50,000 per annum for the benefit of each of the children. The wife offered him £ 1 million for a house in England in which he could reside for life; € 500,000 for a house in Germany for his exclusive occupancy until the children attained their majority and £ 18,000 per annum for the benefit of each of the children until they completed their secondary education. She argued that in all other respects her husband should stand on his own feet; he had willingly signed the agreement but for which there would have been no marriage; all her assets were inherited and were her separate property; there was no matrimonial home, and she was the primary carer of the children.

It was argued, inter alia, that the agreement was a jurisdiction rather than a choice of law clause and was therefore caught by Brussels 1[33], though this was not pursued, and that English law on prenuptial agreements was contrary to human rights, which was dismissed. The key issue nevertheless remained: what, if any, was the relevance of the prenuptial agreement? Baron J held that the agreement was not a valid contract and in any event was »defective« inasmuch as there had been no disclosure by the wife, no negotiation between the parties, the husband had not received independent advice and that the parties had had two children. Nevertheless she held that the fact that the husband had signed the agreement, knowing full well its general import, was a circumstance that should be taken into account and the amount awarded was accordingly circumscribed. The husband was awarded £ 5.56 million plus a sum for

---

33 Council Regulation (EC) No 44/2001 of 22 December 2000 on Jurisdiction and the Recognition of Judgments in Civil and Commercial Matters.

housing in Germany and £ 70,000 by way of annual maintenance for the benefit of the children.

2. The current state of the law

A good summary of the current law (provided by C Sharp) is as follows[34]

> »Pre-nuptial agreements cannot exclude the jurisdiction of the court (or the Child Support Agency).
> Pre-nuptial agreements cannot be specifically enforced nor will agreements to forego claims for ancillary relief amount to valuable consideration (unless subsequently embodied in a court order).
> They will be taken into account as either a relevant circumstance under s 25 (1) or as a matter of conduct under s 25 (2) (g) of the 1973 Act.
> They will not be the sole consideration as the court must consider all factors under s 25.
> The weight to be given to them will be entirely fact dependent, as Wilson J said in *S v S* (and it remains true today), ›[i]t all depends‹.
> There is increasing inclination to give effect to the informed agreement between parties of equal bargaining power to arrange their own affairs.
> The passage of time, changes in circumstances and (in particular) the arrival of children in a relationship may have significant consequences in determining what is fair.«

Notwithstanding this analysis Sharp argues that there is now uncertainty as to when a prenuptial agreement will be upheld and that in consequence recourse will frequently be had to costly litigation which has been described as the »the worst of all worlds«.[35]

III. Should The English Position Be Reformed?

The current law on prenuptial agreements has attracted considerable comment from academics, judges and policy makers and serious consideration is being given to reforming the law.

A key criticism of the current law is that it is paternalistic and anachro-

---

34 C Sharp »Pre-nuptial Agreements: a Rethink Required« [2008] *Family Law* 741 at 747-748). See also M Harper and L Alhadeff »*Crossley v Crossley*: Are Pre-nuptial Agreements Now Binding in England?« [2008] *Family Law* 334, at 336-337.
35 See Hoffmann LJ in *Pounds v Pounds* [1994] 1 FLR 775.

nistic[36]. It has been pointed out that when *Hyman* was decided wives did not then have full legal capacity and it made sense to protect them. Now, however, since they do have full competence and particularly because marriage is regarded as a partnership of equals together with the doctrine of separation of property there should be full freedom for both parties to make their economic arrangements. It has in any event been further argued that the decision in *Hyman* is illustrative of the former law's ambivalence about private agreements when, as one commentary[37] has put it, »the fact that the parties had come to an agreement between themselves was... regarded not as a matter of satisfaction but rather as something which should arouse the court's vigilance«, i.e. to be satisfied that the divorce was not collusive. But again all this has changed: the parties are encouraged to settle their financial affairs amicably. Indeed, post separation financial agreements either made independently or as a result of financial dispute resolution appointment, whilst not strictly binding, are normally followed provided the court is satisfied that each party was properly and independently advised.[38] Accordingly, it can be argued that the law is wrong to treat prenuptial agreements differently. Furthermore, given that some of the sensitivities regarding prenuptial agreements are peculiar to marriage it is not absolutely certain that so-called »pre-cips« will be treated the same way. Yet it surely cannot be right to treat prenuptial and pre-cips agreements differently. That would only compound another awkward comparison, namely, the apparently developing recognition of cohabitation contracts at any rate with regard to financial arrangements contained therein.[39]

In defence of the current position there are a number of so-called *public policy* arguments but, say advocates for reform, they are either unpersuasive or point to other alternatives for dealing with the problem. In the former category is the argument that prenuptial agreements diminish

---

36 See B Clark »Should greater prominence be given to pre-nuptial contracts in the law of ancillary relief?« [2004] *Child and Family Law Quarterly* 399 ; S Harris-Short and J Miles, op cit at 7.9.2 and N Lowe and G Douglas *Bromley's Family Law* (10th edn, 2007) 1013-1014.
37 S Cretney and J Masson *Principles of Family Law* (5th edn, 1990) 359. And now *MacLeod-MacLeod* [2008] UK PC 64, [2009] 1 FLR 641.
38 See eg *Edgar v Edgar* [1980] 3 All ER 887 and *Xydhias v Xydhias* [1999] 1 FLR 683.
39 See *Sutton v Mischon de Reya and Gawor and Co* [2003] EWHC 3166 (Ch), [2004] 1 FLR 837 though note Herring's comment (*Family Law* (3rd edn, 2007) 243) that since there are no redistributive powers following the breakdown of cohabitation between unmarried couples cohabitation contracts cannot be said to be »robbing« the court of such power.

the importance/sanctity of marriage. But as Connell J said in *M v M* this is hardly a strong argument given the high number of divorces. Ironically, it is now being said that an ability to make binding prenuptial agreements could add stability to marriage second time round. In any event such binding agreements could lead to greater certainty and hence to reduced costs in the event of divorce.

One concern commonly expressed about making prenuptial agreements binding is that they could inappropriately transfer the burden of maintaining an ex-spouse away from the individual onto the State. But, so the argument goes, that problem could and should be dealt with by appropriate social security laws. Other issues include the adequate protection of children, the appropriateness of agreements made long ago or where circumstances have entirely changed, and protection of the weaker party. These problems could be solved respectively by dealing separately with children, having so-called »sunset clauses« or by simply relying on standard contractual principles such as duress, frustration and so on. Of course, as many have observed, the danger of making agreements binding is that the uncertainties and arguments are simply shifted onto the validity and meaning of the agreement as opposed to the current settlement issues on divorce – thus negating the argument that prenups lead to greater certainty and thus reduced divorce costs.

A further argument is that English law is simply out of line internationally, not just with the civil systems of continental Europe but also many common law systems as well. Australia, New Zealand have changed their laws relatively recently and Ireland are currently considering doing so.[40] In the European context there is, against the background of freedom of movement so dear to the EU, an arguable need for harmonisation. Is it fair that a couple having made a binding prenuptial agreement in one Member State should on divorcing in England find that the agreement can be totally undone? In his postscript to his judgment in *Charman v Charman*[41] Potter commented

> *»The difficulty of harmonising our law concerning the property consequences of marriage and divorce and the law of civilian member states is exacerbated by the fact that our law has so far given little status to prenuptial contracts. If, unlike the rest of Europe, the pro-*

---

40 See e.g. B Fehlberg and B Smyth »Binding Pre-Nuptial Agreements in Australia: the First Year«, (2002) 16 *International Journal of Law, Policy and the Family*, 127.
And in Ireland, see the Report of the Study Group on Pre-nuptial Agreements, 2007.
41 Ibid, at para [124].

perty consequences of divorce are to be regulated by the principle of needs, compensation and sharing, should not the parties to the marriage, or the projected marriage, have at least the opportunity to order their own affairs otherwise by a nuptial contract?«

Similarly, in *Crossley* Thorpe LJ said[42]

»I would classify, in the circumstances of this case, the contract into which the parties entered...as in many respects akin to a marital regime into which parties enter in civil law jurisdictions in order to provide for the property consequences of a possible divorce. It does seem to me that the role of contractual dealing, the opportunity for the autonomy of the parties, is becoming increasingly important.«

1. The Autonomy Arguments

Echoing Thorpe LJ's reference to the increasing importance of party autonomy is the Law Commission's reference to it in their Report on **Cohabitation** in the context of opt-out agreements from the proposed regime for certain cohabitants.[43] But what does party autonomy mean? A dictionary definition of autonomy is *»freedom to determine one's own actions and behaviour«*. However, autonomy and freedom are relative not absolute concepts. One person's freedom and autonomy might be gained at the expense of another's. In this context, however, for whom should there be autonomy? Is it both parties as a single entity or as two separate entities? In most cases the reality is that the parties act individually rather than as a couple. But if there is really to be autonomy, this would not matter since the parties regardless of whether they are acting jointly or individually should be able to contract as they wish, subject only to the **contractual** safeguard afforded by the doctrine of undue influence (which of course is only concerned with position at the time of making the contract). But whether it would be desirable to end the law's protective role may be debated. Clark argues,[44] that feminist theory might suggest that women would be disadvantaged where there is too heavy a reliance on contractual dealing in family matters, in fact such agreements may advantage or disadvantage either gender. She makes the crucial point that it is difficult to judge whether an agreement is fair or not at the time it is made becau-

---

42   Ibid, at para [17].
43   *Law Com No 307 (Summary)* at 1.16.
44   Op cit, n 34.

se the parties' circumstances might change in the future. This might not seem remarkable – this is a risk in any contract – except that, as we have seen,[45] the English ancillary relief regime is based on fairness at the time of adjudication following breakdown which in turn is simply incompatible with party autonomy. We would argue that in the final analysis autonomy is not as important as protecting the interests of potentially vulnerable parties. Furthermore, since prenuptial agreements are generally only utilised in a small number of cases and usually by those with considerable assets, their reform should not put at risk the English redistributive system based on fairness.

IV. The Reaction of Policy makers

As has pointed out,[46] given that full recognition of prenuptial agreements requires the removal of the statutorily conferred discretion under s 25 of the 1973 Act, reform can and should only be done by Parliament. How then have the English policy makers reacted to these type of arguments?

In its Consultation Paper *Supporting Families*[47] the government itself suggested that prenuptial agreements could usefully be made binding but subject to safeguards, namely, that the parties received independent legal advice before entering the agreement; that there be full disclosure of each parties' assets and property before the agreement was made and that the agreement is made no fewer than 21 days before the marriage. Furthermore, the agreement would not have been binding if there was a child of the family whether **or not** that child was born at the time the agreement was made or where under the general law of contract the agreement would be unenforceable or, finally, where the agreement would cause significant injustice to one or both parties or a child of the marriage. These safeguards are so wide-ranging that most agreements would have difficulty negotiating the hurdle. Indeed the point has already been made that *Ella* and *Crossley* apart, all the English cases referred to would fail to do so. In other words, had the proposed reform been enacted it would have made little or no difference to the current law. In the event the proposal did not find favour apparently mainly because of concern that parties'

---

45 Above at p 396.
46 M Griffin »The Judiciary: Shifting the Constitutional Boundary and Usurping Parliament's Role?« [2008] *Family Law* 550.
47 Home Office, 1998, *Supporting Families*.

circumstances could change as time passed following the agreement so that it would be unfair to keep them to its terms and was abandoned. At one stage the majority of judges of the Family Division proposed that the terms of any prenuptial agreement should be made an additional factor for the court to take into account under s 25 of the MCA 1973. A minority would have gone further and provided that both pre and post nuptial agreements should be presumptively binding.[48] Building on that opinion, Resolution[49] proposed that s 25 be amended so as to provide that agreements should be considered binding »unless to do so will cause significant injustice to either party or to any child of the family«.

While this latter proposal might be useful inasmuch as it would at least potentially harmonise the approach to prenuptial agreements it seems doubtful that any of the decisions cited in this paper would have been decided differently had it been enacted which raises the question of whether any such reform is worth the candle. Evidently, the Law Commission think otherwise for in its *Tenth Programme of Law Reform* (published in June 2008) the English Law Commission announced that it will examine the status and enforceability of marital property and finance agreements made either before or during the course of marriage or civil partnership.[50] One of their arguments for doing so is the view that the fact that prenuptial agreements are not currently binding may deter people from marrying or entering into civil partnerships.

While this last point is not without significance (though one would need evidence of the alleged deterrence) one could certainly take the view that the current English law has the best of all worlds, namely, to accept prenuptials as being a material consideration in deciding how to redistribute the family assets but not to be bound by them so as to prevent the court being able to do justice or more importantly able to avoid injustice between the parties.

---

48 N Wilson »Response of the Judges of the Family Division to Government Proposals (made by way of submission to the Lord Chancellor's Ancillary Relief Advisory Group)« [1999] *Family Law* 159, at 162 – 163.
49 The Solicitors' Family Law Association, 2004.
50 It may be noted that in their Report on Cohabitation (Law Com No 307), the Law Commission had recommended (see paras 5.6 to 5.10) that cohabitation agreements should be enforceable.

V. Conclusions

As has been seen, English law has not developed a notion of family property as such. Instead the courts have wide statutory powers[51] to redistribute the spouses' assets upon divorce which, according to case law,[52] should be exercised according to the principle of fairness judged at the time of the court hearing. Such powers are fundamentally inconsistent with a regime of making prenuptial agreements binding. Although this position on prenuptial agreements is out of line internationally, given that it is now well established that the existence of such agreements is a circumstance that must be taken into account even to the extent that it can be decisive,[53] it is suggested that far from being a case of English eccentricity the current position provides a pragmatic solution that enables justice properly to be done. This is well illustrated, we would suggest, by the post 2000 case law which, with the possible exception of *Ella v Ella*,[54] seems to us to have all been correctly decided. Moreover, once it is accepted that the law should have some protective role, and no-one has suggested that prenuptial agreements should be binding regardless of the circumstances, and that therefore such agreements should be enforceable but with significant safeguards, that would merely reflect the current position. In other words, we would question whether reform along such lines is either necessary or desirable. The most we would concede is that there may be an advantage from the point of view of certainty in amending s 25 of the MCA 1973 to make it clear that the making of a prenuptial agreement **is** a factor that should be taken into account when determining the appropriate ancillary relief. [55]

---

51 Interestingly, in his paper *The Financial Consequences of Divorce in England and Wales* delivered at the 13th World Conference of the International Society of Family Law at Vienna in September 2008, Lord Justice Thorpe, in the context of ancillary relief rather than prenuptial agreements, argued for tighter statutory control of the courts' discretion.
52 Principally *White v White* [2001] AC 596.
53 As in *Ella v Ella* [2007] EWCA Civ 99, [2007] 2 FLR 35 and *Crossley v Crossley* [2007] EWCA Civ 1491, [2008] 1 FLR 1467.
54 Above.
55 To save costs, it might also be worth considering altering the rules so that parties have to justify departing from the terms of a prenuptial agreement as a preliminary issue.

Matrimonial Finances in the Context of the Macanese Legal System: General Principles and Issues[1]

Paula Nunes Correia[2]

I. Introduction

Macao, a former Chinese territory under Portuguese administration, is at the present moment, just like Hong Kong, a Special Administrative Region (SAR) of China, ever since the land was handed over to the People's Republic of China (PRC) on December 20, 1999. Being a SAR implies holding a number of significant differences from the regime of Mainland China. In what the Macanese legal system is specifically concerned, it has been subject to a prior reformation in order to adjust the (Portuguese) laws previously in force to the specific needs of the region and its population. This former movement of adaptation of the laws and regulations was initiated some time after the signature of the Joint Declaration, by both the PRC and Portugal, back in April 1987, to be finished by December 1999.

This being said, even though the legal system presently in force in Macao Special Administrative Region (MSAR) continues to be part of the same model of law formerly applicable – that is the Continental European or Civil Law type, as it is strongly and inevitably inspired in its predecessor, to be precise in the Portuguese legal order compelling in the territory until its return to Chinese sovereignty – it simultaneously bears undeniable singularities.

Political and historical reasons mainly have therefore made possible the subsistence of different legal realities in one same country. Accordingly, we may broadly speak of a »*one country* (China), *two*

---

1 Due to understandable publication requirements, this article corresponds to a reduced version of the paper I have actually presented in Vienna, at the ISFL 13th World Conference.
2 Faculty of Law, University of Macau, China.

(political/economic/social...) *systems³*, three legal orders (Mainland China, Hong Kong and Macao)« principle. Article 2 of MSAR Basic Law provides that

»*the National People's Congress authorizes the Macao Special Administrative Region to exercise a high degree of autonomy and enjoy executive, legislative and independent judicial power, including that of final adjudication, in accordance with the provisions of this Law.*«

My main purpose is to introduce you to some general principles and issues regarding family finances, although essentially restricted to the matrimonial relationship, in the context of the Macanese law. Matrimony produces a variety of personal and non-personal, *maxime* financial, effects. My

---

3 The *One Country, Two Systems* Chinese Constitutional principle, was firstly coined by Deng Xiaoping back in January 1982. Later on, in December, *a new Constitution of the PRC was enacted* (Albert Chan, The concept of »one country, two systems« and its application to Hong Kong, in Boletim da Faculdade de Direito, Universidade de Macau, ano VI, n° 13, 2002, page 123). Article 31 of PRC Constitution *contemplates the establishment of special administrative regions of the PRC, which may practice social systems different from other parts of China* (ibidem, page 123). The Sino-Portuguese Joint Declaration, signed in 1987, regulated the implementation of the principle to the future Special Administrative Region of Macao. Moreover, this principle has been conceived to, somehow, mitigate the effects of a sudden reintegration of the former colonies into China, being applicable for fifty years. As a matter of fact, article 5 of MSAR Basic Law (in force since December 20, 1999) provides that *the socialist system and policies shall not be practiced in the Macao Special Administrative Region, and the previous capitalist system and way of life shall remain unchanged for 50 years*. Other references: Albert Chan, article cited, pages 121 to 139; Francisco Gonçalves Pereira, O processo negocial da Declaração Conjunta – Uma abordagem preliminar, in Boletim da Faculdade de Direito, Universidade de Macau, ano V, n° 11, 2001, pages 63 to 88; Francisco Gonçalves Pereira, A Constituição Chinesa, a Lei Básica, a autonomia de Macau, in Boletim da Faculdade de Direito, Universidade de Macau, ano V, n° 11, 2001, pages 175 to 183; Ieong Van Chong, A Lei Básica da RAEM e a concretização do princípio »um país, dois sistemas«, in Boletim da Faculdade de Direito, Universidade de Macau, ano V, n° 12, 2001, pages 95 to 107; Liu Gaolong, The Legal Status of Macau Special Administrative Region, in Boletim da Faculdade de Direito, Universidade de Macau, ano V, n° 11, 2001, pages 97 to 105; Liu Gaolong, Definição do regime »um país, dois sistemas« na Lei Básica de Macau, in Boletim da Faculdade de Direito, Universidade de Macau, ano VI, n° 13, 2002, pages 141 to 155; Paula Nunes Correia, The Evolution of Matrimony in Macao (China): an Overview, in Pravni Život – Legal Life, Journal for Legal Theory and Practice of The Jurists Association of Serbia, nº 10, volume II, Belgrade, Serbia, 2006, pages 71 to 88; Paulo Cardinal, A questão da continuidade dos instrumentos de Direito Internacional aplicáveis a Macau, in Boletim da Faculdade de Direito, Universidade de Macau, ano V, n° 11, 2001, pages 93 to 96; Pedro Ferreira, Os limites de Macau no contexto da Região Administrativa Especial da República Popular da China após 1999, in Boletim da Faculdade de Direito, Universidade de Macau, ano V, n° 12, 2001, pages 109 to 119.

attention will logically concentrate on the latter. For such purpose I shall start with the reciprocal marital duties emerging from marriage. In spite of being generally classified as personal effects of matrimony, they present different features, as some of these obligations ought to be considered mainly moral, and others have a mixed, or even a clear economic expression. In what the patrimonial effects of marriage are concerned, I shall accordingly follow with a brief presentation on general principles governing the administration of the couple's assets, as well as on those regulating the spouses' debts – for which they can either be jointly or exclusively liable, depending on the type of debt incurred – being both important effects independent from the assets regime. A notice on general principles about matrimonial conventions – both ante-nuptial and post-nuptial conventions – as well as on assets regimes will, naturally, follow. With regard to the matrimonial assets regimes, a reference will be made to the supplementary regime, or participation in acquests regime, as well as to the remaining legally typified regimes: communion in acquests, general partnership and separation regime[4]. Before concluding, I still propose to briefly refer to the spouses' freedom of making a legally valid Will.

II. Matrimonial Finances in the Context of the Macanese Legal System – General Principles and Issues[5]

For a reference, the essential substantive regulation of the following matters is contained in the Civil Code of Macao (MCC), to be more precise in

---

4 In spite of being substantial matters whenever you talk about matrimonial finances, I take the liberty of skipping both subjects – matrimonial conventions and assets regimes – in the present publication, taking into consideration the restrictions mentioned in the first footnote, as well as the fact that those issues have also been part of my presentation at the ISFL 12th World Conference. Therefore, for such matters please refer to *Paula Nunes Correia, New Family Law issues in Macao's return to Chinese Sovereignty*, in *Family Law: Balancing Interests and Pursuing Priorities*, edited by *Lynn D. Wardle & Camille S. Williams*, published by *William S. Hein & Co.* of Buffalo, New York, USA, 2007, pages 44 and 45.

5 Main references: *Francisco Pereira Coelho e Guilherme de Oliveira, Curso de Direito de Família*, volume I, *Introdução, Direito Matrimonial*, 3ª edição, Coimbra Editora, 2003; *Manuel M. E. Trigo, Lições Preliminares de Direito da Família e das Sucessões, (segundo as aulas ao 4°ano do Curso de Direito em Língua Portuguesa no ano lectivo de 1999-2000)*, Faculdade de Direito, Universidade de Macau; *Pires de Lima e Antunes Varela, Código Civil Anotado*, volume IV, 2ª edição revista e actualizada, Coimbra Editora, Limitada, 1992.

its fourth book[6], compelling in the territory just before its return to Chinese sovereignty.[7]

1. Patrimonial Duties Issued from Matrimony

Two fundamental principles govern the effects of matrimony in general: equality concerning the spouses' rights and duties and shared leadership of the family, about which husband and wife must agree on the orientation of life in common, having in consideration the family wellbeing, as well as each other's interests (article 1532, paragraphs 1 and 2 of MCC[8]).

In addition, I would like to inform at once that matrimony is necessarily a heterosexual relationship (article 1462), being homosexual marriage not even considered a non-valid matrimony, but rather juridically non-existent [article 1501, paragraph e)].

In what the spouses' obligations are concerned, there are five marital duties born with marriage, imposing reciprocal obligations on them: respect, fidelity, cohabitation, cooperation and assistance (article 1533 and subsequent). The duties of respect, fidelity and cooperation are mainly moral, while the duties of cohabitation and assistance have more material characteristics[9]. Therefore, I shall mainly focus my attention on the latter. Nonetheless, I shall still dedicate a few words to the former.

Respect is a *residual duty*[10], in the sense that a violation of any of the other four marital duties is also a breach of the duty of respect. As a result, only non-direct violations of the former rights may be considered as an infringement of the latter. This duty involves a duty of respect towards each other's personality, both as a human and a married person, namely preventing offenses to one's physical and moral integrity, honor, image or sensibility (being at once a negative and a positive duty)[11].

---

6   As the Macanese Civil Code follows, just like the Portuguese Civil Code, the *Savigny* plan.
7   The new Civil Code of Macao, approved by the Decree-Law 39/99/M, August 3, is in vigor in the territory since November 1, 1999 (in the terms of article 1 of the Decree-Law 48/99/M, September 27).
8   From now on, if not indicated otherwise, all articles belong to MCC.
9   To avoid possible misunderstandings, I should perhaps clarify that these duties of cooperation and assistance correspond to the *devoirs de assistance et de secours*, respectively, namely of the French Civil Law.
10 *Francisco Pereira Coelho e Guilherme de Oliveira, op. cit.*, page 389. (Translated citation).
11 Offenses to the children or to the in laws, for instance, may also be a violation of the duty of respect.

Fidelity means at once the (negative) duty to keep sexual relations exclusively between spouses, to refrain from intentionally having consummated heterosexual relations with a third person, i.e., adultery. However, infidelity is not synonym for adultery: homosexual relations (normally not regarded as adultery) and relations with a third person that may legitimately make the other spouse or the public suspect the existence of adultery may be as well considered breach of fidelity.

Cooperation is also and mainly a moral duty. Law cannot oblige spouses to love each other, but it does impose on them a duty of mutual help and support, as well as a duty to assume together the responsibilities inherent to the family life that they have founded (article 1535). Spouses have the duty to mutually support each other, in the good and bad moments (first aspect), as well as the obligation to assume together the responsibilities inherent to the family life that they have both established as, for instance, the interest in their children's health and education (second aspect).

Cohabitation[12] means the duty to live with each other, sharing house and having economy in common, involving as well the duty to have sexual relations with each other (*debitum conjugale*). This whole duty means the traditionally called communion of bed, table and lodging altogether (*tori, mensae et habitationis*). The place where spouses live jointly is their **family residence**, which must be chosen with the agreement of both, taking into consideration the necessities of their professional lives and the children's interests, as well as the protection of the unity of life in family. In case of disagreement, the court will determine or modify (depending on the case) the family residence, at the request of any of the spouses (article 1534). I shall naturally concentrate on the two aspects of the concerned duty of cohabitation that may be of economic relevance: communion of table or life in common economy, and communion of housing.

Spouses are reciprocally obliged to share a life in common economy (spending and saving for their common benefit), as the family they have founded is a common project for which they are equally (morally/financially) responsible. They are namely obliged to share their duties for living a life in common, under one same roof and at one same table.

---

12   The duty of cohabitation has some exceptions. It's, for instance, the case when one spouse is in prison or sick in hospital. Cohabitation is suspended during the divorce procedure (article 1631, paragraph 4), and in case the lack of cohabitation is proven any of the spouses may ask for the effects of divorce to be retroactive to the day where cohabitation ceased due to the other spouse's exclusive and predominant fault (article 1644, paragraph 2).

With regard to the aspect of being obliged to share one same lodging, to share one residence in common, the concept of family residence is vital, assuming a particular importance at the moment when the unity of life in family is threatened by the dissolution of matrimony. Actually, family residence is especially protected not only in a divorce situation (imminent, pending or already declared), but also in case of death.

One of the requirements for a divorce by mutual consent consists in the spouses' agreement on the destination of the family residence [besides the agreements on alimony to the spouse in need and on parental authority over minor children, being the case – article 1630, paragraph 2 of MCC and article 1242 of the Code of Civil Procedure (MCPC)] which will be effective from the moment the judge or the registrar proclaim the divorce. The agreement on the utilization of the family residence is also required for the time the divorce procedure is pending (article 1630, paragraph 3). This agreement on the destination of the family residence (namely the right to occupy, to live or reside in it) is mandatory.

In a divorce by litigation, the court can allocate the family residence to any of the spouses (disregard his/her eventual fault), at his/her request, despite the fact of being a common asset or an asset exclusively belonging to the other spouse, taking into consideration the necessities of each of the spouses, the interest of the children and any other reasons that the court intends to attend. The allocation decided by the court is done by means of a tenancy agreement (either imposed on the other spouse, or even on a third party), although subject to a special regime (article 1648, paragraphs 1 and 2, article 1042, paragraphs 2 to 4 of MCC and article 1249 of MCPC).

Finally, in case of dissolution of marriage by death, there is also a special protection of the right to inhabit the family residence by means of a preferential allocation of such right to the widow/widower (article 1942).

At last, the **duty of assistance** comprehends the obligation to contribute for the charges with family life according to each other's possibilities, as well as the obligation to pay for alimony (articles 1536, 1537 and 1856). However, this second aspect only becomes relevant in case a separation occurs. Having Macao's legislator abolished the separation from bed and board or legal separation, this (marital) duty to pay for alimony practically stands now for when a *de facto* separation (separation of spouses) occurs (articles 1856 and 1536, paragraph 2), making no sense, as far as I am concerned, to speak of a duty to contribute for the expenses with family life in such a context, as there is no family life, or communion of life between spouses if they are separated. Differently, while the spouses live together, I would say that the duty to pay for alimony is, in some way, absorbed by the obligation to supply for the charges with family life, having no autonomy vis-à-vis the latter.

With regard to the obligation to pay for **alimony**, the duty lasts for the time the *de facto* separation endures, if the separation is not imputable to any of the spouses, or is equally imputable to both of them (article 1536, paragraph 2). In case the separation is imputable to one, or to both spouses, this obligation, in favor of the other spouse, only stands, in principle, for the spouse considered mainly, or solely at fault. However, under exceptional circumstances and for equity reasons, the court may impose such duty on the innocent, or the least at fault spouse, taking into consideration, particularly, the duration of marriage and the cooperation that the other spouse has rendered to the couple's economy (same article, paragraph 3). This obligation, in what the amount of alimony is concerned, follows the general principles applying to alimony, that is, it depends on the necessities of the creditor and on the possibilities of the debtor. But doubts may arise when it comes to define the necessities of the creditor under such circumstances: should they be restricted to sustenance, lodging and clothing, or should it be granted the same economic and social level that she/he had before the separation occurred (according to the debtor's possibilities, of course)?

With reference to the **obligation to contribute for the charges with family life**, both spouses are obliged, according to each one's possibilities. This duty can be fulfilled by any of the spouses by means of affecting his/her resources to those charges and by the work used up at home or in maintaining and educating the children (article 1537, paragraph 1). This being said, each spouse may fulfill his/her obligation either by means of affecting his/her resources to the charges with family life, or by means of doing the house work, or maintaining and educating the children, or still by doing both, depending on the agreement they have made about the orientation of life in common (*supra*). In case of violation, any of the spouses can demand to directly receive part of the other spouse's income or profits to be determined by the court (same article, paragraph 3).

2. *Administration of the Couple's Assets*

The general principles governing the administration of the couple's assets are as follows: **each spouse has the administration of his/her personal assets** (article 1543, paragraph 1); the two of them, together, have the **joint**

administration of their common assets (article 1543, paragraph 3, 2nd part).

These are imperative rules, which cannot be modified by the spouses by celebrating a matrimonial convention [neither a pre-nuptial, nor a post-nuptial convention – articles 1569, paragraph 1, subparagraph c) and 1578, paragraph 3].

Nonetheless, each of the above mentioned rules has some **exceptions**. Therefore, regarding the first one – each spouse has the administration of his/her personal assets – each of the spouses still has the administration: of the chattels, exclusively belonging to the other spouse, solely used by the former as a work instrument, that is, with which the administrator has a special link [article 1543, paragraph 2, subparagraph e)]; of the other spouse's personal assets, in case of absence or impediment of the latter, that is, if the other spouse is not capable of performing his/her administration for being in a remote or an unknown place, or for any other reason, as long as he/she has not voluntarily and legally empowered a representative to administrate those assets [same article and paragraph, subparagraph f)]; of the other spouse's personal assets if the latter has conferred such powers by means of a mandate [which terms are generally provided in article 1083 and subsequent – article 1543, paragraph 2, subparagraph g)].

Moreover, now regarding the second mentioned rule – according to which both spouses, together, have the joint administration of their common assets – each of the spouses still has the administration: of the chattels, held in common, solely used by the former as a work instrument, that is, with which the spouse administrator has a special link [article 1543, paragraph 2, subparagraph e)]; of the common assets, in case of absence or impediment of the other spouse, that is, if the latter is not capable of performing his/her administration for being in a remote or an unknown place, or for any other reason, as long as he/she has not voluntarily and legally empowered a representative to administrate those assets [same article and paragraph, subparagraph f)]; of the common assets, if the other spouse has conferred such powers of administration by means of a mandate [same article and paragraph, subparagraph g)]; of the incomes received for his/her work[13] [same article and paragraph, subparagraph a)]; of his/her author rights[14] [same article and paragraph, subparagraph b)]; of the common assets brought by him/her into marriage, or acquired for

---

13   In spite of being qualified as a common asset, according to the relevant assets regime.
14   Pls. refer to the previous note.

free after matrimony, as well as of the assets in replacement of the former [same article and paragraph, subparagraph c)]; of the assets that have been donated or left to both spouses excluding the other spouse from its administration, except when the assets have been donated or left in view of the legitime or legal portion of the other spouse [same article and paragraph, subparagraph d)]; finally, each of the spouses also has the legitimacy to practice acts of ordinary administration[15] regarding the assets held in common by the couple (article 1543, paragraph 3, 1st part).

3. Spouses' Debts

Both, **husband and wife, may** legitimately **incur debts without each other's consent** (article 1557, paragraph 1). For the effect of determining the spouses' responsibility (*infra*), the date in which the debts were incurred coincides with that of the fact which has originated them (same article, paragraph 2).

Spouses are **jointly responsible** for the following **debts** (article 1558, paragraph 1): the ones incurred by the two of them, or just by one of the spouses with the other's consent, before or after the wedding and irrespective of the assets regime applicable [same article and paragraph, subparagraph a)]; the debts incurred, by any of them, to pay for the normal charges of family life (implying small debts, like food, clothing, medical fees, and so on, occurring ordinarily or periodically[16]), before or after the wedding and despite the relevant assets regime [same article and paragraph, subparagraph b)]; the ones incurred during matrimony, by the spouse administrator and within the limits of his/her powers of administration (*supra*), for the couple's common (economic or moral) profit (which is not, in principle, presumable – same article, paragraph 3 –, being assessed by the spouse's objective purpose when he/she incurred the debt, and not by the outcome[17]) [same article and paragraph, subparagraph c)]; the debts incurred, by any of the spouses, within the practice of commerce, unless it is proven that they were not made for the couple's common profit, or if either the separation of assets regime, or the participation in acquests regime are in force [same article and paragraph, subparagraph d)]; the

---

15 These acts, unlike the denominated acts of disposition, do not affect the substance of the assets, but are mainly practiced to maintain or preserve the administrated patrimony. Pls. refer to *Carlos Alberto da Mota Pinto, Teoria Geral do Direito Civil*, 3ª edição actualizada, Coimbra Editora, 1996, pages 406 to 411.
16 *Francisco Pereira Coelho e Guilherme de Oliveira, op. cit.*, page 449.
17 *Francisco Pereira Coelho e Guilherme de Oliveira, op. cit.*, pages 451 and 452.

debts impeding donations, inheritances or legacies if, according to the relevant assets regime, the donated or inherited assets become common patrimony [same article and paragraph, subparagraph e) and article 1560, paragraph 2]; the debts incurred before the wedding, by any of the spouses, for the couple's common profit, whenever the general communion assets regime is in force (as, for instance, the wedding party costs), (article 1558, paragraph 2); the debts encumbering common assets, even if their payment is due before the wedding (article 1561, paragraph 1); the debts that encumber personal assets if they are caused by the receipt of the relevant profits and these are considered common according to the assets regime applicable (article 1561, paragraph 2).

Regarding these **debts of joint responsibility**, the following **assets are concerned** (article 1562): under the participation in acquests assets regime, the spouses' personal assets respond conjointly and, whenever the assets of one of the spouses are lacking or insufficient, the assets of the other spouse respond subsidiary [paragraph a)]; under the separation of assets regime, the spouses' personal assets respond conjointly [paragraph b)]; under any of the communion of assets regimes (either general communion, or communion of acquests), the couple's common assets respond for the debts and, whenever these assets are lacking or non-sufficient, the personal assets of any of the spouses respond in solidarity [paragraph c)].

Each spouse is **exclusively responsible** for the following **debts** (article 1559): the ones incurred, by each of the spouses, without the other spouse's consent, before or after the wedding, unless they were incurred to pay for the normal charges of family life, or by the spouse administrator for the couple's common profit and within the limits of his/her administration powers [*supra* – paragraph a)]; those originated in crimes or other facts imputable to one of the spouses, such as indemnifications, sanctions, restitutions, judicial fees or fines, unless those facts, implying simply civil liability, fall under the joint responsibility of both spouses [*supra* – paragraph b)]; the debts that encumber personal assets of one of the spouses, unless they are caused by the receipt of the respective profits and these are regarded as common according to the assets regime applicable [paragraph c) and article 1561, paragraph 2 – *supra*]; the ones encumbering donations, inheritances or legacies, provided that the relevant assets belong exclusively to one of the spouses (article 1560, paragraph 1).

With regard to the **debts of exclusive responsibility** of one of the spouses, the following **rules** are in force: the personal assets of the debtor spouse respond for such debts as well as, being applicable any of the communion of assets regimes, his/her share in the common assets, subsidiary (article 1564, paragraph 1); however, the debtor spouse's work income and his/her author's rights (despite their possible qualification as common assets according to the relevant assets regime) respond simultaneously with his/her personal assets (same article, paragraph 2).

4. Freedom of Testation vs. Legitimate or Forced Heirs: Brief Notice

In what this last subject is concerned, the Macanese legal solutions are not diverse from the ones applicable in many other legal orders, being based on two different ideas: on one hand, the one originated in the Germanic law, according to which the patrimony belonged to the family, being the *paterfamilias* a mere administrator of the assets; on the other hand, the one coming from the Roman law, according to which the patrimony was individually owned, namely implying for the *de cujus* an unlimited freedom of making a testament. However, these two attitudes have developed in a converging sense: the freedom of testation has been, to a certain extent, exceptionally admitted in the former situation; the *officium pietatis* has, somehow, exceptionally restricted the testator's freedom in the latter circumstance[18].

Who are the **legitimate or forced heirs**, to begin with? The answer is: the **spouse**, the **descendants** and the **ascendants**. The spouse and the descendants belong to the 1st class of successors, while the spouse and the ascendants belong to the 2nd class of successors, with a preference for the heirs belonging to the former class. In each class the closest relatives have preference to the ones positioned in a more distanced degree. In principle, the successors in each class succeed in equal shares (articles 1995, 1973, 1974, 1975 and 1976).

The **fraction** of the **patrimony held in reserve** for the legitimate or forced heirs **varies** from a **minimum** of ¼ to a **maximum** of ½, depending on different possible combinations of these heirs as follows. Whenever there are neither descendants, nor ascendants, the spouse alone is entitled to ⅓ of the inheritance (article 1996). The spouse and the children together are entitled to ½ of the inheritance. If there is no surviving spouse, the children are entitled to either ⅓ or ½ of the inheritance, depending on whether there is only one child or two or more children (article 1997). The descendants of the 2nd degree and subsequent (i.e., grandchildren, great-

---

18   Carlos Alberto da Mota Pinto, op. cit., pages 155 to 159.

grandchildren and so on) are entitled to the portion which was reserved for his/her ascendant (who could not, or did not want to accept the inheritance), according to the same general principles above mentioned (article 1998). Finally, the spouse and the ascendants together are also entitled to ½ of the inheritance. However, if there is neither surviving spouse, nor descendants, the ascendants alone are entitled to either ⅓ or ¼ of the inheritance, depending on whether we are referring to the parents, or rather to the ascendants of the 2nd degree and subsequent (i.e. grandparents, great-grandparents, and so on – article 1999).

III. Conclusion

One of the very first notions that we learn about the qualification of family law is that of an institutional law – in the sense that the lawmaker extracts it from the family where it lives and is continuously being produced – along with a particular sensitivity to any change in the environment, that is very prone to develop modifications, namely in accordance with the social, economic, political or even religious progress.

Therefore, in this particular legal field, the debate and interchange of different points of view is estimated to be indispensable for a sane evolution of the subject. At this point, I cannot but express my deepest gratitude to the remarkable effort incessantly and generously developed by the International Society of Family Law, from which everyone may learn and profit, simultaneously implying a significant and definite achievement for humanity as well.

L'Entreprise Familiale dans le Régime Matrimonial Légal Espagnol

Gabriel García Cantero[1]

I. Les Aspects Commerciaux d'après la Réforme Introduite par la Loi de 13 Mai 1981 dans le Régime Matrimoniale Legal en Espagne

L'Espagne, ainsi que la France, l'Allemagne ou l'Autriche et à la différence de l'Italie (C.c. 1942) et du Pays Bas (C.c. 1992), restent-ils encore dans le groupe des pays oú il y a deux Codes pour régler la matière privée (Code civil et Code commerce, Código civil et Código de comercio, B.G.B. et H.G.B.), et de ce fait il s'en suit que leur régime matrimoniale légal garde, de règle, le silence à propos des aspects commerciaux des rapports économiques crées parmi les conjoints pendant la durée du régime, et, notamment, à propos de ce qu'on appelle, en général, *l'entreprise familiale*. Mais en Espagne et après la réforme de 1981 promulguée à la suite de la Constitution de 1978, cette manque de communication parmi ces domaines a pris fin, et en conséquence on trouve dans la loi civile des concrètes références à des institutions commerciales. Laissant de cotê les Droits foraux (c.à.d. les droits civils speciaux en vigueur dans certaines régions), on trouve à ce propos dans le Code civil espagnol deux règles à portée générale; selon l'art 1383:

»*Les conjoints ont le devoir de s'informer réciproquement et périodiquement sur la situation et sur les revenus obtenus dans toute activité économique developpée par chacun d'eux.*«

Cette norme se trouve en rapport avec l'art. 1393-4º qui octroi à chaque conjoint la faculté de demander l'extinction judiciaire du régime légal dans le cas d'inaccomplissement grave et réiteré de ce devoir d'informer l'autre sur les activités économiques qu'il a maintenu pendant que celui-ci a été en vigueur. D'accord à l'art. 1347 núm. 5:

La loi civil qualifie des biens communs (bienes gananciales) *les entreprises crées, pendant la durée du régime légal, par l'un ou*

---

[1] Catedrático de Droit Civil, Émérite de l'Université de Zaragoza, Spain.

l'autre des conjoints moyennant des biens communs. D'autres articles y se rapportent: ainsi l'art. 1362, núm. 4º (qui atribue caractère commun aux frais d'exploitation de cette entreprise familiale); et l'art. 1366 (à propos de la responsabilité des biens communs par l'activité économique d'un conjoint même si celle-là a donné lieu à de responsabilité extracontractuelle).

Plus d'un quart de siècle aprés l'introduction de ces nouveautés légales, l'interpretation de ces articles c'est pas pacifique, même si le Décret-Royale 17/2007, de 9 fèvrier, a réglé pour la prémiere fois la publicité du *protocole familiale*[2], une institution que la pratique avait introduit récemment en Espagne et que la bibliographie sur l'entreprise familiale s'avait enrichie entretemps.

II. Analyse du Devoir Réciproque et Périodique qui Tombe sur les Conjoints à l'Égard de l'Information à propos de leurs Activités Économiques

L'art. 1383 n'avait pas d'antécédent en Espagne dans le régime légal anterieur et cela explique que les prémiers commentateurs de la réforme on essayé d'inscrire ce devoir de renseignement dans le cadre clasique de la communauté limitée des biens existante parmi les conjoints soumis au régime légal. La *sociedad de gananciales* – selon la terminologie traditionnelle de ce régime en droit espagnol – suppose la possible existence jusqu'à de trois patrimoines: à savoir, le patrimoine commun et le propre à chaque conjoint. De ce fait il est possible que leurs titulaires de l'un ou l'autre puissent developper, simultanément à l'existence de la commu-

---

2 Cette institution a été introduite en France par GAULTIER, »Les ›holdings‹ familiales. Perennité et sucession«, 2eme. ed. (Paris 1988), et developpée par NABASQUE-BOUSSIER-RICHEN, La transmission de l'entreprise familiale (Paris 1992). Son but ne serait-il pas de résoudre les problèmes qui pose l'entreprise familiale, mais plutôt de les écarter surtout au moment de la mort du fondateur. En conséquence il offre un caractère interdisciplinaire (civil, commercial, fiscal etc). Dans certains pays la prohibition des pactes succesoraux oblige à donner au protocole familial la valeur juridique d'un engagement d'honneur (ou »gentleman agreement«). On cherche par son moyen de maintenir la cohésion et l'harmonie familiale, la transmission de ce qu'on appelle la »culture de l'entreprise«, ainsi que de compatibiliser les interêts familiaux et commerciaux surtout au moment de la trnsmission »mortis causa« de l'entreprise en facilitant sa gestion (Voyez FERNÁNDEZ GIMENO et Mª José REYES LÓPEZ, »La empresa familiar« (Valencia 2000), p.204 et suivantes).

nauté, des activités économiques indépendantes, et en principe séparés et autonomes. Mais cette indépendance ne pourra pas être totale: en éffet, les bénefices obtenus par l'entreprise appartenant à un seule conjoint et gerée par lui-même deviennent aussi des biens communs, et possedent également la même nature les frais d'exploitation de celle-là selon la loi, et pourtant ils sont à la charge des biens communs. Dans ces cas, on peut s'interroger: comment serait-il possible que les circonstances telles que la réussite économique ou la faillite de l'entreprise privative d'un époux deviennent ignorés par l'autre conjoint? ou quand même, comment la bonne ou la mauvaise réussite des affaires de l'un des conjoints pourriaient rester cachés à l'autre? Pour expliquer cette situation on parle d'une communauté d'interêts parmi les conjoints mariés sous le régime de *gananciales;* mais c'est claire qu'on ne peut pas traiter-les ceux-ci comme s'ils seraient vraiment des membres d'une société.

On a soutenu d'abord que ce devoir d'information ne signifie pas d'autre chose, dans la pratique, que faire part en général de la situation de la marche des affaires respectives, et non plus d'une communication minitueusse et détaillée des bilans, inventaires et aussi de la situation de chaque concrète opération économique en cours; et, d'autre part que ce devoir exige implicitement une demande d'information préalable d'un conjoint laquelle avait été déniée formellement par l'autre, comme la condition pour mettre en fonctionnement le système et la procédure des sanctions juridiques[3]. Sans oublier pourtant les éffets du devoir de garder le sécret dans les affaires tombant sur l'un ou l'autre; ainsi il y aura un motif pour refuser l'information si du fait de transmettre à l'autre les renseignements de nature économique se dérive un danger pour l'informant, pour un tiers ou même pour la société légale[4].

Les renseignements devront en être fournis *périodiquement*, mais on n'indique pas dans la loi la périodicité exigée; il semble raisonnable qu'il y aura, au moins, un *minimum* legal de sorte, par exemple, qu'à la fin de l'année économique, chaque époux devra informer l'autre de la marche de ses affaires; mais en somme, tout cela en dépend des circonstances. D'autre part, l'extinction définitive du régime patrimonial des conjoints semble une sanction legale trop sévère pour l'inaccomplissement de ce devoir; il semble aussi que le conjoint tenu au marge des activités écono-

---

3 Ainsi DE LOS MOZOS, »Comentarios del Código civil«, dirigés par Albaladejo, t. XVIII, vol. 2º, deuxième éd. [Madrid 1984], pág. 383.
4 Selon l'avis de PRETEL SERRANO, »Comentario del Código civil del Ministerio de Justicia« [Madrid 1991] II, pág. 737.

miques de l'autre pourra l'exiger en nature, par le moyen des astreintes introduites en droit espagnol par la nouvelle Loi de Procédure civile de 2000, ainsi qu'il pourra donner lieu aussi à des dommages interêts.

En résumée: il faut reconnaître que la réforme de 1981 sur le régime matrimonial légal a élargie, en général, le domain juridique de la communauté d'interêts économiques existant parmi les conjoints pour atteindre le terrain où, jusqu'à présent, il semblait prévaloir l'interêt individuel. En conséquénce, l'autonomie absolue et sans restrictions de chaque conjoint pour gérer ses affaires, et en vertu de ce devoir, vient d'être limitée dans l'interêt de la famille; en principe, donc, chaque conjoint a droit d'être informé et de connaître en général les résultats de l'activité économique réservée de l'autre. À mon avis l'art. 1383 devra être interpreté dans un sens raisonnablement large, de sorte que l'information devra tomber aussi sur les résultats d'une activité profesionnelle quelconque (laquelle a de règle un caractère privatif d'accord à l'art. 1346 nº 8), et même sur les bénéfices obtenus sporadiquement par exemple, à la Bourse, ou finalement d'un prix importante gagné au Lotto.

III. Le Statut de l'Entreprise Familiale Crée ou Fondée par un Conjoint pendant le Mariage et Moyennant des Biens Communs

1. La liberté de commerce, des gens mariées

Avant la Loi de 1981 les conjoints soumis au régime légale étaient admis à l'exércice du commerce d'accord aux arts. 6 à 10 du Code commerce 1885, promulgué à l'époque oú la femme devrait obtenir civilement la licence de son mari pour contracter en général; ces articles essaiaient de faciliter l'exércice du commerce par la femme mariée en établissant une présomption de consentement du mari quand la femme l'exérçait avant de se marier et continuait à le faire après son mariage sans l'opposition de son mari; ces règles determinent aussi le patrimoine qui devrait répondre finalement des dettes resultant de ces activités. En tout cas il faut rémarquer que ce régime commercial n'est pas d'accord ni au principe constitutionnel d'égalité des conjoints, ni au régime établi par la Loi de 1981, malgré qu'ils restent formellement en vigueur[5].

---

5 Pour FERNÁNDEZ GIMENO et Mª José REYES LÓPEZ, op. cit. pag. 49 et suivantes, cette double régulation ne constitue pas qu'une source des problèmes et ne répond qu'a des reliques historiques très eloignées des besoins actuelles.

D'autre part, c'est claire aussi que les conjoints, pendant le mariage, ils pourront s'integrer et rentrer, à titre personnel, dans toute clase des sociétés civils et commerciales sans que, pour autant, ces sociétes deviennent des *entreprises familiales* au sens propre. Il s'appliquera, cas per cas, le régime géneral de chaque société et simultanément celui de la société de *gananciales*, quant, par exemple à la nature juridique des titres des actions ou des participations appartenant aux conjoints (art. 1352 Cc).

2. L'Entreprise Familiale Prevue à l'Art. 1347, nº 5 du Code Civil

La nouveauté qui répresent l'art. 1347 núm, 5, c'est la fondation ou création d'une entreprise qualifiée de *familiale*, par un conjoint à l'aide du capital commun et normalement comme résultat du travail personnel de celui-ci. Il s'agit d'une conséquence d'appliquer les cas numeros 1º et 2º de l'art. 1347, parce qu'on atribue la nature des biens commun aux produits du travail de chacun et aux revenus des biens privatifs ou des biens communs.

La doctrine accepte les cas suivants:

1. La fondation d'une entreprise familiale par l'un ou l'autre conjoint pendant le mariage et avec des biens qualifiés de communs à l'époque; on pourrait dire que ça serait le cas le plus simple, voire le plus fréquent.
2. La fondation conjointe de l'entreprise familiale par tous les deux conjoints ensemble et au même moment, réalisée aussi moyennant des biens communs;
3. L'adhesion succesive d'un conjoint à l'entreprise familiale crée par l'autre pendant le mariage; et,
4. Le cas spécial de l'entreprise privative crée avant ou après le mariage, avec des biens privés et à laquelle il s'adhère l'autre conjoint avec du capital commun.

Dans les trois premiers cas il y a toujours le travail personnel et le capital commun employé, et pour le num. 4, l'art. 1354 déclare l'existence d'une communauté romaine des biens en proportion aux biens – privés ou communs – apportés.

3. Les Traits Caracteristiques de l'Entreprise Familiale au Sens Stricte

La doctrine souligne que la loi emploi des mots tels que *entreprise* ou *établissement* que le Code civil ne définit pas; ce sont des termes pris du langage courante et pas téchnique, et on accepte que tous les deux font référence à la notion d'*empresa mercantil*, employé au sens objectif, c.à.d. une universalité de fait composée par des biens meubles, immeubles, ou d'autres en vue d'obtenir benefices par son titulaire, et auquelle la loi traite de façon unitaire.

En principe, il semble qu'il serait indifférant la forme juridique adoptée pour établir cette entreprise familiale (par ex. entrepreneur isolé, société civil, ou société irrégulière); la doctrine civiliste et la jurisprudence ont de resèrves pour accepter que ce precepte soit-il applicable aux sociétés commerciaux de capitaux (anonyme ou de responsabilité limitée)[6]. Si le capital apporté a une nature juridique, en partie commun et en partie privée, la loi dispose la création d'une communauté des biens dont le caractère privatif et commun restera en proportion au capital apporté de chaque cotê, (ce qui, le cas écheant, exigera des calculs minutieux).

4. L'Entreprise Familial au Sens Large
Au sens estricte il n'y a d'autres cas d'entreprises »familiales« que les ceux-ci énumérés. Mais au sens large on peut considèrer aussi les cas d'entreprises où ils rentrent d'autres membres de la famille en dehors du conjoints, en apportant, soit son travail, soit l'argent, soit tous les deux (par ex. les enfants, même d'un seule des conjoints), ou des membres de la famille de l'un ou de l'autre conjoint (parents, frères ou soeurs, oncles tantes, neveux, petits enfants etc). Mais ces cas ne sont pas contemplés spécifiquement par le Code civil.

5. Regime Juridique de l'Entreprise Familiale au Sens Stricte dans le C.C
À mon avis, le sens de l'art. 1347 numero 5, signifie que cette entreprise creé et fondée par l'un ou l'autre des époux, ou même par tous les deux ensemble, font partie dorénavant du patrimoine commun selon le régime légale et aussi que les benefices obtenus d'elle sont aussi com-

---

6 À ce propos on invoque l'arrêt de la Chambre Civil de la Cour de Cassation de 18 septembre 1999 qui refuse le cas de création des sociétés avec personnalité juridique différente de celle des associés. Dans ce sens MARTÍNEZ DE AGUIRRE, op. cit. pág. 234. À mon avis on pourra inclure dans l'art. 1347-5º C.c. pas seulement le cas des sociétés civiles irrégulieres, mais aussi les sociétés civiles constitués d'accord au Code civil ainsi que les sociétés commerciaux à caractère personnel (L'arrêt de la même Chambre de 30 avril 2001, refuse aussi la création d'une société anonyme comme entreprise familiale). En conséquence, je considère trop stricte l'opinion exprimée par FERNÁNDEZ GIMENO et Mª José REYES LÓPEZ. op. cit. pg. 38 quand ils soulignent que le regime de l'art. 1347-5ª C.c. s'applique seulement » à toute entreprise qui n'est pas organisée en forme societaire«.

muns, et qu'à la fin du régime tous ces biens rentreront dans le partage. C'est possible, mais il s'avere plutôt rare dans la réalité, que chaque conjoint ait fondé de sa part une entreprise familiale différente et autonome (par exemple, le mari a crée une entreprise agricole et sa femme une autre entreprise d'hôtellerie); dans ce cas il y aura deux patrimoines séparés, tous les deux de nature commune, et dont les bénefices vont aider conjointement de règle à l'économie de la famille[7].

Le régime de cette entreprise familiale au sens estricte pourra en devenir complèxe pendant le mariage. Un cas emblematique il pourrait se présenter quand y travaillent en exclusivité tous les deux époux de sorte que tous les resources de la famille proviennent des benéfices de cette entreprise vraiment *familiale*. Il y a deux questions à considérer: d'un côté, et pendant que l'entreprise se trouve en formation, il est à conseiller que leurs benefices y soient, en tout ou en partie, investis; mais d'autre part, le maintien de la famille devra se faire préférenment avec les bénéfices de l'entreprise familiale. Par la suite, le niveau de vie de la famille va rester probablement lié à la situation financière de celle-là. En Espagne, la nouvelle Loi de 2003 sur la faillite (que la loi appelle *concurso*), en unifiant tous les procédures d'exécution universelle, permet que l'entreprise individuelle familiale y puisse être soumise. En fait cette Loi s'oriente, en cas de faillite, vers l'obtention des accords avec les créditeurs en vue de sauver, à mésure du possible, la vie de l'entreprise en danger.

L'art. 1362-4ª met à la charge de la *sociedad de gananciales*, *les frais de l'exploitation régulière des affaires ou de l'exercice d'une profession de la part de chaque conjoint*. C'est une règle logique parce que l'art. 1347 numero 2, attribue un caractère commun à tous les benefices obtenus soit des biens privatifs soit de biens communs; ce qui ratifie aussi l'art. 1381. *Ubi emolumenta ibi onus.*

En tout cas, et étant donné que chaque conjoint gère indépendamment sa propre entreprise (celle-ci, probablement, fondée avant le mariage et maintenue ce regime après sa célébration), et en même temps il a pu fonder parallèlement une autre entreprise familiale avec de biens communs et dont la direction et gestion il s'occupe aussi, il semble presque inévi-

---

7 Parmi les régles qui établissent le *régime général primaire du mariage*, à l'art. 1318 on dit que *les biens des conjoints sont soumis aux charges du mariage;* et l'art 1362 on décrit celles-ci en détail. À rémarquer qu'en dernièr lieu on mentionne *les frais d'exploitation des entreprises privatives de chaque conjoint* au même niveau que les frais d'acquisition, conservation et jouissance des biens communs.

table l'existence des fréquents rapports entre les patrimoines privés et le patrimoine commun par l'intermédiare de chaque époux qu'il en est sont titulaire. Cela explique le contenu de l'art. 1382:
> »*Chaque conjoint pourra, sans le consentement de l'autre, mais toujours avec sa connaissance, prendre en qualité d'anticipation, des sommes d'argent commun pour ses besoins* (le texte espagnol dit: »tomar como anticipo el numerario ganancial que le sea necesario«) *et d'accord avec les usages et les circonstances de la famille, pour l'exercice de sa profession ou pour l'administration ordinaire de son patrimoine.*«

Cet article semble quelque peu surprenant parce qu'on ne parle pas de sommes reçus en prêt, ni d'obligation de payer les intérêts de la somme prise, ni même de son remboursement, et il a donné lieu à beaucoup des débats[8].

6. D'autres Problèmes de l'Entreprise Familiale. Le Protocole Familiale

Finalement il faut rappeler que tous ces cas d'entreprise familiale au sens stricte peuvent poser pas mal de problèmes au moment de l'ouverture de la succession *mortis causa* de son titulaire, surtout dans le cas où celui-ci a voulu choisir parmi ses enfants celui qui sera le continuateur de l'entreprise. Dans le Code civil espagnol le père titulaire d'une entreprise familiale qui veut l'atribuer *mortis causa* à l'un des enfants, il en pourra disposer de plusieurs mechanismes juridiques, et notamment le partage d'ascendant réglé à l'art. 1056 C.c. qui permet le nommer héritier de l'entreprise familiale sous condition de payer en argent aux autres enfants leur réserve dans un délai *maximum* de cinq années[9].

La pratique a crée récemment ce qu'on appelle le *protocole familiale* et dont j'ai parlé auparavant, qui vient d'être réglé par le Décret Royal 17/2007, de 9 février, dont l'art. 2º le décrit comme l'ensemble des pactes souscrits entre eux par les membres de la société, ou avec les tiers qui maintienent avec ceux-ci des liens familiaux, appartenant à une société qui ne côte pas en bourse, mais dans laquelle ils conservent un intérêt commun, en vue de réaliser un modèle de communication et d'accord

---

8   DE LOS MOZOS, op. et loc. cit. págs. 379-382; PRETEL, commentaire ad art. 1382, op. cit. II, pags. 733-736, qui se fait écho des plusieures opinions doctrinales.
9   Voyez une application à l'entreprise agricole: Teodora F. TORRES GARCÍA, op. et loc. cit. págs, 1656 et suivantes.

unanime dans la prise de décisions, et dans le but de régler les rapports entre famille, propriété et entreprise qui affectent à la société[10].

On veut que ce *protocole familiale* puisse aider à résoudre à l'amiable les conflicts au cours de la vie de l'entreprise familiale parmi les membres de celle-ci et spécialement à la mort du titulaire. Pour cela on a permis l'annotation au Registre Commercial de ces pactes à l'objet de renforcer ses éffets juridiques parmi les obligés et à l'égard de tiers. Malhereusement dans le cours de l'année 2007, à la ville de Barcelona, on a constaté qu'aucun protocole ne s'était inscrit[11] dans dit Registre ce qu'il pourra signifier, au moins initialement, l'existence de quelques méfiances suscités dans la pratique à l'égard de cette publicité du protocole familial.

IV. Quelques Conclusions

Le nouveau régime de la entreprise a reçu certaines critiques pour des motifs différentes. Les rapports avec les règles du Droit commercial ne se considèrent pas ni precises ni adéquats. On ne fait pas aucune référence dans la réforme de 1981 aux différentes types des sociétés commerciales régles par des lois spéciaux, d'ailleurs assez étudiées et commentés par la doctrine commercialiste et qui ont donné l'occasion à beaucoup de jurisprudence. La règle de l'art. 1365-2º, selon laquelle »si l'un des conjoints était commerçant il sera applicable les dispositions du Code commerce«, semble inspiré dans des principes obsolètes comme on a vu auparavant. De la part du Droit du travail on a reçu aussi des critiques pour ne pas en tennir compte la dernière législation de ce genre[12].

Cependant je considère d'entrée très utile la réforme introduite dans le régime legal, même s'il en serait susceptible des plusieurs perfectionnements. Les preceptes analysés supposent la reconnaissance de la réalite sociale représentée par un certain nombre, toujours croissant, des couples mariées en Espagne sous le régime de *gananciales* au XXIéme siècle. De plus en plus les époux s'engagent activement dans la vie économique et créent personnellement des entreprises familiales, surtout des

---

10 Voyez en général FERNÁNDEZ DEL POZO, *El protocolo familiar. Empresa familiar y publicidad registral* [Cizur Menor, 2008].
11 FERNÁNDEZ DEL POZO, op. cit. pg. 12.
12 Voyez FERRANTE, *La empresa familiar creada por los cónyuges en régimen de sociedad de gananciales en el Derecho español. Perplejidades y necesidad de armonización del Derecho civil y laboral*, »RCDI«, noviembre-diciembre 2007, pág. 2559 y ss.).

services à l'aide des nouvelles technologies, soit comme source compleméntaire de leur revenus, soit même comme activité principale. Donc, il semble prévisible que, des plus en plus, les cas établis par la loi de 1981, vont se multiplier dans la vie réelle. À mon avis il ne faut pas craindre à la *commercialisation* de la vie civile par la voie des régimes matrimoniax; par contre, sous quelques aspects, c'est la vie sociale qui est en train de se *commercialiser*. D'autre part, j'en suis d'accord pour mieux répenser, actualiser et harmoniser les rapports entre le Droit civil, le Droit comercial et le Droit du travail, à l'objet d'en éliminer dans ces cas leurs contradictions[13].

Bibliographie

La bibliograhie générale sur le régime légale dans le Code civil est abondante; ainsi parmi les Manuels on peut citer:
› CASTÁN TOBEÑAS- GARCÍA CANTERO, *Derecho civil español, común y foral*, tome V, vol. 1º, 12éme éd. (Madrid 1994);
› LACRUZ et alii, *Elementos de Derecho civil*, IV, *Familia*, 2éme éd. mise au jour par RAMS ALBESA (Madrid 2005);
› MARTÍNEZ DE AGUIRRE et alii, *Curso de Derecho civil*, IV, *Derecho de Familia* (aux soins de MARTÍNEZ DE AGUIRRE) 2éme ed.(Madrid 2008).

Sur la réforme de 1981:
› ÁVILA ÁLVAREZ, *El régimen económico matrimonial en la reforma del Código civil,* »Revista Crítica de Derecho Iinmobiliario«[RCDI], 1981, págs. 1373 et suivantes;
› CANO TELLO, *La nueva regulación de la sociedad de gananciales*, (Madrid 1981);
› EGEA IBAÑEZ, *Empresa o establecimiento mercantil. Bienes gananciales o privativos. Reforma del Código civil,* »RCDI«, 1982, p. 1281 ss.;
› GUILARTE GUTIÈRREZ, *La naturaleza de la actual sociedad de gananciales,*«Anuario de Derecho Civil« [ADC] 1992, págs. 875 y ss.;
› DE LOS MOZOS, *La nueva sociedad de gananciales,*«Revista de Derecho Notarial«[RDN] 1982, págs. 189 y ss.; »Comentarios Albaladejo«, XVIII-2º, (Madrid 1984);
› RAMS ALBESA, *La sociedad de gananciales* (Madrid 1992);

---

13 À propos des rapports avec le Droit du travail voyez les interessants reflexions de FERRANTE loc. cit. pgs. 2576 et ss.

> VALLET DE GOYTISOLO, *En torno a la naturaleza de la sociedad de gananciales,* »Estudios Lacruz«, I (Barcelona 1992),pág. 99 et ss.

Sur les aspects spécifiques traités dans ce rapport:
> AMAT SALAS, *La continuidad de la empresa familiar* (Barcelona 1998);
> CADARSO PALAO, *Sociedad de gananciales y participaciones sociales* (Madrid 1993);
> Mª Isabel DE LA IGLESIA MONJE, *La actividad empresarial de nueva creación por el cónyuge: Su consideración de bien ganancial,* »RCDI«, mayo-junio 2007, págs. 1334 ss;
> FERNÁNDEZ GIMENO, *Los problemas de transmisión de la empresa familiar* (Valencia 1999);
> FERNÁNDEZ GIMENO y Mª José REYES LÓPEZ, *La empresa familiar* (Valencia 2000);
> GARCÍA CANTERO, *Empresa familiar y sociedad de gananciales,* dans le vol.»La empresa familiar ante el Derecho. El empresario individual y la sociedad de carácter familiar« (dir. Garrido de Palma) (Madrid 1995);
> GARCÍA URBANO, »Comentarios del Ministerio de Justicia«, II, *Comentario ad art. 1393,* págs. 763 ss;
> LÓPEZ SÁNCHEZ, *La empresa mercantil y la sociedad de gananciales tras la Ley de 13 de mayo de 1981,* »RJC«, 1981, págs. 1983 y ss.;
> PALAZÓN GARRIDO, *La sucesión por causa de muerte en la empresa mercantil* (Valencia 2002);
> PEÑA BERNALDO DE QUIRÓS, *Comentario ad art. 1347,* »Comentario del Ministerio de Justicia«, II (Madrid 1991) pág. 644 ss.;
> PRETEL SERRANO, *Comentario ad art. 1383,* idem. idem, págs. 736 ss.;
> RAMS ALBESA, *La empresa en la sociedad de gananciales,* dans le volume »Homenaje Roca Juan«, II (Madrid 1984);
> REVERTE NAVARRO, *Sucesión mortis causa en la empresa y sucesión legitimaria (notas al nuevo art. 1056 del Cc)* (Murcia 2004);
> SANCIÑENA ASURMENDI, *Régimen económico matrimonial del comerciante* (Madrid 1996);
> TORRALBA SORIANO, *Comentario ad art. 1347,* dans le volume»Comentario a las reformas del Dereho de Familia«, II (Madrid 1984);
> Teodora F. TORRES GARCÍA, *Una aproximación al art. 1056.II C.c. (posible sucesión mortis causa de la empresa)* ,dans le volume »Homenaje Cuadrado Iglesias« (coord. Gómez Gálligo), II (Madrid 2008) págs. 1652 ss.

Alimony in Divorce in the Italian Legal System

Rita Duca[1]

I. Introduction

Following the dissolution of a marriage in the Italian legal system, alimony plays a crucial role in the economic organisation of the entire family[2]. In Italy financial support for divorcing couples is ruled under Article 5 of Act 898/1970, as amended by Article 10 of Act 74/1987.

This paper aims to clarify some parts of the rules that are particularly difficult to interpret, through an analysis of the differing opinions of scholars and the courts.

The first point regards the consequences of the Italian legislator's decision to give alimony, by means of the new act, a different nature, providing support only for maintenance, abandoning the previous »rewarding« and »compensatory« nature of support.

The second issue refers to the economic conditions of the beneficiary as a measure for the attribution of alimony in the divorce. For instance, while the act refers to a *»lack of adequate means«*, the courts will sometimes interpret this as *»the same standard of living enjoyed during marriage«*, but on other occasions as a *»guarantee of a decent and autonomous life«*.

In the third part, this paper aims to classify the criteria followed by Italian judges on deciding the *quantum* of the alimony in the divorce on a discretionary basis albeit depending upon the economic conditions of the partners, the reasons for the decision, their respective contributions to family life and the length of the marriage.

---

1 University of Palermo, Italy.
2 Some other consequences of a patrimonial nature related to marriage dissolution are: the right to a survivor's pension, the right to a share of the indemnity provision (*TFR*), an allowance from the estate and health care. For further details, see C.A. Viola, *L'assegno divorzile*, published by Giappichelli, Turino, 2004, pp. 63-83.

Finally, this paper will focus on *de facto* couples. The following four fundamental questions will be addressed:
> What is the nature of alimony in divorce in the Italian system?
> When was the acknowledgment of the right to alimony »born«?
> What are the criteria followed by the Italian courts in deciding the »quantum« of alimony?
> What right do *de facto* couples have to alimony?

II. What Is the Nature of Alimony in Divorce?

On the basis of the original formulation of Article 5 of Law 898/1970[3], case law[4] formulated the »composite« nature theory of divorce maintenance, which was given a threefold function: assistance, indemnity and compensation[5]. These three functions recognised by alimony were given equal weight and therefore took into account – in both qualification and quantification - three criteria reconstructed on the basis of these parameters.

The »assistance« function was to guarantee financial assistance for the partner with reduced economic capacity as a result of divorce. The benchmark of this function was to find an imbalance between the economic conditions of the divorcees. The »indemnity« aspect was intended to punish the spouse whose actions resulted in the failure of the marriage and the consequent responsibility to resolve the break in the family. The benchmark in this function was an analysis and evaluation of the reasons that had determined the divorce decision. The third, »compensatory«, function was designed to compensate partners for having contributed, materially and morally, towards the creation of family assets. This function was calculated through the assessment of the personal and economic contributions made by each partner during the marriage.

These three parameters (imbalance in partners' economic conditions,

---

3 Article 5, Act 898/1970 »In its judgement declaring the dissolution or termination of the marriage's civil effects, the court takes into account the spouses' conditions, the reasons for the decision, the personal and economic contributions of each to the family and the creation of capital of each and their combined income. The court looks at all these elements in relation to the duration of the marriage and imposes the obligation for a spouse to provide periodic alimony for the other, when this other is lacking in adequate means and cannot obtain them for objective reasons«.
4 See the leading case(s) *Cassazione* Sect. un., April 26, 1974, n. 1194, in *Foro it.*, 1974, I, c.1335.
5 See G. BONILINI, *Il diritto di famiglia*, vol. I, *Famiglia e matrimonio*, Turino, 1999, p. 635.

the reasons for the decision and the personal and economic contributions made by each during marriage) could also operate as autonomous reasons, independent of each other, for the assignation of alimony. Thus it could shift between assistance, indemnity or compensation, changing nature according to the practical impact of these three elements.

Italian legislature abandoned this particular system, considered a source of excessive judge discretion, in a 1987 reform with the stated intention of creating a singular basis for the determination of the nature of maintenance. The new system enhances and emphasizes the assistance aspect, pushing into the background, but not eliminating, the indemnity and compensation functions.

In the light of the new legislation the problem has essentially reversed: the entitlement to alimony can only be ruled in favour of the partner who lacks an adequate income and can not obtain one for objective reasons. The other two elements were placed as criteria in the calculation of the size of the divorce maintenance. The multi-functional nature of the alimony assignation was thus abandoned and it now recognises only the assistance nature[6], aimed simply at the protection of the weaker partner.

III. When is Acknowledgment of the Right to Alimony Given?

The Italian legislator of 1987 created an alimony based solely on financial assistance and consequently ruled that the precondition for its recognition should be based on the *»lack of adequate means«* of the applying partner. But what must be understood by the expression *»lack of adequate means«*?

The wording of this statute has, in practice, proved difficult and ambiguous, causing numerous problems of interpretation, mainly due to the inaccuracy of the legal parameters provided. Therefore it has been left to the judiciary, with their differing opinions, the arduous task of refining the definition of this concept.

While there is agreement that this »lack« can not be identified with a genuine state of need – scholars and jurisprudence have asked themselves (and come up with different answers) whether their point of reference in assessing this inadequacy of means should be *»the same standard*

---

6 »Divorce alimony which is not based on the existence of a state of need of the other spouse, has a purely assisting role, finding its jusification in the inadequacy of means of claimant spouse.« See the leading case(s) *Cassazione* on May 7, 1998, n. 4617, *Mass.*, 1998, this judgement reflects the position expressed by Cass. Sect. un. No 11490/1990.

of living enjoyed during marriage« or *»the guarantee of a decent and autonomous life«*.

The solution to these two contrasting possible interpretations was given in 1990 by the *Corte di Cassazione*, with four cases discussed in one hearing[7], in which it was established that alimony should presuppose a lack of adequate income to achieve the same standard of living enjoyed during marriage, and not merely economic self-sufficiency. The position adopted by the *Corte di Cassazione* was then consolidated and is now widely accepted.

In light of that judgement and subsequent judicial interpretation, »adequacy of means« should be understood as the economic conditions of the couple during the entire period of marriage until the cessation of cohabitation[8]. The concept of means must necessarily include assets and income of every type and usefulness that can be included as assets for each of the partners.

> *»Since the prerequisite for the granting of alimony is the claimant partner's inadequacy of means - construed as insufficient to guarantee them a standard of living similar to that experienced during marriage - the deciding judge must, in cases of insufficient economic means of the claimant, verify the divorce-caused deterioration of economic conditions«.*[9]

To ascertain the deterioration of the claimant partner's economic conditions, the court must make a comparative and thorough investigation of their former partner's economic situation and assets to detect possible approximate income equality or substantial disadvantage for one of the two parties. In the case of the latter the court establishes the right to receive alimony, making it possible for the partner to maintain a standard of living at least comparable with that experienced throughout their marriage.

The lack of means must also include the impossibility of obtaining them – objective reasons which prevent them from seeking paid employment. These may include advanced age, a precarious state of health or the need to devote themselves to childcare. In this respect, case law is resolute that »the determination of the ability to work should not be made in

---

7   See the leading case(s) *Cassazione* on October 12, 1990, n.11489, 11490, 11491, 11492.
8   Will include the period of legal or *de facto* separation.
9   See the leading case(s) *Cassazione* November 22, 2000, n. 15055, in *Nuovo Diritto*, 2001, p. 567.

hypothetical or abstract realms, but in those of practicality and concreteness[10]«. It should take into account all elements, including the attitudes, skills and any other characteristic of the person, without neglecting any socio-economic, environmental or territorial factor, which may, in context affect their finding of gainful employment.

IV. What Are the Criteria Followed by the Italian Courts in Deciding the »Quantum« of Alimony?

As explained above, the pure assistance theory of divorce is now *jus receptum* in case law. The necessary condition for its concession is that the inadequate means of the claimant must be shown, and all other elements operate only after a positive assessment of this condition, as criteria for the calculation of settlement.

From this it can be concluded that the verification of a spouse's right to periodic alimony from the other is accomplished via a two-pronged investigation[11]:

Firstly, the court must verify the existence of the abstract right by verifying the lack of adequate means of the claimant spouse or objective reasons for the impossibility of finding them, in relation to a hypothetical standard of living analogous to that enjoyed during the marriage, or one that could have been enjoyed based on the economic conditions of both spouses.

In this way, a quantitative sum can be determined that can guarantee the claimant that same standard of living and to get past their situation of economic difficulty, with the fixing of a maximum amount for the payment of alimony.

In the second phase the court will then proceed to the concrete determination of the actual amount of the alimony (the *quantum*), which must be based on a weighted and bilateral evaluation of all the criteria set out by law. These criteria operate on factors of moderation and decrease the

---

10   See the leading case(s) *Cassazione* July 16, 2004, n. 13169.
11   »The determination of the spouse's right to the administration of a periodic cheque from the other should be accomplished through a dual investigation relating to both the right and the quantum, the prerequisite for the granting of alimony is the ability of the spouse to maintain a standard of living similar to that enjoyed during marriage.« See the leading case(s) *Cassazione* on October 29, 1996, n. 9439, *Famiglia e diritto*, 1996, p. 508.

amount considered in the abstract phase, and may even cancel it out if the conservation of standards of living provided by marriage is no longer compatible with them.

The criteria used by Italian courts for the determination of the alimony *quantum* are those set out under section 6 of Article 5 of divorce act:
> The economic conditions of ex-spouses;
> The reasons for the decision;
> Their respective personal and economic contributions to the family;
> Their respective incomes;
> The duration of the marriage.

The criterion of the spouses' economic conditions includes every circumstance that could affect their overall assets. To conduct a proper evaluation, the court must take into account both the »real« income of each spouse, as well as other assets, including real estate (albeit temporarily unproductive of income), since these assets, in addition to their intrinsic capacity to ensure economically important benefits to their owner, represent an asset value that may be suspect to conversion or other use.[12]

From this it can be inferred that the benchmark is comprised of the »*total economic potential*[13]« of the spouses during marriage, covering all economic elements or other elements appreciable in economic terms, with the exception of the income of the burdened spouse, which may impact on the conditions of the parties.

To practically verify the actual economic conditions of the spouses every element must be considered useful, such as the practical abilities of each to work and earn. The court must, in fact, assess the real possibility of undertaking paid employment, in light of every possible environmental or personal factor, taking into account the place where they live, the pay for the type of work, the educational qualifications of the applicant and their psycho-physical condition. In reality, »the opportunity to take on employment must be related to that carried out during the marriage, since any employment other than that carried out previously

---

12 See the leading case(s) *Cassazione* on October 29, 1998, n. 10801, Mass., 1998.
13 »The Supreme Court has in particular pointed out that the benchmark, after the assessment of the claimant spouse's income, is the total economic potential of the spouses during marriage. This is the deciding factor in meeting the applicant's needs and lifestyle expectations, bringing them relief from the more modest standard of living possibly tolerated following divorce.« See the leading case(s) *Cassazione* Civ, sez. I, on April 4, 2002, n. 4800.

can not be considered adequate¹⁴«. For this reason the court should not ignore agreements made during the marriage regarding whether one of the two spouses had decided to renounce work in order to take care of children. Such an agreement not only prevents the work-renouncing spouse from growing professionally, but their decision to deal mainly with the management of the family permits the other spouse to dedicate themselves exclusively to their career.

The reasons for the decision criterion »postulates an investigation into the responsibilities for the failure of the marriage, with a perspective encompassing the entire duration of the marriage¹⁵«. This criterion echoes the old »indemnity« nature of alimony with the intent of »punishing« the spouse who rendered cohabitation intolerable due to their behaviour, breaking the material and spiritual bonds and making their repair impossible¹⁶. The court, in its assessment of the reasons for the decision, is neither influenced by a consensual separation, which says nothing about the causes of intolerability of cohabitation, nor by a previous judgement that may have declared one of the spouses responsible, from which it can cleanly detach. On the contrary, the court must take into account all behaviour after separation that may have caused the breaking of material and spiritual bonds and hindered the reconstruction of the family unit.

The personal and economic contribution to the family's condition is a criterion used in quantifying the alimony which affords the court discretion to adapt the decision to the individual case. The court must take into account all the contributions, both moral and economic, made by spouses towards the maintenance of the family. In other words, the court must consider not only the contributions provided by the spouses that are subject to economic evaluation, but also those provided by a spouse, who, by dedicating themselves to the needs of the family, for example through constant care for children, has encouraged its growth. As a result, case law, in a very recent judgement in 2008, ruled that the court must take into account the contribution to the running of the family provided by the wife/mother in deciding the amount of divorce alimony¹⁷. The contribu-

---

14   See the leading case(s) *Cassazione* on October 17, 1989, n. 4158, Mass., 1989.
15   See the leading case(s) *Cassazione* November 22, 2000, n. 15.055 in New Law, 2001, p. 567; according to Cassation November 22, 1992, n. 11978, in Foro, 1993, I, No Quadri.
16   See the leading case(s) *Cassazione* May 21, 1993, n 3.520.
17   See the leading case(s) *Cassazione* Civ., Sez I, January 14, 2008, n. 593.

tion must be commensurate to the whole married life, including any period of *more uxorio* cohabitation and legal or *de facto* separation[18].

The income of both spouses is the only alimony-determining criterion which has not created excessive difficulty in economic quantification. The objective evaluation of the spouses' incomes is clearly aimed at highlighting the possible existence of economic disparity between the incomes of the ex-spouses.

Finally all the criteria described above must be assessed in relation to the duration of the marriage, to avoid possible parasitic annuity. The duration does not in fact represent merely an element of a quantitative nature, but on the contrary actually evaluates the strength of the spiritual bond between spouses.

In merit, case law tells us that »a short or indeed very short duration of cohabitation, the creation of marital ties for apparently utilitarian reasons or the failure in establishing a material and spiritual communion between spouses can mean the absence of divorce alimony when the marriage, by the will of the applicant for allowance, is only formally established[19]« and an application for divorce is brought after only a short time.

V. What Right Do *de facto* Couples Have to Alimony?

Particularly interesting and delicate is the question that concerns the relationship between alimony and *de facto* family.

Theoretically, the rule in Article 5, paragraph 10 of statute no. 898/1979 stipulates that the obligation to pay alimony ceases with the new marriage of the spouse creditor, because they may be maintained by their new spouse. This last right however does not apply to *de facto* cohabitation, which is why the same rule finds neither analogous nor extensive application. Consequently full equality between the new marriage and *de facto* cohabitation is not possible.

Remarriage brings the divorced spouse into a new and autonomous context of reciprocal rights and care duties and collaboration with the new spouse, and thus involves the annulling of the right to alimony in

---

18 This emphasis on the separation period is due to the importance that we recognize is due to the activities performed by the spouse, who in this period, continues to deal primarily with the care and education of children. See the leading case(s) *Cassazione* April 2, 1985, n. 2261.
19 See the leading case(s) *Cassazione* February 13, 2004, n. 790, in Mass., 2004.

the fullness of the new legal relationship with its fully productive effects, mainly in its assets.

De facto cohabitation, on the contrary, even when showing stability and durability, does not imply, *de jure*, the extinction of the rights and obligations present from the previous relationship[20], even if it means improvements in the beneficiary's economic conditions.

We must therefore ask ourselves if, after the fixing of or the review of alimony, the court should take into account the new circumstances of the divorce beneficiary, now living with another person, and if this support should be adequately and regularly maintained.

In this regard, the prevailing theory believes that non-married relations, episodic and generally devoid of stability, have no bearing on these considerations. The conclusion is radically different however if a relationship approaches the status of a real *de facto* family (a family model which, despite being based on affection rather than legal obligation, is being given increasing legal recognition). In this case, the benefits received or regularly performed, attain value on the legal plane as acts of fulfilment of a natural obligation and change in practice, at least temporarily, the economic status of former spouse.

The increasingly credited case law position that the material assistance given to a divorcee by a *de facto* cohabiting partner, if certain and continuous reflects on the *quantum* and even on the right to alimony insofar as it may reduces or eliminates it completely.

The *Corte di Cassazione* recently boldly reaffirmed this position, ruling that »in the absence of marriage, the right to alimony, remains in principle even if the applicant has entered into *de facto* cohabitation with another person, unless it is proved, by the other ex-spouse, that this cohabitation has resulted in an economic improvement, although not supported by stable legal guarantees, but in fact adequately consolidating and protracting over time, for the entitled beneficiary[21]«.

---

20 V. Franceschelli, reports of fact. Reconstruction of the case and general theory, Giuffrè, Milano, 1984, p.51 et seq.
21 See the leading case(s) *Cassazione* civ., Sez I, January 20, 2006, n. 1179.

Solidarity between Former Spouses – What if Guilt Has Nothing to Do with It?
An Overview of the Connections between the Portuguese Divorce Reform and the Regime of Maintenance Obligations between Former Spouses

Paula Távora Vítor[1]

I. Introduction

Maintenance obligations between former spouses are traditionally considered to be one of the main »consequences« of divorce. Therefore, when the divorce system changes this »consequence« is likely to be affected as well[2].

At the present, maintenance between former spouses is indeed one of the issues addressed by the reform of Portuguese divorce law. The new law regarding divorce has affected the grounds of divorce and, thus, the background for maintenance obligations between former spouses too.

In this article I shall focus on the changes caused in the determination of maintenance obligations between former spouses by the disappearance of the divorce grounded on fault from the new Portuguese divorce system. I shall also try to put into perspective the way which these altera-

---
1 Family Law Center, Faculty of Law at the University of Coimbra, Portugal.
2 By the time this paper was presented in the ISFL's 13th World Conference in Vienna, the Divorce Reform Law was still in the course of legislative procedure. Indeed, the project 509-X had already been discussed in general terms and in specific terms in the Portuguese Parliament. It was approved as Decree 232-X and, in order to enter into force as a law, it had to be promulgated by the President of the Republic. However, the President had given a political veto to this Decree and the Parliament had a new opportunity to re-evaluate it. The President of the Republic had considered that the changes proposed by Decree 232-X could provoke situations in which the spouse that does not fulfill his/her duties unilaterally puts an end to the marriage and obtains benefits, including on a patrimonial level (http://www.presidencia.pt/?idc=10&idi=19017). Nevertheless, although the President of the Republic addressed directly other consequences of divorce, he never referred directly to the issue of maintenance between former spouses. Later on, a new version (Decree 245-X) was approved by the Parliament and in 21st October 2008, it was promulgated by the President of the Republic. The new divorce law, Law n.º 61/2008, was later published in 31st October 2008 and entered into force thirty days after its publication.

tions have redesigned the regime of such obligations. In order to do that, I shall have to determine if, within the context of the former law, the concept of »guilt« was of paramount importance when determining maintenance obligations in the majority of situations and whether the new reform has completely erased it in this field. I believe that this analysis will be a contribution to shed light on the ultimate reasons that ground such maintenance obligations.

II. Guilt and Punishment and the Former Portuguese Divorce System

As far as the grounds on which divorce is applied are concerned, the Portuguese divorce system is considered to be »pluralistic«[3]. This classification is valid in the context of the new divorce system as well as in the context of the previous law. Today, one may find either divorce by mutual consent or divorce without the consent of one of the spouses.

Formerly, one would face the categories of divorce by mutual consent or litigious divorce. According to the previous law, maintenance between former spouses was addressed in a different way by these different types of divorce. Therefore, I shall analyse them separately.

1. Divorce by Mutual Consent

Divorce by mutual consent was, as it is today, jointly applied to both spouses, who do not have to disclose its reason[4]. However, mutual agreement that disclose marriage should be dissolved was not enough. There had to be three additional agreements that concerned the consequences of divorce: the exercise of parental responsibility; the future of the family home; and spousal maintenance[5] (former art. 1775.º, n. 2, of the Civil Code). The latter agreement focused on the issue that this paper discusses.

---

3   This terminology was adopted in Boele-Woelki, Katharina; Ferrand, Frédérique; et al., *Principles of European Family Law Regarding Divorce and Maintenance Between Former Spouses*, Antwerp – Oxford, Intersentia, 2004, p. 13.
4   It is not a motiveless divorce but rather a *divorce* for a reason that is not revealed, one which the law allows to be kept secret. Coelho, Francisco Pereira; Oliveira, Guilherme de, Curso de Direito da Família, Vol. I, 4. Ed., Coimbra, Coimbra Editora, 2008, p. 601 and Oliveira, Guilherme de, Portugal – Family and Succession Law, *in International Encyclopedia of Laws*, Suppl. 29, Kluwer Law International, 2005, p. 122.
5   The property distribution agreement is not demanded, since it would raise many complex questions and turn divorce by mutual consent more difficult. Coelho, Francisco Pereira; Oliveira, Guilherme de, *Curso...cit.*, p. 605 and Oliveira, Guilherme de, Portugal – *Family and Succession Law...cit.*, p. 122.

Before the reform – and after it, in fact – divorce by mutual consent was petitioned in the Civil Registry Office (art. 271.º of the Civil Registration Code) which made it, consequently, as a rule, an administrative proceeding[6], for which the registrar of the Civil Registry was the competent authority. But, what were the powers of the registrar of the Civil Registry as far as the spousal maintenance agreement was concerned?

At a first level, law granted him/her the possibility to scrutinize such agreement[7]. According to former article 2016.º, n. 1, c), of the Civil Code, any of the spouses might be obliged to provide maintenance to the other, given his/her situation of need. The registrar of the Civil Registry (or the judge, in the exceptional situation mentioned in footnote 6) should have to analyse the agreement so as to check if the amount of maintenance settled was a reasonable one, taking into account the circumstances of the case (former art. 2016.º, n. 3 of the Civil Code). This agreement would have to adequately protect the interests of the spouses themselves and their children. If this was not observed, they would be invited to alter it accordingly (former art. 1776.º, n. 2 of the Civil Code).

The second level was the ratification of the agreement. The granting of the divorce depended on it (cf. former arts. 1778.º and 1776.º, 2 Civil Code). Thus, whenever one of the agreements that the law foresaw was not ratified, namely the one that concerned maintenance, it was not possible to decree divorce by mutual consent.[8]

Divorce by mutual consent was (and still is) favoured by Law[9] and, in practice, this type of divorce is the most common. In the year 2006, about 93,9% of divorces in Portugal were by mutual consent.[10] Therefore, main-

---

6   The process was only judicial when the spouses, in the course of a litigious divorce, and during the attempt at reconciliation or at any other moment of the process, agreed to divorce by mutual consent (former article 1774.º, 2 Civil Code, former article 12.º, 1, b) of Decree-Law 272/2001, of 13th October, and article 1407.º, 2 Civil Procedure Code) .
7   In order to do this, the registrar may determine the practice of actions and require any production of evidence (art.12.º, 5, Decree-Law n.º 272/2001, of 13th October).
8   Therefore, when spouses were invited to alter it and they did not do it or they did not do it in a way that such interests were protected, the registrar would not ratify them and divorce would not be granted (former art. 1778.º of the Civil Code). This also applied to the ratification of the other aforementioned agreements.
9   Namely because the parties can always convert the litigious divorce into a divorce by mutual consent and because the judge is legally obliged to seek the spouse's agreement so that divorce is by mutual consent, . Coelho, Francisco Pereira; Oliveira, Guilherme de, *Curso...cit.*, p p. 596 and 597.
10 Instituto Nacional de Estatística, Estatísticas Demográficas, 2008, in 2006 http://www.ine.pt/xportal/xmain?xpid=INE&xpgid=ine_publicacoes&PUBLICACOESpub_boui=16223823&PUBLICACOESmodo=2.

tenance obligations between former spouses have been mostly regulated by agreement between themselves.

In conclusion, within the context of the previous law, the concept of guilt, which was never advocated during the procedure of divorce by mutual consent, was not taken into consideration in order to determine maintenance obligations towards former spouses. As a result, it was not evoked in the vast majority of divorces, which have been divorces by mutual consent.

2. *Lititigous Divorce*

Litigious divorce was applied for by one of the spouses against the other, grounded on a specific cause and petitioned in court. This type of divorce was always judicial.

In the context of the previous law, the structure of litigious divorce in Portugal was a »mixed« one. One might find two different sorts of reasons that reflected diverse conceptions of divorce[11].

One the one hand, there was the violation of the matrimonial duties[12], grounded on the guilt of the spouse that performed it, as long as it would have damaged the possibility of a common living (former art. 1779.º of the Civil Code).

On the other hand, divorce could be grounded on three objective situations (*de facto* separation; absence; alteration of mental faculties) that implied the irretrievable breakdown of the marriage (former art. 1780.º of the Civil Code). Although guilt was not an element taken into consideration, when evaluating the existence of such grounds, both in the cases of absence (former art. 1783.º of the Civil Code) and of *de facto* separation (former art. 1782.º, 2 Civil Code), the judge would have to declare the guilt of the spouses (former art. 1787.º Civil Code), in order to associate specific consequences to it.[13]

---

11   About these different conceptions of divorce, cf. F. M. Pereira Coelho, Divórcio e separação judicial de pessoas e bens, *in Reforma do Código Civil*, Lisboa, Ordem dos Advogados, Conselho Geral, Instituto da Conferência, 1981 and F. M. Pereira Coelho; Guilherme de Oliveira, *Curso...cit.*, p. 617.

12   Portuguese Law presents a list of spousal duties in article 1672.º of the Civil Code: respect, fidelity, cooperation, cohabitation and assistance. This list remains untouched by the divorce reform. However, the violation of any of these duties is no longer ground for divorce by itself.

13   According to Guilherme de Oliveira, »The ›declaration of conjugal guilt‹ should express the result of an overall judgment about the marital crisis, as regards to knowing if the divorce is imputable *equally* to both spouses or *exclusively or predominantly* to one of them«. Oliveira, Guilherme de, Portugal – *Family and Succession Law...cit.*, p. 125.

Even though it was said that Portuguese divorce system had overcome the theory of »divorce-sanction«[14], the idea of punishment was still connected to litigious divorce, even when it did not have its foundations on the guilty violation of matrimonial duties, but it was rather based on the irretrievable breakdown of the marriage.

Guilt played a main role in this system. As a matter of fact, the rules of distribution of property could be altered in the presence of a guilty (or mainly guilty) spouse (former art. 1790.º of the Civil Code), he/she would lose benefits received due to the marriage or in consideration of the marital status (former art. 1791.º of the Civil Code) and the innocent or less guilty spouse was entitled to receive an indemnity for non-patrimonial damages caused by the dissolution of marriage (former art. 1792.º of the Civil Code).

As far as maintenance between former spouses was concerned, the presence or the absence of guilt would be decisive to determine the existence of such obligations in each specific case. Together with the needs of the creditor and the resources of the debtor, these were considered the main elements to take into account in the determination of such obligations.

Of course, the divorcing spouses might manage to reach an agreement concerning maintenance, within the general freedom of settlement.[15] However, because this possibility would not always be feasible within the framework of the litigious divorce, law had to determine who was entitled to maintenance. Hence, a diversity of situations could arise:

> If both spouses were declared equally guilty or none of them was declared guilty, both had the right to apply for maintenance.
> If one of them was considered to be the only guilty party or his/her guilt was considered to be »clearly superior« to the other's, only the innocent or the less guilty spouse held the aforementioned right.

In the special situation of former article 2016.º, n.º 1, b) of the Civil Code, the idea of guilt seemed to be absent. Indeed, this article dealt with situations in which divorce was decreed grounded on the alteration of mental faculties (former art. 1781.º, c) of the Civil Code), an objective ground

---

14 Vide F. M. Pereira Coelho, *Divórcio...*, cit., p. 32 and F. M. Pereira Coelho; Guilherme de Oliveira, *Curso...*, cit., p. 619. Fidélia Proença de Carvalho considers that the theory of »divorce-sanction« was still present in our divorce system when divorce was grounded on fault. Fidélia Proença de Carvalho, O conceito da culpa no divórcio – Crime e castigo, in Comemorações dos 35 anos do Código Civil e dos 25 anos da Reforma de 1977, vol. I, Direito da Família e das Sucessões, p. 589 and 591.
15 F. M. Pereira Coelho; Guilherme de Oliveira, *Curso...*, cit., p. 693.

for divorce, which would exist regardless of any guilty behavior. In such case, only the defendant (the mentally ill person)[16] had the right to apply for maintenance. The law assumed that it could not demand the sacrifice from the other spouse to remain married, since »conjugal life« might no longer effectively exist, but it imposed on him/her certain obligations, including the payment of maintenance.[17]

Finally, the last situation (former art. 2016.º, n.º 2, of the Civil Code) was considered an exception in relation to the aforementioned rule. Even though the element »guilt« was a key to grant or deny maintenance, the Portuguese legislature had considered that »reasons of equity« could be enough to overcome this obstacle under certain circumstances. Therefore, the court would exceptionally grant maintenance to the guilty or the most guilty party or to the spouse who had petitioned for divorce grounded on the alteration of mental faculties of the other.

In order to be able to make such decision, the court would have to take into consideration the duration of the marriage and the collaboration provided by the beneficiary spouse to the couple's economy.

This way, the determination of the liability to pay was strongly related to the concept of guilt. However, one should note that, according to the Portuguese system, once the right to such claim was decided, the guilt would no longer be further considered, namely when determining the *quantum* to be paid.[18, 19]

---

16   M. N. Lobato de Guimarães notices that the breakdown of the common living may be due to one of the spouses, even though he/she cannot be blamed, as in art. 1781.º, c) of the Civil Code. p. 195. Guimarães, M. N. Lobato de, Alimentos, in *Reforma do Código Civil*, Lisboa, Ordem dos Advogados, Conselho Geral, Instituto da Conferência, 1981.
17   F. M. Pereira Coelho; Guilherme de Oliveira, *Curso...*, cit., p. 643.
18   The *quantum* of maintenance to be provided to the former spouse has been a recurrent debate issue. One would find three different opinions regarding such matter. One strict interpretation considered that the former spouse could claim that which is *indispensable* for his/her survival, clothing and board (art. 2003.º, n. 1 of the Civil Code) and also for health and travelling expenses. Others conveyed the idea that maintenance should be kept at *the level to which he/she has been accustomed* during the marriage. Finally, the intermediary position maintained that the former spouse »may aspire to a level of support that puts him/her in a *reasonable situation* – above the survival threshold, but probably below the standard of living that the couple previously enjoyed«. Oliveira, Guilherme de, Portugal – *Family and Succession Law...*, cit., p. 131.
19   According to the studies of the Commission on European Family Law, this is not the case of other systems, as Greece, Italy or Switzerland, where guilt may be considered in order to determine the amount of maintenance. AA. VV., European Family Law in Action, vol. II: Maintenance Between Former Spouses, Katharina Boele-Woelki; Bente Braat; Ian Sumner (eds.), Antwerpen, Oxford, New York, Intersentia, 2003, pp. 133, 135, 138 and Boele-Woelki, Katharina; Ferrand, Frédérique; et al., *Principles of European Family Law...*, cit., p. 75.

III. What if Guilt Has Nothing to Do With It? – The Portuguese Divorce Reform and its Repercussions on Maintenance Obligations between Former Spouses

Since divorce was introduced in Portugal in 1910 it has been a matter subject to frequent changes. Even recently Portuguese legal theory had noticed that the »divorce issue« was still open, even as far as the grounds for divorce were concerned. It had already been questioned if the constitutional »right to free development of personality« (art. 26.º of the Portuguese Constitution) would allow the legal limitations to divorce that the law foresaw.[20]

These ideas followed an European trend. They were also addressed by the Commission on European Family Law (CEFL) when creating the *Principles of European Family Law Regarding Divorce and Maintenance Between Former Spouses*. Such principles strongly inspired the project to reform divorce that has lead to the present law, which I shall analyse regarding maintenance obligations between former spouses.

1. Divorce by Mutual Consent

In the new law, the core of divorce by mutual consent remains untouched. It is still required jointly by both spouses, who do not disclose its cause (art. 1773.º, n. 2 of the Civil Code).

However, the new law has aimed at broadening the number of situations that may follow the procedure of divorce by mutual consent. Indeed, whenever the spouses agree to divorce, but do not agree in any of the subjects that they must regulate, in which the payment of maintenance to the former spouse[21] is included, there can also be divorce by mutual consent.[22] Yet, such divorce is petitioned in court (art. 1773.º, n. 2 of the Civil Code).

In this situation, one will find the judge determining the consequences of divorce, as in a divorce without the consent of one of the spouses (art. 1778.º-A, n. 3 of the Civil Code)[23].

---

20 Coelho, Francisco Pereira; Oliveira, Guilherme de, Curso de Direito da Família, Vol. I, 4. Ed., Coimbra, Coimbra Editora, 2008, p. 590.
21 As well as the regulation of parental responsibilities and the future of the family home (cf. art. 1775.º, n. 1 of the Civil Code).
22 Cf. Boele-Woelki, Katharina; Ferrand, Frédérique; et al., *Principles of European Family Law...*, cit.,p. 31 and 32.
23 Cf. Boele-Woelki, Katharina; Ferrand, Frédérique; et al., *Principles of European Family Law...*, cit.,p. 50.

As a result, divorce by mutual consent is also possible even when spouses cannot agree or cannot entirely agree on the consequences of divorce, namely on spousal maintenance.

In conclusion, maintenance obligations between former spouses will not always be determined by agreement in the divorce by mutual consent, as it happened in the context of the former regime. In fact, there may now be an intervention of the court. Nonetheless, the element of guilt is subject to the same approach – it shall never be considered.

2. *Divorce Without Consent of One of the Spouses*

The new divorce law retains the fundamental scheme of litigious divorce. Nevertheless, the nomenclature has changed into »divorce without consent of one of the spouses«. It is still applied for by one of the spouses against the other, grounded on a specific cause (art. 1773.º, n. 3 of the Civil Code) and petitioned in court.

The main idea of these new rules is to erase the element of guilt from the Portuguese divorce system.

Therefore, divorce without consent of one of the spouses may only be grounded on objective situations[24], since divorce on the basis of fault has disappeared.

Additionally, the declaration of guilt that one would find in the former regime, either for situations of divorce grounded on fault or of divorced based in objective situations, no longer exists.

This solution has also been inspired by the CEFL's *Principles of European Family Law Regarding Divorce and Maintenance Between Former Spouses*, which consider that »eliminating any reference to fault (…) avoids any undesirable investigation into the state of marriage by competent authority and better respect the personal integrity and autonomy of the spouses«[25]. It is stated that the elimination of any reference to fault follows a trend of development of many European jurisdictions.[26]

Does this change have any consequences with respect to the maintenance between former spouses? What is the new regulation?

---

24 These situations are *de facto* separation, absence, alteration of mental faculties and any other facts that, regardless of guilt, may demonstrate the irretrievable breakdown of marriage (art 1781.º of the Civil Code).
25 Boele-Woelki, Katharina; Ferrand, Frédérique; et al., *Principles of European Family Law…, cit.*, p. 55.
26 *Idem.*

2.1 The Principle of Self-Sufficiency

First of all, the new article 2016.º, 1 of the Civil Code opts to spell out statutorily a principle of self-sufficiency[27], although this principle was already present in our system.[28] Indeed, one must not forget that, as far as the determination of the amount of maintenance is concerned, article 2004.º, 2 Civil Code foresees that the possibility of the former spouse to support him/herself has to be considered.

What is the meaning of this statement? Let us not forget the remarks of Pereira Coelho and Guilherme de Oliveira about maintenance between former spouses. According to the authors, this is an increasingly sensitive matter, due to the social and cultural context of western societies, where people remarry more often and the individualistic ideology is becoming dominant, which makes it more and more difficult for the law to impose a post-divorce solidarity.[29] This way, the legislature has to clearly state his/her position and the starting point is, undoubtedly, the idea that each one should support him/herself.

2.2 Right to Apply for Maintenance

Furthermore, the new law determines that either of the spouses is entitled to apply for maintenance regardless of the type of divorce (art. 2016.º, n. 2 of the Civil Code)[30]. In the former article 2016.º of the Civil Code, as it has been mentioned, several distinctions were made, given that there was the declaration of guilt and it was necessary to evaluate it for maintenance purposes. In view of the fact that the new law has erased the concept of guilt, there are no distinctions to be made.

Thus, it seems that, as far as the liability to pay is concerned, the general regime of maintenance obligations shall be applied. Since it is implied in the new solution that guilt is not considered when determining the existence of maintenance obligations, the elements that will be taken into

---

27   As in other European countries and in accordance with Principle 2:2 of CEFL's Boele-Woelki, Katharina; Ferrand, Frédérique; et al., *Principles of European Family Law...*, *cit.*, p. 77.
28   M.N. Lobato de Guimarães notices that, »in a society based in labour, each one should work in order to support him/herself«. Guimarães, M. N. Lobato de, *Alimentos...cit.*, p. 176.
29   Coelho, Francisco Pereira; Oliveira, Guilherme de, *Curso...*, p. 693.
30   This solution has a historical predecessor in Decree of 3rd November 1910 (article 29.º), that stated that any of the spouses was entitled to claim for maintenance. Serra, Adriano Paes da Silva Vaz, Obrigação de alimentos, *Boletim do Ministério da Justiça*, Julho, n. 108, 1961, p. 82, fn. 96.

account will be the needs of the creditor and the resources of the debtor, as it is stated in article 2004.º, n. 1 of the Civil Code [31,32].

2.3 Denial of Maintenance for »Clear Reasons of Equity«

Finally, the new law foresees that, for »clear reasons of equity«, the right to apply for maintenance may be denied (art. 2016.º, n. 3 of the Civil Code).

Which »reasons« are these? Is it a way to open a door to a sanction towards a reprehensible behaviour of the spouse in need? How will it be determined, since there is no declaration of guilt?

In order to answer to these questions, let us analyse the »exceptional hardship clause« to the debtor spouse proposed by the CEFL's Principle 2:6, according to which »the competent authority may deny, limit or terminate maintenance because of the spouse's conduct«.[33]

Indeed, this type of clause is not directly established in the new divorce law, however, it seems that we may find in the new article 2016.º, n. 3 of the Civil Code the same functional meaning as far as the denial of maintenance is concerned.

The CEFL notices that the »hardship should be exceptional in order to avoid the possibility of fault re-entering into the system. This means that not every form of misconduct during the marriage and after the divorce can be taken into account« and only situations »which are so grievous that maintenance cannot or can no longer be expected should play a role«[34].

Thus, according to the CEFL, such clause does not evoke the idea of guilt. Nonetheless, one cannot stop noticing that there may be (and usually are) reprehensible behaviours that are addressed by such rule.

As far as the termination of the maintenance obligation is concerned, one may find a legal rule within our system which expresses a close idea to the second part of Principle 2:6 and which has not been altered by the reform. In reality, article 2019.º of the Civil Code foresees that the maintenance obligation shall terminate if the creditor is not worthy of that benefit because of his/her disapproved moral behaviour. According to M.

---

31 Coelho, Francisco Pereira; Oliveira, Guilherme de, *Curso...*, *cit.* , p. 694.
32 As it is foreseen in Principle 2:3. Boele-Woelki, Katharina; Ferrand, Frédérique; *et al.*, *Principles of European Family Law...*, *cit.*, p. 79.
33 Boele-Woelki, Katharina; Ferrand, Frédérique; *et al.*, *Principles of European Family Law...*, *cit.*, p. 100.
34 Boele-Woelki, Katharina; Ferrand, Frédérique; *et al.*, *Principles of European Family Law...*, *cit.*, p. 103.

N. Lobato de Guimarães, this is a rule that still expresses some sort of »moral censure«[35] that persists despite of the proposed new logic of the system.

As for the determination of the *quantum* of maintenance, among the elements to be taken into consideration, one cannot find any guilt-related factor.[36]

IV. Some Further Conclusion-Like Remarks

What is the meaning of these changes? The CEFL notices that »the existence and the extent of, as well as the weight to be attached to a maintenance claim between the spouses generally depends on an assessment by the legislature as to whether and to what extent the creditor spouse deserves to be protected.«[37]

Until recently, in the Portuguese system, as a common rule, only the innocent or the less guilty spouse *deserved* this protection. Therefore, there was a moral judgement underlying it, which was external to the purposes of the general rules of maintenance obligations of providing maintenance for a person in need.[38]

Maintenance between former spouses was subject to a special regime, where the »primary criterion« to grant maintenance was given by the appraisal of the claimant's behavior: if his/her conduct was not to be censured nor was it to be more censured than the defendant's conduct, then maintenance should be granted. When was the conduct to be censured? When there was guilt.[39]

---

35 M. N. Lobato de Guimarães, *ob. cit.*, p. 208. According to M. N. Lobato de Guimarães, the solution could be given by article 2013.º of the Civil Code.
36 According to article 2016.º-A of the Civil Code, the following elements shall be taken into consideration in order to determine the amount of maintenance: the duration of marriage, the contribution for the couple's economy, the spouse's age, health, professional qualifications and employment ability, the care of common children, the resources and income, a new marriage or *de facto* union and every other factor that may influence the ability to pay maintenance or the needs of the creditor.
37 Boele-Woelki, Katharina; Ferrand, Frédérique; *et al.*, *Principles of European Family Law...*, *cit.*, p. 69.
38 »The fundamental purpose of maintenance after divorce is to provide economic support to the dependent former spouse« Boele-Woelki, Katharina; Ferrand, Frédérique; *et al.*, *Principles of European Family Law...*, *cit.*, p. 69.
39 These are approximately the words of M. N. Lobato de Guimarães. M. N. Lobato de Guimarães *ob. cit.*, p. 196.

The new solution allows any of the spouses (including the one that may have been *de facto* responsible for the marriage's collapse) to receive maintenance from the other.[40] This enlarges the group of people that may benefit from post-divorce spousal maintenance.

However, there is a new logic to take into account. Let us not forget the principle of self-sufficiency. This is a rule that follows the way leading to the opposite direction – it intends to narrow down the group of the beneficiaries as well as the width of the maintenance obligation.[41] Thus, associated with the principle of self-sufficiency, there is the tendency to promote the independence of spouses following their divorce[42,43], which will primarily affect women, since they are the main beneficiaries of post-divorce solidarity.

Therefore, in this new system there is a twofold trend that follows opposite directions – the first one that enlarges the group of beneficiaries whilst the other highlights the importance of reducing it.

This reflects new conceptions regarding the duties of the spouses, which become feebler. On the one hand, if they are not fulfilled, there are no sanctions associated and a spouse, who could be considered the guilty party under the former regime, will now be able to require maintenance from the other. On the other hand, it seems clearer that there is lack of a strong basis to impose solidarity obligations when the family relationship has terminated with divorce.

---

40 »Bearing in mind the CEFL's divorce Principles, there is no justification for making fault a precondition and in any event the clear trend within Europe is to move away from fault« Boele-Woelki, Katharina; Ferrand, Frédérique; *et al.*, *Principles of European Family Law...*, *cit.*, p. 83.
41 The version of article 2016.º-B, n.º 1 of the Civil Code of Decree 232-X stated that, as a rule, maintenance should be granted for a limited period. This solution followed closely CEFL's Principle 2:8, which concerns »limitation in time« .However, this rule could no longer be found in the Decree 245-X, which was the version that later became Law.
42 Boele-Woelki, Katharina; Ferrand, Frédérique; *et al.*, *Principles of European Family Law...*, *cit.*, p. 78.
43 According to Maria de Nazareth Lobato de Guimarães, it is not legitimate to hold someone, as a family member, accountable for the support of other family members, outside the circle of a normal nuclear family. Moreover, the author stresses the idea that it should not be a life-long obligation. Guimarães, M. N. Lobato de, *Alimentos...*, *cit.*, p. 209.

An Analysis of the Rights of South African Women and Children to Maintenance from Husbands and Fathers in African Customary Marriages and Domestic Partnerships

Jan C. Bekker[1]

I. Introduction

The Recognition of Customary Marriages Act[2] (the Act) has not brought about certainty regarding the existence of valid customary marriages. Section 3 lays down certain elaborate requirements, virtually the same as for valid common law marriages. But problems arise from section 3 (1)(b) according to which »the marriage must be negotiated and entered into or celebrated in accordance with customary law«. But for that provision, it would have been absurd to call it a customary marriage at all. This provision makes the customary negotiations and celebrations a statutory requirement for the validity of a customary marriage.

The section 3 requirements are in any event not applicable with retrospective effect. Marriages entered into before the Act came into operation on 15 November 2000 are not subject to the new requirements, obviously because there were no statutory requirements, except in KwaZulu-Natal where the codes of Zulu law laid down certain requirements.[3]

The duty imposed upon the parties by section 4 (1) of the Act »to ensure that their marriage is registered«, does not provide certainty. It implies an *ex post facto* registration. Section 4 (9) moreover provides that failure to register a customary marriage does not affect the validity of the marriage. Any interested person may therefore come afterwards and aver that there was a marriage or there wasn't. That puts the onus on the parties to prove or disprove the existence of a valid customary marriage.

The statutory recognition and mandatory dissolution have put the existence and consequences of customary marriages more than ever in the

---

1 University of Pretoria, South Africa.
2 120 of 1998.
3 KwaZulu Act on the Code of Zulu Law 16 of 1985 and Natal Code of Zulu Law Proc R151 of 1987.

legal arena. It is spawning numerous legal disputes, especially when one of the parties dies or institutes divorce proceedings. The parties choose the most favourable option. If a woman, for instance, wants custody of children born from a relationship, she would prefer to say she was unmarried. But if being unmarried would thwart a claim for maintenance under the Maintenance of Surviving Spouses Act[4] or a claim to succeed intestate, the surviving »spouses« would claim to have been married.

The problem is going to escalate as there are many customary marriages. The number sex, and population group in 2001 were as follows:

	Black African
Male	1 395 751
Female	1 603 670

(Information supplied by Statistics South African on 21 August 2003)

The larger number of female African customary marriages (207 919) is probably indicative of polygynous marriages, but one cannot be sure. There is a possibility that more women than men believe and say they are married by customary law. It is common knowledge that men »emigrate« to industrial centres where they enter into extramarital relationships. They may be reluctant to reveal that they are in fact married by customary law to a wife back home. Mayer[5] devotes a whole chapter to the discussion of what he calls »sexual partnerships«. Pauw[6] remarked that »[l]iving together in concubinage is a common relationship in town and a partner to such union is referred to as *masihlalisane* (let us stay together) or *ishweshwe* (a concubine). Many male immigrants enter into relationships of this kind in town, but it is less common among town-bred men«.

II. Problem of Proving Existence of a Customary Marriage

In former times, marriage in Africa served three major purposes:
> »... the continuation of the lineage group through natural reproduction; the provision of domestic labour by the wife; and as a means

---

4 27 of 1990.
5 *Townsmen or Tribesmen* (1971) 252–269.
6 *The Second Generation* (1963) 135.

by which wider political and economic alliances were established between the families of the wife and that of the husband.«[7]

It followed that marriage was often a matter of family, rather than personal, concern. For that reason a bride was sometimes chosen by the groom's family.

A further characteristics of an African marriage was its private and social nature. It was an arrangement between two families that could be adapted to suit their needs and accommodate the particular situation. It had no precise moment of beginning or termination, sometimes depending on delivery of lobolo in instalments. The marital relationship developed over years, becoming final with the birth of children and full payment of lobolo. Death of the husband did not automatically terminate the marriage, as the families could arrange its continuation by arranging levirate or sororate unions.[8] A wife remained a member of her husband's family. The absence of rigid formalities would not have been problematic in the close-knit communities of the past. People knew one another and proof of marriage was seldom a problem. If the validity was disputed, it could be proved by many events, such as the evidence of go-betweens, family elders and the public rituals of negotiation and integration of the bride with her husband's family. In presentday society, however, people are more mobile and relationships are no longer as close as they used to be. It has not only become more difficult to establish the existence of customary marriages in these circumstances, but there are also more occasions on which it needs to be proved. For a wide variety of reasons, such as claiming maintenance, insurance benefits, subsidised housing and damages for the death of a breadwinner, marital status has to be precisely fixed to comply with bureaucratic requirements.

Many people moreover live in informal relationships – in current legal parlance called domestic partnerships. In the case of Africans when they separate, or one of them dies, the other one may claim to have been married by customary law, or denying that they were, depending on what stance has the most lucrative outcome.

---

7   In sharp contrast to the western concept of marriage: Women and Law in Southern Africa (WLSA) *Uncovering Reality (Excavating Women's Rights in African Family Law)* 5. Undated working paper No 7.
8   For useful accounts of customary marriage in Southern Africa, see: Mönnig (1978) The Pedi 193-4; Schapera A Handbook of Tswana Law and Custom (1955) 130-8.

III. The Male Heir's Duty of Support

The main objective of African customary law of succession was to protect the family and the community against the disruptive effect of death on the integrity of the family.[9] The system of succession facilitated continuation of the family as a corporate entity by making the eldest male descendant of the deceased his universal heir. He succeeded not only to the property, but also to the position, status and standing of the deceased. In the absence of male descendants the estate devolved upon the eldest male ascendant, the deceased's father or uncle.[10] This mode of succession also ensured continuation of the family lineage.

This system was virtually a life insurance policy for the whole family. The heir stepped into the shoes of the deceased and was obliged to maintain all the family members. Every member of the family was entitled to reasonable care and maintenance.

In the *Bhe*[11] case the Constitutional Court has virtually drawn a line through these rules of succession and the concomitant duty of support. The ratio decidendi was that the rule of primogeniture precludes widows and children (including extra-marital children) from inheriting from their deceased father. According to the court the customary heir's duty to support the whole family cannot justify the limitation on the rights of women and children. The court consequently held that the application of the customary law of succession is unconstitutional and invalid.

The judge dismissed the traditional significance of the custom in the following words:

> »*Modern urban communities and families are structured and organised differently and no longer purely along traditional lines. The customary law rules of succession simply determine succession to the deceased's estate without the accompanying social implications which they traditionally had. Nuclear families have largely replaced traditional extended families. The heir does not necessarily live together with the whole extended family which would include the spouse of the deceased as well as other dependants and*

---

9   Bennett and Peart A Sourcebook of African Customary Law for Southern Africa (1991) 379 and 383. See also Mbatha »Reforming the customary law of succession« 2002 SAJHR 260.
10 Olivier *et al* Indigenous Law (1995) 147–148 and Kerr Customary Law of Immovable Property and of Succession (1976) 124–125.
11 *Bhe v Magistrate, Kyayelitsha and others* 2005 (1) BCLR 1 (CC).

descendants. He often simply acquires the estate without assuming, or even being in a position to assume, any of the deceased's responsibilities.«[12]

This judgment may be criticised on various grounds:
1.) The reference to a change in the structure and organisation of modern urban communities is superficial. The judge does not say who and where these »modern urban communities« are. He does not exclude non-urban communities. Urban is a relative concept. There are some 22 million Africans living on communal land.[13] Many more live in informal settlements where there is no clear dividing line between rural and urban.
2.) Many, I venture to say most, African estates are not amenable to disposal in terms of the Intestate Succession Act. The sum total may be a single family dwelling. If it is to be converted into cash for distribution among heirs each one will get a mere pittance. Another estate might consist of a homestead where there are different houses occupied by a conglomerate of family houses that have no economic value. As a collectivity the homestead is simply not for sale. It is the family home.

So the judge has pulled this rug, this epitome of *»umuntu ngumuntu ngabantu«* (translation: a person is a person because of other people) from under the feet of all and sundry for the sake of »modern urban communities«, whatever that might mean.

While one may not deny that male primogeniture perpetuates male dominance and thus inequality the court has thrown the baby out with the bath water. Admittedly there are families no longer structured along traditional lines, but there are many where the blanket application of the European concept of dividing the assets between surviving spouse and children is incongruous. The division may result in little parcels of money and goods having to be distributed. What is more, many family homesteads constitute a family economic unit that cannot be meaningfully turned into divisible cash.

---

12 Para 80 of the case.
13 Sibanda, »The Birth of a New Order and Unitary Land Administration in the Communal Areas of South Africa« Walter Sisulu University Law Journal (2006) 4.

The court, however, left the door open for Parliament to enact a comprehensive scheme that would reflect the necessary development of the customary law of succession.[14] In order that the Intestate Succession Act 81 of 1987 be applied the court added that that Act does not preclude an estate devolving in accordance with an agreement reached among all interested parties, but in a way that is consistent with the Intestate Succession Act.[15]

The Minister for Justice and Constitutional Development recently introduced a Bill in Parliament providing that in appropriate cases an enquiry be held by the Master of the High Court or a magistrate to ensure an equitable division of the estate.[16]

Neither an agreement about division of the estate nor an enquiry would restore the family cohesity nor the heir's duty to care for the family. The judge expressly stated that such families no longer exist in »urban areas«.

IV. Discarded Wives and Other Dual Marriages

According to the judgment in *Nkambula v Linda*[17] the husband's subsequent civil marriage to another woman nullified the former customary marriage. The customary law wives were probably more often than not unaware of the civil marriages, because their husbands left home as migrant labourers and married by civil rights where they worked. They only saw their husbands during holidays when they were back from the city. In some cases all the parties concerned might have been unaware of the consequences of a civil marriage.

This practice legally came to an end on 2nd December 1988 when section 1 of the Marriage and Matrimonial Property Law Amendment Act[18] came into operation. It provided that if a man is married by customary law, he may enter into a civil marriage with that woman only, unless the customary marriage was dissolved.[19]

---

14 Paragraph [122] and [124] at 629 F-G and 630 B-C of the judgment.
15 Paragraph [130] at 631–632C.
16 Clause 5 of the Reform of customary Law of Succession and Regulation of Related Matters Bill [B10-2008].
17 1951 1 SA 377 (A).
18 88 of 1984.
19 No statistics are available but it may be assumed that men nevertheless continued to marry second wives by civil rites. That creates a legal conundrum that cannot adequately be dealt with in this article.

This practice left a substantial number of women »unmarried«. They could claim maintenance from their husbands for children born of the union, but they themselves had no legal claim against their former husbands, except the dubious right provided by s 22 (7) of the Black Administration Act[20] preserving »the material rights of any partner of a subsisting customary union«.

In terms of clause 7 of the Reform of Customary Law of Succession and Regulation of Related Matters Bill[21] these women will have the same rights of succession as the common law widows.

V. Action for Damages Caused by the Death of a Breadwinner

Dependants' actions for damages caused by the death of a breadwinner revealed the anomalies inherent in refusing customary marriage full recognition.[22] In 1963, the legislature intervened by recognising customary unions for purposes of claims for damages for loss of support from any person who unlawfully causes the death of the other partner.[23]

Another consequence of non-recognition of customary marriages was the overriding effect given to civil marriages. The partner of a customary marriage could nullify his or her customary union by entering into a civil marriage.[24] Husbands in particular[25] could easily rid themselves of their customary marriage wives without having a divorce.[26] Conversely, if the spouse of a civil marriage purported to marry another person by customary rites, the second marriage was null and void. It was not deemed biga-

---

20 38 of 1927.
21 [B10-2008].
22 *Santam v Fondo* 1960 (2) SA 467 (A) at 470-4. See Kahn (1960) 77 *SALJ* 279-84.
23 Section 31 of the Black Laws Amendment Act 67 of 1963. See *Mayeki v Shield Insurance Co Ltd* 1975 (4) SA 370 (C) at 373. In *Makgae v Sentraboer (Koöperatief) Bpk* 1981 (4) SA 239 (T) at 247, it was held that the certificate should be produced simultaneously with the issue of summons. In *Dlikilili v Federated Insurance Co* Ltd 1983 (2) SA 275 (C) at 283, the court held that the document had to be based on a register of customary marriages.
24 *Nkambula v Linda* 1951 (1) SA 377 (A). See Peart »Civil or Christian marriage and customary unions: The legal position of the discarded spouse and children« (1983) 16 *CILSA* 39.
25 Although wives, too, could automatically terminate their customary unions by this method.
26 Because the ›discarded‹ wife was put at risk, the legislature intervened again, in s 22 (7) of the Black Administration Act 38 of 1927, to protect ›the material rights of any partner‹ of a subsisting customary union.

mous because customary marriages were not recognised as marriages for purposes of criminal law.[27]

All the discarded wives were left without a claim for maintenance against their former husbands. That is the position to this day. The »material rights« protected by section 22 (7) of the Black Administration Act probably consisted of no more than a right to a »house« in a traditional family home.

Another type of dual marriage that is quite common is a double marriage where parties intend to and unanimously agree to enter into a civil and customary marriage. Coertze[28] found that 26,7 percent of 100 families in an urban township concluded civil marriages after conclusion of customary marriages. The Centre for Indigenous Law found a far higher figure, namely 61 percent in another township.[29]

Discussion with academics and magistrates in the Eastern Cape revealed that in rural areas in that part of the country dual marriages have become a common feature. Couples get married in true customary fashion and thereafter proceed to church or to the local magistrate or Home Affairs official for a civil marriage.

In theory it poses no problem but in fact the parties are tied up in a bipolar situation – socially married by customary law but in a legal technical sense married by civil rites.

VI. Women Trapped between Two Legal Cultures

In customary law the head of a family was always a male person. The family is generally a compound or extended family, consisting of the houses of more than one wife in the case of polygynous marriages and invariably including unmarried children of both sexes and even relatives.

In this set-up the husband was responsible for the care and maintenance of **all** the members of the family. This was simply a factual situation. It was not as if the husband's wife or wives were subordinate to him. They were just part of the family.

---

27   *Sonyane v Rex* 1912 EDL 361.
28   »Die Gesinslewe in Atteridgeville« in Eloff and Coertze *Etnografiese Studies in Suidelike Afrika* (1972) pp 291–334.
29   Vorster (Compiler of report) Urbanites perceptions of lobolo: Mamelodi and Atteridgeville (2000).

In present social circumstances women increasingly fulfil the role of family heads. They are unmarried and include widows, divorcees, never married women and women deserted by their husbands. Some of these family households may extend over three or four generations, without a single marriage having been concluded. It could be described as a new form of extended family, with a matrifocal tendency. This makes the concept of »father family head« in those circumstances meaningless. Bennett[30] stated that the extended family has been destablished so that –

> »...the structure now clearly survives as a traditional ideal, not a reality. This proposition is borne out by various studies which indicate that nuclear families are ubiquitous, and that they are giving way to single-parent units, often headed by women.«

The extent of the female-headed family units may be gauged by reference to Statistics South Africa 2004 data which indicate that in 2001 there were no less than 61% female-headed households in formal housing in South Africa.[31]

If the female family head is 18 years of age, she has all the powers of a major. She would be the guardian of her minor dependants, also her extra-marital children. She would also be liable for the maintenance of all her grandchildren if the parents are unable to do so. If the parents of children born in wedlock are unable to maintain their children the maintenance obligation rests on the children's grandparents. The grandparents are similarly obliged to maintain extra-marital grandchildren.[32] This could place an unbearable burden on female family heads. But she has no control over and no legal responsibility for the other children in her household.

She probably would not be able to represent the members of the household in court or in legal acts outside the household. However, in *Mabena v Letsoala*[33] the court accepted that a mother may negotiate and receive lobolo in respect of her daughter's marriage. This may be an indication that the courts will recognise female family headships in other fields of customary law as well.

---

30 *Op cit* 186.
31 See Department of Social Development Population and Gender Equality in South Africa (undated report).
32 *Petersen v The Maintenance Officer, Simon's Town Maintenance Court* 2004 2 SA 56 (C).
33 1998 2 SA 1068 (T). This judgment cannot be taken as of general application. The negotiations about marriage are between two families. If the bride's father is around the mother may not without more ado fulfil his role.

It may be added that the large and growing female households are a huge social problem. Although men are in theory not indispensable, the customary law caters for male-headed extended families and the common law for nuclear families in which two parents have reciprocal rights and duties.

VII. Domestic Partnerships

South African statistics show that a large number of people live together in domestic partnerships. According to the 1996 census 1 268 964 people described themselves as living together with a partner. The 2001 census estimated that nearly 2,4 million individuals were living in domestic partnerships. Statistical data show that only about 40% of African and Coloured women were married. The 1996 census figures were broken up as follows:

African	1 056 992
Coloured	132 180
Indian/Asian	7 119
White	84 000
Unspecified	8 181

The figures show that dependence-producing relationships are substantial in number and on the increase. The large number of African domestic partnerships may partly be ascribed to migratory labour, which still persists despite the demise of apartheid. It is fairly common for a migratory labourer to have a wife in town and another back home in a rural area.[34] The quandary of women is often a tale of two cities.

This, of course, leaves women on both sides of the fence vulnerable. The wife back home is dependent upon remittances (a typical South African phenomenon) from her husband and the one in town equally needs support, but lacks security, status and a right to demand maintenance. The scenario is pretty grim.

The legislature proposes to remedy this unsatisfactory state of affairs by enacting a law, presently called the Domestic Partnerships Bill [B-2008].

---

34 See S A Law Reform Commission Project 118 Report on Domestic Partnerships (March 2006) pp 28–29.

It provides for registered and unregistered domestic partnerships.[35] The registered ones are of no account for purposes of this article, because a person who is married under the Recognition of Customary Marriages Act may not register a domestic partnership.[36] In the case of an unregistered domestic partnership the parties may, briefly, claim in court:

> Property division and or maintenance after termination of the partnership
> Maintenance after death of a partner, and
> Claim to succeed when the domestic partner dies intestate

The claims would cover claims by or against persons who are married by customary law or civil rites.

There is merit in this proposal to alleviate the plight of domestic partners. In the case of registration, however, one may ask who would register a partnership instead of getting married? If they do marry they have tried and tested ways of ordering their relationship.

As for unregistered ones, the manifestations are so wide and varied that any one could *ex post facto* come along and claim to have been in a domestic partnership or not, depending on what is the most lucrative option. It may lead to cat and dog fights, like those that were virtually a national pastime when one had to prove guilt to obtain a divorce. The circumstances to which a court **must** have regard to resolve an application for division of property or maintenance are exactly those that beg for allegations and counter-allegations. The courts would have to start from scratch to give content to the criteria such as age of the partners. What if it lies anywhere between 18 and 88? The duration? One year? Five years? Fifty years? What about it? The reputation and public aspects of the relationship? Why? The answers would probably be arbitrary - depending on the whims and fancies of the judge concerned.

Every conceivable aspect of the partnership is left at the discretion of a court. There is no indication of how a partnership comes into being nor when. There is no way in which it is legally terminated nor when. No rights and duties are ascribed to the parties while the partnership lasts.

More important perhaps is the fact that the law will dump these untold numbers of human relationships of variable characteristics in the lap of courts that cannot cope with ordinary run of the mill criminals and liti-

---

35 Chapters 3 and 4.
36 Clause 4 of the Domestic Partnership Bill [B 2008].

gants. Where would the Africans, especially the women – the poorest of the poor – ever get the money from to make a court application? A point-blank denial would without more ado place the onus of proof on the applicant. And a simple allegation would put the respondent on the defence.

VIII. Maintenance of Surviving Spouses Act 27 of 1990

This Act provides the surviving spouse who is unable to support him or herself from his or her own means and income with a claim of maintenance against the deceased spouse's estate in an amount sufficient to provide him or her with reasonable maintenance.[37] Here again the claimant will have to prove that he or she was married to the deceased by customary law.

There is also *a lacuna* in the Act. If the claim of a survivor and that of a dependent child compete with each other, claims must, if necessary, be reduced proportionately.[38] There is a possibility that the claims of two or more customary wives may also compete with each other. In such an event this section cannot be invoked for a proportionate reduction. Each one, it would seem, could claim »reasonable maintenance«.

IX. Maintenance when Courts Grant Orders for Dissolution of Customary Marriages

In terms of section 8 (1) of the Act a customary marriage may only be dissolved by a court by a decree of divorce. That, at least, creates some certainty. However, in terms of section 8 (4)(e) a court granting a decree for dissolution of a customary marriage –

> »*may, when making an order for payment of maintenance, take into account any provision or arrangement made in accordance with customary law.*«

The only possible arrangements that come to mind are **isondlo** and return of the wife to her father's family home.

Isondlo is traditionally limited to a beast (nowadays mostly sound-

---

37 S 2 (1).
38 S 2 (3)(C).

ing in a sum of money) as thanks-giving for rearing a child. It is payable when the child is returned to its family. It is by no means maintenance, because it is a once-off payment.[39] There was an effort to equate it with maintenance,[40] but that was, with respect, absurd. A judge could surely not regard it as »an arrangement made in accordance with customary law«.

The other likely »arrangement« is that on divorce a customary law wife is supposed to return to her family home or even to be accommodated with the children in the husband's family home after divorce.[41] While such an arrangement is a possibility it is not a substitute for maintenance. Ironically, the abolition of succession in terms of the rules of male primogenitures may lead men to deny any responsibility for their family members.

X. The Maintenance Act 99 of 1998

In terms of section 2(1) of this Act
»The provision of this Act shall apply in respect of the legal duty of any person to maintain any other person, irrespective of the nature of the relationship between these persons giving rise to that duty.«

That would include customary law wives, but once again proof of the existence of the marriage comes into play. More importantly, the Maintenance Act is nought for the comfort of women. Bennett[42] explains:
»Finally, notwithstanding the threat of criminal prosecutions and garnishee orders, there is a notoriously low level of compliance with maintenance orders. Although subsequent marriages, poverty and unemployment provide a partial explanation, a further consideration is the fact that men are not predisposed to comply. They feel that, once they pay lobolo, they have fulfilled their duties and that they are then entitled to custody of their children with no corresponding obligation to maintain them.«

39　See Bennett Customary Law in South Africa (2004) 282–283.
40　*Hlengwa v Maphumulo* 1972 BAC 58 (NE).
41　See Bekker and Maithufi Maintenance duties of black spouses married by customary law in new dispensation *Obiter* (2003) 450–451.
42　*Op cit* 284.

XI. Conclusion

I am often consulted, especially by women, who are caught on the wrong foot having to prove *ex post facto* that they were or were not married by customary law. I am also often made acutely aware of persons who try to manipulate the system by trying to prove that they were married or not, depending on what suits them.

The problems cannot be solved by bringing domestic partnerships within the ambit of the law. A customary marriage is a marriage in its own right. An effort to resolve the lack of proof by giving effect to »partnerships« would further confuse the issue. Domestic partnerships are but part of the issue. Problems stem from the wide range of factors mentioned above. A remedy might be to make registration a requirement for the validity, accompanied by publicity of the requirement. In that event, more specific regulations prescribing the manner of registration would also be necessary. A discussion thereof would take me beyond the scope of this paper.

As the issues are so many and varied an official enquiry, say by the SA Law Reform Commission, may be justified. In some way or another the question of married – not married and concomitant maintenance obligations should be clarified.

Opsomming

'n Ontleding van die regte van Suid-Afrikaanse vrouens en kinders van gewoonteregtelike huwelike en van saamwoonverhoudings om onderhoud te eis van hulle mans en vaders.

Hierdie artikel ontleed die regte van swart vrouens en kinders om onderhoud te bekom van hulle mans en van die vaders van hulle kinders. Daar is enersyds gewoonteregtelike huwelike waarvan die geldigheid maklik betwis kan word. Andersydis is daar saamwoonverhoudings ingevolge waarvan die partye geen wedersydse onderhoudsverpligrting het nie. Die biologiese vaders van kinders is wel verplig om die kinders te onderhou, maar die afdwinging van dié verpligting is problematies.

Die skrywer doen aan die hand dat die hele aangeleentheid herondersoek word ten einde die leemtes reg te stel.

Alimony on the Margins:
Protecting Homemaking Service in the Public Interest

Lynn D. Wardle[1,2]

I. Introduction: Dentifying Public Interests to Clarify the Confused State of Alimony Theory

The traditional labor division between husband and wife, with the husband as a full-time wage-earner and the wife as a full-time homemaker, no longer characterizes most marriages in the United States or in many of the developed nations around the world. In recent decades the removal of legal and social obstacles to the education, training, professional, career, and competitively-paid employment opportunities for women in the paid-workforce has facilitated a dramatic increase in the number and percentage of married women and single women with children who are full-time employees engaged in paid labor and has led to a notable decrease in the percentage of married women and single women with children who are engaged full-time in homemaking.

For example, the percentage of women over 16 in the workforce in the United States rose by two-thirds, from 36% in 1960 to 58% in 2000.[3] More pointedly, the U.S. labor force participation rates among mothers of all children under 18 rose from 47.4% in 1975 to 72.9% in 2000; among mothers of children aged 6-17 labor force participation rates rose from 54.9% in 1975 to 79% in 2000; among mothers of children aged 3-5 the labor force participation rates rose from 45.0% in 1975 to 71.5% in 2000; and among mothers of children under age 3 labor force participation rose from 34.3% in 1975 to 61.0% in 2000.[4]

---

1 Professor of Law, Brigham Young University School of Law, Provo, USA.
2 The valuable research assistance of Joseph Shapiro, Elizabeth Harnish, and Jacob Ong, and the computer expertise of Becky Swim is gratefully acknowledged.
3 Sandra L. Clark & Mai Weismantle, Women's Bureau, U.S. Census Bureau, U.S. Dept. of Commerce, Census Brief 2000 (2003) available at http://www.census.gov/rood/woo-3pubs/c2kbr-18.pdf (seen 29 August 2008).
4 Bureau of Labor Statistics, U.S. Dept. of Labor, Working in the 21st Century, available at http://www.bls.gov/opub/working/data/chart16.txt (seen 20 August 2008).

One consequence of those labor-force, gender-role and social-expectations shifts has been an erosion of theoretical foundations for requiring the payment of alimony upon divorce. As used herein, the term *alimony* refers to money which a court orders one divorcing spouse (usually the husband) to provide in some specific amount to his former spouse (usually the wife) after the dissolution of their marriage for the support or partial support of the receiving spouse.[5] The old legal justifications for alimony (that the marriage had not formally ended, or the dissolution was due to the »fault« of the husband), ceased to justify alimony upon the adoption of no-fault divorce. As John Eekelaar and Mavis Maclean put it,

> »when the legislature made a definite ... move away from fault-based divorce in 1971, the only rationale for [the award of alimony] collapsed ... The retention of the fiction of the marital support obligation was no longer tenable.«[6]

Likewise, the economic justification for alimony when laws, markets and other social forces severely restricted the employment opportunities of women is no longer valid, either. General economic dependence of wives upon husbands is no longer socially expected, legally encouraged, or economically compelled. Less spousal economic dependence has resulted in reduced and fewer alimony awards.

Justifications for alimony can be categorized as **private** and **public**. The **private** justifications look to protect the private economic interests of the dependent spouse on the basis of legal principles that generally protect fairness in inter-personal financial dealings such as express or implied contract, partnership, unjust enrichment, constructive trust, etc. The waning of alimony has caused some American scholars to suggest creative new theories of private entitlement to alimony.[7] These new private alimony justifications are intellectually fun and interesting; however, they have had no significant impact in preventing or ameliorating a reduction of alimony awards.

The other category of justifications for alimony awards can be called **public** because they attempt to justify alimony on the basis of protecting public interests, not private economic interests of one spouse. The public interests behind alimony are the focus of this paper. Can alimony be justi-

---

5 Christopher L. Blakesley, §32:01-:02, in 3 Contemporary Family Law (Lynn D. Wardle, et al, eds., 1988).
6 John Eekelaar & Mavis Maclean, Maintenance After Divorce 15 (1986).
7 *See infra* note 23.

fied today by reference to any public interests even when private interests do not justify an alimony award?

Some have argued that alimony awards are contrary to the public interest in promoting the productive labor of all employable adults.[8] Promotion of »productive labor« is a widely-accepted social value, especially in affluent western countries.[9] On the surface, an award of alimony to a woman who has chosen to be primarily a homemaker rather than to engage in paid employment may seem inconsistent with public policies promoting »productive labor« of all employable adults. However, this paper argues that homemaking is »productive labor«, and that there are compelling public interest justifications for awarding alimony in cases in which a good faith spouse has engaged in substantially full-time homemaking rather than in employment for pay. Alimony can and should be used as a tool to protect the investment by spouses in critical social functions relating to child rearing and family maintenance that generate social capital.

While the alimony justification issue arises in many countries, this paper analyzes the example of the United States of America. It focuses on married women, particularly married women with minor children. However, the analysis should be transferable to other situations including some married women without children, cohabiting women with children, and to similar post-dissolution spousal support issues in other legal systems.

Part II of this paper describes the alimony conundrum in American family law today. While the law appears to make alimony as readily available, if not more easily awardable, than any time in history, the practice of awarding alimony seems to be restricted and waning.

Part III shows that homemaking is **productive labor** because it serves the public interest in many ways. For example, homemaking service **saves the public treasury enormous costs,** and homemaking service directly generates valuable **social capital** which benefits all members of society. In these and other ways, women who engage in homemaking service rather than paid employment are engaged in **productive labor.** An award of ali-

---

8   The distinguished Professor Herma Hill Kay, for example, opposed alimony because it gave married women an incentive to be financially dependent upon their husbands, which made them vulnerable not only during marriage but especially upon divorce. Dean Kay advocated elimination of alimony (as a goal, at least) in order to force married women to become more self-sufficient. Herma Hill Kay, *Equality and Difference: A Perspective on No-Fault Divorce and It's Aftermath,* 56 U. Cin. L. Rev. 1, 79, 84-85 (1987).

9   For example, government policies offering or protecting limited post-birth child care leave, limiting paid leave to just a few months, or one or two years, clearly illustrate the »productive labor« principle of public policy in a related context.

mony to a full-time homemaker could be justified by the public interest in promoting important productive labor that strengthens the infrastructure of society, even if there were no private economic interest justification for alimony (e.g., if wife's income were sufficient for her needs).

Part IV then shows that many women in America today recognize the value of homemaking services, even if the legal order does not. Already, many American women organize their lives to maximize the time they can give to homemaking service and bypass economic-earning opportunities that would detract from or impair their ability to render homemaking service. However, most of them do so to a limited (not-full-time) extent.

The **margin** referred in the title reflects the reality that few married woman are full-time homemakers today, so the main thrust of the public justification of alimony initially might have application primarily in those marginal cases. However, it also suggests that some women who engage in homemaking on the margins of their private economic production also may be able to show that their less-than-fulltime homemaking service has made significant social contribution worthy of some recognition in the law of alimony.

It is important to clarify what this paper is not suggesting or arguing. It is **not** arguing that all (or any particular) married women or married mothers should be full-time homemakers. How to balance the work-home conflict is a decision every married woman and every mother must make for herself. So this paper does **not** call for the law to dictate or encourage all mothers to be full-time homemakers. However, it argues that women who choose to engage in full-time or significant homemaking service make valuable contributions to the public interest that deserve to be recognized in the law of alimony.

II. The Conundrum of Alimony in Family Law Theory and Practice in America

Today, in the United States of America, alimony is legally available more than ever before. »All states give a divorce court the power to award post-divorce alimony in at least some instances« for at least some period of time.[10] In all states an award of alimony depends upon a showing of need

---

10 J. Thomas Oldham, Divorce, Separation and the Distribution of Property, § 13.04 *Alimony*, at 13-51 (2005).

for financial support by one spouse and the ability of the other spouse to pay such support.[11] In at least thirty-nine states the standard of living while married is a baseline reference point consideration in determining **need**.[12] However, alimony awards have become less common and more temporary. For instance, one study of alimony shortly before the general adoption no-fault divorce revealed that alimony awards were granted in only 15 % of divorce cases.[13] That statistic may also reflect the fact that most divorces occur early in marriage (half of divorces occur in the first six years), before the parties have acquired much in the way of income or assets. Thus, today, alimony is awarded in relatively few American divorce cases, and the alimony awards usually are small or of short duration. As social scientist Constance Shehan and her associates recently wrote:

> »Alimony awards are currently – and have historically been – rare in the US... The portion of divorces in which alimony has been awarded has seldom exceeded 15 %.«[14]

In 1993, Robert Kelly and Greer Litton Fox, two leading expert in the empirical dimensions of American divorce published a very revealing study in 1993 that was based on a sample of 879 divorce cases from Oakland County, Michigan in the early 1980s. The study separated found that in divorce cases involving couples with a single income alimony was awarded in 13.6 % of the cases, while alimony was awarded in divorce cases involving dual income couples less than half that often, in only 6.5 % of the cases.[15] Nearly a decade later, Professor Kelly published another study of alimony (in collaboration with William Rinaman), this time based on national data from the National Survey of Families and Households (NSFH); focusing on respondents who had experienced first divorces between 1977 and 1988 and had dependent children, the study revealed that in only 8.9 %

---

11 *Id.*; see also Blakesely, *supra* note 4, at §32:02; *id.* §32:07; Brenda L. Storey, *Surveying the Alimony Landscape*, 25 Fam. Advoc. 10 (Spring 2003).
12 Linda D. Elrod & Robert G. Spector, *A Review of the Year in Family Law: ERISA, Jurisdiction, and Third-Party Cases Multiply*, 40 Fam. L. Q. 545 (2007); *id.* at 591, Chart 1—Alimony/Spousal Support Factors.
13 *See generally* Lenore J. Weitzman & Ruth B. Dixon, *The Alimony Myth: Does No-Fault Divorce Make a Diffrence?* 14 Fam. L. Q. 141 (1980).
14 Constance L. Shehan, Felix M Berardo, Erica Owens, Donna H. Berardo, *Alimony, An Anomaly in Family Social Science*, 15 Family Relations No.4, Families and the Law 308, 308 (2002).
15 Robert K. Kelly & Greer Litton Fox, *Determinants of alimony awards: An empirical test of current theories and a reflection on public policy*, 44 Syracuse L. Rev. 641, 643 (1993); *id.* at , 679, 681.

of the divorce decrees was alimony (or any comparable ongoing financial obligation other than child support) was awarded.[16] The Internal Revenue Service reports that

> »in 2004, of the 132 million tax returns that were filed, half a million of them had claims on them of having paid alimony to another person (ironically 134,393 less persons claimed receiving alimony the same year).«[17]

The scarcity of alimony awards today illustrates that the historical justifications for alimony are rarely applicable now. For instance,»fault« as a ground for award of alimony seems inconsistent with, if not eliminated by, the universal adoption of no-fault grounds for divorce in America. By the same token, unilateral no-fault divorce belies and subverts the assumption that marriage is a lifelong commitment. Because social and economic changes in the past thirty years have made it possible (and socially preferred) for women to obtain the same kind of jobs that men have, financial need for alimony is less likely. What justification is there for ordering a man to pay his money to support a woman to whom he is no longer married, who has (or is capable of holding) a good job that will provide her with enough income to be self-sufficient?

To resolve that impasse, some legal scholars have made creative theoretical arguments to justify the general or wider award of alimony.[18] Most

---

16 Robert F. Kelly & William C. Rinaman, *The Structure and Prediction of Classes of Divorce Settlements Involving Dependent Children in a National Sample*, 38(3/4) Journal of Divorce and Remarriage 1, 9,11 (2003).

17 Individual Income Tax Returns, 2000-2004, www.irs.gov/pub/irs-soi/04intba.xls, summarized at www.endalimonynow.com (seen 15 August 2008). *C.f.*, Christopher Reynolds, *Reliable Exes*, 26 American Demographics, issue 3, p. 10 (2004) (»According to a recent study published in *American Demographics*, »Current Population Survey information ... reveals that of more than 200 million people who report income, some 453,000 identify that income as coming from alimony payments.«).

18 *See, e.g.*, Ira M. Ellman, The Theory of Alimony, 77 Cal. L. Rev. 1 (1989); June R. Carbone, *Economics, Feminism and the Reinvention of Alimony: A Reply to Ira* Ellman, 43 Vand. L. Rev. 1463 (1990); Carl Schneider, *Rethinking Alimony: Marital Decisions and Moral Discourse*, 1991 B.Y.U. L. Rev. 197 (1991); June Carbone & Margaret F. Brinig, *Rethinking Marriage: Feminist Ideology, Economic Change, and Divorce Reform* 65 Tulane L. Rev. 953 (1991); John C. Sheldon & Nancy Diesel Mills, *In Search of a Theory of* Alimony, 45 Me. L. Rev. 283 (1993); Jana B. Singer, *Alimony and Efficiency: The Gendered Costs and Benefits of the Economic Justifications for Alimony*, 82 Geo. L. J. 2432 (1994); Margaret Brinig, *Comment on Jana Singer's Alimony and Efficiency*, 82 Geo. L. J. 2461 (1994); Margaret Brinig & Steven M. Crafton, *Marriage and Opportunity*, 23 J. Legal Stud. 869 (1994); Ann Laquer Estin, *Love and Obligation: Family Law and the Romance of Economics*, 365 Wm. & Mary L. Rev. 989 (1995); Joan M. Krauskopf, *Rehabilitative Alimony: Uses and Abuses of Limited Duration Alimony*, 21

of these theories and have focused on various economic private interests, and many have used feminist theoretical justifications. The explosion of new theoretical images of alimony has added to the confusion over the purpose and role of alimony today, but has had no discernible impact on the low number of alimony awards.

For example, the American Law Institute's *Principles of the Law of Family Dissolution* recommends liberal redistribution of income streams to equalize income after marriage on a general compensation for lost economic opportunity theory.[19] However, as Allen Parkman has noted:

> »[T]he ALI Principles lacks consistency because it does not provide a logical reason why ex-spouses‹ incomes should be shared just because they were married. Without a clearly defined reason, numerous injustices will occur. For example, a woman who made numerous sacrifices before marriage to acquire important income-earning skills, such as a medical education, will be forced to share her income with a man who did not make similar sacrifices either before or during marriage.«[20]

III. Homemaking is Productive Labor that Promotes Substantial Public Interests

The term »productive labor« is a term of political economy and refers to that which »produces or increases wealth or value« or »(chiefly in Marxist theory): that contributes to production; esp. in *productive forces:* the sources and determinants of productivity, as labour power, ... the skills of the individual worker, etc...«[21] For example, Adam Smith, in *The Wealth of Nations* wrote:

> »There is one sort of labour that adds to the value of the subject upon which it is bestowed: there is another which has not such effect. The former, as it produces a value, may be called productive.«[22]

Fam. L. Q. 573 (1988); Lenore Weitzman, *The Economics of Divorce: Social and Economic Consequences of Property, Alimony and Child Support Awards,* 28 UCLA L. Rev. 1181 (1981).

19 The American Law Institute, Principles of the Law of Family Dissolution, at 785 (2002) (Chapter 5, Compensatory Spousal Payments).
20 Allen M. Parkman, *Bringing Consistency to the Financial Arrangements at Divorce,* 87 Ky. L.J. 51, 55 (1998-99).
21 Oxford English Dictionary Online, *productive, adj.* and *n.,* at 4 (Draft Revision Sept. 2008), available at http://dictionary.oed.com/cgi/entry/50189374? (seen 10 September 2008).
22 Adam Smith, An Inquiry into the Nature and Causes of the Wealth of Nations I. II. iii (1776); quoted in OED, *supra* note 4.

If alimony justification is viewed as a question of public economic interests, it can be posited as inquiring whether homemaking is »productive labor.« The general assumption in western societies is: »No, homemaking is not productive labor.« Ironically, the most influential ideological foundation for the rejection of homemaking service as productive labor lies in the writings of Marx, Engels, and Lenin (rather than any of the capitalist economists whose works explain the economies that have actually liberated workers and married women).

»*In classical Marxist theory, as in early Soviet policy, the transformation of the family was perceived to be essential to the liberation of women. ... It required a shift of functions from the family to the wider society.*«[23]

Marx and Engels foresaw that the future family would be free as women would be liberated from homemaking to participate in »social production.«[24] Engels expressed the core assumption underlying the Marxist view of the family:

»*[T]he first condition for the liberation of the wife is to bring the whole female sex back into public industry, and ... in turn demands that the characteristic of the monogamous family as the economic unit of society be abolished.*«[25]

Engels had compared the position of wives in traditional marriages to that of the proletariat (with husbands in the role of the capitalists) and he anticipated a day when women would be economically independent.[26]

»*Only when this is accomplished [would] a new generation of women grow up, Engels [wrote], who have never known ›what it is to give themselves to a man from any other considerations than real love or to refuse to give themselves to their lover from fear of the economic consequences.‹*«[27]

---

23 Gail Warshofsky Lapidus, Women in Soviet Society 235-36 (1978).
24 H. Kent Geiger, The Family in Soviet Russia 21-22 (1968).
25 Friedrich Engels, The Origin of the Family, Private Property and the State 137-138 (1972), cited in Eleanor Burke Leacock, *Introduction*, in Friedrich Engels, The Origin of the Family, Private Property and the State 43 (1972).
26 Inga Markovits, *Family Traits*, 88 Mich. L. Rev. 1734, 1743 (1990) (book review of Mary Ann Glendon, The Transformation of Family Law: State, Law and Family in the United States and Western Europe (1988)).
27 Leacock, *supra* note 25 at 43, citing Engels, *supra* note 25, at 145.

Lenin, also was »strongly opposed« to the individual household with its »stinking kitchen,« and dedicated to »sav[ing] woman from housewifery.«[28] He wrote that a housewife was

> »a daily sacrifice to unimportant trivialities. ... They are like worms which, unseen, slowly but surely rot and corrode.«[29]

While Communism and Marxism have been generally rejected by liberal democracies, the remnants of this attitude toward homemaking, supplemented by the myopic materialism of consumer-capitalism, still thrives. Yet there is strong evidence to support the conclusion that homemaking is productive labor that benefits society in materially important ways.

1. *Homemaking Service Saves the Public Treasury Significant Costs.*
The value of the service by homemakers to dependent individuals, especially young children, elderly family members, and youth in need of supervision and socialization is hard to quantify. But the fact that if the homemakers did not provide that service, someone else would have to do so, and in many cases (especially involving the less-wealthy) it would be the state. Thus, homemakers save the public treasury a great deal of money by the service they render which relieves the state of having to provide those services at taxpayer expense. The actual monetary value of homemaking services provided by full-time homemakers is highly debated. Recent estimates range from $ 30,000 per year,[30] to $ 117,500 per year,[31] to $ 773,700

---

28 Geiger, *supra* note 24, at 46.
29 Geiger, *supra* note 24, at 46.
30 Women Work! The National Network for Women's Employment. http://www.women-work.org/resources/tipsheets/valuehomemaking.htm (seen 12 September 2008) (replacement value is $30,000 per year) (»This method evaluates homemaking by determining how much it would cost to replace a homemaker with paid workers. All of the homemaker's tasks and the amount of time spent on each are listed in the table on page 1 of this tip sheet. The hourly rate to hire an individual to perform each of these tasks is determined, and the cost is added up.«) One problem with this approach is that does not account for the fact that a homemaker is on call 24 hours a day, seven days a week, which would obviously significantly increase replacement service costs. See also Liz Pulliam Weston. *What's a Homemaker Worth? The Shocking Truth*. MSN Money, http://moneycentral.msn.com/content/collegeandfamily/p46800.asp (seen 12 September 2008) (»The lifetime economic value of a female homemaker who dies at age 30 is currently about $300,000, Schouten said, based on statistics from a seminal study in this area, The Dollar Value of Household Work. Compare that to a 30-year-old who makes the average white-collar wage of $19.86 an hour.«)
31 *Mother's love worth $117,000 per year, study says.* CNN.com/living. http://www.cnn.com/2008/LIVING/worklife/05/09/mom.salary.ap/ (seen 12 September 2008).

per year. [32] That represents the estimated market value of the services performed by the typical homemaker in a typical year. Using even the lowest estimate, it is obivous that many couples could not afford to pay for such services. They would turn to the government for assistance – to obtain the service from the government (such as a government day care provider), or to ask the government to subsidize their cost of contracting for those services. Thus, even if the lowest figure, $ 30,000 per year, were used, the amount of money saved the public by homemakers caring for dependents (especially young children and the aged) instead of public agencies having to care for those dependent young and old citizens, is staggering!

2. *Homemaking Service Directly Generates Valuable Social Capital.*
Homemaking service produces many intangible but very valuable contributions to the public good in the form of the generation of social capital. While a full-time homemaker is not necessary to produce social capital, families with a full-time homemaker in the home appear to generate social capital more effectively than other family forms. That is the glue of society.

> »*A social organism of any sort whatever, large or small, is what it is because each member proceeds to do his own duty with a trust that the other members will simultaneously do theirs. Wherever a desired result is achieved by the co-operation of many independent persons, its existence as a fact is a pure consequences of the precursive faith in one another of those immediately concerned.*«[33]

The family is the first schoolroom, where children learn duty, responsibility, self-control, obedience to the unenforceable, and other virtues necessary for the functioning of democratic society.

The importance of this element of homemaking was recognize and celebrated in the Founding Era of the American nation. American republicans saw »marriage as a training ground of citizenly virtue,«[34] Likewise, »it

---

32 *How Much is Your Mother Worth This Mother's Day? Try $773,700.* http://www.ricedelman.com/cs/pressroom/pressroom_detail?pressrelease.id=9&titleParam=How+Much+Is+Your+Mother+Worth+This+Mother%27s+Day%3F+Try+%24773%2C700%21 (seen 12 September 2008).
33 William James, *The Will to Believe* in The Will to Believe and other essays in popular philosophy 1, 24 (Dover 1956).
34 Nancy F. Cott, Public Vows. A History of Marriage and the Nation, 18 (2000).

served as a ›school of affection‹ where citizens would learn to care about others.«[35] One founding era writer noted that »by marriage ›man feels a growing attachment to human nature, and love of his country.‹«[36] For many »Revolutionary-era leaders, marriage had several levels of political relevance, as the prime metaphor for consensual union and voluntary allegiance, as the necessary school of affection, and as the foundation of national morality.«[37] Families were viewed as »schools of republican virtue.«[38] Homemakers were deemed especially important to the cultivation of republican virtues by the Founding generation. As Linda Kerber has written:

> »*The Republican Mother's life was dedicated to the service of civic virtue: she educated her sons for it, she condemned and corrected her husband's lapses from it. If, according to … [one] commonly accepted claim, the stability of the nation rested on the persistence of virtue among its citizens, then the creation of virtuous citizens was dependent on the presence of wives and mothers who were well informed, ›properly methodical‹, and free of ›invidious and rancorous passions.‹ … To that end the theorists created a mother who had a political purpose and argued that her domestic behavior had a direct political function in the Republic.«[39]*

Michael Grossberg agrees.

> »*By charging homes with the vital responsibility of molding the private virtue necessary for republicanism to flourish, the new nation greatly enhanced the importance of women's family duties. … At times ›it even seemed as though republican theorists believed that the fate of the republic rested squarely, perhaps solely, on the shoulders of its womenfolk.‹*«[40]

---

35 Cott, *supra* note 34, at 19.
36 Cott, *supra* note 34, at 19.
37 Cott, *supra* note 34, at 21.
38 Mary Lyndon Shanley, Review Essay, *Public Values and Private Lives, Cott, Davis, and Hartog on the History of Marriage Law in the United States*, 27 Law & Soc. Inquiry 923, 926 (2002). *See also* Cott, *supra* note 34, at 10.
39 Linda K. Kerber, Women of the Republic: Intellect and Ideology in Revolutionary America 22-30 (1980).
40 MICHAEL GROSSBERG, GOVERNING THE HEARTH: LAW AND THE FAMILY IN NINETEENTH-CENTURY AMERICA 6-9 (1985).

De Tocqueville was also convinced of this when he toured America fifty years after the founding. He wrote: »[T]he American derives from his own home that love or order which he afterwards carries with him into public affairs.«[41] His contemporary social commentator, Vienna educated Francis Grund, emphasized the importance of the republican family for the preservation of the American constitutional system when he observed:
> »I consider the domestic virtue of the Americans as the principal source of all their other qualities. ... No government could be established on the same principle as that of the United States with a different code of morals. Change the domestic habits of the Americans ... and it will not be necessary to change a single letter in the Constitution in order to vary the whole form of their government.«[42]

Thus, there is a constitutional significance of homemaking insofar as it instills republican citizenship virtues in the rising generation. It is of immeasurable public value.

Moreover, homemaking saves the public enormous sums indirectly. For example, divorce is enormously costly, not just for the private parties and families involved, but for the public. A recent study by a Business School professor published by the Institute for American Values and the Institute for Marriage and Public Policy calculates that the public costs – costs to American taxpayers – of family marital break-up and of non-marital childbearing (CBOW), total at least $ 112 billion each year for the USA, $ 70 billion in federal budget costs go to dealing with the consequences of marital break-down and avoidance every year, and family fragmentation costs state and local governments $ 42 billion every year.[43] About five-to-ten percent of the tax burden in most states is attributable to public costs of divorce and nonmarital childbearing. So there is a huge public interest in protecting and strengthening families. That is what homemaking does – fulltime or marginal – it strengthens marriages and families.

Homemaking is consistently shown to have a positive, reinforcing effect upon marriage stability and continuity. A recent study by University of Virginia Sociologist, Dr. W. Bradford Wilcox, provides some evidence.

---

41   Alexis de Tocqueville, Democracy in America, vol. 1, page 304 (New York, Alfred A. Knopf, 1972) (originally published in 1835).
42   FRANCIS J. GRUND, THE AMERICANS, IN THE MORAL. SOCIAL, AND POLITICAL RELATIONS 171 (1837).
43   Institute for American Values, The Taxpayer Costs of Divorce and Unwed Childbearing 5 (Benjamin Scafidi, Principal Investigator, 2008).

Wilcox compared active Evangelicals (who follow traditional family styles more than the other groups), active Mainline Protestants, inactive Evangelicals, inactive Mainline Protestants, and unaffiliated men and families.[44] Active Evangelicals were happier and more satisfied than the families of other or inactive or unaffiliated men, who adhered to traditional family forms only about one-third to one-half as often as the active Evangelicals. He found that the active Evangelicals and active Mainline Protestants are about one-third more affectionate as parents (hugging and kissing and praising their children) than unaffiliated dads.[45] Moreover,

> »[w]ives of active Evangelical Protestant family men report the highest levels of happiness with the affection and the understanding that they receive from husbands, and they are followed fairly closely by wives of active mainline Protestant family men. Wives of unaffiliated family men report the lower levels of happiness.«[46]

Wives of active Evangelical Protestant family men also reported the lowest levels of violence (2.8 percent) of the five groups.[47]

IV. Many American Women Value Homemaking Service and Give It Priority

While trends for the past three decades have shown increasing numbers and percentages of married women working, the most recent surveys suggest that there is a changing attitude toward paid employment by such mothers themselves. For example, a 2007 poll by the Pew Research Center revealed that most American mothers of children under 18 prefer to work only part-time (50%) or to not work at all (30%) rather than full-time employment (20%).[48] Only 16% of all mothers with pre-school aged children (0–4) desired full-time employment. The same poll also reported

---

44 W. Bradford Wilcox & Jennifer A. Marshall, *Soft Patriarchs, New Men: How Christianity Shapes Fathers and Husbands*, Heritage Lectures No. 880, at 4 (June 6, 2005) (58% traditional gender traditionalism among active Evangelicals compared to 44% for active Mainline Protestants, compared to 37% for unaffiliated).
45 *Id.* at 5.
46 Wilcox & Marshall, *supra* note 44, at 5.
47 *Id.*
48 Pew Research Center, *From 1997 to 2007: Fewer Mothers Prefer Full-time Work*, July 12, 2007, available at http://pewresearch.org/assets/social/pdf/WomenWorking.pdf (seen 16 July 2007).

that mothers who were employed rated themselves as significantly poorer parents (only 28 percent rated 9 or 10 out of 10) than part-time (41 percent) or not-employed (43 percent) mothers.[49]

The desire for economic stability explains a large part of the trend toward mothers working during the past three decades. Sociologist Mark Evan Edwards of Oregon State University explains that the movement of more young mothers into paid employment largely reflects the »dramatically changing economic situation« and asserts that »economic uncertainty and fear of downward mobility [have] inspired the adoption of dual earner arrangements.« He correlates the movement of young mothers into paid employment with both the divorce boom in the 1970s and 1980s, and with the economic downturn of that era.[50]

But the employment patterns of married women and mothers reveals their commitment to homemaking. The Bureau of Labor Statistics reports that **women are more than twice as likely as men** to work part time – that is, fewer than 35 hours per week,[51] reflecting greater commitment to gendered homemaking roles and responsibilities. (By 2004 the percentage of women in the workforce working parttime had risen to nearly 26%, the fifth straight year it had risen.)[52] The BLS reported in 2003 that the percent of mothers with children of all ages rose between 1975 and 2000, the percent of women working was lowest for mothers of children under 3 years of age (61%), was next lowest for mothers of children 3-5 (71.5%), and highest for mothers of children aged 6–17 (79%).[53] That tiered-approach also clearly reflects the greater homemaking commitment of America's working women because when children are young more caregiving time is needed. This data supports the claim that American mothers value homemaking and that their homemaking commitments shape their workforce participation.

More evidence of this comes indirectly from the persisting »gender pay

---

49 Id.
50 Mark Evan Edwards, *Uncertainty and the Rise of the Work-Family Dilemma*, 61 Journal of Marriage and the Family 183 (2001).
51 Bureau of Labor Statistics, U.S. Dept. of Labor, Women at Work: A Visual Essay at 3(2003), available at http://www.bls.gov/opub/mlr/2003/10/ressum3.pdf (seen 20 August 2008). (In 2002 about 25% of women worked part-time, while only 11% of men worked part-time).
52 Employed persons by full- and part-time status and sex, 1970–2004, in Workforce Databook, Table 20, available at http://www.bls.gov/cps/wf-databookk-2005.pdf (seen 20 August 2008).
53 Bureau of Labor Statistics, U.S. Dept. of Labor, Working in the 21st Century, chart 16, available at http://www.bls.gov/opub/working/data/chart16.txt (seen 20 August 2008).

gap.« While there are undoubtedly several factors that contribute to the gender pay gap, homemaking commitment to children demonstrably accounts for some of the residual gender pay gap. As the British Equal Opportunities Commission noted, »[m]uch of this is explained by women choosing to take career breaks to have families or opting for lower paid jobs – so called occupational segregation.«[54] A 2004 Report from the U.S. Congress' Government Accounting Office concluded that women's earnings are impaired by their disproportionate role as family caregiver. »[S]ome experts said that some women trade off career advancement or higher earnings for a job that offers flexibility to manage work and family responsibilities.[55] An article in Fiscal Studies in 2006 by Gillian Paull estimated that »among men and women without children, women in full-time work earn just 4.9 % less than men. And they are more likely than men (34.8 % against 33.2 %) to be in supervisory jobs.«[56] So homemaking by mothers clearly accounts for some part of the residual gender pay gap, and the persistence of the gender pay gap attests to the continuing commitment of American working women to giving significant homemaking service.

V. Conclusion: Alimony Law Should Recognize the Public Worth of Homemaking Service

Alimony law theory is in disarray today because lawmakers and legal commentators have failed to recognize the public interests underlying alimony awards, as a general matter, and have failed to specifically recognize the public interest in the »productive labor« of homemaking. By focusing their efforts on trying to manipulate private interest theories, both academics and legislators have overlooked and disregarded the great value of the enormous contributions which homemakers make to society in general.

---

54 Tim Worstall, *Gender Pay Gap, Yet Again*, at http://timworstall.typepad.com/timworstall/2006/01/gender_pay_gap_.html (January 27, 2007) (seen July 20, 2007).
55 *Women's Earnings, Work Patterns Partially Explain Difference between Men's and Women's Earnings*, U.S. Government Accounting Office, October 2003, at 3, available at http://usgovinfo.about.com/gi/dynamic/offsite.htm?zi=1/XJ&sdn=usgovinfo&cdn= newsissues&tm=254&f=10&tt=2&bt=0&bts=0&zu=http%3A//www.gao.gov/new.items/ d0435.pdf (seen 20 July 2007).
56 *The Gender Pay Gap and Children*, Dec. 1, 2006, at http://stumblingandmumbling. typepad.com/stumbling_and_mumbling/2006/12/the_gender_pay_.html (seen 20 July 2007).

It takes more faith to enter, maintain and invest one's life in a marriage today than in earlier times because divorce has become so common in and so accepted by our society, and because our unilateral no-fault divorce laws convey a powerful message about the legal insecurity of marriages. To counter those and other centrifugal forces of modern life, the public interest in marriage needs to be recognized and the contributions of homemakers to »productive labor« and to social capital of society should be legally acknowledged in alimony law.

Finally, it is worth repeating that this paper is **not** suggesting that all (or any particular) married women or married mothers should be full-time homemakers. How to balance the work-home conflict is a decision every married woman and every mother should make for herself with her family. However, this paper does assert and has tried to show that persons who choose to engage in full-time or significant homemaking service make valuable contributions to the public interest that deserve to be recognized specifically in the law of alimony.

New Models of Partnerships – Financial Consequences of Separation

Nina Dethloff[1]

I. Introduction

Family life is changing throughout the world. Growing numbers of couples are living together without being married. Same-sex relationships are widely recognized. Children are being raised by heterosexual or homosexual couples who are married or cohabitating and who are or are not their biological parents. Divorce and separation are also on the rise leading to numerous consecutive marriages and partnerships. Lawmakers all over the Western world have responded to this growing diversity of forms of partnership and family life, thus acknowledging that the traditional family based on life-long marriage between husband and wife with their biological children although not replaced by, has come to coexist with new forms of family units. Three different trends can be discerned which will be considered in turn: New forms of registered partnerships and civil unions have emerged, marriage has been opened to same-sex couples and rules have been enacted for de facto relationships. A comparative analysis of the financial consequences of separation will lead to some conclusions about the state's role in intimate relationships as new forms of family life materialize.

II. Registered Partnership

After more than two thousand years of the monopoly of marriage almost twenty years ago a new legal status was created, that of registered partnerships. As homosexual relationships became gradually more accepted and the number of cohabitating couples increased, the need to recognize legally their relationships arose. Sexual orientation was no longer considered a valid ground for discrimination[2]. Instead of opening marriage to

---

1 Bonn University, Germany.
2 Cf. Charter of fundamental rights of the European Union, art. 21, 2000 O.J. (C 364).

same-sex couples many countries, at least initially, opted for a politically more acceptable path and introduced registered or domestic partnerships or a civil union.

The Nordic countries were the first to allow same-sex partners to enter into registered partnerships, with Denmark leading the way in 1989[3]. Meanwhile, Scandinavia has been followed by many other European countries, such as the Netherlands[4], Germany[5], Switzerland[6], the United Kingdom[7], the Spanish Autonomous Communities[8], the Czech Republic[9], Slovenia[10] and supposedly Hungary as of summer 2009[11].

A great variety of registered partnerships can also be found in almost all other continents: In the United States of America Vermont[12], Connecticut[13], New Jersey[14] and New Hampshire[15] offer civil unions, and California[16], Oregon[17], Washington[18] and the District of Columbia[19] have

---

3 Lov om registreret partnerskab (Lov nr. 372 af 7/6/1989); cf. Craig A. Sloane, *A rose by any other name: marriage and the Danish Registered Partnership Act*, 5 CARDOZO J. INT'L & COMP. L. 189 (1997).
4 Wet van 5 juli 1997 tot wijziging van Boek 1 van het Burgerlijk Wetboek en van het Wetboek van Burgerlijke Rechtsvordering in verband met opneming daarin van bepalingen voor het geregistreerd partnerschap, Stb. 1997, 324.
5 »Gesetz zur Beendigung der Diskriminierung gleichgeschlechtlicher Gemeinschaften: Lebenspartnerschaften«, v. 16.2.2001 (BGBl. I S. 266).
6 »Bundesgesetz vom 18.06.2004 über die eingetragene Partnerschaft gleichgeschlechtlicher Paare« (Partnerschaftsgesetz, PartG).
7 Civil Partnership Act, 2004, ch. 33 (Eng.).
8 Cf. Aragon: Ley 6/1999, de 26 de marzo, relativa a parejas estables no casadas, art. 3; Navarra: Ley 6/2000, de 3 de julio, para la igualdad jurídica de las parejas estables de Navarra, art. 2 No. 2; Catalonia: Ley 10/1998, de 15 de julio, de uniones estables de pareja.
9 Zákon ze dne 26. ledna 2006 o registrovaném partnerství a o změně některých souvisejících zákonů.
10 Zakon o registraciji istospolne partnerske skupnosti (ZRIPS), Stran 6705, Uradni list RS, št. 65/2005 z dne 08.07.2005.
11 For the development see Orsolya Szeibert-Erdös, *Same-sex partners in Hungary: Cohabitation and registered partnership*, 4 UTRECHT L. REV. 212, 217-221 (2008).
12 Act Relating to Civil Unions, No. 91, 2000, VT. STAT. ANN. tit. 15, §§ 1201-1207 (2007).
13 An Act concerning Civil Unions, CONN. GEN. STAT. §§ 46b-38aa to 38pp (2008); cf. J Thomas Oldham, *Developments in the US – The struggle over the creation of a status for same-sex partners*, INT'L SURV. FAM. L. 481, 485-486 (2006).
14 N.J. STAT. ANN. § 37:1-28 (2008).
15 N.H. REV. STAT. ANN. §§ 457-A:1 to A:8 (2008).
16 CAL. FAM. CODE §§ 297-299.6 (West 2007).
17 OR. REV. STAT. ch. 106 (2007).
18 WASH. REV. CODE § 26.60 (2007).
19 The Domestic Partnership Equality Amendment Act of 2006, 2006 D.C. LAW 16-79; Omnibus Domestic Partnership Equality Amendment Act of 2008, 2008 D.C. LAW 17-231.

domestic partnership laws. Registered partnerships or civil unions can also be entered into in several Canadian provinces[20], in some Central and South American countries and regions[21], as well as in New Zealand[22] and an increasing number of Australian territories[23].

Sometimes, such as with the pacte civil de solidarité in France or the Adult Interdependent Relationships in the province of Alberta these new forms of partnership are open to heterosexual couples as well. In those cases they often constitute a framework that confers fewer rights and obligations than marriage, thus creating a sort of mini-marriage for both same – as well as opposite-sex couples. Frequently, however, legislatures have created a legal status that is reserved for same-sex partners. Here the trend is clearly to approximate the status to marriage, thus providing for financial relief, division of property or maintenance upon separation.

III. Same-Sex Marriage

Instead of introducing or after having introduced registered partnerships for same-sex couples a growing number of countries has opened marriage to homosexuals. Registered partnerships or civil unions, even when granting equal rights, have been considered inadequate to put an end to the discrimination of homosexuals, as they create a separate status. Lawmakers therefore choose to replace them by or opt for a gender-neutral marriage. The first country to introduce same-sex marriage was the Netherlands in 2001[24], followed by six other countries so far: Belgium in 2003[25]

---

20 Nova Scotia (Vital Statistics Act, R.S.N.S., ch. 494 (1989)); Québec (An Act Instituting Civil Unions and Establishing New Rules of Filiation, Bill 84, ch. 6 (2002), Explanatory notes); Alberta (Adult Interdependent Relationships Act, S.A., ch. A-4.5 (2002)); Manitoba (Common Law Partners' Property and Related Amendments Act, S.M., ch. 48 (2002); see Caroline A. Thomas, *The Roles of Registered Partnerships and Conjugality in Canadian Family Law*, 22 CAN. J. FAM. L. 223, 244-246 (2006).
21 E.g. Columbia The Domestic Partnership Equality Amendment Act of 2006, 2006 D.C. LAW 16-79; Omnibus Domestic Partnership Equality Amendment Act of 2008, 2008 D.C. LAW 17-231; Uruguay Ley No. 18.246, CM/387, Regulación de la unión concubinaria, 27.12.2007.
22 Civil Union Act, 2004 (N.Z.).
23 E.g. Relationships Act 2003 (No. 44 of 2003), 17.09.2003, Tas. Acts.; Katy A. King, *The Marriage Amendment Act: Can Australia prohibit same-sex marriage?*, 16 PAC. RIM L. & POL'Y 137, 149 (2007); see also Relationships Act, 2008 (No. 12 of 2008), Vict. Acts.
24 Law of December 21, 2000, Stb. 2001, 9.
25 Law of February 13, 2003, Moniteur belge, February 2, 2003, Edition 3, p. 9880.

and Spain[26] as well as Canada in 2005[27], South Africa in 2006[28], Norway and Sweden as of 2009[29]. Massachusetts[30] and California[31] also permit same-sex couples to marry. Elsewhere this issue is currently under debate, for example in Denmark[32].

In many countries the issue of same-sex marriage is highly controversial. Opposition often results from a prevailing religious impact on family law[33]. Voiced in political terms the state is considered to have a fundamental interest in traditional marriage between husband and wife, in particular due to its reproductive function[34]. Constitutional concerns are often raised: Marriage as protected by the constitution is deemed to be the Christian marriage between husband and wife, thus prohibiting same-sex marriage[35].

Conversely, more and more often constitutional law is deemed to **require opening** marriage to same-sex couples. To exclude homosexuals from entering into a marriage is seen as violating the basic premises of individual liberty and equality and considered as discrimination on the ground of sexual orientation. Moreover, even though same-sex partners cannot have biological children together, they frequently raise children together. These can be either the biological children of one of the partners, often conceived through artificial insemination with the consent of the other partner, or foster or adopted children. Same-sex couples therefore often provide care for children in just the same way as opposite-sex partners and fulfil functions similar to those of heterosexual married

---

26   Ley 13/2005, de 1 de julio, por la que se modifica el Código Civil en materia de derecho a contraer matrimonio (B.O.E., 2005, 157).
27   Civil Marriage Act, ch. 33, 2005 (Can.); see generally Wade K. Wright, *The tide in favour of equality: same-sex marriage in Canada and England and Wales*, 20 INT'L J.L. & POL'Y & FAM. 249, 252 (2006).
28   Civil Union Act, 2006, Government Gazette 30.11.2006 No. 29441, Act No. 17.2006.
29   In Norway: Lov om endringer i ekteskapsloven, barnelova, adopsjonsloven, bioteknologiloven mv. (felles ekteskapslov for heterofile og homofile par), Norsk Lovtidend avd I nr 7 2008, LOV-2008-06-27-53; in Sweden: proposition 2008/09:80 Äktenskapsfrågor, adopted on 01.04.2009.
30   Goodridge v. Department of Public Health, 798 N.E.2d 941 (Mass. Acts 2003).
31   *In re* Marriage Cases, 43 Cal. 4th 757 (Cal. 2008).
32   For a comparative overview see Katharina Boele-Woelki, *The legal recognition of same-sex relationships within the European Union*, 82 TUL. L. REV. 1949, 1955-56 (2008).
33   Ben Schuman, *Gods & Gays: Analyzing the same-sex marriage debate from a religious perspective*, 96 GEO. L.J. 2103, 2108-13 (2008).
34   Lynn D. Wardle, *»Multiply and replenish«: Considering same-sex marriage in light of state interests in marital procreation*, 24 HARV. J.L. & PUB. POL'Y 771 (2001).
35   For the German legal situation cf. Entscheidungen des Bundesverfassungsgerichts [BVerfGE] [Constitutional Court] 10, 59, 66; 29, 166, 176; 53, 224, 245.

partners. Thus especially in countries where adoptions by same-sex partners are allowed this argument is raised in order to allow homosexuals to marry. Parents merit the same protection whether they are of the opposite or of the same sex. Such protection is needed throughout the existence of the partnership, in particular if certain benefits are reserved for married couples with children[36]. It is equally important upon the breakdown of the relationship as marriage law provides a legal framework that ensures that the economic consequences of the breakdown are not born by one but by both partners[37].

Mostly the legal status of same-sex marriage is exactly the same as that of opposite-sex marriage, for example in Canada, Spain and Norway. Where fewer rights are granted these usually concern the parent-child relationship. However, there is a noticeable trend to allow not only stepparent or second parent adoptions but joint adoptions of a child not previously connected with either partner. More recently, a number of countries have changed their parentage law: More and more often the homosexual partner who consents to an artificial insemination is considered as legal parent of the child, as is usually the case with the consenting husband of the biological mother. Upon his or her birth the birth mother's partner thus becomes the legal mother of the child without the need for adoption[38].

IV. De facto Partnership

There is a great diversity of legal responses to the problems arising out of the increase in cohabitation: Especially upon separation cohabitating couples often find themselves in a position similar to that of married partners upon divorce. Frequently one partner has contributed to the partnership in a way that leads to a significant economic imbalance between the partners upon separation, for example by making a financial contribution to the other partner's property or education. Especially if a couple has raised children one of the partners has often taken on more of the homemaking work.

---

36 Goodridge v. Department of Public Health, 798 N.E.2d 941, 963-64 (Mass. Acts 2003).
37 *Id.* at 963.
38 See for Sweden: Maarit Jänterä-Jareborg, *Sweden: Lesbian couples are entitled to assisted fertilization and to equal rights of parentage*, Zeitschrift für das gesamte Familienrecht [FAMRZ] 2006, 1329-1330.

When courts have been confronted with requests for financial relief upon separation of cohabitees, they have increasingly invoked concepts such as implied contract, unjust enrichment, partnership or property law or resorted to concepts such as constructive trusts or other instruments of equity to reach a just result upon separation of cohabitees. However, in a growing number of countries this approach has been considered inadequate: The outcome of litigation is hard to predict, the weaker party is often not sufficiently protected and relief is frequently limited to major financial contributions thereby ignoring the contributions of the homemaking party.

Increasingly lawmakers have therefore enacted legislation for de facto relationships which applies under certain conditions, for example after a certain period of living together, without any act of registration. Such legislation can be found in many European countries, such as the former Yugoslavian countries[39], Croatia[40], Slovenia[41], or Serbia[42], Sweden[43] and Norway[44], a number of Spanish Autonomous Regions, namely Catalonia[45], Navarra[46], Extremadura[47] and Aragon[48], and was most recently introduced in Scotland[49]. However, these developments are by no means limited to Europe: Comparable legislation can be found in many South and Central American countries like Brazil[50], Bolivia, Ecuador or Venezuela.

---

39 For an overview cf. Christa Jessel-Holst, *Neue Entwicklungen im Bereich des Familienrechts der jugoslawischen Nachfolgestaaten*, Zeitschrift für das gesamte Familienrecht [FamRZ] 2004, 847-854.
40 Obiteljiski zakon, (Family Act) 14.7.2003; cf. Nenad Hlača, *Neuerungen im Familienrecht der Republik Kroatien*, Zeitschrift für das gesamte Familienrecht [FamRZ] 2008, at 1702; Dubravka Hrabar, Legal Status of Cohabitants in Crotia, *Die Rechtsstellung nichtehelicher Lebensgemeinschaften* 2005, 399-414.
41 Zakon o zakonski zvezi in družinskih razmerjih (Marriage and Family Relations Act) 2003; cf. Viktorija Žnidaršič Skubic, The Reform Of Slovenian Family Law: Property Relations Between Spouses, The International Survey of Family Law, at 367 (2008).
42 Zakon o braku i porodičnim odnosima (Family Act) 24.2.2005.
43 Lag 1987:32 om sambos gemensama hem 1987:232; replaced by Sambolagen 2003:376, in force since 01.07.2003; Maarit Jänterä-Jareborg, *Das neue schwedische Gesetz über die nichteheliche Lebensgemeinschaft*, Zeitschrift für das gesamte Familienrecht [FamRZ] 2004, 1431-1432.
44 Lov No. 45 om rett til felles bolig og innbo når husstandsfellesskap opphører, 4.7.1991
45 Ley 10/1998, de 15 de julio, de uniones estables de pareja.
46 Ley 6/2000, de 3 de julio, para la igualdad jurídica de las parejas estables de Navarra.
47 Ley 5/2003 de 20 de marzo, de parejas de hecho de la Comunidad Autónoma de Extremadura.
48 Ley 6/1999, de 26 de marzo, relativa a parejas estables no casadas.
49 Family Law Act, 2006, Scot. Parl. Acts, sec. 26-29.
50 Lei N° 10.406, 10.1.2002.

In fact it is a world wide trend: Australia[51], New Zealand[52] and Canada[53] have also enacted legislation on de facto partnerships.

The variety of legislation is enormous. The rules differ mainly in two respects: The conditions which must be fulfilled in order to constitute a de facto relationship, and the legal consequences that arise from such de facto relationships, especially upon dissolution of the partnership, be it by separation or by death. When considering the requirements that have to be met in order to constitute a de facto or stable relationship the requisite acts usually define it as a relationship that is comparable to that of a married couple except for the act of formalization. Statutes often refer to partners living together »as if they were husband or wife or civil partners«[54]. When assessing this, the duration of the partnership and the existence of children are of special importance[55]. Whereas initially legislation was limited to cohabitating partners of the opposite sex, more recently statutes also apply to homosexual couples.

There are also significant differences in the legal consequences that arise from such de facto relationships[56]. On the one hand upon separation of cohabitating partners basically the same rules apply as in the case of divorce, thus usually leading to an equal sharing of the matrimonial property and/or to some right to maintenance[57]. On the other hand there are special provisions for cohabitating partners that grant the courts wide discretion in assessing the amount of a compensatory payment taking into consideration whether there have been partnership related gains and losses[58]. Whereas the first concept leads to more legal certainty and foreseeability, thus reducing the potential for litigation, the second one is

---

51 See e.g. De Facto Relationships Act, 1991, N. Terr. Austrl. Acts; Property Law Act, 1974, Queensl. Act, Part. 19; De Facto Relationships Act, 1996, S. Austl. Acts; Relationships Act 2003,Tas. Acts.
52 Property (Relationships) Act, 1976 (N.Z.) as amended on 1.2.2002.
53 Adult Interdependent Relationships Act, S.A. (2002) (Can.); Juliene Payne/Marilyn Payne, Canadian Family Law, 2nd ed. 2006, at 48.
54 Family Law Act 2006, Scot. Parl. Acts, Sec. 25(2).
55 E.g. Property (Relationships) Act, 1984, N.S.W. Acts, sec. 4 (Austl.); for New Zealand cf. Bill Atkin, *Reflection on the New Zealand`s property reforms `five years on`*, The International Survey of Family Law, at 224 (2007); Jenni Millbank, *The changing meaning of »de facto« relationships*, visited Dec. 9, 2008) ‹http://papers.ssrn.com/sol3/cf_dev/AbsByAuth.cfm?per_id=449651#reg›.
56 Nina Dethloff, *Vermögensausgleich bei Auflösung nichtehelicher Lebensgemeinschaften*, Festschrift für Rainer Frank at 81-99 (2008).
57 See e.g. Property (Relationships) Act, 2001 (N.Z.).
58 See e.g. Property Law Act, Queenls. Acts, Sec. 291-2.; De Facto Relationships Act, Tas. Acts, Sec. 16(1)(a) und (c); Family Court Act, W. Austl. Acts, Sec. 205 ZG.

better able to consider the individual circumstances and thereby accomplish justice in every case.

V. Conclusion

What is the state's role when confronted with new forms of family life? As a fundamental principle the freedom of choice should be safeguarded. Modern family law has to respect the individual's and the partners' preferences for different forms of partnerships and family life. At the same time the state has to ensure that the weaker party is protected. Here family law differs significantly from other areas of law. The characteristics of long-term intimate relationships require special measures of protection. Party autonomy cannot be relied upon to the same extent as in commercial transactions where partners bargain at arm's length. Family law has to provide a legal framework that compensates an economic imbalance resulting from the partnership.

Marriage provides a legal framework which typically ensures that upon divorce the economic consequences of the breakdown of the partnership are born by both partners, usually providing for an equal division of the marital property and for the payment of maintenance where one partner has suffered marriage-related detriments. Marriage law can thus be considered as a form of standard contract that obviates the need to negotiate individually the conditions for divorce. As family life has become more varied, ranging from a traditional family with a homemaking partner to dual-income-no-kids partnerships, the statutory provisions should be open to some modification by the parties.

The more marriage laws can be contractually modified, the less pressing the need seems to become to create an additional legal framework for those who can marry, such as a registered partnership with fewer consequences. But even if states choose to introduce such an additional status as an alternative, the need remains to protect the weaker party in cases where no marriage or registered partnership was entered into. The state's role to protect the weaker family member therefore requires provisions for de facto relationships. Where such a relationship equals that of a married couple the same need arises to compensate for a partnership related economic imbalance upon separation.

Finally, family law should not discriminate on the grounds of the partners' sexual orientation. This requires that homosexuals are offered a legal status for their partnership just as heterosexuals are. Marriage provides such a framework for long-term intimate relationships. If states opt for registered partnerships for same-sex couples instead, this status should at least confer the same rights and obligations as marriage. The principle of equality and non-discrimination also requires that legislation on de facto relationships applies to hetero- as well as homosexual couples. Ultimately, the state must respect the parties' choice of family form as well as ensuring the protection of the weaker – regardless of the parties' sexual orientation.

London – The Divorce Capital of the World

Mathew Thorpe[1]

I. Introduction: The 1973 Act

The society last discussed the financial consequences of the breakdown of family relationship in, I think, 1983. My aim therefore is to trace the statutory evolution, or more accurately the absence of statutory evolution, in this area of the law of England and Wales. My focus will be on the financial consequences of divorce for the spouses. There have, during the past generation, been radical statutory innovations, mostly with very poor outcome, for child maintenance but I exclude them from my territory. Similarly I exclude statutory innovation for same sex couples. Nor will I consider the efforts of the Law Commission, so far unavailing, to introduce some semblance of justice for heterosexual cohabitants who experience relationship breakdown.

To make good my primary point that we have suffered, and are suffering, from legislative drift I need to establish the origins of the dominant statutory provisions, section 21–25 of the Matrimonial Causes Act 1973 (hereinafter the 1973 Act). The reform of the law of divorce has always aroused passions and factions in parliament. The Divorce Reform Act 1969 was no exception. Its proposal that no divorce could be granted without proof of the irretrievable breakdown of the marriage was broadly supported, provided it was accompanied by strong safeguards. One was that irretrievable breakdown could only be proved by one of five routes, generally either plucked from the old catalogue of matrimonial offences or, if consensual, earned by a substantial period of separation. The other safeguard was financial protection for the weaker party. Essentially the 1973 Act was the expression of that protection.

In Parliament stronger protection had been sought in the form of a Community of Property Bill, which passed its second reading but was withdrawn by its sponsors on the understanding that the Government

---

[1] Head of International Family Justice for England & Wales and Lord Justice of Appeal.

would meet their demands. However what the Government enacted (the Matrimonial Proceedings and Property Act 1970: subsequently consolidated into the 1973 Act) was not Community of Property but the judicial duty on or after the grant of divorce to fix maintenance obligations and to redistribute assets in the exercise of a discretion lightly directed by a checklist contained in the focal section 25. Furthermore the judge was given an overarching objective which Parliament thus expressed:

»*to place the parties in the financial position in which they would have been if the marriage had not broken down.*«

The sponsors of the Community of Property Bill had been out-manoeuvred by questionable tactics.

How did the judges of that now distant day interpret the new duty? Sensibly they focussed in the majority of cases in the middle range on securing the home or, at least a home, for all the parties, or at least one of them, whether or not there were children of the family. But the concepts of sharing or equality were undreamt of. In rebuffing a Community of Property amendment to the Bill that became the 1970 Act the Lord Chancellor posed the rhetorical question:

»*Are half (the husband's) business assets to be taken away from the business and given to a woman who knows nothing about business?*«

In like vein Lord Denning, the great judge of the day, in rejecting a wife's claim for a share in approximately £ 2,000,000 at modern monetary values resulting from the sale of the husband's family business ruled:

»*(the wife) did not work in (the business) herself. All she did was what a good wife does do. She gave moral support to her husband by looking after the home. If he was depressed or in difficulty she would encourage him to keep going.*«

That did not give her any right to a share in the proceeds. This judicial interpretation of its duty fully accorded with social and popular expectations. Indeed the popular reaction to the outcomes that resulted from the application of the 1973 Act was the conviction that judicial reluctance to investigate marital history resulted in injustice to payers when the payees contribution to the breakdown of the marriage went unreflected in the order.

II. The 1984 Act Amendments

In 1980 the Law Commission published its discussion paper: the Financial Consequences of Divorce: the Basic Policy, and in 1981 published recommendations based on the responses to its paper. These recommendations passed into law by incorporation into the Matrimonial and Family Proceedings Act 1984.

What were the effects of this reform? First the structure and text of the 1973 Act was largely confirmed. But Parliament intended major changes.

1.) the overriding objective was sensibly removed, since it had proved quite impossible of practical attainment. However, I emphasise that no alternative objective was substituted.
2.) the Act imposed a new duty on the judge to terminate financial relationships between the parties as soon after the divorce as was just and reasonable. This in ordinary legal language was the duty to achieve a clean break. To achieve this end the judge was given the additional power to dismiss a claim for periodical payments without the consent of the recipient either at the outset, or on a later variation application, provided so to do would not cause financial hardship.
3.) and no doubt to the disappointment of many litigants spoiling for a fight, the Act restricted the consideration of marital or other misconduct to »such that it would be inequitable to disregard.«

I will now consider how the judges interpreted these statutory reforms. First the removal of an overriding objective without any replacement had the obvious consequence of enlarging yet further the ambit of the judges' discretion. However, the judges reasonably inferred that Parliament must have intended them to craft outcomes that were seen to be fair to each party, even if Parliament had not so stated. But that provided only an elastic aid. Not only did the judge lack an over-arching objective he also lacked a statutorily defined starting point. He might have been left to pluck figures from the air were it not for a judicial aid provided by the dominant family judge of his generation, Ormrod LJ. In *O'Donnell v O'Donnell*[2] in 1975, and in other cases, he introduced the yardstick of the applicant wife's »reasonable requirements«. This concept engendered a science and a professional industry that quantified the cost of the applicant's reasonable requirements by positing the required home or homes,

---

2   [1976] Fam 83.

the required chattels and the required future annual expenditure capitalised by a computer programme approved by the Court of Appeal in *Duxbury v Duxbury*[3]. You will observe that this was the product of judicial necessity and creativity in the absence of clear statutory rules. The Ormrod mechanism survived a generation and I will later come to its demise in 2000 in the case of *White v White*[4].

I will take the other two innovations out of turn because there is little to say about the Parliamentary restriction on reflecting conduct in financial awards. That it remained unpopular can be seen from a section of the Family Law Act 1996 which enlarged the judges discretion to have regard to misconduct. However, since that section is within Part II of the Act it remains dead on the statute book because this Government declined to ordain a commencement date for Part II, a neat way of achieving its repeal.

It is upon the judicial interpretation of the second innovation of the 1984 Act that I intend to dwell at greater length. The purpose and objective of the innovation is clear from the Law Commission's 1981 report from which I have selected the following quotations:

»*There was, however, a wide-spread feeling amongst those who commented on the Discussion Paper that greater weight should be given to the importance of each party doing everything possible to become self-sufficient, so far as this is consistent with the interests of the children; and we believe that the statutory provisions should contain a positive assertion of this principle.*«

»*The court has, under the existing law, power to make orders for a limited term, and this power is sometimes exercised when it is felt that a spouse (usually the wife) needs some time to readjust to her new situation but could not or should not expect to rely on continuing support from her husband. We think that it would be desirable to require the courts specifically to consider whether an order for a limited term would not be appropriate in all the circumstances of the case, given the increased weight which we believe should be attached to the desirability of the parties becoming self sufficient.*«

»*Nevertheless, the response to the Discussion Paper showed strong support for the view (with which we agree) that such finality should*

---

3   [1987] 1 FLR 7.
4   [2001] 1 AC 596.

be achieved wherever possible, as for example where there is a childless marriage of comparatively short duration between the husband and a wife who has income, or an earning capacity, or in cases of a longer marriage, where there is an adequate measure of capital available for division.«

»The response to the Discussion Paper indicated wide support for the view that the court should be more clearly directed to the desirability of promoting a severance of financial obligations between the parties at the time of the divorce; and to give greater weight to the view that in the appropriate case any periodical financial provision ordered in favour of one spouse (usually the wife) for her own benefit – as distinct from periodical payments made to her to enable her to care for the children – should be primarily directed to secure wherever possible a smooth transition from marriage to the status of independence. We believe that this general objective should be embodied in the legislation.«

The judgments in the Court of Appeal in the early wake of the reform fully recognised this objective. Waite LJ in the 1986 appeal of *Tandy v Tandy*[5] said:

»The effect of the legislation, as now amended, is thus to give effect, whether on the making of the original order or on a subsequent application to vary it, to what has become loosely known as the »clean break«, a term which is perhaps now used in a wider context than when it first appeared. The legislative purpose, that is to say, is to enabled the parties to a failed marriage, wherever fairness allows, to go their separate ways without the running irritant of financial interdependence or dispute. For better-off families that can and will normally be achieved by a capital lump sum paid in satisfaction or commutation of the right to be maintained on a periodic basis. The legislation clearly contemplates, however (and there is no dispute as to this) that there will be circumstances in which fairness to one side demands, and to the other side permits, a severance of the maintenance tie in cases where no capital resources are available.«

---

5   [1988] FCR 561.

However, the law governing financial provision for the applicant wife has from its statutory inception in 1857 been strongly marked by paternalism. Adult autonomy is overshadowed by the court's concern to make the applicant financially secure. In families of substantial worth the judges were comfortable to opt for the route of »clean break«, where financial security for the wife could be immediately achieved from the outset. But where the route to »clean break« involved an assessment of future probabilities expressed in an order for periodical payments only for a term of years, the paternalistic instincts inhibited the judge from confining the applicant's support to such a fixed term. Still more inhibited was the judge in imposing a fixed term declared to be absolute in that it was incapable of extension by subsequent application. This inhibition is well illustrated by a long series of appeals in the 1990's culminating in the judgments of Ward LJ in $C\ v\ C^6$ and $G\ v\ G^7$.

My own conviction is that the social policy that underlined the Law Commission's recommendation was wise. The time had come to move at least gently away from paternalism and to encourage financial independence post divorce. The continuing monthly credit to one bank account and debit to the other sustains an emotional and psychological relationship and interdependence inconsistent with the dissolution of the marriage. The 1984 amendment introduced the question: should the applicant achieve financial independence at the end of a fair term and not the question will the applicant achieve it. Without the spur of a fairly judged terminus the recipient might be either tempted to avoid the challenge or inhibited by psychological dependence from establishing or re-establishing an earning power. Thus when the case of *McFarlane* reached the Court of Appeal consolidated with the case of *Parlour*[8], in each the applicant's obligation to achieve financial independence, and the courts duty to order periodical payments only for such term as would enable the recipient »to adjust without undue hardship«, led to judgments that expressly required the recipients to achieve financial independence by means of periodical payments for a limited term of years that far exceeded their needs in those years. In the case of Mrs McFarlane we restored an order of £ 250,000 per annum, reduced by the High Court Judge on first appeal, but limited to an extendable five year term. That put the onus on the recipient to apply for

---

6   [1997] 2 FLR 26.
7   [1997] 1 FLR 368.
8   [2005] Fam 171.

an extension before the end of the term if circumstances had prevented her from achieving the goal which we had set for her.

Mrs McFarlane appealed to the House of Lords where her case was consolidated with the appeal of Mr Miller, who challenged an award of £ 5,000,000 to his wife at the end of a brief marriage, an award which we had upheld in the Court of Appeal. It will be seen that whereas the consolidated appeals in the Court of Appeal raised the same issue the consolidated appeals in the House of Lords raised very different points.

Mrs McFarlane succeeded in her appeal, in that the House of Lords removed the five year term expressing the annual payment of £ 250,000 to be during joint lives or until her remarriage. Thus effectively the onus to initiate a further application, and to achieve a clean break, was transposed to the husband who retained the right to apply for the termination of her order with or without further capital payment.

The consolidation of appeals raising separate points has resulted in House of Lords judgments that do not consider in any depth the essential difference of view as to the construction and application of Section 25A of the 1973 Act. I would say, as you might expect, that the solution preferred by the House of Lords insufficiently reflects the reform of the 1984 Act and the objective so clearly stated in the Law Commission's recommendations.

Having analysed the judicial response to the amendments introduced by the 1984 Act I return to my principal theme: Parliaments attempts to modernise the law in the last decade of the twentieth century and the first decade of the twenty-first century.

III. Subsequent Legislative Inertia

The need for modernisation can be traced to:
1.) the growing sense that the paternalistic approach was increasingly inappropriate in a world in which 50 % of marriages ending in divorce have lasted for only nine years.
2.) the allied sense that the parties to a marriage should have the contractual freedom to provide for the financial consequences of divorce.
3.) judicial and practitioner frustration at the enormous and disproportionate costs bills in contested applications.

This reality could undoubtedly be partially ascribed to the width of the judicial discretion and the consequent impediment to negotiated settlements. It was often said that a specialist practitioner, asked by his client what she might expect to be awarded by the court, would reply: it depends which judge we get on the day.

The problem of costs bills disproportionate to the sum in dispute could be partially traced to lax and antiquated procedures largely uncontrolled by the court. Accordingly in 1992 a committee of judges and practitioners came into spontaneous being to seek procedural reforms. I chaired the committee which was, after much initial suspicion, embraced by the Ministry of Justice (then the Lord Chancellor's Department) and officially adopted as the Lord Chancellor's Ancillary Relief Working Group (hereinafter the Working Group) its proposed reforms were initially piloted in trial courts and then in 2000 universally applied. They have been an unqualified success, introducing firm judicial case management throughout the process, complimented by a full blown financial dispute resolution appointment before any trial is directed.

In February 1998 the responsible Minister announced the Government's intention to modernise the law »to deliver a greater sense of certainty for the parties...«. Thereafter the Working Group was asked to deliver urgent advice to the Lord Chancellor as to the course of modernisation, having particular regard to the formulaic approach introduced in Scotland by the Family Law (Scotland) Act 1985. The report, and subsequent discussions with the Ministry's Family Policy Division, led to the publication of the Ministry's proposals in a Home Office White Paper: Supporting Families – October 1998. In sum, the first proposal was for the introduction of rational rules for the division of family assets in limitation of judicial discretion and the second was to give legislative force to pre-nuptial contracts.

In 1999 the Government published the responses to the two major proposals in the White Paper with which this paper is concerned. Those responses were relatively few but broadly supportive. The next step would surely be the drafting of a bill, given the Governments stated priority. The cynic might have preferred to forecast that the Government would shy away from reform in any area traditionally emotive and unlikely to advance the Government's popularity. The cynic would have been right. The reform was abandoned. Why and in consequence of what debate we may not know since the Government has maintained silence and vouchsafed no information whenever taxed.

Dissatisfaction with this outcome has been almost universal amongst specialist judges and practitioners. The judges have deplored the denial of clear statutory rules or principles. The practitioners have repeatedly presented their cogent arguments for legislative legitimacy for pre-nuptial contracts.

IV. Judicial Reform

Into this legislative vacuum entered the House of Lords. The case of *White v White* involved a farming family. The High Court Judge awarded the wife a cash sum to exit the farming partnership which we substantially increased in the Court of Appeal. Both parties applied for permission to appeal to the House of Lords. The applications were granted, perhaps surprisingly, since the House had never previously entertained a quantum appeal in this field and there was then no family law specialist in the Court. The outcome was sterile for the family. Both appeals were dismissed. The appellants together had incurred costs totalling half a million pounds in procuring this negative outcome. They may have taken little consolation from the fact that the House of Lords revolutionised the way in which judges thereafter exercised their ample discretion. Gone forever was the practical mechanism of reasonable requirements, which by the turn of the century was seen to embody gender discrimination. In came the principle of equality. Or did it? In the leading speech of Lord Nicholls, equality was not a presumption (that would be to usurp the role of the legislature) nor a starting point but rather a cross check to ensure that the tentative outcome was fair. This formulation was, perhaps not surprisingly, critically received. It was a confusing formulation and not one that much advanced the quest for clear principles to limit the judicial discretion. It is to be noted that the only other speech was from Lord Cooke who would have made equality a principle, but the other three members of the Court preferred Lord Nicholls' approach.

The continuing need for statutory modernisation I articulated in my judgments in *Cowan v Cowan*[9] and in *Lambert v Lambert*[10]. In the latter case the Court took a stride along the road to equality which had been signposted in Supporting Families and articulated as I have described in *White v White*.

---

9 [2002]FAM97.
10 [2003]1FLR139.

The House of Lords returned to the task of modernising the law governing the financial consequences of divorce in the appeals of *Miller* and *McFarlane* which I have already introduced[11]. By then the House had been strengthened by the elevation of the distinguished family lawyer, Baroness Hale of Richmond. Thus there were fully reasoned judgments from Lord Nicholls, Baroness Hale, Lord Mance, and Lord Hope[12]. Three principles emerged to limit the exercise of the trial judges discretion: equality (or sharing), needs and compensation. In needs there was nothing new but difficulties result from its inter relationship with compensation. Then much expert time has been spent in analysing differences of expression, particularly between the judgment of Lord Nicholls and that of Baroness Hale, in the definition of matrimonial assets. Again the judgments have been critically received by specialist practitioners who see more extension than restriction in manoeuvres that attend the negotiation and preparation of complex cases. For a fuller examination of these appeals I refer to the English chapter in the 2008 edition of the International Survey of Family Law by Mary Welsted at 61. I am in complete agreement with her conclusions, particularly:

> »*it is time for the Government to finally grapple with this unsatisfactory state of affairs. It is essential that English law is brought into line with those jurisdictions where married adults are treated as such, where they are permitted to make enforceable agreements and in default of such agreements, they have the certainty of knowing that matrimonial property, strictly defined as such, will be divided in a way clearly defined by statute.*«

We speak with the same voice. In the post *Miller* and *McFarlane* appeal of *Charman v Charman*, the Court of Appeal re-emphasised the case for statutory reform[13]. Whether we shall be heeded seems most doubtful.

In her final sentence Mary Welsted writes:

> »*the Law Commission should be requested to conduct a thorough review of the law and produce a draft bill for enactment by Parliament.*«

What was the Working Group is now the Money & Property Sub-Committee of the Family Justice Council. Throughout the last twelve months and

---

11 *[2006] 2AC 618.*
12 [Lord Hoffmann did not give a reasoned judgment].
13 [2007] 1 FLR 1246 at 106.

more the Committee has urged the Law Commission to include this area of the law in its next work programme. The Law Commission has decided not to do so, no doubt mindful of the relationship between their labour and the prospects of Government commitment. However, at least it has decided to tackle the lesser, but still important, question of pre-nuptial contracts. That there is judicial support for a clear movement away from paternalism to adult autonomy is not in doubt. The Committee has fully supported the case presented by the specialist practitioners association, Resolution. In the recent appeal of *Crossley v* Crossley[14] I have shown my support.

V. Parliament and the Judges

That this Government has shirked the responsibility to modernise our laws governing maintenance and the property consequences of divorce can not be denied. More particularly it has failed to ensure Parliamentary debate and determination of the principles that would thereafter govern the exercise of judicial discretion. This conclusion is fortified by the Government's readiness to modernise on purely practical levels. Over the past generation personal pension plans have become a major ingredient in the mixture of assets comprising the family fortune, particularly where the breadwinner generates a massive annual income. The 1973 Act conferred no power on the judge to invade that territory, which remained the sovereignty of the breadwinner. The case of *Brooks v Brooks*[15] allowed the judges to call for the enlargement of their powers so that part of the accumulated pension value could be diverted for the benefit of the applicant. The Government swiftly responded with the Welfare Reform and Pensions Act 1999, amending the 1973 Act to introduce first the power to earmark and then the power to split the breadwinners pension in to two separate funds, one for each.

An obvious consequence of the Government's failure to promote legislation has been the intervention of the House of Lords. It may be asked whether this intervention has been legitimate. The constitutional boundary between what is judicially permissible and judicially presumptuous is one that, as a family lawyer, I find hard to discern. In 2000 Lord Nicholls

---

14   [2008] 1 FLR 1467.
15   [1996] AC 375.

declared that to introduce a presumption of equality would go beyond the permissible bounds of statutory interpretation. Yet six years later he took the plunge. In *Bellinger v Bellinger*[16] the majority in the Court of Appeal and the judges of the House of Lords refused to extend judicially the legal definition of marriage, although declaring a refusal of a trans-sexual's right to marry a breach of the rights by the European Convention of Human Rights. Yet the distance travelled by the House of Lords by way of *White v White* and on to *Miller* and *McFarlane* has resulted in a fundamental change in our law. Concepts to determine outcome have been introduced that nowhere appear in the statute. As I have illustrated, those concepts would have been summarily rejected in the Parliament of 1969 that passed the statute. That the shift is not just conceptual is easily illustrated by the recent case of *Charman*. The judge, applying the House of Lords authorities, awarded the applicant wife £ 48,000,000. In our Court her Counsel, in responding successfully to the husband's appeal, conceded that under the former yardstick of reasonable requirements she would have received about £ 20,000,000. As families become increasingly bi-national and mobile the ambition of the wife, and the dread of the husband, is the assessment of her financial application by a London judge.

It may also be asked whether the intervention of the House of Lords has been beneficial in the sense that it has improved the quality of justice for those many couples that now experience divorce. The answer from the public at large would surely reveal a gender divide: affirmative from payees and negative from payers. Viewed more objectively the answer might be that, whilst the judicial elite have striven to improve the quality of justice, underlying their conclusions are social policy concepts. Whether they are shared by those who legislate, we do not know. We can assume that, at a point where the policy values of judges and legislators divide sufficiently sharply, Parliament will intervene with a reforming statute. The Law Lords are an assembly of the greatest legal intellects available in any age and are there to settle the law. Their qualification to settle issues of social policy is not so evident. However in so far as solutions emerge from, or are influenced by, innovation in broadly comparable jurisdictions the House of Lords is best placed for comparative study. It appears as if some of the concepts introduced in *Miller* and *McFarlane* derived from earlier legislation in New Zealand.

---

16 [2003] 2 AC 467.

VI. The European Dimension

Any judgement on the benefits of the reforms crafted by the House of Lords cannot be confined to their domestic impact, as would have been permissible in 1969 when the statute was born. Almost 40 years later England is no longer an island but a piece in a global jigsaw. London is perhaps the most cosmopolitan of all cities. Some harmony between the laws of states with broadly comparable economic and social conditions is obviously desirable. This is not simply aspirational for we are one of the twenty seven member states of Europe. There is, of course, wide divergence in the national laws of the member states but harmonisation of laws regulating marital property regimes and the property consequences of divorce is impeded by the singularity of our laws contrasted with the civil law states of Europe. Modernisation of our law should, I believe have regard to this dimension and to our responsibility to aid European harmonisation in this field, a field of ever increasing significance as the percentage of marriages between nationals of different states and as the mobility of couples within Europe increases. Article 3 of Regulation Brussels II bis provides that of the several states likely to hold jurisdiction to dissolve a marriage only that first seised exercises it. This provision, admirable in simplicity, becomes crucially significant if London awards are not only at a much higher level but also achieve that level by ignoring the marital property regime that the couple chose at the outset.

In our jurisdiction the grant of the decree and the consequent financial award are not severable. The paternalistic root ensures that either party has the right to bring financial applications to judgment on or after the grant of divorce. This paternalism created the only exception to our rule that divorce and financial award are not severable. Under Part III of the 1984 Act a wife divorced in another jurisdiction may, under generous jurisdictional rules, bring ancillary relief applications here, if granted permission so to do. The provision was designed to meet hardship to a woman domiciled in England but divorced in a foreign state whose laws offered her little or no financial relief. In the European context the survival of this statutory provision must be questionable. Should the English wife who married a Belgian under a marital regime of separation be able to bring a claim in London when dissatisfied with the judicial award in Brussels?

The Common Law solution to these problems prior to the Brussels Regulation was the doctrine of forum conveniens. The classic illustration of the operation of the doctrine in the European context is the case of *de*

Dampierre v de Dampierre[17]. The judges in the Court of Appeal had allowed the French wife to bring her financial claims against the French husband in London. The House of Lords held that France was the more convenient forum. The husband therefore escaped the spectre of a London award. This doctrine is still applied where the other jurisdiction engaged is not a European member state and its continued application is vital to avoid injustice. The decision of the European Court of Justice in *Owusu*[18] must not be allowed to prevent the use of the doctrine, particularly where two common law jurisdictions are engaged.

The effect of the reforms introduced by the House of Lords could be said to amount to something close to community of property, rejected by Parliament in 1969 but cautiously advanced by the Law Commission in its 1973 report: First Report on Family Property – A New Approach. Were Parliament now to debate the desirability of introducing a marital property regime of community in some shape or form, the advantage to be gained by moving closer to our European partners would surely be weighed.

A less radical reform that would lessen the divide would be to give legislative effect to pre-nuptial contracts. This would involve some departure from another ancient root of our law, namely that parties may not by contract oust or limit the jurisdiction of the Court to grant financial relief on divorce. But this traditional principle, like paternalism, seems to have little remaining utility in the modern world. Adults should be free to contract at the point of marriage for the financial consequences of future divorce. This freedom, which would have been considered contrary to moral principle and to devalue the institution of marriage, seems to me to be urgently required, given the average duration of marriage in the modern world. The freedom would of course be subject to limits and safeguards which it would be for Parliament to set.

VII. Conclusion

A stern prosecutor might accuse the judges of trespassing on to legislative territory and, where Parliament has pointed a way, of not always following the sign post. It is clear that in 1984 and again in 1996 Parliament signalled that misconduct should more often and more obviously be reflect-

---

17 [1988] AC 92.
18 [Case C-128/01].

ed in any fair outcome. Perhaps the judges have adopted the Nelsonian response. Arguably the judges have not given the emphasis to terminating financial interdependence that Parliament intended. Where Government has chosen not to introduce statutory reform, presumably for rational policy reasons albeit not expressed, the judges should not themselves have introduced such radical change without any evidence of underlying social policy such as would be available to the Law Commission and to Parliament. The prosecutor might also query the benefits of judicial intervention in fields of social rather than legal science. The intervention results in four separate speeches which specialist practitioners can mine for nuggets to suit their case or for inconsistencies. Similarly judges have to wrestle with the application of law reformed in such un-parliamentary language. Undoubtedly the cases in the House of Lords have not produced greater certainty or predictability. Thus the negotiation of settlement is no more straightforward and it is the lawyers rather than the litigants who are the principal beneficiaries of these decisions.

In defence it can be said that the merits of the reasonable requirements mechanism had long outlived the values of the society for which it was created. Lord Nicholls, coming to the issues without the assumptions and traditions of a specialist in the field, in clear language and with farsighted vision crafted approaches and solutions for modern times. The process which he initiated, he and the other judges carried forward with great intellectual clarity some six years later. In a rapidly changing world perhaps evolution is necessary with that sort of frequency. Certain it is that Parliament will never be able to legislate with any regularity or frequency. Thus the judges are providing a vital function, ensuring that the law in a field of great social significance keeps pace with changing times.

I doubt that a jury composed of the eminent and diverse scholars of the ISFL would return an unanimous verdict of these issues.

Acknowledgements

I have already acknowledged the help that I received in drafting this paper from Mary Welsted's chapter in the 2008 Survey of International Family Law. However, I have not acknowledged the very great reliance that I have placed on the work of Doctor Stephen Cretney. In particular I have drawn on his Blackstone lecture of May 10th 2003 (The Family and The Law - Status or Contract [2003] CFLQ 403) and on his Magnum Opus: Family Law in the Twentieth Century (Oxford University Press: 2003). Finally, in considering the judges interpretation of the power to order a clean break introduced by the 1984 Act, I have drawn on the 2008 paper of Martin Pointer QC: Meal Tickets for Life? 1984 and All That.

Des Solidarités dans les Couples Séparés

Hugues Fulchiron[1]

> *Precariousness is increasingly marking out the life of couples (married or not). At first sight, the marriage is the only legal framework offering a real protection in the event of dissolution. Social and legal contemporary developments nevertheless make the analysis far more complex.*
> *Based on a survey conducted within the court of Lyon by the Family Law Center, this study of legislation and case law highlights a double mutation in France:*
> ➢ *Whatever the form of cohabitation might be (marriage or else), the consequences of separation are still moderated by a minimum of solidarity, though its goals and modalities have changed. This solidarity is no longer the prorogation of a legal and moral obligation that would maintain the link between the partners. It rather demonstrates the clear desire to ensure a minimum of fairness between them. Thus, this minimum of solidarity illustrates more a concern for justice to the parties at the very moment of the separation than the will to sustain a link.*
> ➢ *Although all kind of couples are concerned by this minimum solidarity, it is gradually reducing to a limited solidarity. It neither provides a partner with a guarantee of maintenance any more, nor (even less) does it give rise to an expectation to the preservation of his standard of living. In any case, this minimum solidarity only tends to facilitate the acceptance of the dissolution by the parties*

Deux phénomènes marquent en profondeur le droit contemporain de la famille: la multiplication des couples hors mariage et celle des sépara-

---

[1] *Hugues Fulchiron, Université de Lyon, Professeur à l'Université Jean Moulin Lyon 3, Directeur du Centre de droit de la famille.* L'auteur tient à remercier Renaud Daubricourt, allocataire de recherche et chercheur au Centre de droit de la famille, ainsi que M.E. Folleas, S. Giboulet, F. Matricon, M. Milesi et Th. Collin, étudiants en master de droit de la famille, qui ont réalisé l'enquête sur laquelle s'appuie cet article.

tions et des recompositions familiales. La vie des couples est de plus en plus marquée par la précarité: le constat vaut pour les couples non mariés (qu'ils vivent en union libre ou qu'ils aient opté pour un partenariat enregistré) comme pour les couples mariés[2]. Dans ces différentes hypothèses, les modalités de la rupture et les conséquences qu'en tire le droit sont des plus instructives. Elles révèlent la différence de nature entre les diverses formes d'unions: *»Dis moi comment tu meurs, je te dirai qui tu es«*. Ainsi en est-il en droit français pour la rupture du partenariat enregistré, le Pacs: liberté de la rupture, intervention facultative et secondaire du juge, absence de règles précises gouvernant la liquidation des intérêts communs, tout témoigne du »désengagement« de la loi et, corrélativement, de la liberté laissée aux individus, pour le meilleur et pour le pire[3].

Si mariage et partenariat, et, dans une moindre mesure, union libre, se rejoignent pendant la vie commune, les différences éclatent lors de la rupture: à première vue, seul le mariage assure la protection du plus faible[4]. La supériorité du mariage en tant que régime protecteur se traduit notamment par les règles qui gouvernent la liquidation des intérêts communs des époux et l'aménagement de leurs relations patrimoniales après la séparation. Ainsi en droit français, seul le mariage ouvre-t-il droit à »maintenance«. Le mariage serait-il le seul statut du couple susceptible d'assurer un peu de solidarité dans les couples désunis? En vérité, la situation est beaucoup plus complexe.

Certes, le mariage ouvre la voie à la solidarité entre époux divorcés, mais les évolutions légales et jurisprudentielles contemporaines l'érodent peu à peu. Rien de surprenant à cela: ce n'est que la conséquence d'autres évolutions; évolutions politiques et sociales (les femmes ont acquis une certaine autonomie financière et la France connaît un taux très important de femmes mariées qui continuent à travailler après la naissance des enfants), évolution des mœurs et des mentalités (on divorce de plus en plus tôt et de plus en plus souvent)[5], évolution du mariage lui-

---

2   Pour un aperçu chiffré, cf. F. Prioux, »Vive en couple, se marier, se séparer: contrastes européens«, *Population et sociétés*, INED, avril 2006: plus de 40 divorces pour 100 mariages en France, en 2003. 115 000 divorces ont été prononcés en 2001, 155 253 en 2005 (*Annuaire statistique* du Ministère de la Justice, 2007). En 2007, 260 000 mariages seulement ont été célébrés G. Pison, »La population de la France en 2007«, *Population et société*, INED, 2008).
3   Cf. Ph. Malaurie et H. Fulchiron, *La famille*, Defrénois, 3ème éd. 2009, n°350 s.
4   *Mariage, conjugalité, parenté, parentalité*, H. Fulchiron (dir.), Dalloz, à par. 2009.
5   En 2001, la durée moyenne des mariages était de 14,9 années; elle était de 14,2 en 2005. L'augmentation du nombre des divorces dans les dix premières années du mariage est

même (qui n'est plus conçu comme une »assurance pour la vie«, mais comme une séquence, que l'on rêve sans fin, dans une vie de plus en plus longue):[6] toutes évolutions qui ne peuvent que retenir sur la solidarité entre époux divorcés.

A l'inverse, le régime des partenariats enregistrés tend à s'aligner en droit civil comme en droit fiscal sur celui du mariage: le Pacs, dit-on en France, se »matrimonialise«, ce qui bien sûr retentit sur les conséquences de la séparation. Plus les effets attachés à l'union se renforcent, moins la séparation peut n'être qu'une séparation »sèche«. Certaines formes de solidarité naissent ou renaissent.

En fait, en cette matière comme dans bien d'autres, les sociétés occidentales vivent un moment de transition: les anciennes solidarités s'effacent, de nouvelles solidarités émergent, dans d'autres champs, sous d'autres formes, avec une autre intensité.

Pour tenter de rendre compte de l'évolution des solidarités lors de la séparation du couple, on partira de deux postulats:

> *postulat n°1*: quelle que soit la forme de vie en couple, les conséquences de la séparation sont tempérées par un minimum de solidarité, même si les modalités et les finalités en ont changé: elles ne sont plus le prolongement d'une obligation juridique et morale qui lierait le couple au-delà de la rupture; elles manifestent plutôt le souci d'assurer un minimum d'équité entre les époux ou les concubins lors de la rupture. Ce minimum de solidarité traduit donc moins la permanence du lien qu'un souci de justice au moment et au moment seulement de la séparation.

> *postulat n°2*: si cette solidarité minimum concerne tous les couples, elle se réduit peu à peu à une solidarité minimale. Elle n'offre plus une garantie de subsistance et moins encore l'assurance d'un maintien du niveau de vie. Le rêve du législateur français de 1975 s'est évanoui, face à la montée de divorces de plus en plus nombreux et de plus en plus précoces. Pour les unions en mariage comme pour les unions hors mariage, cette solidarité minimale, tend seulement à faciliter le »passage« de la rupture.

---

significative (cf. *Annuaire statistique de la Justice*, 2007, préc.: 40 675 sur 115 388 divorces prononcés en 2001; près de 64 000 sur 155 353 en 2005).

6 Sur ces évolutions, cf. not. I. Thery, *Le démariage*, éd. O. Jacob, 1993.

I. Une Solidarité Minimum

Deux sortes de mécanismes tendent à assurer dans les couples séparés un minimum de solidarité. La forme la plus classique en est l'obligation alimentaire au sens large, et ses substituts que sont, pour prendre l'exemple français, la prestation compensatoire après divorce, *i.e.* l'octroi d'une somme d'argent en un plusieurs versements ou l'abandon de bien en pleine propriété ou en usufruit pour atténuer les conséquences de la séparation. Mais il faut aussi tenir compte des règles du partage des biens entre époux séparés et, plus généralement, des règles qui gouvernent la liquidation des intérêts communs du couple lors de la rupture : par ce biais aussi le législateur ou le juge peuvent assurer directement ou indirectement un minimum de solidarité.

1. Pensions et Prestations

Les changements du droit français en la matière sont tout à fait significatifs. Ils témoignent des transformations de la conception du mariage et du divorce; ils traduisent l'évolution de la place et du rôle de la femme dans la famille et dans la société; ils reflètent la complexité des relations entre solidarités interindividuelles au sein de couple et de la famille et solidarités collectives.

Légalement, la métamorphose est radicale. La césure est intervenue avec la loi du 11 juillet 1975 relative au divorce, dont les orientations ont été non seulement confirmées mais accentuées par les lois ultérieures[7].

Avant 1975, le droit français connaissait la traditionnelle »pension alimentaire«, traduction du devoir de secours qui liait les époux au-delà de la rupture du mariage. La survie de l'obligation alimentaire entre époux était subordonnée à l'innocence du conjoint bénéficiaire, *i.e.*, dans un système qui ne connaissait que le divorce pour faute, à l'absence de torts à sa charge. De nature alimentaire, la pension tendait à assurer un minimum de ressources au conjoint débiteur. En pratique, le système s'accordait bien avec une société où relativement peu de femmes mariées continuaient à travailler après le mariage et où le divorce risquait de laisser l'épouse sans ressources propres.

Rompant avec la tradition, la loi du 11 juillet 1975 créa la prestation compensatoire. Le procès fait à la pension alimentaire est connu: injus-

---

[7] Lois du 30 juin 2000 et du 26 mai 2004, cf. Ph. Malaurie et H. Fulchiron, *op. cit.*, n°785 s et réf. cit.

tice d'un système qui faisait dépendre les moyens de vivre de la femme des fautes dans le divorce, défauts de paiement des pensions qui laissaient l'épouse sans ressource et ne faisaient que raviver les conflits après divorce, inadéquation de l'objet même de la pension alimentaire (le nécessaire) avec les besoins comme avec la réalité. Détachée, sauf exceptions, des torts dans le divorce, la prestation compensatoire change de finalité: elle tend à compenser, autant qu'il est possible, la disparité créée par le divorce dans les conditions de vie respectives des époux (art. 270 c. civ.)[8].

Il n'est donc plus question de survie du devoir de secours né du mariage[9]. La prestation compensatoire tente sinon de garantir aux époux, notamment à la femme, le maintien de leur niveau de vie, du moins d'atténuer la chute de niveau de vie qu'entraîne bien souvent le divorce. Son montant est évalué forfaitairement en fonction des besoins et des ressources de chacun au jour du divorce et dans un avenir prévisible, en tenant compte de différents paramètres, notamment des choix de vie effectués par les époux pendant la vie commune (le fait, notamment, que la femme ait arrêté de travailler ou ait ralenti sa carrière professionnelle pour s'occuper du foyer et des enfants)[10]. Ce forfait, est évalué une fois pour toutes; sa révision est exceptionnelle: son règlement intervient »pour solde de tout compte«.[11]

Les modalités de paiement de la prestation compensatoire traduisent cette nouvelle conception: elle s'exécute en principe sous forme de capital (somme d'argent, abandon d'un bien en pleine propriété ou en usufruit). Le versement d'une rente, viagère ou temporaire, est l'exception.[12] Par ses

---

8   J. Carbonnier, *Droit civil, Introduction, Les personnes, La famille, l'enfant, le couple*, PUF, 2004, n°608 et réf. cit.
9   En 1975, le devoir de secours entre époux survivait dans un seule hypothèse: celle du divorce imposé à un époux innocent qui ne peut ou ne veut pas divorcer (on pensait surtout, à l'époux malade). L'autre époux peut obtenir le divorce, mais il doit en assumer toutes les conséquences et, notamment, respecter l'obligation de secours contractée dans et par le mariage. La règle a été supprimée par la loi du 26 mai 2004: dès lors que l'on reconnaît un véritable droit au divorce avec l'ouverture du divorce pour altération définitive du lien conjugal, il ne saurait être question de maintien des droits et devoirs nés du mariage.
10 Art. 271 c. civ.
11 Cf. *Droit de la famille*, P. Murat (dir.), Dalloz, 2008.
12 La révolution réalisée en 1975 n'a pas toujours été comprise par le juge. Par deux fois, en 2000 et en 2004, le législateur a dû intervenir pour en confirmer les orientations. Il a ainsi réaffirmé que la prestation compensatoire s'exécutait en principe sous forme de capital (dont il a diversifié les formes et assoupli les modalités de paiement); le juge ne peut recourir à la rente qu'à titre exceptionnel, »par décision spécialement motivée, en raison de l'âge ou de l'état de santé du créancier ne lui permettant pas de subvenir à ses besoins«; et il ne peut s'agir que d'une rente viagère.

finalités comme par ses modalités, la nouvelle prestation compensatoire marque donc une rupture: d'un devoir de solidarité fondé sur un engagement pris lors et par le mariage (pour le meilleur et pour le pire), le droit français est passé à une solidarité »atténuée«, liée à un souci d'équité. Il ne s'agit plus de garantir un minimum vital mais d'assurer un équilibre minimum entre les anciens époux.

Deux points méritent cependant d'être soulignés. D'une part, le pourcentage de prestations compensatoires demandées et accordées en pratique est relativement faible (cf. *infra*). D'autre part, il n'existe aucun mécanisme comparable pour les couples non mariés. Est-ce à dire que dans l'immense majorité des séparations, tout esprit de solidarité a disparu? En réalité, l'idée que le partage de la vie commune entraîne un minimum de solidarité en cas de rupture passe par d'autres canaux, notamment par la recherche d'un minimum d'équité dans le partage des biens acquis pendant la vie commune.

2. Partage des Biens Acquis Pendant la Vie Commune

Il est un moyen très efficace, même s'il peut être plus discret, d'assurer l'équité lors de la séparation: redistribuer les richesses du couple, notamment les biens acquis pendant la vie commune. Tel est le cas pour les couples »statutaires« avec le régime de communauté d'acquêts, régime légal des époux français, mais aussi avec les présomptions d'indivision qui, dans le Pacs, atténuent le principe de séparation de biens. Tel est le cas également lorsque le juge intervient en équité pour corriger l'injustice des dispositions contractuelles prévues par les époux ou par les partenaires, ou pour pallier l'absence de toute règle de répartition entre concubins vivant en union libre.

2.1 Le Jeu des Régimes Légaux

En France, les époux qui se marient sans faire de contrat de mariage se placent sous le régime de la communauté de biens: tous les biens acquis ou créés pendant le mariage sont en principe communs, quelque soit celui qui les a acquis ou créés, et ils seront partagés comme tels lors de la dissolution du mariage. C'est dire que, hors les exceptions prévues par la loi (cf. par exemple les biens reçus en héritage ou les biens acquis avec des biens propres), l'enrichissement de chacun profite aux deux époux. Les effets du régime communautaire, accentués par les règles de preuve du caractère propre ou commun des biens considérés, avec notamment une présomption de communauté, traduisent une certaine vision du mariage: le mariage est le partage d'une vie, partage des efforts de chacun, partage des richesses (et des dettes) acquises pendant la vie commune.

De façon assez surprenante, cette vision se retrouve plus ou moins dans le Pacs, même si les règles sont *a priori* inverses[13]. Sauf stipulations particulières de leur pacte, les partenaires Pacsés sont soumis à un strict régime de séparation des patrimoines: chaque partenaire conserve la propriété personnelle des biens dont il était propriétaire au jour de l'enregistrement du Pacs; il est seul propriétaire des biens acquis par lui en son nom pendant la durée du Pacs (art. 515-5 c. civ.), étant précisé que si l'autre a contribué à cette acquisition, il a, mais il a seulement, une créance contre son partenaire: chacun pour soi. Mais lors de la liquidation, la solidarité que l'on avait chassée par la porte revient par la fenêtre, à travers les règles de preuve: il appartient en effet à chaque partenaire de prouver, par tous moyens, le caractère personnel de tel ou tel bien. A défaut, le bien sera réputé indivis et partagé par moitié (art. 515-5 al. 2 c. civ.). C'est dire qu'une partie de l'enrichissement du couple bénéficiera aux deux partenaires, car sauf pour les biens les plus importants (un immeuble par exemple), il est peu probable que l'un des partenaires se soit ménagé la preuve de sa propriété exclusive. Indirectement, le »régime légal« du Pacs garantit ainsi un minimum d'équité entre partenaires par le partage des biens acquis ou mis en commun pendant la vie commune[14].

Il est cependant des cas où le simple jeu des règles légales ne permet pas d'assurer un tel partage: celui d'époux mariés sous le régime de la séparation de biens, celui de partenaires qui par contrat ont opté pour un régime séparatiste renforcé ou celui de simples concubins vivant en union libre. Mais même dans ce cas, l'idée que la vie commune est source d'un minimum de solidarité est la plus forte: il appartient aux juges de trouver les mécanismes juridiques qui permettront de l'assurer.

---

13   Cf. Ph. Malaurie et H. Fulchiron, *op. cit.*, n°405 s.
14   Par ailleurs, le législateur a mis en place un mécanisme qui peut lui aussi rétablir un minimum d'équité dans le partage (art. 515-7 al. 10 *in fine*: les créances d'un partenaire contre l'autre peuvent être compensées avec les avantages que le créancier a pu retirer de la vie commune, notamment en ne contribuant pas à hauteur de ses facultés aux dettes contractées pour les besoins de la vie courante. Un partenaire ne peut ainsi (trop) s'enrichir aux dépens de l'autre. Quant aux partenaires qui, au contraire, souhaiteraient plus de partage, la loi leur offre un régime alternatif, l'indivision conventionnelle.

2.2 L'Intervention du Juge en Équité

Pour garantir un minimum d'équité, le juge français utilise essentiellement trois instruments empruntés au droit commun: la société créée de fait, l'enrichissement sans cause et, au besoin, l'octroi de dommages intérêts.

Lorsque des époux, des partenaires ou des concubins exercent en commun une activité, en dehors de tout cadre légal, cette activité peut recevoir la qualification de *société créée de fait*, et sera liquidée comme telle, avec partage de l'actif entre les intéressés, dès lors que sera prouvée l'existence des trois éléments constitutifs d'une société: des apports mutuels en capital ou, plus souvent, en industrie, une contribution aux bénéfices et aux pertes, l'intention de s'associer pour le succès de l'entreprise commune[15]. Soit par exemple deux époux mariés en séparation de biens; le mari exerce une profession libérale ou commerciale; la femme l'aide dans sa profession sans être rémunérée; lors du divorce, le fonds libéral ou commercial est un bien propre du mari; en principe, la femme n'a droit à rien, bien qu'elle ait contribué au développement du fonds: si elle prouve l'existence d'une société créée de fait, elle aura droit à sa part dans la société. Il en va de même pour deux concubins ou deux partenaires qui seraient associés dans une entreprise ou plus généralement dans un projet commun.

À l'évidence, le recours à une telle technique a quelque chose d'artificiel, même si les juridictions françaises, notamment la cour de cassation, sont très vigilantes sur la qualification. Mais il permet d'assurer un minimum d'équité.

Le même souci se traduit dans l'utilisation, plus fréquente et plus généreusement admise, de l'*enrichissement sans cause*. Le concubin, le partenaire ou le conjoint qui a collaboré à l'activité de l'autre sans rémunération[16], qui a réalisé des travaux dans un immeuble de l'autre ou qui a sacrifié sa vie professionnelle pour s'occuper de sa famille, peut demander une indemnité correspondant à la plus faible des deux sommes représentant l'enrichissement de l'un et l'appauvrissement de l'autre. Encore faut-il prouver l'existence de l'enrichissement et de l'appauvrissement (plus value ou dépense évitée pour l'un, perte ou manque à gagner pour l'autre), et surtout l'absence de cause (par ex. l'obligation de contribuer

---

15 Cf. Ph. Malaurie et H. Fulchiron, *op. cit.*, n°331 et réf. cit.
16 Et qui n'a pu établir l'existence d'une société créée de fait: l'action fondée sur l'enrichissement sans cause a un caractère subsidiaire. Cf. A. Gouttenoire, »Collaboration familiale et enrichissement sans cause«, *Dr. famille*, 1999, chron. n°19 et réf. cit.

aux charges de la vie courante, l'obligation d'éducation des enfants etc.). Certes, le succès de la demande est incertain, mais la multiplication des actions sur ce fondement prouve par elle-même la nécessité de ce genre de mécanisme »compensatoire«.

Les *demandes de dommages intérêts* semblent *a priori* s'inscrire dans une tout autre perspective. Certes, il n'y a aucune faute à rompre le concubinage ou le Pacs, et la loi reconnaît aujourd'hui un véritable droit au divorce. Mais les circonstances dans lesquelles la rupture intervient ou la violation des obligations contractées peuvent ouvrir droit à dommages intérêts. Or il apparaît que les juges ont parfois tendance à utiliser les dommages-intérêts pour compenser les »pertes« subies par un conjoint ou par un concubin. Le législateur donne d'ailleurs l'exemple avec, en cas de divorce, les dommages intérêts de l'article 266 c. civ[17]. Il y a là encore altération d'un mécanisme de droit commun au service de l'équité[18].

Doctrine et jurisprudence disposent d'autres instruments, tels que les libéralités par exemple. Tous tendent au même but: assurer, quelque soit le mode de conjugalité, un minimum de solidarité, en équité, dans la rupture. Mais ce minimum n'est ou, dans le mariage, tend à devenir, un minimum seulement: la solidarité minimum n'est qu'une solidarité minimale.

II. Une Solidarité Minimale

Si les mécanismes évoqués tendent à assurer en équité un minimum de solidarité, l'évolution des modes de vie en couple, la multiplication des séparations en mariage et hors mariage, les transformations du statut de la femme, le changement des mentalités, ne sont pas sans influence sur les modalités et, plus fondamentalement, sur les finalités de cette solidarité. Il ne s'agit plus que d'une solidarité minimale, cantonnée dans le temps, cantonnée également dans son montant. En témoignent à la fois les données théoriques et les données pratiques.

---

17 Art. 266 c. civ.: »*Sans préjudice de l'application de l'article 270*« (droit à une prestation compensatoire) »*des dommages intérêts peuvent être accordés à un époux en réparation des conséquences d'une particulière gravité qu'il subit du fait de la dissolution du mariage soit lorsqu'il n'avait lui-même formé aucune demande en divorce, soit lorsque le divorce est prononcé aux torts exclusifs de son conjoint*«.

18 Cf. A. Gouttenoire, « Responsabilité civile et rupture unilatérale du couple », in Des concubinages, droit interne, droit international, droit comparé, Mélanges en l'honneur de J. Rubellin-Devichi, LITEC, 2001, p. 257 s. et réf. cit.

1. Evolutions Théoriques

En matière de divorce la création de la prestation compensatoire en 1975 constitua, comme on l'a souligné, une véritable rupture. Une seconde révolution est en cours: la marginalisation de la prestation compensatoire. A ce phénomène correspond, en creux en quelque sorte, l'absence de tout débat sur la création d'un système parallèle pour les partenaires ou pour les concubins.

1.1 La Marginalisation de la Prestation Compensatoire

Parler de »marginalisation« est assurément ambigu. En fait, l'idée s'impose peu à peu que la rupture, ou plutôt le risque de rupture, est inhérent à la vie de couple. Le divorce n'est pas un accident, mais un risque »normal« du mariage: une probabilité (statistique) que les époux doivent prendre en considération lors de l'union[19].

Dans cette perspective, les évolutions du droit français trouvent une certaine logique, avec la disparition du devoir de secours, expression d'une obligation alimentaire entre époux qui survit à la dissolution du mariage, avec la création de la prestation compensatoire et la volonté réaffirmée d'un paiement en capital, pour solde de tout compte, quitte à en fractionner le paiement[20] et, en cas de décès du débiteur, le principe légal d'une charge qui ne passe aux héritiers que dans les limites de la succession[21].

Le législateur tend ainsi à bannir, autant que possible, les liens entre époux divorcés, ce non seulement par souci d'éviter les conflits, mais aussi parce que la rupture doit être une vraie rupture juridique. On retrouve ici l'idée selon laquelle le mariage est certes un engagement pour la vie, mais qu'il est désormais dans sa nature d'être précaire: il peut être rompu à tout moment (un peu comme un CDI)[22] et cette rupture met fin aux droits et aux devoirs qui en étaient nés: paradoxalement, du moins en apparence, le mariage survit mieux à la mort d'un époux qu'au divorce.

Bien plus, même l'idée, si forte en 1975, selon laquelle la prestation compensatoire tend à garantir, autant qu'il est possible, le maintien

---

19 La France ne connaît pas encore d'assurance divorce, mais le risque pourrait bien être assuré un jour.
20 Art. 274 c. civ. Cf. *supra*
21 Art. 280 c. civ.
22 Contrat de travail à durée indéterminée, dont la rupture est relativement libre, à la différence du contrat de travail à durée déterminée (CDD) dont la rupture est strictement encadrée.

d'un certain niveau de vie à la femme divorcée, s'efface peu à peu. Avec le triomphe du paiement sous forme de capital et le rejet de la rente, la prestation compensatoire apparaît plus comme une sorte de compensation forfaitaire temporaire, que comme un moyen de compenser dans la durée la chute du niveau de vie entrainé par le divorce: elle s'affiche de plus en plus comme un instrument, provisoire, de stabilisation et/ou de redémarrage.

En d'autres termes, la pension alimentaire de 1975 et même, dans une certaine mesure, la prestation compensatoire après 1975, étaient marquées par l'idée de perpétuité du mariage, elle-même héritée du principe d'indissolubilité du lien matrimonial. Aujourd'hui, il en va tout autrement: au moment du divorce, la loi et le juge favorisent, autant que possible un rééquilibrage; mais, avant tout, on solde les comptes. En poussant à l'extrême, on serait tenté de dire que le nouveau modèle serait le suivant: chacun reçoit sa part lors de la liquidation du régime matrimonial, part à laquelle on ajoute quelque chose, pour »lisser« la chute du niveau de vie ou permettre le redémarrage; mais au-delà, il appartient à chacun de reconstruire sa vie, seul ou avec un nouveau conjoint, partenaire ou concubin.

Confirmation de cette évolution peut être trouvée, en négatif, dans l'absence de tout débat sur la création éventuelle d'un équivalent de la prestation compensatoire dans les couples non-mariés.

1.2 L'Absence de Tout Débat sur une Transposition du Système de la Prestation Compensatoire dans les Couples Non-Mariés

Lors des débats sur le Pacs en 1999 et en 2007, il n'y eut pas de refus de créer une »prestation compensatoire« au nom de la différence de nature entre mariage ou partenariat, ou au nom de la différence de degré dans l'engagement, etc: il n'y eut pas de rejet car il n'y eut pas de discussion, faute de revendication.

Pourtant, l'idée en soi n'a rien d'absurde. Dans le Pacs comme dans l'union libre, il y bien vie commune partagée, mise en commun de moyens, parfois sacrifice de l'un (la femme) pour garantir l'équilibre du foyer et l'éducation des enfants. Et dans le Pacs, le législateur français, en 1999 et plus encore en 2005, a multiplié les rapprochements avec le mariage, pendant la vie commune et après le décès, à tel point que l'on parle aujourd'hui de l'existence d'un véritable statut commun du couple, constitué d'un ensemble de droits et de devoirs personnels et patrimoniaux qui varient moins dans leur nature que dans leur intensité.

Que l'on n'ait même pas imaginé de créer un mécanisme parallèle à la prestation compensatoire confirme l'idée que celle-ci n'est plus que la survivance du passé. A cet égard, les nouvelles formes d'union pourraient constituer une sorte de »modèle« d'évolution pour le mariage: modèle marqué par le déclin de la solidarité non pas pendant la vie commune, mais après la séparation. Lors de la rupture, chacun prend ce qui lui revient et tente de reconstruire sa vie. Chacun pour soi.

Déclinantes dans le couple, les solidarités familiales continuent en revanche à rayonner dans les rapports entre parents et enfants. Mais peu importe alors que les parents soient mariés ou non.

Cette évolution théorique se traduit-elle dans les faits? Constate-t-on un recul des prestations compensatoires après divorce?

2. Evolutions Pratiques

La réponse à la question est délicate car il existe, paradoxalement, très peu de données sur le sujet en France[23]. Pour tenter de se faire une idée plus précise, le Centre de droit de la famille de Lyon a mené une enquête systématique sur les décisions de divorce rendues en 2007 par le tribunal de grande instance de Lyon. Certes, il ne s'agit que d'une photographie très partielle de la réalité, à un moment donné et en un lieu donné (il n'est pas exclu que, comme dans d'autres domaines, il existe des particularismes locaux et une »doctrine« judiciaire propres à la juridiction lyonnaise); de plus les données disponibles sont encore partielles[24]. Les premiers résultats sont cependant riches d'enseignements.

On ne peut tout d'abord qu'être étonné par *le faible nombre de prestations compensatoires*: elle n'est prévue, par les parties dans leur convention ou par le juge dans sa décision, que dans 16,14% des cas[25] (ce qui correspond à peu près à la moyenne nationale: une prestation compensatoire dans un divorce sur huit[26]). Le chiffre est d'autant plus significatif

---

23 Pour quelques données chiffrées, cf. E. Roumiguière, *Des prestations compensatoires sous forme de capital et non plus de rente*, Infostat Justice, n°77, nov. 2004. Adde par ex. la revue A.J. Famille 2008, *Prestations aliments, données chiffrées*, n°7, 2008, p. 306 s. ou le panorama dressé pour les cours d'appel de Nîmes et de Montpellier par Y. Zemrak, *Les prestations compensatoires*, Revue de jurisprudence régionale, 2008, n°11, p. 113 s. Adde, sous l'angle de la révision des prestations compensatoires, l'étude de C. Moreau, E. Severin et B. Munoz-Perez, *Les prestations compensatoires à l'épreuve du temps*, Ministère de la Justice, sept. 2006.
24 Ont été analysées l'ensemble des décisions de divorce prononcées par le tribunal de grande instance de Lyon en 2007, soit 4209 décisions.
25 695 dossiers sur 4209.
26 Statistiques du Ministère de la Justice, cf. Infostat, nov. 2004 préc.

que les demandes sont elles-même relativement peu nombreuses: elles n'apparaissent que dans 20,67% des dossiers. Certes, il conviendrait d'approfondir l'enquête pour mieux comprendre les raisons de ce petit nombre de demandes: n'y a-t-il rien à compenser, n'y a-t-il rien pour compenser, les compensations patrimoniales se font-elles parallèlement, à travers le partage des biens et la prise en charge des dettes ? Quoi qu'il en soit, si la question occupe l'attention des juges et des avocats, et qu'ils y consacrent une grande partie de leur temps car les négociations sont souvent difficiles et les conflits très aigus, on est loin d'un mécanisme qui jouerait dans une majorité de divorces.

Il conviendrait également de distinguer les hypothèses où les époux s'accordent sur l'existence et le montant de la prestation, dans le cadre d'un divorce par consentement mutuel ou dans le cadre d'une convention que les époux, passant par une procédure de divorce »contentieux«, soumettent à l'homologation d'un juge d'une part (soit 54,67% des dossiers prévoyant une prestation compensatoire), et celles où il existe sur ce point un vrai conflit entre les époux et qu'ils demandent au juge de le trancher, d'autre part (45,32% des cas). En l'état actuel des données fournies par l'enquête on peut seulement relever que les prestations sont proportionnellement plus nombreuses dans les divorces contentieux que dans le divorce par consentement mutuel: près de 62% alors que les divorces contentieux représentent moins de 47% de l'ensemble des divorces.

On est également frappé par le petit nombre de refus: près de 80% des demandes sont exaucées. Les rejets interviennent essentiellement en raison de l'absence de disparité (ou de disparité qui n'aurait pas été démontrée par le demandeur); est parfois mis en avant la durée trop courte de l'union; dans un seul dossier le juge utilise la clause d'équité de l'article 270 c. civ. qui lui permet de refuser d'octroyer une prestation lorsque le demande en est formulée par l'époux aux torts exclusifs duquel le divorce est prononcé, «au regard des circonstances particulières de la rupture«.

Tout aussi remarquable, est le *montant relativement faible en moyenne des prestations accordées*, même si quelques cas particuliers pourraient en donner une fausse image[27]. Ainsi, la médiane du montant des prestations compensatoires versées sous forme de capital ou de capital renté[28]

---

27   Les 2 millions d'euros accordés dans un dossier par les juges lyonnais ou les 1,5 million sur lequel se sont entendus les époux dans une autre affaire.
28   i.e. un capital versé par fractions, cf. art. 275 c. civ.

(*i.e.* la forme »normale« d'exécution de la prestation compensatoire)[29] pour tous types de divorce est de 25 796 Euros[30].

Quant aux prestations accordées, par exception, sous forme de rente[31] (12,81 % des cas), leur montant s'élève en moyenne à 750, avec là encore de fortes disparités (maximum: 5000 Euros pour des revenus mensuels de 13 500 Euros; minimum: 150 Euros...). Les montants restent donc, en moyenne assez faibles: la rente offre plus un complément de ressources que la garantie du nécessaire[32].

Il est vrai que les chiffres doivent être analysés avec prudence car leur fiabilité est loin d'être parfaite. D'une part en effet, il n'existe pas en France de barème permettant d'évaluer les prestations compensatoires de façon cohérente: jurisprudence et législateur s'opposent fermement à l'usage de tels instruments. D'autre part, malgré les efforts du législateur, la connaissance exacte du patrimoine des époux reste insuffisante: le juge est loin de disposer toujours d'une vision précise de la situation[33].

Il serait intéressant de savoir si cette stagnation est particulièrement nette ou non lorsque la prestation prend la forme d'un versement en capital, fût-il fractionné, et si son montant est plus important, comparativement, lorsqu'elle se traduit par l'abandon d'un bien en pleine propriété (le plus souvent l'immeuble ou une quotte part de l'immeuble dans lequel vivait et doit continuer à vivre la famille). Il est en tout cas significatif que, selon les chiffres du Ministère de la Justice, dans 87 % des cas, la soulte due par l'époux créancier au titre du partage de communauté compense l'intégralité de la prestation due par l'autre. Cette concordance n'a rien de fortuit: la prestation tend moins à compenser une disparité objectivement appréciée qu'à solder les comptes entre les ex-époux.[34]

---

29 Les juges lyonnais respectent les consignes du législateur: 87,19 % des prestations sont accordées sous forme de capital.
30 Selon les données réunies par le Ministère de la Justice en 2004, la moitié des prestations sous forme de capital (soit 72,6 % des prestations) avaient un montant supérieur à 21 499 Euros lorsqu'elles étaient versées sous forme de capital en numéraire; 10 % dépassaient 80 000 Euros. Le montant du capital était légèrement moins élevé quand il était payé en plusieurs versements successifs (18 460 Euros), cf. Infostat, nov. 2004 préc.
31 16 % des cas seulement selon les chiffres du Ministère de la Justice, Infostat nov. 2004, préc.
32 Selon les données du Ministère de la Justice, la moitié des rentes ne dépassaient pas 305 Euros, 10 % seulement étaient supérieures à 1040 Euros.
33 Ce que confirme l'enquête menée auprès du TGI de Lyon: qu'il s'agisse de divorces par consentement mutuel ou de divorces contentieux, le juge est loin de disposer d'une connaissance exhaustive du patrimoine des époux, ni même de leurs revenus.
34 Cf. Infostat, nov. 2004 préc.

La suite de l'enquête menée auprès des juridictions lyonnaises et une analyse plus approfondie de ses résultats devraient permettre de se faire une idée plus précise de la situation.

Les couples changent, les solidarités évoluent. Au juriste d'être attentif à ces métamorphoses et à ne pas rester les yeux fixés sur des étoiles mortes.

Part III – Children

Family Finances through German Support Laws: Effects of Child Support Priority

Barbara Willenbacher[1]

I. Introduction

The aim of the reform of the child support law in Germany was primarily to reduce child poverty and consequently also children's need for social welfare. This emphasises the priority of the child's well-being, and can be compared with the »children first« campaigns in Common Law states in the 1990s. In this respect, a comparison of the reform of child support in the USA, England and Wales, and Germany is useful at the outset.

The advantages of this system can be seen in the USA in the collected and increased payments of child support in numerous cases and in the fact that as a consequence, the income of many single-parent households had risen above the poverty line. As the regular completion of high school and uptake of employment of adolescents of divorced parents is positively influenced by regular child support payments, it should follow that more regular and increased child support payments improve the labour market situation of adolescents from divorced marriages. On a further positive note, it is highlighted that the collection of support refinances a part of the social welfare that is paid out.

Comparable effects were apparent through the reforms of child support law 1991 in England and Wales, which have since been partly revised[2]. The income of persons from the middle classes entitled to support was particularly affected by the new regulations, without the household income of the female support recipients being at the same time correspondingly improved. Through the state collection of support payments, needs-dependent social welfare benefits were dropped (*Marsh/Ford/Finlayson 1997*). The new regulations brought about, similar to in the USA, a situation in which the income of single parents not dependent on so-

---

[1] Faculty of Law, Leibniz University Hannover, Germany.
[2] by the child maintenance and other payments bill.

cial welfare was increased, without, however, creating similar incentives for single parents to emancipate themselves from social welfare (*Bryson/ Ford/White 1997*). In actual fact, the employment rate of single mothers did not rise; only the drawing of supplementary social welfare decreased slightly in the group of single mothers who were already in employment and who, on the advice of the support agency, were in a position to increase the weekly amount of hours worked by two hours[3]. An increase in the rate of support payments or the level of support given was, in contrast to the USA, not achieved.

While in the USA, England and Wales, the implementation of the subsidiarity principle was at the forefront of the reform considerations, the state recourse to private support obligations has long been institutionalised in the Federal Republic of Germany.

II. The German Support Laws

In Germany, by contrast, the focus is 2008 on considering the interests of the subsequent families. However, all reforms draw on the fostering of the child's wellbeing through the safeguarding of child support payments.

Germany's justice minister deems the reform of child support law of 2008 to be one of Germany's fundamental social policy reforms, as it placed divorced and non-married mothers on equal footing. Up until this point, the period of time for drawing childcare support for non-married mothers was limited to the care of children aged 0–3, while divorced mothers were able to draw childcare support on a more long-term basis.

Bases for claims Before 2008	2008
Difference between divorced and non-married mothers	No difference
No obligation to work for divorced mothers/ child 0-8 years	No obligation to work for mothers/ child 0–3 Exception due to child well-being: No care possibility

---

3   due to benefit reference levels.

Part-time/child 8–12	—
Full-time/child 12–15	—
Unmarried mothers child 0–3	—

At the same time, the precedence given to the first divorced ex-wife, which was institutionalised through the divorce law reform of 1977 as a continuance of the gender contract during marriage, was abolished, and the compensation of the socially weaker spouse in the support law was weakened. This is achieved among other things through the changed ranking of obligees: Ranked in first place are minors and qualifying non-minors, in second place resident parents and in third place spouses or ex-spouses who possess support entitlements due to other bases for claims. Through the narrower time limitation of care support, the likelihood increases that other bases for claims have to be realised earlier on: namely entitlement due to unemployment or *Aufstockungsunterhalt (compensation payments)*, which are of lower priority.

Ranking Before 2008	2008
I. Children, children and their mothers	I. Children
Priority of 1st ex-wife	—
II. Other bases for entitlement	—
Equality of the wives	II. Mothers of children 0–3 Ex-wives following long marriage
III. Other bases for entitlement	III. Other bases for entitlement
Equality of the wives	(Equality of the mothers)

III. Socio-Legal Reality

The reform of support law of 2008 strengthens the »self-responsibility« of spouses and distributes the risks of impairment of human capital through non-employment or part-time employment at the expense of those who have taken this risk as long as this is not classified as limited by child-rearing or a long-lasting marriage. This enables conflicts to occur in the support process regarding reasons for forgoing full-time employment in the past. The fact that interruptions in employment can no longer be compensated in the long term regarding their effects on the course of income is not taken into account (*Baumgärtner 2003*).

The reform draft explicitly invokes the social scientific investigations into the reality of child support and family change. With the increase in non-marital births and serial monogamy, the loss of importance of marriage, the changed attitude towards post-marital obligations in terms of legal policy is legitimised. At the same time, in 2007, the Federal Constitutional Court, with the help of the construction of the care entitlement of the child analogous to the (albeit since revised) English child support law (*Wikeley 2006*), reformulated the care support of the mother of this child and placed a time limitation on it, also applying this limitation to divorced mothers. This paradigm also renders existing divorce and separation contracts as non-effective.

Investigations from the Anglo-Saxon domain show that above all women from the upper middle class fall down the social ladder through separation and divorce (*Hetherington 2002*). Compared to the social status of the father, their children also descend the social ladder as adults, as the neighbourhood, school and education are no longer financed in accordance with the marital standard. This also applies for the financing of part-time work of the mother through additional maintenance, even though, according to *Amato* (2007), it is precisely part-time work which otherwise ensures an optimal development of children and adolescents in dual career families.

The poverty of single parents can only be eliminated through full-time employment, but since 1972, this has been on the decline for mothers of children under 6 in Germany (5th family report). Thus, the poverty rate of single parents amounts to 31% (43% in the former East German states) (*The Social Situation in Germany 2008*). The full-time employment of mothers in Germany lies below that for Austria and Switzerland. For all countries it is the case that single parents, more so than married mothers, have to put up with untypical and poorer working conditions, and despite a desire for full-time employment, have to accept part-time work (*Engelbrecht/Jungkunst 2001*). Therefore, in contrast to men, the income of single mothers reduces considerably following separation, in general by 37 %. (*Gender data report 2005*). And while men are able to recoup the loss of income following separation after one year, the woman's loss of income remains permanent. This can be attributed among other things to the consequences of past breaks in employment (*Beblo/Wolf 2002*).

Although the rate of persons receiving support following divorce has decreased, with support constituting the main source of income for 11 % of West German single mothers and 1 % of East Germans, the legal disputes regarding spousal support have not decreased. In 2006, 72 291 spousal support actions (in relation to 191 707 divorce cases 2006 at the family court) were instituted in Germany, of which only a minority were settled through the divorce. The majority of proceedings are conducted after separation and divorce. Generally speaking, the proceedings serve purposes of amending, reducing or abolishing spousal support payments. According to the most recent family law investigations, only 5 % of divorced mothers receive spousal support (Proksch 2002). In 1975, the rate amounted to 25 %, and following the introduction of the 1st marriage law reform of 1977decreased 1980 to 20 %, contrary to the expectations of critics (*Voegeli/Willenbacher 1993*). Consequently, in comparison to other countries, e.g. Australia, Germany today has low rates of spousal support (*Fehlberg 2004*).

Child support too, despite the purported greater readiness to pay of the obligors, is only regularly paid in two third of cases; in one third of cases it is paid irregularly or less: mainly the payments do not occur at all (*Forsa 2002*). Generally speaking, attempts to collect payment through judicial means do not improve the situation. And the successive increases in payments envisaged in the guidelines are not observed. Legal conflicts regarding child support, moreover, take place in 100 % of cases (*Willenbacher, Müller-Alten, Diekmann 1986*).The payment of spousal support did not reduce child support payments as the group of debitors paying regularly child support in the higher income groups equally pay spousal support. The lower income groups – paying less than the guidelines impose – are generally not liable to pay spousal support (*Forsa 2002*).

Since the reform of the support law came into effect, support proceedings in family courts have – according to practitioners – risen considerably, and some family courts oppose the obligation of mothers to take up employment again once the child is over 3 years old. Legal scholars have developed theoretically new age group models in order to replace the old models of jurisdiction. The first decisions confirm the anticipated regulations by the legal scholars, which assume no schematic duty to work full-time once the child is aged 3 and above. Rather, it is argued with regard to the child's well-being that full-time employment is not yet appropriate. This also applies for non-married mothers. The federal high court supported (18.3.2009) the obligation to work full time for the mother of a seven year old child.

If one considers the rationale the behind reform of child support law, it is apparent that the above-mentioned social scientific studies on the reality of child support and family change have not been completely adopted. For instance, the increased frequency of divorce is drawn on without, however, taking into account the fact that the frequency of divorce of marriages with children turns out to be lower.

The frequency of remarriage[4] is referred to, but the different chances of remarrying for women without children – compared to women who bring children with them into the marriage – is disregarded. The same applies for »repartnering« without marrying. However, this logic does not apply to men.

Equally, the high number of unmarried parents is pointed out, without giving mention to the high number of marriages of these parents.

Moreover, the increased employment of mothers is emphasised, without mentioning the high proportion of part-time work, which does not correspond to the legislator's ideas regarding the appropriateness of full-time work, staggered according to the age of the children. The restrictive opening hours of German kindergardens hinder additionally working hours flexibility.

And the higher unemployment rate of single mothers is also ignored. Women with children arrange their employment oriented towards their children's care needs, irrespective of family status. In many Western countries, women remain in part-time employment for longer than is envisaged in models from the legal profession. This means that the majority of women would theoretically have an entitlement to additional care support, or with increasing age of the children, (the divorcees) would be entitled to *Aufstockungsunterhalt (compensation payments.)*

---

[4] Although the gender gap between men and women in terms of the rate of remarriage has disappeared.

The legislator's perceptions do not correspond to the demographic data in Germany. When children are aged 3–15 years, the majority of mothers work part-time, followed by being a housewife in West Germany. The federal states differ considerably in this regard; only in the former East German states is full-time employment predominant for mothers of kindergarten and primary school children. In West Germany, by contrast, part-time work prevails. And in West Germany, for all age groups, being a housewife occupies second place.

Do single parents, who can only be saved from poverty by full-time employment, then behave differently? The answer is no. In contrast to Switzerland and Austria, the employment rates turn out to be lower – irrespective of the family status. The unemployment rates are particularly high; higher than those of married mothers. The rate of mothers who are housewives only decreases when the children are over 6 years old.

The social risks after separation and divorce are gendered:
> The increased employment rates of mothers conceal the fact that mothers are in many cases employed part-time and are not geared towards increasing or recovering human capital, and the increased employment figures are based, moreover, on unusual working hours and consist of precarious employment relations.
> The traditional pattern according to which the man holds the higher professional position is nowadays only realised on average in half of West German couples. In the middle class, a more long-term obligation to pay child support in the framework of the post-divorce support can be assumed, for the employment rate of wives decreased during the marriage in relation to the level of the husband's income. And only here does the uptake of employment not lead to a loss of entitlement to support in relation to the marital standard of living.
> An obligation to care for children by the non-resident parent following separation does not exist, as judgements on visitation rights show.
> A higher percentage of men liable to pay child support enter into new relationships following the separation.
> In order to avoid jeopardising social peace, mothers do not demand increases in child support.
> Lacking child support payments are generally not attributable to other maintenance obligations of the obligor; half of women entitled to support do not call in post-marital support and 50% of the remainder with support entitlements to not receive them.

> Single parents constitute the largest group of households living below the poverty line. Moreover, this group has increased in size in Germany in the last decades, while the strengthened collection of child support in the USA has led to a reduction in the rate of poverty of single mothers.

IV. Simulation

Due to the division of labour between the sexes, the model types developed by jurisdiction so far will be situated in social terms and the effect of the reform of support law will be modelled using case scenarios in accordance with the new rank order of persons entitled to support.

Provided that 85% of all children from divorced marriages grow up with the mother, the following constellations emerge:

Scenario I
A father liable to pay maintenance, in his second marriage with an non-employed wife without children, can no longer deduct the maintenance for his second wife from his income, and in the case of a so-called *Mangelfall* (situation in which the income of the non-resident parent is not sufficient to cover their self-maintenance and the child support) would have to pay a higher child support to his children, provided that they are minors or qualifying non-minors[5].

Scenario II
The divorced woman entitled to support is forced to take up employment herself earlier on, and in the so-called *Mangelfall*, the minor children receive a higher or the full child support. However, the child support turns out lower – in comparison to the standard support before the reform. Moreover, the support obligor, in contrast to the spousal support, can offset the child support against tax to a lesser extent, such that for this reason, the sum of the full child support turns out to be lower (in comparison to the full child support calculated before the reform. However, if there is no *Mangelfall*, i.e. the income of the support obligor would be sufficient to finance the child care maintenance and child support, the bur-

---

5   children 18-21 years old in educational or vocational training living in the household of one parent.

den on the support obligor decreases. The question arises of whether this can be balanced out through *Aufstockungsunterhalt (compensations payments)*.

Based on the new legal situation, a so-called *überobligatorische*[6] employment will be assumed more rarely (when due to the children, no employment, be it full or part-time, can be demanded), meaning that this income can no longer remain unconsidered, with the consequence that the *Aufstockungsunterhalt* can then be dropped or cut. Moreover, in this case, the second and first wives are given equal status in the ranking, meaning that the *Aufstockungsunterhalt* would also be proportionately cut back for this further reason. This also applies for the support due to unemployment. And in Germany, the unemployment rate of single mothers, at 15–20%, is at a high level compared with Switzerland and Austria.

Scenario III
The father liable to pay maintenance has further children from a second relationship, with the consequence that first of all, priority in terms of child support is given to all minor and non-minor qualifying children, followed by child care maintenance for the mother of a child under 3 years. In these cases, only if there is a high income would an *Aufstockungsunterhalt* for the divorced mother of the children from the first relationship be likely.

Scenario IV
Fathers providing childcare are generally employed on a full-time basis to a considerably greater extent, meaning that the question of child care maintenance for fathers rarely arises.

Scenario V
Unmarried mothers (provided that 95% of all non-marital children live in the household of their mother)

As, generally speaking, almost 60% of all unmarried mothers go on to marry the father of their child (*Vaskovics 1994/Bien 1998*) and 30% marry another man, those mothers who had only a short or no relationship with the father of their child will benefit from the support reform. Here, the rate of females drawing child care maintenance should be increased. In this regard, the child care maintenance is then oriented to the income sta-

---

6 when no employment is imposed by the law – the income by full-time or part-time emloyment is not taken into account when spousal support is calculated.

tus of the mother prior to the birth. Only in the cases in which the parents of the child cohabited for some time, which is above all the case in the former East German states, is the support then geared towards the joint standard of living.

In multi-father families (*Schneider 2001*), the sum is spread across the respective fathers. Support for a new, childless wife can now no longer be deducted from the income of the support obligor, and in a similar care situation the support would be proportionately divided between the mothers. As a high percentage of unmarried mothers cohabit with men other than the father of their child, the question arises of the reduction of support due to economic savings.

Now, women who draw welfare benefit will in the future be forced to claim child care maintenance. The child care maintenance of unmarried mothers should not free them from dependency on Hartz IV unemployment benefit, as in addition, public transfer payments remain necessary. This means that the household income of unmarried mothers should not considerably increase in these cases.

V. Summary

In *Mangelfällen*, the reform of support law leads to higher child support payments and will consequently lower children's need for welfare in Germany. However, this only applies when child care maintenance for the respective parent is not owed at the same time. In such cases, the discontinuation of child care maintenance should in general barely change the total sum that is paid, or reduce it.
Only if there is a higher income of the obligor does the reform lead to a significant reduction in household income of single divorced mothers, and here, the need for welfare of the divorced parent rather than the children, could in return be increased:

1.) Due to the low flexibility of the labour market and narrow kindergarden hours, the unemployment of single women should be further increased,
2.) Due to the ranking of entitlement to support owing to unemployment,
3.) Due to the reduction of recognition of income from *überobligatorische* employment,
4.) Due to the proportionate consideration of the costs of full-time care and the share in visiting costs,

5.) Due to the deduction of possibly increased child support payments from welfare rates.

Hence, the utilisation of public funds by single divorced mothers will increase. For irrespective of whether the single women are entitled to support, they only increase their employment in combination with improved child care possibilities. In particular, divorced mothers with children aged 3-9 years will have to accept an additional financial impact in order to secure the care of their children. Therefore, losses in household income of divorced middle-class mothers will be expected – a phenomenon which, according to *Amato* (2007), leads to an endangerment of the children's development chances. Although these groups did not remain in a position of poverty for long due to their professional qualifications, as the socioeconomic panel in Germany proves, according to Amato, even short-term encroachments on household income can have negative effects. So far, in contrast to the USA, children from divorced marriages in Germany show no social downward mobility. This might possibly change in the future, for in California, the family law reforms have considerably increased the downward mobility of children (*Gruber 2004*).

The need for welfare of unmarried mothers of kindergarten children aged 3-6 could, by contrast, be reduced, or the burden on the public purse could be partly eased. The socioeconomic situation of divorced and unmarried mothers is consequently more strongly aligned at a lower level.

Approximately two thirds of child support in Germany are paid regularly, a third irregularly as mainly the obligors are not able to pay (*Andreß 2003/Forsa 2002*). For the majority the child support might be slightly reduced due to the changed forms of calculation, in the second it will not change. The high poverty rate of single women in Germany is therefore not expected to be reduced from a cross-country comparison. The pressure on single parents in terms of the arrangement of employment is increasing, as is the pressure to keep career breaks as short as possible.

Comparable to the reforms in the USA and England, the legislator might have intended, through the securing of support payments for children, to create an incentive in order to facilitate the uptake of low-waged jobs so as to improve the income level of single parents. As support is offset against social welfare payments, in spite of support paid, the income effect is absent in the case of drawing social welfare. Only the combination of support and income from gainful employment increases the household income. Comparable to this is also the possibility to refinance social welfare costs in the case of unmarried mothers and in the case of increased child support payments for female unemployment benefit recipients.

References

- *Hans-Jürgen Andreß:* Die wirtschaftlichen Folgen von Trennung und Scheidung. Stuttgart 1999.
- *Hans-Jürgen Andreß* et al.: Wenn aus Liebe rote Zahlen werden. Wiesbaden 2003.
- *Australian Institute of Family Studies:* Why study Attitudes to Child Support? Melbourne 2005.
- *Anna Aizer:* The Impact of Child Support on Fertility, Parental Investments and Child Care and Child Well-Being. In: Journal of Human Resources 2006 p.28–71.
- *Paul Amato:* Together alone. Cambridge (Mass.) 2007
- *Doris Baumgärtner:* Frauen im mittleren Erwerbsalter. Bern 2003.
- *Sabine Berghahn:* Neue Chancen für geschiedene Frauen. Ffm 1992.
- *Walter Bien* (Eds.): Kind ja, Ehe nein. Opladen 1998.
- *Walter Bien, Jan Marbach* (Eds.): Partnerschaft und Familiengründung. Opladen 2003.
- *Walter Bien, Angela Hartl, Markus Teubner* (EDs.): Stieffamilien in Deutschland. Opladen 2002.
- *Katharina Boele-Woelki* u.a.: Principles of European Family Law Regarding Divorce and Maintenance Between Former Spouses. Antwerpen 2004.
- *Katharina Boele-Woelki* u.a.(Eds.): European Family Law in Action, Vol. III: Parental Responsibilities. Antwerp 2005
- *Jonathan Bradshaw, Jane Millar:* Lone Parent Families in the UK, London 1991.
- *Margaret Brining:* Economics of Family Law. Cheltenham 2007.
- *Alex Bryson, Reuben Ford, Michael White:* Making Work pay. London HMSO 1997.
- *Bundesamt für Statistik: Sozialberichterstattung* Schweiz. Neuchatel 2002.
- *Bundesministerium für Familie, Senioren, Frauen und Jugend:* Genderdatenreport. 2005.
- *Bundesministerium für Umwelt, Jugend und Familie.* Österreichischer Familienbericht 1999
- *Bundeszentrale für politische Bildung:* Die soziale Situation in Deutschland. 2008.
- *Carole Burgoyne, Jane Millar:* Enforcing Child Support, in: Policy and Politics 1994, p.95–104

> *Laurence Charton:* Beginn und Auflösung der ersten Lebensgemeinschaft in der Schweiz. Neuchatel 2000.
> *Pierre-Andre Chiappori* and *Yoral Weiss:* Divorce, Remarriage and Child Support. Foerder Institute for Economic Research 2006.
> *Child Support Agency:* National Client Satisfaction Survey 1995. London 1996.
> *Jocelyn Crowley:* The Politics of Child Support. New York 2003.
> *Gwynn Davis/Jacqueline Barron/Julie Bedward:* Child Support in Action. Oxford 1998.
> *Helene Dearing:* Why do mothers working longer hours in Austria than in Germany. In: Fiscal Studies 28, p. 463-495.
> *Lu Decurtius, Peter C.Meyer:* Väter und Scheidung. In: FamPra 2002, p. 48-66.
> *Nina Dethloff:* Gutachten: Unterhalt, Zugewinn, Versorgungsausgleich. Deutscher Juristentag 2008
> *Deutscher Bundestag*; 5. Familienbericht 2005
> *Deutscher Bundestag:* Siebter Familienbericht. 2008
> *Greg Duncan et al.:* Armuts- und Sozialhilfedynamiken in Europa und Nordamerika,
> Bremen, ZES Arbeitspapier Nr.11/92, 2002.
> *John Eekelaar:* Regulating Divorce, Oxford 1991.
> *John Eekelaar:* Third Thoughts on Child Support, In: Family Law 1994, p.99-102
> *Jutta Engelbrecht, Maria Jungkunst:* Wie bringt man Beruf und Kinder unter einen Hut? In. IAB Kurzbericht 2001
> *Enquete* ‚étude de l'histoire familiale'.In: Insee 1999
> *Reuben Ford, Jane Millar:* Private Lives and Public Responses. London 1998.
> *Forsa:* Unterhaltszahlungen für minderjährige Kinder in Deutschland. Stuttgart 2002.
> *Irwin Garfinkel* et al. (Hrsg.): Child Support Assurance, Washington 1992.
> *Irwin Garfinkel:* Assuring Child Support, New York 1992.
> *Irwin Garfinkel* et al. (Hrsg.): Social Policies for Children. Washington 1996.
> *Irwin Garfinkel* u.a.: Fathers under Fire. CASE 1998.
> *Timothy Grall:* Custodial Mothers and Fathers and Their Child Support. In: Current Population Reports 2007. P60-234
> *Alison Graham/Emma Knights:* Putting the Treasury First. London 1994.
> *Jonathan Gruber:* Is making divorce easier bad for children? In: Journal of Labor Economics 2004, p.799-833.

> *Martin Halla:* Unterhalt, Obsorge und Scheidungsanwälte. Econ Papers 2005.
> *Eileen Mavis Hetherington:* For the better or for the worse. New York 2002
> *Heinz Hausheer, Annette Spycher:* Unterhalt nach dem neuen Scheidungsrecht. Bern 2001.
> *Regula Hinderling:* Verschulden und nachehelicher Ehegattenunterhalt (Schweiz/USA). Basel 2001.
> *Stephen Jenkins, Elizabeth Symons:* Child Care Costs and Lone Mother's Employment Rates. Institute for Social and Economic Research, Working Paper 95-2, Essex 1995.
> *Rainer Kemper:* Das neue Unterhaltsrecht. Neuwied 2008.
> *Kita-Check* 2008
> *Thomas Klein, Wolfgang Lauterbach* (Eds.): Nichteheliche Lebensgemeinschaften. Opladen 1999.
> *Thomas Klein, Johannes Kopp* (Eds.): Scheidungsursachen aus soziologischer Sicht. Würzburg 1999.
> *Thomas Klein* (Hrsg.): Partnerwahl und Heiratsmuster. Opladen 2001.
> *Thomas Klein, Jan Eckhard:* Fertilität in Stieffamilien. In: Kölner Zeitschrift für Soziologie und Sozialpsychologie 2004, p. 71-94.
> *Karin Kurz:* Das Erwerbsverhalten von Frauen in der intensiven Familienphase. Opladen 1998.
> *Nadine Lefaucheur:* Mutterschaft, Familie und Staat. In: Geschichte der Frauen, eds. by Georges Duby, Michelle Pierot. Frankfurt 1995, p.463-483.
> *Doris Lucke:* Rechtssoziologie, Familiensoziologie und Familienrecht. In: *Horst Dreier* (Ed.): Rechtssoziologie am Ende des 20 Jahrhunderts. Tübingen 2000, p. 86-114.
> *Eleanor Maccoby, Robert Mnookin:* Dividing the Child. Cambridge (Mass.) 1992.
> *Sarah MacLanahan, Gary Sandefur:* Grwoing up with a Single Parent. Cambridge (Mass.) 1994.
> *Mavis Maclean, John Eekelaar:* The Parental Obligation. Oxford 1997.
> *Mavis Maclean:* The Making of the Child Support Act, In: Journal of Law and Society Vol.21 1994, p.505-519.
> *Steve Mckay, Alan Marsh:* Lone Parents and Work. London 1994.
> *Jane Millar, Andrea Warman:* Family Obligations in Europe. London 1996.
> *Jane Millar:* Family Obligations and Social Policy. In: Policy Studies 1996, p.181-194.

> *Thomas Piketty:* The Impact of Divorce on School Performance: Evidence from France 1968-2002.Centrte for Economic Policy Research, London 2002.
> *Lore Peschel-Gutzeit:* Unterhaltsrecht aktuell. Baden-Baden 2008.
> Astrid Pfennig (Hrsg.): Families and Family Policies in Europe. Ffm 2000.
> *Maureen Pirog, Kathleen Ziol-Guest:* Child Support Enforcement and Policies, Impact and Questions. In: Journal of Policy Analysis and Management 2006, p. 943-990.
> *Roland Proksch:* Rechtstatsächliche Untersuchung zur Reform des Familienrechts. Köln 2002
> Referentenentwurf des *Bundesministeriums des Inneren:* Entwurf eines Gesetzes zur Änderung des Unterhaltsrechts 2006.
> *Norbert Schneider:* Alleinerziehende. Weinheim 2001.
> *Ingeborg Schwenzer:* Nachehelicher Unterhalt. In: Ingeborg Schwenzer (Ed.): Scheidung. Bern 2005, p. 221-321.
> *Ingeborg Schwenzer:* Ehegattenunterhalt nach der Scheidung. In: Aktuelle Juristische Praxis 1999, p.167-177.
> *Constance L. Shehan* et al. : Alimony. In: Family Relations 2002, p.308-316.
> *Bruce Smith, Ruth Weston:* A Snapshot of Contemporary Attitudes to Child Support. Melbourne 2005.
> *Isabelle Stadelmann-Steffen:* Policies, Frauen und der Arbeitsmarkt. Wien 2007.
> *Statistik Austria* 2008
> *Statistisches Bundesamt:* Statistisches Jahrbuch 2006. Wiesbaden 2006.
> *Statistisches Bundesamt:* Haushalte und Familien 2006. Fachserie 1, Reihe 3. Wiesbaden 2008.
> *Statistisches Bundesamt:* Familiengerichte 2006. Fachserie 10, Reihe 2.2. Wiesbaden 2006.
> *Wolfgang Steegmann-Kuhn, Barbara Seel:* Einkommensdiskriminierung und frauenspezifische Erwerbsbiographie.Aachen 2004.
> *Laszlo Vaskovics* u.a.: Lebenslagen nichtehelicher Kinder. Bamberg 1994.
> *University of Wisconsin-Madison/Institute for Research on Poverty:* Child Support Enforcement Policy and Low Income Families. 2000.
> *Wolfgang Voegeli/Barbara Willenbacher:* Children's Rights and Social Placement. In: International Journal of Law and the Family 1993, S.108-124.
> *Harald Werneck,* (Hrsg.): Psychologie der Scheidung und Trennung. Wien 2003.
> *Nick Wikeley:* Child Support. Oxford 2006.

> *Stephan Wullschleger:* Die Unterhaltspflicht der Eltern. In: *Ingeborg Schwenzer* (Ed.):: Scheidung. Bern 2005, S.895–962.
> *Barbara Willenbacher:* Stellungnahme zur öffentlichen Anhörung des Rechtsausschusses am 12.Juni 1986. In: Protokolle des Rechtsausschusses, Protokoll Nr. 54.
> *Barbara Willenbacher, Lutz Müller-Alten, Jörn Diekmann:* Die Nutzung des gerichtlichen Angebots zur Regelung von Ehescheidungsfolgen. In: Zeitschrift für Rechtssoziologie 7 1986, p.168–190.
> *Barbara Willenbacher, Wolfgang Voegeli, Lutz Müller-Alten:* Auswirkungen des Ehegattenunterhaltsrechts in der Bundesrepublik Deutschland. In: Zeitschrift für Rechtssoziologie 8 1987, p. 98–113.

The Financial Impact of Relocation Disputes: Empirical Evidence from Australia

Patrick Parkinson[1]

I. Introduction[2]

Relocation disputes are some of the most difficult issues for family court judges to decide.[3] There are also acrimonious policy debates about whether there should be a presumption for or against relocation and how the needs of the children to have a relationship with their parents can be reconciled with a primary carer's desire to live where she or he chooses.[4] In those debates, the gender issue is unavoidable, because it is almost always women who want to move and men, the non-resident parents, who oppose that move.[5]

One issue which has so far attracted very little attention is the impact of the process of disputing relocation issues on the wellbeing of children. Children can suffer in various ways through the litigation process – not only through the stress and anxiety associated with uncertainty about the future, and exposure to ongoing parental conflict, but also through the impact on the family of the litigation costs. Children's wellbeing is to a considerable extent affected by the level of financial resources in the home of their primary carer.[6] This is one reason why child support is so

---

1 Professor of Law, University of Sydney, Australia.
2 This research was supported under Australian Research Council‹s Discovery Projects funding scheme (project number DP0665676).
3 D. Duggan, »Rock-paper-scissors: Playing the Odds with the Law of Child Relocation« (2007) 45 *Family Court Review* 193; T. Carmody, »Child Relocation: An Intractable International Family Law Problem« (2007) 45 *Family Court Review* 214.
4 See e.g. Family Law Council, *Relocation* (Canberra: Commonwealth of Australia, 2006).
5 See e.g. C. Ford, »Untying the Relocation Knot: Recent Developments and a Model for Change« (1997) 7 *Colum. J. Gender & L.* 1; J. Behrens, »U v U: The High Court on Relocation« (2003) 27 *Melbourne University Law Review* 572; M. Weiner, »Inertia and Inequality: Reconceptualizing Disputes Over Parental Relocation« (2007) 40 *UC Davis Law Review* 1747.
6 P. Amato & J. Gilbreth, »Nonresident Fathers and Children‹s Well-being: A Meta-analysis« (1999) 61 *J. Marriage & Fam.* 557 at 564; S. McLanahan, »Father Absence and the

important.[7] One implication of analysing the relocation problem in this way might be that in selecting the legal rules or principles that should be applied to relocation cases, a rule which promotes settlements ought to be preferred to one that does not, in order to promote the best interests of children generally.

1. The Need for Empirical Research

In order to find a way forward in terms of public policy on relocation, empirical research concerning the real experience of families is critical to ground the debates on a sure foundation of shared knowledge and understanding of the issues. There is very little such empirical information. There is some evidence concerning the impact of parental moves on young adults,[8] although the findings of that research are hotly contested,[9] and some expert commentary on the issues based largely upon general psychological knowledge.[10] While the available literature reviews and commentaries are helpful, there is a need for rigorous empirical research on the experience of parents and children who are involved in relocation disputes to analyse various dimensions of the problem.

Welfare of Children« in M. Hetherington (ed), *Coping with Divorce, Single Parenting and Remarriage: A Risk and Resiliency Perspective* (Lawrence Erlbaum, 1999) pp.117, 130-35.

7   J. Bartfeld, »Child Support and the Postdivorce Economic Well-Being of Mothers, Fathers, and Children« (2000) 37 *Demography* 203; J. Bradshaw, »Child Support and Child Poverty« (2006) 14 *Benefits* 199; D. Meyer & M. Hu, »A Note on the Antipoverty Effectiveness of Child Support among Mother-Only Families« (1999) 34 *J. Human Resources* 225; L. Argys, E. Peters, J. Brooks-Gunn, & J. Smith, »The Impact of Child Support on Cognitive Outcomes of Young Children« (1998) 35 *Demography* 159.

8   S. Braver, I. Ellman, & W. Fabricius, »Relocation of Children After Divorce and Children's Best Interests: New Evidence and Legal Considerations« (2003) 17 *J. Fam. Psych.* 206.

9   See e.g. C. Bruch, »Sound Research or Wishful Thinking in Child Custody Cases? Lessons from Relocation Law« (2006) 40 *Fam. L.Q.* 281 at 308-09.

10 See e.g. W. Austin, »Relocation, Research and Forensic Evaluation: Part I: Effects of Residential Mobility on Children of Divorce« (2008) 46 *Family Court Review* 137; W. Austin, »Relocation, Research and Forensic Evaluation: Part II: Research in Support of the Relocation Risk Assessment Model« (2008) 46 *Family Court Review* 347. See also J. Wallerstein & T. Tanke, »To Move or Not to Move: Psychological and Legal Considerations in the Relocation of Children Following Divorce« (1996) 30 *Fam. L.Q.* 305; J. Kelly & M. Lamb, »Developmental Issues in Relocation Cases Involving Young Children: When, Whether and How?« (2003) 17 *J. Fam. Psych.* 193; R. Warshak, »Social Science and Children's Best Interests in Relocation Cases: Burgess Revisited« (2000) 34 *Fam. L.Q.* 83.

2. The University of Sydney Study

In order to help fill the knowledge gaps about relocation disputes, our team from the University of Sydney is conducting the world's first prospective longitudinal study of relocation disputes.[11] We are also collaborating with a New Zealand team based at the University of Otago that is conducting similar relocation research in that country.

The research program was designed to explore how parents and children deal with the aftermath of relocation disputes over the long-term. We are exploring such questions as what happens, if the relocation occurs, in terms of children's experiences of changing home, school and community? Is the planned level of contact between parent and child maintained? What happens in terms of the extent of cooperation between the parents? If the relocation is not permitted, how well does the resident parent adapt to this disappointment? How do the children fare? These and other such issues are being explored longitudinally through both qualitative and quantitative methodologies.

We recruited our sample of parents and children mainly by writing to family lawyers all over Australia. Lawyers were asked to identify relocation disputes which had been resolved in the 6 months prior to receiving the letter from us. The criterion for inclusion in the study was that a client had come to see them for advice concerning a relocation dispute. The intention was to capture all cases where a parent had sought legal advice concerning the dispute even if it was settled without engaging in significant litigation. The family lawyers were asked to send a brochure to any clients that were involved in a relocation dispute, and if a client wished to participate they would contact the researchers directly. The researchers have gained considerable cooperation from the family law profession in Australia. Cases in our cohort have come from all over the country. Most parents were interviewed within a few months of the resolution of the relocation dispute, one way or the other. In a small number of cases, they were interviewed prior to finalisation of the dispute, where, for example, they were awaiting the judgment or the case was on appeal.

The first wave of interviews has now been completed. This paper examines the financial impact of relocation disputes, and how the cost of travel affects both resident and non-resident parents if the relocation is allowed.

---

[11] Chief investigators are the author, Dr Judy Cashmore (a developmental psychologist), and the Hon Richard Chisholm (a former Family Court judge). Judi Single is the research associate.

It then explores some policy implications of these findings for the substantive rules on the resolution of relocation disputes. The findings of the Australian study cannot be understood without some background on the context in which these relocation disputes are determined in Australia.

II. Setting the Scene: The Australian Context

1. Distance and Demographic Factors

Relocation is a major issue in Australia, not least because of the size of the continent. From Sydney to Perth (an east-west route) is more than 4,000 kms by road, and it is more than 3,000 kms from Darwin to Adelaide (a north-south route).[12] The distance between other major cities is also measured in the hundreds and thousands of kilometres. Even within one state, such as New South Wales or Queensland, travelling between two towns may involve distances that are the equivalent of crossing several countries in Europe. That means that for many people at least, the relocation of a primary carer to another part of Australia may make it very difficult indeed for the other parent to see the child unless he moves as well, or they can afford frequent plane travel.

Australia is also a nation of migrants. The proportion of the population who were born overseas increased from 10% in 1947 to 24% in 2000.[13] Currently, the Australian population has a net gain of one international migrant every 2½ minutes.[14] Thus a substantial proportion of all Australian residents are either first or second generation Australians. One reason for such high levels of overseas' born residents is marriage between a foreign national and an Australian resident.

2. The Australian Law on Relocation

In parenting disputes, courts are guided by the principle that the best interests of the child are the paramount consideration. There are no specific statutory provisions on relocation. In the case law, there is neither a presumption for nor against relocation. The parent who wishes to move does not bear any onus of proving that the relocation is reasonable. The court must examine not only the primary caregiver's proposal to relocate

---

12 See http://www.sydney.com.au/distance-between-Australia-cities.htm.
13 Australian Bureau of Statistics, International Migration, 2002: http://www.abs.gov.au.
14 See population clock at http://www.abs.gov.au, last accessed April 6th 2009.

but also whether the non-resident parent could relocate as well.[15] This reduces the gendered nature of the issues in relocation cases.

However, following the enactment of major amendments to the *Family Law Act 1975* in 2006,[16] there is now a greater legislative emphasis on the importance of maintaining the involvement of both parents following separation. In determining what is in the best interests of the child, the primary considerations are the benefit to the child of having a meaningful relationship with both parents and the need to protect the child from physical or psychological harm from being subjected to, or exposed to, abuse, neglect or family violence.[17] Judges also need to consider whether equal time, or »substantial and significant time«, are in the best interests of the child and reasonably practicable in cases where the parents will share equal parental responsibility.[18]

While there are some significant differences of approach between judges on how to apply the amended law to relocation cases,[19] the overall intent of the legislation is clearly to promote a greater degree of shared parenting in appropriate cases, and this has implications for relocation disputes. Overall, the consequence of the 2006 changes has been that it is now harder to relocate than it was before.[20]

III. Outcomes of the Relocation Dispute

The findings reported in this chapter are based upon the outcomes of interviews with 80 adults, 40 women and 40 men. Thirty-nine women participants (including one grandmother who was the primary carer) wanted to move, and one non-resident mother opposed the father's move. The 40 male participants were all opposing the ex-partner's move. There were 9 former couples, so 71 different cases over all. Sixty-eight cases have been

---

15 This was an issue highlighted by the High Court of Australia in *U v. U* (2002) 211 C.L.R. 238.
16 *Family Law Amendment (Shared Parental Responsibility) Act* 2006.
17 *Family Law Act 1975* s.60CC(2).
18 *Family Law Act 1975* s.65DAA.
19 For a full analysis, see P. Parkinson, »Freedom of Movement in an Era of Shared Parenting: The Differences in Judicial Approaches to Relocation« (2008) 36 *Federal Law Review* 145.
20 P. Parkinson, »The Realities of Relocation: Messages from Judicial Decisions« (2008) 22 *Australian Journal of Family Law* 35; P. Easteal & K. Harkins, »Are We There Yet? An Analysis of Relocation Judgments in Light of Changes to the *Family Law Act*« (2008) 22 *Australian Journal of Family Law* 259.

resolved. Three are still unresolved. In 65% of the resolved cases (44/68), the applicant was allowed to move with the children either by judicial decision or by consent. In 58% (21/36) of the cases in which there was a judicial determination, the applicant was allowed to move with the children. This is a little higher than in the reported cases since July 2006.[21]

In two cases where the outcome was that the mother was not able to take the children, she left anyway, leaving the child, (in each case a primary school age girl), in the care of the father. Four fathers chose to relocate to the same place as the mother. The fact that a relocation was permitted did not mean it happened. Two women who were allowed to relocate decided in the end not to go through with it – even after a full trial. By the time of the interview a few months after the resolution of the dispute, two had returned to live where they were before.

IV. Low Rates of Settlement

About 53% of cases were resolved by judicial determination (36/68). In family law disputes, generally only 6% of cases in which litigation is commenced are resolved by judicial determination,[22] with an unknown number of cases being resolved by negotiation and mediation without either parent commencing litigation. Many of the cases that did settle were resolved very late in the litigation process, either resolving shortly before trial, or during the trial. The term »consent« often signifies not only agreement, but willing agreement. However, in this study, consent often meant reluctant acquiescence or resignation.

There is no reason to believe that the findings of this study are unrepresentative. Practitioners were asked to identify any case where there was a relocation dispute. Had this been a general sample of parenting disputes in Australia, one might have expected that the cohort would have been distributed fairly evenly along the dispute resolution continuum, with many cases being settled without the need to commence litigation at all;

---

21 In reported decisions since July 2006, when the reforms came into effect, the relocation has been allowed in 53% of cases: Parkinson, n.17 above. A few of the participants interviewed in our study had matters decided before the introduction of the new laws, when relocations were more likely to be permitted.
22 House of Representatives Standing Committee on Family and Community Affairs, *Every Picture Tells a Story: Report of the Inquiry into Child Custody Arrangements in the Event of Family Separation* (Parliament of Australia, Dec. 2003) p.6.

others settling quite early in the litigation process; others still being resolved after court-based dispute resolution efforts; others still being settled once much of the evidence had been gathered, and in particular after a Family Report had been obtained; more cases being settled at the door of the court or after the trial had commenced, and the remainder, a small minority of the whole, being determined by a judge.

The very low settlement rate in relocation cases has a number of explanations which probably operate together. The first is that there is little middle ground between the two parents' positions on which to base a compromise. In most parenting disputes, there is a middle ground in terms of the amount of time the children spend with each parent, or which school the children will attend. Even if the compromise is reached reluctantly on both sides, most parents eventually find some compromise because it is better than the stress and expense of litigation. Often good legal advice on the prospects of success can promote settlements.

However, relocation cases tend to be different. There is little middle ground. The choices in relocation disputes typically are binary choices: either the primary carer will move or she will not, either the non-resident carer will move to be in the same location as the primary carer or he will not. There is some room for negotiation and agreement, for example, over who will bear the travel costs if the relocation occurs. However, that presupposes acceptance of the parent's move. The option for the non-resident parent of relocating as well, or accepting longer periods of holiday contact rather than regular face-to-face time on weekends and perhaps during the week, may well not be at all attractive compared to the preservation of the status quo. The resident parent may also be too invested in the desire to relocate – and to the destination specified – to come up with some other alternative such as delaying the move for a few years, moving somewhere else but less far, or not moving at all. Webcam, telephone and email are also options for communication, but in our interviews with non-resident parents, these were not seen as adequate substitutes for the experience of family life with the children through regular physical contact, involving overnight stays.

Even cases that are difficult to compromise can be resolved without the need to go to trial, if the prospects of success for one side or the other are perceived to be poor. There are numerous factors that can lead a litigant (or his or her advisers) to the conclusion that the prospects of success are not good. The law itself is one major factor in assisting litigants and their advisers to make a realistic appraisal of their prospects of success. However, the more discretionary the system of justice, the less the law signals the outcome. In Australia, during the period of this study, the appellate courts offered very little guidance, if any, about how relocation cases were to be resolved in the light of the changes to the law in July 2006, and very few appeals have succeeded. A great deal of discretion is left to trial judges to determine the case according to their individual assessment of what is in the best interests of the child. The only rule is that there are no rules.[23] Significant variations in outcome can be seen between regions.[24] This unwillingness to lay down guidelines – the reasons for which may only be speculated upon – may well be making it much harder to resolve these already difficult cases than would be the case if clearer guidelines were articulated. A third possible explanation for the low settlement rate is that cases involving relocation are disproportionately cases in which the parents are highly conflicted and find difficulties in reaching child-centred compromises. That is, the desire of one parent to relocate may have been a response to the difficulties of working together with the other parent. Conversely, in a situation where the non-resident parent is motivated by a need to dominate and control the primary carer, the planned relocation – itself a form of escape – will be strenuously resisted. While this was undoubtedly a feature of a few cases in this study, an analysis of the reasons given by 39 mothers for the move indicates that only 6 said that their main motivation was to get away from the other parent and only 3 gave as the main reason that they were escaping violence or control. The main reasons for wanting to relocate were returning home, moving for the sake of a new relationship and being closer to other family members.

V. The Legal Costs of Relocation Disputes

We asked participants to estimate what their legal costs were. These costs were only for that participant and excluded any amounts they were required to pay of the other party's costs. The normal position in family law cases in Australia is that each litigant pays his or her own costs but in certain instances, a costs award may be made against the losing party. The legal costs in our study varied considerably. Twelve participants reported

---

23   Parkinson, n.19 above.
24   Parkinson, n.20 above.

legal costs of $ 100,000 or more, with the highest estimate being between $ 450,000 and $ 500,000.

The median cost of all cases in the cohort was $ 40,000 per participant, with a mean of $ 62,500. These do not represent completely the final figures for the cohort as three cases remain unresolved. The high median cost of the cases is largely a reflection of the fact that so many cases were litigated through to judicial determination, and that many of the cases resolved by consent were not settled until very late in the litigation process. Tables 1 and 2 provide information on the median, mean and highest costs in the cases that went to judgment and those that settled, separately.

Cost of cases resolved by judicial determination

Median	$ 45,000
Mean	$ 66,172 (SD = $ 80,040)
Highest	$ 450–500,000

Cost of cases resolved by consent

Median	$ 30,000
Mean	$ 54,700 (SD = $ 60,170)
Highest	$ 220,000

A confounding factor in estimating legal costs was that for a minority of interviewees, the issue of relocation arose around the same time as, or soon after the separation. At this time, one might expect that lawyers would be advising on other issues to do with the separation, as well as the parenting issues. Getting a divorce in Australia can usually be done without legal assistance, and so this would not have been likely to add much to the legal costs. However, disputes concerning division of property (a highly discretionary process in Australian law) may well have added significantly to the overall legal costs. It is impossible to disaggregate the different legal expenses in such cases because conferences with lawyers, and letters passing between lawyers, might well deal with all the issues in dispute, or at least more than one issue.

In order to test this, we examined 50 cases in which the relocation issue clearly arose as a discrete dispute, at least one year after the separation, and compared the costs of this group with the group for whom the relocation issue arose within 12 months of separation. We found that there was no statistically significant difference between the two groups. This suggests that even in the cases where the relocation dispute arose in the immediate aftermath of separation, or within a reasonably short time thereafter, it was the relocation dispute itself which was the main driver of legal costs. Nonetheless, as well as the relocation dispute itself, some cases involved interim proceedings or collateral proceedings related to parenting matters. For example, the most expensive case involved international child abduction proceedings resulting in the return of the mother and child to Australia, followed by the relocation decision. The legal disputes in this case began soon after separation.

The high legal costs in this cohort of course reflect the fact that most participants were recruited through private lawyers. However, a few participants had some level of legal aid funding or represented themselves for some of the proceedings.

To put the overall legal costs in perspective, the average weekly ordinary full-time earnings in Australia in February 2007 was $ 1070.40 per week or $ 55,661 per year.[25] The median legal costs overall were thus in the vicinity of 74% of annual earnings for employees in ordinary full-time work. However, there are differences between the socio-demographic profile of parents who have separated (even paying parents) and those in the general community. Figures from the Child Support Agency (which is estimated to have data on 94% of separated parents in Australia[26]), indicates that the median and mean income levels of payers are significantly lower than for the general population. In June 2006, the median income of all payers was $ 23,981. This includes a substantial number who are in receipt of income support payments from the Government, due to unemployment or disability. For those who filed tax returns (and were more likely therefore to be in employment) the median taxable income was $ 35,408.[27]

There is no reason to believe that the costs of litigation in relocation cases are all that different from other family law disputes that are litigated. By way of comparison, a study of 47 bills of costs in family law matters (mostly property cases) found that the median cost of these disputes per litigant was $ 10,389 up to and including the stage of pre-hearing confer-

---

25 The statistics on average weekly earnings are available at the Australian Bureau of Statistics: http://www.abs.gov.au.
26 See Ministerial Taskforce on Child Support, *In the Best Interests of Children* (Canberra: Commonwealth of Australia, 2005) p.77.
27 Child Support Agency, *Child Support Facts and Figures 2005-06* (Canberra: 2006) pp.28-29.

ence, and $ 23,804 from that time until the end of the case. This is a total of $ 34,193 for those cases that went to trial.[28] Most of the bills of costs in this study were from 1991–1994, with a range from 1988–1996.[29] Allowing for inflation between the time that the two sets of data were collected, and that a few participants in this study had legal aid or represented themselves, the costs of the cases that went to trial are broadly comparable.[30] What makes relocation so different from all other family law disputes is that comparatively so few cases are able to be settled. The cumulative cost to families, and indirectly to children's wellbeing, is thus vastly greater than for other kinds of family law dispute.

VI. How Was the Litigation Funded?

There were a variety of ways in which parents funded the litigation. The most common way was by using capital assets, in particular, selling property or using the family home as security for the payment of the legal fees. Another major source of funding was from family members who either lent the money or gave it outright. One man funded his litigation through an inheritance he received after his father committed suicide. He had a shared care arrangement and was fighting to keep his child in the area. Another used a compensation payout.

The very high legal costs participants had to meet, relative to income, was a major source of distress. Participants spoke of being financially ruined as a result of the litigation, in some cases losing all the capital they had acquired, or going into severe debt. Eleven participants had to sell the family home as a result of the legal costs.

VII. The Costs of Travel

A further issue in assessing the financial impact of relocation disputes is the cost of travel if the relocation goes ahead. Some judges have sought to resolve the tension between a meaningful relationship and the right

---

28 G. Pesce, »Analysing the Structure of Litigation Costs« (2002) 16 *Australian Journal of Family Law* 1.
29 Personal communication with the author, 13 November 2008.
30 In Pesce's study (n.28 above), there were 47 bills of costs. Thrity-five were in relation to financial matters, 4 to non-financial matters and 8 had a mixture of matters. Forty cases went to trial and 7 were settled.

to freedom of movement by allowing relocation, but with onerous travel requirements in order to spend face-to-face time with the other parent. For example, in one case in the study,[31] a mother applied to move with her young daughter from a regional town on the border of NSW and Victoria to a town in the outback of Queensland. The child was 2 ½ at the time of decision. The mother and father had not lived together. The judge allowed the relocation but ordered that the child should see the father for a week in every month. This means that for 9 months of the year the mother must travel to the town from where she came and spend a week facilitating the child spending time with the father. For 3 months of the year the father has reciprocal rights to spend time with the child in rural Queensland, a right he had not regularly exercised.

In another case, a relocation was permitted for a 2 year old child who moved from the Gold Coast to rural Victoria, a distance of about 1,700 kms. Every 13 days she travels to visit her father in Queensland for an 8 night block. The mother typically travels to the Gold Coast to give the child to the father, travels back, and returns to collect the child.

While the greatest frequency of contact is ordered when the children are not yet of school age, regular contact, despite vast distances, was a common outcome where the mother was allowed to relocate. In some cases this meant weekend travel for school-age children, leaving on a Friday evening and returning on a Sunday evening, as well as travel during school holidays. This raises many issues, such as the burden of travel on the children. Another is the cost of travel. Table 3 indicates how the travel costs were distributed between the parents in 34 cases where the relocation was permitted, took place, and in which contact was occurring. It will be seen that there is no clear pattern of practice in this area in Australia.

Table 3: Travel costs – allocation of responsibility between parents

Shared approximately equally	17
Relocating parent pays all	4
Non-relocating parent pays all	3
Relocating parent pays most	5
Non-relocating parent pays most	5

---

31 Reported under the pseudonym, *Mazorski and Albright* [2007] FamCA 520.

In situations where the travel is between capital cities on the east coast of Australia, there may be relatively inexpensive airfares available at certain times. However the times that children are most likely to travel – Friday evenings, returning Sunday evenings, and at the beginning and end of school holidays – are peak periods for plane travel, and only the most expensive flights may be available. The costs are not only in the children's airfares. Young children are likely to have to be accompanied by a parent, and if the visit is for a significant period, then two adult return airfares and one child's return airfare are likely to be involved in order to facilitate each visit for one child. In a situation, for example, where the child's primary carer is responsible for the travel, she may have to travel to the other parent's home and then return to her own because of her work commitments, and then at the end of the visit, fly back again to collect the child. These costs are ameliorated somewhat if it is feasible for children to travel between two airports on their own, being taken to the plane by one parent and being met off the plane by the other.

The cost of travel for some parents in our study was very substantial indeed. In one case, for example, the mother estimated it cost her $ 15,000 per year. A number of other parents estimated costs in terms of many thousands of dollars. In many cases, the costs of travel may well be unsustainable over the long-term, particularly after the financial impact of the litigation costs. This may lead to a breakdown in the arrangements for the child to spend time with the other parent. In one case, for example, a father consented to his British-born former partner returning to live in the UK with two children aged 8 and 12 on the basis of court orders that he would see his children three times a year in Australia and once per year in the UK. The mother was to bear the cost of travel to Australia. Her plan was to fly with the children from the UK to Australia, where the father would meet them at the airport. The mother would return straight away to the UK. She would then fly back to Australia to collect the children and return again straight away to the UK. Thus, for every trip of the children to Australia, there would be four return airfares. On the first occasion that the children were due to come out to Australia this is what occurred; but prior to the next occasion, the mother sent the father an email to say that she was not bringing the children to Australia as she could not afford it.

VIII. Conclusion

Many jurisdictions have approached the relocation problem by avoiding rules or presumptions and relying on the standard that the best interests of the child are treated as paramount. This may or may not be accompanied by much appellate guidance on the way in which the best interests of children are to be discerned in relocation cases.

However, a statutory rule which provides for the determination of cases according to the best interests of the individual child may well be contrary to the best interests of children generally. Jon Elster has drawn a distinction, in this context, between act-utilitarianism and rule-utilitarianism.[32] An example of this might be child abduction, in which a rule that provides for individualised determination of cases according to the best interests standard, and which emphasises the importance of maintaining the status quo, may be contrary to the wellbeing of children generally by failing to deter unlawful removal of children. The rule that promotes the greatest happiness for the greatest number of children might not be the same rule that would lead to the greatest happiness for a particular child who is the subject of a court case.

The evidence from our empirical study in Australia at least, is that the indeterminacy of the best interests principle, in its application to relocation cases in Australia, could be operating adversely to the interests of children generally. This is because the »transaction costs« of those individualised determinations are so high. The financial devastation that so many families experience is likely to have a significant impact on children's wellbeing, because children's adjustment to separation and divorce is affected by the level of economic security or insecurity in the home of the primary carer.

This research illustrates the dangers of a content-free best interests principle. While the individual cost of litigating cases through to judgment may not be any greater than in other family law disputes about parenting or property, it is the very high rate of cases going to trial and the cumulative cost thereof that ought to trouble policy makers about relocation disputes. The data from this study suggests there is a need for appropriate preventative measures in relation to relocation disputes. This includes Parliament or the courts giving much better signals about the

---

32 J. Elster, *Solomonic Judgments* (Cambridge University Press, Cambridge, 1989) pp.144-45.

cases when relocation is likely to be permitted and the cases in which it is more likely to be refused.[33] There are also significant issues about how much children should travel if a relocation does occur, how the costs should be met and by whom, and why the costs should be distributed in that way.

There has been little attention paid to the financial aspects of relocation disputes and the impact of different rules and standards on the prospects of settlement. This empirical study in Australia points to the importance of these issues, and the need for different jurisdictions to know how the rules, standards and processes of the courts impact upon the parents and children who come before them.

---

33 For proposals in relation to Australian law, see Parkinson, n.19 above.

Regulation of Parenthood – Deregulation of Marriage

Hege Brækhus[1]

I. Introduction

Marriage is a very ancient institution, which has been updated only partly over the centuries. The world has changed in many ways. A big change is the change from a non-monetary economy to a money-based economy. Money now plays a central role in almost all parts of life. Marriage has in a sense been left behind in the old non-monetary economy: the system of marriage presupposes that work within marriage is done not for pay, but only in exchange for housing, food and other kinds of maintenance. Women in marriage are in a sense left behind in a sort of feudal system.[2]

1. Problems in Families

Marriage can be demanding. Economic dependency is a problem for the female spouse. This is closely linked to the division of work in marriage, which leaves the unpaid work at home to the wife. Love may disappear, but economic dependency may mean that wives do not file for divorce even if they do not want to stay in marriage.

Moreover, divorcing is also risky. Violence might escalate; the financial situation may be more clear, but often less advantageous; and the burden of care may come to be distributed even more unequally. The situation of divorced wives is quite similar to the situation of single mothers who have never been married, although the situation of single mothers is generally even more difficult.

Today laws regulate the relation between parents and children. Children are also affected by legislation on marriage and divorce, however, because it affects their parents. When mothers suffer economic problems after divorce, children are also affected because most of them live with their mothers.

---

[1] *University of Tromsø, Norway.*
[2] For the classic statement of the »feudal« nature of the family, see Olsen, The Family and the Market: A Study of Ideology and Legal Reform. 96 Harv. L. Rev. 1497, 1516–1520, 1531–1532 (1983).

For fathers, the loss of contact with their children after divorce is often a problem, even when the fathers have been given joint parental responsibility and visiting rights to promote such contact.

Family law is not a question of nature, but man-made. Why do we not make laws that make marriage and divorce more advantageous for all those involved-women, men and children?

2. Gender Equality in Families

We have a general legal principle about gender equality both in international law and in most national law systems. This means that women and men are to be treated alike or that if they are treated different they should be treated equally well. So far these principles and equal rights laws are applied only in the public sphere, which means working life, schools and universities, organizational life and other parts of society open to the public.

In the private sphere, by which I mean family life and the relation between friends and neighbours, the claim for equality has been seen to be no business of the state authorities, because most legal regulations on equality except family and private relations. This is remarkable because of the fact that many women spend most of their lives in this sphere. It is not only legislation on equality that excepts family and private relations, but also human rights law. Human rights provisions frequently protect the right to privacy, which means that public authorities are not supposed to control or regulate this area of life.[3] These exemptions for private life are part of the explanation why family life is still a place for subordination of and violence against women and children. The same attitude towards the private sphere may be the reason why family law is not updated to safeguard equality for women in the family. I will claim that inequality and subordination are actually in accordance with and upheld by family law. How is it that states are claiming not to interfere with family life and at the same time maintain laws that very much do so?

In principle there are limits to the right of privacy. It is illegal to beat one's spouse and in most countries also illegal to rape her. We know from statistics and from newspaper reports that violence in marriage is a huge problem. We also know that the police in many countries do too little to deter these assaults.

---

3   See e.g. The European Convention for the Protection of Human Rights and Fundamental Freedoms art. 8.

My claim is that violence in the family is only the tip of the iceberg when it comes to women's subordination to men in marriage. There are surely many intermediate levels of exploitation and abuse of power between assault and battery and a happy marriage.

Many will agree that the fundamental premises for inequality between men and women in society at large are to be found in the organisation of family life. Why then do we not fight subordination where it came into being?

I want to give some numbers to show that men and women do have very different economic situations. Even if Norway is said to be the country where the gender equality has come furthest,[4] inequality is still evident. Even if 68% of Norwegian women have an income from work (for men this number is 75%), they still earn on average 40% less than men per year. Part of this is because they work shorter hours as 43% of the working women work part-time (for men this number is 12%). Hourly income remains 15% lower for women than men.

3. Two Inconsistencies in Family Law

The first inconsistency is the discrepancy between the obligation to care and the obligation to earn a living. Every one of us has a responsibility for our own life. Therefore we are supposed to earn a living. We are however also responsible for taking care of our children. Care for children is so much work that in most families the care-giver experiences her care-work as a serious hindrance to earning a normal income and making a living. This is in no way a merely theoretical problem. Most mothers find that their careers and their economic independence crumble during the time that their children are small, while fathers continue to develop their careers without any hindrance.

To secure some degree of freedom inside the family, more and more women use their right to engage in paid work in the public sphere to the extent possible, taking the needs of their family into account. This has made women relatively independent compared to earlier times, and it has made divorce a realistic option for women.

Money provides freedom and independence. Independence gives dignity. Dependency creates subordination, which could be said to be contrary to our standards of citizenship and democratic participation, and certainly contrary to equality.

---

4 See World Economic Forum, The Global Gender Gap Report 2008.

The second inconsistency is a discrepancy between the claim that marriage should be a life-long commitment and the claim that love should be the basis for marriage. It is however only in the last few centuries that marriage is supposed to be built on love. Historically, arranged marriages have been most prevalent.[5] It is of course a good thing that people who love each other are allowed to marry. There seems to be very little concern whether love remains part of marriage, however, as the years pass. The customary view seems to be that married people are happy together as long as they are not divorced.

Many politicians and philosophers in the 18th century expressed the fear that the demand for love in marriage would ruin marriage as an institution.[6] Marriage continued to be a stable institution, however, because the legal system made wives almost totally dependent upon the economic support of their husbands.

It took another two centuries before the fears of the 18th century philosophers began to be realized, after women gained some degree of economic independence through their work in the market during the last half of the twentieth century. It was then that the philosophers' predictions about love destabilizing marriage seemed to have some basis. Compared to earlier times, the divorce rate has exploded.

There is certainly a connection between women's relative economic independence and the divorce rate. The economist Ian Smith writes:

> »*If the percentage of married women in paid employment is high in a particular country, the accompanying low gains from a typical marriage and the relative financial independence of women are mirrored in a high rate of marital breakdown. Indeed the correlation between female economic independence and divorce is visible in many traditional cultures. ... When divorce is financially feasible for women, they make use of the legal provisions for marital dissolution.*«[7]

The divorce rate has risen more or less proportionally with the relative income of the wives compared with their husbands. This is not a very pleasant message from women about their marriages. It seems obvious

---

5 See Stephanie Coontz, Marriage, a History, 2005, 123–124..
6 See Stephanie Coontz, Marriage, a History, 2005, 149–154.
7 See Ian Smith, European divorce laws, divorce rates, and their consequences, in The Law and Economics of Marriage & Divorce, edited by Antony W. Dnes & Robert Rowthorn, 2002, 217–218.

that love must have disappeared from many marriages, even if the marriage was initially based on love. The logic of this suggests that more divorces may come if women's economic opportunity and economic independence increase further. This might very well happen, because equal rights in the labour market is a strong political demand in Western countries. If and when the struggle for equal rights and equal pay in the marketplace achieves more success, an even greater number of women could choose to leave marriage.

There is however probably a parallel development going on. Marriage itself changes over the generations because young men perceive and accept that young women expect more freedom and equality in marriage than earlier generations. Because of this, marriage itself may become more equal for men and women, and thus the need to break out of marriage could decrease. After all, it is nice to stay together.

II. Family Law Today

What functions should marriage fill today? Of course, very many. I will point out three that I find essential: economy, care and love. These three are certainly woven together, but I will try to say something about each of them.

Marriage cannot be fully understood without also understanding the dissolution of marriage, and thus the role of economy, care and love in divorce is important. Clearly in the situation of divorce we have to consider the need for money and care. Love is certainly also part of a divorce. In most cases this is because love has disappeared.

1. Economy

Marriage has a financial impact on its actors. For many women marriage determines their way of life, because marriage is a major source of funding for their lives. Women can still count on marriage for their financial needs. For men marriage can be seen as an economic obligation, but it is probably worthwhile, because it can secure both their needs for care and intimacy and the raising of their children. In addition to this, they are in charge of the family because they are in control of the use of money.

I have studied family law in a number of countries; and even if there are many differences, there tend to be more similarities. An important similarity is that the breadwinners are in different ways almost always able to control the income, directly by the laws of some countries and indirectly in other countries by keeping the money in certain separate accounts.[8] The extent of maintenance prescribed by law may vary, but wives in general are left without realistic legal options if the providers do not fulfil their obligations. The problem in case of enforcement is the same everywhere in the sense that legal provisions are useless because a lawsuit in an ongoing marriage for most people is unthinkable. This means that it is up to the breadwinner to decide how maintenance is to be practised.

Even if some countries grant wives quite extensive economic rights during marriage, the breadwinner will nevertheless retain a superior situation in the marriage as long as the wife has poor economic expectations on divorce.

Housewives in marriage often do a considerable load of work in exchange for little more than their housing, food and clothing. Most people would say that such women are acting very altruistically, which sounds noble and perhaps like something we should encourage.

But is this how it really is? The economist Gary S. Becker who has analysed the economics of marriage presents a very different view. He says:

> »... the scarce resource ›love‹ is used economically, because sufficient caring by an altruist induces even a selfish beneficiary to act as if she cares about her benefactor as much as she cares about herself.«[9]

According to Becker, it is the husband who is the altruist in the family because he provides for the family without really having to.[10] The wife acts »as if she cares about her [husband] as much as she cares about herself« only because she has no choice. When we see it this way, the role of the housewife in the family is certainly nothing to be proud of. Rather, the housewife is someone we need to liberate.

Cohabitation is not regulated by law like marriage, and people are free to choose cohabitation over marriage. This does not however solve the problems of marriage and divorce. There are two reasons for this. The first is that people seem to adopt most of the standards of marriage when

---

8 See Grace Gantz Blumberg, Community Property in California, Second Edition 1993, 460–461.
9 Gary S. Becker, A Treatise on the Family, 1981, 179.
10 This view is shared by West, who points out that women's apparent altruism in the private sphere is in the first instance driven by fear. See Robin West, Caring for Justice, 1997, 114.

they live together without formal marriage. In the case of break up of the relationship women with no cohabiting contracts experience even less protection in regard to economic security than married women in the same situation.

If cohabiting couples try to improve the conditions for the female when she is taking care of their children, the law will most often hamper their attempts. In most countries courts will refuse to accept and enforce a labour contract between parents concerning care for their children. Some countries deny cohabitating people the rights that married couples have, even when there is a contract that attempts to give exactly those same rights.[11]

It is difficult to understand why courts do not accept such contracts. They probably see family law as a kind of monopoly conditions for couples. Family law is the most advantageous regulation women can expect when it comes to motherhood. If so, this is really a way of keeping patriarchy in place.

Married mothers have the right to maintenance. The reason for this right is to compensate for the loss of income in connection with the care of children. It is therefore quite illogical that maintenance in many countries ends at divorce. The care-work is still there, often more than before the divorce.

Some mothers get alimony from the former spouse. Mothers who have never been married do not even have the possibility for that. In some countries single mothers are entitled to social security benefits. It is however a fact that the economic status of single mothers normally is very poor, while their responsibilities are extensive.[12]

This regulation is far from logical. Why is it that unmarried fathers are essentially exempted when it comes to the financial part of care?

2. Care

Children, the sick, and elderly persons need care. Traditionally the major part of this care has been provided by women in the family and thus outside of the public economy. Women's unpaid care-work has great impact on the economy of the whole society in the sense of increased welfare and wellbeing for its members.

---

11 This is the case in Sweden. See Anders Agell, Äktenskap Samboende Partnerskap, 2end ed. 1998, 232.
12 Even in Norway where single parents are entitled to social security benefits single mothers make up a clear underprivileged group, see Jan Lyngstad, Randi Kjeldstad and Erik Nymoen, Foreldreøkonomi etter brudd, Statistics Norway 2005/21.

Parents have a legal obligation to raise and care for their children. Formally the obligation is placed on both fathers and mothers, but in practice it really falls only on mothers, because fathers are seen as the main breadwinner in the family. Thus many mothers have to forgo their chance for a secure economic base of their own, a dilemma that almost no fathers will experience.

Apart from the loss of income women experience when staying out of paid work, a new report from the Norwegian government shows that women's care for children is one of the main reasons for the wage-gap between men and women, as women statistically get a lower income per hour for their work in the market for each child they give birth to, while the income of the fathers increases a little with each child. In Norway as much as 20% of the pay-gap in the public sector and 40% in the private sector is caused by the care for children.[13]

One might ask why almost all this care-work is done by women. It is of course about gender roles, but it is also about economics. As long as men get higher salaries than women, the family as a unit will profit from a division of work in which the women do the necessary care-work while the man brings money to the family.

Law gives the prerequisite for this: Husband and wife are viewed as one unit both in regard to care and economy. If the law had instead treated husband and wife as two separate units, this division of work would not have the same support in law. If the division of work had been understood instead as a private arrangement between two people, each of whom would otherwise be equally responsible for all the care work involved in raising their children, the division would be recognized to be a bad deal for the person doing almost all the care work without receiving any proper payment from the other party.

Because of the economic dependence that women's care for family members in the family creates, most women want to minimise the care work and maximise the work out of the home. In this way, care for children often is given a lower priority, which may leave some children with too little care. Television and newspapers frequently present reports about teachers having to care for their pupils' wellbeing, which easily could come at the cost of the education of all children.

In the Western societies care is squeezed both in private homes and in public service, in private homes because it is not paid and in public

---

[13] See NOU 2008: 6 Kjønn og lønn, 63–64.

services because it is poorly paid. It is however the responsibility of family law to secure children the care they need.

When society gets into arguments about marriage, supporters of marriage tend to point to marriage as the best place for children to be raised. The statement seems to presuppose that marriages are happy, which of course could happen, but very often marriages are not happy.

When people argue for strengthening marriage for the sake of children, they sometimes argue that the legal regulation of marriage should prevent divorce. Women's economic independence seems however to have come to a point where this no longer is possible, at least not through restrictive legislation on divorce. Trapping spouses in unhappy marriages is anyway questionable and negative. Besides, when parents are unhappy and want to part, marriage is probably not good for children either.

It is easy to agree that it is better for children that their parents are happy and together, than fighting, lonely and unhappy. Happiness can flourish without legal regulations. It would seem reasonable to expect or hope that legal regulation would tend to improve the quality of marriages. Legal regulation of marriage as we know it, however, does not create happiness and harmony. On the contrary, marriage law creates position of power and subordination.

When we talk about care it is about care for children, the sick, and elderly persons. This is what the breadwinner pays for through maintenance. Why is it then that maintenance in many countries is discontinued when there is a divorce? Some say that it is because the husband no longer receives the service of the wife. I think this view is outdated. Fathers in our time should be a caring resource for their children even if they are the main breadwinners of the family. Wives with children should not do care work for a man in addition to the heavy burden of work that raising the children represents. After divorce the father might do even less care than he did before, and the wife even more than she did in marriage. In that case, the consequence should be that the pay from the husband to the wife should increase rather than decrease. When the opposite is prescribed by legislation in most countries, there must be some reason, some different view of maintenance. In Norway the leading family law textbook says that support has to be discontinued on divorce because the community between the spouses no longer exists.[14] What does this mean? The work and care has suddenly disappeared as the main reason for support.

---

14   See Peter Lødrup and Tone Sverdrup, Familieretten, 5th ed. 2004, 93.

The obvious change is that the couple is no longer sharing bed and table, which means that their intimate relation is finished. Could it be that it is not work but intimacy and sexual services that men are paying for in marriage, and not the important work of care? If this is the case, it is really serious, and at the sacrifice of the dignity of the wife.

3. Love

Our love life is extremely important to us. In earlier days the challenge was getting married to the person you loved. A large body of literature focuses on variations on this subject. Romeo and Juliet is certainly part of that literature. In our culture this is no longer a big problem. Young people can choose whomever they want to marry. The problem now is how to keep love in marriage, or how to escape marriage when love is gone.

Marriage could be said to be the legal regulation of erotic love. Traditionally intimacy had to be practiced inside marriage and no other places.

When entering into marriage the parties have to give their vow of love. But is love something that could be given by a vow? Is love controlled by our free will? It may of course happen that people who love each other in a moment of intimacy promise to do so forever and ever. This is a private vow and often given in a sense of exaggeration. A public vow is different. It is something that society expects, and that people therefore could believe is possible. If it is not possible, a public demand for such a vow must be considered unethical. In my opinion society should not require or encourage vows that people cannot control by will.

The law professor Lloyd R. Cohen has identified the problem with the marriage vow. He says:

»*The vow is a promise not to be in love with one's spouse but rather to act toward them in a manner that displays love, honour, and respect.*«[15]

It is relieving to hear that love in marriage is normally only good behaviour. But because this is about erotic love, this kind of love also has a physical side. Love as part of marriage is supposed to be a sexual relation. If spouses are supposed to behave as if they loved each other, many certainly extend their sex life even if one or both of them really do not want to. It is alarming to have a system where people are encouraged to practice sex

---

15 See Lloyd R. Cohen, Marriage: the long-term contract in The Law and Economics of Marriage & Divorce, edited by Antony W. Dnes & Robert Rowthorn, 2002, 11.

as a matter of good behaviour. For most of us real love is a premise for sex. If sex is practised only as good behaviour it is close to sexual assault.

Fatherhood is a function of marriage and hopefully a function of love. In marriage the husband of the mother will become the legal father when a child is born, even if someone else is the biological father. This is called the presumption of legitimacy. Fatherhood through marriage is a very ancient legal consequence of marriage.

I question this ancient way of creating fatherhood at a time when full knowledge about human DNA is available. In Norway the knowledge about the DNA has resulted in an amendment of the family legislation saying that presumed fathers, including married ones, can contest fatherhood whenever they like. The background for this statutory rule is that it seemed impossible to prevent legal fathers from re-examining biological fatherhood by means of DNA-tests. In practice, fathers tend to do so when they or their wives file for divorce. This has resulted in a group of grown-up persons loosing the father they grew up with and whom they always had seen as their father. In my view this is offensive for the people loosing their legal fathers, and ridiculous as a legal system.

The answer to this is that biological fatherhood ought to be stated in a secured way from the beginning through DNA testing for all children and parents. This would also equalise children, mothers, and fathers regardless of marriage or cohabitation, which seems to me must be a good thing.

4. Summing Up

Marriage has certainly three important functions, economy, care and love, but none of them is very well protected by law. The result is that mothers are dependent not only in marriage, but certainly also on marriage.

When it comes to fatherhood, children are not well protected. When children are adopted or are the result of sperm donation, Norwegian children at least have the right to know this and who their biological fathers are, as soon as they reach adulthood (18 years). The right to know about genetic origin is important. This is somewhat contrary to fatherhood settled in accordance with the presumption of legitimacy. Here we know that a certain percentage of children have a legal father who is not the biological father, and this is part of the legal system even now when we have access to reliable methods to identify the biological father.

III. Towards a Fair Family-Legislation

1. The Direction of Family Law Reforms in Recent Years

When we look for change, it is interesting to consider the direction that reforms in family law have taken in resent years.

First there has been a significant change towards more liberal divorce laws. The rhetoric is that people who do not want to stay in marriage should not be forced to do so. One way of interpreting this is that love is no longer a condition only when entering into marriage, but an expectation all throughout the marriage. As shown above, however, many will stay in marriage for economic reasons.

Traditionally states have given some economic compensation for the extra costs for families with children, through tax reductions. Benefits such as tax reduction however function as an extra profit for the breadwinner and therefore as a strengthening of the traditional power and structure in the family. In recent years, at least in the Nordic countries, the states have contributed more directly to the homemaker through social security benefits for caregivers, e.g. very good maternity benefits. These benefits are given not only to married caretakers, but to all carers independent of their status of marriage. These contributions are very important to many caregivers, but they are not large enough to secure economic independence in families.

A very interesting reform in the Nordic countries is the so-called father's month. Here a certain part of the paid maternity leave is reserved for the father.[16] Parents have for many years been encouraged to share the paid maternity leave, as this was an obvious option in the regulation of maternity benefit legislation. The result has however been the same as the joint responsibility to care for children, the mother took it all. After the father's month was introduced the percentage of fathers taking maternity leave raised from about one percent to about ninety percent.

If we take a broad view on family law, we might include reforms that have facilitated women's and especially mother's participation in paid work. Access to affordable kindergartens and equal rights in the labour market are important.

---

16 For the time being the »father's month« is six weeks in Norway. It will probably be extended in the future.

Finally we have seen reforms securing contact between children and parents with whom they do not live. This is about joint parental responsibility and extended visiting rights.

Summing this up, we can say that family law reforms point towards independence between parents and separate rights for fathers and mothers. This development is obviously in accordance with the actual needs of fathers and mothers. The development points towards more regulation when it comes to parenthood and less regulation when it comes to marriage.

But even so, the old system of joint responsibility for care and economy for spouses is still the core of family law.

2. The Need for Change

As we have seen, family law makes women subordinates to men in the family by means of distribution of obligations and rights. Even if the subordination is less obvious after divorce, the structure of obligations and rights is even clearer. This is the case, even in a time when gender equality is a fundamental principle of the legal system.

We need a change in family law so that the legal system can contribute to making family life good and equally good for all members of the family both in ongoing marriages and after divorce.

3. Premises for Change

To reach equality in families I point out five premises for legal changes:
1.) Parents doing care work must be guaranteed a fair share of money.
2.) Both mothers and fathers must participate in the care of children
3.) There must be sufficient time for care.
4.) Children must not be discriminated against because of the relation between their parents.
5.) Marriage must be voluntary not only when it is entered into, but all the time.

Nothing of this is in place today, and this causes much stress for men, women and children when it comes to marriage and divorce.
1.) What is a fair share of money today? First of all: It is not what it was a hundred years ago. Today it should be something to live from. It should be secured by law like other wage claims or pecuniary claims. It should in no way depend upon the good will of a provider, and it should be proportional to necessary work done in the family both during marriage and after divorce.

2.) Mothers are the ones who provide children with their daily needs. Even if most fathers do take care of their children from time to time, many fathers experience that it is only after divorce that care as a duty is expected according to law. All children need however contact with their fathers, and mothers need time to develop their skills in the market. Family life would function better if care were a real obligation not only for mothers and divorced fathers, but for all fathers.

3.) The tension between care and earning an income that women experience today has its costs. Very often care is compromised. To bring fathers into care-work will probably not change this because fathers even more than mothers find their identity through work in the market. In this picture law has to protect a minimum of parental contact with children.

4.) The UN Convention on the Rights of the Child art 2 (1) says that children should not be discriminated against because of the status of their parents. Today single mothers in almost all countries are in a difficult economic situation. This is because fathers are less or not at all economically responsible for the care preformed by the single mothers. In my view this is a systematic economic discrimination against children because of the status of their parents.

5.) What is a voluntary marriage? It should be a marriage where there is no economic dependence. Women today are much less dependent on their spouses than they were a hundred yeas ago, but they are still dependent. The laws on marriage in all countries are organised in a way that presupposes that the wife is taking care of the children and that the husband supports the family. In all countries this creates dependency. In case of divorce the maintenance is terminated and often replaced by nothing, which makes the situation even worse. Today women with children are at least to some degree dependent both in marriage and on marriage.

IV. Deregulation of Marriage

If we define marriage as an intimate relation between two people, which is recognised by society, then I think we will always have some kind of marriage. People like their relations to be recognised, and people like to marry. Marriage is also about connection and maybe tradition, family and commitment.

All this can be preserved without making marriage an institution built on dependency and subordination. It is about time marriage is favouring women as much as men. As my analysis above has argued, this is not likely to happen as long as married couples are treated as one legal and economic unit in the law.

Marriage is an arrangement between two grown up and fully liable people. The spouses are of course important to each other as long as their marital alliance is working. Because of this, there might be some need for privileges when it comes to representing each other in different situations e.g. in hospital when illness is preventing on spouse from making proper decisions. I would say that all of us need another person to be one's significant other in these situations. Maybe also people who are not married ought to have the right to point out a person for such purposes.

Apart from this, I can see no need for legal protection for spouses without children. This means that each of the spouses must take full responsibility for their economic needs. If they want to practise a division of work, this would be a totally private arrangement, neutral to family law, but of course of possible interest to the tax authorities.

One justification for marriage as a legal institution has been the felt need to establish a binding fatherhood for children. The presumption of legitimacy was a relatively reliable way for doing this because marriage meant sexual fidelity at least for women. After our discoveries regarding DNA, the presumption of legitimacy is no longer necessary nor is it a rational way of establishing of fatherhood. DNA testing for establishing of fatherhood opens the way for equal treatment of all parents in this relation.

V. Regulation of Parenthood

If a married couple gets children, the need for legal regulation rises considerably. Today economic arrangements in marriage are actually maintained because of the need for care for children. Children however have the same needs independent of their parent's relation to each other. Therefore it is not only married parents that will be in need of legal regulation. It is equally important or maybe even more important, to give adequate legal regulation to parents who are not married, both cohabitating parents and parents who live apart.

1. *Equal and Separate Responsibility for the Care of Children*

To the extent that private care for children is necessary, each parent should be equally responsible for the care-work. It is then important that the responsibility can be transferred to others, even the other parent, only by paying for it according to a labour contract governed by labour law or a service contract governed by the laws of contract. This is important because we know that making care the »joint responsibility« of the parents, creates a bias in favour of a division of labour that contributes to inequality and oppression. A strict division of responsibilities between the parents is particularly necessary for parents who do not live together. Here we must remember that care for children is work around the clock, at least when children are very young.

Parents who do their part of the care themselves, certainly pay for it by the work they do. Parents who let others take over their part of care should therefore be paying properly. This will secure for caregivers who take over the responsibilities of care from a parent not only income, but also the right to social security benefits in case of sickness or old age. In this way also a mother who takes over the responsibility of the father will have some social protection.

Parents who cannot afford to pay others to do their part of the work will have to do the care-work themselves. This will be a completely new situation for fathers because even fathers with a low income and many children are used to having someone else take care of their children without them having to pay for the care. Mothers, on the other hand, will find the situation familiar because almost all mothers have experienced the dilemma between earning money and taking care of children.

2. *Equal and Separate Responsibility for the Support of Children*

In this setting each parent will be equally able to earn an income in the market. We must then presuppose that they are able to earn a living for themselves. In addition to this they must be able to earn enough to pay their half of the financial cost of raising their children.

In this way mothers must be real breadwinners and will have to care about their career in the same way fathers do. Employers on the other hand will have no reason to discriminate or justification for discriminating against women in the market on the ground of being secondary when it comes to economic obligations in the family.

3. Minimum Standards for Contact between Parents and Children

If both parents choose to pay somebody else to do their part of the care for their children in order to be able to prioritise a career in the market, the contact between parents and their children could be very little. To secure equal standards for mothers and fathers in this relation, we probably need some legal regulation.

Most legal systems already have some standards for visiting rights for parents who do not live with their children after divorce. This could be used as minimum standard for all parents, married or unmarried to secure the need of children.

In Norway customary visiting rights for parents after divorce now include one day per week (after work), every second weekend, Christmas or Easter holiday and two weeks during summer holidays. If we imagine this as a standard for all parents, fathers and mothers, married or unmarried, this means that children actually is taken care of by their parents two days a week (after work), every weekend, all Christmas and Easter holidays and four weeks during summer holidays. This is probably more contact with parents than many children experience today, but of course, if this is seen as too little, it is possible to make a somewhat extended version.

4. Divorce as a Normalized Part of Life

The turning point for children is normally the break-up of the family, which often gives the feeling of loss. This is probably difficult to avoid, but it can be normalised in many ways, first of all by making divorce a normal part of adult life. Even if divorce can be difficult for children, it will confirm also to them that their parents are free, and that divorce is the best possible option.

The absence of a parent for a period of time is not the same as a loss of a parent. Nobody claimed that fathers working in overseas trade were lost fathers. They were merely not there. Maybe we can make divorce as natural for children as the circumstance that parents have to stay away from home because of work.

Children need and want both parents. Both fathers and mothers do normally want to stay in contact with their children. Resent years' legal reforms are clearly pointing towards more equal rights here for both parents after divorce. The high rate of divorce calls for some way to limit the cost for the parent who has to move away and also to limit the burden of responsibility for the parent staying with the children, and not least the cost for children.

The loss however is not always there. Even if there are many reports saying that fathers loose contact with their children after divorce, there are also other tendencies. Some reports actually claim that many children see their fathers more after divorce even if they live with their mother.[17] This also points in the direction as argued above, that we have to regulate how much contact parents and especially fathers are supposed to have with their children not only after divorce, but also during marriage.

The important thing for children is that law secures their relation to both parents independent of how the relation between the parents is. If the contact between parents and children is regulated independently of the relation between the parents, the change from unmarried to married and then to divorce would imply almost nothing when it comes to rights and responsibilities.

If also the rules for financial support for children could be continued after divorce, there would be very little to fight about upon divorce, and economy would not be an argument for staying in marriage. The need for funding is the same after divorce as it was during marriage, even if the costs may rise somewhat.

5. Eliminating Dependency Could Mean Strengthening of Marriage

One of the main complaints about marriage is about subordination and dependence due to the traditional division of work in marriage. Probably this kind of degrading of women in marriage is one reason why so many wives file for divorce. If we can fight this, we might as well fight divorce, and secure more harmonious marriages.

VI. Conclusion

Work and income are linked together as mutual performances in the market, but within the family work is not paid. Here the right to money is linked to the status of marriage. Other intimate relations, such as cohabitation, are treated very much the same way as marriage.

To avoid the dependency that the current system creates all responsibilities and rights have to be equally shared by the parents, independent of the relation between them and we have to let work, not status, become the basis for the right to economic benefits.

---

17 See Carol Smart and Bren Neale, Family Fragments, 1999, 59.

If the only legal regulation of family life is the regulation of parenthood, we could imagine a system where there will be no dependence in marriage, and no difference in financial status related to marriage, divorce or single parenthood. Parenthood is after all what is important for society to protect.

Economic responsibilities for children independent of intimate relations between the parents will also secure the economic needs for all children.

Everything, except the interest of patriarchy, points to a development where care for children should be shared between the parents. One benefit among these could be equal conditions in the labour marked and therefore a development towards equal pay.

A system like this will support many young fathers' claim for the right to see more to their children after divorce. This will be easy to accept also for mothers when the same responsibilities are practiced also during marriage.

Care is a right, but it must of course also be a duty for fathers independent of their relation to the mother. This might change another inequality between men and women in our society. That is the consequences of sexual behaviour. For women the risk of pregnancy has been part of their sexual life. All women know that responsibilities follow directly from giving birth. Men on the other hand have a second opportunity by choosing not to marry the mother. The problem could of course also be that the mother does not want to marry the father. Both problems could be solved by giving all fathers full responsibility for their children simply because they are fathers. The risk caused by sexual activity would then be more equally shared by men and women, and maybe we would experience men more virtuous about their sexuality.

If mothers are paid for all the work they do, they will own property in the same way that fathers do, and so there should be no need for sharing of property at divorce.

The big social and economic dividing line in society will then be between parents and people without children rather than between men and women. Parents, both mothers and fathers will be partly prevented from full labour market participation (or pay properly for care), and therefore both mothers and fathers will be economically disadvantaged. The need for society to compensate economically will be more evident and probably also easier to understand and approve.

Love cannot be regulated by law. Love has to be free. If we want to go beyond behaving as if we loved, we need to accept this. This means that marriage law in no way should be a hindrance for divorce neither in terms of legal procedure nor in economic terms.

I am not the only one to advocate this view. Fineman has come to the same conclusion and gave this expression to her view:

»*The pressing problems today do not revolve around the marriage connection, but the caretaker-dependent relationship. In a world in which wives are equal partners and participants in the market sphere, and in which the consensus is that bad marriages should end, women do not need the special protection of legal marriage. Rather than marriage, we should view the parent-child relationship as the quintessential or core family connection, and focus on how policy can strengthen this tie.*«[18]

References

> Agell, Anders, *Äktenskap Samboende Partnerskap*, 2end ed. 1998
> Becker, Gary S., *A Treatise on the Family*, 1981
> Blumberg,Grace Gantz, *Community Property in California*, Second Edition 1993
> Cohen, Lloyd R., *Marriage: the long-term contract*, in The Law and Economics of Marriage & Divorce, edited by Dnes, Antony W. & Rowthorn, Robert, 2002
> Coontz, Stephanie, *Marriage, a History*, 2005
> Fineman, Martha Albertson, *Why marriage?* 9 Virginia Journal of Social Policy & the Law, Fall, 2001
> Lyngstad, Jan, Kjeldstad, Randi and Nymoen, Erik, *Foreldreøkonomi etter brudd*, Statistics Norway 2005/21.
> Lødrup, Peter and Sverdrup, Tone, *Familieretten*, 5th ed. 2004
> Olsen, Frances, *The Family and the Market: A Study of Ideology and Legal Reform*, 96 Harvard Law Review, 1983
> Smart, Carol and Neale, Bren, *Family Fragments*, 1999
> Smith, Ian, *European divorce laws, divorce rates, and their consequences*, in The Law and Economics of Marriage & Divorce, edited by Dnes, Antony W. & Rowthorn, Robert, 2002
> West, Robin, *Caring for Justice*, 1997

---

18 See Martha Albertson Fineman, Why marriage? 9 Virginia Journal of Social Policy & the Law, Fall, 2001, 245.

Documents
- NOU 2008: 6 *Kjønn og lønn*
- The European Convention for *the Protection of Human Rights and Fundamental Freedoms*
- UN Convention on the Rights of the Child
- World Economic Forum, *The Global Gender Gap Report 2008*

Time is money? – Child Support for Children With Alternating Residence in Sweden

Anna Singer[1]

I. Introduction

Children need time with their parents. They also need economic support. This constitutes a dilemma for most parents. The everyday struggle to make time and money suffice is even more complicated for parents who have separated. It is all too common that they have problems cooperating; in many instances the problems are caused by disputes concerning where the child should spend his or her time, and how to allocate responsibility for the child's economic needs.[2]

It is estimated that there are 500,000 children in Sweden whose parents are separated.[3] Every year, around 50,000 children experience their parents' separation. Against this background, it is desirable to have regulations that clearly state how the parents are to share responsibility for the economic maintenance of the child after separation. Such regulations should provide solutions that are seen as just and predictable; they should be easy to apply, both by parents and the authorities; and finally, they should encourage good relations and contact between children and parents. The question is whether the current regulations do this. It is easy to get the impression that it is not the division of the costs for the child that has been the legislator's focus. In many instances, the regulations concerning child support have been used primarily to encourage separated fathers to have contact with their children after separation. A good example of this is the regulation concerning the deduction of mainte-

---

1 Associate Professor at Uppsala University, Faculty of Law, Sweden.
2 See e.g. Ryrstedt, E., Familjerätt och stöd till barnfamiljer, (*Family law and support for families with children*) JT 2004–05 p. 598 f.; Socialstyrelsen (*The National Board of Health and Welfare*), Växelvis boende. Att bo hos både mamma och pappa fast de inte bor tillsammans (*Alternating residence. To live with both mum and dad even when they are not living together*), 2001, p. 21; RFV Analyserar 2003:1 p. 57.
3 SCB (*Statistics Sweden*), Barn och deras familjer (*Children and their families*), 2006, p. 270.

nance payments with regards to costs related to visitation. The more time a parent spends with a child not permanently living with that parent, the less money is to be paid by way of maintenance.[4]

That the time spent with the child – and not necessarily the money spent on the child's needs – affects the maintenance to be paid means that time, in some obscure way, has become the same as money. The most direct relationship between time and money in this context may be found when the child has alternating residence. In such a situation, no maintenance at all needs to be paid according to Swedish law. The child's different economic needs are thought to be covered merely by the time spent with each parent. That mothers and fathers have different incomes, different responsibilities and different relationships with the child is not considered. Hence, one of the core questions behind conflicts between separated parents – i.e. who is paying for what? – is ignored. By not regulating maintenance when the child has alternating residence, the legislator fails to provide economic security for all children with separated parents, regardless of living arrangements, and also neglects to provide conflict solutions and guidelines as regards how the parents should act. Consequently, the interests of the child are not given full protection; something that ought to be a primary goal for legislation concerning children.

In this article, a number of requirements that ought to be fulfilled by child support regulations where a child has alternating residence with both parents will be identified and analysed.[5]

II. Alternating Residence

Alternating residence for children with separated parents has become increasingly popular in Sweden over the last few decades. In 1992/1993, an estimated 4 per cent of all children with separated parents had alternating residence with both parents. In 2005, it was estimated that 21 per cent of the approximately 500,000 children living in Sweden with separated parents were living alternately with both.[6] There are reasons to believe

---

4 The Parental Code, Chapter 7, Section 4.
5 The subject of alternating residence in Sweden has been previously addressed by the author in Singer, A., »Active parenting or Solomon's justice? Alternating residence in Sweden for children with separated parents«, Utrecht Law Review, Volume 4, Issue 2 (June) 2008 pp. 35-47. <http://www.utrecht lawreview.org>
6 SCB (*Statistics Sweden*), Barn och deras familjer (*Children and their families*), 2006, p. 270.

that the numbers are even higher today. The older the child, the more common it is for residence to be alternating. In addition, it is estimated that approximately 10 per cent of children with separated parents live permanently with one of the parents, but stay with the non-resident parent for periods of time exceeding what could be labelled as traditional visitation, i.e. more than every other weekend and every other holiday.

Alternating residence is, in most cases, the result of an agreement between the parents. However, in 1998 the law on custody and residence was changed, introducing the possibility for the court to order joint custody and alternating residence, even against the will of one parent, if it was considered to be in the best interest of the child.[7] The only other limitation set down in relation to such decisions was that joint custody and alternating residence could not be ordered against the will of both parents. The message sent by this amendment to the law was no doubt that alternating residence is a solution generally considered to be in the best interests of the child. It was also put to use by the courts.

A follow up of this change to the law was undertaken by the National Board of Health and Welfare in 2000.[8] The aims were to find out how alternating residence was put into practise; its advantages and disadvantages; and how children were influenced by alternating residence. The results indicated that when the parents were in agreement on this kind of living arrangement it worked out quite well, also for the children. There were, however, also indications that economic questions could be problematic.[9] Similar conclusions were drawn in a subsequent investigation by a government committee in a report published in 2005.[10] The committee underlined the importance of carefully judging the circumstances in the individual case before deciding on alternating residence, regardless of whether this was decided by the parents themselves or by the court. As a reminder to the courts, it was emphasised that alternating residence should not be

---

7   Prop. (*Government Bill*) 1997/98:7 Vårdnad, boende och umgänge (*Custody, residence and access*).
8   Socialstyrelsen (*The National Board of Health and Welfare*), Växelvis boende. Att bo hos både mamma och pappa fast de inte bor tillsammans (*Alternating residence. To live with both mum and dad even when they are not living together*), 2001.
9   Socialstyrelsen (*The National Board of Health and Welfare*), Växelvis boende. Att bo hos både mamma och pappa fast de inte bor tillsammans (*Alternating residence. To live with both mum and dad even when they are not living together*), 2001, p. 7.
10 SOU (Government Report) 2005:43 Vårdnad – Boende – Umgänge. Barnets bästa, föräldrars ansvar. (*Custody – Residence – Access. Best Interest of the Child, Parent's Responsibility*).

decided when the parents had difficulties cooperating and should not be used as a way to create something adjacent to the equal sharing of a child between the parents.

In 2006 – in response to the government committee report from 2005 – the government changed the regulations concerning court decisions in relation to custody and residence. The possibility to decide on joint custody and alternating residence against the will of one of the parents was limited somewhat, but the government saw no reason to abolish the possibility altogether.[11]

Regardless of the changes made to the law in 2006, alternating residence has become a widely accepted form of living arrangement for children with separated parents. The efforts of the Swedish legislature in recent centuries, to emphasize the importance of parents taking joint responsibility for their children after separation has no doubt contributed to this. Many parents have also found this way of organising life after separation very satisfying. Alternating residence is seen as a way to give the child natural and unrestrained contact with both parents in the different events of everyday life; something that is not possible to achieve when the child lives with one parent. It is fair to assume that alternating residence is here to stay.

However, a prerequisite for a functioning arrangement is no doubt that the parents can cooperate. As is well known, economic matters are often a source of conflict between separated parents. Despite this, there are no legal grounds for obliging a parent to provide special maintenance payments where the child has alternating residence with both parents. Both parents are assumed to cover their part of the maintenance when spending time with the child. The consequence is that a parent, who would be obliged to pay special maintenance if the child was living permanently with the other parent, will in some instances prefer alternating residence in order not to pay. On the other hand, the parent who would receive the maintenance payments for the child will, in some instances, be opposed to alternating residence because of the loss of maintenance. The risk of a conflict between the parents is thus obvious.

---

11 Prop. (*Government Bill*) 2005/06:99 Nya vårdnadsregler (*New Custody Rules*) pp. 52–53.

III. Child Support and Alternating Residence

1. Defining Alternating Residence

In legal terms, there are some differences between alternating residence and extended visitation. A court decision on residence can only be made when both parents have legal custody of the child and will state that the child is to live with both of them.[12]

Visitation, on the other hand, can be determined regardless of the custodial status of the persons involved, i.e. when both parents have custody, but also if one of them has sole custody.[13] In reality, the differences between alternating residence and extended visitation might not be visible, since it is possible to decide that the child shall reside permanently with one parent and visit the other parent 50 per cent of the time.

In practice, it has been determined that when both parents have custody and the child spends more than 40 per cent of the time with one parent and slightly less than 60 per cent of the time with the other, it is alternating residence.[14] It the child spends less than 40 per cent of the time with one of the parents it will be considered to be visitation.

The practical implications of whether the child has alternating residence or is just visiting with one parent become apparent when determining child support.

2. The Calculation of Child Support

The possibility for a child to receive maintenance payments from the parent who is not living with the child is of great importance for the child's economic situation. It is well known that single parent families are among those families with children that have very limited economic resources. Single mothers have a lower disposable income than single fathers.[15] It is also of some significance that around 30 per cent of a single parent's disposable income consists of social benefits. For single mothers, this percentage is almost 37 per cent.[16] Against this background, it is clear that a system that contributes to the just division of responsibility between

---

12 The Parental Code, Chapter 6, Section 14 a.
13 The Parental Code, Chapter 6, Section 15 a.
14 See e.g. Supreme Court decision NJA 1998, p. 267 and Court of Appeal decision RH 1993:64.
15 Ds (*Government memorandum*) 2004:41 Ekonomiskt utsatta barn (*Economically exposed children*) p. 112 ff.
16 SCB (*Statistics Sweden*) Income distribution survey 2005.

the parents where it concerns the child's economic needs is essential and desirable.

According to the Parental Code, parents are to provide maintenance for the child according to what is reasonable, having regard to the needs of the child and their combined resources.[17] The child's need for support is, in practise, calculated schematically according to (not binding) guidelines issued by the National Board of Health and Welfare.[18] Older children are considered to have greater economic needs than younger ones. Hence, the maintenance will be higher for older children. Each parent should bear a share of the costs for the child, proportional to his or her economic ability. For example, if a parent earns 80 per cent of the total combined income of both parents (after deductions are made for taxes, cost of living and housing), that parent should pay 80 per cent of the costs for the child's support; i.e. cover 80 per cent of the child's economic needs. The other parent, who earns 20 per cent of the total combined income of the parents, should, in turn, cover the remaining 20 per cent of the child's economic needs.

Parents living with the child, generally fulfil their maintenance obligation by taking care of the child and catering for the child's needs in day to day life. A parent not permanently living with the child should pay an allowance for maintenance, regardless of whether he or she has custody or not.[19] The obligation to pay maintenance can be determined by means of an agreement between the parents, or by the court.

A basic precondition for obliging a parent to pay maintenance allowance is, thus, that the parent is not living permanently with the child. A parent living with the child can, however, be compelled by the court to provide special maintenance payments if he or she neglects the duty to maintain the child. In practise, this option is never used, seemingly because it is assumed that a parent living with the child cannot neglect this duty – it is »automatically« fulfilled through the daily contact!

According to the wording of the law, there are no legal grounds for obliging a parent to provide special maintenance payments when the child has alternating residence with both parents, since the child is considered to live permanently with both. It is tempting to explain the lack of a legal possibility to have maintenance payments established against the will of one

---

17 The Parental Code, Chapter 7, Section 1.
18 Socialstyrelsen *(National Board of Health and Welfare)*, Allmänna råd *(General guidelines)* 1986:9.
19 The Parental Code, Chapter 7, Section 2.

parent with reference to the fact that alternating residence has increased rapidly during recent years; in other words, that the legislator has not had time to address the problem. This, however, does not seem to be a plausible explanation. Other questions concerning the welfare of children have been addressed by the legislator in less time. Instead, the underlying thought seems to be that there is no need to regulate this by legislation since both parents can be assumed to fulfil their duty to support the child economically by virtue of their actual care of the child. Grounds for such an assumption may be present when both parents are living on a similar economic level, i.e. when each parent earns approximately 50 per cent of their combined total income; when they share the child's costs equally; and finally, when they cooperate. If one of the parents has a greater economic capacity – which means that he or she, according to the main rule, should cover a greater portion of the child's economic needs – there is limited support for the assumption that the costs for the child are naturally divided between the parents according to the main rule of the law. For instance, the parent who has the child for 60 per cent of the time, and who is supposed to cover 20 per cent of the child's economic needs, often finds it difficult to manage. At the same time, the parent who is supposed to cover 80 per cent of the child's economic needs cannot automatically be expected to do this during the remaining 40 per cent of the time, thus compensating for the costs that are to be covered when the child is with the other parent.

3. Critique of the Current Regulation

The basic principle that parents should share the maintenance of the child between them in proportion to their income does not directly correspond to the idea that alternating residence automatically regulates the duty to pay child support. Such a relationship nevertheless seems to be behind the existing rules, or rather, lack of rules. Even so, it should to be obvious that such an assumption is not a useful basis for the distribution of the child's costs between the parents. Despite the theoretical and logical bases for the critique regarding the lack of regulation in relation to maintenance where the child has alternating residence, it could be argued that this is not a problem in practise. Indeed, there seems to be some support in favour of this position. The fact is that we have heard very little about maintenance in situations where the child has alternating residence. Could this be a sign that all is working well? Currently, we know very little about this. As was mentioned above, some limited research has been done on alternating residence, focusing mainly on the social aspects of this living arrangement for children with separated parents.[20] However, very little attention has been paid to the economic aspects of alternating residence. That there have been few court cases concerning maintenance where the child has alternating residence can be easily explained by the fact that it is not possible to receive a court decision on maintenance in these cases; hence, there are no such disputes. It is not likely that the question arises in court cases concerning residence either. An objection to alternating residence from one of the parents, with reference to the loss of maintenance payments, would be unlikely to carry great weight. Alternating residence is almost exclusively determined on the ground that it gives the child an opportunity to develop close and good contact with both parents. Economy has little to do with it and references from one parent regarding the loss of maintenance would only cast a bad light on that parent!

There is however, support for the suspicion that the lack of regulation is a problem. Anecdotal evidence indicates that the division of costs for the child is a source of conflict between parents who have chosen alternating residence. It has also been reported that economic considerations can be decisive for choosing or rejecting alternating residence.[21] The parent who should bear a greater portion of the costs for the child benefits from alternating residence, while the parent with less economic capacity has reasons to refuse in order not to avoid losing the child support. In this context, it should be noted that there are gender aspects to be considered. A great majority of parents paying maintenance are fathers, since it is the mothers who very often take care of the children after separation. Fathers, in general, also have higher incomes than mothers. Hence, fathers generally have more to gain from the lack of regulation and consequently from choosing alternating residence as a way to avoid paying maintenance.

There are, thus, several reasons that motivate at least a review of the regulations on the division of child support where the child has alternating residence. Contact between the child and both parents after divorce should, of course, be encouraged and alternating residence can facilitate this. But time is not money. The encouragement of contact between the child and his or her parents should not be made at the expense of one parent having to support the child on means that are not sufficient, and out

---

20 See research quoted above in Part II Alternating residence.
21 See e.g. Socialstyrelsen (*The National Board of Health and Welfare*), Växelvis boende. Att bo hos både mamma och pappa fast de inte bor tillsammans (*Alternating residence. To live with both mum and dad even when they are not living together*), 2001, p. 30.

of fear of losing the ability to have the child for half of the time. The promotion of good contact between the child and parent should not sacrifice the protection of the child's economic interests.

IV. A Just Division of Child Support

1. Maintenance and Time Together – Different Entities

Alternating residence is considered to be an optimal way of giving a child close and good relations with both parents after a separation. It is, of course, important to encourage contact between a child and both parents after separation. But it is also important that a child is provided for economically. Regulations that accomplish a correct division of the costs for a child between the parents, according to their ability to pay, ought to be advantageous for several reasons. Such regulations can be assumed to contribute to good cooperation between the parents and thereby also to good contact between the child and the parents.

It is, however, essential to keep contact and economic responsibility separate since they are two different aspects of parenthood. It has been argued here that it is not realistic to assume that the basic principle of division of the costs for the child in relation to what is reasonable, having regard to the needs of the child and the combined resources of the parents, is automatically fulfilled when the child has alternating residence. A parent with 80 per cent of the total income cannot be expected to cover 80 per cent of the child's needs during 40 per cent of the time. Such assumptions are clearly not functional when regulating maintenance for children. If the purpose is to achieve a correct division of children's costs between the parents according to their ability to pay – something that probably facilitates cooperation between the parents – the starting point should be the actual economic needs of the child, and the question of who is fulfilling them.

2. Separation Is Costly

A well functioning system requires a close connection to the reality that is being regulated. All too often it seems that it is the concern for the parents' economic situation that is at the center of the legislator's attention. But it is important to keep in mind that it is the child's economic needs that ought to be addressed. It is fair to assume that children with alternating residence have greater economic needs than children living in one home.

They will basically need double of everything in a home – in other words, two homes – if alternating residence is to function well. Other expenses for the child, such as traveling expenses, will in many cases also increase with alternating residence. These factors are often neglected when using abstract and standardized methods to estimate the economic needs of children. A just system for child maintenance must be built on the actual economic needs that the child with alternating residence has, not the theoretical costs for a child living with only one parent. It will be more costly to give the child two homes than one!

3. Parents Take Different Responsibilities

In order to find a just system for the division of costs between the parents where it concerns child maintenance, it would also be useful to clarify how parents actually divide the costs between them. It cannot be assumed that each parent covers 50 per cent of the child's economic needs when they have the child for 50 per cent of the time. In other words, it is not certain that each parent pays for every other winter overall or pair of gym shoes. If considering the case that one parent should cover 80 per cent of the child's needs, the picture becomes even more unclear. On many occasions, one of the parents will also be obliged to pay certain costs, such as day care fees or costs for leisure activities; costs that are not connected to actual care. This will be, in many instances, done without any consideration as to what part of the cost that parent, in the end, should actually bear. Furthermore, it is not unrealistic to assume that one of the parents, in practise, takes care of certain expenses, such as clothes, regardless of the time spent with the child.

4. Rational to Divide the Expenses

Even if one could assume that the parents, between themselves, share the cost of the child in proportion to their economic ability, independently of the time spent with the child, it is not a given that this is the best solution. It could be economically rational to give one parent responsibility for certain costs that are independent of actual care, such as clothes, fees for leisure activities, or day care. In this way, it would also be possible to minimize double expenses that might otherwise occur because one parent does not know what the other one has paid for. The remaining costs would be those required for covering the daily needs of the child; costs that should be distributed between the parents according to the time spent together with the child.

5. Children Need Time and They Need Money!

It is not an easy task to construct a well functioning system for the division of child maintenance between the parents where the child has alternating residence. A reasonable starting point is that less conflict between the parents about economic matters after a separation enhances cooperation between them; something that can be assumed to facilitate better contact between the child and both parents. The system should therefore be perceived as just and predictable by the parents and it should not be conflict-creating. Moreover, it should encourage amicable agreements and the rules should be easy to apply.

Apart from the technical questions concerning the design of the regulation, at least three different issues must be addressed: The principles for the division of the costs for the child between the parents; the determination of what costs, not least the increased costs for the child that flow from having two homes, should be divided; and finally, how to encourage contact between the child and both parents after separation.

Alternating residence is, if it functions, a good way to give the child natural and unrestrained contact with both parents in everyday life. But it is not a solution that should be chosen or rejected for economic reasons – time is not money when we are talking about children.

New Child Maintenance Obligations in Croatia: More and More Being a Concern of the Public Law and Less of the Civil Law

Branka Resetar[1]

I. Introduction

After 20 years, i.e. on 1st January 2008, new provisions of the 2003 Family Act came into force in Croatia representing a reform in the field of family law maintenance.[2]

The reform was enticed by new research, according to which about 48.7% of Croatian debtor parents (hereinafter: non-resident parents) did not fulfil their obligation of settling child maintenance claims. Moreover, about 43,000 children aged up to 18 are estimated not to have been provided with child maintenance.[3]

Modifications in the field of maintenance obligations which came into force on 1st January 2008 can be divided into the following categories: a) modifications regarding the method of child support calculation b) modifications regarding the instruments of enforcement c) modifications regarding reinforcing the state role of settling an advance for the support of children.

The goal of the above modifications is primarily modernization, i.e. simplification and acceleration of court proceedings with respect to making decisions on maintenance obligations and to achieving efficiency of the instrument of enforcement. The secondary goal of the reform is fulfilling the constitutional and international obligation of the state to protect the child ensuring material conditions necessary for exercising the right to a decent living standard, particularly when parents are not affected by the right.[4]

---

1 Faculty of Law Osijek, Croatia.
2 The official gazette of the Republic of Croatia no.107/2007.
3 Draft of the Act on the Amendments of the Family Act, Zagreb, May 2007, p. 2, Retrieved August 25 2008, from http://www.vlada.hr.
4 Convention on Children's Rights (Article 27):
   »1. States Parties recognize the right of every child to a standard of living adequate for

The scope of this paper is representing the new Croatian maintenance law, wherein the first part includes a short overview of the maintenance obligations prior to the reform of 2007 and the second part outlines fundamental modifications of the court proceedings concerning maintenance obligations, pointing out those elements which give the legal relation between parents and children more features of the public law. Taking account of recent research on the connection between maintenance and contact with children, the concluding part puts an emphasis on my own assessment of possible effects of the Croatian reform of the maintenance obligations on personal contacts between the child's parents as well as between the child and the non-resident parent.

II. The Child's Right to Support Pursuant to the 2003 Family Act – Prior to the Reform of 2007

According to the 2003 Family Act[5], child support regulations have maintained most of the provisions of the 1978 Marriage and Family Law Act adopted when Croatia was part of the former Yugoslavia. The child's right to be supported by its parents has kept being based on the parent constitutional and legal obligation to support children (Art. 63 para 1 of the Croatian Constitution, Art. 98 and Art. 209 of the 2003 Family Act). This parent obligation and simultaneously right to support minor children originates from parental responsibilities, although in case of discharge of parental responsibilities, the obligation stays (Art. 212 of the 2003 Family Act). Parents are obliged to support major children if they proceed with their regular education and for a year subsequent to the completion of their education as well as if they are incapable of working due to an illness or a mental or physical disability (Art. 210 of the 2003 Family Act). Pursuant to the 2003 Family Act, the identity of the persons that have the legal obligation to support a child and the hierarchy according to which

---

the child's physical, mental, spiritual, moral and social development.
3. States Parties, in accordance with national conditions and within their means, shall take appropriate measures to assist parents and others responsible for the child to implement this right and shall in case of need provide material assistance and support programmes, particularly with regard to nutrition, clothing and housing.
The Croatian Constitution (Art. 62):
»The state is liable for protecting....children and the young, and for ensuring....material and other conditions aimed at promoting the right to a decent life.«

5 The official gazette of the Republic of Croatia, no. 116/2003, 17/2004, 136/2004.

they are obliged to pay the maintenance, have not been amended by the reform. Thus, the hierarchy stays as follows: parents (Art. 98 and Art. 209), grandparents (Art. 216), and, finally, step-parents (Art. 215).

The court is, according to the 2003 Family Act, obliged to *ex offo* issue an order on supporting minor and major children who are still under parental responsibility when making decisions on divorce and annulment of marriage (Art. 300) as well as on maternity or paternity (Art. 301). Those provisions have not been comprised by the reform of 2007, too.

However, what the reform of 2007 has introduced is a new method for child maintenance calculation. Therefore, it is necessary first to describe the method having been in use prior to the reform of 2007.

Before 2007, courts had used to determine maintenance obligations in advance according to the *Nemo pro praeterito allitur* principle. That way, the obligation of child support started to have been calculated from the day of initiating court proceedings on maintenance obligations.[6] That had usually brought to circumstances whereat there was no formal duty to pay maintenance on behalf of the non resident parent for the time after the non-resident parent had moved out and divorce or maintenance proceedings had not been initiated. The same problem had existed on the occasion of additional determination of paternity or maternity wherein maintenance obligations could be defined only after the day of initiating court proceedings concerning judicial determination of paternity or maternity.

The legal method for child maintenance calculation used before the reform of 2007 had been complex and had used to be implemented according to the following order: 1. first, court had determined the child's needs in every particular case, taking account of the child's age and need for education (Art. 232 para 1 of the 2003 Family Act), 2. then, it had evaluated the financial abilities of the parents, bearing in mind all the earnings and actual possibilities of making money, the parents' needs and the legal obligations of supporting other persons (Art. 231 para 3 of the 2003 Family Act), 3. finally, it had determined the total amount of money necessary for supporting a child, giving credit to the resident parent who had invested means and labour in child-rearing and, thus, reducing the previously defined amount for maintenance (Art. 233 of the 2003 Family Act). The reduced amount had represented the maintenance obligations of the non-resident parent.

---

6 Korać, A., Maintenance in: Alinčić, M., Hrabar, D., Jakovac-Lozić, D. i Korać, A., Family Law, Narodne novine, 2006, p. 444.

That way, the law omitted to calculate the value of labour and care of the resident parent invested in a child into maintenance obligations. Although such evaluation of labour and care was and has been inappropriate, it was inevitable since the final amount of support had been reduced on account of labour and care invested in a child by the resident parent. Such an individualized manner of determining the child's needs and the parents' financial abilities had been, on the one hand, preferable and just but, on the other hand, it had caused significant inconsistence in judicial practice and long and complex judicial proceedings.[7]

Enforcement of orders had used to be carried out when requested by the resident parent despite the fact that Art 234 of the 2003 Family Act foresaw the possibility of a social welfare service initiating it. However, this possibility could not force a social welfare service to do so. That is why the resident parent had to hire a lawyer for initiating enforcement of orders and judicial proceedings with respect to the criminal act of failing to pay child support (Art. 209 of the Criminal Act[8]). One must bear in mind that at the time there was no free legal aid in terms of initiating legal proceedings related to child maintenance. The obligation of the state to provide resident parents with advance for the maintenance of children through social welfare services had also existed prior to the reform of 2007 but it had not been consistently implemented in practice.

Apart from the 2007 amendments (influenced by the German law) concerning judicial methods for determining the amount of maintenance for minor children, the new reform has reinforced the duties of the state to, by means of court and social welfare services, *ex offo* intervene with respect to orders on minor child maintenance. That issue will be presented in the next chapter in detail.

---

[7] Rešetar, B., Some issues of determining child maintenance, Collected papers of Zagreb Law Faculty, Vol. 54, No. 5, p. 940-967.

[8] Criminal Act (Art. 209):
»Avoiding employment, changing workplaces and residences, misappropriation of property or any other way of escaping settling child support claims determined by the law, implies a pecuniary penalty or imprisonment lasting up to three years.«

III. Reform of the Child's Right to Maintenance Pursuant to the 2007 Family Act

The reform of maintenance obligations from the 2007 Family Act is divided into three segments:
a.) proceedings with respect to determining child maintenance,
b.) enforcement of orders on maintenance,
c.) emphasizing elements of the public law in the field of child maintenance.

1. Legal Determination of Minor Child Maintenance
The procedure of determining minor child maintenance has been shortened and simplified according to the German legal system.[9] Two new principles have been introduced to the Croatian law.

The first enables retroactive settlement of minor child maintenance claims. Accordingly, the non-resident parent of a minor child who has failed to pay maintenance is liable for paying maintenance retroactively for a time span of up to five years (Art. 209 of the 2003 Family Act).

The second principle has been taken from the German law and refers to legal equalization of care, protection and education of a minor child ensured by the resident parent with pecuniary amount of maintenance provided by the non resident parent (Art. 233 of the 2003 Family Act). Moreover, the Croatian legislation has, similarly to the German counterpart (Regelbetrag-Verordnung), determined guidelines for three age categories – children up to 6, children from 6 to 12 and children from 12 to 18, aiming at defining a minimum percentage of the average Croatian salary intended for child maintenance (17% for the first category, 20% for the second and 22% for the third). The court may discretely determine bigger amounts of money for maintenance if the child's needs are greater or in case of better financial status of parents since the status of the children should correspond to the status of the parents (Art. 232 para 3 of the 2003 Family Act). If a debtor has got more children that need his maintenance (Art. 232 para 5 of the 2003 Family Act) or a child has been receiving its

---
9   Dose, H.J., Gerhard, P., Gutdeutch, W., Haußleiter, O., Pauling, D., Scholz, H. und Thalmann, W., Das Unterhaltsrecht in der familienrichterlichen Praxis, Verlag C.H. Beck, München, 2000; Luthin, H., Mindestbedarf des minderjährigen unverheirateten Kindes, Zeitschrift für das gesamte Familienrecht, 6/01 and Henrich, D., The Reform of German Child and Parent Law on the Background of European Legal Development, European Journal of Law Reform, Vol. 2, No. 1, 2000.

own income which shall contribute to the maintenance (Art. 211 of the 2003 Family Act), the court may order lower child maintenance but not lower than ½ of the minimum support.[10]

Introducing the principle that equalizes the care of the resident parent with the maintenance or support of the non-resident and preparing guidelines for determining minor child support have contributed to the simplification and acceleration of proceedings in the Croatian legal system.

At the very first session of judicial proceedings, the court shall *ex offo* issue an order on interim measures regarding an appropriate amount of maintenance after the other party has been given an opportunity to present their standpoint on the issue. Interim measures can also be determined if the other party has not made their observations but the circumstances require an urgent order on them (Art. 305 of the 2003 Family Act).

The new regulations are aimed at simplifying and accelerating legal proceedings but every determination, reduction or increase of maintenance contribution require contested proceedings, regardless of the existence of a dispute between parties. Only in cases the parties have made a maintenance agreement at a social welfare centre, contested proceedings are not necessary but such a situation happens very rarely. Therefore, with respect to the Croatian legal system, one should *de lege ferenda* consider introducing an administrative method for determining maintenance or a method for determining maintenance pursuant to the rules of uncontested proceedings, which is the case in most contemporary legal systems.

2. Enforcement of Maintenance Claims

Enforcement titles are as follows: maintenance agreement that can be made at a social welfare centre or before court[11], order on interim measures or court order on maintenance.

The court that has issued an order on maintenance or interim measures on minor or major children under parental responsibility, is obliged to *ex offo* carry out enforcement procedure, unless maintenance contribu-

---

10 Korać, A., Maintenance in: Alinčić, M., Hrabar, D., Jakovac-Lozić, D. i Korać, A., Family Law, Narodne novine 2006, p. 480-481.
11 The Croatian legislation has recognized the importance of a non-conflict way of settling disputes and enabled making maintenance agreements at social welfare centres or before court (Art. 230 of the 2003 Family Act). Agreements made otherwise could not be deemed as enforcement titles.

tion will be settled by means of the debtor's income or salary, pension or similar regular income pursuant to a debtor's written consent (Art. 236 of the 2003 Family Act).

Besides the court, a social welfare centre is *ex offo* obliged to initiate enforcement procedure within 15 days after reception of a court order if the court had not done it before (Art. 234 of the 2003 Family Act).[12]

Enforcement procedure may encumber up to ¾ of the salary or other parents' earnings (3/4 of the average salary in state adminstration (Art. 232 para 2 of the 2003 Family Act)).

Maintenance claims are privileged and have priority over all other claims, notwithstanding the period of time of their origin (Art. 232 para 3 of the 2003 Family Act).

In case a debtor deliberately prevents enforcement, he shall be charged with a lack of fulfilling the legal obligation of paying maintenance contributions, which is deemed as a criminal act. Also, a social welfare centre is liable for initiating criminal proceedings (Art. 237 of the 2003 Family Act).

IV. Elements of the Public Law in the Field of Child Support

This part lists the elements of the public law included in the 2003 Family Act, starting from initiating court proceedings with respect to determining minor child maintenance to final satisfaction of child's need for a decent living standard.

No matter whether there is a parent claim for child support or not, the court is obliged to *ex offo* issue an order on supporting minor or major children under parental responsibility every time when it decides on divorce or annulment or marriage (Art. 300), and when it decides on maternity or paternity (Art. 301). At the very first session of judicial proceedings, the court shall *ex offo* issue an order on interim measures regarding an appropriate amount of maintenance in case it considers that there is a need for it (Art. 305 d. and Art. 355).

If a parent does not initiate court proceedings regards determining maintenance (e.g. mother of an extra-marital child), then a social welfare centre is obliged to *ex offo* do it on behalf of the child (Art. 234).

---

[12] The court is obliged to forward every court order or maintenance agreement to a social welfare centre that keeps records on that issue (Art. 235 of the 2003 Family Act) in order to undertake further action for settling maintenance claims.

In order to determine the financial status of a debtor parent, governmental bodies such as the Ministry of Finance – tax administration, the Ministry of Interior, the Croatian Pension Fund, the Financial Agency and others are liable for providing information on the debtor's income (Art. 230 para 5).

The court shall *ex offo* initiate the enforcement procedure (Art. 236), and if it omits to do it, then the same duty has a social welfare centre (Art. 234 para 2).

Upon reception of a maintenance agreement, an order on interim measures or an order on child support and after a maintenance agreement has been made before a social welfare centre, the centre is obliged to render a written warning to both parents. The written warning is aimed at reminding the resident parent that they have to inform the social welfare centre about the lack of paying maintenance contribution by the non-resident parent partly or in its entirety and in such cases the child has the right to state advance.[13] On the contrary, the debtor parent is warned that failing to fulfil the obligation of child maintenance is a criminal act and, in case of settlement of advance by the state, the state shall initiate procedure of cost return against the debtor (Art. 237 of the 2003 Family Act).

A social welfare centre shall file criminal charges against the debtor parent within 15 days after notice on the lack of paying maintenance contribution partly or in its entirety have been received (Art. 237 para 4).

The Croatian Bar Association have been providing free legal aid since December 2006, all in terms of initiating and managing judicial proceedings regarding minor child maintenance.[14]

The above court and social welfare service duties reflect the fact that the state has taken over from the resident parent the right and duty to initiate maintenance proceedings, enforcement of orders and filing criminal charges against the debtor parents with respect to minor children. That way, the Croatian legislation intends to give the parent-child relation that basically belongs to the field of private law more elements of the public law and thus limit the influence of parties in such issues.

---

13 The conditions for state advance appear after the debtor parent has failed to pay maintenance contribution for a consecutive period of time longer than six months or if they have paid less than three contributions within a period of nine months (Art. 352 of the 2003 Family Act).
14 Retrieved September 02 2008, from http://www.hok-cba.hr.

V. Connection between Maintenance and Contacts

The connection between child maintenance and contact between a child and the non-resident parent is controversial.[15] On one hand, in most states formal legal doctrine seeks to prohibit connections between contacts and money,[16] and on the other hand some jurisdictions have recognized connections between contacts concerning child and child maintenance, taking account of shared care in the calculation of child maintenance liability (Australia, New Zealand and North America).[17]

However, many believe that child maintenance and contact rights are tied together in terms of what it means to be a parent. A parent who fails to support his children, at least when he/she has the financial capacity to do so, may in popular perception no longer be entitled to maintain a contact with his minor children if the resident parent objects.[18]

Here, the emphasis is not on showing the connection between contacts and maintenance in different legal systems but on the connection between maintenance and frequency of contacts existing according to the latest sociological researches. At the same time, there is the question whether a reinforced role of the state in exercising the child's right to be supported may soothe the hostile attitude towards the resident parent on the occasion of forcible settlement of maintenance claims or criminal charges.

There have been a number of UK and USA studies showing that fathers who pay child support maintain contact with their children to a great extent.[19] The same results have been offered by research according to which

---

15 Gilmore, S., Re B (Contact: Child Support) – horses and carts: contact and child support, Child and Family Law Quarterly, Vol. 19, No. 3, 2007, p. 357.
16 However, if a non resident parent with contact rights failures to pay maintenance, the other parent may believe that he/she can retaliate by informally cutting off the parent's contact rights or making it more difficult. Even though this tactic has no legal validity, it is nevertheless likely to be faster, cheaper, and more effective than court enforcement. Mnookin, R., Maccoby, E., Dividing the Child – Social & Legal Dilemmas of Custody, Harvard University Press, Cambridge, Massachusetts, London, 1997, p. 45.
17 Gilmore, S., Re B (Contact: Child Support) – horses and carts: contact and child support, Child and Family Law Quarterly, Vol. 19, No. 3, 2007, p. 358.
18 Mnookin, R., Maccoby, E., Dividing the Child – Social & Legal Dilemmas of Custody, Harvard University Press, Cambridge, Massachusetts, London, 1997, p. 145-46..
19 Maclean, M. and Eekelaar, J., The Parental Obligation, Oxford: Hart, 1997 and Smyth, B., Sheehan, G. and Fehlberg, B., Patterns of parenting after divorce, Australian Journal of Family Law, Vol. 15, p. 1-36. Quoted according to Trinder, L., Beek, M. and Connolly, J., Making contact – How Parents and children negotiate and experience contact after divorce, Available at www.jrf.org.uk.

payment of maintenance and contact frequency as complementary aspects of a non-resident father's role have been influential.[20] One of the recent researches have shown that the non-resident parent contact with children and economic support are consistently associated with each other at various stages before and after divorce or separation.[21]

Secondly, another recent American research shows that the increasing percentage of fathers who paid at least some child maintenance is crucial for interpreting the growth of non-resident father-child contact. Statistical analysis does not demonstrate causality. Perhaps increased payment of child maintenance was the sole cause of fathers' greater contact with children, but the same statistical results would be obtained if contact increased maintenance compliance (reverse causality) or both changes were produced by a third unmeasured variable. Authors suspect that the major policy initiatives of the 1980s and 1990s, which helped to improve non-resident fathers' child support compliance, also helped to create (and reflected) a growing cultural expectations that non-resident fathers should be more involved in their children's lives economically and socially.[22] There is one interesting observation – while more stringent legal enforcement of child support payment may have increased father contact, other evidence shows that less adversarial dispute resolution about child custody also increases contact. A randomized trial found that the mediation versus the adversarial legal settlement of custody disputes caused significant and substantial increases in non-resident parent-child contact 12 years later.[23] Furthermore, dozens of scientists have shown that the quality of parent-child relationships and the conflict between parents are the most important predictors of psychological problems in children.[24]

---

20 Stephen, E.H., Freedman, V.A. and Hess, J., Near and far: Contact of children with their non-resident fathers, 20 Journal of Divorce and Remarriage, 171–191; Arditti, J.A., Child support noncompliance and divorced fathers: Rethinking the role of paternal involvement, 14 Journal of Divorce and Remarriage, 107–19 and Furstenberg, F.F., Nord, C.W., Peterson, J.L. and Zill, N., The life course of children of divorce: Marital disruption and parental contact, 48 American Sociological Review, 656–68. Quoted according to: Wilson, G.B., The non-resident parental role for separated fathers: A review, International Journal of Law, Policy and the Family 20, 2006, 286–316.

21 Wilson, G.B., The non-resident parental role for separated fathers: A review, International Journal of Law, Policy and the Family 20, 2006, p. 289.

22 Amato, P.R., Meyers, C. and Emery, R. E., Changes in Nonresident Father Contact from 1976 to 2002, Family Relations, (forthcoming).

23 Emery, R.E., Laumann-Billings, L., Waldron, M., Sbarra, D.A., and Dillon, P., Child custody mediation and litigation: Custody, contact, and co-parenting 12 years after initial dispute resolution. Journal of Consulting and Clinical Psychology, 69, 323–332.

24 Emery, R.E., The Truth about Children and Divorce, Viking Penguin, New York, 2004, p. 68.

It can be concluded that more efficient and stringent collection of child maintenance together with reinforcing elements of the public law might have multiple effects: a) satisfying child's need for support, b) removing one source of conflict between parents and c) indirectly increasing contacts between child and non resident parent.

VI. Conclusion

New provisions of the Croatian 2003 Family Act have modernized legislation in order to accelerate and simplify judicial proceedings as well as to regulate new instruments of efficient collection of maintenance contribution. At the same time Croatia fulfils its constitutional and international obligation of protecting the child and providing them with the material assistance and support programmes necessary for exercising their right to a decent living standard.

Obligatory notice regarding non-settlement of maintenance contribution, instituting maintenance proceedings, enforcement of orders, criminal proceedings *ex officio*, representing the child in maintenance proceedings free of charges as well as state advance for the support of children are some of the important new instruments which imply the public law more than the civil law.

Bearing in mind the connection between paying maintenance contribution and non-resident parent – child contacts as well as damage that may arise to a child due to conflicts between parents, it seems that the Croatian legislation is making the right steps transforming child maintenance into a concern of the public law more than of the civil law, being, simultaneously, on the verge of finding the right solution for the contact concerning children, their welfare and best interests.

The Child's Right to Two Parents:
Facilitating and Financing Joint Parenting

Annette Kronborg[1] and Christina G. Jeppesen de Boer[2]

I. Introduction

The article takes its starting point in a description of the development of the legal regulation of parental authority – from focusing on **marriage and fault** to an emphasis on **individual rights and parents' duty to co-operate**. On this background, we ask for a critical approach to the consequences of the actual mode of regulation; i.e. the massive volume and number of procedures, imposed upon parents in order to ensure individual rights and co-operation. We point out that this matter has not been addressed by the European Court of Human Rights (the Court). We then turn to a description of the simplicity of the Danish child maintenance system and compare it with the regulation of parental authority in order to inspire a rethinking of the latter with a focus on the benefits of more simple modes of regulation. Unfortunately, it seems the development is going in the opposite direction, which we illustrate by finally describing a recent reform of the Danish Act on Parental Responsibility[3] which as a novelty in Danish law introduced a provision concerning the transportation of children in connection with contact.

II. Parental Authority

The upcoming of individual rights are seen as being **at the expense of** a legal regulation, where parental authority – i.e. responsibility and power as to care-giving and decision-making – is delegated from the state to the unmarried mother or the married couple, and where fault could exclude

---

1 Associate Professor, Copenhagen University, Denmark.
2 Utrecht University, The Netherlands.
3 Lov 2007-06-06 nr. 499 Forældreansvarslov.

one of the holders of authority. Today fault is not a criterion for the exclusion of any of the holders, and it is very difficult to obtain sole parental authority – whether the parents were married or not. Thus, the regulation of parental authority is not suitable as a remedy to protect a primary caretaker from conflicts with the other parent. We understand this weakening of parental authority as the end of a development taking its starting point in the **household** governed by the Roman civil law doctrine of patria potestas, and ending with the individualization of the relationship between the state and the individual. A development that goes from conceiving the family as an association – to the dissolvement of this concept into a number of relationships based on either genetics or contracts. In a period after the doctrine of patria potestas was abolished in the name of gender equality (about 1925 in Denmark), marriage law remained founded in tradition and a fault-based regulation. The end of marriage as a basis for the regulation of the parent-child relationship took place around 1985 in Denmark. From then on only individual rights were left.[4] The family soon after became the family of negotiation. The individual right – also of the unwed and non-cohabitant father – was substantiated as a right to participate in the negotiations, reflected in the legal regulation as a duty of both parents to co-operate. Hereby more parents were given access to begin procedures.

The present duty to co-operate covers not only the duty to co-operate in relation to the child's right to two parents, it also covers the duty to participate in the many different and more or less formalized procedures of co-operation; i.e meetings with the other parent, the use of child experts, mediators and other officials. This duty is not as easy to define as are the criteria for obtaining divorce – these criteria being previously accepted as legally decisive in the parents' conflict. Rather like the definition of the principle **of the best interests of the child**, the definition of the duty to **co-operate** depends on the specific situation and prevailing societal norms. It is not to be interpreted in fact-finding-procedures, but is produced within the procedures themselves. Thus, »the duty to cooperate« takes its starting point in participation rather than in the case, and the procedures now contain two tracks; one track of settlement and if unsuccessful, the subsequent one of judgment. Consequently, new functions and

---

4 An exception was the child expertise developed as an authority in family law during the middle of the 20th century. This was only to be for some few decades until the authority was transferred to the individuals.

understandings have been added to the procedures. This development has resulted in an increase of procedural law concerning the parent-child relationship – and for parents who are not capable of solving their conflict it may involve an increase in the volume of procedures. During the last decade, alternative dispute resolution has been introduced as part of both the administrative (settlement) and public court system. The development from parental authority to individual rights has introduced the term **parental responsibility** which is now contained in the title of the Act on Parental Responsibility. The term **responsibility** has a clear political reference. One should take responsibility for one's individual conflicts. This is prestigious. Presently, the overall legal distinction in Danish law concerning the parent-child relationship is whether or not there is a conflict. The law no longer presents an ideal of how the legal relationship should be formed, as long as the parents solve their conflicts themselves. Illustrative is the fact that parents who do not live together (anymore) are free to agree to the allocation of parental authority (sole/joint) and that a private agreement on contact is directly enforceable.

The main ratio of the regulation is to motivate the parents to make their own solution, aimed at creating more equality than can possibly be obtained through enforceable law because of the child's well being. This motivation is sought through a general increase of rights to the non-resident parent and an emphasis upon negotiation. The uncertainty of a legal decision may also work as a motivation to the parents. Legislation now no longer provides parental authority as the decisive instrument to protect the family against its own conflicts – rather it unites the stronger parents who fulfil their duty to co-operate with those parents who are incapable of fulfilling this duty, united in the wording that **a child has a right to two parents**. We believe the regulation is not suitable to protect those who need protection from the conflict with the other parent in order to be able to care for the child. What tradition did in earlier centuries was to motivate people to enter into marriage. This is no longer the aim, but there is still a societal need to emphasize and encourage parents' responsibility towards their children. This can no longer be obtained by referring to tradition or marriage – both sources of law have lost their legitimacy in the process of modernization and equality. Thus, encouragement of parental responsibility is sought through the instalment of **procedures** – legitimate and acceptable because of the apparent equality and non-discriminatory quality of such procedures. However, the volume and number of procedures simultaneously leave the system vulnerable to a critique based on the welfare of the individual child. The idea of justice is equality, but the equality does not address the child's circumstances, instead it addresses the parents' freedom to make their own arrangement. We understand this development as a part of the process of individualization and believe that it implies a need to emphasize the state's responsibility to assess and decide how many and how enduring procedures families have to live with, when the parents are not able to settle their conflicts.

III. The Burden of Procedures

In this part, we will comment on the Court's case law with a focus on the Court's lack of a critical approach towards how burdensome the procedures are to the individuals. Our first example is a case against Denmark which received substantial public attention in Denmark, however not for the reasons we find important. The case is the so-called Jon-case, referring to the name of the boy.[5] As to the facts: A parental authority case between Jon's parents was pending before the Danish Supreme Court. The mother, who was the sole holder of parental authority, requested that Jon (12 years old) would be admitted to the State Hospital's Child Psychiatric Ward since it was clear that he did not want to stay with her. The Court concluded »that the hospitalisation of the applicant did not amount to a deprivation of liberty within the meaning of article 5, but was a responsible exercise by the mother of her custodial rights in the interest of the child.« The reason why a psychiatric ward seemed to be a reasonable solution in the given situation depended upon the insecurity linked to the outcome of the case. Either Jon was allowed to stay with his father according to his own wishes or there was to be made some plan for Jon's integration in his mother's family. Such an integration could harm Jon if his father would eventually win the case. Thus, the Court focused upon the mother's exercise of her parental authority. By this focus the Danish state was acquitted. What the majority of the judges did not focus on was how the parental authority case was handled by the Danish legal system. We believe that this would have been a relevant focus (today even more so) because the continuing process of individualization involves a risk of an increase in the burdening of the family with conflicts and procedures. This case placed Jon's life on standby for the duration of the procedures. The case was brought to the natio-

---

5   Nielsen v. Denmark (28. November 1988. Series A no. 144).

nal lowest court in November 1982 and ended at the national highest court in August 1984. The national court system cannot be viewed to have been slow considering that the case was tried at three levels. Even though it may not have been slow – seen from the perspective of the legal system - it may have been a very long period of uncertainty to the family; uncertainty cannot generally be considered to be a constructive force in family life. The dissenting judges in the Court engaged in the parental authority case but they did not take a critical view on procedural questions related to the case. Instead some of the judges took the odd position that since Jon's father eventually won the case, the Danish government was to be criticized. This is an odd position since at the moment of bringing Jon to the hospital the parental authority case was still pending and not to be predicted.

A second example of a non-critical approach of the Court containing even a validation of the procedures are three cases – called Sommerfeld, Sahin and Hoffmann – all against Germany.[6] They all concerned fathers, who were denied contact with their child. The Court's approach was in favour of sufficient (in the sense not enough) national procedures and hereby supported the national developments of the vision of the negotiating family.[7] The Court articulated the question of

»whether, having regard to the particular circumstances of the case and notably the importance of the decisions to be taken, the applicant had been involved in the decision-making process, seen as a whole, to a degree sufficient to provide him with the requisite protection of his interests.«

Whether or not the father had been sufficiently involved is – by the Court – expressively transformed into a matter of whether or not the child has been sufficiently involved in the procedures. A judgment denying a father contact should not be made without a certain amount of procedures. The volume of procedures increases if the child does not want contact. Hereby the judgments respect the image of the family as a number of equal mem-

---

6   Sommerfeld v. Germany (application no. 31871/96), case of Sahin v. Germany (application no. 30943/96), case of Hoffmann v. Germany (application no. 34045/96).
7   See *Jonas Christoffersen* «Fair Balance – A study of the Principles of Proportionality, Subsidiarity and Primarity in the European Convention of Human Rights« Forthcomming, chapter 4.3.2.1.4. The view is that the Court has not been very mindful of the role of proceduralisation as an instrument to advance the effective protection of the ECHR in domestic law. In K.A. v. Finland (application no. 27751/95) the court made it clear that proceduralisation is viewed as an instrument designed to enable the Court to exercise its substantive review.

bers with individual rights and turn national law into the form of pedagogy. Thus, what law calls fact-finding is turned into something more powerful – pedagogical involvement with the family – as if the national legal process could somehow teach the family how to be a family and make the children benefit from contact.[8] Fact-finding is something one has to live with to obtain justice while pedagogical involvement may be understood as something positive like welfare work. With this approach there seem to be wide limits for procedures in a very sensitive sphere concerning the parent-child relationship. To sum up, the individualization may increase the procedural burden of the families, but also seem to turn the image of procedures into something fruitful thus failing a critical approach.

A third example of not being critical to the procedural burden upon the family is when the **quick return** mechanism according to the Hague Child Abduction Convention of 1980 is defended with the argument that the quick return only decides the jurisdiction of the custody case, and that the best interests of the child will be looked after in the subsequent hearing.[9] Consequently, the increase of procedures related to the hearing on the merits involving the return of the child, is not addressed critically but rather used as an argument in favour of the international regulation of child abduction. The **quick return** mechanism puts the child right in the middle of the procedures demanding the physical removal of the child. We believe the **quick return** mechanism places the burden of creating an international legal order of co-operating states on the wrong shoulders – namely those of children and parents in conflict.

We now turn to the Court's judgments in child abduction cases. We argue that the Court's approach may be understood as a support to build an international legal order based on the **quick return** mechanism. Thus, the Court fails to develop a general approach to the balancing of individual interests in family law. Instead it sets a standard for enforcement of a decision of **quick return** of the child by judging the states for being too slow and inefficient.

In the child abduction cases all the family members are covered by the European Convention on Human Rights art. 8 (respect for family life). Hereby we understand that the petitioner (the parent left behind) is mentioned in paragraph 1 and the other members in section 2 with reference

---

8   See for an analysis of the three judgments, *Annette Kronborg* and *Idamarie Leth Svendsen* »Children's right to be heard – The interplay between Human Rights and National Law« in »Family Life and Human Rights« edited by *Peter Lødrup* and *Eva Modvar*, 2004.
9   The design is later adopted and developed in an EC regulation, (no. 2201/2003).

to protection of other individuals' rights (the abductor and the child). The Court's arguments are very much the same in the different cases. In the Sylvester-case[10] the Court's assessment was as follows: Firstly, it notes that a child abduction case is covered by art. 8 and the states have positive obligations to protect family life. With reference to the Ignaccolo-Zenide v. Romania-case[11], the Court found that

»*the positive obligations that Article 8 lays on the Contracting States in the matter of reuniting a parent with his or her child must be interpreted in the light of the Hague Convention, all the more so where the respondent State is also a party to that instrument, Article 7 of which contains a list of measures to be taken by States to secure the prompt return of children.*«

This argument may be understood as an approval of the **quick return** mechanism set up in the Hague Convention and hereby the Courts' assessment indirectly sustains the **quick return** mechanism. The Court continues by describing the states' duty as not being absolute, since the reunion of a parent with a child who has lived for some time with the other parent may not be able to take place immediately and may require preparatory measures to be taken. Similar to this argument – with a main rule and an exception – the **quick return** mechanism is not absolute in the Hague Convention. The Court continues by arguing, that concerning enforcement, the national authorities are obliged to take all the necessary steps to facilitate execution as can reasonably be expected in the special circumstances of each case. The Court must strike a fair balance between the interests of all persons concerned and the general interest in ensuring respect for the rule of law. Subsequently, the Court deals with the application of coercion and the importance of swiftness, and then turns to the possible change of circumstances after the national decision of the return of the child has been made. The Court accepts that a change in the relevant facts may exceptionally justify the non-enforcement of a final return order.

However, having regard to the State's positive obligations under Article 8 and the general requirement of respect for the rule of law,

---

10 Case of Sylvester v. Austria (Applications nos. 36812/97 and 40104/98) judgment 24. July 2003. The latest judgment with a similar reasoning is from 8. January 2008 in the case of P.P. v. Poland (Application no. 8677/03).
11 Case of Ignaccolo-Zenide v. Romania (Application no. 31679/96) judgment 25. January 2000.

> *the Court must be satisfied that the change of relevant facts was not brought about by the State's failure to take all measures that could reasonably be expected to facilitate execution of the return order.*

It is difficult to understand the argument as the Court's directive of balancing the involved interests because it excludes the child's interests from the balancing of interests in case the state is to be blamed for a delay.[12] The state's margin of appreciation may explain why the Court does not elaborate on all the family members' interest. Anyhow, case law gives the impression that the child's interests are not fully recognized. In the Ignaccolo-Zenide v. Romania-case a dissenting judge mentions the children's right to be heard and in the Maire-case[13] the UN convention on the rights of the child are mentioned shortly. In the Paradis-case it was strongly argued that the abductor should not be able to benefit from her wrongful behaviour although the Court did not consider the children's interests which may run against the Court's argument.[14] In this case – as opposed to the Sylvester-case – the petitioner to the Court was the child-abductor, who did not want to return her children. Thus, in our opinion, the mentioned case law does not succeed in developing an approach to the balancing of interests in order to improve the legitimacy of European family law. Instead the Court joins the international efforts to build national and international, sufficient legal orders which involve a procedural burden represented by the **quick return** mechanism to some families.

Thus the Court has not developed a critical approach neither in the Nielsen-case nor in the German contact cases nor in the child abduction cases. Furthermore, we understand the individualization as involving an increase of the child's participation in the procedures as presented in the UN convention on the rights of the child. We ask for a critical approach of legal designs which increase the amount or volume of procedures in conflicts between parents.

---

12 The argument is repeated in the following case: Case of Monory v. Romania and Hungary (Application no. 71099/01) Judgment 5. July 2005.
13 Case of Maire v. Portugal (Application no. 48206/99) judgment 26. June 2003.
14 Paradis and Others v. Germany (Application no. 4783/03).

IV. Child Maintenance

According to Danish law,[15] parents who do no not live with their children are obliged to pay child maintenance.[16] In 1970 child maintenance was no longer an integrated part of the divorce case but was removed from the regulation of marriage to the regulation of parenthood in order to obtain administrative standardization – the latter being the ratio of the regulation. The criteria to decide the amount to be paid are few and exact. The first criterion is the number of children of the non-resident parent. This is uncomplicated since legal paternity is decided and registered at the time of a child's birth. It is of no importance whether or not the other children are living with the non-resident parent. Thus, only obligations towards other children count. It is not relevant whether or not the father is married or living with a partner. The second and last criterion is the non-resident parent's gross earning. The non-resident parent's disbursements are not relevant and the finances of the parent with care are of no relevance.

The simplicity of the system gives the impression that duties towards one's children are privileged duties compared to one's other duties. The simplicity of the two criteria implies that the child maintenance regime as such is very little involved with the specific family life, but is of such a general character that it is easy to understand as a diagram. You just need to know the number of your children and your gross earning – and the diagram will tell you how much you are obliged to pay to the parent with care. The parents are allowed to make their private arrangement on child maintenance and take what ever they want into consideration. Nevertheless, as far as we know the issue typically does not play a central role in the parents' dispute on contact arrangements. The issues are kept apart in the regulation and to our experience this is also typically the case in parents' handling of their conflicts.

The Danish **Statsforvaltning** (an administrative authority) with appeal to the Ministry of Justice sets the amount and, if the parents cannot arrange subsequent payments between themselves, the municipality will, on application from the parent with care, take over the collection and payment of maintenance. The enforcement system is part of the Danish

---

15   Lovbekendtgørelse 2003-05-15 nr. 352 om børns forsørgelse, senest ændret ved L 2005-06-24 nr. 542
16   See Danish law on child maintenance in the following study: http://php.york.ac.uk/inst/spru/research/summs/childsupport.php

tax-system. The cases do not go to court. This is one of the reasons for the regimes' efficiency.[17]

The standard and minimum amount of maintenance is based on a parent with an average income. In 2008 it is DKK 969 + 125 = 1094 (145 Euro) per month per child. The DKK 969 is tax deductible for the non-resident parent. Levels above standard + 200% are uncommon. The system is administered by – and integrated with – the social benefit system, which is based on universal rights of individuals to basic care and protection. The municipality of the parent with care can advance the standard amount and recover it from the non-resident parent. The child maintenance regime is designed to ensure the maintenance of the **child** – different from other areas of regulation of social benefits, where the reduction of the client's dependence on social assistance is often a central aim. No account is taken of the child's former way of life and policy does not try to preserve it. The parent with care may be dissatisfied when the agency award makes it impossible to maintain e.g. a private school enrollment or continued residence in the family home – but it is of no relevance to the legal decision. The only matter of individual circumstances that is considered relevant is aimed at protecting the economic interests of non-resident parents in that both lower earning and higher earning non-resident parents are protected by the criteria used to set the amount of the obligation itself.

The parent with care is protected from having to depend on the non-resident parent by the system of social benefits and advance payments. Furthermore, the efficiency of the system derives from the use of administrative solutions, rather than the courts – and the fact that both advance payments, collection and social benefits are provided by the one-stop shop of the municipality. The Danish child support system sets up predictable and explicit boundaries between the financial responsibilities of state and families. While parents are responsible for the maintenance of their children, the state is more concerned directly with securing the child's subsistence level by benefits targeted at the parent with care. Thus, in Denmark the principle of subsidiarity (the family coming before the state) is less marked, while the principle of solidarity (society's concern for its citizens) is more marked. The maintenance regime buffers the influence of family. At the same time, the system does not recognise the

---

17 The historical reason may be understood with reference to the Danish autocracy from 1660 with the king as the sovereign. According to the Danish constitution the king is the executive power and it does to some extent explain the distribution of power between the court system and the executive power today.

principle that children should be able to continue their childhood unaffected after the parents' break up.

In comparison with the characteristics of the regulation of parental responsibility, as described above, the advantages of the child maintenance regime may be depicted as follows: The legal procedure is not a great personal burden to the parents. It does not relate to an individual assessment of the best interests of the child. There is no involvement of child experts and there is no duty to participate in meetings. Consequently, the conflict is solidly framed by the diagram and the case is about fact-finding. The maintenance regime thus distances itself from the specific family life, and is based upon predictability as a quality. As regards the relation between the parents there seems to be no idea of justice – and there is no pursuit of equality or reaction to fault. The regulation of parental authority on the contrary does not frame or distance itself from the specific family life or the conflict between parents, but requires full participation and cooperation from the parents – and to some degree, from the child. Equality takes priority over predictability as a central value.

V. Transportation of Children

In 2007 a provision concerning the division of transportation costs and responsibility was introduced as part of the new Act on Parental Responsibility. It is part of the regulation of contact. It stipulates that:
»*The **Statsforvaltning** may take a decision about transportation of the child in connection with contact and may divide the costs.*«[18]

The provision is part of the development towards equality between the parents. Earlier the non-resident parent was responsible for the transportation while the new act holds both parents equally responsible. Another new provision holds both parents responsible for the contact arrangement.[19] These two new provisions have resulted in a new practice; the main rule is that the non-resident parent is responsible for picking up the child – and pay the expenses – while the parent with care is responsible for the child's return and the expenses incurred. An exception can be made if the incomes of the parents differ considerably. At the same time a new

---

18 Forældreansvarsloven § 21, stk. 3.
19 Forældreansvarsloven § 19.

provision was introduced in welfare law administered by the municipalities, providing that both parents may apply for financial support to cover transportation expenses. Before then, only the non-resident parent was responsible for all transportation costs and only he/she could apply for financial support.

The new provision is to be understood in the light of the aim: To motivate parents to co-operate. The guidelines to the Act on Parental Responsibility state that:[20]

> »It is the purpose, that this will contribute to parents' sticking to their responsibility of making contact work, and make parents consider whether contact will work out in case of relocation.«

Four pages of guidelines follow and a yearly regulation of the amount deciding whether or not a parent's income is to be considered low. Relocation may have the consequence that the parent who moves to a more distant location will have to pay more than an equal share of the costs. [21]

The regulation illustrates how the political efforts of creating equality between parents are carried out through an optic of parents as co-operating. The aim of the regulation is not to hold the parents responsible for half of the transportation – but to give them an equal position in their efforts of making their own private arrangements. The regulation also explicitly relies upon the powers of the parents' freedom – aiming at making them co-operate thus implementing equality as far as possible. This is not a regulation based on the power of enforceable law only. The regulation bears the values of equality, freedom and democracy (understood as negotiation and co-operation) which are thus values favoured by the legislature.

On the contrary, the regulation of child maintenance is not based on equality. The regulation of decisions on transportation in relation to contact compared to the child maintenance regime is not typical. According to the latter the disbursements of the parents are of no relevance except from the non-resident parent's disbursements to his other children. Therefore the focus on costs of transportation differs from the general lack of interest of the maintenance system in what type of costs the parents may have. This is the first attempt in the Act on Parental Responsibi-

---

20 Vejledning nr. 9860 af 06/09/2007 samværsvejledning afsnit 6.1.
21 From case law, see TFA 2008.497. The mother and the child moved to the Faroes and the mother was obliged to pay 2/3 of the costs for the child's contact with his father in Denmark.

lity to explicitly bring the parents' finances forward, making the parents co-operate. Thus, the costs of transportation are part of the equality and co-operation ratio while other costs are part of the standardization ratio – with respectively a close and a distant approach to the family.

VI. Concluding Remarks

The individualization of family law involves the upcoming of a new kind of risk to the family which is the burden of procedures. We argue that this has not been given proper attention in Danish family law or in the Court's case law. Rather the opposite is true – it has been given a positive validation. We find it unfair and inhuman that primary caretakers who need protection from their conflicts with the other parent are met by a mode of regulation that aims at producing co-operating parents. Therefore, we are critical to the new provision on transportation and the embodied values. We prefer family conflicts to be better framed by substantive law as the Danish regulation of child maintenance instead of a regulation which distribute the burden of procedures to the most vulnerable part of primary caretakers – in the name of freedom, equality and democracy.

Mamma Mia! The Never Ending Story of the Economic Support of the Adult Child in Italy

Salvatore Casabona[1]

I. Introduction

A famous song of an Italian singer says: you want to do like Americans, but who gives you the money to buy Camel cigarettes? You take it from your mother's purse!

The state of art of adult children in Italy is something hybrid between the desire to protect at all costs individuals and, on the opposite side, the necessity to cut the umbilical cord with the family of origin.

Rereading M. Planiol,[2] a leading commentator of Code Napoleon, and in particular his observation towards the article 203, he stated in 1900 that rearing a child is above all to educate it to all events, giving it primary education as the lack of it means that a man is poorly prepared to earn a living in modern society.

So it is fundamental in our modern society of XXIth century of mass media, ever new technologies, melting pot cultures and hyper specialist know-how to wonder what would be a primary education that prepares a person to earn a living and what should be the extension (temporal and material) of the parental duty of educational and financial support.

Crisis of Italian labour market, the higher level of specialization required, difficulties in finding a job not only push young people to more advanced studies than postsecondary school but also constitute a practical conditioning in their free choices and life autonomy; so even if young people are intellectually mature and ready for a job, nevertheless too often they are not able – for economic reasons – to leave their own families.

Today, most western societies have imposed a duty to maintain one's minor children – whether legitimate or illegitimate – until he or she is full

---

[1] Faculty of Political Science - Palermo, Italy.
[2] M. PLANIOL, *Traité élémentaire de droit civil : conforme au programme officiel*, 1900–1901, no. 1680, Paris.

of age; this duty is laid down in statutes or civil codes and it is enforceable by a parent, the state or, in certain circumstances by the child. Nevertheless the increased importance of postsecondary education – associated by an increase in its costs – in preparing persons to earn a living results today self evident, but the students who attend advanced education are quite often over eighteen years of age and thus beyond the statutory major age in most jurisdictions.

Although parents generally assist their children who attend the post secondary school, children from families who have suffered a marital dissolution are less likely to receive assistance with educational expenses from their parents. So the question is: Does there exist a specific obligation upon parents to pay the expenses for and advanced education of a young adult child[3] or not? Does there exist a specific parents' obligation to maintain their children, even independently from educational needs or not?

Let me face these questions dividing the answer in three parts: the regulation's profile of the problem; the judicial process of interpretation or better the creation of the rules; some conclusions about what in my opinion is the meaning and the consequences of Italian legal and judicial perspective.

II. The Italian Statutory Law

The answer offered by Italian statutory law represents a good expression of a peculiar widespread mentality and of a legal framework oriented to the protection of a crucial role and social functions of familial institution. Let's pay attention on art. 30 § 1 of the Italian Constitution:

>*»(1) It is the duty and right of parents to support, instruct and educate their children, including those born out of wedlock«.*

Furthermore I'd like to point out Art 147 of the It. Civil Code:

>*»The state of matrimony requires from both the husband and wife the duty of supporting, raising and educating their children, keeping in mind their natural abilities, their inclination and aspirations.«*[4]

---

3 For a comparative perspective, see A. QUADRUCCI, *Il diritto al mantenimento del figlio maggiorenne. Note di diritto comparato*, in Famiglia, 2003, n. 1.
4 See A. MIRANDA, *Scelte esistenziali ed educative dei minori in diritto inglese ed italiano*, in Rass. Dir. Civ., 1986, n. 4, pp. 1022 ss.

The above mentioned legal duty is independent from the persistence of parental responsibility (»potestà genitoriale«)[5] in the sense that, once it ceases with major age or with the emancipation of the child (art. 316 It. Civil Code),[6] duty to educate and maintain does not terminate, resting upon parents, if the child is not yet economically independent.

The spouses must fulfil this obligation in proportion to their respective means and according to their trade or household working ability. When the parents do not have sufficient means, the other legitimate or natural ascendants, in order of proximity, are bound to supply to the parents the means necessary in order that they may fulfil their duties towards the children.[7]

The situation towards children does not change with the divorce, so that the parent the child lives with has the right to economic contribution and support by the divorced husband/wife.[8]

---

5   M. ALLARA, *Le nozioni fondamentali del diritto civile*, Torino, 1958 p. 431; F.D. BUSNELLI, Intervento in *Questioni di diritto di famiglia* (atti dell‹incontro tenuto a Camerino il 24-25 aprile 1976), Napoli, 1976, p. 85; A. GIARDINA, *I rapporti personali tra genitori e figli alla luce del nuovo diritto di famiglia*, in Riv. trim. dir. e proc. civ., 1977, p. 1375; N. SCANNICCHIO, Leggi civ. comm., 1987, 116. Dissenting opinion in A.C. PELOSI, *La patria potestà*, Milano, 1965, cap. VI, 27; N. PONTICELLI, *L'assegno di mantenimento tra indipendenza economica e principio di indipendenza economico-professionale*, in Giust. Civ., 2003, p. 1. In the case of divorce art. 155 It. Civil Code, § 2, stated that: »(...) the judge ruling on the separation of the parents adopts the decisions pertaining to the children for their exclusive material and moral interest. The judge evaluates the possibility for the minors to be given in custody to both parents or identifies the parent to whom the children are to be given in custody, determines the time and modalities for their stay with each parent, and also fixes the amount and modalities pursuant to which each parent must contribute to the support, care, instruction and education of the children (...)«, § 3: »parental authority is exercised by both parents. The decisions of major interest for the children on instruction, education and health are taken in agreement between the parents, keeping into account the capacities, the natural inclination and the aspirations of the children«; finally art. 6, L. n. 898/70 states that the duties ex art. 147 rest upon the parents also if they remarry and the measure and modalities of this obligations is established by the judge.
6   Following art. 390 It. Civil Code the only form of emancipation is possible when a children older than sixteen years get married with the authorization of the Court.
7   Art. 148 It. Civ. Code, § 1: »The spouses must fulfil the obligation contemplated in the preceding article in proportion to their respective means and according to their trade or household working ability. When the parents do not have sufficient means, the other legitimate or natural ascendants, in order of proximity, are bound to supply to the parents the means necessary in order that they may fulfil their duties to the children«
8   Art. 155 - quinquies It. Civ. Code: »The judge, evaluating the facts, may order in favor of the children of major age not being economically independent, the payment of a periodic amount (...)«.

Turning on the concrete situation in which the adult child could be, it is possible to distinguish two main hypotheses: 1. the child, not economically independent, has not finished his education yet, and he/she is attending to postsecondary school or to university; 2. the child finished own education, but he/she has not sufficient means to live on her own as well.

III. The Judiciary

Judiciary equates the adult children not yet economically independent, with the minor children, imposing on the parents a specific duty to maintain and consequently a duty to bear the expenses of education: in this case, judges have held that the importance given to the welfare and necessities of offspring justifies the temporal extension of parental support duty even longer than the studying period: then duty of maintenance does not finish but changes, becoming duty of alimony (regulated by art. 433 at seq.).[9]

The surviving of child support is nevertheless conditioned by the absence of the child's »fault« in not taking advantages of the opportunities offered by the family or by the lack of a negligent behaviour in looking for a job or in refusing it without a »reasonable cause«.

However the formulas »fault« or »reasonable cause« are open to a various and not always uniform judicial interpretation.

It was recently held – for example – that a twenty-five years old daughter who passed only half of her examinations at university and who is not yet economically independent has no »fault« (and was consequently entitled to ask her parents the university expenses) considering the ordinary amount of time needed for a middle minded student to have a degree in biology in Italy.[10]

It's similar with the choice of a twenty-nine years old son of middle upper class with a degree in law and LLM in USA to refuse several jobs for continuing his post university education. It was considered »reasonable« and in line with his social status, personal inclination and economic expectations.[11]

---

9 Corte Cass. 28 June 1994 n. 6215; Corte Cass. 02 July 1990 n. 6774; Corte Cass. 05 June 1990 n. 5384.
10 Corte Cass. 07 April 2006, n. 8221.
11 Corte Cass. 3 April 2002 n. 4765 see the comment of M. D'AURIA, *Ancora sulla durata dell'obbligo di mantenimento dei figli ai sensi dell'art. 147 c.c. La «colpa» del figlio maggio-*

On the contrary, in an other case the Court of Cassazione held, that an adult daughter, partially invalid and not yet disposing of a degree, who had refused her father's concrete work proposals (working in a shop), could not request the maintenance of her parents on the ground that the job proposed was not in line with her aspiration, attitudes and studies (physiotherapy.)[12]

In the same direction, it was held that a child who had a degree in law, a LLM in USA and who was admitted to the New York State bar, lost the right to be maintained because he was already able and ready to work, to earn a living, and consequently to maintain himself.[13]

It is evident from the above mentioned cases, that the discretionary power of the judges plays a decisive role in deciding whether the conditions to obtain financial support from parents are fulfilled: valuation of ontological characteristics of adult child (natural abilities, inclination and aspirations); consideration of his behaviour (indolence or reasonable justification behind his incapacity in sustaining himself?);[14] interpretation of external context (like family financial capabilities; social context in which the adult child grew up, state of labour market in a certain place and in a certain moment).[15]

---

renne e l'assenza dalle aule giudiziarie dell'art. 315 c.c. Riflessi in materia di onere della prova, in Giur. It., 2003, p. 45.

12 Corte Cass. 06 November 2006, n. 23673.
13 Corte Cass. 03 November 2006, n. 23596.
14 Corte Cass. 21 February 2007, n. 4102; Corte Cass. 19 January 2007, n. 1146 Corte Cass 18 January 2005 n. 951; Corte Cass. 02 December 2005, n. 26259; Corte Cass. 3 April 2002, n. 4765; Corte Cass. 28 June 1994 n. 6215; Corte Cass. 11 December 1992 n. 13126; Corte Cass. 3 July 1991 n. 7295; Corte Cass. 29 December 1990 n. 12212; Corte Cass. 10 April 1987 n. 3570; Corte Cass. 19 March 1984 n. 1862; Corte Cass. 2 September 1996 n. 7990; Corte Cass. 11 December 1992 n. 13126; Corte Cass. 3 July 1991 n. 7295; Corte Cass. 29 December 1990 n. 12212; Corte Cass. 26 January 1990 n. 475; Corte Cass. 10 April 1985 n. 2372; Corte Cass. 19 March 1984 n. 1862; Corte Cass. 7 November 1981 n. 5874; Corte. Cass. 25 May 1981 n. 3416; Trib. Palermo 21 October 1989.
15 Corte Cass. 7 July 2004, n. 12477; Corte Cass. 25 July 2002 n. 10898; Corte Cass. 18 February 1999 n. 1353; Corte Cass. 4 April 1998 n. 2392; Corte Cass. 7 May 1998 n. 4616; Corte Cass. 27 November 1996 n. 10538; Corte Cass. 2 September 1996 n. 7990; Corte Cass. 28 June 1994 n. 6215; Corte Cass. 11 December 1992 n. 13126; Corte Cass. 3 July 1991 n. 7295; Corte Cass. 29 December 1990 n. 12212; Corte Cass. 26 January 1990 n. 475; Corte Cass. 28 June 1988 n. 4373; Corte Cass. 10 April 1987 n. 3570; Corte Cass. 19 March 1984 n. 1862; Corte Cass. 28 January 1974 n. 215; Trib. Genova 9 December 1998; Trib. Orvieto 16 November 1994 n. 241; Trib. Messina 9 September 1984; Trib Genova 2 December 1980.
On this point see in litterature: O. FITTIPALDI, *Figli maggiorenni di coppie divorziate: addio tentazioni da »mantenuti a vita«*, in D&G, 2005, n. 6; S. MORELLO, *I rapporti perso-*

IV. Conclusion

In conclusion, in family law, the distance from the law in books and the law in action[16] is evident: the characteristics of simplicity, uniformity and predictability of statute rules (good for commercial and tort relationship) do not always correspond with domestic relations that are heavily diversified, highly mutable and unforeseeable in long period.[17]

Furthermore, in family law matters, the dialog between legal rule and moral rule does result particularly complex, as pointed out the

»*translation of even clear moral obligations into legal rules does not always follow, however, and the link between moral discourse and legal regulation is specially complex in family law.*«[18]

---

nali tra genitori e figli, in Dir. Famiglia, 2003, n. 3, p. 791; F. TESCIONE, *Mantenimento ed »automantenimento« dei figli maggiorenni: una linea di confine in continuo mantenimento*, in Dir. Famiglia, 2003, n. 2; A. DE CUPIS, *Brevi osservazioni sulla durata dell'obbligo di mantenimento del figlio maggiorenne*, in Scritti in memoria di Giuffrè, II, Milano; A. NATUCCI, *Mantenimento del figlio maggiorenne*, in L'autonomia dei minori tra famiglia e società, Milano, 1980, 414; L. FERRI, *Diritto al mantenimento e doveri dei figli*, in Dir. fam., 1983, 357; M. DOGLIOTTI, *Diritto del figlio maggiorenne al mantenimento e obblighi del genitore, in applicazione dei principi costituzionali*, in Giur. mer., 1976, I, 200; M. BESSONE, *Diritto al mantenimento del figlio maggiorenne e direttive dell'art. 30, comma 1, Cost.*, in Giur. it., 1975, I, 2, 621; G. STELLA RICHTER, A. SGROI, *Delle persone e della famiglia*, in Commentario del codice civile, Torino, 1967, 604; G. FERRANDO, *Principi costituzionali e diritto al mantenimento del figlio maggiorenne*, in Dir. fam., 1977, 626; M. FINOCCHIARO, *L'obbligo di mantenimento della prole non può essere illimitato*, in Guida dir., 2002, n. 17, 38; W. RIEDWEG, *Mantenimento del figlio maggiorenne non economicamente autosufficiente*, in Fam. e dir., 1997, 62; L. CAVALLO, *Sull'obbligo del mantenimento del figlio di genitore divorziato e sulla relativa cessazione*, in Giust. civ., 1991, I, 3036; G. CERCEO, *Il dovere dei genitori di mantenere i figli non cessa quando essi raggiungono la maggiore età*, in Giur. mer., 1981, 624; A. FALZEA, *Il dovere di contribuzione nel regime patrimoniale della famiglia*, in Riv. dir. civ., 1977, 609.

16 R. POUND, *Law in books and law in action*, in Am. L. Rev., 1910, n. 44, p. 12
17 Generally speaking, about the restricted role which legislation has played in developing law in the western law, A. WATSON, writes in *Legal evolution and legislation*, in BYU L. Rev., 1987, p. 379: »Several factors contribute to this phenomenon: once enacted, legislation is slow to be repealed even though it outlives its usefulness; there are several fields in which legislation could drastically change the structure of law but in which lawmakers are not interested in legislating; legislation has generally lacked the continuity of any particular political, social or economic message; and legislators often reject what would be revolutionary proposals. Thus, though legislation potentially can be most radical mode of changing law, and though it does at times make radical, even revolutionary, changes in law, the history of legislation's role in western world demonstrates its failure to live up to that potential«.
18 L. E. TEITELBAUM, *Intergenerational responsibility and family obligation: on sharing*, in Utah L. Rev., 1992, p. 785.

Statutes do not represent the entire law, nor do the judicial decisions, nor the definitions of legal doctrines given by scholars.

The Italian legal framework and the judicial tracks about the adult children's right to be maintained reveal a silent trend to pass on the difficulties of labour market on families that consequently become a sort of social shock-absorber.

The obvious risk is that the »adult child«, scared by hardness of life, could decide to comply with the child's definition seeking the protection of more and more tired (and older) parents.

Child in a Single (Absent) Parent Family: Maintenance and Family Home

Gordana Kovaček-Stanić[1]

I. Introduction

Family law financially protects the child in a single (absent) parent family using different legal measures. The absent parent is under the obligation to take care of the child by paying the child maintenance. In contemporary family law systems the institution of family home gains importance. Housing needs of the child and stability of housing are important factors in deciding on the rights to reside in family home. The children are particularly vulnerable in the course of divorce or during separation of their parents. One of the factors which might help them to overcome this stressful situation is staying in a family home and retaining the same social environment.

In Serbian law the parental rights and obligations depend more on the fact if the parents live with the child or not, then on the marital status of the parents (divorced, separated, never married). If parents do not live together there are two different types of the exercise of parental rights: joint and sole (independent, autonomous) parental rights. Parents exercise parental rights jointly and consensually when they do not cohabitate, if they conclude an agreement on joint exercise of parental rights, and if the court finds that this agreement is in the best interest of the child, (Art 75/2 Serbian Family Act 2005).[2] The type of the exercise of the parental rights influences the parental maintenance obligation. If parents exercise parental rights jointly they consensually decide on the child maintenance. If one of them exercises parental rights autonomously, then parents are entitled to make an agreement, or if not, the court will decide on child maintenance.

---

1 Faculty of Law, University of Novi Sad, Serbia.
2 The Serbian Family Act was adopted by the National Assembly on 17 February 2005 and entered into force eight days after publishing, but its implementation began on 1 July 2005, hereinafter referred as FA, *Official Journal of the Republic of Serbia* 18/2005. The draft of the Family Act was prepared by a drafting committee with Professor Marija Draškić as the coordinator, and myself as one of the members of this committee.

In recent years the number of minors affected by their parents' divorce in Serbia was: in 2004 – 5,000; in 2006 – 4,300. In 2006 77 % of minor children were entrusted to their mother's care, 18 % to their father's care. The divorce rate was in 2004 – 1.2 per 1,000 inhabitants; in 2005 – 1 per 1,000 inhabitants; or in 2004 – 210 per 1,000 marriages; in 2005 – 197 per 1,000 marriages (which means every fifth marriage was divorced). In 2005 22,5 % children were born outside the marriage (about 16,000).[3] There is no official statistical data of the number on children born outside the wedlock who live (or not) with both parents (if parents cohabitate). Thus, it is questionable how many children born outside the marriage are entitled to child maintenance from the non-residential parent.

II. Child's Maintenance

1. Who is Entitled to Child's Maintenance

The minor child has a right to maintenance from his/her parents, (Art 154/1 FA). The age of maturity is 18 years in Serbian law. If the minor child has income or his/her own property, there is a duty to partially provide for the needs of his/her maintenance, but this obligation is subsidiary to the duty of his/her parents, (Art 154/3 FA). As the child at the age of fifteen gains the right to work, he/she could earn wages. The child is entitled to work with the written consent of the parents, adopter or guardian, if such employment will not endanger the health, morals or education of the child, or if the employment is not otherwise prohibited by law (Arts 24/1, 25/1 Labour Act).[4]

Besides a minor child, the adult child is also entitled to maintenance in certain situations (Art 155 FA). First is the situation when an adult child is incapable to work and lacks sufficient means of maintenance. The adult child is then entitled to maintenance from his/her parents during this period. The second situation relates to education. An adult child who regularly attends school has the right to maintenance from his/her parents in proportion to the parents capacities, up until the age of twenty-six. However, unlike the maintenance of the minor child the FA provides for a protective clause regarding the maintenance of an adult child. The FA

---

3   *Annual Statistic of Republic of Serbia* 2006, pp 79, 90; *Annual Statistic of Republic of Serbia* 2007, pp 83, 94.
4   Labor Act 2005, *Official Journal of the Republic of Serbia* No. 24/2005.

provides that an adult child does not have the right to maintenance if the acceptance of his/her request for maintenance would represent a clear injustice to the parents. It is an issue for judicial discretion to define clear injustice in each particular situation.

In the Supreme Court of Serbia judgment from December 11, 2007 (No Rev. 3216/07) the Court was of the opinion that there is no clear injustice in this case.[5] The son who is a student at the University of Belgrade younger than 26 years claimed for a maintenance from his father. The father is 100% disabled and fully deprived of legal capacity. During the proceedings the court examined the income of the father, his needs, the son`s income and needs and finally determine 25% of father's income to be the maintenance amount. The father's legal representative objected to the son's claim to maintenance on the ground of clear injustice. The Supreme Court was of the opinion that the fact the father is 100% disabled and fully deprived of legal capacity did not affect his obligation to maintenance his son.

Croatian Family Act (amendments of 2007) extends the rights of an adult child to maintenance from his parents to situation of unemployment after the child finishes school.[6] The right to maintenance lasts for one year (Art 210/2). Besides, Croatian Family Act (amendments of 2007) specifies that regular schooling also exists in situation when a student due to justifiable reasons, such as illness or pregnancy, is not able to fulfill his/her obligation in current academic year (Art 210/5). These novelties improve the protection of an adult child. They seem to be acceptable for the Serbian law as well, since unemployment is a major problem in Serbian economy.

2. *Amount of the Maintenance:*
   Criteria and Manner for Determination

In Serbian system, maintenance is to be determined in accordance with the needs of the maintenance beneficiary and the capacities of the maintenance benefactor. The needs of the maintenance beneficiary depend on his/her age, health, education, property, income, and other circumstances that significantly contribute to the determination of the amount owed as maintenance (Art 160 FA). Child's needs cover the wide range of poten-

---

5   *Bilten sudske prakse* Okružnog suda u Novom Sadu 13, 2008. (Court practice bulletin of *District Court in Novi Sad*), pp 72–73.
6   Family Act, *Official Journal of the Republic of Croatia* »Narodne novine« 116/2003, 17/2004, 136/2004, 107/2007.

tial needs, starting form existential to educational, cultural and social needs. UN Convention on the Rights of the Child 1989, which Yugoslavia has ratified and is binding upon Serbia, stipulates that the child, among others, has a right to rest and leisure, to engage in play and recreational activities appropriate to the age of the child and to participate freely in cultural life and the arts (Art 31).[7]

The capacities of the maintenance benefactor depend on his/her income, the possibility to get employed and earn wages, his/her property, his/her personal needs, obligation to maintenance other persons and other circumstances that significantly contribute to the determination of maintenance.

The Family Act of Serbia 2005 stipulates a minimal amount of maintenance as a cut off point which the court should take into account while determining maintenance in each particular case. This sum is compensation for foster children under foster care which foster parents gain from the state, periodically determined by the ministry responsible for family protection, in accordance with law.

Another major innovation of the Serbian Family Act 2005 in the matters of child maintenance is the rule which states that the amount of child maintenance must enable the child to maintain at least the same standard of living as the parent – maintenance benefactor (Art 162/3 FA). This provision is accepted in order to prevent the situation in which parent–benefactor pays the amount of the maintenance much lower then his/her actual capacities are, as a consequence of impossibility of the beneficiary to prove benefactor's income and property. In a lot of cases impossibility of the beneficiary to prove benefactor's income and property is due to existing gray economy in Serbia.

In comparative law the level of the maintenance is defined as a sum depending on specific facts: the number of children-maintenance beneficiaries, the age of the children, etc. For instance, in Russia, the level of maintenance for children cannot be lower than the amount provided by law in terms of percentage of income and/or other revenue of the parents. For one child, this amount is one quarter, for two children it is one third, for three or more children it is half of the income and/or other revenue, (Art 81 Family Code 1995).

---

[7] Law on Ratification of the Convention on the Rights of the Child, *Official Journal of the Social Republic of Yugoslavia* 15/90.

Croatian Family Act (amendments of 2007) stipulates the minimum sum for monthly child maintenance in terms of percentage of average monthly salary in Croatia. This percentage is 17% for a child up to 6 years, 20% for a child from 7 to 12 years, 22% for a child from 13 to 18 years (Art 232/4). In a specific circumstances these percentages might be lower.

In Germany the Child Maintenance Act 1998
»*sets out two means of calculating maintenance for all children: First, individually calculated maintenance in terms of par. 1610 I, II, BGB, and, secondly, set maintenance under par. 1612a BGB a.a. which minors can claim from parents not living in the same household as them. Set maintenance is a maintenance payment reflecting the age of the child and calculated from the average of what parent is able to pay and the average of what the child's needs. It is set out in a statutory order of the federal government.*«[8]

Recently (2007),
»*the Bill makes provision for a statutory definition of the minimum amount of child maintenance by applying the tax-free allowance for minor children to the revised s 1612a.*«[9]

In Serbian law maintenance is generally determined as pecuniary obligation; may also be determined in other terms, but only if the maintenance benefactor and beneficiary so agree (Art 161 FA). The later could be, for example, if a benefactor produces or trades goods which the child needs.

The maintenance beneficiary may, at his/her own choice, request that the amount of maintenance be determined as a fixed monthly amount of money or as a percentage of the regular monthly pecuniary income of the maintenance benefactor. If the amount of maintenance is determined as a percentage of the regular monthly pecuniary income of the maintenance benefactor (salary, compensation of salary, pension, royalties), the amount of maintenance, generally, may be no less than 15% and no more than 50% of the regular monthly pecuniary income of the maintenance

---

8   Rainer Frank, Parentage Law Reformed, *The International Survey of Family Law*, A. Bainham (ed.), 1997, p 174.
9   Kathrin Kroll, The Reform of German Maintenance Law, *The International Survey of Family Law*, B. Atkin (ed.), 2007, p 91, Nina Dethloff, Kathrin Kroll, Strengthening Children's Rights in German Family Law, *The International Survey of Family Law*, B. Atkin (ed.), 2008, p 121.

benefactor, less the amount of taxes and contributions to compulsory social insurance (Art 162 FA). The possibility to constitute the amount of the maintenance in percentage was introduced in Serbian law in 1993, in the time of hyperinflation, as fixed sum was loosing its value on the daily basis.[10]

3. Other Legal Mechanisms

The agreement between parents on child maintenance is another legal mechanism which helps exercising the right of the child to maintenance. FA favours parental agreements regarding parent-child relations, consequently also regarding maintenance. In the situation of divorce by mutual consent spouses are obliged to provide a written divorce agreement, which governs the exercise of parental rights and a written agreement on the division of joint property. The agreement on the exercise of parental rights may be in the form of an agreement on joint exercise of parental rights or an agreement on independent exercise of parental rights (Art 40 FA). The agreement on independent exercise of parental rights includes an agreement on child's maintenance. In the divorce by an action (if the marriage relations are seriously and permanently disturbed or if the cohabitation of the spouses cannot be objectively realized), during the mediation procedure, in the settlement phase the court or institution implementing the mediation procedure is to endeavor that the spouses reach an agreement on the exercise of parental rights and an agreement on the division of joint property (Art 241 FA).

Another legal mechanism which helps in exercising the right of the child to maintenance regards proceedings on maintenance. An action for the maintenance of a child may also be initiated by the guardianship authority (Art 278/3 FA). The guardianship authority is the body which performs family protection, family aid and guardianship. The guardianship authority is authorized to initiate the maintenance proceedings in order to protect the child, per instance in the situation when the parent is not doing so. Procedure is always particularly urgent. The first hearing is to be scheduled within eight days from the filing of the action to the court, while the second instance court is obliged to render a decision within fifteen days following the day the appeal was delivered to court, (Art. 280 FA). Besides, there is a rule which states that the court is not

---

[10] Article 310a and 310b Law on Marriage and Family Relations, *Official Journal of Republic of Serbia* 22/93, 25/93, 35/94.

bound by the claim for maintenance, meaning the court is authorized to make a decision on child maintenance which is different from the claim (Art 281 FA).

The maintenance payment is privileged according to the Serbian Act on Execution Procedure 2004.[11] Such payment is one of the first to be paid if real property is sold in execution procedure, just after execution procedure costs (Art 140).

An important question regarding child maintenance is in what period the child is entitled to maintenance from the absent parent. The dominant view in Serbian law and theory is that the right to maintenance payment exists for the period after the claim for maintenance is submitted to the court. It is not possible to claim maintenance retroactively. On the other hand, according to the Amendments on Croatian Family Act (amendments of 2007), the parent who had an obligation to pay for the maintenance to the child not living with him/her and who failed to do so, is obligated to pay the reimbursement to the child retroactively from the moment the obligation came into existence until the claim for the maintenance is submitted. If the claim is not submitted within five years after the obligation has entered into force, the claim is precluded by statutes of limitation (Art 209/2,3).

In Serbian family law a child's right to maintenance has priority, if there is more than one maintenance beneficiary (Art 166/4 FA). It is similar in comparative law perspective. For instance, in Germany the 2007 Bill introduces changes to the priority system.

»The claims of minor children as well as those of adult children – if unmarried, not yet 21 years old, still living with their parents and attending school – ranked first.«[12]

In other fields of law, inheritance and criminal law, the right to maintenance is also protected. In the Serbian Inheritance Act 1995 is stipulated that the heir looses the right to inherit if he/she has severely violated his/her maintenance obligation towards the deceased (Art 4/1–4). According to Serbian Criminal Code 2005, the failure to pay for the child maintenance is a criminal offense (Art 195).[13]

---

11 Act on Execution Procedure, *Official Journal of the Republic of Serbia* 125/2004.
12 Dethloff, Kroll op. cit. 2008, p 129.
13 Inheritance Act 1995, *Official Journal of the Republic of Serbia* No. 46/1995; Criminal Code *Official Journal of the Republic of Serbia* 85/2005 (the penalty could be fine or imprisonment from three months to three years).

III. Family Home

1. Serbian Law

In Serbia, the habitation is regulated by the Housing Act 1992. However, the previously adopted law, the Habitation Act 1990, amended the habitation regime.[14] This law provided a possibility to purchase an apartment that was socially owned, and therefore the housing right was substituted by the ownership title on the apartment. (The regime of housing right on the socially owned apartment, which was predominant until 1990 paid a respect to the family needs since these were one of the preconditions to determine who was going to be awarded the right of housing.) The Housing Act does not regulate any special right to family home in the situation of termination of marriage. Thus, the spouse who lives with the children can find himself in an inconvenient situation, when the apartment is the property of the other spouse or when both parents are the owners of the apartment but the apartment is not big enough to satisfy the needs of the parents and children, neither by sale or by the division of the apartment. After 1990 a right to a permanent lease has substituted the right of housing on the socially owned apartment. The provisions concerning the lease do offer sufficient protection to a family. It has been prescribed that after a divorce, the spouses may agree on the issue who is going to continue to use the apartment in the capacity of the lessee, and if they do not reach an agreement, the court is to decide in a non-contentious procedure. The court shall take into consideration the following criteria when rendering a decision: housing needs of the divorced spouses and their children, who of the spouses is the apartment lessee, financial and health condition of the spouses, etc. (Art 35/4).

The Serbian Family Act 2005 has regulated for the first time the right to reside (*habitatio*), in favour of a minor child and a parent who exercises the parental right. The minor child and a parent who exercises the parental right have the right to reside in the apartment owned by the other parent, provided that they do not possess a vacant apartment and provided that such a decision would not constitute a clear injustice for the parent who is the owner of the apartment, (Art 194 FA). The reason for drafting such a provision is an obligation to provide the child with such a protection and care, which is necessary for his or her welfare (Art 3 par 2 of the Convention on the Rights of the Child).

---

14 Habitation Act, *Official Journal of the Republic of Serbia*, no 50/92; Habitation Act, *Official Journal of the Republic of Serbia*, no 12/90.

The aim of the provision concerning the right to reside is to solve an inconvenient habitation situation in which the child and parent who exercises the parental right may come, especially after a divorce. In a discussion before the Serbian Parliament, at the time when this law was on the agenda, there was an objection to this solution, stating that it was constitutionally unacceptable being a limitation of the ownership right. However, on one hand, the law recognizes other cases of the limitation of ownership, and on the other hand if we analyze the solutions that exist in the comparative law, we may conclude that the family home has a specific legal regime in many foreign legal systems. That relates especially to the capitalist countries, in which the ownership is untouchable legal concept, one may say.

In one decision concerning the right to reside the Supreme Court of Serbia reviewed a decision of the lower court according to which it would be unjust to the defendant to constitute the right to reside in favour of his minor child, and reversed the decision as wrongful. The fact that the apartment was a gift to the defendant from his mother does not constitute ground for the implementation the legal standard »clear injustice«. Legal standard »clear injustice« does not concern how ownership right is constituted, but rather the entire situation of the defendant. It would be clearly unjust if the right to reside would be constituted. This would concern his health, social status, or other circumstances which he could not improve by his own actions. The fact that the defendant was psychologist with a full time job, and other circumstances in this case did not indicate the existence of the clear injustice to the defendant.[15]

2. Comparative Review

In the comparative perspective there are diverse legal grounds to constitute rights of the child to reside in family home. For instance, in England it is possible to decide the home to be held on trust for sale in equal shares of the parents, with sale postponed until the children of the family reach a certain age (the »Mesher order«), the other decision might be the outright transfer in the home to the custodial parent, etc.[16]

---

15 Decision of the Supreme Court of Serbia Rev. 1594/06 from November 29, 2006, *Bilten sudske prakse Vrhovnog suda Srbije* 06/4 (*Bulletin of Court Practice of Supreme Court of Serbia*).

16 John Dewar, *Law and the Family,* Butterworths, London, Dublin, Edinburgh, 1992, pp 329–333.

In France if one of the spouses is the owner of the matrimonial home, after the divorce the court can establish the lease in favour of the other ex spouse. This happens when one of the parents exercises the parental authority, or if the parents jointly exercise the parental authority, and one or more children have the residence in the family home.[17]

In Italy matrimonial home is preferably assigned to the spouse who takes care of the children. This is also the case in the regime of separate property, regardless of the fact who is the owner of the house or an apartment. The house would remain to the spouse who takes care of the children until non-employed children live in the house.[18]

In Austria a marital home which was owned by one spouse before marriage, can form part of the property to be divided in the course of divorce, the need of a common child may be a valid reason to consider such property in the division procedure.[19]

In Switzerland the court has power to issue rules for the future use of the family home, on the basis of the situation of the family, especially the children, by way of right to residence fairly limited in time (presumably at the latest until the youngest child living with his mother attains 18).[20]

In Greece one of the spouses may be given exclusive use of the family home by court, if, for reason of equity, the special circumstances of the spouses and the interest of the children make it necessary, regardless of rights of ownership or possession.[21]

IV. Conclusion

Family law financially protects the child in a single (absent) parent family using different legal measures. The absent parent is under the obligation to take care of the child paying child maintenance.

---

17 Art. 281-1 Code Civile, L. no. 87-570 du 22. juill. 1987, Dalloz, 1986–87.
18 Roberta Ceschini, Asset Distribution in Italy on Marriage Breakdown, International Family Law 1999. 129, Marina Timoteo, Family Law in Italy, *Family Law in Europe*, London, Dublin, Edinburgh, Butterworths, 1995, pp 288–289.
19 Bea Verschraegen, Family Law Reforms in Austria from 1992 to 1999, *The International Survey of Family Law*, A. Bainham (ed.), 2001, p 42. The reform in 1999, the Law amending Marriage Law, Art 82, par 2 Eherechts-Änderungsgesetz BGB1, I 125/1999, p 35.
20 Oliver Guillod, A new Divorce Law for the New Millennium *The International Survey of Family Law*, A. Bainham (ed.), 2000 p 361, Article 121 Code Civile.b. Reform from 1998, Federal Act of June, 26 1998, reforming Civile Code, RO 1999 1118ff, p 357.
21 Efie Kounougeri-Manoledaki, Family Law in Italy, *Family Law in Europe*, London, Dublin, Edinburgh, Butterworths, 1995, p 208 Art 1393 Code Civile.

The major innovations of the Serbian Family Act 2005 in the matters of child maintenance is the rule which states the amount of child maintenance must enable the child to maintain at least the same standard of living as the parent – maintenance benefactor. The other innovation is introducing the legal standard »minimal amount of maintenance«, which is the amount of remuneration for foster children or persons in family placement. In comparative law the level of the maintenance is defined as a sum depending on specific fact: the number of children-maintenance beneficiaries, the age of the children, etc.

In Serbian law the agreement between parents on child maintenance is one of the legal mechanism which helps exercising the right of the child to maintenance. Another legal mechanism which helps in exercising the right of the child to maintenance regards proceedings on maintenance (an action for the maintenance of a child may also be initiated by the guardianship authority, the proceedings are particularly urgent, the court is not bound by the claim for maintenance). The maintenance payment is privileged in execution procedure: such payment is one of the first to be paid if real property is sold in execution procedure, just after execution procedure costs. Besides, a child's right to maintenance has priority, if there is more than one maintenance beneficiary. In other fields of law, inheritance and criminal law, right to maintenance is also protected (the heir looses the right to inherit if he/she has severely violated his/her maintenance obligation towards the deceased, failure to pay the maintenance is a criminal offence).

Housing needs of the child and stability of housing are important factors in deciding on the rights to reside in family home. The Serbian Family Act 2005 has regulated for the first time the right to reside (*habitatio*), in favour of a minor child and a parent who exercises the parental right. The minor child and a parent who exercises the parental right have the right to reside in the apartment owned by the other parent, provided that they do not possess a vacant apartment and provided that such a decision would not constitute an obvious injustice for the parent who is the owner of the apartment.

In the comparative perspective there are diverse legal grounds to constitute rights of the child to reside in family home: trust for sale in equal shares of the parents, with sale postponed until the children of the family reach a certain age or the outright transfer in the home to the custodial parent (England); the lease in favour to the other ex spouse, if one of the parents exercises the parental authority, or if the parents jointly exercise the parental authority, and one or more children have the residence in the family home (France); matrimonial home is preferably assigned to the spouse who takes care of the children, regardless of the fact who is the owner of the house or an apartment, until in the house live non-employed children (Italy); the need of a common child may be a valid reason to consider a marital home which was owned by one spouse before marriage as a property in the division procedure (Austria); the right to residence fairly limited in time, presumably at the latest until the youngest child living with his mother attains 18 (Switzerland); one of the spouses may be given exclusive use of the family home by court, if the special circumstances of the spouses and the interest of the children make it necessary, regardless of rights of ownership or possession (Greece).

The Maintenance of the Children: Alimony Fund as the Saving Grace?

Vesna Rijavec[1] and Suzana Kraljić[2]

I. Introduction

Maintenance is the legal duty of the parents and the legal right of the children. Already in the Constitution of the Republic of Slovenia[3] (CRS) the parents have legal obligation to maintain their children (article 54 sec. 1 CRS). As CRS, regarding the exact regulation of relations between parents and children, leaves the implementation of the to the law, we have to look for the provisions referring to maintenance of children in the Marriage and Family Relations Act (MFRA).[4] MFRA is the fundamental act defining maintenance, as it determines the persons entitled to maintenance and the persons obligated to provide such maintenance, as well as the conditions needed for the right to maintenance. In Slovenian law maintenance has the character of a strict personal right and duty, as it is not possible to transfer it to another person neither in time of living nor in case of death, i.e. by succession since by the death of the entitled or the obliged person this right or duty, respectively, ends.[5] The basic aim of maintenance is the benefit of the child. As in the case of neglecting the payment of maintenance by the obligated parent the benefit of the child may be endangered, in 1997 the Alimony Fund of the Republic of Slovenia (AF) was established. The fundamental purpose of AF is to at least partly lower the financial deficit met by the parent, where the child lives, and also the child, for whom the other parent does not pay determined or set maintenance.

---

1 Faculty of Law, University of Maribor, Slovenia.
2 Faculty of Law, University of Maribor, Slovenia.
3 Uradni list RS, št. 33I/1991-I; 42/1997; 66/2000; 24/2003; 69/2004; 69/2004; 69/2004; 68/2006.
4 Uradni list RS, št. 69/2004 (uradno prečiščeno besedilo ZZZDR – UPB 1).
5 Geč Korošec M./Kraljić S., Unterhalt nach dem Recht der Republik Slowenien, in: Schwab D./Henrich D., *Familiäre Solidarität, Die Begründung und die Grenzen der Unterhaltspflich unter Verwandten im europäischen Vergleich, Beiträge zum europäischen Familienrecht*, Verlag Ernst und Werner Gieseking, Bielefeld 1997, p. 200.

II. Main Origins of Children's Maintenance in Slovenia

The parents are obligated to maintain their children up to maturity (until the age of 18). In accordance with their capabilities and possibilities, the parents have to provide the child living conditions necessary for their development. If the child visits a regular education (even, if the child is inscribed in part-time studies), the parents are obligated to maintain the child after maturity, but up to the completed 26th year of age, maximally. If the child is younger than 18 years (but older than 15 years), and the child is visiting a regular education (up to 26 years of age) gets married or lives in cohabitation, the parents are obligated to maintain he/she only, if the child can not be maintained by the spouse or cohabitant (article 123 MFRA). If the parents were deprived from the parental right (this is the most radical reaching in the parental right), this parent is still obligated to pay maintenance (article 125 MFRA).

Maintenance is determined based on the needs of the entitled person and the material and financial capabilities of the obligated person (article 129 MFRA). In the determination of maintenance of the child, the court of justice has to respect the interest of the child, so that the maintenance is adequate for the guaranteeing of a successful physical and psychological development of the child. Maintenance has to encompass the costs of the child's necessities for living, especially the costs of residence, food, clothing, shoes, custody, education, upbringing, leisure time, entertainment and other needs of the child (article 129a MFRA).

The parents have the possibility to agree on the maintenance and then to propose to the court of justice to settle on such proposal in non-litigious proceeding. If the court of justice establishes that the proposal is not in line with the interests of the child, the proposal is rejected. Today, the competence for deciding on the maintenance of children has been transferred to the courts of justice, while in the past it was possible to conclude an agreement in front of the centre for social work. The parents can also conclude a settlement regarding maintenance of the children (article 412 sec. 2 Civil Procedural Act (CPA)).[6]

---

6 Uradni list RS, št. 73/2007 (uradno prečiščeno besedilo ZPP – UPB 3).

III. Statistical Date about the Children's Maintenance

In spite of the fact that the MFRA contains very clear provisions on the maintenance of children, in Slovenia many problems are met in practice.

Number of maintenances in classes regarding the amount of maintenance (status 10.4.2008[7])

Amount of maintenance in Euro	Number of maintenances
up to 20	435
from 20 to 40	2.028
from 40 to 60	5.390
from 60 to 80	10.040
from 80 to 120	20.873
from 120 to 200	16.280
from 200 to 400	3.683
over 400	217

Number and amount of the maintenance regarding the act, with which the maintenance was determined (status 10.4.2008[8])

Procedure with which the maintenance was determined	Number of maintenances	The amount of the maintenance		
		highest	lowest	average
The agreement concluded on the centre for social work	21.132	904,32	0,47	95,82
Judicial settlement	16.902	1.333,25	0,00	114,45
The judicial decision	20.210	1.358,59	0,01	126,41
Enforceable notarial deed	723	514,00	5,33	85,62
Together	58.967	Average		111,35

---

7 See www.mddsz.gov.si/si/statistika/prezivnine (12.9.2008).
8 See www.mddsz.gov.si/si/statistika/prezivnine (12.9.2008).

The average maintenance in Slovenia is approximately 111,35 Euros. In practice, we have 435 maintenances lower than 20. Here, it has to be stressed that such low amounts have been determined in the past, when the agreement on the maintenance still could be concluded in front of the centre for social work and there were no demands for an increase of maintenance. Today, as the court of justice decides on the amount of maintenance, it is impossible to settle legally on such a low amount since this would not be likely with the best interest of the child. Conclusions of agreements on maintenance in front of the centre for social work were not always appropriate since, no lawyers were usually present (smaller centers for social work frequently do not have any lawyer employed). In order to protect the interests of the child, a good knowledge of constitutional principles, acts, international conventions and last, but not least, morality, is necessary. The person concluding an agreement on maintenance frequently did not have an according legal knowledge.

We can positively establish that in comparison with 2006 the number of maintenance within the four highest classes has increased, while the number of maintenance in the four lowest classes has fallen (e.g. in 2006 there were 11.388 maintenances in the class from 120 to 200 Euros, while in 2008 there were already 16.280). Also the average amount of maintenance has increased. In 2006 it was around 80 Euros, in 2008 it is 111, 35.

Number of maintenances based on the age of the child (status 10.4.2008)[9]

Age of the child	Number of maintenances
up to 6 years	11.986
from 6 to 14 years	20.132
from 14 to 18 years	11.780
over 18 years (if regular education)	12.818

In the academic year 2006/2007, in Slovenia there were almost 116.000 students (compare with pupils in year 2007/8 167.168 pupils). This means that the students represent approximately 5, 7 % of the total population of Slovenia (in March 2008, 2.028.630 inhabitants lived in Slovenia). Since there are increasingly more students, the courts of justice are facing an

---

9 See www.mddsz.gov.si/si/statistika/prezivnine (12.9.2008).

increase in claims for maintenance after the age of 18. The determination of maintenance was made by the courts of justice in 12.818 cases, which means that 11,05 % students receive maintenance determined based on a ruling by the court of justice.

IV. Problems of Non-Paying the Maintenance

In Slovenia, based on unofficial data, in a third of the cases where maintenance of children is determined, there is a lack of paying or avoiding of payment of maintenance present. Lack of payment of maintenance means that the burden of maintenance is totally transferred to the parent, where the child lives. Since by the lack of payment of maintenance, the child is put in an essentially worse financial position and by this his/her interest is violated. The state tries to ease these consequences in founded cases a little bit. By replacing the maintenance, the state paying the maintenance via the AF helps children with a legal title (jurisdiction, settlement, agreement concluded in front of the centre for social work) giving them the right to maintenance, but not obtaining maintenance by the legally obligated person. The majority of debtors of maintenance are the fathers, who avoid the payment of maintenance in different ways:

1.) *Illegal labor:* since the debtors are not in a regular working status, their wages is not paid to them to their bank account, but »on the hand«. Therefore, the creditor (the child) can not claim execution from the income since they are not evident and the debtor formally does not have any;

2.) *Transfer of ownership:* the debtors transfer their ownership of his property (e.g. cars, house, real estate) to their parents, brothers, sisters, new partners. As result, they do not own personal property or real estates of larger value, from which the creditor (the child) can compensation;

3.) *Debtors change their employer:* every employer has the duty to send the conclusion on the execution to the new employer and to inform the court of justice on this, when the working relation of the debtor ends. Employers mainly ignore their obligation put on them by the conclusion on the execution. Mainly, this is the consequence on their negligence and the irregularity of the documentation, but it is also important that the court of justice which could sanction such an employer fails to do so.

4.) *Debtors change the residence, depart abroad:* RS has not yet coordinated its procedures with some countries, based on which the Ministry of Justice sent the proposal for execution to the other states. This is regulated only with the states of former Yugoslavia. For the enforcement of maintenance, the creditor should hire a lawyer abroad, who should create a proposal for execution and obtain data on the debtor's residence, on his employer, etc. Since the services of lawyers are very expensive, the creditors mainly do not seek to engage foreign lawyers for this purpose.[10]

V. The Alimony Fund

Alimony Fund of the Republic of Slovenia (AF) was established on 9.5.1997 based on the Guarantee and Alimony Fund of the Republic of Slovenia Act (GAFA),[11] and entered into force on 18.10.1999.

The basic activities of AF are directed towards the enforcement of the right to compensation of maintenance of children that were granted maintenance by a judgement, contemporary order or an agreement in front of the centre for social work, when the persons obligated to pay maintenance do not pay, and the execution of the debts from the legal representatives of the child. The basic aim set by the foundation of AF was to motivate the persons obligated to pay maintenance by free will, just by its existence. The non-payment of maintenance was, and today still is, a big problem in the RS.[12] Therefore, through the activities of AF, it is meant

---

10 Remarks on the Second Report of the Republic of Slovenia on the adopted measures for the realisation of the Children Rights Convention, June 2003, remarks were prepared by SEECRAN – South East European Child Rights Action Network in cooperation with non-governmental organisations, p. 33.
11 Uradni list (Official Gazette) RS, no. 78/2006 (officially cleansed text of ZPJS – UPB 2).
12 In Penal Code of the Republic of Slovenia (Uradni list RS, no. 55/2008) article 194 defines non-payment of maintenance as criminal act:
»*(1) Who does not pay maintenance to a person, who he or she has to maintain by law and the maintenance of whom is determined by an executable title, in spite of being capable, is to be punished with prison up to one year. (2) If, due to an act from the previous section, survival of the person entitled to maintenance is endangered or could be endangered, or if the criminal is avoiding to pay maintenance, he or she is to be punished with prison up to three years. (3) If the court of justice files a verdict on probation, it can burden the person, who committed an act from first of second section of this article, with the regular payment of maintenance, and it may order that the person has to pay the outstanding maintenance or other awarded obligations from maintenance.*«

to reach the consciousness that the right to maintenance is a fundamental right of the child that does not live with its parents.

AF helps children to enforce their right to receive compensation for maintenance by the help of their legal representatives and gives advice for the decisions on the execution of these rights. The persons obligated are motivated to pay maintenance or regulation of relations towards the child's legal representatives.

1. Pre-Conditions for the Reception of Compensation for Maintenance

GAFA determined the conditions that have to be fulfilled for the payment of compensation for maintenance. The basic guideline of AF are the benefits of the child that are neglected by the non-payment of maintenance, sometimes even to the minimum of existence from the point of the material pre-conditions. In order to prevent abuse, the conditions for the obtaining of the right to payment of compensation for maintenance are clearly determined.

1.1 Legal Base for Payment

The base for the payment of compensation for maintenance is given, when maintenance was determined by a valid judgement or contemporary order by the court of justice or an agreement in front of the centre for social work, respectively, and is not paid by the obligated person or is not regularly paid.[13]

1.2 Non-Payment of Maintenance

It is valid that the obligated person does not pay maintenance, if it is not paid within in three months in a row or if it is not paid regularly, respectively. This means that in the last twelve months, the obligated person owes at least three average monthly maintenances.

1.3 Citizenship or Permanent Residence

The person entitled to compensation for maintenance is only a child, who is a citizen of the RS and has a permanent residence in the RS.

13　More about enforcement titles see Rijavec V., Izvršilni naslovi, ki se lahko potrdijo kot EIN - postopek v izvorni državi, In: *Evropski pravni prostor in izvršba,* Maribor, 2006, p. 22; Rijavec V., Das internationale Zwangvollstreckungsrecht am Beispiel Sloweniens, *Evropski pravnik* 1/2007, p. 63-88.

1.4 Foreign Citizens

Also a child without citizenship of the RS, who is a foreign citizen, is entitled to compensation for maintenance, but it has to have permanent residence in the RS and a bilateral agreement between the states has to say so, or under the condition of reciprocity.

1.5 Limitation of Age

The right to compensation for maintenance lasts up to the completed age of 15 or 18, respectively, if the child does not enter a labour relation. The right to maintenance is proven by a confirmation on the enrolment into school that has to be presented by the entitled person at the beginning of the new school year. By this, an essential difference regarding the time aspect of entitlement to maintenance is given. Namely, MFRA determines that the parents, as a rule, are due to maintain their child up to the age of 18. This duty may be prolonged also above the limit of the child's age of 18, if the child is regularly visiting school. In this case, parents are due to maintain their child up to the end of studies or up to the age of 26, at the latest, respectively. Regarding the mentioned, children regularly visiting school after the age of 18 without receiving, or without regularly receiving maintenance that they are entitled to, are neglected.

1.6 Failure of Execution

For the actual payment of compensation for maintenance, another condition has to be fulfilled: execution has to fail or the proceeding of execution has to be unfinished, and since the application for execution, more than three months have to be passed.

1.7 Impediments

The act encompasses also impediments (negative pre-conditions) or names circumstances, respectively, when the child is not entitled to compensation for maintenance, in spite of the conditions mentioned above, i.e.
> a child living in a common household with the person obligated to maintenance;
> a child given to foster care;
> a child placed to an institution due to education, schooling or training, and care is mainly free of charge (article 21č GAFA).

2. Proceedings for the Obtaining of Compensation for Maintenance

Proceedings for compensation for maintenance begin based on an application. On the first level, AF decides upon the right to compensation for maintenance. Ministry of labour, family and social affairs decides about complaints against decisions by AF. In conflicts against decisions by the ministry, the Administrative Court of the Republic of Slovenia decides. The complaint against the decision, by which the ending of the right to compensation for maintenance was established, does not hold back the execution of the decision (article 22 GAFA).

3. Amount of Compensation for Maintenance

In the determination of compensation for maintenance the age of the child and the amount of maintenance determined by a valid judgement, contemporary order or agreement made in front of the centre for social work are respected. The amount of compensation for maintenance is adjusted to the living costs and at the moment amounts to:

Age of the child	Amount of compensation for maintenance
for a child up to the age of 6	66,88 Euro
for a child between the age of 6 and 14	73,57 Euro
for a child above the age of 14	86,94 Euro

When maintenance is lower than the legally determined compensation, the child is entitled to compensation for maintenance equal to the amount of the determined maintenance by the court of justice, contemporary order or agreement, respectively. Compensation for maintenance is not paid, if the amount of compensation for maintenance is lower than 8,35 Euros. It is paid, when common multi-monthly amount is exceeding this sum. The condition of age is fulfilled in the month, in which the child reaches a certain age. The child shall obtain the right to compensation for maintenance according to the law from the first day of the following month from the filing of the application. Compensation for maintenance is paid by AF to the legal representative of the child until the 15th of the month for the running month.

The limitation of age is one of the essential differences between maintenance and compensation for maintenance. The right to compensation for maintenance, namely, is limited until the age of 18, while the right to maintenance is prolonged over the age of 18, but until the age of 26 at the latest, provided that the child is visiting school regularly.

4. Ending of the Right to Compensation for Maintenance

Right to compensation for maintenance ends:
> based on the demand by the child's representative;
> based on the demand by the person obligated to maintenance, if he or she proves that all due maintenance was paid and that maintenance was paid for two months in advance or financial means have been deposited at the court of justice for the benefit of the child, or if duty of maintenance was taken over by a debtor of the obligated person;
> if the conditions for the right to compensation for maintenance are not fulfilled any more (article 21f GAFA).

5. Registers on Compensation for Maintenance

For the collection, processing, forwarding and use of personal data from the lists of personal data, the provisions of the act regulating protection of personal data are used, if no other act determines something different. AF leads a register on compensation for maintenance for the use of execution of AF's tasks and statistical or scientific purposes. Register on compensation for maintenance contains personal data on the child, legal representative and the obligated person:

> *register on the child contains:* personal name; birth data; unique citizen's register number; address of residence; locally competent centre for social work; citizenship; data on common household; amount of maintenance; employment; eventual foster care, placement into an institution; paid maintenance in the last year before the filing of the application according to months; paid maintenance in the time of recognition of the right to compensation for maintenance;
> *register on the legal representative* contains: personal name; unique citizen's register number; number of the bank account, savings account or non-resident account of a foreign citizen; address of residence, where the mail should be sent to.
> *register on the person obligated to maintenance* contains: personal name; birth data; unique citizen's register number; address of residence; citizenship; data on common household; employment; data on income and property (article 27č GAFA).

Data needed in the proceedings of acknowledgement of compensation for maintenance are obtained on the applicant, the children, the legal representative of who is the applicant and for who he or she is filing the applica-

tion and the person obliged to maintenance, directly from the applicant. The applicant may send only data on personal name, birth data, data on permanent or contemporary residence and employment on the person obligated to maintenance. Other data are obtained by AF. AF may obtain data from existing registers on personal data from the managers of:
> the ministry of internal affairs – data on common household from the central register of inhabitants, data on ownership of a motor vehicle, data on a status;
> the ministry of labour, family and social affairs and the centre for social work – data on the sending to foster care, on the amount of maintenance;
> the ministry of education, science and sports – data on a placement into a educational institution;
> the institution for pension and invalidity insurance of Slovenia – data on insured on the paid insurance, security upgrade and other;
> the institution for health insurance of Slovenia – data on insured, included into health insurance;
> the institution of the Republic of Slovenia for employment – data on paid compensations from the title of insurance for the case of unemployment, financial support, scholarships;
> the geodesic administration of the Republic of Slovenia – data on the amount of land register income;
> banks and savings banks – data on open bank accounts, running and other accounts;
> the Bank of Slovenia – on open bank accounts of the users;
> the Clearing depots stock company – data on ownership of shares;
> the bankruptcies or employers of debtors (article 27d GAFA).

6. Claims

A very important field of work of AF is the collection of claims from the obligated persons. Here we must stress, that the compensation isn't a new obligation of the person who is obligated to pay the maintenance. It is just the substitutional fulfilment of the obligation which have been determined, for example, by the judgement.[14]

AF collects also debts of the legal representatives who received means from AF without a base. AF independently leads proceedings of collection

---

14 I Up 269/2003 - Judgement of the Administrative Department of the Supreme Court of the Republic of Slovenia (13.1.2005).

against the obligated persons from the beginning of the existence and by the help of lawyers, who lead proceedings on behalf and on the account of AF. Such an organisation of leading of proceedings of collection demands a principle of economic handling of the AF means, as execution proceedings are connected to high costs. The number of cases with an involvement of lawyers is lowering from year to year. AF files most of the execution proposals and claims by the help of the employees of AF. Employees of AF quickly and effectively obtain data needed for a proposal for execution by investigations and proper connections with external institutions, as there are the central register on inhabitants, institution for health insurance of the Republic of Slovenia, the ministry of internal affairs, the Clearing depots stock company and others.

In spite of this, cooperation with lawyers is still needed in some cases. Filing of execution proposals against debtors is running in all the country. Besides this, a legal regulation is demanded by AF, after which certain actions may be taken as representatives in front of the court of justice exclusively by lawyers.

By judicial collection, the AF tries to reach at the obligated persons that they start to pay existing obligations, together with the activities of prior collection. It is mainly about activities before the beginning of judicial collection, where the informing of debtors on the state of debts belongs to, in order to make them conscious of their obligation and to make them start to pay their debts and maintenance.[15]

AF files executive proposals to the executive departments of the courts of justice in all the RS. Most of proceedings are very demanding and long lasting. The success of collection is strongly influenced by the fact that debtors of AF mostly are very difficult to be subject to enforcement, as they do not dispose of income or property. In 2005 AF succeeded to collect 24,7 % in comparison with payments in the same year.

On the day of the payment of compensation for maintenance, AF becomes creditor of the legal representatives in relation to the persons obligated to maintenance, and this up to the amount of paid compensation, increased by the calculated interest and costs of proceedings.[16] On 31.12.2005 AF showed claims against 3.173 debtors or persons obligated to maintenance, respectively.

---

15   Guarantee and Maintenance Fund of the Republic of Slovenia, Annual Report 2005, p. 23.
16   See also VS06447 – Judgement of the Civil Department of the Supreme Court of the Republic of Slovenia (7.2.2002).

About subrogation and entrance of AF into position of the child as creditor, the AF has to inform the person obligated to maintenance and present proper documents for proof of this to him or her. AF is liberated of payment of judicial taxes for payment of claims being transferred to it. Means obtained by the payment of claims are the income of AF and the AF is due to collect them.

By the payment of the debts by rations gives the person obligated to maintenance the possibility to pay rations in financially acceptable amounts. AF may allow the obligated person, if he or she is unemployed and has not other income, on his or her demand a delay or payment in rations of the claim, but not longer than for a period of six months. AF may also cancel debts of an obligated person in total or partly, when execution was without success or execution does not promise any successful collection of claims (article 28a GAFA).

In deciding upon the cancellation of a claim, based on all documents in the file, the AF evaluates the present running of execution, possibilities for the collection in the future and the amount of costs of executive proceedings. Decisions on cancellations are made once a year, as a rule, at the end of the fiscal year. The authorised employee of the financial sector prepares documentation in connection with claims against the obligated person, by the help of the employee taking care of collection of debts from the title of paid compensations for maintenance, and decides, whether conditions for the cancellation of the claim are fulfilled. Based on the proposal on the cancellation of the claim, the director of AF decides by decision. Based on the final decision on the cancellation of the claim, AF takes back the proposal for execution in the proper part.[17]

Form the mentioned derives that the agreement on the dynamics of payment of debts demands a great measure of understanding of the reasons for the non-payment of maintenance and the judgement, whether it is about relatively lasting or eventually a debtor's contemporary inability to pay. The obligated person has to attach proof to the demand for a delay or payment of debts by rations, from which derives that he or she is unemployed and that there is no other income.

Proof is especially: a confirmation on the enrolment into the register on employment seekers; a confirmation on the enrolment in the register of unemployed persons; a register on state of property; decision on in-

---

[17] General Conditions of Business of the Public Guarantee and Maintenance Fund of the Republic of Slovenia, Uradni list RS, no. 78/2002, articles 41 to 45.

come for the last year; copy of the land register on an eventual ownership of land.[18]

AF relies also on all facts and evidence in connection with employment and property state of the person obligated to maintenance that he or she obtained alone in the time of proceedings. All income named based on Parental Protection and Family Benefit Act[19] for the establishment of the right to child support is respected. Director of the AF decides upon the demand by the person obligated to maintenance by decision, based on the proposal by the commission.

In the case of death of the person obligated to maintenance, AF may cancel the claim for the payment for the obligated person's heir, if the payment would be in contradiction with the benefit of the child, who would be awarded the right to compensation for maintenance by a decision by AF, and if the heir agrees with the cancellation of the claim. Director of AF also decides on the cancellation of the claim, based on the commission, and AF withdraws the proposal for execution in the correspondent part.

VI. Conclusion

The basic aim of AF is to lower the consequences suffered by children due to non-payment of maintenance by the parent, where the children do not live on the one hand. On the other hand, the purpose of AF is the influence on the persons obligated to maintenance, who have and still today do avoid payment of agreed or determined maintenance for their children. In spite of that there are still many open and unsolved questions. One of the fundamental ones is based on the payment of maintenance to children, who are visiting school after maturity. According to MFRA they have the right to maintenance up to the age of 26 under the condition of regular education. Compensation for maintenance is paid only up to the age of 18, what means that children being educated are shortened twice: as from the side of the parent not paying maintenance, as well as from the side of the state that did not have to take care of the widening of this right until the child's age of 26. A further weakness is that AF only pays compensation for maintenance. This is especially expressed, when main-

---

18   General Conditions of Business of the Public Guarantee and Maintenance Fund of the Republic of Slovenia – article 34.
19   Uradni list RS, no. 110/2006 (officially cleansed text PPFBA – UPB 2); 10/2008.

tenance is much higher than the paid compensation. In spite of the cases of named lacks, we must not neglect the importance of the basic purpose of AF, i.e. that the children being most affected due to non-payment of maintenance are supported.

Financial Provisions and Child Equality

Andrew Pote[1]

I. Introduction

The present economic conditions of rising fuel and food costs, increased inflation, and zero economic growth for the last quarter in Britain for the first time in sixteen years, make it an appropriate time to be examining the Law relating to Financial Provisions and Child Equality. I just remind you at this point that I am talking about the Law as it applies in England and Wales. Other parts of the United Kingdom e.g. Scotland and Northern Ireland have similar but different law, practice and procedure, and I am not qualified to talk about those neighbouring jurisdictions.

I am going to explain how we are working at present in England and Wales in a fragmented system in respect of financial provision provided for children by absent parents. The law practice and procedure in this area is very complex and full of exceptions and caveats. Given the limited time I have to speak to you I am only going to talk to you in broad principles, and cannot cover every area in great detail. But of course, I will be more than happy to answer your questions or carry on further discussions whenever you see me around.

However, I am talking primarily about the different approach taken to cases where the children are born to parents that are or were married to each other as opposed to cohabiting or who had a casual sexual liaison. I will also describe how administrative decisions for child maintenance work through the Child Support Agency.

Given the amazing fact that the charity »Save the Children« claims that one in three children in the U.K. lives in poverty, with one in ten living in severe poverty, (with the highest level found in London) it is not surprising that in 2004 the housing charity »Shelter« claimed that one million children in Britain were suffering »devastating« health and education problems because they lived in crowded, unfit or emergency accommodation.

---

[1] Chambers 13KBW, London and Oxford, United Kingdom.

The breakdown of family life contributes to this sad indictment on our society and our Government's aim to end child poverty by 2020 will need a massive shift in the way resources are distributed to give any chance of this being achieved. Living on the poverty line is defined as being part of a household with an income of less than 60% of median income, the mid point of the scale of national earnings which in April 2007 stood at £ 23,764 pre tax. However, the Joseph Rowntree Trust has just published research which suggests that a single person needs an income of £ 13,000+ to have a minimum standard of income. So a family of four on 60% of £ 23,764, i.e. £ 14,258 is bound to struggle especially as the national minimum wage for a 40 hour week is only £ 11,921.

The law on financial provision for children has a significant role to play in this area but it is my opinion that a more robust approach is required and that a chance to deal with some of the problems of child maintenance payments payable by absent parents has been missed by the decision to replace the Child Support Agency (state run body) with a new organisation called the Child Maintenance and Enforcement Commission. Until the Child Support Act 1991 jurisdiction for child maintenance lay with the courts. However, this all changed because it was thought that too many absent fathers were not contributing to the upkeep of their children and were leaving the tax payer to financially bring up their children through state benefits. The Family Law Bar Association (of which I am a member) and some family law solicitors called for the restoration of the jurisdiction of the courts on the basis that administrative assessment has never worked and never will. The Child Support Agency is currently chasing £ 3.3 billion owed to single mothers and its backlog of cases stands at 300,000. An application for state benefits has an automatic application for an assessment.

II. Financial Provision for Children between Separated Parents

Basically there are four ways that financial provision is made for children between parents who do not live together:

1. Agreements
By private agreement between the parents without an application to the Child Support Agency or the courts (these agreements can be relevant for subsequent applications to the court).

2. Child Support Agency

Assessments by the Child Support Agency only in the form of periodical payments based on a percentage of net income of non resident parent, applicable whether the child's parents were married to each other or not. The percentages payable are:
- 1 Child: 15%
- 2 Children: 20%
- 3+ Children: 25%

The maximum payable is limited and net income over £ 2000 per week is ignored. Any top-up has to be applied for through the courts.

It is only the income of the non resident parent that is relevant, not the income, or lack of it, of the resident parent, capital assets available from either parent or the needs of the child.

But an allowance by way of percentage deduction from the net weekly income is made for the fact that a non – resident parent has other children living with him who are his children or those of the partner he lives with. The percentages are:
- 1 Child – 15%
- 2 Children – 20%
- 3+ Children – 25%

For example a man with a weekly net income of £ 600 lives with his wife and three children. 25% or £ 150 is deducted and he then would pay 15% of £ 450 to his mistress for his child born to her. This would be £ 67.50 per week as opposed to £ 90 if he did not have any other children.

However, the calculations are completely unaffected by the income of the wife who say may also be in receipt of £ 600 net per week as against the mistress who may be on state benefits.

If an assessment is possible the courts can only make orders for child maintenance if the parties agree in writing the amount payable. If the absent parent lives outside the country the Child Support Agency does not have the power to act and the jurisdiction is left with the courts.

In respect of the above, section 2 of Child Support Act 1991 states:
> »Where in any case which falls to be dealt with under this Act, the Secretary of State is considering the exercise of any discretionary power conferred by this Act, he shall have regard to the welfare of any child likely to be affected by his decision.«

3. Divorce Proceedings

For a child of the family, i.e. child born to parents who were or have been married to each other, or a child treated as a child of the family, court orders in ancillary relief proceedings under the Matrimonial Causes Act 1973 (the financial claims in divorce proceedings).

There were 128,534 divorces in 2007 in England and Wales, and although this was a 3% drop on 2006 and the lowest number since 1976, it still affected 117,193 children aged under 16. Of these nearly two thirds were under 11 years old, and a fifth under five.

The average legal costs of ending a marriage in the courts is about £ 13,000 and the need in most cases is for the family home to be sold to purchase either two smaller properties or provide the funds to reach a settlement, whether by consent or imposed by the court.

»It shall be the duty of the court in deciding whether to exercise its powers or and, if so, in what manner, to have regard to all the circumstances of the case, first consideration being given to the welfare while a minor of any child of the family who has not attained the age of eighteen.«

»As regards to the exercise of the powers of the court in relation to a child of the family, the court shall in particular have regard to the following matters –
> the financial needs of the child;
> the income, earning capacity (if any), property and other financial resources of the child;
> any physical or mental disability of the child;
> the manner in which he was being and in which the parties to the marriage expected him to be educated or trained;«

»As regards the exercise of the powers of the court against any party to a marriage in favour of a child of the family who is not the child of that party, the court shall also have regard –
> to whether that party assumed any responsibility for the child's maintenance, and, if so to the extent to which, and the basis upon which, that party assumed such responsibility and to the length of time for which that party discharged such responsibility;
> to whether in assuming and discharging such responsibility that party did so knowing that the child was not his or her own;
> to the liability of any other person to maintain the child«.

4. Children Act Proceedings

For children whose parents are not and have not been married to each other as well as those that have, court orders pursuant to section 15 and Schedule 1 Children Act 1989. This is important as about 44% of children in the United Kingdom are now born to unmarried parents.

Schedule 1 of the Children Act enables a Court to make maintenance orders, secured maintenance orders, lump sum orders, settlement and transfer of property orders for the benefit of children under the age of 18 years and is extendable to cover tertiary education and school fees orders. However, the position is clear that the resident parent cannot have any direct or separate benefit from any order made. Courts are alive to any attempt for financial claims by a resident parent being »dressed up« as claims for a child. However, the Courts have recognised the responsibility, and other sacrifice, of the unmarried parent (generally the mother) who has to be the primary carer of the child. The carer should have control of a budget that reflects her position and that of the father, both social and financial.[2]

When making an order the Court will take the following into account:
> the parents respective incomes, earning capacities, property and other financial resources that they currently have and are likely to have in the foreseeable future;
> the financial needs, obligations and of both parties currently and in the foreseeable future;
> the child's financial needs;
> any physical or mental disability of the child;
> the manner in which the child was being or has expected to be educated and trained;
> the child's welfare generally – although this is not a paramount issue, as it is under other sections of the Act e.g. when deciding the residence of a child or contact with the non – resident parent.

Lump sum payments can cover a wide range of matters including reimbursement for past expenditure reasonably incurred in connection with a child's birth and maintenance. In Re S (Child Financial Provision) [2005] 2FLR 94 the phrase »for the benefit of the child« was given a wide construction. In this case, the mother obtained money to enable her to travel to Sudan where the child lived with the father because that visit was for the child's benefit, as well as the mother's.

---

2   Re P (Child Financial Provision) [2003] 2FLR 865.

There are numerous examples of decisions where settlement of property is ordered during the child's minority to provide suitable housing, but the equity in the property reverts back to the absent parent once the child in question reaches his or her majority in the appropriate share.

III. Conclusion

The problem that gives rise to inequality is that in cases under the Child Support Agency Divorce Proceedings and Children Act Proceedings, different principles are being applied, in the different circumstances.

The Child Support assessment is only looking at the absent parent's net income. There is no question of need, and capital assets and housing resources are not taken into account. If the parents are married then these issues can be looked at in the ancillary relief proceedings but if there is no marriage then they will not be.

Schedule 1 applications are relatively rare and for a number of reasons. But because there is currently no provision for financial relief in English law for unmarried cohabiting couples on relationship break-up they are the last chance of securing adequate financial arrangements for children. The financial duties and responsibilities towards children can be too easily avoided as the arrears figure of £ 3.3 billion chased by the Child Support Agency shows. It is not fit for purpose and is rightly being reformed. But the replacement of it by a new state administrative based agency will I believe do little to address the real underlying problem. There will be a greater emphasis on promoting agreements but what is really required is a low cost easily accessible court remedy where all the financial needs of the child can be considered in all the circumstances of the case with the same rules applied whether the child is born in wedlock or out of it.

The concept of a percentage of net income is a good starting point but should be capable of being departed from in cases where a child has special needs e.g. mental or physical disability or educational needs. Private education in England is a growth area. The fact that a father's children by his wife have been educated privately should be an important factor in how his other child, by his mistress, is educated. Equally, capital assets are important e.g. a non-resident parent may have a large amount of equity in his house which he could borrow against to provide a lump sum. This could be used to help meet a child's own housing need.

To many resident parents a regular certain payment per week or month is exactly what is needed, but to others a lump sum payment is required to meet immediate costs of housing, health treatment or education.

No one system meets every case fairly but the current system does not treat children equally and is in need of reform.

Part IV – Financial Planning and Responsibilty

New Features of Hungarian Matrimonial Property Law in the Draft of a New Civil Code

András Kőrös[1]

I. Historical Antecedents

In Hungary, as in the majority of Eastern-European countries during the so-called socialist period, family law was separate from civil law, considered as a special branch of law, and the rules pertaining to families were placed in a separate code, dissociated from other norms of civil relations. The Family Law Act of 1952 – which was the first comprehensive codification of this field of law – came into being when the rapid demise of private property was the official ideology in the socialist states, and hence matrimonial property provisions of the Act were insufficiently regulated.

The Family Law Act of 1952 introduced a mandatory matrimonial property regime which was close to the limited community of property system – property owned by each spouse before marriage or acquired during the marriage by gift or inheritance as well as the assets for purely personal use constituted separate fund, all other properties and acquisitions fell to the common fund – and fixed that statutory matrimonial regime cannot be excluded neither totally nor partially by contract. Despite the deficiencies of the regulation, it must be stressed that the lawmaker was striving to create such a community property law that would take into consideration the equal rights of the parties in the marriage, and the differences in the earning potential of men and women, as well as the activities of the wife in the household and childrearing. These principles were not generally accepted in Western European family laws in that time in contrast to Eastern Europe, at least on the formal level.

Soon after the Family Act had entered into force, legal practice showed that the matrimonial property law provisions, written in only five articles, were not satisfactory even in a world where private property played a diminishing role in economic life. First, judicial practice tried to fill the

---

[1] Supreme Court of Hungary, Budapest.

gaps, and later on, the legal principles developed by the courts received a regulation in law, in the articles of 1974 and 1986 amending the Family Act. However, in 1986, there were new developments in economic relations, and the law acknowledged the possibility of entering into property contracts that had been abolished in 1952. Thus partners getting married and spouses acquired the right to deviate from the statutory community property regime by mutual agreement. Still, the provisions of community property contract were regulated too laconically, perhaps therefore parties rarely took advantage of undertaking it. The changes of attitude could be recognized in the rule of the Family Act saying that the measures of the Civil Code should be properly applied to the spousal property issues. It denotes that the amendment of the Act tried to strengthen the elements of civil law in family relations, due to the strengthening of the economic function of the family and the increasing significance of accumulation of property in families. Naturally, the families' main source of wealth was the professions and work-related benefits.

In the course of the past two decades significant changes occured in property relations, their importance, the magnitude of private property, and the direct or indirect participation of individuals in business life. The profound economic and social changes since the collapse of communism in 1990 have brought such changes in the area of civil relations that their legal coherence requires framing a new Civil Code. The Draft of the New Civil Code, which was prepared on the basis of a Governement Resolution in 1998, integrates the broadest possible range of private law regulations stipulated in specific laws, among others, the regulations of family law. Thus the substance of family law will be incorporated in the Civil Code as a separate Book of the Code. (In structure the Hungarian Code is inspired by the Dutch Civil Code. Therefore the Hungarian Code will be broken into five Books, Family Law, the subject of my contribution being one of them).

II. The Principles of the New Family Law Book

An integration of the body of family law into the Civil Code raises more questions than would be raised by adjusting the amended Family Law Act to today's circumstances. The peculiarities of the social relations regulated by family law necessitate that certain fundamental principles which are characteristic for family relations but typically differ from civil law will

be formulated in the preamble of the Book on Family Law. There are four main principles drawn up by the codifiers considered as the guidelines of the law-practice:
> the protection of the family relationships,
> the protection of the child's interests,
> the principle of equality of the spouses,
> the principle of equity and the protection of the weaker party.

From the perspective of matrimonial property law the last two principles are the relevant ones. In Hungary, similarly to other Eastern-European countries, problems such as granting spouses equal rights or improving the position of a housewife were resolved in the 1950s. The common administration and disposal of the common fund and equal distribution of the common assets form the basis of the Hungarian law. There is no need to change these fundamental principles even if the regulations become much more fine-tuned than at present. Moreover, as regards the disposition over the property, some European laws differentiate between property serving the every-day life of husband and wife, including the commonly inhabited dwelling either in joint or separate ownership, and property serving professional occupation and participation in business. Such a role is unknown in current Hungarian law and there is a particular need to regulate this issue in a more real-life and differentiated way.

The principle of equity and protection of the weaker party could serve in practice as a legal balance between the requirements of autonomy of the spouses and the solidarity between them. The current law knows the so-called »fairness clause« in matrimonial property relations which gives the court an opportunity to deviate from the strict application of the statutory provisions if either of the spouses should gain unfair advantages by it. The New Family Law Book intends to ensure the harmony of these main principles in family law matters in general.

III. Main Features of the New Regulation in the Draft

The Draft preserves **community property as a statutory system** given 50 years of tradition, but its regulation will be radically broadened. The regime remains actually a limited community of property system in which the sphere of separate property is regulated in compliance with international practice (as mentioned). The sole exception is that any profit from separate property realized during the marriage belongs to the spouses' common property. However, any increase in the value of the separate property does not alter its status (e. g. the interest of a share belongs to the common property, the increase of the value of a share enriches the separate fund). The new law adds to the separate property the non-property damage compensation as a personal grievance of the respective spouse, too.

The Draft contains detailed rules on the charges and debts of the spouses which cannot be found in the current rules. As regards the liability of the spouses towards third parties for the transactions involving one of them, there is a rebuttable presumption that the other consented. This means that the transaction is binding on both spouses even if one of them was unaware of said transaction. It is not binding only if the party opposing the transaction can prove that a third party was aware of the lack of his/her consent at the time it was concluded. However, conveyance of the matrimonial dwelling and putting common assets at the disposal of a business association require the effective consent of the spouses.

Differentiating between »business property« and any other property of the spouses has significance in several aspects. The assets necessary for profession or assets for business fall under the exclusive administration of the respective spouse, but he/she is obliged to inform the other spouse on the effectiveness of the business. After the termination of marital cohabitation the spouse may dispose exclusively of the assets of his/her professional or business activities, even if those have been acquired from a common source. (Naturally, it doesn't influence his/her obligation of payment at the distribution). Where one of the spouses was a member of a business association, but has received his/her business share during the marriage, the non-member spouse may request the division of the share by contract or via court action, unless the foundation deed of association provides otherwise.

The Draft attributes particular importance to the self-determination of spouses in family matters, including property issues. For the sake of ensuring this fundamental principle, spouses acquired the right to deviate from the rules of the statutory matrimonial property sytem by concluding a **matrimonial property contract**. The current law contains only one sentence about the substance of the contract, saying that »the spouses may decide on deviating from the provisions of this Act, which property should be joint or separate properties«. The new Family Law Book devotes a whole Chapter to the institution of the spouses' settlement containing generally optional rules.

Basically, a matrimonial property contract can have two types of content. One is the acceptance of statutory property regime, deviating from the general rules included in the law on some issues (e.g. the objects of common or separate property, compensation claims between the spouses during the marriage and after divorce, administration and disposal over common property). The other is to stipulate another type of property law system. (Deviation in details, naturally, may also occur in the area of the optional property law systems).

The new law regulates two types of property systems as optional: **community of accrued gains** and separation of property which can be chosen by spouses in their agreement. The first one resembles the German »community of surplus« regime. The essence of this system is that the property of the spouses remains separate property during the marriage: each spouse is free to administer his/her own assets. Upon the termination of marriage the spouses share the increase of each other's wealth (the so-called accrued gains). The spouse with a larger surplus has to compensate the difference by giving half of the difference to the other. Under the terms of the Draft the compensation may be either monetary or the division of the surplus property in kind. The rules of the system try to protect the share of both of the spouses in accrued gains. When the debts of one spouse exceed the share of the other spouse, the court has the power – at the request of the other spouse – to terminate the contract and separate the properties of the spouses. This is not automatic, but may follow when the party indebt cannot produce a security deposit.

The **separate property system** provides the almost complete financial independence of the spouses. The marriage itself actually does not bring any change to their property situation. However, even in the case of separation of property, it is necessary to define the minimum duty of the parties, while contractual liberty of the parties may not infringe upon basic family-protection interests (e. g. the rights of the child or the solidarity between the spouses). Therefore, it will not allow for any avoidance of the costs of the common lifestyle and any non-participation in the offspring's financial care or any unilateral disposal over the rights of spouses to live in the matrimonal home. Additionally the contract may not aim at any encroachment upon creditor's rights. Moreover, the ban on infringement upon »sound morals« is established in family law, which serves as a general rule in the Hungarian Law of Contracts, too.

The principle of »**protection of the family home**« calls for special provisions for the disposal over the common dwelling without respect to the fact that it is common or separate property. The family law provisions determine separately the issues of settlement of dwelling use by the spouses in case the settlement is based upon joint agreement. However, the judge is entitled to deviate from the way of settlement of the use of the dwelling as written in the contract, in the interest of assuring the right of the use of the matrimonial home for the child, who is a minor.

The new Code holds that matrimonial property agreement can contain a provision also in the case of death, and to this extent the spouses may have a joint will. However, such joint-will provisions in the contract should lose their legal force when the spouses have or one of them has a child subsequently, following the agreement.

As regards the **formal requirements** of the contract, the new Family Law Book preserves the current law that the contract is valid only if a notary or a lawyer has certified it. A new element of the regulation is that the contract can be enforced against third parties only if it has been entered into the national registry of property law contracts supervised by the National Chamber of Hungarian Notaries. It would be the foundation of a more efficient protection of creditors versus the *mala fides* »internal property movements« of the spouses.

IV. Conclusion

The Draft of the New Family Law Book regards the preservation of well-balanced family life one of the most important human values which recognises the freedom and autonomy of the members of the family. Equality, autonomy, solidarity and protection of the weaker party (primarily the minor) are the pillars upon which the modern family regulation has to be built. Allow me to express the hope, as one of the experts who has elaborated the text of the new family law regulations in Hungary, that these features would be implemented in the functioning of matrimonial property rules, too.

References

› Szakértői javaslat az új Polgári Törvénykönyv tervezetéhez [Draft of a New Civil Code for Hungary: an Expert Proposal] - edited by Lajos VÉKÁS, Complex – Walters Kluwer Group, Budapest 2008.
› Masha ANTOKOLSKAIA: Harmonisation of Family Law in Europe. A Historical Perspective – Chapter 17. Matrimonial Property Law – Intersentia, Antwerpen-Oxford, 2006.
› Orsolya SZEIBERT-ERDŐS: The Role of Self-Determination in Hungarian Family Law Primarily Concerning Matrimonial Property Settlements – in: The Role of Self-Determination in the Modernisation of Family Law in Europe, Edited by Míquel MARTÍN-CASALS and Jordi RIBOT, Documenta Universitaria, Girona 2006, pp. 129–148.
› Márta DÓCZI: Hungarian Matrimonial Property Law – in: The International Survey of Family Law, 2003 Edition, general editor: Dr. Andrew BAINHAM pp. 209–215.
› Emilia WEISS: Remarks on Certain Aspects of the Codification of Family Law, 1-2 Acte Juridica Hungaria (2002) pp. 175–204.

The Economic Consequence of Divorce in Japan Trend in No-Fault Divorce and *Rikon Isharyo* (Solatium by Divorce) Scheme

Fumiko Tsuneoka[1]

I. Introduction

The aim of this paper is to describe the economic consequence of divorce in the light of *solatium theory* in Japan and to contribute to the discussion about the marital property distribution and alimony regime under the no-fault divorce system.

No-fault divorce, which was introduced during the 1960's and the 1970's mainly in the western countries, is founded upon the modern concept that the termination of a marriage results from irretrievable marital breakup, but not necessarily from the spouse‹s misbehavior. The reform of maintenance or alimony accompanied this »divorce by irretrievable breakup of marriage« movement, so those economic adjustments by divorce were also considered to be assessed without regard to marital misconduct.

However, through this revolutionary change, it has been pointed out that no-fault divorce regimes do not always satisfy the spouses, particularly in economic respects. In many countries, the new alimony or property distribution system impoverishes wives while heavy economic burdens sometimes weigh husbands[2]. Moreover, although the law abandoned the consideration of fault factors in deciding the economic order by divorce,

---

[1] Professor of Law, Faculty of Law, Dokkyo University, Japan.
[2] For example, in the United States, it is pointed out that the law in most states during the 1960s'-1970's divorce reform disfavored awards of alimony. However, the lawmakers and the courts began to take a positive attitude toward alimony in the 1980s as the divorce rate rose and the poor economic position of divorced women and their children became more widely known. At the same time, it is also recognized that the divorced spouses are now not only the rich people but also the blue-collar workers. The husband cannot always afford both to pay alimony for the divorced wife and to maintain his new family. See *LESLIE JOAN HARRIS, LEE E. TEITELBAUM & JUNE CARBONE, FAMLIY LAW 433 (3rd ed., 2005); IRA MARK ELLMAN, The Theory of Alimony, 77 Cal. L. Rev. 1, 48 (1989)*.

these factors still seem to remain or to revive in some jurisdictions in order to achieve equitable distribution of marital property or appropriate spousal support[3]. Even where marital fault may not be taken into account, the spouse is often allowed to claim for marital torts to compensate moral damages caused by misbehavior of the other spouse, which used to be an element of alimony[4].

In Japan, the economic consequence of a divorce is major concern of the parties as well as in other countries. On the other hand, with respect to the legal system of dealing with the economic problems of divorce, Japanese marriage-divorce law is unique in that it experienced complete renovation under the influence of the General Headquarters of the U.S.A in 1947, two years after the end of World War II. With this historical background, Japan already got innovative provisions then, which included a modern no-fault divorce concept and an equitable distribution system of marital property. Moreover, we have long developed a *solatium theory* in order to satisfy the concrete need of the divorced spouses. This paper focuses on that solatium by divorce scheme in Japan and would aim to contribute to the comparative study on the economic reconstruction of the dissolved families in the era of the no-fault divorce.

II. The No-Fault Divorce Regime and the Economic Consequence in Japan

1. The Introduction of Solatium by Divorce Under the Meiji Civil Code

The family law before the reform in 1947 was under the *Meiji* Civil Code (enacted in 1898). With respect to the divorce law, it allowed both a divorce by agreement (Art.808) and a divorce by judicial decree (judicial divorce) which was based on the fault divorce concept (Art.813)[5]. As the *Meiji* Civil Code was based on the patriarchy system, the judicial divorce contained several unequal grounds between the husband and the wife. For example in the case of adultery, the misconduct of the wife was a simple reason to

---

[3] See LYNN D. WARDLE & LAURENCE C. NOLAN, FUNDAMENTAL PRINCIPLES OF FAMILY LAW, 742 (2002).

[4] ROBERT G. SPECTOR, *Marital Torts: The Current Legal Landscape*, 33 Fam. L. Q. 745 (1999).

[5] Art. 813 provided the fault-based grounds such as adultery, punishment, cruelty, serious insult and desertion, one no-fault ground of »missing for not less than three years«, and one ground related to the patriarchal family system (»dissolution of adoption of the son-in-law«).

divorce her by the husband, while the husband was claimed for divorce by the wife only when he was punished for fornication, but not when he just committed adultery (see Art. 813).

When we see the economic order by divorce, the *Meiji* Civil Code had no provision for property division or spousal support after divorce. Customarily, the husband paid consolation money (*Tegirekin*) to the wife when the couple got divorced. However, as *Tegirekin* was not a legal system, it was not subject to the judicial force in case of default in payment by the husband. Moreover, the customary payment itself had been made only in some places in Japan, not countrywide. Even if it was paid, the amount was not enough to support a living after the divorce for most of the wives. Many divorced wives were forced to maintain themselves with a minimum wage work or to become dependent on their own relatives. The economic situation of the divorced wives was extremely severe under the *Meiji* Civil Code.

The courts recognized the problem that divorce without financial treatment was unfair and harsh to the wife who was socially and economically in a poor position. After ten years of the enactment of the *Meiji* Civil Code, the Supreme Court found a solution to this problem by applying the tort theory in order to allow the divorced wife to claim for solatium (*Rikon Isharyo*) for the mental, emotional damage she suffered from divorce[6]. Although the amount was not always enough, the solatium by divorce had worked as the major means to save the wife from an economic disaster after divorce until the law reform in 1947.

2. Divorce Grounds in the Reformed Civil Code and the Trend toward No-Fault Divorce

2.1 Divorce Grounds in the Current Civil Code

In the reform of 1947, the legislators made a complete reexamination of the family law of the *Meiji* Civil Code under the influence of GHQ. The divorce grounds and the economic order by divorce were ones of the major objects of this renovation. They were reformed with the concept of gender equality and independence of the spouses from each other (see Civil Code Art.2). With respect to the divorce grounds, it provides a divorce by judicial decree (Art.770) along with a divorce by agreement (Art.763) as the *Meiji* Civil Code did. The grounds for a judicial divorce consist of two fault

---

6   *Daisinnin* Supreme Court, March 26, 1908, *Courts Reports (civil cases) vol.14, sec.7, p.340*.

grounds (adultery, desertion), two traditional no-fault grounds (missing, insanity), and one no-fault ground of an irretrievable breakup of marriage[7]. These grounds include no discrimination between the husband and the wife in their application.

Divorce by agreement is the most common form of divorce in Japan[8]. However, as the actual number of divorces has been rising for decades, the significance of a judicial divorce increases. When the spouses agree on the dissolution of the marriage but they have difficulty in making an agreement on the distribution of marital property or maintenance after divorce, they may take the way of judicial divorce. Furthermore, particularly facing the cases that the faulty spouse claims for divorce against the no-faulty spouse's will and the latter firmly refuses divorce, the courts have developed the idea of non-fault divorce under the divorce ground of Civil Code art.770 (1) (v).

2.2 »Grave Cause Making it Difficult to Continue the Marriage« in Art.770 (1) (v)

The current Japanese Civil Code had a seed of pure no-fault divorce right at the start of the 1947's reform as it introduced the divorce ground of irretrievable breakup of the marriage in art.770 (1) (v). It provides that either husband or wife may file a suit for divorce if there is any grave cause making it difficult to continue the marriage. Specifically, this provision allows the spouse to get divorced from the other one without determining who is at fault. This is based on the idea of a pure no-fault divorce in its words and the courts are to give the divorce decree whenever they recognize that the marriage is irretrievably broken up.

However, the word of »grave cause making it difficult to continue the marriage« is abstract and unclear about its concrete conditions, so the courts have exercised acting discretion in interpreting and applying

---

7 Art.770 sub-sec.(1) provides that »only in the cases stated in the following items may either husband or wife file a suit for divorce: (i) if a spouse has committed an act of unchastity; (ii) if abandoned by a spouse in bad faith; (iii) if it is not clear whether a spouse is dead or alive for not less than three years; (iv) if a spouse is suffering from severe mental illness and there is no prospect of recovery; or (v) if there is any other grave cause making it difficult to continue the marriage.«

8 About 90% of the divorcing couples take the way of divorce by agreement (see *http://www1. mhlw.go.jp/ toukei/rikon_8/repo3.html*). Neither the judiciary nor other governmental agency intervenes in this procedure. The spouses are able to divorce themselves simply by the agreement and the registration at the family register office (Civil Code Art.763, 764).

art.770 (1) (v). The typical »grave cause making it difficult to continue the marriage« is a sort of fault grounds like domestic violence, cruelty and bitter spendthrift habits, or no-fault based ones like impotence and incompatible temperaments. However, the dispute where views have mostly divided is whether the divorce claim filed by the faulty spouse may also be allowed against the faultless (or less faulty) spouse's will when the marriage is irretrievably broken up under art.770 (1) (v)

2.3. The »Passive Breakup of Marriage« (*Shoukyokuteki Hatan-syugi*) and the »Active Breakup of Marriage« (*Sekkyokuteki Hatan-syugi*)

The Supreme Court of Japan has long given a narrow interpretation to art.770 (1) (v) and has held the position that the court should not allow the divorce claim filed by the spouse who had committed marital misconduct. Only the spouse who was not responsible for the breakup of the marriage had been entitled to claim for divorce there. The leading case was *Husband v. Wife* in 1952[9] where the husband had been separated from his wife for five years and had lived with another woman and their child. He filed a divorce suit under art.770 (1) (v) with the reason that there was a grave cause which made it difficult for him to continue the marriage with his wife. As dismissing the suit, the Supreme Court stated that it was selfish of the husband to claim for divorce, because he engaged in misconduct and got separated from the wife by his own motion. It further said that if the court allowed divorce in this case, it would not only be extremely bitter for the wife, but also give the people motivation for unprincipled misbehavior.

The emphasis on morality in the society and the respect of fidelity between the husband and the wife was essential to the Supreme Court's standpoint. Moreover, it also considered the protection of the faultless wives who were poor economic actors in society and then were likely to be forced into an economic disaster by a divorce decree against their will. As the courts and the society supported these views, the 1952's case had been the fixed precedent for handling the divorce suits filed by the faulty spouse for a long time[10].

---

9 Supreme Court, Third Petty Bench, February 19, 1952, *Supreme Court Reports (civil cases) vol.6, sec.2, p.110*.
10 See Supreme Court, Second Petty Bench, November 5, 1954, *Supreme Court Reports (civil cases) vol.8, sec.11, p.2023*; Supreme Court, Third Petty Bench, December 14, 1954, *Supreme Court Reports (civil cases) vol.8, sec.12, p.2143*.

This precedent of the 1952's Supreme Court decision is called the »passive breakup of marriage« rule in Japan, because only the spouse who is not responsible for the breakup is entitled to claim for divorce with the reason of an irretrievable breakup of the marital relationship. The upholders of this rule emphasized the respect for the bond of marriage, moral sense among the people and the protection of the wife against the husband who was committing a misconduct. They applied the principle »against abuse of rights«, »clean-hand« or »good faith« as the legal basis for their arguments.

However, the requirement for divorce in art.770 (1) (v) is that there is a grave cause making the continuation of the marriage difficult. When the court dismisses the divorce claim under this provision, it primarily has to declare that there is no such grave cause, or that the marriage is not irretrievably broken up and the continuation of the marriage is expected. Simply emphasizing fidelity or morality would not be enough to satisfy the reason of dismiss of the divorce claim by the faulty spouse when the marriage of the parties is deadlocked for years.

Under this consideration, many counterarguments have been made against the »passive breakup of marriage« rule. They insist that the divorce claim filed by the faulty spouse should be allowed as well as the claim filed by the faultless spouse, when the marriage is irretrievably broken up. This view is called the »active breakup of marriage« rule.

2.4. Pure No-Fault Divorce Regime under the
»Active Breakup of Marriage« Rule

As the divorce reform in the United States and European countries was introduced to Japan in the 1960s and the 1970s, many authors insisted that it was against conscience of the people to force the husband and the wife to be bound to the broken marriage. They also emphasized the importance of allowing the faulty spouse to get divorced from the other faultless spouse and to create a new relationship with another partner.

The sentiments of the courts began to shift from the »passive breakup of marriage« to the »active breakup of marriage« along with the literatures. The Supreme Court came to pass the divorce decree for the faulty spouse under the specific condition that his or her misconduct occurred after the marriage had already broken up by the reasons other than his or her fault[11]. Furthermore, the drastic change was made in 1987 by the

---

11   Supreme Court, First Petty Bench, October 24, 1963, *Monthly Bulletin on Family Courts vol.16, sec.2, p.36*; Supreme Court, Second Petty Bench, May 21, 1971, *Supreme Court*

Supreme Court Grand Bench[12] which clearly expressed the turn to the »active breakup of marriage« rule by allowing the divorce suit filed by the husband who had broken the marital relationship irretrievably by his own misbehavior[13].

In this case, the husband had deceived his wife with another woman. After he got separated from the wife and began to live with the woman and her children, he filed the divorce suit. However, the court refused his claim under the »passive breakup of marriage« rule (This first divorce suit was filed shortly after the above *Husband v. Wife* in 1952). The husband asked the wife to divorce him by agreement repeatedly after he had lost the suit, but she firmly kept refusing it. After 36 years of separation, the husband filed a divorce suit against the wife again. The Tokyo District Court and the Tokyo High Court dismissed it following the precedents. However, the Supreme Court decided to reverse them and to allow the divorce claim filed by the husband who had caused the irretrievable breakup of marriage by his own fault.

What is remarkable about this decision of the Supreme Court Grand Bench is not only that it shifted to the »active breakup of marriage« rule. It also presented three conditions for applying this rule in order to protect the faultless spouse (particularly the wife) from falling in hardship by being divorced against her will. Specifically, the Grand Bench stated in the reasons that the divorce claim by the husband should not be dismissed only because it was filed by the faulty spouse, when

› »the separation of the couple stretched over a substantially long period in comparison with the age of both of the spouses and the period that they had lived together before the separation,«
› »the couple have no dependent child of them,« and
› »there are no particular circumstances which would be really against the sense of justice, such as that divorce would make the faultless spouse extremely wretched in the mental, social or economic respect.«

We may say that this decision set Japanese divorce law to the pure no-fault divorce system because the court would allow divorce filed by the faulty spouse when the marriage is proved to be irretrievably broken up by the

---

Reports (civil cases) vol.25, sec.3, p.408.
12 The Supreme Court of Japan holds the Grand Bench formed by all of the fifteen Justices when it changes its own precedent. Court Act Art.10 (3).
13 Supreme Court, Grand Bench, September 2, 1987, *Supreme Court Reports (civil cases) vol.41, sec.6, p.1423.*

period of time of separation. The courts have been since shortening this separation period[14] and now the lower courts may allow divorce with the six years separation[15]. About the requirement of »no dependent child«, the Supreme Court has also loosened it in the later case and passed the divorce decree while the couple had a high school child[16].

However, with respect to the third condition of the 1987's Grand Bench, the courts have been deciding more carefully whether there are particular circumstances which are really against the sense of justice or not. Specifically, while this condition lists the mental, social and economic hardship of the other spouse as a reason for the courts to refuse the divorce decree, the concern about the economic circumstances is the center of the divorce practice. For example, when the wife received public assistance and there were practically no prospects that the better-off husband would make property division or pay support enough for the living of the wife and their dependent child, the Supreme Court dismissed the divorce claim filed by the faulty husband[17]. On the other hand, the court allowed divorce in the cases that there were substantial prospects that the faulty spouse could afford to provide property or support for the other spouse[18] or that the other spouse (here the husband) had his own earnings enough to support himself[19].

Viewing these cases, while the 1987's Supreme Court decision opened up a pure no-fault divorce regime to Japanese divorce law, it is closely tied to the financial condition of the faultless spouse. The divorce decree is practically dependent on whether the economic order by divorce is fully made or not.

---

14 The Supreme Court allowed divorce by eight years separation in 1990. Supreme Court, First Petty Bench, November 8, 1990, *Monthly Bulletin on Family Courts vol.43, sec.4, p.72.*

15 Tokyo High Court, June 26, 2002, *Hanrei Jiho (Law Cases Reports) number1801, P.80.*

16 Supreme Court, Third Petty Bench, February 8, 1994, *Monthly Bulletin on Family Courts vol.46, sec.9, p.59.* In this case, the faulty husband has been supporting the wife and the child, while the couple had been separated since the child was three years old.

17 Supreme Court, Third Petty Bench, March 6, 1990, *Monthly Bulletin on Family Courts vol.42, sec.6, p.40.*

18 Supreme Court, Third Petty Bench, September 7, 1989, *Courts Reports (civil cases) num. 157, p.497; supra* Supreme Court, Third Petty Bench, February 8, 1994, *Monthly Bulletin on Family Courts vol.46, sec.9, p.59.*

19 Supreme Court, First Petty Bench, December 8, 1988, *Monthly Bulletin on Family Courts vol.41, sec.3, p.145.* The wife committed misconduct in this case and filed the divorce suit against the husband who earned 4,000,000 yen a year.

3. The Economic Order by Divorce and Solatium Theory

3.1 Solatium by Divorce under the Meiji Civil Code

The Meiji Civil Code had no provision about the economic order by divorce. The customary payment of consolation money (Tegirekin) by the husband did not satisfy the divorced wife's needs in terms of the amount of money, nor in terms of the legal system (see II. 1.).

The courts recognized the hardship of the wives without financial treatment, so the Supreme Court affirmed the application of the tort theory to compensate for the wife's damage in its 1908's decision . In this case, the wife claimed for solatium for the mental, emotional damage by reason of the husband's cruelty and serious insult, which were also the reasons of divorce decree filed by the wife. While the amount was not always enough and the compensation was limited to the damages caused by particular misbehavior of the faulty husband, the solatium by divorce worked as the major pecuniary treatment for the divorced wives after this decision until the law reform in 1947.

3.2. »Distribution of Property« under the Current Civil Code art.768

In the reform of 1947, the legislature expressly provided that the spouse has the right to claim for »distribution of property« at divorce (Civil Code Art. 768). About the meaning of »distribution of property«, the provision refers just to division of marital property; however, it also requires taking »all other circumstances« into account by distribution of property[20]. Concerning what »all other circumstances« suggests, art.768 lists no concrete situations like the necessity of support for the other spouse or compensation for damages caused by marital misconduct, so it leaves it to the discretion of the courts. However, the legislature's intention lied in that »distribution of property« included not only division of marital property, but also spousal support and solatium by divorce[21]. Upon this understand-

---

20 Art.768 (1) (2) provides that one party to a divorce may claim a distribution of property from the other party and (3) states »the family court shall determine whether to make a distribution, and the amount and method of that distribution, taking into account the amount of property obtained through the cooperation of both parties and all other circumstances.«

21 *Supreme Court General Bureau, THE MATERIALS REGARDING THE DIET ABOUT THE REFORM OF CIVIL CODE, p.487, 1953.*

ing, the courts have decided »distribution of property« comprehensively, but substantially considering three elements of property division, spousal support and solatium.

3.3 The Nature of Solatium by Divorce

With respect to the nature of solatium by divorce, the legislators of the current Civil Code art.768 regarded it as a penalty to the faulty spouse who had caused the divorce[22]. The Supreme Court confirmed this view in *Wife v. Husband* of July 23, 1971[23]. It stated in the reasons that solatium by divorce was not the damages for the individual unlawful act such as violence or cruelty which was the ground of breakup of the marriage, but the compensation for the mental damage of the other spouse who was forced to determine on divorce by the misbehavior of the faulty spouse[24]. Furthermore, the Court showed an eclectic position in order to explain the relation of solatium by divorce to »distribution of property« of art.768 because the tort nature of solatium was legally different from property division or spousal support at divorce. The Supreme Court stated about it as follows:

Distribution of property at divorce aims division of marital property and spousal support after divorce; these elements do not necessarily require the fault of the spouse (here the husband) against whom the other spouse (here the wife) claims for distribution. About the fault of the husband, the wife has the right to claim for solatium separately even after she got »distribution of property«. However, on the other hand, as the court is allowed to decide »distribution of property« by considering all the circumstances under art.768 (3), it may also decide it inclusively with solatium for the wife. When the divorce court decided »distribution of property« including solatium by divorce and the wife further files a suit for solatium at another district court, the latter court should examine whether her damage was fully compensated by the previous »distribution of property«. If the previous »distribution of property« did not include solatium or, even if included, when it was not sufficient to compensate her mental damage, the court may order the husband to pay solatium to the wife with the reason of tort.

---

22 *Supra Supreme Court General Bureau, p.558.*
23 Supreme Court Second Petty Bench, July 23, 1971, *Courts Reports (civil cases) vol.25, sec.5, p.805.*
24 About the damage the spouse suffered from individual violence or cruelty, she may file a tort suit under Civil Code art.709 and 710 separately from the divorce.

Following this precedent, the courts in Japan have taken the element of solatium into account in calculating and deciding »distribution of property« while they also allow the other spouse to file the tort claim for solatium independently.

3.4 Trend to Pure No-Fault Divorce and the Role of Solatium by Divorce

As the no-fault divorce revolution began in the 1960s in Europe, America and other countries, several academics argued that the economic protection of the divorced spouse should be made simply by property division under the equal distribution rule and compensatory or rehabilitative maintenance in Japan as well. They state that solatium by divorce is to be refused in the no-fault divorce regime; even if the divorce suit is filed by the faulty spouse against the faultless spouse's will, the court should award the divorce decree when the marriage is irretrievably broken, and without allowing solatium by divorce.

However, against the forward literatures, the courts take the conservative standpoint on the economic order by divorce. It is still the established precedent in Japan to allow solatium by divorce in faulty cases. Furthermore, the courts sometimes hold solatium in great account in order to pass the divorce decree under the »active breakup of marriage« rule. Viewing the above Supreme Court Grand Bench decision in 1987 (see II 2.4.), the case was remanded to Tokyo High Court in order to examine whether there was particular circumstances which would be really against the sense of justice, especially in the economic respect. The court ordered the husband to pay 150,000 dollars of solatium by divorce along with 100,000 dollars of spousal support in exchange for divorce, while the husband had already gifted the marital residence to the wife during separation[25]. It is quite a high amount in comparison with the average of solatium in Japanese divorce practice, which is from 20,000 dollars to 30,000 dollars[26]. By ordering a fairly large amount of property division and spousal support, the court takes well into consideration economic protection of the wife after divorce here. Furthermore, it awarded the additional large amount of solatium to the wife, which was expected to solace the wife's mental pain about being forced into divorce under the pure no-fault regime based on the »active breakup of marriage« rule. We may say from this decision of the

---

25   Tokyo High Court, November 22, 1989, Hanrei Jiho *(Law Cases Reports) num. 1330, p.48.*
26   Cf. *http://www.courts.go.jp/sihotokei/nenpo/pdf/B19DKAJ25˜27.PDF*

remanded Tokyo High Court that while the idea of pure no-fault divorce is prevailing, the need of compensation of the other spouse's pain caused by divorce is still not disregarded by the courts in Japan. The appropriate economic order by divorce is the key to allow the divorce claimed by the faulty spouse (see II.2.4.); however, it does not only mean property division or material maintenance of the other spouse's livelihood after divorce but also includes substantial compensation of his or her mental damage caused by divorce. Moreover, what supports this practice is theoretically the independence of solatium by divorce from property division or spousal support in its legal nature, and practically the comprehensive discretion of the courts in deciding »distribution of property« under »all the circumstances« (Civil Code Art.768)[27] in Japanese divorce law.

III. Conclusion

Japanese divorce law have given a positive role to the solatium by divorce as the measure to achieve justice for the faultless spouse under the no-fault divorce regime of the »active breakup of marriage« rule. This approach may look to be quite different from the other countries' system where the element of punishment to the faulty spouse has been excluded from alimony or any other economic adjustments at divorce under the concept of clean-break. However, it is often pointed out that through the establishment of the pure no-fault divorce regime, the conflict and hostility of the parties has shifted from the divorce itself to the economic consequences of divorce. This is a problem common to all the countries which have steered for the drastic change of the divorce law in these forty years.

The economic security of the society is closely connected with the stability of individual families. It is hoped that the development of the economic order by divorce and *solatium theory* in Japan may contribute to the discussion to seek for the compatibility of the independence with the economic protection of the divorcing spouses in the era of the no-fault divorce regime.

---

27 Supra Supreme Court Second Petty Bench, July 23, 1971, *Courts Reports (civil cases)* vol.25, sec.5, p.805.

Achieving Economic Equality at the End of Marriage and Other Relationships: Not All Is Fair in Love and War

Mark Henaghan[1]

I. Introduction

[2]There is »no actual equality when the husband is left with the ability to earn a significant income and the wife is left with little or no ability to earn a living« said the then President of the New Zealand Court of Appeal, Richardson P, in *Z* v *Z (No 2)*.[3] Mrs Z was married to Mr Z for 28 years with three children produced and cared for. When Mr and Mrs Z first married Mrs Z, then a secretary, was earning more than her husband who worked in a government department. After five years of part-time work at home and looking after the children, Mrs Z became ill. For the rest of the marriage Mrs Z cared for the children, looked after all the household duties and supported Mr Z in his career. Mr Z left the government department in 1987 to join a large international accountancy firm. At the time of separation in 1994, Mr Z was earning NZ $ 300,000 and Mrs Z was on a benefit of NZ $ 17,000. Mrs Z received half of the matrimonial property (her share came to NZ $ 500,000), but the overall result was not equal because of the large disparity in earning capacity.[4]

Z v *Z (No 2)* exemplifies what Baroness Hale said in *Miller* v *Miller; McFarlane* v *McFarlane*,[5] that a

> »... strict adherence to equal sharing would lead to a rapid decrease in the party's, who carried out the primary care of children, standard of living and a rapid increase in the breadwinner's.«

---

1 Professor and Dean of Law, University of Otago, Dunedin, New Zealand.
2 Thank you to Emily Acland and Heidi Gray, LLB (Hons) students for their research assistance. Thank you to Karen Warrington for producing the manuscript.
3 [1997] 2 NZLR 258.
4 The Court of Appeal did award Mrs Z a share in Mr Z's partnership in a large accountancy firm even though the partnership was personal to Mr Z and could not be sold or transferred to anyone else. The value of the share in the partnership was settled out of Court.
5 [2006] UKHL 24, [2006] 2 AC 618, [2006] 1 FLR 1186 at para 142.

Mrs McFarlane was a solicitor in a leading firm of solicitors in London who interrupted her career to bring up three children. Mr McFarlane was an accountant who continued his career throughout the marriage. The marriage ended after 11 years. During the marriage the husband's net income grew from £ 272,000 to £ 579,000 in the year of separation and £ 753,000 the year after separation.

Baroness Hale has coined the phrase »relationship generated disadvantage« to explain this phenomena of one partner's earning capacity growing while the other partner plays the support role of looking after the children. The phrase »relationship generated« assumes that the difference in earning capacity between the parties is because of the relationship and not some other factor like the particular talents of Mr Z and Mr McFarlane.

This paper uses a partnership analysis to substantiate the positions taken by Richmond P and Baroness Hale, considers the objections to and rationales for this approach and concludes with the best way to deliver economic equality at the end of marriage or other relationship in the nature of marriage.

II. A Partnership of Equals

In 1965 the Beatles and the Beach Boys were all the rave. The Vietnam War had been underway for three years. A New Zealand judge, Sir Owen Woodhouse, who had returned from the Second World War, in the case of *Hofman* v *Hofman*[6] made the statement that

> »marriage is really a partnership of equals ... a partnership of a very special nature ... a joint enterprise.«[7]

This was a radical statement at that time. Traditional notions of property law were the norm. Whoever acquired the property had the best claim to it. Woodhouse J's philosophy was that relationship property legislation is not »part of the law of property« but rather is »social legislation« to support the »ethical and moral undertakings« that men and women take on when they marry and essentially it is part of ensuring »the equal status of women in society.«[8]

---

6   [1965] NZLR 795.
7   Ibid at 798.
8   *Reid* v *Reid* [1979] 1 NZLR 572 at 580.

The New Zealand parliament put Woodhouse J's aspirations into legislation in the Matrimonial Property Act 1976. This Act, which applied only to marriage, recognised that marriage is a partnership and that husbands and wives make equal contributions to it.[9] The Act did not deliver on this underlying principle. Only the family home and chattels were strongly presumed to be shared equally as long as the marriage had lasted for more than three years.[10] Other property acquired during the marriage could be shared unequally if one partner clearly made a greater contribution to it.[11] The Act defined what contributions to a marriage partnership were.[12] These included non-monetary contributions such as care of children, the management of the household, the performance of household duties, the giving of assistance or support to the other spouse and the forgoing of a higher standard of living. The provision and payment of money were also counted as contributions. The Act explicitly said that there is

»*no presumption that a contribution of a monetary nature is of greater value than a contribution of a non-monetary nature.*«[13]

But, the tug of money was irresistible to the courts.

The case of *Reid v Reid*[14] exemplifies the bias towards monetary contributions. Mr and Mrs Reid were married for 21 years. Mrs Reid brought up four children of the marriage and supported Mr Reid. Mr Reid was a successful businessman who built up a company to the value of NZ $ 500,000. The majority of the Court of Appeal held that Mr Reid's contribution was one and a half times that of Mrs Reid. Cooke J held that his contribution was three times that of Mrs Reid. Mr Reid used his business talents, but is he any different from a husband who uses his talents and accumulates a small amount of matrimonial property? Mrs Reid played her role in the partnership by bringing up the children. Mr Reid won twice over – not only did he obtain more than half the matrimonial property (60%) but because he had been able to develop his talents through the division of labour in the household, he also built the basis for his future prosper-

---

9   The long title to the Matrimonial Property Act 1976 said that the Act was »to recognise the equal contribution of husband and wife to the marriage partnership.«
10 Section 11 Matrimonial Property Act 1976.
11 Section 15 Matrimonial Property Act 1976.
12 Section 18 Matrimonial Property Act 1976.
13 Section 18 Matrimonial Property Act 1976.
14 [1979] 1 NZLR 572 at 589.

ity whereas Mrs Reid would have to start from scratch in the workforce.[15] An analysis of all the decisions in the New Zealand Court of Appeal under this Act shows that monetary contributions were given more weight than non-monetary ones.[16]

From the 1st of February 2002 family property disputes in New Zealand have been governed by the Property (Relationships) Act 1976. The new law was enacted by updating the previous Act, hence 1976 still remains in the title. This Act put the brakes on judicial discretion. All property acquired during a marriage or living together relationship (which includes same sex relationships), that lasts more than three years, is to be shared equally.[17] The equal contributions of husbands and wives and living together partners are now reflected in a presumption to equally share the property they have acquired together.

III. Achieving an Equal Result

The Property (Relationships) Act 1976 introduces a further principle – that a just division of relationship property has regard to the economic advantages and disadvantages to the spouses or de facto partners arising from their marriage or de facto relationship or from the ending of their marriage or de facto relationship.[18] Provision is made in the machinery of the Act for a court to redress what is termed »economic disparity«.[19] To achieve this the court must find that the income and living standards of one spouse or partner are likely to be »significantly« higher than the other. This must be »caused« by the division of functions in the marriage or relationship. For example the fact that one partner has given up the opportunity to earn money in the paid workforce to look after the children. In these circumstances a judge has a discretion, if the judge considers it just, to compensate the economically disadvantaged party by ordering the other party to pay a sum of money out of their share of relationship

---

15 Hardie Boys J »Judicial Attitudes to Family Property« (1995) 25 Victoria University of Wellington Law Review, 31-41 at 36 emphasises this point.
16 Mark Henaghan and Nicola Peart, »Relationship Property Appeals in the New Zealand Court of Appeal 1958-2008: The Elusiveness of Equality« in Rick Bigwood (ed) *The Permanent New Zealand Court of Appeal: Essays on the First 50 Years*, Hart Publishing (UK) in press to be published in 2009.
17 Section 11 Property (Relationships) Act 1976.
18 Section 1N(c) Property (Relationships) Act 1976.
19 Section 15 Property (Relationships) Act 1976.

property or to transfer some of their share of relationship property to their spouse or partner.

The rationale for the disparity provision is that marriage and de facto relationships are partnerships of equals. The contribution each partner makes to the partnership, whilst they may be different, are to count equally. At the end of the marriage or relationship if the contributions are equal then the result in terms of economic well being should also be equal. Total economic equalisation is not the goal. The provision is activated where the economic outcome is substantially different.

IV. Objections to the Disparity Provisions

Past benefits are not taken into account. By past benefits is meant the provision of material well-being during the marriage or relationship. For example, the partner who is earning provides the money for the home while the other partner who brings up the children »benefits« from having a roof over their head provided. However, at the same time the earner »benefits« from their partner caring for their children and providing support to the earner's career. In the partnership each is benefiting the other by making different but equal contributions to the joint enterprise. The benefits are equal.

The earner may argue that they have suffered the loss of spending time with their children which they are not compensated for in the same way the child carer is compensated for their time out of the paid workforce. This is not an argument to deny the carer their loss of earnings which is real to them. Nor is it an argument to automatically compensate the earner by giving them compensatory time with their children. That would be to treat children as relationship property.

The earner may argue that the reason that there is a disparity between what they earn and what their partner, who has cared for the children, can earn is their individual talent and has nothing to do with the marriage partnership. This objection denies that marriages or relationships are joint enterprises. The Property (Relationships) Act 1976 provides a mechanism for such individuals.[20] They can contract out of the partnership provided they and their partner receive separate legal advice and

---

20 Part 6 of the Property (Relationships) Act 1976, ss21-21T Property (Relationships) Act 1976.

both agree that disparity in income and living standards will not be compensated.

A disparity award may be criticised for reinforcing economic dependence by the child carer after the relationship or marriage is over. This is a matter of perspective. The child care, home maker partner is not dependent, they are being compensated for the fact that their role in the partnership has disadvantaged them economically while at the same time it has advantaged the other party.

A related objection is that a disparity provision penalises partners who work and bring up children. This does not necessarily follow. If the work that is taken on is part-time and less than what could be done without the care of the children, then the division of functions are still causing economic disparity. If the capacity to earn during the marriage has been enhanced whilst bringing up children then there is no economic disparity at the end.

V. How the Disparity Provision Works

Mr and Mrs X married in 1982. Both won accountancy prizes at university. In 1989, with the birth of their first child, Mrs X stopped working to take care of the child. Another child was born in 1992. During the marriage Mr X completed an MBA (Master of Business Administration) and became a high earner. When the marriage ended in 2003 NZ $ 7.5 million worth of assets had been accumulated. These were divided equally because they had all been accumulated during the marriage. Mr X earned NZ $ 7.7 million in salary over the last five years of the marriage. The wife was working part time earning NZ $ 10,000 per annum. Mrs X sought NZ $ 1.72 million in disparity to compensate her for the disadvantage she had suffered by being out of the paid workforce and for the advantages she had helped create by supporting Mr X in his endeavours to enhance his earning ability.

The Family Court was not sympathetic to Mrs X's claim.[21] Judge Clarkson held that while there was a significant disparity of income between Mr and Mrs X at the end of the marriage there was not a significant difference in likely living standards because the amount of relationship property (NZ $ 7.5 million) when divided would provide a comfortable living for both. However, it is not how comfortable the living standards will be

---

21 X v X [2006] NZFLR 361.

but whether there will be a significant difference which must follow if one partner has a significant difference in income earning capacity.²²

Judge Clarkson further ruled that the disparity in income between Mr and Mrs X was not caused by the division of functions in the marriage but rather that it was a matter of »choice rather than necessity«²³ that Mrs X had come out of the paid workforce to care for the children. The husband's »extremely high skills«²⁴ were given sole credit by Judge Clarkson for his high income.

Rodney Hansen J in the High Court appeal held that the division of functions in the marriage was the dominant cause of the economic disparity. It was a

> »*classic case of a man being given full rein to develop his career and maximise his earning potential while his wife puts her career on hold.*«²⁵

Underlying Judge Clarkson's analysis in the Family Court, that was unsympathetic to Mrs X, were the objections that are commonly raised about provision of economic disparity. Judge Clarkson commented that Mrs X already had benefits and advantages from the marriage. She had had a high standard of living during the marriage and with the benefit of half the assets she could live off the investments without having to work again. Judge Clarkson feared that payment of compensation would place a »premium on the role of the caregiver«.²⁶ None of these considerations are relevant to the core issue which is that marriages and relationships are joint enterprises whereby each partner makes their contributions. These contributions are counted as equal, but economic results will not be equal if one partner has helped enhance the earning ability of their partner while their own earning ability has decreased.

---

22   Rodney Hansen J in the appeal to the High Court accepted that there was significant difference in both income and living standards. *X* v *X* [2007] NZFLR 503 (HC).
23   [2006] NZFLR 361 at para 149.
24   Ibid at para 143.
25   *X* v *X* [2007] NZFLR 503 at para 120.
26   [2006] NZFLR 361 at para 160.

VI. The Conundrums of Compensation

1. *What Is It For?*

Even though the Property (Relationships) Act 1976 introduces the principle that a just division of relationship property has regard to the economic advantages and disadvantages arising from the relationship or marriage, the courts have looked only at disadvantages when awarding compensation. The New Zealand courts have focused on compensation for loss of opportunity to establish a career. When Mrs X went back to the Family Court[27] to claim her compensation she was not awarded the NZ $ 1.72 million in disparity she asked for. Instead she received NZ $ 240,000 which amounted to 3.5 % extra of the relationship property. This amount was calculated by the Court starting from what was termed a »but for« income. This is the income it was estimated Mrs X would have been earning had she not been at home caring for the children. The Court then deducted 50 % for future contingencies such as Mr X may lose his job or suffer ill health. Another 10 % was deducted for the uncertainty of the »but for« test given it was an estimation. The Court then worked out the number of years it would take Mrs X to get back to her full earning capacity. Mrs X was entitled to the compensation to cover those years. The overall amount was halved on the basis that it was relationship property and all such property is shared. This is questionable, the amount was for compensation, it was not relationship property.

In the only case so far in New Zealand to go to the Court of Appeal where economic disparity was an issue the Court took a conservative approach.[28] Mrs M and Mr B were married for 22 years and there were two children of the marriage. Mrs M's income had supported Mr B during the marriage for a year while Mr B took pupillage as a barrister in London. This pupillage enhanced Mr B's career. When the children arrived Mrs M became a full time homemaker back in New Zealand. All the relationship property, which included an amount (NZ $ 225,000) for Mr B's share as a partner in a law firm, was shared equally. At the time of the break up, Mr B was earning NZ $ 600,000 per annum. Mrs M was given a compensatory award of NZ $ 75,000, by Allan J in the High Court,[29] which was not disturbed by the Court of Appeal. Robertson J[30] said that a

---

27 *X* v *X (Quantum)* [2008] NZFLR 512.
28 *M* v *B* [2006] 3 NZLR 660.
29 This amount was based on Mrs M's likely earning ability of NZ $ 70,000-NZ $ 90,000 p.a.
30 Above n26.

»s15 award does not permit a court to exercise a broad and unfettered discretion to redress economic disparity.«

The President of the New Zealand Court of Appeal, William Young P, observed that
> »loss of earnings remains real even though her capital base has been improved.«[31]

The lawyer for Mrs M, Deborah Hollings QC, argued that
> »the husband has 'gained' a secure, high, long term income to some extent as a result of the wife's ›contributions‹ for which she has not otherwise had just recompense.«[32]

This is the advantage part of the principle of doing justice economically at the end of a relationship. New Zealand judges have ignored this part of the principle. Hammond J described[33] Mr B's income as »naturally occurring« which
> »has little or nothing to do with what was brought about by the particular circumstances of the marriage.«

The focus only on disadvantages (the loss of earnings) and the ignoring of advantages (the increased earning capacity of the other partner) has meant that the awards for disparity in New Zealand have generally been low.[34]

Lord Nicholls of Birkenhead in *Miller* v *Miller*; *McFarlane* v *McFarlane*[35] said the
> »parties may have arranged their affairs in a way which has greatly advantaged the husband in terms of his earning capacity, but left the wife severely handicapped so far as her own earning capacity is concerned. Then the wife suffers a double loss, a diminution in her earning capacity and the loss of her husband's enhanced income.«

---

31 Ibid at para 205
32 Ibid at para 273 cited in Hammond J's judgment.
33 Ibid at para 274.
34 The NZ $ 240,000 in *X* v *X (Quantum)* [2008] NZFLR 512 is the highest award in the reported cases. The next highest is NZ $ 138,000 in the High Court case of *P* v *P* [2005] NZFLR 689.
35 [2006] UKHL 24, [2006] 2 AC 618 [2006] 1 FLR 1186 at para 13.

Two decisions of the English Family Division, when discussing compensation for disparity in income and living standards at the end of a marriage, have focused on the »enhanced income« of the earner. The disadvantage of lost career prospects was dismissed by Bodey J in *CR v CR*[36] as a basis for compensation because it was »far too speculative.«[37] This has been born out in the New Zealand experience with wide ranging differences between judges[38] in how they approach making awards for lost career prospects. Bodey J went on to say that the wife's forfeiture of career prospects (which were described as ordinary) were compensated for by the fact of equal division of the family property. Bodey J concluded that it would be unfair to ignore the large income imbalance between the husband and wife at the end of the marriage. The husband was earning £ 1 million per annum net and the wife, who was 51, was receiving £ 100,000 per annum from the husband for her support. The husband had paid rent of £ 90,000 for lease of a property inhabited by the wife. The wife had not been in the paid workforce for 9 years. The »domestic infrastructure« and »support«[39] provided by the wife in the marriage was acknowledged as enabling the husband through »talent and hard work«[40] to have the future income of £ 1 million per annum net.

The earning capacity of the husband was created by the »contributions, lifestyle and spadework of the parties during the marital relationship« according to Charles J in *H v H*.[41] It was a »fruit« or »product of the joint endeavours of the parties during the marital partnership.«[42] The contribution is by giving the earner more time to spend at work (and often more time for leisure recovery) whilst the homemaker attends to the household labour.

So, compensation for a disparity in income and living standards at the end of a marriage or living together relationship is for the loss of develop-

---

36 [2008] 1 FLR 323.
37 Ibid at para 92.
38 The differences are spelt out in J Miles, »Dealing with Economic Disparity: An Analysis of Section 15 Property (Relationships) Act 1976 in *Property (Relationships) Act 1976* [2003] NZ Law Rev 535-568.
39 Above n34 at para 93.
40 Ibid at para 93.
41 [2007] EWHC 459 (Fam) [2007] 2 FLR 548 at para 111.
42 Ibid at para 111. Mrs H was awarded an extra million dollar of property as compensation. Ira Mark Ellman in »Do Americans Play Football?« *International Journal of Law Policy and the Family* 19, (2005) 257-276 at 265, 266 uses the concept of »relational duties« to describe the joint endeavour in a marriage. The American Law Institute's *Principles of the Law of Family Dissolution: Analysis and Recommendations* classifies this as a loss of »marital living standards« at section 5.04.

ing a career (the disadvantage) and for the contribution to developing the other partner's career (the advantage).[43]

2. How to Compensate

The House of Lords in *Miller v Miller; McFarlane v McFarlane*[44] awarded Mrs McFarlane £ 250,000 per annum for her needs and to compensate her for the disadvantage she had suffered by being out of the workforce while the husband had established a career worth £ 753,000 net per annum. There was no time limit put on the award. Mr McFarlane would have to go back to Court if he wanted it to be curtailed. The American Law Institute's *Principles of the Law of Family Dissolution: Analysis and Recommendations* makes provision for a periodic or lump sum payment when awarding compensation for loss of living standards and loss of earning capacity.[45]

The advantage of periodic payments is that they can be adjusted if the payer's or the payee's circumstances change. The disadvantage is described eloquently by Lord Justice Thorpe

»*the continuing monthly credit to one bank account and debt to the other sustains an emotional and psychological relationship and interdependence inconsistent with the dissolution of the marriage.*«[46]

Conceptually, disparity claims are about the future and the past. The disparity is in the future yet it is based on past contributions. The past has generally been dealt with by awards from capital and the future by awards from income. Given this mixture of the past and the future, there is no reason why compensatory payments cannot come from both capital and income.

In New Zealand at the moment compensation can only be awarded out of relationship property (capital). Maintenance payments (income) can only be paid to meet reasonable needs and not to compensate.[47] Reasonable needs does take into account the living standard during the mar-

---

43 The English Law Commission consultation paper released in May 2006 *Cohabitation: The Financial Consequences of Relationship Breakdown* recommends the terms economic advantage and disadvantage as a principled way to resolve the financial consequences of relationship breakdown.
44 [2006] UKHL 24, [2006] 2 AC 618, [2006] 1 FLR 1186.
45 Sections 5.04 and 5.05.
46 »London – The Divorce Capital of the World of Family Law« at para 17, paper presented at the 13th World Conference of the International Society of Family Law, Vienna, Austria, September 16–20, 2008.
47 Sections 63 and 64 Family Proceedings Act 1980.

riage and relationship.[48] There is an obligation to assume responsibility for one's own needs within a »reasonable« time which will vary in the circumstances depending on the ages of the spouses, the duration of the marriage or relationship, the effects of being out of the workforce and the ongoing responsibility for care of children.[49]

A problem with maintenance as the only remedy to compensate is that it requires the payer to have a sufficiently high income to be able to pay it. It is possible to have disparity in low income families. For example in $B \vee B^{50}$ there was a disparity finding of NZ $ 6,000 in a low income family between the husband's and wife's incomes.

An advantage of having the option of being able to use income as a means of compensation is that in some situations there may be a large disparity in income and living standards but very little relationship property (capital) with which to compensate,[51] because for example all the property is in a trust. Therefore the courts should have access to both income and capital when awarding compensation.

3. How Much?

The New Zealand courts have not agreed on a formula for calculating the amount of compensation.[52] Bill Atkin has described their attempts as judicial »plucking out of the air«.[53] It has lead to a new field of valuation whereby valuers give evidence of what they think the non-earner has lost. This is a very costly exercise for the litigants with no consensus about what should be taken account of in making the valuation.[54]

Baroness Hale said in *Miller v Miller; McFarlane v McFarlane* that the goal of a compensatory award is to give both parties »an equal start on

---

48 Sections 63(2)(c) and 64(2)(c) Family Proceedings Act 1980.
49 Section 64A Family Proceedings Act 1980.
50 [2004] NZFLR 653. A sum of NZ $ 16,000 was awarded to be paid as compensation out of relationship property.
51 Bill Atkin, Economic Disparity – how did we end up with it? Has it been worth it? [2007] NZFLJ 299 at 302 points out this problem.
52 J Miles, »Dealing with Economic Disparity: An Analysis of Section 15 Property (Relationships) Act 1976« [2003] NZ Law Rev 535–568 discusses the various formulas that have been used.
53 Bill Atkin, »Courts Trudge Through Statutory Sludge« (2002) Butterworths Family Law Journal, 31–32 at 32.
54 Judge Jan Doogue, »Sections 15 and 15A of the Property (Relationships) Act 1976 – six years on: certainty or uncertainty« [2007] NZFLJ 282–288 – »the guiding principle... is to take a broad brush approach« at 288.

the road to recovery.«[55] An »equal« start in that case would have been to divide the £ 753,000 net income of the husband in half. That was not done because full equalisation may not be practicably possible.

The Family Court of Australia's case *Pethridge v Pethridge*[56] provides the basis for a solution of how to calculate out the amount of compensation for disparity. Mr and Mrs Pethridge were married for 22 years with three children of the marriage including twins. The wife worked part time during the marriage. At the end of the marriage the husband earned A$ 644,000 per annum and the wife A$ 36,000 per annum. In deciding what the distribution of marital property should be the Australian Family Law Act 1975 gives the Court a wide discretion with a wide range of factors to be taken account of which includes the financial and non financial contributions to the marriage, children and the property.[57] Because of the vast difference in income and the fact the wife's »parenting and home maker role had enabled the husband to build experience and seniority for which he is now well renumerated...«[58] the wife was awarded 70% of the matrimonial property and the husband 30% (A $ 310,500).

The strength of the approach in *Pethridge v Pethridge* is that where there was a significant difference at the end of the marriage in income earning capacity, the Judge was able to award a significant difference in property distribution to compensate. The decision was made easier by the fact that Mr Pethridge's new partner was independently wealthy. The difficulty with the decision in *Pethridge* is the discretionary nature of reaching the result and the wide list of factors that had to be worked through.

A guiding principle in the New Zealand Property (Relationships) Act 1976 is that matters should be resolved in an »inexpensive, simple and speedy« manner.[59] The current open discretion in deciding compensation and the use of valuers has made disparity cases expensive, complex and slow. The move to a strong presumption of equal sharing of all property acquired during a marriage or relationship has created certainty and predictability. The disparity provision comes into play when there is a »significant« difference in economic disparity. Significant could be defined as more than a 10% difference in income at the end of the marriage or relationship. The difference will be because of a mixture of the home maker being out of

---

55 [2006] UKHL 24, [2006] 2 AC 618, [2006] 1 FLR 1186 at para 144.
56 [2008] Fam CA 775.
57 Section 79 Family Law Act 1975.
58 Above n54 at para 123.
59 Section 1N(d) Property (Relationships) Act 1976.

the paid work force, the support of the home maker and the talents of the earner. Rather than try and tease out how each of these factors has contributed to the disparity, which would inevitably be a matter of impression, it is simpler to have a rule that a court can order 5, 10, 15 or 20% extra of the relationship property to compensate for disparity. The degree of disparity would determine where the award is made. Mr X was earning NZ $ 1.54 million per year compared to Mrs X NZ $ 10,000 (154% more). Therefore Mrs X should have received as compensation the maximum of 20% more of the property (NZ $ 7.5 million) which is NZ $ 1.5 million.

Mr McFarlane was earning £ 753,000 and Mrs McFarlane was not earning. The maximum of 20% would apply which would have come to £ 600,000 compensation (the property was worth £ 3 million). Overall Mrs McFarlane would receive £ 2.1 million of the £ 3 million worth of property. This would not prevent a maintenance claim by Mrs McFarlane to meet her everyday needs.

The reason for the 20% more ceiling, (which would lead to a 70/30 split of the relationship property) is that any more than that is not likely to be politically acceptable, even though large earners can overcome the difference in property settlement quite quickly. The 20% difference maximum gives some deference to the argument that some of the difference is because of the talents of the earner. It also takes account of future contingencies such as the earner's health and termination of work.

Where there is insufficient relationship property to compensate then the court can award the same proportions (5, 10, 15, 20%) of the earner's net salary for a fixed period of time as the means of compensation. It would be possible to combine both methods, for example if the disparity warrants a 20% difference it could be done by 10% extra of the relationship property and 10% of the salary for a period of time. The preference should be for it to be done though the division of the relationship property to encourage a clean break.

My proposal will not lead to full economic equality but it will lead to quicker, more predictable results which will give larger compensation amounts to the non earner than are currently being awarded. It will be one further step on the path to achieving economic equality at the end of the joint enterprise of marriage or living together as a couple.

Elderly Dependency, Family Caretaking and Law in Portugal

Maria João Romão Carreiro Vaz Tomé[1]

I. Introduction

This essay seeks to contribute to the larger vision within which Portuguese contemporary society reflects on policy and law in relation to aging and the elderly. The elderly must not be considered only as a burden on society, but also as a resource which can contribute to society's well-being. Both the state and the society are called to reflect on the challenges of contemporary aging.

The policy debate on the contemporary challenges of the elderly and family caretaking in Portugal is at stake. The debate includes various different threads on inquiry including globalization and its transformative effects on the workplace, the transformation of contemporary familial structures and its effects on the work of taking care of elderly dependents, and the so-called »feminization of poverty.«

We live in an era of change and controversy with respect to family values. Family law reflects the fragmentation of family ideology. No significant consensus emerged on the broad lines of the last family law reforms. The issue is the choice between competing moral principles. There are two competing visions of the family: one grounded in longing for the stability usually connected with a two-parent heterosexual family, and another based on recognition of the many changes in family form and structure. It can be urged that while a dominant theme of family policy debates in the closing decades of the last century was the need for family law to accommodate the reality of unconventional family life, the emerging theme in the opening of the 21st century is the need to define the limits of that accommodation.

The demographic changes make it difficult to ignore aging and elderly caretaking. Old people are found in all societies, but in very different proportions. Portuguese society faces the steady increase in adult life expec-

---
[1] Portuguese Catholic University School of Law, Porto, Portugal.

tancy associated with the growth in the number of older people, the weakening in labour-force participation of the elderly because of the trend to earlier retirement[2] and the decline of the birth rate[3]. Furthermore, changes in family reveal different problems and needs and render caretaking more difficult.

Which adjustments are necessary to help the family to meet its caretaking responsibility? What are the appropriate roles of the family and the state in bearing elderly dependency economic burdens?[4] It is submitted that to understand what reinforces the risk for a caretaker to lose income when caring for the elderly we must take into account the links between the labor market organization, the family structures and the welfare state institutions. In fact, most jobs and social security systems are still based on the model of the employee with a non-working spouse who looks after the family and runs the household. Of central importance is the convergence of societal and familial interests in adequately addressing dependency.

Presently, family structures sustain more the state and the economy than vice versa. Ignoring family needs and caring for dependency frustrates the achievement of gender equality. The failure to accommodate the labour market to caretaking can be catastrophic.

Regarding the role of the marital family in social law, we take into account its caretaking function and its use by the state as a proxy for desirable outcomes in social policy[5]. Carework and the burdens that caretakers bear as a result of their caretaking are taken into account.

---

2 In view of the decline in population of working age in the next future, and of its consequences on the size of the labour force, there is a policy concern to include the people aged 55 and over in the workforce.
3 In 2007, around 17, 4 % of the population in Portugal were aged 65 and over and around 15, 3 % were aged under 15. The »old-age dependency ratio« (that is, the ratio of the number of people 65 or older (nonworkers) to the number of people 15 to 64 years old (workers)) was 25.3 per cent in 2004. In 2006, this »old-age dependency ratio« was translated into an ageing rate of 114 per 112 individuals aged under 15. Between 1990 and 2005, life expectancy at 65 increased for both women and men. This affects household circumstances. The proportion of women increases with age and there are more women than men aged 65-74 living alone. See www.cidm.pt.
4 See MARTHA ALBERTSON FINEMAN, *The Autonomy Myth: A Theory of Dependency*, The New Press, New York, London, 2004, at xvii-xviii; MAXINE EICHNER, *Review Essay: Dependency and the Liberal Polity: on Martha Fineman's The Autonomy Myth*, 93 *California Law Review* 1285, 2005, at 1289.
5 See MARTHA ALBERTSON FINEMAN, *The Public and Private Faces of Family Law: Progress and Progression in Family Law*, 2004 *The University of Chicago Legal Forum* 1, at 4-5.

If the traditional breadwinner-married-to-caretaker model fails to take account of the ways many individuals now live, and the universal breadwinner model fails to consider elderly dependency, on what conception should the welfare state be premised?

A relevant policy question concerning the family should be how the law can support individuals in caring relationships. Should the law recognize the care provided and received by others rather than family members? It is also important to the design and functioning of a work-based social security system to define what should count as work. Its meaning should be shaped by the underlying teleological justifications for linking work to transfer eligibility.

One significant axis of controversy concerns the appropriate respective roles of the family and the state in bearing elderly dependency burdens. In past times, family members provided reciprocal care to each other through an unspoken intergenerational pact. Parents cared for children during dependency, and, in turn, children cared for parents during their old age.[6] In fact, in a patriarchal family, there is constant intergenerational association, and often coresidence, within a family. The modern social state serves some of the purposes that family units and larger voluntary social networks have served historically.[7] Yet, the family continues to bear much of the burden associated with dependency.[8] Whether the role of the family should expand or shrink is a subject of much debate.

It is relevant to point out that society's feasible choice set does not comprise an unlimited spectrum that runs from the extreme of no dependency assistance at all to the other extreme of completely socialized assistance. Because unaddressed dependency is extremely costly to society as a whole, society has committed itself to provide at least a minimal level of public support for dependents that lack personal or familial resources.

Two approaches occupy opposite ends of the spectrum of possible cost-sharing arrangements between the family and society. The first approach (the »family-first support« model) views the state's role as limited to patch-

---

6 See LEE ANNE FENNELL, *Relative Burdens: Family Ties and the Safety Net*, 45 *William & Mary Law Review* 1453, 2004, at 1474.
7 See MARY ANN GLENDON, *The Transformation of Family Law, State, Law, and Family in the United States and Western Europe*, The University of Chicago Press, Chicago, London, 1989, at 294.
8 See MARY ANN GLENDON, *The Transformation of Family Law, State, Law, and Family in the United States and Western Europe*, The University of Chicago Press, Chicago, London, 1989, at 306.

ing holes in familial support networks, so that assistance is supplied to a dependent individual only where familial arrangements are insufficient or absent. It places costs of elderly care on the family whenever the family is capable of providing that care. However, this model retains a role for public assistance to dependent individuals when familial resources are absent or inadequate. In the opposing model, the state provides an additional safety net for certain categories of dependent individuals regardless of their familial resources or arrangements.

Two normative criteria feature the dependence cost allocations debate: efficiency (which involves minimizing the overall cost of dependency and its treatment throughout society) and distributive justice (which relates to the fairness of the distribution among members of society of the cost of dependency and its treatment).

Typically, at least three parties are deeply interested in whether dependency is adequately addressed: the dependent individual, the dependent individual's family, and the state. The family is typically bound to its dependent members by love and other forms of interdependency, but the state is also invested in the care of its citizens.

II. Family Relationships

The legal concept of family is found in Article 1576 of the Civil Code. It considers as sources of legal family relationships marriage, parenthood, affinity and adoption. This is a legal-technical concept of family. However, Portuguese law takes into account larger and less technical notions of the family, which are valid within certain domains or for certain effects. Thus, social security law and lease law makes resort to the concept of »family aggregate«.

Under a legal approach, the family is composed by a group of individuals but it is not itself a legal person. Taking into account the interests of the individuals, their autonomy and independency, the law has eliminated most references to the family's interest or good. This does not mean that in some cases the law does not acknowledge it as holder of its own interests as different from the individual interests of the members of the group. The normative modern marriage is an economic partnership built on sharing principles (Article 1671 of the Civil Code).

III. The Traditional Family

The family preferred by the legal system is rooted in history. However, several of today's families are not traditional in structure. The number of families meeting the traditional family model has steadily declined. Thus, some current laws to a certain extent reflect value judgments about the ideal family structure instead of the reality of how people live. This misalignment hurts those who conform to the traditional structure as well as those who do not[9].

In fact, at the heart of the social system, the notion of family evokes an image of the traditional patriarchal household with the male breadwinning father as its head. The sources of gender inequality in social systems arise from regimes based on a traditional concept of the family where the husband is the breadwinner, and the wife is seen as the economic dependant whose social security entitlements are derived through the husband. Inequality also arises from the non-recognition of caring for the elderly as economically valuable work. The concept of family as recognized by social law has not changed much over time. Social rights are essentially based on a traditional dependency model, and, thus, are also of little use to modern couples.

It is urged that the option of a single income family has disappeared, since most families require the income of two wage earners simply to stay in place in real income terms. Nevertheless, the allocation within families of care giving responsibilities has not changed much over time. No matter how much money women make or how much value they place on their careers, they retain the majority of the caretaking responsibility. This caretaking responsibility in turn leads to less market work, less social benefits and increased dependency for women[10].

---

9   See MARIA JOÃO VAZ TOMÉ, *O direito à pensão de reforma enquanto bem comum do casal*, Coimbra Editora, Coimbra, 1997, at 128 ff; MARIA JOÃO VAZ TOMÉ, *O direito à pensão de reforma (por velhice) no divórcio – Algumas Considerações*, Seminário »Direito da Segurança Social«, Tribunal de Contas, Lisboa, 2000, at 150 ff.

10 See MARTHA ALBERTSON FINEMAN, *Masking Dependency: The Political Role of Family Rhetoric*, 81 Virginia Law Review 2181, 1995, at 2200; MARTHA ALBERTSON FINEMAN, *The Neutered Mother, the Sexual Family and Other Twentieth Century Tragedies*, Routledge, New York, London, 1995, at 164-166, 227; JENNIFER R. JOHNSON, *Preferred by Law: The Disappearance of the Traditional Family and Law's Refusal to Let It Go*, 25 Women's Rights Law Reporter 125, 2004, at 125-126, 129; MARIA JOÃO VAZ TOMÉ, *A esquecida conexão patrimonial entre o Direito da Família e o Direito da Previdência Social*, Comemorações dos 35 anos do Código Civil e dos 25 anos da Reforma de 1977, Coimbra Editora, Coimbra, 2004, p.526 ff, 529 ff; VIVIAN

Women perform the great majority of paid and unpaid care work in Portuguese society, and political, cultural and social expectations shape the lives of the many women who will provide this care. Women's caretaking responsibilities make them economically vulnerable. A woman who devotes herself to the caring for an elderly dependent may herself become dependent on another or others for resources to support herself and her charge.

Despite the fact that many families now have two earners, very little workplace restructuring has taken place to support elderly caretaking.

Domestic arrangements that do not conform to the family unit are on the rise. More and more individuals are living alone than in past decades. Divorce rates are increasing.[11] The number of persons marrying is also in decline.[12] The increase in civil marriage[13] is connected with the rise in the number of second and subsequent marriages. But it also masks a change in the understanding of marriage: there is been a cultural shift in

---

HAMILTON, *Mistaking Marriage for Social Policy*, 11 *Virginia Journal of Social Policy & the Law* 307, 2004, at 318, 362-365.

11   In 2007, there were 25 255 divorces, which makes 2, 4 divorces per 1000 inhabitants compared to 2, 2 divorces in 2006. See INSTITUTO NACIONAL DE ESTATÍSTICA, *Estatísticas Demográficas – 2007*.

It is interesting to point out the new divorce law (Law 61/2008 of 31st October). The legislature adopts a »pure« no fault divorce system. The law establishes a compensation obligation that is partly based on the theory that traditional marriage operates on a »gendered division of labour«. It looks at the individual contributions of each spouse to the marriage. Thus, if the contributions of one spouse to the household is significantly larger that it was expected to be according to a proportionality criterion, because he or she mostly considered the family interest to the detriment of his or her individual interests and as a consequence suffered relevant property damages, that spouse is entitled to a compensatory award (Article 1676 (2) of the Civil Code). It is submitted that if the marriage dissolved through no fault of either spouse, some return on the investment is considered to be appropriate.

Furthermore, the law embraces the concept of rehabilitative alimony. Alimony is now awarded only to help the financially impacted spouse to become self- sufficient and should be a temporary measure (Article 2016 (1) of the Civil Code). It is a consequence of the clean break principle. The presumption behind rehabilitative alimony is that it will eventually help the supported spouse obtain steady employment and learn to survive. The spouses' marital standard of living is not considered (Article 2016-A (3) of the Civil Code). Although the legislature intended to eliminate fault, it allows misconduct to be taken into account in a clause of negative equity (Article 2016 (3) of the Civil Code) which prevents the needy spouse from receiving alimony in case that it is shocking imposing the alimony obligation on the other spouse.

12   See www.cidm.pt.

13   In 2007, there were 4, 4 marriages per 1000 inhabitants compared to 4, 5 marriages in 2006. In 2007, 22 895 of the 46 329 marriages were civil marriages. See INSTITUTO NACIONAL DE ESTATÍSTICA, *Estatísticas Demográficas – 2007*.

which marriage is seen more as a terminable contract rather than a lifelong commitment.[14] The median age for marriage has risen.[15] The ability of the family to carry out the tasks for which society relies on it has been dramatically altered by changes in family structure, in the labour force participation of women[16], and in the nature of dependency itself. The modern two-earner family with children, and the single-parent family in particular[17], must rely more on outside support systems for dealing with their dependent members than the homemaker-breadwinner household, which has now become atypical. And while the pool of available caretakers within the family has been shrinking, the composition of the group in need of care has altered to include far fewer children and far more elderly people than it did before.[18]

---

14 In 2007, the second marriage rate was 22.9 per cent. See INSTITUTO NACIONAL DE ESTATÍSTICA, *Estatísticas Demográficas – 2007*.
15 In 2007, the average age in first marriage was 29.7 years for women and 32.2 for men. The average age at which young people leave home has tended to rise over time for both men and women. See INSTITUTO NACIONAL DE ESTATÍSTICA, *Estatísticas Demográficas – 2007*.
16 It is interesting to point out that in 2006, the women's employment rate was 62.3 per cent compared to 73.8 per cent for men's. Moreover, the percentage of employed women with part-time jobs was only 15.9 per cent. Furthermore, women also earn less than the similarly situated men. In 2004, their remunerations were 80 per cent of men's. In addition, earnings of men tend to increase with age, at least up to the age of 50, but this is less the case for women. This in part reflects the smaller rate of women than men in senior positions. Women earn less than men even when they have been in the job for a similar length of time. Indeed, as in the case of age, the wage gap tends to widen the longer women and men have been in the same job. Finally, in 2006, the female unemployment rate was 9.0 per cent and the male rate was 6.5 per cent. See www.cidm.pt.
17 In 2001, the rate of monoparental families was 11.5 per cent. See www.cidm.pt.
18 In 2007, there were 9,7 live births per 1000 inhabitants compared to 10,0 in 2006, much less than the rate of 2.1 per cent which is required to maintain the population constant. See INSTITUTO NACIONAL DE ESTATÍSTICA, *Estatísticas Demográficas – 2007*.
    See MARIA JOÃO VAZ TOMÉ, *Family Law and Family Values in Portugal*, in *Family Law and Family Values*, edited by Mavis Maclean, Hart Publishing, Oxford and Portland, Oregon, 2005, at 333–335.

IV. Recognizing Family Look-Alikes: Quasi-Family Relationships: People That Live in a »Common Economy Relationship« (Law 6/2001 of 11th May)

It is not just the law that confers on the nuclear family its status.[19] In fact, the law has been to some extent one of the most flexible of Portuguese normative institutions, offering the promise of more flexible models of the family than many other normative systems.

One set of challenges to the current preference for the traditional family is the concept of quasi-family to include other groups that »look like« families; these challenges argue that these entitlements should be conferred because they perform the same function of fulfilling the emotional and material needs of their members.[20] This argument seems to confer some benefits to some non-family groups.

The family is seen as the place for distributive justice, the place for inter-individual and inter-generation solidarity. Other groups that »look like« a family may also be considered as the place for distributive justice and solidarity.

1. A Functional Model

This approach encourages a functionality test, which recognizes relationships of any form that function like a family. A functional family member can be seen as someone who takes care of somebody on a daily basis, and provides affection and financial support. This family can be said as a social unit capable of fostering relationships characterized by intimacy, trust and mutual affection.

There has been employed a functional approach to the family in order to obtain for alternative familial benefits usually reserved for the marital family. This approach questions whether an unconventional relationship shares the essential characteristics of a traditionally accepted relationship; if so, the unconventional relationship should receive equivalent benefits.

---

19 See MARY ANN GLENDON, *The Transformation of Family Law, State, Law, and Family in the United States and Western Europe*, The University of Chicago Press, Chicago, London, 1989, at 291, 293; JAMES A. SONNE, *Love Doesn't Pay: The Fiction of Marriage Rights in the Workplace*, 40 *University of Richmond Law Review* 867, 2006, at 871, 943–944.

20 »It is widely accepted that significant changes occurred in family behaviour in western societies during the last quarter of the twentieth century«. See JOHN EEKELAAR, *Personal Obligations*, in *Family Law and Family Values*, edited by Mavis Maclean, Hart Publishing, Oxford and Portland, Oregon, 2005, p. 1.

In fact, care giving and economic support benefit society whether performed within or outside of the marital relationship.

Examples of these types of reforms include people that live in a »common economy relationship«.

2. A Dependency Model

This approach could advocate a structure to accommodate elderly dependency through the recognition that caretakers' functions of nurturing require resources. Thus, the new »family line« would be around dependency: the elderly, the terminally ill, and the disabled – all inevitably dependents.

3. People that Live in a »Common Economy Relationship« (Law 6/2001 of 11 May)[21]

The emergence of different legal quasi-family relationships shows the development of a new morality that is beginning to inform family law that rests focused on connection, care, and commitment to other individuals, but also contains problematic notions of choice. For this purpose, the state has deemphasized the family form.

Others who are not couples but are in defined »common economy relationships« have been granted a more limited set of rights and obligations under some laws than people living in a de facto union. Through the enlargement of the circle of relationships recognised by law, regulation has been extended to groups of people sharing habitation.

There is a kind of a pattern of coresidence, which has some clear benefits. It neither condemns people to lonely old age nor deprives the young of the wisdom of the aged.

According to the law, the concept of »common economy relationship« is applied where people live in community of table and home for more than two years and have established a life in common as far as mutual help and share of resources are concerned (Article 2(1)). It may be constituted by people either linked or not by family ties, by people of the same or of different sex, by two or more people. At least one of the members has to be 18 years old (Article 2(2)). The law also protects the situation of two individuals of different sexes that do not have sexual relationships, as well as those situations of three or more individuals that share the same space

---

21 See FRANCISCO PEREIRA COELHO, GUILHERME DE OLIVEIRA, *Curso de Direito da Família, Volume I,* Coimbra Editora, Coimbra, 2008, at 94 ff.

and share the living costs. Mutual help or share of resources is required. It is not necessary that people share their incomes and resources; it is sufficient that they live in a community of mutual help where they contribute to the living expenses. These are situations that are not restricted to the community of economy, but also have regard to the share of material, sentimental, social, human resources among other things. They are protected in labour law, tax law, and protection of the common residence and transmission of the lease contract upon the death of the tenant member is granted (Articles 4(1) (e) and 6). In fact, upon the death of the partner whose name is on the lease, the award possession of a rented home is granted to the other partner, in the light of the interests involved (Article 1106 of the Civil Code).

In case of death of the owner of the common residence, ordinary rules are not applied. The non-owners are entitled to both the right to dwell in that property for five years and the right to prefer on its sale (Articles 4 (d) and 5). This rule is not applicable where there are ascendants and descendants that have lived with him or her for one year and intend to continue living there, where there is a will stating the opposite, where there are descendants under 18 that do not live with the dead but do need the house to live.

The benefits given to the individuals are translated into rights to holidays (Article 217 (5) of the Labour Code), to absenteeism (Article 227 (2) of the Labour Code; Article 203 of the Labour Code Regulation) and leave (Article 43 (5) of the Labor Code, Article 71 (8) of the Labor Code Regulation, Article 99 of the Labor Code Regulation, Article 44 of the Labor Code) in both the public (Article 4 (1) (a)) and the private (Article 4 (1) (b)) sectors, in terms equivalent to those enjoyed by married couples. In addition, those tax benefits which are applicable to spouses also apply to »living in a common economy relationship« with some adjustments (Articles 4 (1) (c) and 7).

However, the law establishes some impediments to the acknowledgment of »living in a common economy«: a contract which implies living in the same house, a working relationship, the existence of a common economy for temporary and specific purposes, and physical or psychological coercion of any individual (Article 3).

In some public law areas, where family membership is at stake, the family is envisioned as an economic, rather than a legal, entity. Therefore, living in a »common economy relationship« was legally considered in social law, labour law and tax law.

The demographic changes of the past century make it difficult to ignore caregiving. Things have changed so much over the past few decades with regard to family formation and functioning that traditional expectations for the family have been challenged. It can be said that family law and social law should recognize the care provided and received by other people rather than family.

Therefore this regulation may be viewed as a way of accommodating dependency. In fact, elderly dependency, culturally assigned to the family, is privatised. Neither the state nor the labour market directly contribute to or assist in the necessary caretaking – that is done in the privacy of household. The burdens of economic support and caretaking are allocated within the household based on the perceived roles its members play. This assignment of burdens within the household operates in an inherently unequal manner; the uncompensated tasks of caretaking are mainly placed with women.

From a functional perspective, this new institution could be used as a complement to the state to care for the dependency of the elderly. It should be concerned with the elderly dependents that need protection. Caretaking should be valued and biological and economic connections should not be of paramount importance. It should accommodate demands of inevitable and derivative dependency and adequately protect the nurturing unit of caretaker and dependant in tax law, inheritance law, social security and welfare laws, and etc. A kind of »care giving family« would be a protected space, entitled to special treatment by the state.

The »common economy relationship« can be seen as an embryonic support to individuals who create caring relationships.

Economic support is essential to dependent caretaking. There is a public interest in these functions whether they are performed both within and outside of the marital family.

In fact, with old people living longer, the costs to relatives or nonrelatives of providing the elderly with goods and services are incurred for a longer period. By sharing a house with a relative or a friend, elderly people have access to the potential support which living with other people implies.

In addition, by considering wealth in real and not merely pecuniary terms, household production, like elderly caretaking, is an important source of wealth.

By supporting more pluralistic personal relationships and conceptions of care, family law could also transform gender itself.

V. Collective Responsibility Models

1. The Relevance of Care Work

Work is central to many areas of law, including social law. However, work is not easy to define. Yet it is essential to the design and functioning of a work-based welfare system. Work should be understood contextually, its meaning shaped by the underlying normative justifications for linking work to social benefits.

Caring has individual importance, as for many people, providing it entails some of life's greatest commitments and personal rewards. Caring has also universal importance, since individuals could not survive or flourish without it. Caring has societal and economic importance, because it provides the foundation for society's institutions and reproduces families, communities and society itself, while contributing greatly to the national economy. Caring has ethical importance, since it is an essential virtue to a democratic society. Finally, elderly caretaking is a productive activity.

2. Societal Responsibility Models

It can be said that the egalitarian family is the solution to the problem of women's subordination and economic vulnerability. Such a family would »encourage and facilitate the equal sharing by men and women of paid and unpaid work, of productive and reproductive labour«[22].

On the contrary, private responsibility alone is unlikely to provide a complete basis for addressing elderly care concerns. The result of this structure is that elderly are viewed as a family rather than a societal responsibility. Moreover it is argued that the gendered nature of the traditional family will be resistant to the most radical transformations. The ideal of the egalitarian family is fundamentally insufficient to overcome the gendered and unequal nature of the marital family. In addition, attaining equality in the marketplace, one of the goals of the egalitarian couple,

---

22 See JOAN WILLIAMS, *Unbending Gender: Why Family and Work Conflict and What to Do About It,* Oxford University Press, Oxford, New York, 2000, at 232; SUSAN MOLLER OKIN, *Justice, Gender, and the Family,* Basic Books, USA, 1989, at 171; MAXINE EICHNER, *Review Essay: Dependency and the Liberal Polity: on Martha Fineman's The Autonomy Myth,* 93 California Law Review 1285, 2005, at 1295–1296; NANCY FRASER, *Justice Interruptus: Critical Reflections on the »Postsocialist« Condition,* Routledge, New York, London, 1997, at 47–48; MARY ANNE CASE, *How High the Apple Pie? A Few Troubling Questions about Where, Why, and How the Burden of Care for Children Should Be Shifted,* 76 Chicago-Kent Law Review 1753, 2001, at 1756.

potentially leaves the family without available caretakers. »Shared« caretaking between spouses has remained illusory – whether or not both partners work, women perform most domestic work[23].

Public support must be deemed an integral part of any solution to the issue of care work that takes the goal of substantive sex equality seriously. Achieving substantive sex equality requires state support of care work[24].

But what kind of public support? It can be said that there are two different types of public support[25]. According to the so-called »direct subsidy« approach, the state directly subsidizes caretakers for performing care work in family settings. In accordance with the so-called »public integration« approach, the state accommodates societal institutions like the labour market to the demands of caretaking.

Both of these models are a departure from the model that has dominated social policy, which is constructed on a particular vision of social organization. It is based on the presumption that citizens should and do live in families comprised of a breadwinner married to a caretaker, and their children. Most of the programs developed on this model sought to replace the breadwinner's wage in the event of unemployment, sickness, disability, or retirement.

Events in recent years have at least partially forced the demise of this breadwinner-married-to-caretaker model. The increased entry of women into the labour market and the fact that many jobs no longer pay enough

---

23 See MARTHA ALBERTSON FINEMAN, *The Autonomy Myth, A Theory of Dependency*, The New Press, New York, London, 2004, at 171, stating that »we must reject the notion that the problem of work/family conflict should be cast as the problem of a lack of equal sharing between women and men of domestic burdens within the family. We have gone down that road and it is a dead end. Our arguments for reform must now acknowledge that the societally constructed role of mother continues to exact unique costs for women«. See JOAN WILLIAMS, *Unbending Gender: Why Family and Work Conflict and What to Do About It*, Oxford University Press, Oxford, New York, 2000, at 235; MAXINE EICHNER, *Review Essay: Dependency and the Liberal Polity: on Martha Fineman's The Autonomy Myth*, 93 *California Law Review* 1285, 2005, at 1296–1297.

24 See MARTHA ALBERTSON FINEMAN, *The Autonomy Myth: A Theory of Dependency*, 2004, at 201–202; JOAN WILLIAMS, *Unbending Gender: Why Family and Work Conflict and What to Do About It*, Oxford University Press, Oxford, New York, 2000, at 235; NANCY FRASER, *Justice Interruptus: Critical Reflections on the »Postsocialist« Condition*, Routledge, New York, London, 1997, at 53–54.

25 See MARTHA ALBERTSON FINEMAN, *The Autonomy Myth, A Theory of Dependency*, The New Press, New York, London, 2004, at 263; MARTHA ALBERTSON FINEMAN, *Cracking the Foundational Myths: Independence, Autonomy, and Self-Sufficiency*, 8 *American University Journal of Gender, Social Policy and the Law* 13, 2000; MAXINE EICHNER, *Review Essay: Dependency and the Liberal Polity: on Martha Fineman's The Autonomy Myth*, 93 *California Law Review* 1285, 2005, at 1303–1304.

wages to support a family have been responsible for some recognition that this model does not conform to the far more varied groupings in which people now live their lives. Some thinkers propose a model that presumes everybody should be a breadwinner. However, in adopting this new »universal breadwinner« model, social policy fails to take account of elderly dependency and to give caretaking the support it both requires and merits.

Yet if the traditional breadwinner-married-to-caretaker model fails to take account of the ways many citizens now live their lives, and the universal breadwinner model fails to take account of elderly dependency, on what alternative conception should the social system be premised? The direct subsidy approach holds that caregivers should continue to provide care in much the same way that caregivers in the traditional breadwinner-married-to-caretaker model did. Job structures are not required to change, and care giving is still to be performed largely by family members in private homes. The difference between the traditional model and this approach is that now caregivers will receive money for their work from the state. In contrast, the public integration approach, calls for the state to structure societal institutions in ways that enable citizens to integrate the roles of both caregiver and breadwinner into their lives. This approach therefore requires significant changes to the labour market. It replaces the old model of the breadwinner married to the caretaker with one in which citizens are each, individually, both breadwinners and caretakers.

Unlike the old breadwinner-married-to-caretaker model and the modern universal breadwinner model, both the direct subsidy and public integration models have the virtue of public support for caretaking and contribute to the achievement of sex equality. In addition, they likely allow women to achieve financial equality and better combat the destructive myths about care. Moreover, they render possible the coexistence of the caring and breadwinning roles and ensure that dependents' needs are met.

VI. Conclusion

Gender neutrality continues to dominate the legal arena. Recognition of difference is deemed suspect based on the fear of reinforcing problematic and hierarchal stereotypes, thereby undermining headway in women's equality. Furthermore, the normative appreciation for sameness of treatment as a proxy for equality makes recognizing difference unpalatable.

However, these concerns are also used to justify avoiding the recognition of gender difference even when such recognition is essential to alleviating hardships that women face. The caretaker role must be affirmatively recognized and revalued to give caretakers the dignity they deserve commensurate with the important societal contributions they provide. Caretaking provides an important and needed contribution to society by supporting elderly dependents.

Despite the tremendous public interest in elderly dependents' care, the state's efforts to directly support dependent caretaking, irrespective of the family structure within which it occurs, have been anaemic. The rhetorical importance placed on elderly caretaking stands in stark contrast to family support policies.

The marital family is the locus for economic support of dependents in what can be seen as a privatized system of wealth redistribution. The family's caretaking and economic functions are closely related. Economic support is essential to caretaking; the economic well-being of all its elderly dependents, therefore, should be of primary concern to the state. Ignoring the emerging family needs can be disastrous to both the family and society.

Public support must be an essential component of any solution to the carework issue. Since changes in family form and functioning make caretaking and managing elderly dependency more difficult, policymakers should promote the adjustments that are necessary in order to help the family to meet its caretaking responsibility.

The state could deemphasize family form. It could also introduce programs that directly bolster elderly caretaking and the economic supports that make such caretaking possible.[26] The state, irrespective of the economic resources, should employ several of family-friendly structures: for example, job-supported paid elderly caretaking leave, economic familial support, and universal elderly care. Payroll tax could be used to finance these benefits and expanding social security to include families impoverished by elderly caretaking, thus »addressing a societal problem at a societal level.« To further ensure the economic security of the elderly, the state should also make modifications to the welfare, social security, and tax systems. These could include combining the welfare and social security

---

26   See MARTHA ALBERTSON FINEMAN, *The Autonomy Myth: A Theory of Dependency*, The New Press, New York, London, 2004, at 200, 261-262; MARLENE SCHMIDT, *Family Friendly Policy and the Law: Germany: Employment, the Family, and the Law: Current Problems in Germany*, 27 *Comparative Labor Law and Policy Journal* 451, 2006, at 451.

systems into a system that ensures that dependents and their caretakers receive a level of support and increasing elderly tax credits for caretakers.

The state should support care work in a manner that would allow citizens to combine caretaking responsibilities with work in the labour market, or at least directly subsidize such care work in private homes.

Working time arrangements do not seem to provide much support for people with caring responsibilities. In Portugal, over 90% of women work fixed or staggered hours. Flexible working-time arrangements have a key role to play in rendering possible to individuals with elderly dependency responsibilities to pursue a professional career. Some types of working arrangements may be considered, such as fixed or staggered hours, working time banking, flexible working time arrangements, and other.

Ignoring caring for elderly dependency frustrates one of the goals embraced by family law over the past thirty years: the achievement of gender equality within the family.

The state should take seriously into account the redistribution of care work between the sexes. The political goal that women and men should have equal opportunities and roles in occupational life and in family tasks does not harmonize with welfare policies based on a single breadwinner model.

Self-Determination and State Intervention: A Balance for Protection of the Reserved Portion of the Estate in the 2002 Brazilian Civil Code in the Light of New Family Arrangements[1]

Cláudia Elisabeth Pozzi[2]

I. Civil Law and Family in Modern Society

Self-regulation of the individual's private life is one of the characteristics of the modern-day family. It is this principle that sets the scenario for a critical analysis of the legal impasses this freedom of choice may create for second families; thus, this article proposes an analysis focused on self-determination within the domestic environment and the protection of the patrimony of the reserved portion of the estate of the new families' members.

1. The Transformations of Family and Private Space

Tolerance of a certain diversity in the field of family law (marriage; post-marriage following divorce and family re-composition; births outside marriage; single parenthood; unmarried status; de facto partnerships; single status and the right not to have children) is indicative that pluralism within family law is not a new concept (Lemouland, 2007). This in effect gives space to the idea that people have yet to free themselves from traditional family patterns characterized by marriage, sexual and spatial co-habitation with children.

On the legislative level, the new juridical relevance criterion of subjectified relations between individuals and the institution of family represents a fundamental moment in history (Furgiuele, 1987), as the defense of new rights within the family ambit enables a readjustment capable of addressing the desire for a more democratic and just order (Giddens, 1993) through the integration of fundamental rights into the sphere of the

---

1 I wish to thank Fundação para a Ciência e Tecnologia, Portugal, for the financial support to my participation in the 13th World Conference of the International Society of Family Law, *Family Finances*, Vienna, Austria, September 16–20, 2008.
2 University of Coimbra, Portugal.

citizens' private lives. This is one of the main shifts that family law has undergone.

Concomitant to these alterations, the freedom to establish contracts within family law represents the practical application of these opening remarks on the empowerment of the individual (Grossi, n/d) to negotiate and re-negotiate conjugal agreements in accordance with the subjective interests of the parties (division of assets, bequests, testaments) and in relation to parenthood (adoption, forms of establishing guardianship and child visits and use of reproductive biotechnologies).

Such declarations prove to be effective and valid provided they do not conflict with constitutional decrees, and as long as the content of such contracts falls within the family ambit, which the parties are unable to determine due to the public interest in private relations with regard to equality and the dignity of those involved (Perlingieri, 1986). The State's intervention regulates, therefore, in the private sphere: monogamy, the prohibition of incest, responsible parenthood and the forbidding of the use of human embryos in assisted reproductive techniques; and in the patrimonial sphere it regulates: property arrangements, prenuptial agreements and restrictions on the freedom to act in donation contracts among ascendants, descendants and spouses and in regard to protection of the non-disposable part of the family economy.

Central to this tendency to subjectify juridical-family relations is the fragmentation of the centrality of codifying laws in Western legal systems (Irti, 1979). This being a reflection of legislative pulverization effected through micro-systems (Perlingieri, 1997) with autonomous rights hierarchically articulated in the constitutional text and the constitutional principles and human rights representing a hermeneutic guide in order to guarantee historical and juridical unity of the whole system (Perlingieri, 1986). Or, a shift from the centrality of the Civil Code as society organizer to a constitutional interpretive axis.

The penetration of values in family rights resulting from the fundamental rights of human dignity and the intimacy of family life (Oliveira, 2008) provides a link between the internal order and the universalization of basic human rights (Arnaud, 1998) in admitting the intersection of normative rules of familiar life internally and externally linked to a worldwide contemporaneity (Allard & Garapon, 2006), in which the **commerce of judges** implies knowledge transmission especially through the influence of international courts on local courts, resulting in the transcendence of traditional legal boundaries.

This exteriorization of family relations that surpass civil codification offers an example of the characteristics that constitute the internal normativeness of each country, leading to complexity in the modern day justice system (Pocar & Ronfani, 2007), based on the social and ethical function as a condition of being in the private world and having the family ambit being filtered through a family law system open to new normative sources.

There is space for behavioral and transformational changes of intimacy interposed with the democratization and universalization of law (Santos, 2002), international court decisions, treaties, human rights conventions (Giacco, 2006); characteristics that tend to redefine traditional assumptions of family law.

By transcending its boundaries Civil Law feeds on the tendency to adopt (not without resistance from the dominant legal culture) pluralism (Fachin, 2000) in contrast to the positivist view of the juridical dogma (classical) that proclaims the law to be a closed, self-referential system, that relies on limited sources as strictly laid down in the law (Corapi, 1986). The law is subjected to family realities that are brought about through other forces (social, cultural, economic, scientific and anthropological) and whose own forms of family relations cannot be dismissed once they exist in effect.

Not without cause, the defense of the idea that family presents itself as an **intrinsic institution**, intrinsically self-referential by virtue of possessing an **intimate and proper juridical order** pre-existent to law, incorporating the family into the social reality (Xavier, 2008).

2. New Arrangements and Legal Perspectives

From this perspective, a clash occurs within the unitary model of the heterosexual matrimonial family that continues to be hierarchically privileged in the Brazilian juridical order. Such was the orientation of the Brazilian Civil Code of 1916: legitimate family and illegitimate family; legitimate offspring and illegitimate offspring.

With the 1988 Constitution, pluralism in the family circle appears for the first time thus admitting familiar entities as a family category (with a certain hierarchical prevalence of marriage), causing an interpretive outcry over the principle of extended equality before the law regarding the family circle.

It was not until the promulgation of the 2002 Civil Code that family law was reshaped by the constitutional text and by jurisprudence, which tended to assign equal rights to marriage and in de facto partnerships (Law n. 8,971/94 and Law n. 9,278/96).

Following 2002, although a greater proximity existed between families constituted within and outside civil marriage, in inheritance rights there was a complete differentiation in terms of the form of patrimony transfer, thus representing the persistence of the unitary and hierarchical model in the current legal arrangement.

There are many gaps or omissions in Brazilian family law: there is no legal provision for homosexual unions and *de facto* socio-affective parenthood does not encounter legal support.

The new forms of affective relations in recomposed families open the way for diversity in kinship and pluri-parenthood (Le Gall, 2003), which render the traditional family structures inapplicable (Théry, 1998). Civil law has nothing to say on family diversity and clearly displays its failure to adapt to current realities (Fachin, 2002).

This point is important because even though civil marriage accounts for the vast majority of conjugal relations, there is the need to underline a tendency towards diversification of this model. *Civil Registry Statistics for 2007*[3] demonstrate this assertion. In 2007, although there were 916,006 marriages in Brazil, 2.9 per cent higher than in 2006 (889,828), the numbers of dissolutions (direct divorces and separations) reached 231,329. In other words, for every 4 marriages there was one registered dissolution. There is a preponderance of marriage between single people (83.9 per cent) with a tendency for this type of arrangement to decline over the last 10 years (90.1 per cent in 1997). There is also a growing proportion of marriages between divorced and single people, especially divorced men and single women (7.1 per cent) and marriages between two divorced spouses (2.5 per cent).

Family recomposition is one of the characteristics of current marital relations, broadening the variety of affective situations of parenthood and the types of family structure. *Social Indicators of 2007*[4] offer data on the growth of one-person families (10.7 per cent) and the single-parent family (18.1 per cent), the vast majority of which are under the financial responsibility of women (89.2 per cent). This fact is representative of the changes in the domestic domain in regard to gender relations and indicative of the economic reproduction difficulties of those families in which almost half of them (42.6 per cent) are composed of children under the age of 16 and living (47 per cent of them) with ¾ of a minimum salary per capita[5].

---

3 *Statistics of Civil Registry 2007*/Brazilian Institute of Geography and Statistics.
4 *Social Indicators 2007*/ Brazilian Institute of Geography and Statistics.
5 The minimum salary in 2008 was R$ 415,00, approximately 130 Euros.

II. The Economic Protection of Families: The Non-Disposable Part of Patrimony

Tension between self-determination in the private sphere and state intervention in the legal protection of the rights of heirs to the family patrimony is located in this context of contemporaneity of civil law, associated with the internationalization of types of knowledge which engage in dialogue (Fachin, 2000) and with the normative pluralism of sources concerning the understanding of family grouping.

However, the democratization of personal life and self-determination of individuals have an economic counterbalance (Commaille, n/d): the division of matrimonial patrimony after divorce, the formation of recombined families and added fragilization of female single-parent families that have the sole custody of minor children in 90.64 per cent of divorce and separation cases[6].

The patrimonialization of private legal relationships still enshrined in the 2002 Brazilian Civil Code is perfectly combined with the oldest civilist tradition that continues to center on the family as constituted by marriage, and on legitimate parenthood. However, this protection, that has been the stage of profound social exclusions, paradoxically and through the imperativeness of the norm that imposes economic limitations on self-determination in the private and patrimonial life of families, becomes an important mechanism of family reproduction following conjugal breakdown, specifically in view of the inadequacy of family-supportive public policies and the fragilization of female-led single-parent families.

Freedom of contract in the private sphere integrates with these presuppositions of family self-regulation, especially sales and purchase contracts and donations between ascendants and descendents or between spouses. In the first case, as it is a compulsory contractual transfer between the parties, there are no legal restrictions to the juridical business. The law merely demands the duty, under penalty of nullification, that an express agreement exists on the part of the remaining descendents and spouse (article 496, Civil Code)[7].

In the hypothesis of donation, the discipline of this contract occurs with greater strictness since it is a free transaction between the parties.

---

6   *Statistics of Civil Registry 2007*/Brazilian Institute of Geography and Statistics.
7   All the following mentioned legal dispositions are from the Civil Code of 2002 (Law n. 10,4067/2002).

It is valid only if it preserves the inheritance rights of the necessary heirs (article 1845 prescribes that: **The necessary heirs are descendants, ascendants and the spouse**), applying only to the disposable portion of the patrimony that constitutes half of the inheritance assets (article 1846) following the deduction of the deceased's debts and funeral expenses.

By way of tempering this legal imposition (Lôbo, 2003) it is admitted that the donor may expressively dispense with collation if he/she donates to the necessary heir his/her available share (article 2005), either by using the appropriate legal instrument or by means of testament (article 2006).

It is worth mentioning that other acts may also be considered as an anticipated use of the reserved portion of the estate, such as those denominated extraordinary expenses used in the upbringing and education of children, as well as in payment of debts and indemnifications resulting from illicit practices by minor children under the parent's civil responsibility (article 2002).

These restrictions on the married person's freedom to make donations or who has necessary heirs at the time of juridical transaction pose the question of self-determination in the private sphere in the context of new family configurations. This is the specific issue that will be addressed below.

1. The Brazilian Civilist Tradition

Protection of the reserved portion of the estate extends to the family constituted by marriage and by parenthood, the latter being consanguineous or by adoption. The family traditionally depicted in Brazilian legislation is of nuclear and heterosexual nature, with biological parenthood, even though this is at odds with existing variations in family types.

This failure to adapt within the legal regime perpetuates a model of the present family in the systematization of the juridical institutions of donation, legitimate succession and of collation in regard to necessary heirs, that generates situations of conflict within the Brazilian legal system that reveal in their nature the persistence of exclusion and discrimination (against illegitimate families) that are frequently the source of litigation to be dealt with by the Courts.

Recomposed family relations, and in the case of socio-affective parenthood, do not exactly fit in with the codified model of family patrimonial protection, and specifically the latter (socio-affective children) by reason of not being legally inserted within a family, do not enjoy protection guaranteed by law. By law, inheritance rights are attributed in a descending straight line, to biological and adoptive children (article 1829, I).

Brazilian civil legislation, within a centenarian tradition in existence since the 1916 Civil Code, provides for the protection of family patrimony in the juridical institutions of donation and testaments in the case of existing necessary heirs, which prior to the present Civil Code was restricted to descendants but which currently has been extended to spouses.

The importance of this institution lies in the fact that it guarantees to the descendants and to the spouse equality in the transfer of family patrimony, specifically the reserved portion of the estate (Monteiro, 2003), which, as previously mentioned, consists of half of the patrimony of the donor and/or testator, measured at the moment of disposal, *inter vivos* (donation) (article 544 of the Civil Code) or *causa mortis* (testament) (articles 1846, 2002 and 2004).

The self-determination of the patrimony title-holder to freely dispose of, benefit from or to transmit their possessions, is limited (in the cases of acts of generosity or liberality) to the other half, i.e. the denominated disposable share (article 2005). Unrestricted transmission is only applicable in this kind of share relative to acts of a compulsory nature, provided that they do not result in the diminution of the patrimony or in cases of donation of the disposable share, where an express dismissal of collation occurs.

The principle of equality is fundamental in the inheritance system of modern law, presuming that the donations made between ascendants and descendants or between spouses are anticipations of the respective hereditary quotas. The act of heirs restituting to the estate any advantages they may have received in life for the sake of equal division is known as collation (Beviláqua, 2000). Collation imposes the duty on beneficiary heirs to share equally any part of the inheritance received in advance with the other necessary heirs, after the death of the donator occurs (Veloso, 2003).

There are then three legal requisites for the occurrence of collation: the occurrence of donation of ascendant to descendant or of one spouse to the other; participation of the endowed or **donatary** in the inheritance of the donor and any dispute over the reserved portion of the estate succession between the endowed and other necessary heirs (Gomes, 204); and equality between all children over the reserved portion of the estate thus preserved.

Donations made to the descendants and spouse constitute an advance payment in life of the appropriate share of the inheritance (article 544) which, upon the death of the donor, requires the necessary presentation of equivalence to these possessions previously transmitted, when drawing up the inventory of the deceased donor's patrimony, by means of collation (article 2003).

2. *Solution of Conflicts Presented to the Courts*

In what follows we verify how the Brazilian Justice system has dealt with these conflicts between what the law stipulates and the diversity of family composition by analyzing the decisions of one high court, the Supreme Court of Justice, and two State Courts (Rio Grande do Sul's Court of Justice and São Paulo's Court of Justice).

2.1 Recombined Families, de facto Partnerships, Homosexual Families and Co-Habitation

Firstly, the phenomenon of family recomposition raises the question of private self-determination allowing the existence of post-divorce marriage and creating new situations for the law. With this, the recent amendment to the Brazilian Civil Code, which establishes the privileged position of the spouse as a necessary heir, has created an area of impasse, given that when it comes to assessing the donor's or testator's patrimony, there could occur a disparity of spouses (ex-spouse and surviving spouse) corresponding to different moments in the donor's affective and conjugal life.

Traditionally, if a donation occurs during the period of marriage between spouses that draws on the reserved portion of the testator's estate, or again, when donation from the division of property takes place within the ambit of an agreement drawn up at the time of consensual divorce, upon the death of the testator the surviving spouse should collate the donation when the deceased's inheritance process begins, so that the inherited portions can be shared equally among all the necessary heirs with whom she/he would compete (descendant, ascendant or even new spouse).

Here, the *vexata quaestio* is: it may be that the beneficiary, who had received an advance on the reserved portion of the estate, is no longer qualified as an heir – for example, as a consequence of divorce, no longer being the deceased's surviving spouse. How can the portions/shares be adjusted among the necessary heirs if this previous beneficiary is no longer an heir? The matter of the donation is a perfectly legal and settled affair whereby the beneficiary spouse cannot be compelled or obliged to restitute the donation since he/she is no longer the spouse of the deceased and therefore has no claim to any succession rights. The law as it stands renders equalization between the hereditary portions impossible, resulting in a situation of disparity among the spouses as time goes by, who in effect no longer maintain that civil status.

In recombined families, the existence of an ex-spouse, who has benefited from the inheritance, and the surviving spouse, has yet to find a jurisprudential solution. Nevertheless, any donation made during the course of marriage, separation or divorce cannot violate the reserved portion of the estate protected for other necessary heirs (article 544)[8]. This decision states that the goods or property can only be presented for the purpose of verifying whether the value of the donation does not exceed the disposable portion, rendering it inofficious and resulting in the necessary reduction of the part that exceeded the reserved portion of the estate (articles 549 and 2007). However, this fact no longer has the proper effect of equalizing shares of inheritance between the necessary heirs.

In the light of this situation, it could be that the beneficiary ex-spouse, often based on agreement in judicial separation or divorce, maintains a position of privilege in relation to the surviving spouse who married the deceased divorced testator, insofar as, in the quality of necessary heir, he/she could not reclaim the collation of previous assets bequeathed to the ex-spouse in order to equalize the shares of the reserved portion of the estate, given that the ex-spouse does not qualify as necessary heir of the deceased by virtue of previous rupture of the conjugal society. They would merely be able to invoke the nullification of the possessions that exceed the reserved portion of the estate, by reason of those being inofficious. In contrast, where a donation or testament has been made in favor of the present spouse, these should be computed so as to ensure that they do not violate the reserved portion of the estate of children born prior to the union, in which case there could be a reduction of the provisions.[9]

This leads to the conclusion that two quite different disciplines exist in recombined families: donations to an ex-spouse cannot be collated in the sense of equalizing the reserved portion of the estate in relation to the deceased's spouse by virtue of the non-existence of further legal bonds between them (marriage rupture); but with regard to donations to the current spouse, these can always be collated in relation to children born in a previous marriage in view of the perennial bond of kinship in parenthood.

---

8   Superior Court of Justice, Special Recourse n. 154948, on 19.02.2001.
9   Rio Grande do Sul's Court of Justice, Appeal n. 70012360478, on 14.09.2005.

In second place, cohabitation (de facto partnership) present in the Brazilian ordinance since the Federal Constitution of 1988, in matters of succession displays inequalities when compared with marriage. If the legislation sought, within the scope of the relations of family rights to bring the institutions closer, there exists a complete misalignment within the area of succession rights, since surviving partners do not enjoy equality of rights in relation to the surviving spouses (article 1790). Between a couple, the affective relations have differentiated impacts on succession, resulting in a certain primacy accorded to the institution of marriage depending on the model used: formal (marriage) or informal (cohabitation or stable union).

One of the profound inequalities resides in the fact that the surviving partner is not a necessary heir (article 1845) and in consequence does not have the right to demand the collation of donated estate to other necessary heirs, for although the partner is still an heir that can compete with co-heirs, he/she cannot request collation.

Such limiting norms are not observed in other areas that deal with patrimonial questions between partners. In these areas the jurisprudence is more conciliatory: the welfare rights of the surviving partner in receiving pension upon death[10] or in receiving indemnity from life insurance[11]. Something that is not repeated or copied within the family and succession rights where profound lines of distinction exist between different family types and which generate considerable variation in verdicts on these rights.

However, there are decisions that recognize the equality between marriage and cohabitation and that consequently impose the right to collate, be it on the part of the other necessary heirs or the surviving partner, over the possessions donated by the author of the inheritance[12].

To a larger degree of exclusion, partners of the same sex do not enjoy family rights in the discipline of the new Civil Code; there exists a legal gap for such relations while only heterosexual couples are legally protected. Frequently, the rights of homosexual couples are under juridical tutelage[13], a manifest contrast between the absence of a legal text and

---

10 São Paulo's Court of, Justice, Offenders Attachments n. 670174-1/4, on 18.10.2005.
11 São Paulo's Court of Justice, Appellation with Revision n. 187.159.5/9, on 12.07.2005.
12 This is the position of the large majority of decisions enacted by Rio Grande do Sul's Court of Justice, but does not represent the majority position in relation to other Brazilian State Courts.
13 In particular, social and patrimonial rights of distinct origin of family law, as in the case of partition of assets acquired in constancy cohabitation in the proportion of participation of each party.

the application of law. This lack of legal support in the family field means that the large majority of Brazilian courts dismiss these petitions as being without foundation.[14]

Co-habitation is also not recognized as a union that institutes rights in the family ambit (article 1727). The acts of liberty suffer legal restrictions: a married person cannot donate to (article 550) or bestow on (article 1801, III) the concubine under the threat of nullification of the act. From this relation unrecognized by family law, patrimonial effects on the patrimonial division occur solely if an effective economic participation in the acquisition of the patrimony is proven (Summation 380 of the Supreme Federal Court).

2.2 Matrimonial, Extra-Matrimonial and Socio-Affective Parenthood

Constitutional equality of all children leads to equality in the family arena. The descendants, even those born outside the marriage or recognized following the death of the donor, enjoy isonomy and should collate the reserved portion of the estate in the event it was advanced.[15] The same applies to descendants excluded from succession by illegal acts committed against the deceased ascendant (articles 1816 and 1961) once their representatives assume such incumbency.

True that in the case of blood kinship, according to case law understandings already consecrated, even those recognized or born following free actions of the progenitor would have the right to seek an equal share of the reserved portion of the estate in inventory once the ascendant is deceased.[16] The reference here is death; it does not matter if donations were made to children conceived in different periods, there is the right to seek equality of hereditary shares of all necessary heirs at the time of the testator's death.

As such, although disparity may occur in life in terms of transmission of ascendant patrimony to descendants in the form of donation, following the death of the donor, technically all heirs (descendants) have identical rights in the division of the deceased's estate by reason of isonomy of all children.

14　This is the position adopted by many of the Justice Chambers of São Paulo's Court of Justice as expressed in the Civil Appellation n. 266.853-4/8, of 28.11.2002, by not conferring succession rights to the surviving partner of a homosexual partnership.
15　São Paulo's Court of Justice, Appellation with Revision n. 534.239-4/4, on 27.06.2008.
16　Superior Court of Justice, Special Recourse n. 730483, on 03.05.2005.

However, there remains the question of the value to be collated. Article 1792 of the 1916 Code contained a rule through which the collation was made based on the value of the goods/property at the time of donation; and this text remains in the present Code. In the existence of an advanced payment from the reserved portion of the estate to some children, when it comes to collation the existing basis is to compute values at the time the advance occurred (which could have taken place decades earlier!), the equalization in conferring the reserved portion of the estate is not fully realized.

In a retrospective evaluation, the perpetuation of inequality between the descendents is indeed possible. Even more so if we consider that the descendant had benefited in life from the advanced inheritance and that they would need to account for interests gained over things subject to collation- goods/property (article 2004, § 2).

Such a disparity occurs in cases of reconfiguration of kinship in the domestic space as in the case of adoption and children born outside marriage (Yngvesson, 2007), that commonly bid for this right to equalization of the parts of the reserved portion of the estate.

The latter, if not recognized by the progenitor, should propose a *post mortem* process of paternity or maternity investigation, in addition to an inheritance petition or the opening of an inventory with a request for collation in the case of partial or total donation of goods and property in order to have rights to the ascendant's patrimony. The inheritance being a patrimonial right, the proscriptional deadline to litigate against the estate is ten years. After this period, one can only seek the establishment of parenthood, this being a fundamental right of identity and therefore cannot be proscribed.

A worse scenario occurs in the case of socio-affective parenthood where the problem is further amplified. This type of parenthood has no legal status in Brazil. However, Courts do recognize, though not unanimously, affective parenthood ties where no blood ties between ascendant and descendant exist. This is the case of *»Brazilian-style«* adoption which consists of providing false information in the public registry of births of the child as if they were biological and of **foster children** or **apparent status parenthood.** Realities which, although not yet systemized under Brazilian law, are extremely common in ethnographic studies that describe the circulation of children within informal networks of community solidarity (Fonseca, 2006).

Case law disagreement over the matter is enormous. The logic of the judicial order is geared to typical cases. It is understood that a socio-affective relationship is spontaneous, leading to juridical effects, voluntarily assumed by the parents through legal or »Brazilian-style« adoption. This one has created juridical effects in the family arena but there remain many judicial controversies.

However, a person raised in a situation of apparent status is unable to insist upon judicial recognition of the situation. It remains a duty of the parents to regularize the affective link, thus generating legal consequences. In this line of interpretation, it is understood that »*taking apparent status of children as apt to constitute legal bond is taking a non-authorized step in our order*«[17].

For this reason, it can be concluded that the law creates asymmetries between people depending on the types of ties or bonds they establish among themselves. Traditional family arrangements are privileged, while the line of interpretation is left open for each court whether or not to recognize the diversity of concrete situations experienced by families.

III. Conclusions

It appears to be a tradition of juridical thinking to create inequalities between individuals when it relates to the universe of private relations and, especially, the family ambit and consequently, succession rights. Nowadays, after more than a century, the 2002 Civil Code still maintains in its structure juxtaposing forms of family that enter in conflict: the immobility of the traditional family type, with all the guarantees, against the mutability of practices and experiences of conjugality and parenthood, with graded guarantees.

Freedom to make use of patrimony on behalf of a third party or within the family is of juridical relevance in permitting economic mobility under new conjugal and parental arrangements, especially in cases of marriage dissolution agreements and future recompositions. The fundamental pillar of guaranteeing dignified continuance and survival in the form of cogent norms for the regulation of family economies does not fully cover the new family arrangements.

It is a contradiction that bears evidence to the crisis of a judicial model that can no longer remain exclusive and unitary, widening the structural divisions historically present in Brazilian society (Faria, 1988).

---

17   Rio Grande do Sul's Court of Justice,, Court Appellation n. 70019810704, on 27.07.2007.

Contrasts between reality and the norms, inequalities legally posed among families, leading to the need for juridical thinking in the family field in order to recognize and guarantee plurality in private life and the integration of such diversities of affective modes of living within the complex of norms of family protection, thus render effective »*the normative relevance of constitutional principles and the application – directly or indirectly – of the proper principles in intersubjective relations*« (Perlingieri, 2008).

References

> Lemouland, J. J. (1997). Le pluralisme et le droit de la famille, post-modernité ou pré-déclin, *Recueil Dalloz*, *18* (Chronique), 32–41.
> Allard, J. & Garapon, A. (2006). *Os Juízes na Mundialização*. A nova revolução no direito. Lisboa: Instituto Piaget.
> Arnaud, A. J. (1998). Internationalisation des Droits de l'Homme et Droits de la Famille. De la globalisation au postmodernisme en droit. In Arnaud, A. J. *Entre modernité et mundialisation. Cinq leçons d'histoire de la philosophie du droit et de l'État*. Paris: LGDJ, (pp. 77–104).
> Beviláqua, C. (2000). *Direito das Sucessões*. Campinas : Red Livros.
> Commaille, J. (s/d). Une sociologie politique du droit de la famille. Des référentiels en tension: émancipation, institution, protection. http://www.reds.msh-paris.fr/communication/textes/comail1.htm (10.10.2007).
> Corapi, D. (1986). Lo studio e l'insegnamento del diritto privato comparato nelle Università italiane, *Rassegna di diritto civile*, *2*, 437–445.
> Fachin, L. E. (2000). *Teoria Crítica do Direito Civil*. Rio de Janeiro: Renovar.
> Fachin, L. E. (2002). Transformações do direito civil brasileiro contemporâneo. In Ramos, C. L. S. et al. (Org.). *Diálogos sobre direito civil. Construindo a racionalidade contemporânea*. Rio de Janeiro: Renovar, (pp. 41–46).
> Faria, J. E. (1988). *A crise do direito numa sociedade em mudança*. Brasília: Editora Universidade de Brasília/UNB.
> Fonseca, C. (2006). Da circulação de crianças à adoção internacional: questões de pertencimento e posse. *Revista Pagu*, *26*, 11–43.
> Furgiuelle, G. (1997). Condizioni umane protette e nuovi diritti individuali nella famiglia dei diritti europei, *Rassegna di diritto* civile, *87*(1), 82–99.
> Giacco, M. L. (2006). La famiglia in Italia tra normativa europea e legislazione regionale, *Il Diritto di Famiglia e delle Personne*, *XXXV*, 1948–1957.

> Giddens, A. (1993). *A Transformação da Intimidade. Sexualidade, Amor, Erotismo nas Sociedades Modernas*. São Paulo: Editora da Universidade Estadual Paulista/UNESP.
> Gomes, O. (2004). *Sucessões*. 12ª Ed. Rio de Janeiro: Forense.
> Grossi, P. (s/d). A formação do jurista e a exigência de um hodierno *repensamento epistemológico*. http://ojs.c3sl.ufpr.br/ojs2/index.php/direito/article/viewFile/1731/1431 (05.06.2008).
> Irti, N. (1999). *L' età della decodificazione. L'età della decodificazione vent'anni dopo*. Milano: Giuffre.
> Le Gall, D. (2003). Filiations volontaires et biologiques. La pluriparentalité dans les sociétés contemporaines, *Neuropsychiatrie de l'Enfance et de l'Adolescence*, *51*(3), 118-123.
> Lôbo, P. L. N. (2003). *Comentários ao Código Civil. Parte Especial. Das várias espécies de contratos. (Arts. 481 a 564)*. São Paulo: Saraiva.
> Monteiro, W. B. (2003). *Curso de Direito Civil*. 37ª Ed. Direito das Sucessões. São Paulo: Saraiva.
> Nevares, A. L. M. (2002). Entidades familiares na Constituição: críticas à concepção hierarquizada. In Ramos, C. L. S. et al. (Org.). *Diálogos sobre direito civil. Construindo a racionalidade contemporânea*. Rio de Janeiro: Renovar, (pp. 291-315).
> Oliveira, G. (2008). Pósfácio. In Oliveira, G. & Pereira, T. S. (Org.). *O Cuidado como Valor Jurídico*. Rio de Janeiro: Forense, (pp. 395-396).
> Perlingieri, P. (1986). L'incidenza dell'interesse pubblico sulla negoziazione privata, *Rassegna di diritto civile*, *4*, 936-949.
> Perlingieri, P. (1986). L'interpretazione della legge come sistematica ed assiologica, *Rassegna di diritto civile*, *4*, 1012-1032.
> Perlingieri, P. (1997). *Perfis do Direito Civil. Introdução ao Direito Civil Constitucional*. Rio de Janeiro: Renovar.
> Perlingieri, P. (2008). *O Direito Civil na Legalidade Constitucional*. Rio de Janeiro: Renovar.
> Pocar, V. & Ronfani, P. (2007). *La famiglia e il diritto*. Bari: Laterza.
> Santos, B. S. S. (2002). Direito e Democracia: a reforma global da justiça. In Pureza, J. & Ferreira, A. C. (Org.). *A Teia Global: Movimentos Sociais e Instituições*. Porto: Edições Afrontamento, (pp. 125-176).
> Théry, I. (1998). *Couple, Filiation et Parente Aujourd'hui. Lê droit face aux mutations de la famille et de la vie privée*. Paris: Editions Odile Jacob/La Documentation française.progenitor
> Veloso, Z. (2003). *Comentários ao Código Civil. Parte Especial. Do Direito das Sucessões. (Arts. 1.857 a 2.027)*. São Paulo: Saraiva.

› Xavier, R. L. (2008). *Ensinar Direito da Família*, Porto: Publicações da Universidade Católica.
› Yngvesson, B. (2007). Parentesco reconfigurado no espaço da adoção, *Cadernos Pagu*, 29, 111–138.
› Other References
› Superior Court of Justice. http://www.stj.gov.br/portal_stj/publicacao/engine.wsp
› Justice Court of Rio Grande do Sul. http://www.tj.rs.gov.br/
› Justice Court of São Paulo. http://www.tj.sp.gov.br/
› *Statistics of Civil Registry 2007*/Brazilian Institute of Geography and Statistics. http://www.ibge.gov.br/home/estatistica/populacao/registrocivil/2007/registrocivil_2007.pdf
› *Social Indicators 2007*/Brazilian Institute of Geography and Statistics. http://www.ibge.gov.br/home/estatistica/populacao/condicaodevida/indicadoresminimos/sinteseindicsociais2007/indic_sociais2007.pdf

Legal Protection of the Survivor of a Couple in French Family Law

Odile Roy[1]

I. Introduction

Since 2006,[2] the French Civil code, no longer draws distinction between legitimate and illegitimate filiations, and children's rights are identical whether their parents are married or not.[3] But, whether couples are married or not remains essential because of considerable differences, especially with regard to property rules.[4]

In the particular example of where the union is dissolved by death, the surviving member of the couple is not legally protected in the same way depending on whether they were married or not.

In France, marriage is only allowed between a man and a woman.[5] Of course, since 1999[6] same sex couples may decide to choose a legal status, the »*pacte civil de solidarité*«, currently called *PACS*, open to all couples,[7]

---

1 Maître de Conférences en droit privé, Centre d'Etudes Juridiques Européennes et Comparées, Université Paris Ouest Nanterre La Défense, France.
2 *Ordonnance n° 2005-759 du 4 juillet 2005*, entered into force on July 1st, 2006, recently ratified by Parliament: the bill of ratification, loi n° 2009-61 du 16 janivier 2009, brings some modifications without changing principles of this reform.
3 In 2008, 52 % of births are outside marriage. Cf. *Insee : bilan démographique 2008.* http://www.insee.fr/fr/themes/document.asp?ref_id=ip1220
4 Significant also are extra patrimonial consequences: for instance, only married couples may adopt a child (cf. Civil code art. 346). See, O. ROY, « *Le modèle français : évolutions et résistances face au pluralisme familial* » *in Réflexions sur le pluralisme familial,Presses universitaires de Paris Ouest, Coll. Sciences juridiques et politiques,* to be published in 2009.
5 Cass. 1re civ., 13 mars 2007, *D*. 2007, p. 935, obs GALLMEISTER, p. 1389, rapp. PLUYETTE et p. 1395, note AGOSTINI; *Gaz. Pal.* 2007, *jur.* p. 1073, rapp. PLUYETTE et p. 1090, avis DOMINGO; *JCP G* 2007, act. n° 136, obs. FAVIER; *Dr. famille* 2007, *comm.* n° 76, note AZAVANT; *AJ famille* 2007, p. 227, note CHÉNÉDÉ ; *LPA* 2007, n° 142, p. 19, note MASSIP.
6 *Loi n°99-944 du 15 novembre 1999,* modified by *loi n°2006-728 du 23 juin 2006* (Civil code, art. 515-1 to art. 515-7)
7 This status may only be chosen by two people living together in a »couple« relationship, but not by people who simply cohabit, such as sibling living together: in order to enforce the prohibition on the incest, *Pacs* is forbidden between close family members (Civil code, art. 515-2).

same sex or not[8]. But, although the survivor of a »*pacsé*« couple is better protected than the survivor of two cohabitants (»*concubinage*«), he or she is not as well protected as a surviving spouse.

Could this be considered like a discriminatory treatment? If you read the judgment delivered on April 29th, 2008 by Grand Chamber of the European Court in the case of Burden v. the United Kingdom, you could think so.

In this case, the applicants were two unmarried sisters, living together all their lives in a house they inherited from their parents. Both in their eighties, each one had made a will leaving all her property to the other sister. They complained that, when one of them died, the survivor would be required to pay a heavy inheritance tax, unlike the survivor of a marriage or of a British civil partnership who is currently exempt from charge.

Claiming they are victims of discriminatory treatment, they relied on Article 1 of Protocol N°1 taken in conjunction with Article 14.

The Grand Chamber observed that the relationship between siblings was of a different nature to that between married couples and homosexual civil partners under the British Civil Partnership Act 2004, because those unions were forbidden to close family members. The reference so made for the prohibition on the incest means that this Partnership status, as marriage and the French *Pacs*, may be chosen only by two people living together in a »couple« relationship, but not by people who simply cohabit.

> »*The fact that the applicants had chosen to live together all their adult lives, ..., did not alter that essential difference.*«[9]

As with marriage, the Grand Chamber considered that the British civil partnership, conferring a particular status on those who expressly and deliberately decided to enter it, set these types of relationship apart from other forms of co-habitation.

> »*Rather than the length or the supportive nature of the relationship, what is determinative is the existence of a public undertaking, carrying with it a body of rights and obligations of a contractual nature.*«[10]

---

8   More and more couples are attracted by *Pacs* (+ 25 % par an), in particular heterosexual couples: so, among all *pacsés* couples (more than 500 000 since 1999), the proportion of same sex couples was 25 % in 2002, but only 6 % in 2008; besides, if the number of marriages has a tendency to decrease, the number of heterosexual couples bound by marriage or *Pacs* steadily increase with the passing years. *Insee : bilan démographique 2008*, quoted above note 3.
9   § 62, CEDH 29 April 2008, Burden v. the United Kingdom.
10 § 65, CEDH 29 April 2008, Burden v. the United Kingdom.

The Grand Chamber considered that there could be no analogy between married and Civil Partnership Act couples, on one hand, and heterosexual or homosexual couples who just chose to live together, on the other hand.

Also, in this case, the absence of such a legally-binding agreement between the two sisters rendered their relationship of co-habitation, despite its long length, fundamentally different to that of a married or British Civil Partnership couple.

The Grand Chamber concluded that the applicants could not be compared to a married or Civil Partnership couple. It followed that there had been no discrimination. What can we deduce from this case with regard to the French law?

It is certain that the survivor of a couple neither married nor *pacsé* is in the worst situation,[11] but a couple of »*concubins*« who chose to stay free of any status cannot complain about an absence of legal protection.

On the other hand, should not legal protection of the surviving member of a couple benefit those who chose such a binding agreement as marriage or *Pacs*? Failing that, isn't it discrimination?

In spite of recent reforms in 2006 and 2007 which moved the *Pacs* closer to marriage, only the surviving spouse benefits from a legal protection whereas the *pacsé* partner will be protected only if such was the will of the deceased.

We can observe such a difference both in the transmission of the deceased's possessions (II) and in the preservation of the survivor's home (III).

II. The Transmission of the Deceased's Possessions

Concerning the transmission of the deceased's possessions in favour of the survivor; the equality about inheritance tax (1) must not lead someone to forget that the surviving partner is not an heir (2).

1. The Equality about Inheritance Tax

About inheritance tax, *pacsés* partners could not claim they are victims of a discriminatory treatment:

---

11 The survivor is not an heir of the deceased and if he or she is designated as a legatee by a will, the inheritance taxes are 60%.

Inheritance tax schemes usually follow the order of succession, although in certain countries, such as France, the surviving spouse is granted a more favourable tax exemption than any other category of heir. But, since 2007,[12] the fiscal situation of the survivor of a couple is henceforth identical if this couple was married or *pacsé*:[13] for deaths occurring since August 22nd, 2007, the surviving spouse or *pacsé* partner is exempt from inheritance taxes.

From January 1st, 2008, if someone married or *pacsé* wishes to anticipate the transmission of his or her possessions by donations to the other member of the couple, the donee benefits from the same fiscal advantage (exemption of charge to a threshold of 76 988 euros, and taxes at progressive rates above this threshold) whether he or she is the spouse or the *pacsé* partner.

But, as it is easy to break a *Pacs*,[14] the legislator wanted to avoid that some couples decide to *Pacs* themselves only for the time to make a donation in fiscally advantageous conditions: then, in order to avoid fraud, the fiscal advantage is questioned if the *Pacs* is broken-up before the end of the year following that of its conclusion for any other reason than the marriage of the partners between them or the death of one of them.

Apart from this particular rule intended to limit fraud, the tax system is thus identical and if we keep to this precise question of inheritance taxes, as in Burden's case, no discrimination exists.

Nevertheless, the fiscal favour can benefit to someone *pacsé* only if such was the will of his or her *pacsé* partner.

---

12 *Loi n° 2007-1223 du 21 août 2007 en faveur du travail, de l'emploi et du pouvoir d'achat* (so-called *loi TEPA*).

13 Let me add moreover that, according to the same law, from January 1st, 2008, two siblings being in the same situation than the two sisters in the case of Burden v/ The United Kingdom, would be also exempted from inheritance taxes; this law indeed exempts from charges the brother or the sister surviving if the following three conditions are combined:
 – first one, he or she has to be, at the time of the death, bachelor, widower, or divorced;
 – second one, he or she must be, at the time of the death, 50-year-old or affected by an infirmity;
 – and finally, he or she was constantly taken up residence with the deceased during five years having preceded the death.

14 *Pacs* is dissolved by the death or by the marriage of partners or of one of them, but *Pacs* can also be dissolved by a joint declaration of the partners or even by unilateral decision of one of them (Cf. Civil code, art. 515-17).

2. *The Difference about Quality of Heir.*
Indeed, only the surviving spouse, contrary to the surviving *pacsé* partner, has the quality of heir.

2.1 The Spouse
On one hand, the spouse is an heir as long as he or she is not divorced (and thus even if he or she is actually separated, or during the procedure of divorce), and he or she cannot be pushed aside from the succession by any of the other heirs of the deceased (art. 756, Civil code).

The 2001 reform[15] strikingly increased the surviving spouse's rights in the succession:

Whereas in Common Law systems there is traditionally freedom of testamentary devolution, in Civil Law systems the order of succession is generally established by statute or code, with some particularly privileged categories of heirs being granted automatic rights to a portion of the estate, the so-called »*réserve*«, which cannot be modified by the deceased's will. In France, the reservating heirs are the descendants (art. 913, Civil code), and if there is no descendant, the spouse of the deceased (art. 914-1, Civil code). Ascendants are no longer reservating heirs since the coming into force of the 2006 reform.[16]

> In front of descendants, the surviving spouse inherits a quarter in full property, and can prefer the whole usufruct if there are only common children (art. 757, Civil code). The spouse, in this case, is not a reservating heir and then could be disinherited, but we shall see later on that his or her home will nevertheless be protected. Besides, if the deceased had left a legacy to the surviving spouse, this last one benefits from a special available quota which can concern even the usufruct of the descendants' *réserve* (art. 1094-1, Civil code).
> If there is no descendant, the spouse is, henceforth, reservating heir for a quarter in full property and cannot be thus deprived of this minimal part. But his or her rights are, as a rule, much superior: in front of father and mother of the deceased, who are entitled each to a quarter in full property, the spouse collects an half in full property, and even three quarter if only the father or the mother survived (art. 757 -1, Civil code).

---

15   *Loi n°2001-1135 du 3 décembre 2001*, coming into force on July 1st 2002.
16   *Loi n° 2006-728 du 23 juin 2006,* reforming successions and *Pacs*, coming into force on January 1ST 2007.

Except the very exceptional case of a kind of legal »*droit de retour*« allowing to get back some possessions of family in favour of siblings of the deceased, in case of predeaths of the father and the mother (art 757-3, Civil code), the spouse inherits from the whole succession in front of other relatives of the deceased (art. 757-2, Civil code).

2.2 The *Pacsé* Partner

On the other hand, the *pacsé* partner does not inherit from his or her partner. The surviving partner, as a simple »*concubin*«, can come to the succession only by virtue of a will indicating him as legatee.

> - If the dead partner had no child, he or she could henceforth give or bequeath his or her possessions to his or her partner without limits because the *réserve* of the parents in the ascending line was eliminated by law in 2006.[17]
> - If the dead partner had children, the freedom to give or bequeath to his or her partner will collide with the reserve of the descendants, and whereas the surviving spouse benefits in this case from a special available quota (art. 1094-1, Civil code), the generosities made in favour of the *pacsé* partner will be limited to the usual available quota (art. 913, Civil code).

It is thus unmistakable that the unified tax measures are not enough to provide to the surviving partner the same rights as to the surviving spouse. Besides, this latter benefits from a better protection of his or her home.

III. The Home of the Survivor of the Couple:

Married or *pacsés* couples are protected in a very uneven way whether it is concerning rights of habitation and use or concerning preferential attribution of accommodation and furniture.

1. The Rights of Habitation and Use of Housing and Furniture

Concerning rights of habitation and use of housing and furniture, the protection is not the same for the surviving spouse and for the surviving *pacsé* partner.

---

17 Cf. supra note 16

1.1 The Spouse

In favour of the surviving spouse, the legislator of 2001[18] organized a kind of maintenance which allows to preserve his or her home and minimal resources.

First, the surviving spouse benefits, during one year from the death, of the free habitation and use of the home that he or she occupied effectively as main accommodation at the time of the death, as well as the furniture, included in the succession, furnishing this home (art. 763, Civil code).

This temporary protection of the living environment can work if the accommodation belongs fully or partly to the succession, and even if it is a lease (which the rent will then have to be paid off by the succession). Qualified as »direct effect of the marriage«, this right is a mandatory rule and the surviving spouse can thus not be deprived of it neither by deviating contractual provisions, nor by a will in favour of a third person.

Let us add that only the surviving spouse benefits from two other means of protection to maintain his or her living conditions:

> Failing a contrary will expressed within the framework of an authentic testament by the deceased, the surviving spouse benefits from a life right of habitation on the accommodation and a life right of use on the furniture concerning home he or she occupied effectively as main accommodation at the time of the death (art. 764, Civil code). Even when the deceased had bequeathed this house to somebody else, the spouse may stay in this home freely for all his or her life if this legacy was not expressed within the framework of an authentic will but within the framework of a will written, dated and signed by the testator.[19]

> Besides, the succession of the predeceased spouse owes a maintenance allowance to the surviving spouse if he (or she) is in the need (art. 767, Civil code).

1.2 The *Pacsé* Partner

The surviving *pacsé* partner is not as well protected in spite of the latest reforms:

Since 2006,[20] when the *Pacs* is dissolved by the death of one of the partners, the Civil code (art. 515-6 paragraph 3) allows the surviving partner to

---

18 Cf. supra note 15.
19 This will written, dated and signed by the testator, so called "testament tolographe", remains perfectly valid (Civil code, articles 969 and 970) but the legatee will benefit from the right to use this property only after the death of the surviving spouse.
20 Cf. supra note 16.

benefit too, during one year after the death, from a temporary protection of his or her accommodation and furniture, but here the rule is not a mandatory rule. This protection will work only if the deceased partner did not decide to deprive the surviving partner of this temporary right.

But this limitation is obvious: this protection could not be a mandatory rule because the partner who would like to prevent this could do so by terminating the *Pacs*. Indeed, as well as the possibility of terminating their union unanimously, a *Pacs* can also be dissolved by the unilateral decision of one of the partners.[21]

This possibility of one-sided rejection without control of the *pacsé* partner, aroused principal criticism by comparison with marriage, thus limits the efficiency of the protection.

For those who have the choice between marriage and *Pacs*, it is the price of the freedom. On the other hand, for same sex couples who cannot choose marriage, it could be considered discriminatory treatment.

2. *The Preferential Attribution*

Concerning the preferential attribution of full property of the home (accommodation and furniture), differences also exist.

2.1 The Spouse

The Civil code allows the surviving spouse, or each heir, owner of an undivided part of the deceased's possessions to ask for the preferential attribution of full property of the home that he or she occupied effectively as main accommodation at the time of the death, as well as the furniture furnishing this home, or the company in which he or she works (Civil code, art. 831 and following ones.).

Article 831-3 concerns preferential attribution in favour of the surviving spouse, of the full property of the home that he or she occupied effectively as main accommodation at the time of the death, as well as the furniture furnishing this home. The first paragraph of this text clarifies that, in this case, preferential attribution in favour of the surviving spouse is »*de droit*« what means that the judge has no discretion (power of appreciation); then, if the surviving spouse asks the allocation of the property of this accommodation he or she will obtain it. The second paragraph adds that rights resulting from this preferential attribution cannot prejudice to life rights of habitation and use that spouse may exercise in virtue of article 764.

---

21   Cf. supra note 14.

2.2 The Pacsé Partner

Since the law of June 23rd, 2006, the Civil code (art. 515-6 paragraph 2) grants to the surviving partner the profit of the provisions of the first paragraph of article 831-3: this means that the surviving partner may also obtain preferential attribution of home that he or she occupied effectively as main accommodation at the time of the death, without any power of appreciation of judge.

But even there, the protection of the surviving *pacsé* partner is far from equal to that of the surviving spouse:

> - First, not being an heir of the deceased, the partner is less likely than the surviving spouse to be the owner of an undivided part of this accommodation.
> - Besides, even if the surviving *pacsé* partner is the owner of an undivided part of this accommodation, the preferential attribution of full property of it can work in favour of the surviving partner only if the deceased partner expressly foresaw it in his or her testament: this last condition limits clearly the reach of the rule.

IV. Conclusion

Finally, States, in principle, remain free to devise different rules in the field of taxation policy and French rules on inheritance tax could not be considered, following the Burden case, as discrimination.

However, in spite of the recent reforms, the surviving *pacsé* partner is not as well protected by law as the surviving spouse; he or she can only be protected if such was the will of the deceased partner. This may be considered the price of the freedom, and freedom is not easily compatible with mandatory rules.

It does not raise problems for heterosexual couples who have the choice between *Pacs* and marriage (and the great majority of *pacsés* couples are heterosexual couples[22]). But, as far as homosexual couples have, at least at the moment, no right to get married, this more limited protection may be considered discriminatory treatment.

---

22   Cf. supra note 8.

Legitimate Portion and other Techniques of Protection of Surviving Spouses and Children.
A Comparison between Civil Law and Common Law Systems

Andrea Fusaro[1]

I. Comparative Scholarship in the Area of Succession Law

We know that succession law must be analysed within a broader context, as it fulfils both an economic and social function. It regulates, respectively, the transfer of wealth upon a person's death on the basis of the principle of testamentary freedom and protects the family as a social unit[2].
In connection with social and economic evolution in the last decades, succession law has changed almost everywhere:
»*over the course of the twentieth century, persistent tides of change have been lapping at the once – quiet shores of the law of succession*«[3].

Comparative scholarship has highlighted these changes[4] through research normally pursued according to the »functional-typological method«[5], in order to identify typical solutions to legal problems in different systems.

The succession law has long been considered one of the more indigenous branches of the law[6], so that according to the traditional view a more harmonized or unified succession law is neither feasible nor desirable[7].

---

1 Professor of Comparative Legal Systems- Faculty of Law- Univ. Genova, Italy.
2 M.J.DE WAAL, *Comparative Succession Law*, in M.REIMANN – R.ZIMMERMANN, *The Oxford Handbook of Comparative Law*, Oxford Univ. Press, Oxford, 2006, p.1071, 1072.
3 J. H. LANGBEIN, *The Nonprobate* Revolution *and the Future of the Law of Succession* (1984) *Harvard L R* 1108.
4 M.J.DE WAAL, *Comparative Succession Law*, in M.REIMANN – R.ZIMMERMANN, *The Oxford Handbook of Comparative Law*, Oxford Univ. Press, Oxford, 2006, p.1071, 1097.
5 K. ZWEIGERT – H. KOETZ, *Introduction to Comparative Law* (trans. Tony Weir, 3 rd. edn, 1998), 25.
6 W. PINTENS, *Grundgedanken und Perspektiven einer Europaeisierung des Familien -und Erbrechts* – Teil 1, (2003) 50 *Zeitschrift fuer das gesamte Familienrecht*, 329, 331.
7 A.VERBEKE – Y. HENRI LELEU, *Harmonization of the Law of Succession in Europe*, in A. HARTHKAMP, M. HESSELINK, E. HONDIUS, C. JOUSTRA, E. DU PERRON (eds.), *Towards a European Civil Code* (3rd edn, 1998), 335.

This assumption has been challenged by many authors, who have noticed that the fifth book of the German Civil Code on the law of succession carried out a reform where different local traditions were mixed.[8]

Comparative research has focused on how inheritance rules have been influenced by the changing definition of family.[9] They have verified a trend that strengthens the position of the surviving spouse at the expense of children and further relations, shifting towards a »horizontal law of succession«[10].

The trend toward unity has been detected in the sphere of forced succession, which often interacts with family law; so that the harmonization is the result of common social developments, not of a deliberate state policy.[11] Indeed, the increased life expectancy has changed the function of succession law. Descendants are now often relatively old when they get the assets, so that inheritance has lost the role of providing them with the means to make a successful start in professional life. Furthermore, in recent times, the change in the nature of wealth, due to the growth in the importance of financial assets and human capital, has also transformed patterns of succession.[12]

II. Testamentary Freedom and its Possible Limitations.

There appears to be a wide acceptance of the proposition that no system – at least in western legal tradition – actually recognizes unlimited testamentary freedom.

The principle of forced succession is deemed to be based on »social« considerations:

> »...*practically speaking, forced succession means succession within the family – to the wife, children, or other dependants. Forced suc-*

---

[8] D. LEIPOLD, *Europa und das erbrecht*, in *Europas universale rechtsordnungspolitische Aufgabe im Recht des dritten Jahrtausends: Festschrift fuer Alfred Soellner* (2000), 647.
[9] S.M. CRETNEY, *Reform of Intestacy: The best We Can Do?*, (1995) 111 LQR 77; P. BUSER, *Domestic Partner and Non-marital Claims against Probate Estates: Marvin Theories Put to a Different Use* (2004) 38 *Family Law Quarterly* 313.
[10] W. PINTENS, *Die Europaeisierung des Erbrechts* (2001) 9 *Zeitschrift fuer Europaeisches Privatrecht* 628.
[11] M. J. DE WAAL, *The Social and Economic Foundations of the Law of Successions*, (197) 8 *Stellenbosch* LR 162, 163.
[12] J. H. LANGBEIN, *The Twentieth-century Revolution in Family Wealth Transmission* (1988) 86 *Michigan L R* 722.

cession imposes upon the testator the obligation to care for members of his/her family before satisfying any other desires and needs. In a sense, it converts private property at death to family property«.

On the contrary, testamentary freedom can be defended on economic grounds:

«...the principle of gift, since it exalts the volition of the property holder, is consistent with free market economics...Individuals as holders of private property may dispose of it as they see fit. The principle of gift can be called economic. Despite the paradox that a gift is not an economic system and is presupposed by it«[13].

It is very well known that civil law countries protect spouses and children by granting them the legitimate portion[14]: they are entitled to a fixed portion of the deceased's net estate – whole, or limited to a part, for instance movable property[15] – irrespective of any will; the law gives them the automatic right, apart from their wealth or need, which is considered only to award alimony (which is also awarded to the divorced spouse). In France this right is called »la reserve héréditaire«[16], in Germany »Pflichtteilsrecht«; they have different roots, which are linked to the different degree of penetration of the Roman law in France and in Germany during the middle ages. The French law comes from ancient German tradition, the German law from Roman law tradition.[17] In addition, in some legal systems the surviving spouse is entitled to reside in the family dwelling and is granted the right to use household furnishings[18]; in others, widows and children may claim temporary rights of alimentary nature.[19]

On the contrary, English law does not recognize preferential treatment to any of them on a fixed basis: it allows the judge the power to allot what

---

13 L. M. FRIEDMAN, *The Law of the Living, the Law of the Dead: Property, Succession and Society* (1966) 29 *Wisconsin LR* 340, 353.
14 Like Scotland.
15 Succession Scotland Act 1964, of which Scottish Law Commission is promoting a reform: *Discussion Paper on Succession*, n. 136, august 2007.
16 Y.-H. LELEU, *La Réserve héréditaire en droit francaise et en droit luxembourgeois*, in *Examen critique de la reserve successorale, Tome II Droit Belge*, Bruylant – Bruxelles, 1997, 81.
17 H. COING, *Zur Entwicklung des Pflichtteilsrecht in der Zeit des 16–18 Jahrhunderts*, in *Gedaechtnisschrift fuer W. Kunkel*, Frankfurt am M., 1984, 25 ss.
18 Art. 763 French Code Civil ; Art. 540 Italian Civil Code.
19 Art. 767 French Code Civil; Par. 1969 BGB on »Dreissigster«; Succession Scotland Act 1964; Par. 2 – 204 UPC on «family allowance».

he considers appropriate to the »dependants« in accordance with a statutory scheme.[20] The divergence between the common law and the civil law approach has often been stated as a piece of conventional wisdom[21], but the American approach on this issue is somewhat closer to that followed in civilian jurisdictions.[22] In the USA, the role of legitimate portion is played – with some differences – by forced inheritance, in connection with separate property regime;[23] indeed in the USA – where succession law is not a federal issue – the situation varies state by state, and in some we find a legitimate portion in favour of the surviving spouse, not the children[24].

III. Two Patterns of Protection Against Disinheritance: Fixed Share and Discretionary Maintenance

An almost unlimited testamentary freedom has been recognized in English law, even though the presence of the trust:
> »makes dynastic and financial sense in one's lifetime to transfer majority shareholdings in companies to trustees to manage for the benefit of one's spouse and descendants rather than allow small minority shareholdings to pass absolutely to each of one's heirs«[25].

In the twentieth century the legislature introduced »family provisions«[26], allowing discretionary maintenance claims by the persons proving to be

---

20 B. HANOTIAU, *Rapport sur la reserve en droit anglais et en droit americain*, in *Examen critique de la reserve successorale, Tome II Droit Belge*, Bruylant – Bruxelles, 1997, 255.
21 M.A.GLENDON, *Fixed Rules and Discretion in Contemporary Family Law and Successions*, in *Tulane Law Review*, 60 (1986), 1165.
22 M. A. GLENDON, *Transformations of Family Law. State, Law, and Family in the United States and in Western Europe*, Chicago – London, 1989, 243; A. ZOPPINI, *Le successioni in diritto comparato*, in *Tratt. Dir. Comp.*, dir. da R. Sacco, Utet, Torino, 2002, 72.
23 J. H. LANGBEIN – L. W. WAGGONER, *Redesigning the Spouse's Forced Share*, in *Real Property, Probate and TrustJ.*, 22(1987), 310, »It is essential to understand that American forced – share is entirely a consequence of the separate – property regime for marital property«.
24 Except for Luisiana.
25 D. HAYTON, *The problems of Diversity*, in D. HAYTON (ed), *European Succession Laws*(1998), 1,8.
26 Last statutes: *Inheritance Family Provisions Act* 1938; *Inheritance Provisions for Family and Dependents Act* 1975, as amended by the *Law Reform (Succession) Act* 1995 and the *Civil Partnership Act* 2004. Under the Act 1975 the list of applicants is as follows: the surviving spouse or civil partner of the deceased; a surviving former spouse or former civil partner of the deceased who has not remarried or registered a new civil partnership, a surviving cohabitant of the deceased, opposite sex or same sex; a child of the deceased; a person treated by the deceased as a child of the family relation to any marriage of the deceased; a dependant of the deceased.

economically »dependant« on the deceased. Under the Inheritance Act 1975, the list of applicants is as follows: the surviving spouse or civil partner of the deceased; a surviving former spouse or former civil partner of the deceased who has not remarried or registered a new civil partnership, a surviving cohabitant of the deceased, opposite sex or same sex; a child of the deceased; a person treated by the deceased as a child of the family in relation to any marriage of the deceased; a dependant of the deceased. The court has to be satisfied about the presence of »reasonable standard provision« for the applicant, and can award to the surviving spouse approximately half the value of the property, as in divorce. Keeping in mind the situation of the dependant, the court can take one more of the following financial provisions: an order for periodical payments or the income from the estate, a lump sum, a transfer or a settlement of the property.

The notion of legitimate portion is entrenched in systems which follow the civil law pattern, with differences regarding both the rules and the range of beneficiaries.[27] With regard to the rules, in some countries – like in France before 2007,[28] and the other systems influenced by the French civil code, amongst which Italy – the legitimate portion is the right to a share of a part of the deceased's estate, while in others – such as Germany – it is a credit.[29] The first solution hinders the circulation of immovables which are left by will or intestate succession, or by gift, because of the risk of claims on the assets by the members of the family who are protected through the rules on the legitimate portion.

We find different rules even in relation to the estate object of the share, as it normally encompasses gifts and sometimes even more, such as purchasing for amounts inferior to the actual value. In the circle of the beneficiaries, children and spouses are always mentioned, while parents are in a subordinate rank; the consistency of shares varies from system to system[30], and the surviving spouse receives different protection. Sometimes inheritance schemes are influenced by matrimonial property

---

[27] D. HAEINRICH, *Familienerbrecht und Testierfreiheit im europaeischen Vergleich*, in D. HENRICH – D. SCWAB(eds), *Familienerbrecht und Testierfreiheit im europaeischen Vergleich* (2001), 372, 380.

[28] Y.-H. LELEU, *La Réserve héreditaire en droit francaise et en droit luxembourgeois,*in *Examen critique de la reserve successorale, Tome II Droit Belge*, Bruylant – Bruxelles, 1997, 81.

[29] R. FRANK, *Erbrecht*, Verlag C.H. Beck, Muenchen, 2007, 255 ss.

[30] In Germany the Pflichtteil is one half of the amount which the applicant would have received if the deceased had died intestate and the applicant would have qualified as a successor. In France and in Italy the shares vary depending on the number of descendants.

regimes.

In the USA, the surviving spouse is the most favoured. Subsequent to the almost complete abrogation of dower[31] and courtesy, in the middle of the last century, separate property states adopted the elective share, the option given to claim a fixed part of the total estate; to remedy »frauds on the widow's share«, states disregard pre – death transfers or adopt the »augmented estate« introduced by the 1969 provisions of the UPC. According to the 1990 Uniform Probate Code[32] intestate succession rules the widow/er is entitled to the entire estate, and he/she are the only ones protected from intentional disinheritance by the deceased, in all but one state (Luisiana).

The number and importance of wills has decreased in the USA in last decades in favour of some substitutes[33], as also indicated in the »Uniform Non-Probate Transfers on Death Act«[34].

Illinois probate law – like many others – preferred to ignore non marital children, eventually this exclusionary rule was challenged; the United States Supreme Court declared it unconstitutional, warning that states have to adapt inheritance law to reflect the evolution of family structures. Nonetheless, after more than twenty-five years not all states recognize inheritance rights to the members of non-traditional families: they rarely include surviving partners in the circle of beneficiaries.

IV. Recent Developments.

In Germany, the legitimate portion is criticised on the basis of different grounds[35], including the impact of increased life expectancy on the pat-

---

31 Dower assigned the widow one-third interest I inheritable realty owned by the husband. It exists updated in some states: Arkansas, Kentucky, Michigan and Ohio. See R. C. BRASHIER, *Inheritance Law and the Evolving Family*, Temple Univ. Press, 2004, 14: »... *First, dower interfered with the state's interest in promoting free transferability of land....Second, because dower originally applied only to real estate, the protection it afforded against spousal disinheritance steadily diminished as intangible personalty... increasingly replaced real estate...«.*
32 The first edition of the UPC was approved in 1969 by the National Conference of Commissioners on Uniform State Laws.
33 J. H. LANGBEIN, *The Nonprobate Revolution and the Future of the Law of Succession* (1984) *Harvard L R* 1108.
34 A model proposed in 1991 and adopted by 44 states.
35 D. HAEINRICH, *Familienerbrecht und Testierfreiheit im europaeischen Vergleich*, in D. HENRICH – D. SCWAB(eds), *Familienerbrecht und Testierfreiheit im europaeischen Ver-*

ters of succession[36], and some scholars went as far as to argue that the present regime could be unconstitutional. The Bundesverfassungsgericht did not uphold this opinion[37], but the debate on the point is lively[38], and a proposal to modify certain articles of the German civil code has recently been prepared by the German Ministry of Justice [39].

In the USA and in other civil law countries forced inheritance has been under pressure for a long time[40], as its premises appear outdated. American commentators complain that inheritance rights are often assigned to the surviving spouse independent of a minimum duration of the marriage, and despite the fact that the spouses may have been in the midst of divorce proceedings, or their relationship is falling apart[41]. Criticism is also levelled regarding the substantial neglect of the homemaking efforts of the spouse. These are not recognized at the same level as in a divorce settlement.

The 1990 provisions of UPC-amended in 1993 – shared the view of marriage as a gender-neutral economic partnership[42], connecting the presumed contribution of the surviving spouse to the length of the marriage, but balancing this approach with a support component, which recommended that no less than 50,000.00 dollars be assigned. Further criticism comes from academic research on family firms: they have found that inheritance law may constraint investment in firms, underlying the opportunity to allow the testator to bequeath the largest possible fraction of his estate to a single child.[43]

In continental Europe something new has recently appeared. Between 2001 and 2006 France has adopted reforms[44] – which introduced many

---

gleich (2001), 372, 380.
36 K. W. LANGE, *Die Pflichtteilsentziehung gegenueber Akkoemminglingen de lege lata und de lege ferenda* (2004) 204, *Archiv fuer die civilistische Praxis*, 804.
37 BVerfG, 19. 4. 2005, *Fam RZ* 2005, 872.
38 M. SCHOEPFLIN, Verfassungsmaessigkeit *des Pflichtteilsrechts und Pflichtteilsentziehung, Fam RZ*, 2005, 2025.
39 »Entwurf eines Gesetzes zur Aenderung des Erb- und Verjaerungsrechts«, Referententwurf des Bundesministeriums der Justiz, 10. 4. 2007.
40 K. KUCHINKE, *Ueber die Notwendigkeit, ein gemeineuropaeisches Familien – und Erbrecht zu schaffen* , in *Europas universale rechtsordnungspolitische Aufgabe im Recht des dritten Jahrtausends: Festschrift fuer Alfred Soellner* (2000), 589.
41 R. C. BRASHIER, *Inheritance Law and the Evolving Family*, Temple Univ. Press, 2004, 10.
42 C. H. WHITHEBREAD, *The Uniform Probate Code's Nod to the Partnership Theory of Marriage*, in *Probate Law J.*, 11 (1992), 125.
43 A. ELLUL, F. PANUNZI, M. PAGANO, *Inheritance Law and Investment in Family Firms*, available in SSRN, Working Paper Series.
44 Loi *2001-1135 du 3.12. 2001 »relative aux droits du conjoint survivant et des enfants*

changes: the protection of the surviving spouse was strengthened[45]; the number of the beneficiaries was reduced, excluding the parents from the circle of those entitled to the legitimate portion; the legitimate portion was turned into a money claim, which has become a credit[46]; the rule against inheritance contracts was relaxed[47]; the prohibition of the »fideicommissary substitution« was removed to allow broader inheritance planning.[48]

V. Legal Transplants.

The advantage of a fixed share rule is certainty, and its main disadvantage is rigidity

> »...A court – based discretionary system is very flexible. The award can take into account many factors such as the length of marriage or civil partnership, the conduct of the parties, the needs of the claimant, the nature of the estate and the needs of

---

adulterins et modernisant diverses dispositions de droit successoral«: F. BELLIVER e J. ROCHFELD, Drit successoral. Conjoint survivant. Enfant adulterin. Loi 2001-1135 du 3 decembre 2001, in Rev. trim. dr. civ., 2002, Chron., 156,. Reform of divorce: art. 22-XII l. n. 2004-439 du 26. 5. 2004. Loi n. 2006-728 du 23.6. 2006 «portent réforme des successions et des libéralités«: J. CARBONNIER, P. CATALA, J. de SAINT AFRIQUE, G. MORIN, Des liberalités. Une offre de loi, Defrenois, 2003; Ph. MALAURIE, Examen critique du projet de loi portant réforme des successions et des liberalites, in Defrenois, 2005, 38298; M. GRIMALDI, Premières vues sur la réfome des successions et des liberalités(loi n. 2006 728 du 23 juin 2006), in Recueil Dalloz, 2006, n. 37, 2551 ; D. VIGNEAU, Le reglement de la succession . Observation sur le projet de loi portant réforme des successions et des liberalités, in JCP N, 2006, I. 1144; Ph. MALAURIE, Préface, in M.-C. FORGERARD, R. CRONE, B. GELOT, Lé nouveau droit des successions et des libéraliés. Loi du 23 juin 2006. Commentaire & formules, Defrenois, Parigi, 2007; Id., Les successions. Les libéralites , Defrenois, 2006. 97; Id., La réforme des successions et des libéralités, in Defrénois, 2006, p.1319 ss.

45 Par.756, 757 French Civil Code. P. CATALA, Proposition de loi relative aux droits du conjoint survivant, in Dalloz,2001, Actual, 862.

46 Par. 923 French Civil Code. : P. CATALA, Prospective et perspectives en droit successoral, in Sem. Jur. Ed. Not., 2007, 55 ; Y. – H. LELEU, Suggestion de loi visant à introduire le principe de l'égalité en valeur dans les réglements successoraux, in Examen critique de la reserve successorale, Tome III Propositions, Bruylant – Bruxelles, 2000, 25.

47 Par. 929 French Civil Code. I. DURIAC, La renonciation anticipée à l'action en réduction, in Recueil Dalloz, 2006, n. 37, 2574.

48 Par 1048 »Liberalité graduelle« French Civil Code. N. PETERKA, Les libéralités graduelles et résiduelles, entre rupture et continuité, Recueil Dalloz, 2006, n. 37, 2580. Par. 1075 »Liberalités Partages« R. LE GUIDEC, Les libéralités – partages, in Recueil Dalloz, 2006, n. 37, 2584.

the beneficiaries....The award may take the form of a lump sum, transfer of property or periodical payments and can be tailored to the particular estate in question«. Nevertheless, it is well known that »the main disadvantages of a court – based system are uncertainty and inconvenience. ...a discretionary system can provoke litigation... This is likely to involve the re-opening of any matrimonial and family discord with distasteful affirmations of past conduct« [49].

The scheme based on fixed rules, in the French amended version, is perhaps the solution which adapts to other civil law systems, such as Italy, which nowadays are aiming to reform the legitimate portion[50]. This pattern is better adapted to the judiciary system[51], where we can see a link between the different position of the judge in the two areas. In the English legal system the role of the judge is quite superior, as the judge is reputed to have more discretion in deciding disputes. In civil law jurisdictions and under American law, the legislator has strived to avoid judicial discretion, though nowadays judges have some limited discretion:

»legislators believe it is neither wise nor feasible to grant American probate judges the pervasive discretion to decide who is and who is not in the family for each estate that comes before them. Untempered judicial discretion could lead to wildly inconsistent and unpredictable outcomes, reducing public confidence in the probate process. Also, a discretionary system permitting individually tailored solutions would demand far more resources than does an objective system«[52].

Reputed scholars brought forward the abovementioned arguments, assuming that fixed share schemes match with continental Europe. The recommendation is not to follow *the English discretionary maintenance claims model.*[53] According to the recent French reform, self determination

---

49 Scottish Law Commission, *Discussion Paper on Succession*, n. 136, august 2007, 46, where to Scottish legislator is recommended the fixed share scheme.
50 G. AMADIO, *La successione necessaria tra proposte di abrogazione e istanze di riforma*, in *Riv. Not.*, 2007, I, 803; S. DELLE MONACHE (ed.), *Tradizione e modernità nel diritto successorio. Dagli istituti classici al patto di famiglia*, Cedam, 2007.
51 R. CHESTER, *Should American Children be protected against Disinheritance*, in *Real Property, Prob. & Trust J., 32 (1997), 405*, promoting judiciary pattern.
52 R. C. BRASHIER, *Inheritance Law and the Evolving Family*, Temple Univ. Press, 2004, 7.
53 M.A.GLENDON, *Fixed Rules and Discretion in Contemporary Family Law and Successions*, in *Tulane Law Review*, 60 (1986), 1185; A. ZOPPINI, *Le successioni in diritto com-*

can be enhanced, in order to allow the child to give up inheritance rights, to set up effective, generation-skipping, succession planning, with an eye to advance the position of handicapped descendants – especially once the prohibition of »fideicommissary substitution«[54] – has been removed, and to help investment in family firms.

The fixed share pattern should also work for spouses, provided that self determination is improved in this area of the law as well.[55] The share of the surviving spouse should depend on the length of the marriage, following the American UPC scheme.

Finally, the legitimate portion should be replaced with a cash value,[56] in order not to hinder or restrict the alienability of immovable disposed by will or gift.[57]

---

parato, in *Tratt. Dir. Comp.*, dir. da R. Sacco, Utet, Torino, 2002, 94.

54 P. DELNOY, *Organisation d'un régime de dévolution successorale conventionelle permettant d'assurer la survie d'une enfant handicap,* in *Examen critique de la réserve successorale, Tome III Propositions,* Bruylant – Bruxelles, 2000, 25.

55 This rule is recommended by Scottish Law Commission, *Discussion Paper on Succession,* n. 136, august 2007, 51.

56 G. GABRIELLI, *I legittimari e gli strumenti a tutela dei loro diritti,* in S. DELLE MONACHE (cur.), *Tradizione e modernità nel diritto successorio. Dagli istituti classici al patto di famiglia,* Cedam, 2007, p. 115.

57 Y. – H. LELEU, *La réduction et le rapport en valeur. Réflexions critiques en vue d'une réforme législative,* in *Examen critique de la réserve successorale, Tome III Propositions,* Bruylant – Bruxelles, 2000, 213.

Family Business: The Need for a General Framework

Mireia Artigot-Golobardes and Laura Alascio-Carrasco[1]

I. Introduction

Family owned businesses are of a special nature. In many cases, corporate and family relations intertwine, and the operation of these businesses is often directly affected by personal and family affairs.[2] These businesses thus merit particular consideration.

The study of family business as a special kind of business began in the 1960's and 1970's,[3] but there is still no unique definition of family business. Sometimes, the concept of family business overlaps with the definition or characteristics of small or medium enterprises. However, family businesses are not all small or medium businesses, and all small or medium businesses are not family businesses.[4] Family businesses are very diverse in size,[5] and they take on a wide variety of corporate structures, from partnerships to closely-held corporations to limited liability companies or corporations. Furthermore, some are publicly traded on stock markets while others are closely-held by their shareholders.

---

1   Both at Universitat Pompeu Fabra, Barcelona, Spain.
2   Kelin E. GERSICK, Joahn A. DAVIS, Marion McCOLLOM HAMPTON, Ivan LANGSBERG (1997), *Generation to Generation: Life Cycles of the Family Business*, Harvard Business School Press, Boston, p. 4 (discussing nepotism, sibling rivalry, and unprofessional management).
3   Tagiuri and Davis developed a three-circle model to represent the interactions between family and businesses. The three-circle model describes the family business system as three independent but overlapping subsystems: business, ownership, and family. See Tagiuri, R., Davis, J.A. (1982). Bivalent attributes of the family firm. Working Paper, Harvard Business School, Cambridge, Massachusetts. Reprinted 1996, Family Business Review IX (2) 199–208.
4   José Javier PÉREZ-FADÓN MARTÍNEZ (2005), *La empresa familiar: fiscalidad, organización y protocolo familiar*, CISS, Bilbao. At 18.
5   For example, Spanish family businesses are typically smaller than the average size of European family owned business. See Ramón ADELL RAMÓN (1998), »El acceso de la empresa familiar a los mercados de valores«, *Alta Dirección*, núm 202, pp. 49–55. At 49.

This diversity of characteristics makes it difficult to provide a uniform concept, definition or description of what family businesses are[6] and therefore to conceptualize the general challenges they face. The problems presented by a sole person business working with a family member are not the same as the ones presented by a publicly traded corporation with a majority of stock owned by a few family members. And the challenges presented by a closely-held company with shareholders who are family members are significantly different than the ones faced by a publicly listed corporation the stock of which is traded on a stock market. Further, businesses are not subject to the same incorporation requirements and regulations when incorporated in the U.S., in Europe or in Japan; neither are individuals. Therefore, family businesses do not fit into a corporate structure, corporate size, ownership and management structure or specific industry.

Despite the difficulty of tracing a concept that could help explain and define what family businesses are, the literature has highlighted some characteristics commonly shared by family businesses irrespective of their diversity.[7]

First, the ownership of family businesses is generally structured around individuals who are related by a family relationship. This does not necessarily mean that family businesses are owned solely or completely by family members. There could be other shareholders, but family businesses are generally owned, or the majority of stock is owned, by individuals belonging to a certain family.[8]

Second, the management of family businesses is generally held by family members who own the majority of the company's stock.[9]

Finally, family businesses generally have a long-term intent to participate in the market if possible, in the hands of the founding family. Family businesses do not generally have short-term goals of incorporating the

---

6 Francisco VICENT CHULIÀ (2000), »Organización jurídica de la sociedad familiar«, *Revista de Derecho Patrimonial* 5/2000, pp. 21–48. At 21.
7 Some have described family business as business where ownership, management and intent of permanence overlap. See Francisco VICENT CHULIÀ (2000), »Organización jurídica de la sociedad familiar«, *Revista de Derecho Patrimonial* 5/2000, pp. 21–48. At 29. See also José Javier PÉREZ-FADÓN MARTÍNEZ (2005), *La empresa familiar: fiscalidad, organización y protocolo familiar*, CISS, Bilbao. At 18.
8 José Javier PÉREZ-FADÓN MARTÍNEZ (2005), *La empresa familiar: fiscalidad, organización y protocolo familiar*, CISS, Bilbao. At 18.
9 This management structure should not be understood as a ban on external members to participate in the business board but the majority of the board members belong to the family who at the same time owns the business.

business in order to sell it for profit or to obtain a high short-term return on the investment. For the most part, family businesses intend to remain in the market and be able to capture a share of the market of their industry and to continue under the control of the family members.

However, family businesses face specific challenges that condition their structure and possibilities of success. This article provides a study of the specific challenges faced by family businesses from a corporate, family and inheritance law perspective. In light of the major importance of family business in European and in U.S. economies,[10] the absence of a global framework for family owned businesses is surprising. The definition of family business that will be used in this paper will be based on the above-mentioned characteristics of ownership, management and long-term business goals that will allow us to lay out the specific family business challenges that can be addressed through a regulatory framework.

The next three sections of this paper develop the three major challenges presented by family business: Section 2 focuses on corporate law questions, Section 3 presents the effects on family business of the interaction between family law and corporate law, and Section 4 discusses the effect of inheritance law on the transfer of family businesses to the next generation. As mentioned above, these issues have not been addressed globally by legislators. As will be presented below, corporate managers have tried to create mechanisms to overcome such problems, but they have been largely unsuccessful because most of the problems derive from the imperatives of family and inheritance law. Section 5 develops a response to the lack of general framework for family businesses provided by private practitioners: the family law protocol. The last section of the paper includes brief conclusions.

---

10   Numbers vary because the lack of a commonly shared definition of what family businesses are makes calculations difficult. In countries such as Spain 65 to 80% of total of business are family business and their output amounts to 15% of the Gross Domestic Product (GDP) while they create between 65 to 70% of the total employment, employing more than 700.000 people. Further, 22% of the Spanish biggest thousand corporations may be considered family businesses. The U.S. shows similar figures: 35% of the biggest 500 U.S. corporations are family businesses that generate 42% of the employment of the U.S. economy. This information is available at the website of the Instituto de la Empresa Familiar – the Spanish Family Business Institute (http://www.iefamiliar.com/organizacion/datos.asp).

II. Fitting into Corporate Law: Corporate Challenges of Family Businesses

Family businesses are companies incorporated and structured as any other corporation. They generally share with other types of businesses such goals as maximizing profits, ensuring viability, and growing and consolidating positions within a given industry. So the fact that businesses are owned and managed primarily by family members does not make them particularly different from other businesses in these respects. For that reason, corporate law does not consider family businesses as a special kind of business needing special regulation.

However, corporate structure, management, and the availability of external financing are especially sensitive issues for family businesses. In fact, these issues may explain why it is often so difficult for family businesses to survive beyond the first generation, unlikely to survive beyond the second, and almost impossible to survive beyond the third.[11]

1. Finding the optimal corporate structure of family businesses.

Family businesses may be formed under any of the company or corporate structures available under corporate law: They may be individual or single-person companies or adopt a corporate form that enables corporate founders to enjoy limited liability.[12] Deciding the optimal structure and legal form of a family business will have important consequences, both legal and economical, on the creation of the business, its development, management, transfer, and its prospect of success.[13]

In the past, small family businesses were generally formed as individual or single-person companies. While this form is still used, the uncertainties of the market and the difficulties of success have tended to push even small family businesses toward limited liability structures that protect private assets. Most businesses nowadays – including family business

---

11 The Spanish Instituto de la Empresa Familiar – the Spanish Family Business Institute – quantifies this information stating that 11 % of the family businesses who are members of the Spanish Family Business Institute are in the first generation, 36 % of them make it to the second, 25 % to the third, 21 % to the fourth, 4 % to the fifth, 2 % to the sixth and 1 % to the seventh generation. This information is available at http://www.iefamiliar.com/organizacion/datos.asp.

12 José Javier Pérez-Fadón Martínez (2005), *La empresa familiar: fiscalidad, organización y protocolo familiar*, CISS, Bilbao. At 23.

13 José Javier Pérez-Fadón Martínez (2005), *La empresa familiar: fiscalidad, organización y protocolo familiar*, CISS, Bilbao. At 23.

– are structured as either limited liability companies or as corporations.[14] Furthermore, family businesses tend to be closely-held.[15]

The differences between limited liability companies and corporations are significant. Limited liability companies are closed companies, which means that their stock is not traded in a stock market. They are therefore less liquid, as shareholders are allowed to sell their shares only to other shareholders or to third parties that the other shareholders agree on. Further, personal characteristics of shareholders are relevant because the corporate charter may place restrictions on who may own the company's stock, limiting ownership, for instance, to individuals as opposed to other companies or corporations. Corporations, on the other hand, have shareholders that receive stock certificates and elect board directors that adopt the major corporate decisions but do not engage in the day-to-day management of the corporation, which is the responsibility of corporate officers.[16] Corporations may be closely-held, in cases where stock is not publicly traded, or they may be public corporations, where stock is traded on a stock market and therefore freely transferable between shareholders, who do not necessarily have to be family members.

2. *The Management of the Family Business:*
   The Difficult Balance between Family and Business

Finding an equilibrium between business managers and stock owners, who are at the same time family members, is especially relevant in the case of family businesses. Deadlock situations resulting from disagreements among family members[17] present a serious threat to management and can result in complete collapse, with obvious consequences for the position of the business in the market.

Family businesses generally have three major kinds of management options available:[18] First, managers and directors may themselves be family members and simultaneously shareholders. A second design is one where

---

14 Frank H. EASTERBROOK & Daniel R. FISCHEL, *The Economic Structure of Corporate Law*, 228–252, Harvard University Press, Cambridge (1991).
15 José Manuel CALAVIA MOLINERO (1998), »Aspectos societarios de la empresa familiar: raíces históricas y nuevas opciones«, *Alta Dirección*, núm 202, pp. 409–16. At 410.
16 Frank H. EASTERBROOK & Daniel R. FISCHEL, *The Economic Structure of Corporate Law*, 228–252, Harvard University Press, Cambridge (1991).
17 José Manuel CALAVIA MOLINERO (1998), »Aspectos societarios de la empresa familiar: raíces históricas y nuevas opciones«, *Alta Dirección*, núm 202, pp. 409–16. At 412.
18 José Manuel CALAVIA MOLINERO (1998), »Aspectos societarios de la empresa familiar: raíces históricas y nuevas opciones«, *Alta Dirección*, núm 202, pp. 409–16. At 414.

both management and directors are individuals external to the family. Finally, management may be a mixed system under which certain managers are members of the family and others are external to the family. Needless to say, regardless of the chosen corporate structure, whenever family members can serve as business managers, it is important to establish minimum standards and requirements for these positions in order to avoid having them filled by non-professional or non-qualified family members.[19]

It is beyond the scope of this paper to present the advantages of one management structure over another. However, management structures that favor the inclusion of non-family members either exclusively or jointly with family members would seem the best way to preserve some separation of the two often conflicting institutions in play here: on one side, the family and the personal and emotional conflicts it entails, and on the other side, the business, where certainty, efficient decision-making processes and serious management decisions are generally the formula for success. Markets seem to perceive positively the introduction of mechanisms by which family and business are as separated as possible.[20]

3. *The Access to Capital Markets:*
   A 21st Century Challenge for Family Businesses

In today's corporate world, finding financial sources and attracting external investors is key for the success of a company. Capital stock, necessary for starting the business, is not enough for financing the often valuable investments businesses need to make and profits or corporate assets are not generally totally re-invested in the business. Shareholders claim their dividend and systematic re-investment is not a long-term option. Therefore, it is part of the daily life of a business to go to investors, financial institutions or the stock market to obtain additional financing.

Family businesses are not excluded from this phenomenon: they need external financing, obtain financial sources beyond family members and, sometimes, even go public in a stock market for this purpose.

Obtaining external financing is not easy for family business for several reasons. First, as mentioned above, even though it is not possible to talk about a unique corporate structure of a family business, the corporate

---

[19] INFORME DE LA PONENCIA DE ESTUDIO PARA LA PROBLEMÁTICA DE LA EMPRESA FAMILIAR (543/000005), Boletín Oficial de las Cortes Generales – Senado VII Legislatura. Serie I: Boletín General, núm. 312 de 23 de noviembre de 2001, pp. 1–40. At 39.

[20] José Manuel CALAVIA MOLINERO (1998), »Aspectos societarios de la empresa familiar: raíces históricas y nuevas opciones«, *Alta Dirección*, núm 202, pp. 409–16. At 414.

form mostly used by family business is the limited liability company.[21] This structure implies that the company is closely held and that the personal conditions and qualities of shareholders are important. Further, there is generally no market for the shares that are sold to either other shareholders or to approved third parties (often other family members). Additionally, because of the illiquid condition of the shares, it is difficult to determine a share value since they are not publicly traded and therefore there is no market price for them. All these factors discourage external investors from financing or from becoming shareholders of this kind of businesses.

Second, because of the family relationships generally inherent in the daily life of a family business, external investors may be dissuaded from investing and instead look for more flexible and open business structures.

Third, one of the goals of investors is generally short-term profits on their investment. As mentioned above, this strongly contradicts one of the essential elements of family businesses that aim at permanence and continuity of the shareholders and board members.

All these elements represent specific difficulties of family businesses for finding external finance sources. There have been proposals to improve the situation and create mechanisms to facilitate the access of family businesses to external investors. One proposal is to create investment funds that could commit to mid-term investments in exchange for tax benefits.[22] However, this has not yet been tried.

In order to avoid having to negotiate individually with each potential investor, one of the most common processes used to have access to external financing is listing the company on a public market.[23] Going public affects not only the way the company is financed but also the personality and often the character of the company given that there will have to be new management structures and new shareholders to whom it will be necessary to share information and control.[24]

---

21 Frank H. EASTERBROOK & Daniel R. FISCHEL, *The Economic Structure of Corporate Law*, 228–252, Harvard University Press, Cambridge (1991).
22 See Informe de la Ponencia de Estudio para la problemática de la empresa familiar. Ponencia del Sr. José Manuel Lara Bosch, President of Planeta Publishing Group. At 3.
23 When a company lists its shares on a public exchange, it will almost always issue additional new share so that it can raise extra capital. This new issuance is particularly important because the money paid by investors for these newly-issued shares is directly received by the company and not to the other shareholders, as it happens when shares are bought and sold in a public stock market.
24 Ramón ADELL RAMÓN (1998), »El acceso de la empresa familiar a los mercados de valores«, *Alta Dirección*, núm 202, pp. 49–55. At 52.

The process of going public is not easy for any company because it entails a determination of the price at which shares will be offered, involves a potential change in the corporate management, and eventually entails a decrease of control by company owners, which in the case of family businesses are generally family members. However, public offering can be a step toward achieving higher corporate growth, increasing corporate transparency, providing liquidity to shareholders, facilitating access to information about the companies' market value, diminishing control and ownership of the company's founding members, giving a better image to the company, and representing that the company is increasing its activities or volume level.

It does not seem possible to establish a moment or situation when issuing a public offering will be attractive for all family businesses. It is often said, however, that this moment tends to come when a family business moves toward ownership by different branches of the family.[25]

As mentioned above, corporate law issues are not specifically problematic for family businesses. Given the interaction, and often overlap between family and business, the personal law of the different family members will be of crucial importance especially in two areas of special relevance for the viability, success and potential transfer of the family business to the next generation: family law, which will be the topic of the next section and inheritance law, which will follow.

III. The Effect of Family Law on Family Businesses: A Difficult Overlap

When talking about businesses and the challenges they face, it is generally only necessary to look at corporate law requirements – together with tax law – to determine what are the steps needed to be taken in order to create, manage and develop a business. However, family businesses entail an additional requirement given that the personal laws of family business owners may directly impact the ownership structure of the family business. This becomes particularly apparent in a family crisis.

As mentioned earlier, family businesses are generally structured as separate legal entities with ownership divided between shares owned by

---

25 Ramón ADELL RAMÓN (1998), »El acceso de la empresa familiar a los mercados de valores«, *Alta Dirección*, núm 202, pp. 49–55. At 55.

family members.[26] In the moment of a family divorce, depending on the marital regime in force, shares, returns, dividends or profits could be subject to division. Thus, legislation affecting the economic marital relations and the content of separation agreements may have a direct impact on the ownership structure, management, and potential success of family businesses. In some states, such as Spain and the United States, plurilegislative systems mean that family businesses may need to consider a variety of marital property regimes to which they might be subject. An important division in these systems is between separate property and community property regimes.

Under a separate property regime, there is a legal presumption that individual assets and income generated by such assets belong to whichever spouse paid for them, earned them or has title to them. Therefore, these assets are not subject to division with the other spouse. Despite the separation of property and the presumption of property title, this does not necessarily mean a complete separation of property between spouses given that there are certain payments or compensations, such as equitable distribution of property, alimony and spousal support payments, that need to be made in order to avoid inequitable results. In contrast, community property regimes create a legal presumption that all income and assets acquired by either spouse during marriage belongs to both of them in equal shares. Therefore, whenever there is a marital crisis, property will be divided equally between spouses.

The effects of marital economic regimes have been significantly mitigated with the possibility of premarital agreements and separation agreements. But even in cases where these kinds of agreements are adopted, economic disputes between spouses may arise with respect of the share to which they are entitled or the value attributed to a certain asset.

Family businesses, as any other economic asset, may be a private good – if created before marriage – or a marital good – if business was created during marriage.[27] This qualification is crucial for the prospect of the family business because that will determine whether family businesses may be subject to distribution between spouses or may generate compensation rights from one spouse to the other. Further, there may be problems regarding the economic value of the family business or regard-

---

26 Law 7/2003, of April 1st, of Limited liability company »Nueva Empresa«. See Fernando CURIEL LORENTE (2001), »La sucesión de la empresa familiar en el derecho civil aragonés«, XI Encuentros del Foro de Derecho Aragonés, pp. 86–139, 96.

27 See Informe de la Ponencia de Estudio para la problemática de la empresa familiar at 28.

ing the increase of value and the form of payment of the compensation to the non-business spouse.[28] When all these issues collide, family businesses may become non-manageable.

IV. Organizing the Transfer and Future of the Family Business: The Effect of Inheritance Law on the Succession of Family Businesses

The third and last key issue that differentiates family businesses from other businesses is the impact of inheritance law on them. Inheritance law is of special importance for family businesses for two major reasons: First, organizing the succession of family businesses is key to the future of the company given that the lack of planning can result in the business disappearing. Second, inheritance law imposes rigid and burdensome limitations to the scope of decision of individuals when organizing their succession that inherently affect the organization of the succession of the business.

The organization of the succession of family businesses is crucial so that the continuity, stability and therefore future prospect of the business is granted.[29] Companies need continuity and stability and interruptions can be very harmful. It is well settled in the literature that in order to minimize the risks presented by the transfer of the family business to the next generation, the succession should be as planned as possible. Business owners should work out succession plans that allow successors to take over immediately upon an owner's death or retirement.

A second issue of special relevance regarding the succession of the family business is that its stock and therefore its value is part of the decedent's estate. Inheritance laws generally establish mandatory shares in the form of a percentage of the estate that the law determines compulsory for the decedent's issue, if any; for the surviving spouse of the decedent, if any; or jointly, depending on the inheritance law applicable to the decedent. A family business is not contemplated as a unity and therefore is not especially protected by the legal system in that respect. Therefore, the family business is one of the assets that may be subject to the widow/widower's and to the decedent's issue inheritance rights.[30]

---

28 Ana FERNÁNDEZ-TRESGUERRES GARCIA, Esquema para la redaccion de un protocolo familiar, pp. 161, 164.
29 See Fernando CURIEL LORENTE (2001), »La sucesión de la empresa familiar en el derecho civil aragonés«, XI Encuentros del Foro de Derecho Aragonés.86–139. At 106.
30 See Fernando CURIEL LORENTE (2001), »La sucesión de la empresa familiar en el dere-

Mandatory shares or economic rights of the decedent's surviving spouse over a certain percentage of the estate is of major importance for the ownership structure and eventually for the success of family businesses for several reasons: first, because issues regarding the valuation of the stock in family businesses – that are generally closely held corporations – may arise; second, because heirs who are not awarded the family businesses will be entitled to compensation.[31] If the decedent's estate has not enough assets to effectively pay such compensation and the payment is done with stock of the family business, its ownership structure and potentially management structure will be affected. Third, inheritance law imposes liability for outstanding debts to the decedent's heirs who may not always be the business successors. One could consider whether such debts should be born by the heirs or by the business successors.[32]

Hence, the future of the family business, as an important asset of the decedent's estate may be seriously jeopardized when inheritance laws are applied.

V. How to Overcome Such Problems Faced by Family Businesses?

As described above, family businesses present special challenges that are inherent to their personal structure and the legal context applicable to the individuals who at the same time are its owners. What is needed is a framework that would facilitate the foundation, development and transfer of family businesses. The current legislation, however, does not provide this.

Family business owners have sought such a framework and have suggested the creation of a statute of family business that would encompass all the characteristics and special needs a family business has in order to facilitate and enhance its performance. Even though legislatures have recognized of the importance of such businesses,[33] there are very few leg-

---

cho civil aragonés«, XI Encuentros del Foro de Derecho Aragonés.86–139. At 104.
31   The ownership structure of family business and the percentage of stock owned by the decedent will influence in the incentives to invest in the family firm. See A. ELLUL, M. PAGANO, F. PANUNZI, »Inheritance Law and Investment in Family Firms«, ECGI – Finance Working Paper No 222/2008.
32   See Fernando CURIEL LORENTE (2001), »La sucesión de la empresa familiar en el derecho civil aragonés«, XI Encuentros del Foro de Derecho Aragonés.86–139. At 101.
33   Ramon BLASI PUJOL, »El protocol familiar com a instrument apte per pactar la compensació econòmica per raó de treball de l'article 41 del Codi de Familia«, Revista Jurídica de Catalunya, 2006 (3), 707–728, at 712. See also Family Business Institute.

islative initiatives, at either the European or the domestic level.[34] Up to today, legal systems have not generally incorporated specific measures to facilitate family businesses to address their specific challenges[35] beyond those facilitating and simplifying family business bureaucracy.[36] Hence, the rules applicable to family business are the general regulations applicable to any company.[37]

In light of the absence of legislative initiatives and the limitations of current corporate law to deal with such issues and provide solutions to these challenges, professionals – especially law firms – have created private law instruments in order to fill the void. These instruments are called Family Protocols and while they are not yet in general use, their adoption is growing significantly.[38]

The Family Protocol[39] is an agreement between family members used to coordinate their behavior and their relationship with the business it-

---

[34] At the European level it is worth noting the Commission Recommendation 94/1069/EC, of 7 December 1994, on the transfer of small and medium-sized enterprises, O.J. L 385, 31/12/1994 P. 0014- 0017. The Reccomendation may be found at http://eur-lex.europa.eu/LexUriServ/LexUriServ.do?uri=CELEX:31994H1069:EN:HTML.

[35] José Javier PÉREZ-FADÓN MARTÍNEZ (2005), *La empresa familiar: fiscalidad, organización y protocolo familiar*, CISS, Bilbao. At 41.

[36] For example, in Spain, in 2003 Congress passed a new law regulating limited Liability companies – and not specifically family businesses – whereby business where provided with new and simplified bureaucratic procedures regarding the companies' registration, administrative procedure requirements, accounting rules, relationship with public administrations, tax deferrals as well as introducing the possibility of conducting some of such procedures through email. See Law 7/2003 of April 1 (RCL 2003,903) de la sociedad limitada nueva empresa amending Law 2/1995 of March 23 (RCL 1995, 953) of Limited liability companies. Despite not being directly aimed for family businesses, such regulation will definitely have an impact on the requirements they will be subject to and the often too burdensome burocracy companies are faced, especially in continental Europe.

[37] José Javier PÉREZ-FADÓN MARTÍNEZ (2005), *La empresa familiar: fiscalidad, organización y protocolo familiar*, CISS, Bilbao. At 15.

[38] In fact, the Spanish Family Business institute states that only 25% of the biggest Spanish family businesses that represent 8% of the Spanish GDP, have a family protocol. See http://www.iefamiliar.com/organizacion/index.asp.

[39] The origin of family protocols should be found in shareholder agreements of close companies in the United States. Family Protocols is a contract parallel to the articles of incorporation drafted in order to coordinate the decision making process of the company The family protocol may include this kind of regulation (and it often does) but it has a broader scope. See Jorge Alberto RODRÍGUEZ APARICIO (2004), »El protocolo familiar«, a VV. AA. *El buen gobierno de las empresas familiares*, Thomson-Aranzadi, Navarra. At. 295; Francisco VICENT CHULIÀ (2000), »Organización jurídica de la sociedad familiar«, *Revista de Derecho Patrimonial 5/2000*, p. 38; José Javier PÉREZ-FADÓN MARTÍNEZ (2005), *La empresa familiar: fiscalidad, organización y protocolo familiar*, CISS, Bilbao. At 43.

self.⁴⁰ It is a set of rules⁴¹ that originally the founder and all other family members that own the business will sign, and, will consider whether and how to include new members in the future.⁴²

There are authors that have suggested that a Family Protocol is a legal instrument that despite not being legally binding provides credibility and mutual trust to the parties entering into it.⁴³ Hence, its existence does not guarantee the intended coordination without the concurrence of the willingness of all family members to comply and enforce its provisions. For this reason, the Protocol is sometimes referred to as a »game of promises«.⁴⁴ Others, however, view the Protocol as no more than a management tool because it creates the idea of belonging to an entrepreneurial family while serving as a guide to anticipate potential problems and set out ways of solving them.⁴⁵

We read Family Protocols as a non-enforceable instrument with a flexible content depending on the needs of each family and business.⁴⁶ Hence, its effectiveness will depend on the commitment of all parties of the protocol to comply with them and its content, form and nature of Family Protocols will vary from one business to the other or from one family to another: each family designs it to suit their own needs.⁴⁷ When drafting a Family Protocol, family members meet and decide the direction of the

---

40   José Javier Rodríguez Alcalde y Maribel Rodríguez Zapatero (2006), »El protocolo familiar: un juego de promesas«, *La Notaría,* núm 33, p. 13.
41   Some authors (Ana Fernández-Tresguerres García (2002), »Protocolo familiar: un instrumento para la autorregulación de la sociedad familiar«, *Revista de Derecho de Sociedades*, vol. 2, núm. 19, p, 90) refer to it as a »code of conduct« as it provides the guidelines that family members engaged in the business must follow in order for it to run smoothly.
42   Jorge Alberto Rodríguez Aparicio (2004), »El protocolo familiar«, a VV. AA. *El buen gobierno de las empresas familiares*, Thomson-Aranzadi, Navarra, p. 298.
43   See José Javier Rodríguez Alcalde y Maribel Rodríguez Zapatero (2006), »El protocolo familiar: un juego de promesas«, *La Notaría,* núm 33, pp. 13–24, at 16.
44   José Javier Rodríguez Alcalde y Maribel Rodríguez Zapatero (2006), »El protocolo familiar: un juego de promesas«, *La Notaría,* núm 33, p. 13.
45   Ana Fernández-Tresguerres García (2002), »Protocolo familiar: un instrumento para la autorregulación de la sociedad familiar«, *Revista de Derecho de Sociedades*, vol. 2, núm. 19, pp. 90.
46   Ramon Blasi Pujol, »El protocol familiar com a instrument apte per pactar la compensació econòmica per raó de treball de l'article 41 del Codi de Familia«, *Revista Juridica de Catalunya*, 2006 (3), 707–728, at 714.
47   Ana Fernández-Tresguerres García (2002), »Protocolo familiar: un instrumento para la autorregulación de la sociedad familiar«, *Revista de Derecho de Sociedades*, vol. 2, núm. 19, pp. 89–113. At 91.

business and the relationship between the family and the business.⁴⁸ The depth, content and rigidity of the Protocol will have two contradictory effects because while it will provide certainty to family members about the content of their agreement, it will also introduce difficulties in amending it and in being able to involve external non-family members to the management of the business.⁴⁹

The substantive content of the Protocol can roughly be divided into two categories: personal and family law related provisions and corporate law provisions. Most Protocols will begin with the history and values of the family and the business⁵⁰ that will determine the goals and objectives of the business.

Personal and family related provisions refer basically to family law and inheritance law types of clauses and are used to ensure that the property of the shares stay within the family. With respect to family law clauses, protocols generally include the duty of all married business owners to enter into marital agreements in order to establish a separate property regime⁵¹ or to alter the community property regime in order to avoid the business shares becoming part of the marital property subject to division. One of the major problems presented by this kind of clause is that the Protocol is *res inter alia*, that is, if the spouse who is not a business owner is not a signing party of the protocol, then he or she is not bound by it. The question that arises in these cases is whether a business owner could be held liable for breach of the provisions of the Protocol in cases where his or her spouse is not willing to enter into a marital agreement. Additionally, even in cases where the non-business spouse agrees to enter into a

---

48   Francisco VICENT CHULIÀ (2000), »Organización jurídica de la sociedad familiar«, *Revista de Derecho Patrimonial 5/2000*, pp. 21–48. At 30.
49   This contradiction could result in a vicious circle in which it would lose liquidity in the market making in less attractive for external investors that, in turn, would make the company even less liquid. See A. ELLUL, M. PAGANO, F. PANUNZI, »Inheritance Law and Investment in Family Firms«, 40, SSRN Working Paper.
50   Jorge Alberto RODRÍGUEZ APARICIO (2004), »El protocolo familiar«, a VV. AA. *El buen gobierno de las empresas familiares*, Thomson-Aranzadi, Navarra, p. 299.
51   Ana FERNÁNDEZ-TRESGUERRES GARCÍA (2002), »Protocolo familiar: un instrumento para la autorregulación de la sociedad familiar«, *Revista de Derecho de Sociedades*, vol. 2, núm. 19, p. 92: When the default marital property regime is community property two major issues arise: 1) Liability of the community property for debts of one of the spouses: the community property is held liable for the debts of the spouses so the shares could be compromised, should the non-owner spouse become indebted. 2) Title of the shares: in case of divorce the spouses are entitled to half of the community property. This means that in cases where there were not sufficient assets, the shares could be transferred to the non-owner spouse.

marital agreement, the question will be whether specific performance of the clauses of the Family Protocol is available as a remedy for breach.

Regarding inheritance law clauses, Family Protocols often include clauses in which a business founder promises to appoint one of his or her children as heir so this child can continue with the business.[52] In most legal systems, however, this type of clause is unenforceable as against inheritance law principles of freedom of the testator until the end of his or her life.[53] Other legal systems do allow succession contracts in which the testator agrees on the heir **before** death. Because of their contractual nature, these succession contracts are irrevocable unilaterally and therefore will be binding both for the testator, who will not be able to appoint someone else as heir, and for the appointed heir, who will not be able to repudiate the decedent's estate.[54] As it can be easily foreseeable, the key to this kind of contracts is the game between appointing a son or daughter as heir or heiress while at the same time the rest of issue waive some of their inheritance rights.

The third type of clause usually included in the Protocol is a corporate law clause. This may be classified in two types:
1.) restrictions on share transfers in the form of personal conditions or minimum percentages of shares to transfer and
2.) management related clauses that may recommend the formation of management bodies such as a Family Council that may be composed by family members that do not necessarily need to be business owners.

Family Protocols are becoming more and more popular in Spain to organize the interaction between family and business. Their popularity appears to result from their private nature, which addresses the needs of entrepreneurial families. However, their short history and the lack of

---

52 Ana FERNÁNDEZ-TRESGUERRES GARCÍA (2002), »Protocolo familiar: un instrumento para la autorregulación de la sociedad familiar«, *Revista de Derecho de Sociedades*, vol. 2, núm. 19, p. 99.
53 For example, in some legal systems such as Spain and France) it is specifically forbidden any contracts whose object is a future inheritance right. Article 1271 of the Spanish Civil Code.
54 This is the case of Germany, and also Spain, a pluri-legislative state in which autonomous communities with historical civil law regimes allow this kind of contracts. In particular, the newest reform of the Catalan inheritance law is particularly permissive with inheritance contracts. See Joan EGEA FERNÁNDEZ (2007), »Protocol familiar i pactes successoris: la projectada reforma dels heretaments«, *InDret* 3/2007.

judicial opinions interpreting them make their enforcement and effectiveness questionable. It remains to be seen how this will play out in the future, but there is clearly room for improvement, and when the protocols are challenged in court, judges will establish their nature, content and enforceability. This should help family members and business managers make future decisions about Protocols. Moreover, if the use of the protocol is spread to a majority of companies, it may be the case that the legislature finally sees a need to step in with comprehensive regulation.

VI. Conclusions

Family businesses face specific challenges that significantly differentiate them from other kinds of business and that unequivocally determine their position in the market and influence their prospects and potential success. The overlap of corporate law, family law and inheritance law in the creation, evolution and transfer of family businesses makes it necessary to provide a general regulatory framework that would address the specific challenges that these businesses face. The private sector has already attempted to provide a solution to these issues through Family Protocols, but success has been limited because of the corporate, family and inheritance mandatory regulations that cause such Protocols to be of a non-binding nature.

The adoption of a general legislative framework that would help family businesses address these specific challenges is urgent in light of their weight in the industries of many economies.

The Planning of Succession in International Family Business Recent Developments in Germany

Roland Krause[1]

I. Challenges for Succession Planning

1. Introduction

Family entrepreneurs face an unavoidable succession dilemma: they must make strategic decisions about transitioning ownership of the family business. The main alternatives are either to sell the company to someone outside the family or to make arrangements for an interfamily succession. In the latter case, there are many transition modes, e.g., through a gift of shares, a will or a mixed marriage/succession contract. The choice of the succession mode here is the outcome of an interaction process between generations, with civil and tax laws determining the transactions costs of the different succession alternatives. Almost 90% of all Family Business Succession Plans fail in the third generation.[2] This is known as the **Buddenbrooks principle**, according to which a fortune is destroyed at the latest by the time it falls into the hands of the third generation.[3] This is considered to be due to the finding that the descendants realize that they are going to inherit a fortune, but are at the same time unfortunately not at all interested in or committed to the company. Perhaps the single most important element in the success or failure of a family business is the relationship among key members of the business family.[4]

Most businesses can survive the threats of competition, economic cycles, changes in technology etc., but the deterioration of interpersonal relationships will devastate the business and tear apart any or all of the

---

[1] Lecturer, Dept. of Civil Law, Insurance Law and International Private Law, Freie Universität Berlin, Germany.
[2] *Harris, Jeff* Small Business Informer, 22.08.2007 – www.sbinformer.com
[3] *Huber,* Germany's inheritance tax disputes continue, 03.02.2004, Credit Suisse online – emagazine.credit-suisse.com
[4] *Bengel, Manfred* Unternehmen vererben – Rechtliche Strategien für die geregelte Unternehmensnachfolge in: Internationale Familienunternehmen, Rödl, Scheffler, Winter (ed.) C.H.Beck, München 2008.

family ties. Family businesses are unique because, in addition to the usual technical business and estate planning issues, the business is interrelated to a multitude of family factors.[5] Lack of planning does lead in many cases to high tax demands and the division of the family assets or the destruction of the life‹s work of the testator and disputes among family members. This lack of preventative provisions can only be corrected after death to a very limited degree. A targeted transfer of assets cannot be rendered possible with such corrections. The following text concentrates on successions of ownership within the family. It illustrates the nature of this intergenerational problem and discusses how a specific legal system – in this case the one present today in Germany – influences the choice of succession. Although succession problems are universal, transition methods which are in fact adopted do vary around the world as each country has its own tax system. This influences the choice of laws in international successions.

2. *Definition of Family Business*

There exists at present no standard definition for a family business. However, main criteria include:

1.) a strong link of a family with the business through the owner by means of the capital being held by the family or the management through family members;
2.) strong influence of the family with regard to strategic decisions of the company;
3.) the intergenerational desire to maintain the business as an asset within a small circle of owners (the family) and to guide the development of the business, including the naming of a successor.[6] The term »Family Business« usually evokes the image of a small firm with the owner and his spouse running the business. However, the reality in the 21st century is quite different. Among the Top-100-firms in Germany, 38 are family-owned. These firms include *Porsche, BMW, Aldi, Langenscheidt, Quelle, INA (Schaeffler), Haniel, Beisheim, Bosch, Bertelsmann*.[7]

---

5 *Ambrecht*, California Trusts and Estates Quarterly, published by the Estate Planning, Trust and Probate Section, Vol. 4, No. 3, Fall 1998. http://www.taxlawsb.com/resources/FamBus/enterpri.htm
6 Landtag von Baden-Württemberg, Bericht der Mittelstandsenquete, Drucksache 12/5800, Stuttgart 2000.
7 http://www.familienunternehmen.de/top500/

Certain key values may be found to differ in »*family*« companies when these are compared to »*regular*« companies. A long term focus is usually aimed for vs. a shareholder-value strategy on a quarterly or yearly basis. Non-listed companies are not obliged to make their results public, even on a yearly basis. This allows for a long-term tactic. A closer look at the balance sheet of many family businesses reveals that a high liquidity and a high rate of accrued gains are predominant. This results in a low ratio of external capital.

3. Market Share and Problems
Family businesses comprise 80-90% of all business enterprises in North America; 50% in Spain and 80% in Germany.[8] Family-run businesses employ 57.3% of Germany's workers. About one third of family businesses in Germany are expected to turn to the next generation over the next 5 years. By 2010, most of the closely-held and family businesses will lose their primary owner due to death or retirement. 25% of senior generation family business owners have not completed any estate planning »other than writing a will« while eighty percent want the business to stay in the family whereby it is only twenty percent who are confident that it will ever happen.[9]

Problems faced by the family business regarding succession include the need to maintain the ownership of the business in the family circle, to find a suitable heir capable and interested in running the business.[10] There are good reasons why succession planning is one of the most challenging to-dos on a family business owner's checklist. To begin with, the stakes are high – so high in fact, that most family businesses fail to negotiate the transition – and are thus sold either to pay taxes or because no one in the family is willing or able to take over here.[11] Management succession planning frequently faces the problem of too many offspring wanting the top job. When that happens, current leadership often has to dispense with the ideal of giving everyone equal power and to offer controlling interest to the person or persons best suited for a particular job. On the other hand, it is possible that no-one from the next generation is interested in or capable of

---

8   For a worldwide overview see *Klein* p. 1-14, in Internationale Familienunternehmen, Rödl, Scheffler, Winter (ed.) C.H.Beck, München 2008.
9   *INSTITUT FÜR MITTELSTANDSFORSCHUNG BONN*, Press notice 05g/2007 www.ifm-bonn.org
10 *Huber/Sterr-Köln*, Nachfolge in Familienunternehmen, p. 1, Stuttgart 2006.
11 *Bengel*, p.227.

leading. In that case, the owner may have to go outside the firm itself and find the best-matched candidate. Additionally, the communities of stakeholders involved in the process can be numerous and are often in conflict. Other perils to the family business are the risk of forced sale of the family business due to: divorce, succession tax payments and litigation on succession, especially in regard to the portion of the estate reserved. The compulsory portions of a testator's estate are a particular problem in Germany in the event of death.[12] The example of a standard case of a businessman with three children may illustrate this. Only one of the children wishes to join the family business. However, if the father dies, the other two children will still be entitled to their compulsory portions (**Pflichtteil**). If they insist on payment of their inheritance, this could put serious liquidity strains on small and medium-sized enterprises.

4. *Establishing a Succession Strategy*

There are, on the other hand, numerous advantages for international family companies. Common core values are a key factor of success in expanding internationally, since coordination costs are lower than in non-family-owned businesses.[13] A family network abroad helps to maintain cultural unity in the company, enabling compensation of distance from the main company in a country overseas through family ties.[14] Attorneys, accountants, and financial advisors often focus exclusively on the tax and legal aspects of transfer strategies. They seldom address the underlying emotional and psychological issues that are involved.[15] To find a solution for the next generation, it will be necessary to redefine the family's and the company's strategy. What do they want to do together? Who are their clients? What are their resources? What could they do better than their competitors? It is crucial to establish first the shared values of the family, and thus the family's shared dream in general, before coming to the vision for the family business. This translates into strategy and at the last step to the structure. The details of the dispositions *mortis* causa shall primarily reflect this structure with regard to civil and company law and in a second step shall be optimized with regard to tax considerations.

---

12 Bengel, p. 240.
13 Klein, p. 14.
14 Rödl, Christian, Rechtsformwahl internationaler Familienunternehmen in Internationale Familienunternehmen, Rödl, Scheffler, Winter (ed.) C.H.Beck, München 2008.
15 Ambrecht, cf. supra.

II. Tools of Transmission

Succession entails three aspects: management, ownership, and taxes. Ownership succession is usually split off from management succession because next-generation members may want to retain their equity in the business, but not take on any significant operating roles at the company.[16] The current owner may want to give exactly equal shares to everyone, but those who work in the business may feel they are entitled to more. Likewise, those who don't work in the business may feel the same way about their own shares. After all, they may reason, they're not drawing salaries, so they should get a bigger share of dividends and profit-sharing. Furthermore, those not participating in the succession of the company (the spouse or children not continuing the family business) may have a legitimate interest in compensation. This compensation may be settled with assets of the private property of the testator or through transfer of company assets upon death, a usufruct on those assets or regular lifelong pension payments. Tax implications will determine the exact choice of the compensation payment.

Different tools of transmission are used for family enterprises which include property or production sites abroad. While careful succession planning is a long process, usually taking several years for a transition to the next generation, emergency measures should be taken even at a young age of the family business owner as a mere precaution. A standard emergency precaution is a power of attorney post mortem.

1. Power of Attorney Post Mortem

A power of attorney acknowledged before a notary public is valid as such; it does not cease upon death of the principal according to German law, § 672 BGB[17]. It may also be established as a pure **power of attorney post mortem,** thus having effect only after the death of the principal. It serves as a mere precaution for ad-hoc measures. It is most commonly used for transactions which are time-critical after the death, such as sales of stocks or bank transactions. In an international context, the use of this power of attorney is doubtful. In most countries, any power of attorney ceases to be valid upon death of the principal. Although a choice of law

---

16   *J. O.Hutcheson* www.businessweek.com 30 July 2007.
17   For a translation of the German Civil Code cf. http://www.iuscomp.org/gla/statutes/biblstat4.htm

may be expressed in the power of attorney, it will not be widely accepted abroad. In Spain for example, a power of attorney **post mortem** will not be recognized since this was at one time a common means of avoiding succession tax by means of prescription.

2. Joint Will

If the family business constitutes the main source of income and has been created by the spouses jointly, a joint will (known in German as **gemeinschaftliches Testament**) may be written down. Married couples can establish a **Berliner Testament**, a special form of joint will together with binding destination of the property to the surviving spouse and, upon his or her death, to the children.[18] Therein it is often the case that the spouse who survives the other may not change or may only reduce the testament. Such clauses should be taken up however only after consultation with the Civil Law Notary as they may lead to profound result if incidents, unforeseen to the spouses, incur. After the death of one spouse, a mutual testamentary disposition of the other spouse can, generally speaking, not be revoked anymore and remains binding.[19] However, if the surviving spouse renounces the inheritance, he is free to change his will, § 2271 II l BGB. A joint will does not guarantee the continuity of the family business since the children may still claim their forced portion of the inheritance.

3. Contract on Inheritance

The testator may conclude a contract of inheritance (**Erbvertrag**) with another person (not just the spouse), § 2274 ss. BGB.[20] The contract of inheritance requires notarisation.[21] The testator may also make binding bequests in the contract of inheritance. It is through this contract, with the participation of the children as prospective heirs with right to a forced portion of the family business, that further binding dispositions such as a pre-distribution of assets may be combined with a rejection – from the future heir – of his right to a forced portion of the estate (**Pflichtteilsverzicht**).

---

18   *Frieser* in Handbuch des Fachanwalts für Erbrecht, Chapter 1, 543, Wolters Kluwer 2005, München.
19   http://legal-succession.com/pages/er/er-germany2.html
20   http://dejure.org/gesetze/BGB/2274.html
21   § 2276 BGB, http://dejure.org/gesetze/BGB/2274.html

4. Prior Heir / Subsequent Heir

The classical instrument of maintaining the family business in the family for several future generations is a last will containing the nomination of subsequent heirs. A testator may leave his estate to a **Vorerbe** (prior heir) and a **Nacherbe** (subsequent heir) in the way that a person first becomes heir after someone else, at a particular time or the occurrence of a particular event, the later being referred to as the subsequent heir, § 2100 BGB. In the usual case, maybe the family house and all business-related assets go to A for life, and when A dies, then to B. The institution is similar to the English »settlement«.[22] The particularity is that both prior heir and subsequent heir are heirs of the testator for a certain time, thus being single heir of the testator for a certain time. The prior heir's own right to dispose of the items in the estate is subject to restrictions (§§ 2112–2115 BGB) and he is obliged to hand over the estate to the subsequent heir in such a condition as accords with proper administration, § 2130 BGB.

This construction enables the exclusion of certain persons from the estate (mostly the new spouse after the death of the testator) and it protects the estate against the claims of forced portions as it is considered separate property from the spouses. It is furthermore useful for young entrepreneurs who do not yet know who they might be able to appoint as a successor as their children are still under age. Together with detailed instructions for the executor of the will, a sucession strategy for minors as final heirs of the business can be established this way.[23]

5. Family Holding

The most common form elected in Germany for a family business is the »**GmbH & Co. KG**« mostly for succession tax reasons (see below III). This popular fusion of a private partnership and joint stock company is suitable for entrepreneurs wishing to combine limited liability, with the advantages of a privately orientated corporate structure. The general partner is the private limited company (GmbH), which bears liability solely to the extent of its share capital. The limited partners are individuals; they form a private limited partnership (KG) with calculable liability. While the KG does have advantages tax wise, there needs to be not only at least one owner with limited liability (Kommanditist), but also at least one with unlimited liability (Komplementär). According to German

---

22 *Fisher*, The German Legal System, 3rd Edition, p. 89.
23 *Bengel*, p. 232.

Tax law (§§ 12 para. 6 Erbschaftsteuergesetz and § 9 Bewertungsgesetz), a participation in a foreign company is valued with its common value. However, foreign capital companies, real estate property and production sites may be considered for inheritance tax purposes with their German tax balance value. The European Court of Justice considers the different evaluation of foreign and domestic business property for succession tax purposes contrary to Art. 54 and 56 of the EU-Treaty.[24] Therefore it is generally highly advisable to opt for capital companies rather than personal companies in the structuring process of the international family business. Futher, a relocation of the headquater is also easier to accomplish.

6. Family Foundation

If the purpose is to keep the company intact, a German family foundation (**Familienstiftung**[25], § 80 BGB ss.) might equally be considered suitable. There are no direct tax advantages to this, but if a company is brought into such a foundation and the founder lives for another ten years, no forced portions of the estate can be claimed by the heirs. The company will then belong to the foundation. Of course, this means that the father/mother must while still alive overcome any resistance on the part of the children.[26] The motives for establishing a foundation are as numerous as their forms and the determination of aims. In connection with the transfer of assets to a foundation the question must be asked to what extent provisions for the benefactor and his family can be made possible through the foundation and which consequences this may have concerning tax on income and the substance of property. Besides the transfer of assets against provision payments the testator (more precisely, the benefactor to the foundation) may set up the reserved usufruct to basic and capital assets, as well as classical beneficiary payments and employment relationships with the foundation. The first two methods for provisions are relevant for the taxation of the transfer of the assets already, whereas beneficiary payments and employment relationships are only of interest within the framework of the regular taxation.[27]

---

24 ECJ 17.01.2008, C-256/06 (*»Jäger«*).
25 Familienstiftung established through *Gesetz zur Modernisierung des Stiftungsrechts* in 2002.
26 Familienunternehmen: Recht, Steuern, Beratung, p. 236 *Hannes/Kuhn/Brückmann* (ed.), Berlin 2007.
27 Seibold, Die Versorgung des Stifters und der Stifterfamilie bei Vermögensübertragung auf eine gemeinnützige Stiftung, Familienstiftung oder Doppelstiftung und deren ertrag- und substanzsteuerlichen Auswirkungen, Diss 2008, p.XV http://www.opus-bayern.de/uni-wuerzburg/volltexte/2008/2801/

6.1 Two Models of Foundations

Two models are possible since 2002: A **Family Foundation** with the main aim of participation in the family business through holding the shares and distribution of the annual surplus to more than 50% to the family members or a **non-profit foundation** which must aim at distributing its earnings to a very narrow, specific non-profit goal.[28]

6.2 Taxation of Foreign Foundations and Trusts

Income of foreign family foundations, associations and trusts is attributed to the founder/settlor or the beneficiaries regardless of a distribution of trust funds. Thus, these persons are discriminated in relation to founders and beneficiaries of German family foundations who are only taxed if they receive funds. The German supreme tax court had fixed the premises, under which a family foundation has been set up and endowed effectively under the gift tax act.[29] Even if a foundation has been effectively set up and endowed in terms of foreign law, the transfer of assets may not be taxed if the founder has reserved himself special powers, so that the foundation cannot effectively and legally dispose of the funds. Such special powers can for example be the right to instruct the board of directors of the foundation concerning the administration of assets, the right to claim the reassignment of funds, the possibility to change the articles or to recall members of the board at any time. However, foundations within the European Community are excluded from January 2009 onward.[30] This entails a considerable improvement for founders, settlors and beneficiaries of a trust located in the EU or the EEA. They will be only taxed if they actually receive funds and thus will be prevented from »double taxation«. Foundations and trusts under Liechtenstein law do not fall under the newly created dispositions for lack of exchange of information.

Recent discussions about fiscal transparency caused the OECD to publish a greylist on fiscal transparency. Amongst the European countries listed are Switzerland and Liechtenstein as they have committed to the internationally agreed tax standard but have not yet substantially implemented in this area.

---

28 § 58 No. 5 AO [Abgabenordnung, German Fiscal Code] regulates the taxation of the non-profit foundation.
29 BFHE 217, 254 of 28. June 2007.
30 § 15 Abs. 6 Außensteuergesetz, reformed on 25. Dezember 2008, effective 1. Januar 2009 (Art. 39 Abs. 1, 8 G vom 19. Dezember 2008) http://bundesrecht.juris.de/astg/__15.html

III. Inheritance Tax reform of 2009

In Germany, inheritance tax is conceived as a tax that accrues by way of succession, that is, the inheritor must pay tax on the assets received. As of January 1, 2009, a reform of inheritance tax legislation[31] exempts family homes and business enterprises from taxation under certain circumstances.[32] The reform has a major impact on all future inheritance and gift cases related to Germany or German citizens.

1. Unfair Discrimination of Real Estate Property

Until 2006, German real property was generally subject to the inheritance tax, yet very low assessments of the value of real estate lowered the tax burden significantly. The Federal Constitutional Court vitiated the regime as being unconstitutional.[33] Germany's Constitutional Court ruled that the present system for calculating the tax was unfair since it taxed the transfer of real estate property more favorably than the transfer of cash instruments, such as stocks.[34] If one followed the idea of the ability-to-pay principle in this context, it would no doubt have been worth considering integrating inheritance tax into income tax – while at the same time reducing the tax rates and offering appropriate deferral options. The starting point was considering how to improve the general taxation conditions for inheriting a business, in order to strengthen and preserve companies and to safeguard jobs. This is an important matter for family-run industrial SMEs, which have been waiting for this reform for three years. The Federal Constitutional Court ruled that by 31 December 2008 the legislators must remedy the unconstitutional unequal treatment in the valuation of individual types of assets, otherwise inheritance tax will cease to be collected. However, as inheritance tax has been abolished in some of the neighboring countries, demands for a abolition had been voiced. Valuations Above all, new approaches to the values were needed in the areas of business assets and real estate.

---

31 Gesetz zur Reform des Erbschaftsteuer- und Schenkungsteuergesetz, Dec. 31, 2008, BUNDESGESETZBLATT [BGBl.] I at 3018, § 13, available at http://bundesrecht.juris.de/erbstg_1974/BJNR109330974.html

32 *Palmer,* Global Legal Monitor 25.03.2009 http://www.loc.gov/lawweb/servlet/lloc_news?disp3_1159_text

33 (Bundesverfassungsgericht, Nov. 7, 2006, Docket No. 1 BvL 10/06, available at http://www.bundesverfassungsgericht.de/entscheidungen/2006/11.

34 For an overview of Inheritance in Europe: http://www.agn-europe.org/htm/firm/news/ttf/2008/inheritance.pdf

2. New Exemptions and Valuation Rules

The major changes are: new valuation rules for business assets, agriculture and forestry assets, stocks, and real estate; broader general personal allowances; a partial tax exemption for the transfer of a company; and tax exemption for owner-occupied real estate. The new, 2009 legislation taxes real estate at market values, but exempts the heir of an owner-occupied family dwelling from inheritance tax if the decedent was his spouse, parent, or grandparent. The exemption applies only if the heir lives in the house for ten years, and, for children and grandchildren, only 200 square meters (2,150 square feet) of a single home or condominium are exempted.

The exemption for the heir of a business attempts to preserve domestic business or agricultural enterprises and domestic employment. If, over a seven-year period, the heir pays out wages amounting to 650 percent of the annual payroll at time of death, 85 percent of the inheritance tax is waived. If, over a ten-year period, the heir pays out 1,000 percent of the annual payroll at time of death, the entire inheritance tax is waived. These exemptions, however, apply only if the financial assets of a business do not exceed certain percentages.[35] In any event the provisions on keeping the business in operation are very restrictive, even though they are linked with a reinvestment clause. Furthermore, the tax-exempt portions have been raised. Most property inherited and used by spouses and children will remain free of inheritance tax. The spouse is entitled to a tax-free portion of 500.000 Euros while children receive 400.000 Euros tax-exempt.[36] Civil partners receive the same tax allowance as do spouses. Even though Class Two (**Steuerklasse II**) recipients, i.e. siblings, nieces, nephews, divorced spouses, step parents, parents-in-law and children-in-law, will generally benefit also from a general increase of the personal exemption amount from 10,300.00 Euros previously now up to 20,000.00 Euros, this will be generally be overcompensated by the steep increase of inheritance tax rates for Class Two recipients up from previously 12 through 40 percent to now 40 through 50 percent, so in most cases the German government will take a significantly deeper tax bite in the case of Class Two recipients after December 31, 2008.

---

35 *Palmer* op. cit.
36 *Kessler / Eickie*, Tax Notes Int'l, January 19, 2009, p. 233

3. Preferential Treatment for Shares

Besides agricultural and forestry property as well as business assets, it is also shares in corporations which will qualify for the preferential treatment in case of a shareholding of more than 25%, including pools of share-holders. However, the assets named only qualify for preferential tax treatment if no more than 50% of the relevant assets are qualified as »passive« non-operating assets (e.g. real estate let to others, widespread shareholdings). Apart from that, »passive« assets must have already been part of the transferred business 2 years before the transfer to be part of the privileged property. Foreign business property is subject to the preferential treatment as long as the property is effectively connected with a permanent establishment in a state of the European Union. The preferential treatment of shares in corporations requires that the company's seat or effective place of management is located in Germany, the European Union or the European Economic Area. The sale or abandonment of a business as well as a private withdrawal of essential assets within the following 15 years after the transfer will cause a complete loss of the tax privilege and thereby trigger a subsequent taxation. However, an exemption is made if the sale of an independent division of the business or of essential assets is not aimed at the retrenchment of the business.

IV. Conclusion

The reform of the Inheritance Tax 2009 is a clear relief for family-run businesses, and necessary to keep and safeguard jobs in Germany. After all, one of the most prestigious and prominent tasks of the government in this legislative period has found its way to the tax code. With the Reform of the Inheritance Tax and Valuation Law, the German Government is attempting to bring about a constitutional valuation of all categories of assets which will comply with the ruling of the Federal Constitutional Court. The new law brings much legal certainty for heirs of family businesses, even though some questions regarding the sum of salaries and the holding period remain.

Fiddler on the Roof: On the Ambiguity of Family Finances

Bea Verschraegen[1]

I. Who does What? Who gets What?

»Family Finances« as a multiscalar issue which addresses various aspects of transfer of services, goods and financial contributions among the family members, of third parties to family members and of family members to third parties, coincides with the global crisis. This crisis is certainly not limited to economic bottlenecks; it embraces also social, legal and political topics.

The discussion on whether law reflects reality – in many cases it does not – is not new. Family law and its development very much depends on **politics**, it also depends on the willingness of human beings to fit in with given legal structures, and – as e.g. in *Macao*[2] – on historical events. Family law has very much become an area of »**evasion of the law**« and of »**political opportunism**«. Law reforms to some extent have reacted to the need of people, they also mirror to some extent international, national, regional pressures and the influence of lobby groups. However, each reform ought to be based on **interdisciplinary research** and ask for the causes of certain developments, such as e.g. a high percentage of illegitimate children or of one parent families – e.g. in *Brazil*[3] – in order to understand the society it wants to rebuild or adapt.

Some States, such as *South Korea*[4], have introduced a vast system of legal rules and invest huge amounts of money in order to **integrate** immi-

---

[1] Convenor, Full Professor at the Universities of Vienna, Austria, and Bratislava (Uninova), Slovakia.
[2] For a synopsis of financial issues within the family under Macanese law see *Nunes Correia*, Matrimonial finances in the context of the Macanese Legal System: General principles and issues, 415–426.
[3] See *Groeninga*, An Interdisciplinary Approach of Family Finances, 133–142.
[4] *Keum Sook Choe*, Study on Legal and Financial Support for Multicultural Families in South-Korea, 143–159.

grants and to **stabilise** multicultural families that face enormous problems of different nature (economic, legal, educational, social etc). Here, the belief that a highly regulatory mechanism will influence and actually change developments in society that are regarded as undesired seems to be predominant.

In his opening speech, *Frank*[5] mentioned that from a comparative perspective blood relationship and marriage, by and large, seem to play a key role in order to claim a right to support. This holds also true for inheritance rights. Rights of the surviving spouse have been strengthened in industrialised states. However, inheritance rights cannot be appraised without also considering the property regime at stake. Lacking a marital relationship, inheritance rights can be created by will, though in this case, inheritance tax may deviate considerably from that provided for »privileged persons«, such as married couples and children. Statutory inheritance law usually takes a formal approach and does not distinguish between rich and poor heirs, between those who had a close or a distant relationship with the deceased person, or any other individualised concept. Hence, it is increasingly questioned, whether the distribution of the estate as provided by statutory law really reflects the »last will« of the deceased; the tendency seems to be that the strict formal approach is more and more modified by material considerations. The former are indeed used as an argument to defend either the mandatory share on the one hand or the testamentary freedom on the other.

It is hard to analyse and compare the **interplay** of support-marital property-inheritance issues. In most cases, specific rights will correspond to marital relationships and offspring, but the development of family, property and inheritance law demonstrates that this is not necessarily the case. It is argued very often that **formal** criteria tend to **reduce transaction costs**. For example, if a mandatory share can only be denied on the ground of specific criminal acts, then, indeed, it does not make sense to invoke proceedings because the heir never was friendly with the deceased; or, if grounds for divorce do not consider faulty behaviour – often they do so in spite of a so-called »no fault-system«[6] – costs may considerably increase when the law entails a **hardship clause** and one party thus tries to invoke

---

5 *Frank*, Introductory Lecture – Family Solidarity in Support and Inheritance Law, 1–21.
6 See *Verschraegen*, Chapter 5 »Divorce«, »Grounds for Divorce and Selected Consequences«, in Drobnig/Zweigert/Glendon (Eds), Vol. IV, International Encyclopedia of Comparative Law (2004) 1–91.

faulty behaviour or economic need that must be compensated, or **fault** may come into play when the quantum needs to be assessed and/or **equity** is a decisive factor.[7] At this stage, the court may, but need not, confer goods from one party to the other or force one party to make material provision (support or income) for the other. These compelling transfers[8] may be considerable.

No consensus is reached on the issue whether and on which basis **material support** should be provided for a party when the relationship broke down. Two very different principles prevail: »**family solidarity**« (»insurance against future risks«) on the one hand and the »**earned-share and compensation approach**« (compensation for former investments of assets and efforts) on the other. What is considered »fair« needs to be assessed according to reality: we are facing low marriage, but high divorce rates. Therefore, the second alternative seems to be more adequate. It can apply to married couples, couples living together, persons assuming responsibility whether they are relatives or not. Adequacy stands here

---

7   Support upon divorce under *Italian law* has the primary aim to assist the weaker party; its indemnity and compensation functions come into play only subsidiarily. In practice, support by the other spouse is due in case of lack of inadequate income to achieve the same standard of living enjoyed during marriage, and thus encompasses mere economic self-sufficiency. The term »adequacy of means« is to be understood in a broad way and stands not only for money, but also for everything with money value, including assets, immovable property and income of every type. The quantum involves an investigation into all possible influencing factors, including the responsibility for the marriage breakdown. If the creditor takes up a de facto cohabitation with a third person, he/she does not necessarily lose the support awarded; it is rather up to the debtor to prove that the cohabitation economically improves the situation of the support creditor (*Duca*, Alimony in divorce in the Italian Legal System, 439–447 [441, 442, 445, 447]). This view underlines the individual character of support upon divorce as a consequence of the dissolution of the status »marriage«. Similarly, *Portuguese law* abolished divorces based on faulty behaviour, and support upon divorce is characterised by the »principle of self-sufficiency«, thus reducing »family solidarity« after dissolution of the marriage. For »clear reasons of equity«, i.e. in cases of exceptional hardship, support upon divorce may be denied (*Vítor*, Solidarity between Former Spouses – What if Guilt has nothing to do with it? An Overview of the Connections between the Portuguese Divorce Reform and the Regime of Maintenance Obligations between Former Spouses, 449–460 [457 f]). Possibly not only economic factors are decisive here, as the Civil Code of *Portugal* provides, that no support is due, when the creditor is not worthy of such a benefit because of his/her disapproved moral behaviour (*Vitor*, 449 [458 f]). Hence, it may well be that the self-sufficiency level is decreased if such a behaviour seems decisive. The question is, whether in such cases society would assume the economic responsibility.
8   *Eekelaar*, Partners, Parents and Children: Grounds for Allocating Resources across Household, 23–32.

for »justice«. How »justice« is done, however, remains a question of dispute. Some systems are based on the »earned share principle« allocating an »equal share« or a »reasonable share«, others rely on »compensation«.[9] With regard to *England and Wales* Eekelaar[10] is of the opinion that only in case of compensation is the claimant under a duty to mitigate the loss. However, experiences in other systems show that quite some means are invested by mitigating parties to use gaps in or exceptions provided by the law to argue the »earned share principle« to their advantage.

Finally, one may ask whether the duty to compensate for the disadvantages is **personal** or **social** by nature. It is claimed[11] that such obligations should remain personal: the person who is better off must compensate for the disadvantages. I wonder whether this also applies to all risks of the labour market in times of global crisis. In addition, compensation of disadvantages actually only is of interest where a party is in the position to compensate at all, and this is a minority.

In response to the **changing labour market** and the need for planning of eventual **changes** of and in **family relationships** (e.g. in case of divorce, separation, disagreement, offspring) and **estate planning** for family businesses, some legislators,[12] among them the *Spanish* legislator, took into

---

9 It can be regarded as a matter of policy, when courts turn to a broad interpretation of rules in order to protect the weaker spouse upon divorce. Hence, the construction of the law on the distribution of property taking »all other circumstances« into account, when deciding on divorce, embraces claims of different legal nature (distribution of property, spousal support upon divorce, and »solatium« as a tort issue in order to compensate the other's spouse pain and distress caused by the divorce itself). See *Tsuneoka*, The Economic Consequence of Divorce in Japan. Trend in No-Fault Divorce and *Rikon Isharyo* (Solatium by Divorce) Scheme, 683-694. The application of the »solatium theory« in practice reflects the concern about the economic situation of the wife upon divorce, and of justice as a general concern. If the spouse who caused the breakdown of the marriage files for divorce based on irretrievable breakdown, fault or at least causality between behaviour of the claimant and breakdown of the marriage comes up, which leads in practice to the right to compensation. It is argued, then, that compensation does not really fit into the picture of a no fault-divorce: not only because the fault-issue plays a role as such, but also because the courts have wide discretion when they appreciate distribution of property under all the circumstances and can fix the quantum of the solatium as different in nature from the property division and spousal support, freely (*Tsuneoka*, 683 [694]).
10 Eekelaar, 23 (30).
11 Eekelaar, 23 (32).
12 *Artigot-Golobardes/Alascio-Carrasco*, Family Business: The Need for a General Framework, 761-776.

account the rising number of such **businesses**.¹³ It is legitimate to ask whether a general framework is needed or desirable, as family law and succession law entail mandatory provisions which cannot be amended by agreements or unilateral acts. This would be an interdisciplinary task of i.a. family, succession, corporate, labour and tax lawyers, of lawyers with expertise in the field of public and social (security) law, and presumably of psychologists and therapists. *German* law for example offers a whole range of possible (and legal) instruments to deal with family businesses.¹⁴ Yet, allegedly they all become a victim of the »Buddenbrooks principle« and disappear in the third generation.¹⁵ In order to avoid this, the German legislator has, among other precautions, amended its inheritance tax law, which is said to be »a clear relief for family-run businesses, and necessary¹⁶ to keep and safeguard jobs« that comprises around 80% of all enterprises in *Germany*.¹⁷

A strong **interrelation** of law, politics, economy, labour market, ethics, the (welfare) State and society is present in the context of **caretaking of elderly**. This also touches upon the gender issue. By way of example, *Portugal* is claimed to lack any substantial vision for the growing number of the elderly population and the care it needs. A setting might be the family unit, special institutions or the »common economy relationship«.¹⁸ As the need for care and assistance is not only of special concern to *Portugal*, but also of general concern, States should take this into account and subsidise in different ways (e.g. social benefits, tax cuts, nursing leave, flexible working hours, combination of the welfare and the social security system, redistribution of work within the family setting etc).¹⁹

---

13 Each spouse – contrary to the situation in *Serbia* for example – has a right to be informed on the business activities of the other; the surplus is part of the community property, and since 2003 the family enterprises can be included in insolvency procedures, see *García Cantero*, L'entreprise Familiale dans le Régime Matrimonial Légal Espagnol, 427–437 (429, 433).
14 See *Krause*, The Planning of Succession in International Family Business. Recent Developments in Germany, 777-788.
15 *Krause*, 777.
16 *Krause*, 777 (786 f, 788).
17 *Krause*, 777 (779 and n. 8).
18 Introduced in 2001 with specific rights and obligations, not limited to family members or persons with an intimate relationship, see *Vaz Tomé*, Elderly Dependency, Family Caretaking and Law in Portugal, 709–724 (717).
19 *Vaz Tomé*, 709 (720 ff).

II. Family solidarity

But what »family solidarity« stands for is open to debate. What is to be regarded as a »family« at all in the first place? And what is meant by »solidarity«? Generally speaking, it means the economic responsibility of close relatives for one another, including responsibility of adult children towards their (grand-) parents (»intergenerational family solidarity«[20]). If this responsibility is not voluntarily assumed, some advocate immediate **enforcement** of support duties in order to strengthen family solidarity. Yet, formal duties invite **evasion strategies**. The ideal formula still to be found is how to stimulate private (formal or informal) support without losing the support of welfare services. Some States provide for tax reliefs, grants for home caring, specific »compensation« by the estate for the carers etc.[21]

Support obligations of parents towards their children are based on the principle of family solidarity. If this principle for one reason or the other fails, the question arises whether States owe a »basic minimum standard of care« to each child. *Farrugia*[22] comes to the conclusion that there is a vast tension between the best interest of the child (as guaranteed by international and national laws) on the one hand and the public interest to intervene on the other hand. She supports such a minimum standard in theory at least for children that are removed from parental responsibility and placed under the care of the State and criticises (together with the UN Committee of the CRC) that e.g. in *Malta*, the *UK* and *Northern Ireland* »appropriate assistance in the performance of their child-rearing responsibilities, and notably to those families in a crisis situation due to poverty« seems to be lacking.[23] It is therefore claimed that either States should act on their own initiative to pursue debts incurred by parents who cannot or will not pay maintenance on the children or the children themselves should be given independent access to civil justice instead of letting the taxpayer assume such costs.

---

20 See *Ribot*, Family law and intergenerational family solidarity – Should there be enforceable maintenance rights vis-à-vis adult relatives?, 33–47.
21 *Ribot*, 33 (41).
22 *Farrugia*, State Responsibility in Enforcing Maintenance Obligations towards Children, 71–84.
23 *Farrugia*, 71 (79).

South Africa is a particularly interesting example of how the State (courts and legislator) reacts to **different forms of family life** and what **degree of solidarity** with regard to **support** is expected.[24] It seems that no coherent system of responsibility exists, which would allow to derive principles which are applicable to all persons of a family unit who are dependent, in need and who contributed to the family unit. This applies especially to large groups of poor persons with a low level of literacy and a high level of dependency (heterosexually) cohabiting with another person, but also to those whose marital position underlies religious law, such as Muslim marriages. Within these family units contributions are made and dependency is great, but when it comes to the recognition of rights applicable to other family units, such as heterosexual or same-sex monogamous marriages/partnerships, more specifically duties of support, intestate succession and property rights, the courts shift the responsibility to the legislator. According to some authors, a **functional approach** based on the **right to equality, dignity and non-discrimination** would allow to include »non-conventional family forms«[25] and, hence, to recognise contributions within the family unit.

The 2008 Draft of the *Czech* Civil Code, which entails family law in its second part, is said to be based on »family and (post) partnership solidarity and private law responsibility«.[26]. Protection of cohabitants upon separation to a very limited extent is provided for, but the child seems to have the right to enjoy the same living standard as before the separation of his/her parents and the mother can claim child support to cover that standard. Maintenance upon divorce is limited to the necessary support and not limited by time, or should – in case of faulty behaviour of the debtor – cover the same living standard but is limited by time.[27] Whether and

---

24 See *Sinclair/Davel*, Evolving Family Forms and the Duty of Support in South African Law, 85–97.
25 *Sinclair/Davel*, 85 (97).
26 *Králíčková*, Legal protection of unmarried and divorced mothers in the Czech Republic, 281–291 (291). The law in force partly reflects the *Czechoslovak* family law which followed the *Soviet* approach (under *Soviet* law maintenance during marriage and upon divorce was regarded as »a bourgeois survival of the past« and »incompatible with the ideology of proletarian state«, see *Khazova*, Family Law in the Former Soviet Union: More Differences or More in Common?, in Antokolskaia [ed.], Convergence and Divergence of Family Law in Europe [2007] 97 [98 f.]), and to some extent introduced changes in maintenance and marital property law in 1998 (*Králíčková*, 281 [286]).
27 *Králíčková*, 281 (289).

to what extent the expected amendments of the Civil Code will transform the »**feminisation of poverty**« into »**family solidarity**« remains to be seen.

III. Differentiation or Equalisation?

Prevailing models that either support the equalisation of the mutual obligations of cohabitants and married partners[28] or are strongly opposed to such an approach are challenged e.g. by *Lifshitz*.[29] He presents principles for a third, so-called »**new liberal model**«, that takes into account the existing models, but points out the »liberal state's responsibility to create a variety of spousal institutions« and thus takes a »**pluralistic approach**«.[30] Cohabitation is, then, to be regarded as a separate social and legal institution with a selected package of rights and duties. Those spousal rights and obligations that are designed to encourage a certain (marital) behaviour or reflect »society's ethos« with regard to marriage, such as marriage properties, should not apply to cohabitation, whereas rules on the protection of weaker and dependent family members should. Further, where marriage law is based on the express or presumed intention of the parties, it should not apply to cohabitation, if the parties deliberately did not want to get married in the first place. However, where marriage law is designed to provide justice, prevent exploitation, protect children etc, it should apply to cohabitation. Finally, commitments of cohabiting couples ought to be qualified as individual, which implies the couples' rights of exit. The pluralist approach further allows distinguishing, among the different kinds of relationships, among »trial marriage«, »regular cohabitation«, »relational cohabitation«, »exploitation cohabitation« and »same-sex cohabitation,« each of which has different legal consequences.[31] The new model thus introduces a **differentiated approach** to different family structures, each of which with appropriate and specific rights and obligations. The details are still under review. Hence, one can only suppose that

---

28 *Greece* elaborated a bill as of September 2008 which provides for nearly the same rights to heterosexual couples as married couples have and no distinction is made between legitimate and illegitimate children, see *Agallopoulou*, Financial consequences of cohabitation between persons of the opposite sex according to Greek law, 293–304 (302).
29 *Lifshitz*, Married against their Will? A Liberal Analysis of Western Cohabitation Law, 305–320.
30 *Lifshitz*, 305 (318 ff).
31 *Lifshitz*, 305 (319 f).

according to this model, e.g. the *Italian* rules on the »family enterprise«[32] would apply to longstanding cohabiting couples, whereas according to the prevailing *Italian* opinion they do not. The legislator of *New Zealand* treats marriages, registered civil unions (heterosexual and same-sex) and de facto couples alike when it comes to the application of »equal property sharing regime«.[33] The Property (Relationships) Act 1976 entails no definition of a »de facto relationship«, but (non-exhaustively) lists a number of factors that shall be taken into account, thus vesting in the court a large measure of discretion.[34] On the issue of **property division**, the court has hardly any discretion: Basically, the property is to be divided equally,[35] unless the couple contracted out of the Act, which is **retroactively** applicable.[36] However, it is claimed that the courts, when applying the law as it stands, do not achieve equal treatment of spouses.[37] It is argued, that a **fix rule to compensate for disparity**[38] might lead to greater legal certainty and less costly procedures.[39] *Sweden* provides for a **minimum level of protection** of a financially vulnerable party upon dissolution of a relationship between **cohabitants**. However, only the joint dwelling and household goods acquired for joint use by the cohabitants can be shared (equal share system); money, savings, other items are not subject to division.[40] It is claimed that economically speaking, it lies within the »logic of cohabitation« that cohabitants form a »work, consumption and investment unit« even when finances are treated separately. In *Norway* co-ownership is therefore established on the basis of the cohabitants' indirect contri-

---

32 *Insigna*, *De facto* Family and Family Enterprise in the Italian Legal System, 321-328.
33 *Briggs*, The Formalization of Property Sharing Rights For De Facto Couples in New Zealand, 329-343.
34 *Briggs*, 329 (332, 334).
35 *Briggs*, 329 (337).
36 *Briggs*, 329 (338 f): If one applies the »relationship generated disadvantage«-principle, which implies that the difference in earning capacity between the parties is due to the relationship and not to other factors such as particular talents (of the breadwinner), and, based on a strong presumption of equal sharing of all property acquired during marriage or relationship, if one takes both the capital as well as the income in order to make a compensatory award when there is a significant disparity in earning capacity at the end of the marriage or relationship.
37 *Henaghan*, Achieving Economic Equality at the End of Marriage and Other Relationships: Not All Is Fair in Love and War, 695-708.
38 E.g. 5, 10, 15 or 20 % extra of the relationship property.
39 *Henaghan*, 695 (707 f): the 20 % margin seems still politically acceptable, it also acknowledges that a part of the difference may be due to the talents of the earner and takes into account future contingencies such as his/her health and termination of work.
40 *Brattström*, The Protection of a Vulnerable Party when a Cohabitee Relationship Ends – An Evaluation of the Swedish Cohabitees Act, 345-354 (347).

bution in form of domestic work or payment of current expenses.[41] But this **retrospective** model is apt to create disputes which imply litigation costs. The same seems to apply to a **future-oriented compensation** model, because retained benefits and economic losses caused by the relationship must be assessed.[42] Therefore, glancing at *New Zealand*, *Sweden*, the Principles of the Law of Family Dissolution of the *American Law Institute*, and at the main rule of *Schwenzer's* Model Family Code, the relationship as the basis for obligations and rights is advocated for *Norway*: only assets acquired during the relationship should be subject to equal division, at least in relationships with short duration.[43]

IV. Marriage or Divorce: What is the greater Risk?

The **short duration of relationships** in general is not only reflected in statistics and in the overwhelming number of contributions to this book, it also influences **legal theory** on marriage and divorce: **Breakdown** of a relationship seems to have become (directly or indirectly) a »**normal risk**« that couples should calculate on. Upon dissolution or separation »family solidarity« in the sense of »life long insurance maintaining the marital standard«, therefore, seems to lack its proper foundation. According to *French* law, merely a »minimum of equity« at the time of separation or divorce seems adequate; the quantum should only ease the transition from the relationship to its dissolution.[44] Compensatory claims (»prestations compensatoires«), several decades ago still »alimony pensions« (»pensions alimentaires«), are apparently – and most probably due to very different factors – seldom claimed in practice and the amount is surprisingly low (or perhaps high in relation to the income); they are not available to non married couples.[45] When it comes to the distribution of property – with different rules for married couples and »pacsés« – the actual outcome, due to

---

41 *Sverdrup*, An Ill-fitting Garment: Why the Logic of Private Law Falls Short between Cohabitants, 355–368 (360, 368).
42 *Sverdrup*, 355 (363).
43 *Sverdrup*, 355 (368).
44 *Fulchiron*, Des Solidarités dans les Couples Séparés, 517–531 (519, 522).
45 *Fulchiron*, 517 (522), whose Center of Family Law analysed the case law 2007 of the Tribunal de Grande Instance of Lyon (see 528 ff), also mentions the caveats (local limitation, limited period of time, lacking further information on the economic situation of the couple, missing information on other »compensating« instruments, such as payment of debts, distribution of property etc.

rules of evidence, may be similar.[46] Some adjustment is further achieved by applying instruments of »droit commun«, such as the non-commercial partnership (»société créé de fait«), unjust enrichment and damages.[47] But, at the end of the day, each spouse/partner is considered to assume his/her life on his/her own. If at all, then family solidarity is mirrored in the relationship between parents and children, independent of matters of form with regard to the couples' relationship.[48]

V. Nothing but Costs!

Policy principles may cause considerable costs of varying nature. For example, **support claims** by (grand-) parents against their (grand-) children may lead to an alienation between the relatives, the ones in need may be forced to claim support first before they can rely on welfare benefits. Persons caring for the elderly may face disadvantages in their career and independency.[49] When it comes to the question whether it is cheaper to support families and their children in need than to remove the children from home and finance alternative care, the **preservation of the children's family structure** e.g. in *South Africa* seems to be the cheaper alternative.[50] Prevention and early intervention programmes aim at preserving the family structure of the child, at the development of appropriate parenting skills and the capacity of parents and care-givers to safeguard the best interests of their children, thus avoiding the removal of the child from the family unit.[51]

Inter-country adoption involves high costs, such as translation fees, administrative expenses, costs for medical examinations, costs charged by children's homes and other supplying institutions, travel and accommodation expenses. In the *Netherlands* such **transaction costs** are no longer deductable from the tax. In addition, there is a growing concern on inter-country adoption as a »commodity trade« which turns out to be to

---

46 For details see *Fulchiron*, 517 (523).
47 *Fulchiron*, 517 (524 f).
48 *Fulchiron*, 517 (528).
49 See *Ribot*, 33 (39).
50 *Van der Linde*, The extent of the state's duty to support family life through prevention and early intervention programmes: A reflection on the Children's Act 38 of 2005, 99–113.
51 *Van der Linde*, 99 (102).

the detriment of the children. The minimum level of protection provided for by the Hague Convention on Protection of Children and Co-operation in respect of Inter-country Adoption cannot be guaranteed anymore. As demand exceeds supply, abuse and child trafficking are likely and the best interests of the child risk becoming a subsidiary concern. Hence, **social costs** (e.g. children sold by their parents or simply taken away; corruption) are extremely high.[52] It is, therefore, suggested in the *Netherlands* that i.a. prospective adoptive parents should rather focus on foster care and that the original families ought to be supported in order to facilitate the return of their children.[53] But international standards do have an impact on the adoption policy, e.g. in *Romania* and *Poland*, and have led to control mechanisms and a reduction of inter-country adoptions.[54] The same may, in the future, apply to the *USA* as a significant importing country, where the Hague Convention was adopted on April 1, 2008.[55]

Relocation costs, including litigation costs and their impact on the property of each parent, travel costs of parents and children, stress, distress and influence on the child's wellbeing in general – social costs – of children due to the distance from one parent and to the regular travelling over long distances etc, led to »the world's first prospective longitudinal study« in *Australia* by the University of Sydney.[56] Relocation disputes involve »**transnational**«, »**transaction**« and »**social costs**«. Parents find themselves in a polarised position: one – in the study usually the mother – wishes to move, the other is opposed to such a move, so chances to achieve a friendly settlement are scarce.[57] The issue is of utmost importance in *Australia* due to its size and migration background. Lacking any legal provision on relocation itself, courts apply the principle of the best interest of children as a paramount consideration and achieve different outcomes. Amendments of the Family Law Act 1975 in 2006 emphasising the importance of involvement of both parents after separation resulted in fewer relocations.[58] The study suggests that the best interest principle ought to be put

---

52 *Bagan-Kurluta*, Adoption in a globalized world, 215-231 (217).
53 *Van der Linden*, What Price Should be Paid for a Child? Financial Aspects of Inter-country Adoption, 195-214.
54 *Bagan-Kurluta*, 215 (217 ff).
55 For more international details see *Bagan-Kurluta*, 215 (225 ff).
56 See *Parkinson*, The financial impact of relocation disputes: Empirical evidence from Australia, 553-567.
57 *Parkinson*, 553 (559).
58 *Parkinson*, 553 (556 f).

into concrete forms in order to signal the parties involved on a possible outcome of their case and hence reduce the enormous transaction costs.[59] A similar wish is expressed by a *Swedish* expert, who indicates that around 21% of the estimated 500.000 children in Sweden are **alternatively living** with both parents.[60] Those children spend more or less the same amount of time with each parent. This leads to the result that no child support is paid, although it may be assumed that the costs are not divided equally, but may even be higher than if the child would mainly live with one parent. Especially single mothers are affected; they have usually very limited economic means and approximately 37% of their disposable income consists of social benefits.[61] The costs mentioned concern the infrastructure of the child, travel costs, clothes, costs not connected to actual care, fees for leisure activities etc. At present, *Swedish* law does not deal with child support in the context of **alternating residence** and presumably costs that emerge independently of the child's presence are not thought of. A regulation dealing with this issue should entail principles on the division of these costs, determine the costs due to two homes, and means to encourage contact of the child with both parents.[62]

»One in three children in the *U.K.* lives in poverty, with one in ten living in severe poverty«.[63] The Child Support Agency is trying to collect £3.3 billion owed to single mothers and has a backlog of cases amounting to 300.000.[64] When it comes to the assessment of child support, the law in *England and Wales* distinguishes between couples that are or were married to each other and parents that are, were or never were cohabiting. In the former category just the income of the non resident parent is considered, whereas neither the actual income of the resident parent, nor the capital assets of either parent or the needs of the child play a role; in the latter case that applies to 44% of children in the *U.K.* Account is taken of both incomes, resources and earning capacities, the financial needs and obligations of both parents, the financial needs and any other special needs of the children, including their education and training, and

---

59 *Parkinson*, 553 (566).
60 *Singer*, Time is Money? – Child support for Children with alternating residence in Sweden, 591–601 (592).
61 *Singer*, 591 (595).
62 *Singer*, 591 (601).
63 *Pote*, Financial Provision and Child Equality, 665–671 (665).
64 *Pote*, 665 (666).

the welfare of the child in general.[65] The Child Support Agency is to be replaced by a new (administrative) organisation, namely the Child Maintenance and Enforcement Commission, but it seems that what is really needed is **low cost access to courts** that consider **all the circumstances of the case** independently of the status (legitimacy/illegitimacy) of the child in order to treat all children equally.[66]

Child support in *Croatia* has very much become a matter of **public concern**. The reasons for recent reforms in this direction were that around half of the debtors would not pay child support, part of them probably deliberately. Therefore, the *Croatian* legislator modified the system of support calculation, taking *German* law as an example, introduced **ex offo procedures** of child enforcement, and reinforced advance payments by the State.[67] Child support debts can since the 2008 reform be claimed retroactively for a period of up to 5 years. By and large, the system is said to be more simple and efficient than it used to be; courts and social welfare centres cooperate in child support matters, the debtor may be criminally prosecuted for not fulfilling his/her maintenance obligation; governmental bodies are obliged to provide information on the income of the debtor, and the *Croatian* Bar Association has been providing free legal aid in child support matters. It is presumed that the **State's intervention** will also have a positive impact on the relationship between the parents on the one side as well as between the non-resident parent (child support debtor) on the other.[68] The (**transaction** and **social**) **costs** for these interventions remain unknown, but one may hope that they really turn out to be in the best interest of the child. *Danish* law has a different focus: parents (here: upon divorce and separation) have the individual right and duty to co-operate in child related matters, which lead to massive amount of procedures in order to ensure their rights and duties, at the **financial** and **social costs** of the parties involved. The **process of »individualisation«** risks increasing family conflicts and the number of procedures.[69] The child support system seems simple, but is claimed to

---

65   *Pote*, 665 (667, 669).
66   *Pote*, 665 (665, 670).
67   *Resetar*, New Child Maintenance Obligations in Croatia: More and More being a Concern of the Public Law and Less of Civil Law, 603–613.
68   *Resetar*, 603 (607 ff).
69   *Kronborg/Jeppesen de Boer*, The child's right to two parents: Facilitating and financing joint parenting, 615–627 (616 ff).

focus too much on data, such as the number of children and the gross earnings of the child support debtor. Lacking an agreement between the parents on child support, the quantum is fixed by the administrative authority and enforcement procedures are taken care of by the municipality that works – so it is claimed – very efficiently. To the parents' relief they are not really involved in the procedure, nor are their actual family life or the best interests of the child.[70] Predictability is a major feature of this approach. This also holds true for the division of **transportation costs**. Both parents are liable equally to pay such costs, but the law has in fact another aim it wants to pursue: to give the parents an equal position upon bargaining their own arrangements as a direct consequence of their freedom of contract.[71] By and large, a regulation in the frame of (private) substantive law – as is the case for child support – is neatly preferred to a system which presupposes equal bargaining power, needed to fulfil the duty of co-operation in matters, such as pursuing individual rights and duties and transportation costs.[72] Child maintenance under *Serbian* law constitutes an adjustable minimum sum up until the age of 26 of the child; it should enable the child to maintain at least the same standard of living as the debtor, and **cannot** be claimed **retroactively**. A major problem when proving the income of the debtor is the **gray economy** in *Serbia*.[73] In times of hyper-inflation, child support can, since 1993, also be expressed in percentage. Several procedural safeguards are aimed at quick and efficient enforcement of child support (e.g. guardian authority that may initiate proceedings; the privileged character of child support claims in enforcement procedures etc).[74] In order to protect the child and the resident parent upon divorce, *Serbian* law introduced in 2005 the right to reside in the house owned by the non resident parent, unless this would constitute a »**clear injustice**« to the owner.[75] This innovation aims at the protection of the minor child and the resident parent with custody; it seems, therefore, that the right to reside is most probably limited in time.

---

70 *Kronborg/Jeppesen de Boer*, 615 (623 ff).
71 *Kronborg/Jeppesen de Boer*, 615 (625 ff).
72 *Kronborg/Jeppesen de Boer*, ibidem, 615 (627).
73 *Kovaček-Stanić*, Child in a single (absent) parent family: maintenance and family home, 637–648 (640, 643, 648).
74 *Kovaček-Stanić*, 637 (642 f, 648).
75 *Kovaček-Stanić*, 637 (644).

Child maintenance in *Slovenia* is regarded as a **personal duty** of the parents in the benefit of their child. Yet, quite some non-resident parents do not pay child support, at least not regularly, and apply a whole range of »**evasion techniques**«, such as pursuing illegal labour on the gray market, transferring their property to other persons, changing working place, and/or their habitual residence.[76] The aim of the Alimony Fund of the Republic of Slovenia is to partly compensate for losses of support, to enforce child support compensation claims, to advise creditors of child support, and to motivate debtors to provide child support deliberately.[77] The main difference between child support and compensation for child support is not only the quantum, but also its limitation with regard to the child's age. Child support may be due, depending on the need of the child and income of the debtor as well as on further education of the child creditor, up until the age of 26, whereas compensation for child support is limited to the age of 18.[78] This leads to the result that children who want to pursue further education are often forced to give up that idea or to work during their studies. This problem is, of course, not limited to *Slovenia*, quite to the contrary. Many other States provide loans to the children that once they are settled on the labour market must be paid back. In *Slovenia*, the burden of maintenance seems to rest on the resident parent and on the child at stake.

Supranational organisations (UN, Hague Conference, EU) have been dealing with the harmonisation of Private International Law. The **cross-border recovery of child maintenance**[79] for example is an issue which involves **transaction and social costs** at the same time. Apart from operational problems (e.g. effectiveness of transmitting and receiving agencies; location of the maintenance debtor etc) due to i.a. the heterogeneous nature of the different legal sources, lack of a central parent locator system, high (transaction and/or social) costs for time-consuming translation and for maintenance creditor who are in need of maintenance are involved. In some areas, Central Authorities are an excellent option, in others, possibly such as cross-border maintenance recovery, their effectiveness may not always be evident.

---

76   *Rijavec/Kraljić*, The Maintenance of the Children: Alimony Fund as the Saving Grace?, 649–663 (653 f).
77   *Rijavec/Kraljić*, 649 (654 f).
78   *Rijavec/Kraljić*, 649 (656).
79   *Curry-Sumner*, International Recovery of Child Support: Are Central Authorities the Way forward?, 175–193.

The **enforcement of child support** is a prominent paradigm of **transnational costs**. This is due to the procedures which vary from country to country, also within the *United States*, and to the lack of administrative cooperation mechanisms between governments that assure the actual establishment and enforcement of support orders.[80] The new Hague Convention on Family Maintenance[81] provides i.a. that child support orders are provided free of cost to the applicant; it therefore reflects a strong *US* policy which, however, holds that child support is and remains a **private obligation** of the parents. The high migration rate and family members with different nationalities or domiciles in different parts of the world mirror what is called the »global family«. It is said that the Hague Convention has great **redistributive potential**.[82] The work in the field of family law done by Hague Conference which culminates in the creation of a centre for international judicial and administrative cooperation in order to protect families and children thus considerably helps to **reduce transaction, transnational and social costs**. However, different approaches of *common law countries* and the *civil law countries* exist with regard to jurisdiction, applicable law and the enforcement of judgments.[83] Due to fundamental dichotomies the *USA* do not have the intention to ratify the Protocol on the applicable law. In addition, no agreement was achieved in The Hague on the issue of modifications of the original support order. Therefore, it is hoped that the administrative cooperation system[84] will work efficiently, and thus will be able to realise its redistributive potential.

Although the question whether **homemaking services** should in the **public interest** have an impact on the assessment of support upon divorce (alimony) concerns many legal systems, it was addressed by *Wardle* for the *United States*.[85] Admittedly, when turning to inevitable daily homemaking servic-

---

80 *Estin*, Transnational Family Finances and the United States, 233–242.
81 Hague Convention on the International Recovery of Child Support and other Forms of Family Maintenance (no 38; 2007), signed by the *USA* on November 23, 2007, by Burkina Faso on January 7, 2009 (as of May 1, 2009).
82 *Estin*, 233 (240).
83 *Spector*, The Hague Convention on the International Recovery of Child Support and other Forms of Family Maintenance: Divergent Private International Law Rules and the Limits of Harmonisation, 243–255 (246).
84 See Art 10 para 1 lit e & f and Art 10 para 2 lit b & c providing that an application through the Central Authorities includes an application from a debtor or creditor to modify an existing maintenance order. *Spector,* 243 (247, 249, 255).
85 *Wardle*, Alimony on the Margins: Protecting Homemaking Service in the Public Interest, 475–490.

es, one may indeed sometimes feel encouraged to cite *Lenin*, who wrote that a housewife was »a daily sacrifice to unimportant trivialities... They are like worms which, unseen, slowly but surely rot and corrode«,[86] especially when balancing »the work-home conflict is (regarded) a decision every married woman and every mother must make for herself«.[87] But the point is that some family members (probably usually women) do assume household tasks and thereby indeed save the public treasury huge amounts of money, services that otherwise will or might be provided at taxpayer expense[88] and/or at the expense of working opportunities, the income of the spouses, and/or the children. Some legislators do take into account such services in that in addition to support upon divorce the property is to be distributed equally or equitably. Looking at the economic reality today only a very small number of divorcees is able to pay support upon divorce in addition to child support and both sides often end up with no property to distribute at all. The enormous **public costs** of marital break-up and non-marital child-bearing assumed by the State resp. the taxpayers[89] surely also cover cases in which it might also be in the public interest that the marriage is terminated and/or the children are taken care for in another setting.

State interest may well be considered more important than the »**social costs**« in the context of **expulsion of foreign nationals** who have illegally settled in a country and established a family. In *Japan* for example, »State interest« is focussed on the acceptance of skilled workers, not so much – as is claimed[90] – on the fulfilment of legal obligations of the ICCPR and the CRC, such as respect of family life and securing the best interests of the child. Hence, foreign nationals, who have been living and illegally working in unskilled jobs in *Japan* and established a family unit, are systematically expelled from the country, in order to enhance skilled work and to decrease the risk of terrorist acts. Hereby it is taken into account that family members with different nationalities are sent back to their country of origin which implies the splitting up of the family at stake. »Social costs« in cases like these are tremendously high and considered to be the entire responsibility of the family at stake.

---

86 Cited by *Wardle*, 475 (483).
87 See *Wardle*, 475 (478 and 490).
88 *Wardle*, 475 (483).
89 *Wardle*, 475 (486 f).
90 See *Fu*, Expulsion of Irregular Foreign Residents from Japan. The Right to Family Unification and the Best Interests of the Child, 161–174.

Transaction and **social costs** are involved when it comes to **(alternative) dispute resolution**. The *Australian* experience with »Legal Resolution Services™« seems to show a reduction of transaction and social costs. Parties share the costs of Consultants and/or the Settlement Facilitator; they get expert advice within a mediation framework at an early stage (»first step approach«) and thus have an option not offered by the judicial system.[91] Cost-sharing is, of course, only fair, if parties have more or less the same income; LRS™ is only possible, if the parties have an income at all. It is hard to say whether this model is of interest in other countries, where average parties have very little money, lack expertise and are reluctant to use similar services, if they can enjoy free basic legal advice and where mediators may receive state benefits for the mediations of e.g. family cases.

VI. Allocation of Risks and Resources

One of the parameters to analyse the extent of **personal risks** within the family is the support obligation. The tendency is to limit such obligations to a certain age and/or to a certain degree of relationship.[92] This does not necessarily imply that needs beyond these borders are automatically to be considered as social ones. They basically remain personal risks. Only when persons in need cannot provide for their own support anymore and a responsible support provider is lacking, will the society assume this risk. But what happens, if society faces a global crisis? Will this strengthen the »principle of subsidiarity of welfare benefits«? Is it probable that support obligations – by principle – be limited to parents and persons in loco parentis?[93]

Support duties of **adult children** towards their **elderly parents** are a nice example of the interplay of **personal responsibility** and **social responsibility**. The exact borders of each burden depend on many factors and are often[94] summarised with »**redistribution of resources in a given society**«.

---

91 *Campbell*, Legal Resolution Services™ and its interface with ADR: An Australian Perspective, 115–132 (118).
92 See *Ribot*, 33-44.
93 See *Schwenzer*, Model Family Code (2006) 166.
94 See *Ribot*, 33 (44).

Allocation of resources also plays a role in other contexts: **Survivor's benefits** (in *Belgium*) traditionally are based on an »adult worker«-model. In this model it is assumed that the surviving spouse and children should be able to receive the benefits because they were dependent on the income of the deceased.[95] The clear consequence of such allocation of benefits is, then, to reduce the benefits, if there was no dependency, in which case there is no »**social risk**« to be compensated. However, few cases will correspond to this situation. Because even if there are two bread-winners the average family will usually have no surplus. In addition, a whole range of tasks within the family (and the household) must be handled. Presumed that two bread-winners divide these tasks equally, the surviving partner must now assume the entire (non-paid) tasks. Some regard the **coverage of balancing work and family life** as a »**new social risk**«.[96] Authors mirror this plea against the *Belgian* divorce and maintenance reform law 2007 which attempts to cover new social risks in that it takes into account the changed attitude towards marriage and divorce. Divorce is since then basically independent of any fault and (time limited) maintenance as **compensation** for the financial risks occurring as a result of the loss of the breadwinner is due, if there is a surplus of income and a need of the other spouse. In this respect the survivor's pension scheme seems more generous than the allocation of support upon divorce in child raising cases, but also more generous than the unemployment benefit scheme, which does not exempt the parent from employment. The **interplay** of dependency of adults and children of other persons, of the state and of employment demonstrates that there is a »**gap**« between **personal possibilities** and **socio-economic feasibility**. Yet, it is argued that social security measures (e.g. survivor's pension) should not go any further than private compensation mechanisms (e.g. time limited support upon divorce) in order to harmonise the private and social systems of support.[97] Such a system must presuppose that the state guarantees employment which covers the needs of the persons in question.

The **preservation of the child's family environment** in *South Africa* for example is regarded as a primary responsibility of the parents, if the child is living in the family, whereas the State is primarily responsible, when

---

95 *Alofs/Hoop*, The sustainability of survivor's and divorce benefits in the adult worker model: incorporation of new social risks, 49-70.
96 *Alofs/Hoop*, 49 (54 ff).
97 *Alofs/Hoop*, 49 (66).

the child does not. However, attempts are made to strengthen the **rights of the child** with corresponding **duties of the State**.[98] The fulfilment of such duties involves huge amounts of money and at present only the lowest implementation plan can be implemented.

Not specifically limited to *Germany*, but claimed by one scholar for *States* (in general) is the recognition of the **principle of freedom** of individual choice as to the **form of living together,** be it within a marriage, a registered or unregistered heterosexual or same-sex partnership resp. cohabitation; in any case the State should ensure the **protection of the weaker party**.[99] This requires **regulation** in any case, whereby distinctions for example along the lines of what was suggested by *Lifshitz*, including the relatively short period of cohabitation, are worth to be considered.

Whether **cohabiting couples**, especially women with children, ought to be **protected** upon breakdown of the relationship, is probably a question which arises everywhere and is answered controversially. If emphasis is laid on the status, such as marriage or partnership, and the principle of autonomy of individuals, protection, if at all, can for example in *Canada/Quebec*, only be found in remedial constructive trust and unjust enrichment in order to obtain quasi-matrimonial property rights. This situation is regarded as unfair and inadequate, if the couple has common offspring. Then, the best interest of the child should prevail over the importance of status in order to distribute the property and to allocate support as upon divorce.[100]

Looking at the **consequences of divorce and separation**, marriage increasingly becomes a »**normal**« **personal risk**, be it at the expense of the weaker party or at that of the other party, who may face difficulties in assuming further responsibilities based on a new relationship. In order to reduce the rate of child poverty and to cut down expenses in the field of social welfare, the *German* legislator placed in his »**fundamental social policy reform**« divorced and non-married mothers on an equal footing.[101]

---

98 *Van der Linde*, 99 (105).
99 *Dethloff*, New Models of Partnerships, 491–499 (498 f).
100 *Goubau*, Division of Family Assets and De Facto Conjugality: the limits of a free choice approach, 271–279 (274, 279).
101 See *Willenbacher*, Family Finances through German Support Laws: Effects of Child Support Priority, 535–551 (536).

The **principle** of »**self-responsibility**« was strengthened and the risks of impairment of human capital through lacking employment or part-time employment were redistributed. Research in the field of social science in *Germany* reveals that in cases where the non-resident parent can neither cover his own maintenance not the support of the child (so-called »Mangelfall«) the law in force leads to an increase of child support, provided no support upon divorce (alimony) is due. Whereas if the debtor has a higher income the income of the (middle-class) support creditor (single divorced mother) significantly decreases (at least during a certain period of time) and the need for social welfare and probably the risk of lower chances of development of the children may well increase. Along with this, the **pressure** on **single parents** with regard to employment is rising.[102]

Italian case law reveals that the risk of finding a job on the **labour market** by adult children gradually has become one of the parents to maintain their children beyond the stage of advanced education, provided the child bears no fault by neglecting the opportunities offered by the family, and the child is not negligent in that it looks for a job or does not refuse it without a reasonable cause.[103]

VII. Modern Times or Postmodernism?

The possibility to change the marital property regime by contract is not only based on the **principle of contractual freedom**, but also reflects the **liberty of couples** to organize property aspects of their family life according to their individual wishes and needs. *Serbia* (re -) introduced the concept of »marriage contract«, by which cohabitants and married couples can regulate their property relations.[104] This has been criticised for several reasons, i.a. because the **weaker party** is not sufficiently protected, and because such **contractual freedom** is said to be contrary to *Serbian* tradition and to disturb the harmony of emotional relations.[105] Interestingly, financial regulation within the family on a contractual basis seems to be

---

102   *Willenbacher*, 535 (544 f).
103   *Casabona*, Mamma mia! The never ending story of the economic support of the adult child in Italy, 629–635.
104   Draškić, Financing the Romance: Marriage Contract in the Serbian Family Act, 381–393 (390).
105   Draškić, 381 (392).

at odds with »emotional« relationships, such as marriage and cohabitation, whereas it is accepted and deemed necessary that the state provides for legal rules in order to protect the parties.[106]

Prenuptial agreements (agreements made before marriage on the assets in the event of divorce or separation) are not binding in *England and Wales*. Family assets are governed by ordinary rules governing property law which is based on the doctrine of separation of property. Courts decide upon divorce on the distribution of property according to the needs generated by the relationship of the parties, compensation for relationship-generated disadvantages may be due as well as sharing the fruits of the matrimonial partnership of equals.[107] Some argue that *English* law is **paternalistic** and **anachronistic** and parties should have **full freedom** to make their economic arrangements; others advance **public policy** arguments.[108]. Based on an analysis of the case law, and measuring it against the Consultation Paper »Supporting Families«, *Lowe/Kay* drew the conclusion that, by and large, the outcome of the cases would not have been different, if prenuptial agreements would have been binding indeed.[109] Instead, they advocate basically sticking to the current law and eventually accepting prenuptial agreements as a material considering in deciding

---

[106] Some argue that marriage in Western societies, e.g. *Norwegian* law promotes subordination and dependency of women. It is claimed that today, marriage should fulfil three functions, notably economy, care and love. In order to achieve these goals, women should be economically independent; fathers should be obliged to care for their children as mothers do, and love ought to be understood as good behaviour towards each other. Fatherhood as a consequence of the »presumption of legitimacy« is in times of DNA outdated; *Braekhus* claims that biological fatherhood ought to be tested in all cases, all the more since *Norwegian* law gives (*Norwegian*) adopted adult children and those that were conceived as a result of sperm donation the right to know their male parent. Finally, it is claimed that marriage ought to be deregulated, because there seems to be no need for it, at least as long as the couple has no offspring; whereas the relationship between parents and children, independent of marriage, ought to be ameliorated and provide for equal responsibilities and duties. In general, divorce ought to be considered a »normal part of life«. See *Braekhus*, Regulation of Parenthood – Deregulation of Marriage, 569–589 (579, 582 ff).

[107] *Lowe/Kay*, The Status of Prenuptial Agreements in English Law, 395–413 (397).

[108] E.g. prenuptial agreements would diminish the importance/sanctity of marriage, or, by contrast, could add stability to marriage and introduce greater certainty and reduce costs; such agreements would shift the burden of maintaining from the individual to the state; protection of children and weaker party might be questioned; the validity, fairness and meaning of the agreement made before the marriage might be at stake upon divorce etc, see *Lowe/Kay*, 395 (408 ff).

[109] *Lowe/Kay*, 395 (411).

the distribution of family assets. By contrast, LJ *Thorpe* is of the opinion that contractual freedom under *English* law not only corresponds to the needs of **modern times** and of harmonisation in the European context,[110] but prenuptial agreements as an example of such freedom would also reduce procedural costs considerably, and, thus, serve the litigants more than their lawyers.[111]

In 2005, an optional (contractual) marital property regime of »sharing of accruals« (separation of property with the equalisation of surpluses« was introduced in *Poland*[112]. It is claimed to be a response to the **changed attitude of spouses in modern times,**[113] in which spouses increasingly get involved with **commercial activity**. This called for protection of the **weaker spouse**, usually the woman, who may not have the same job opportunities as her husband, can claim half of the surplus but does not face claims of the other spouses' creditors.[114] Whether the goal of the *Polish* legislator in times of global crisis and crashing down of businesses is actually fulfilled, seems doubtful.

Tradition, opportunism, simple personal need, ignorance or whatever it may, be lead to **legislative acts** that miss the point and also evoke **evasive reactions** of persons addressed by such acts. The *South African* Recognition of Customary Marriages Act 1998 seems to be a striking example of legal uncertainty and decrease of protection formerly to some extent provided by customary law.[115] Increased regulation and bureaucratic requirements are in contradiction with social reality of customary marriages for many reasons, most importantly because the occasions on which such marriages must be proved have increased. The economic means of (usually) women to prove what needs to be proved, lack in nearly all cases. **Law and policy distort social structures**, if they introduce piecemeal reforms without an overall view on society. One among many examples shall dem-

---

110 *Thorpe*, London – The Divorce Capital of the World, 501–516 (508 ff, 514).
111 *Thorpe*, 501 (509, 515).
112 *Stępień-Sporek*, Sharing of accruals as the best solution for marriage?, 369–379.
113 According to *Mandia,* Principles, deviations therefrom and consequences of formal and non-formal relationships, 259–269, cohabitation was introduced in *Albania* in 2003 due to the »fanatic mentality« (of whom is not indicated, though).
114 *Stępień-Sporek*, 369 (377).
115 *Bekker*, An Analysis of the Rights of South African Women and Children to Maintenance from Husbands and Fathers in African Custormary Marriages and Domestic Partnerships, 461–474.

onstrate what is meant. Customary law – so it seems – used to combine succession rights with duties of support: The eldest male descendant of the deceased used to become the universal heir and it was his duty to support the entire family. According to the Constitutional Court, however, customary law of succession is unconstitutional and invalid, if succession rights of women and children are limited. However, it may well be that more than 20 million *Africans* living on communal land, with each extended family living in a single dwelling, the family home, must face a »*Western* concept« of what family is all alike that is transplanted to them independently of realities of customary law, and thus enhances their poverty and legal insecurity.[116] It seems that also a »*Western* concept« of »law« is applied, which necessarily invites to evasion strategies, because »law« is also »customary law«. A wide variety of human relationships have developed, registered, unregistered, parallel to a customary or a civil marriage and it seems questionable whether the envisaged introduction of a domestic partnership model can grasp what is law in customary law.[117]

Contrasting **familial rights and duties** to **succession rights** (especially the »reserved portion«) of the »traditional family« to those of other forms of living together reveals contradictions in *Brazilian* law that have historical reasons, but may also, by reason of policy, be regulated differently or remain unregulated. All problems related to **family re-composition** and **self-determination**, including the freedom (at least among adults) to live according to one's own wishes albeit possibly with no or little legal consequences in civil law, also have **economic** consequences.[118] These differ depending on the form of living together resp. alone. **Re-composed families** may face less property or capital to inherit, because the former spouse was given a donation as an anticipated reserved portion, or, as the case may be, because children out of previous relationships question donations to the spouse of the re-composed family.[119] In addition, the values and principles underlying family rights and obligations must not necessarily concur with those applicable in inheritance law. Cohabitation may well have legal consequences, but may be neglected in inher-

---

116   *Bekker*, 461 (465).
117   *Bekker*, 461 (471, 474).
118   *Pozzi*, Self-Determination and State Intervention: A Balance for Protection of the Reserved Portion of the Estate in the 2002 Brazilian Civil Code in the Light of New Family Arrangements, 725–740.
119   *Pozzi*, 725 (733).

itance law, by e.g. not giving a cohabitant a reserved portion as the surviving spouse has. This leads to the result that the surviving cohabitant cannot challenge donations to other necessary heirs. Other relationships, e.g. same-sex couples, although a certain transfer of goods and/or services may occur, are not regulated by law.[120] There are other situations which seem to call for a certain degree of recognition in family and succession law, notably those concerning children, more specifically in **socio-affective parenthood**. What is called for by an *Italian* expert is the legal relevance of constitutional principles and their application to intersubjective relations.[121] Whether it is the aim of constitutional principles to embrace such relations seems questionable, though. Surely, when arguing on the basis of the principle of equal treatment, the mere existence of a variety of life forms and styles does not yet render them comparable.

French law.[122] differentiates in family and succession law between married couples, pacsés and cohabitants.[123] It is argued that at least those pacsés, who cannot marry, as *French* law stands at present, notably same-sex pacsés, are discriminated against in inheritance law and with regard to the protection of the home, including the use of the furniture, because different rules apply to married couples resp. the surviving spouse on the one hand and to pacsés resp. the surviving pacsé on the other. Although it is acknowledged that the **binding legal nature** and the **corresponding rights** and **obligations differ**, the different treatment of those who cannot opt for marriage should be regarded as **discriminatory**.[124] To what extent certain models such as the *French* one on the legitimate portion with its scheme based on fixed rules are apt for recommendation or even legal transplant in other legal systems[125] can, in my opinion, not be judged in general without taking into account the effect of such transplants in the legal system at stake.

Equality of spouses, family solidarity and **protection of the weaker party** are pillars upon which the Hungarian draft of the New Civil Code, more

---

120 *Pozzi*, 725 (733 f).
121 *Pozzi*, 725 (738).
122 *Fusaro*, Legitimate Portion and other Techniques of Protection of Surviving Spouses and Children. A Comparison between Civil Law and Common Law systems, 751-760 (757 f).
123 *Roy*, Legal Protection of the Survivor of a Couple in French Family Law, 741-749.
124 *Roy*, 741 (749).
125 See the discussion in *Fusaro*, 751 (758 ff).

specifically of the family (property) law provisions are built.[126] The Draft takes into account the economic and social changes of *Hungarian* society, the increase of private property and the involvement of individuals in business life.[127] The legal property system is that of community property; parties may by matrimonial property contract deviate from the statutory system and opt for either »community of accrued gains« or »separation of property«.[128] The latter has limits to contractual freedom, though: Basic family interests, such as the welfare of the child, the solidarity principle, should not be infringed upon. The separation of property shall, therefore, not be of any influence on the costs of family life, child care and upbringing included. In addition, the family home is protected in that independent of any agreement between the parties the judge can accord the right to use the matrimonial home by the residing parent and the child until the age of majority of the child.[129]

VIII. Conclusions

Contractual freedom, equality, self-determination, family solidarity, protection of the weaker party[130] etc are advanced as leading principles of (postmodern?) family law. However, marriage has become a risk, divorce is a risk; we end up with nothing but costs and extreme poverty. Conclusions that remind us in many ways of *Hieronymus Bosch*, who himself, for as much as we know, led a »bourgeois« and apparently happy life. But *Bosch* does not help us any further, unless we want to relax and enjoy his extraordinary masterpieces.

However, in the family law context little time remains to relax. We need to rethink basics and remind ourselves of the social, political, cultural, economic and legal context people are living in. Interdisciplinary and multiscalar research is needed and yet a lot is »in«, but nowadays unfortunately not family law. What the 13th World Conference of the ISFL demonstrated

---

126 *Kőrös*, as one of the experts for the elaboration of the *Hungarian* draft on family law, in: New Features of Hungarian Matrimonial Property Law in the Draft of a New Civil Code, 675-681.
127 *Kőrös*, 675 (676).
128 *Kőrös*, 675 (678 f).
129 *Kőrös*, 675 (679 f).
130 Surely not only women and children.

is that we ought to be quite careful with equalisation and legal transplant. In one country it is claimed that the State should withdraw from private life, in another it is argued that the State should intervene. In yet another country broad discretion of the courts is endorsed, whereas others call for concrete norms. Some advocate equality, others equity. Some wish to compensate for what occurred in the past, others want to anticipate what will happen in the future.

Personally, I am of the opinion that is seems wise to differentiate instead of equalise, because different situations and needs ask for different solutions and responses. Whether marriage should be the starting point to measure the legal and economic position of persons living in other forms or situations may be questioned. This is not so much because marriage, in many parts of the world, increasingly tends to become a »minority project«. I rather have the impression that not all the consequences of marriage have been adapted to what it is today: A model elaborated to last for life and – in many legal systems with considerable consequences – whereas the simplicity of its dissolution contrasts the model and to some extent its consequences. Turning to other forms of living together, like registered partnerships that (may) have »status« character too; they all are terminable unilaterally, but, from a comparative point of view, with varying consequences in different branches of law (e.g. family law, succession law, tax law, social law etc). At least in highly industrialised countries I would favour basically that every couple living together primarily assumes a personal risk and their chances consist of »partnership« and mutual support during the partnership.

Children and elderly persons are another issue. Humanity and independence begin when children are healthy, receive a good education and have actual job chances. This is an individual responsibility and also one of society at large, independent of the children's status. Elderly people, soon a majority in many states, are in need too. But here, the »Buddenbrooks principle« – of course not as in *Thomas Mann*'s novel (merely) representing the »Bourgeois« family – should apply in that (adult) children should be given a chance to look after themselves and their children and not be burdened by a duty to take care of their parents. This is, in my opinion, primarily a task of the society. The tendency seems to go in the other direction.